CIVIL WAR STORIES

CIVIL WAR STORIES

40 of the Greatest Tales about the War Between the States

LAMAR UNDERWOOD

Guilford, Connecticut

An imprint of The Rowman & Littlefield Publishing Group, Inc.
4501 Forbes Blvd., Ste. 200
Lanham, MD 20706
www.rowman.com

Distributed by NATIONAL BOOK NETWORK

Copyright © 2018 by Lamar Underwood

British Library Cataloguing in Publication Information Available

Library of Congress Cataloging-in-Publication Data

Names: Underwood, Lamar, editor.
Title: Civil War stories : 40 of the greatest tales about the War Between the States / Lamar Underwood.
Description: Guilford, Connecticut : Lyons Press, 2018. | Includes bibliographical references.
Identifiers: LCCN 2017058429 (print) | LCCN 2017057678 (ebook) | ISBN 9781493032013 (e-book) | ISBN 9781493032006 (hardcover : alk. paper)
Subjects: LCSH: United States—History—Civil War, 1861–1865—Anecdotes. | United States—History—Civil War, 1861-1865—Personal narratives. | United States—History—Civil War, 1861–1865—Sources.
Classification: LCC E655 (print) | LCC E655 .C494 2018 (ebook) | DDC 973.7—dc23
LC record available at https://lccn.loc.gov/2017058429

♾™ The paper used in this publication meets the minimum requirements of American National Standard for Information Sciences—Permanence of Paper for Printed Library Materials, ANSI/NISO Z39.48-1992.

Printed in the United States of America

CONTENTS

CONTENTS

Contents

Acknowledgments

The editor would like to thank Lisa Purcell for the contribution of eight chapters to this work. Presented with her own introductions to the stories, they are identified with her name at the start of each chapter.

INTRODUCTION

THE BLOODIEST SINGLE DAY OF BATTLE IN AMERICAN HISTORY TOOK PLACE ON SEPTEM-
ber 17, 1862—beside a Maryland creek called Antietam that fronted the village of
Sharpsburg. Following the battle, in late September photographer Mathew Brady staged
a special exhibition at his New York gallery. He called the event "The Dead of Antietam."
The photographs presented also included those of Brady's assistants, Alexander Gardner
and James F. Gibson.

The close-up images of dead men sprawled on the battlefield—sometimes in gruesome tangled clusters, with dead horses nearby—were unlike anything ever seen by the
public. Among other comments, a reporter for the *New York Times* wrote, "Mr. Brady
has done something to bring to us the terrible reality and earnestness of the war. If he has
not brought bodies and laid them in our door-yards and along [our] streets, he has done
something very like it."

Strong words, those. I present them here in the hope that the chapters of this book
will bring to you a similar mood, as the words of actual veterans of the war describe what
they saw and felt during the fighting. This volume cannot offer the photographs of Mr.
Brady and his talented assistants, but it has been my goal to bring the realities of the Civil
War into your thoughts with prose that achieves the same searing revelations of pain and
loss, of hardships almost beyond description. And, as the *Times* reporter commented, "the
earnestness of the war."

In the four long years of fighting that ended with the Union saved, the sacrifices of
the soldiers and their officers in both blue and gray took place on a horrific scale. One
can throw every noun, adjective, and phrase that comes to mind at the images that flash
through our minds: Hunger. Thirst. Pain. Separation from loved ones. Fatigue beyond
description. Doubt and worry about incompetent leaders and their orders. Loss of hope
and ever seeing home again.

Finally, there is death itself. For the religious faithful—and there were many on both
sides—the end came as a release from what literally seemed to be hell on earth. For most
soldiers, every step forward toward the guns of the enemy was made possible by the slim
hope, conviction even, that those who fell would be the "other guys."

For some, as revealed in countless accurate descriptions of the fighting, a total breakdown of will and courage took place. They fled in open panic. Or sometimes they found ways to malinger, hang out on the fringes where the firestorm did not reach, act as if they were just moving slower than the advancing troops. Words like *duty, honor, country*—the West Point mantra—were meaningless to men numb with fear, men to whom survival at any cost seemed more important than any orders ever issued.

For officers, whose shoulders carried the responsibilities of giving those orders, duties required far more than just showing up and doing what they were told. Their decisions on where, when, and how to place and use their troops were heavy ones, with death and surrender the cost of blunders. And no matter how effective the battle plans and orders, they had to be carried out with officers leading the way on the field. In the Civil War, officers up to the rank of general were casualties in mind-boggling numbers. Lieutenants, captains, majors, colonels. They were wiped out by hailstorms of bullets and artillery bursts.

Even the generals did not always walk away after the battles. Many were fatally wounded on the battlefields, including the Confederate's legendary Stonewall Jackson, shot by one of his own nervous pickets as he inspected the forward lines during the battle of Chancellorsville.

Jackson was Robert E. Lee's "right arm," as General Lee described their relationship. With Jackson gone, Lee faced unforeseen challenges in reorganizing his army and leading its operations. In the chapters ahead, Lee's agonizing decisions are presented with vigor and details. He has plenty of general-officer company. The bold strokes and blunders of generals on both sides of the struggles, including Ulysses S. Grant, form the background of battles described by the men who fought them.

The revelations about General Lee described in the stories I have been reading give your editor a runaway train of thought. If Robert E. Lee had not turned down Lincoln's offer to lead the Union army, the war would have been much, much shorter under Lee's skills and leadership capabilities. And Robert E. Lee, not Ulysses S. Grant, might have been elected president of the United States. Instead, Lee resigned his commission and walked away from his West Point heritage and years of Union army service. Why? He said he could never raise a sword against his beloved Virginia, which had joined the secession. What loss of life and bloodshed could have been prevented had he stayed with the Union? We'll never know.

The memoirs of many surviving Civil War veterans, from all ranks and all walks of life, were published in the late 1800s and early 1900s. These selections form a large body of the works presented here. As your editor, I have found the experience of discovering them to be both engaging and illuminating. There are scenes in these works that burn into consciousness like great clarion calls, saying, "Remember . . . remember . . . these are things we endured, so that our nation might live."

Anyone interested in history, particularly military history, and fortunate to be in the position of editing a book such as this, calling the shots on stories selected, would probably choose some other stories—stories not presented here. I regret leaving out any readers' favorites, but have no worries at all on all the chapters before you here.

By reading them, you will experience as closely as possible what service was like in the Civil War, for the blue and the gray, for the generals and the men, for the folks at home who faced challenges, sometimes horrific, of their own. There is far more in these accounts than memories of the action. These writers often bare their souls in describing their feelings and motivations. There is anger and commitment here on both sides that help us understand "the terrible reality and earnestness of the war."

—Lamar Underwood

EDITOR'S NOTE

THE STORIES THAT FOLLOW, EXCERPTED FROM FULL BOOKS, ARE PRESENTED WITH THEIR original spelling and punctuation largely untouched. Spelling errors will be apparent, such as *Pittsburg* for *Pittsburgh*. Also, readers should be aware that in some cases the writers have incorrect dates. In all cases, the numbers of troops in the various encounters have not been validated to historical accuracy. They are given as written and have suspect accuracy in some cases. At the time most of these stories were written, paragraphs sometimes ran on for pages. The editor has inserted paragraph breaks in appropriate spots to provide a break from the monotonous grayness of the long-running original paragraphs.

—Lamar Underwood

CHAPTER I

In the Ranks
By Reverend R. E. M'Bride

R. E. M'Bride recalls his experiences as a private soldier in the Army of the Potomac in this excerpt from his book In the Ranks: From the Wilderness to Appomattox Court-House, *published in 1883. From a quiet Pennsylvania town to the battlefields and hospitals of this savage war, "Robbie" M'Bride, as he was known as a soldier, not yet a reverend, survived the war and returned home to tell the story of the fighting as seen "In the Ranks."*

—LAMAR UNDERWOOD

"WAR!"

It is a little word. A child may pronounce it; but what word that ever fell from human lips has a meaning full of such intensity of horror as this little word? At its sound there rises up a grim vision of "confused noise and garments rolled in blood."

April 12, 1861, cannon fired by traitor hands, boomed out over Charleston harbor. The dire sound that shook the air that Spring morning did not die away in reverberating echoes from sea to shore, from island to headland. It rolled on through all the land, over mountain and valley, moaning in every home, at every fireside, "War! War! War!"

Are we a civilized people? What is civilization? Is it possible to eliminate the tiger from human nature? Who would have dreamed that the men of the North, busy with plowing and sowing, planning, contriving, inventing, could prove themselves on a hundred battle-fields a fiercely warlike people? The world looked on with wonder as they rushed eagerly into the conflict, pouring out their blood like water and their wealth without measure, for a sentiment, a principle, that may be summed up in the one word—"nationality." "The great uprising" was not the movement of a blind, unreasoning impulse. A fire had been smoldering in the North for years. The first cannon shot that hurtled around the old flag as it floated over the walls of Fort Sumter shook down the barriers that confined it, and the free winds of liberty fanned it to a devouring flame.

The Yankee—let the name be proudly spoken—as he turned the furrow, stood by his work bench, or listened to the jarring clank of his machinery, had mused with heavy heart and shame-flushed cheek how a haughty, brutal, un-American spirit had drawn a line across the land, and said, "Beyond this is not your country. Here your free speech, free labor, and free thought shall never come." While this line was imaginary, he had waited for better days and larger thought to change the current of the times; but when it was transformed into bristling bayonets and frowning cannon, the tiger rose up within him, and with unquestioning faith he took up the gauge of battle. Men talked of the "cold blood of the North." That blood had surged impetuously through the veins of warrior freemen for a hundred generations. Here in the New World it had lost none of its vigor. The sturdy spirit that in other years ruled the hand that wielded the battle-ax, still ruled, when the hand was employed in subduing mountain and prairie.

The North was averse to war, because it was rising to that higher civilization that abhors violence, discards brute methods, and relies on the intellectual and moral. Such a people, driven to desperation, move right forward to the accomplishment of their object with a scorn of cost or consequences unknown to a lower type. Hence it is that the people of the North, without hesitation, grappled with a rebellion the most formidable ever successfully encountered by any government.

Turning away from a half million graves, wherein they had buried their slain, their bravest and best beloved, they forgot all bitterness for joy that peace had come. No people in the world had greater reason for severity than the victors in this strife. War, willful, unprovoked, without the shadow of justification, had been thrust upon them. This had been preceded by a series of usurpations the most unblushing ever endured by a free people. These were a part of the plan of a band of traitors, who had plotted for years to overthrow the existing order of things, and establish an empire with human slavery for its chief corner-stone.

The "Golden Circle," with its center at Havana, Cuba, its radii extending to Pennsylvania on the North, the isthmus on the south, and sweeping from shore to shore, was the bold dream of the men who plotted the destruction of the American republic. Their object was pursued with a cold-blooded disregard of all right, human and divine, worthy of the pagan brutality of the Roman Triumvirate. Prating about the "Constitution" with hypocritical cant, they trampled upon every safeguard of popular liberty, and at last, in defiance of even the forms of law, plunged the people of the Southern States into a war with the government, which, even if successful in securing a separation, could only have been the beginning of woes, as their plans would develop.

But notwithstanding the heinousness of the accomplished crime, not a man was punished. It is doubtful whether popular opinion would have approved the punishment of even the arch-traitor, Jeff Davis. The common sentiment was expressed by the oft-repeated verdict: "Enough of blood has been shed." Whether this was wise or not it is vain to inquire. Perhaps the future will vindicate the wisdom of the generous course of the government. Thus far it has seemed like folly. The South has shown a persistent vindictiveness unequaled in the history of any people, a cruelty toward the helpless victims of their hate that is shameful to the last degree. The cowardly assassination of political opponents, the brutal murder of black men, women, and children, has been defended openly or covertly by pulpit, press, and platform. If any disapprove, their voice is not heard in condemnation of the wrong. This may have resulted partly from the fact that many of the people of the North, notably many so-called statesmen, ignored common sense and gave way to gush and sentiment. There is nothing gained in this prosy world by calling black white. The leaders of the rebellion were guilty of the horrible crime of treason, and we baptized it something else. The result is manifest to all who are not willfully and wickedly blind to the facts.

Yet it is the part of duty to hope for the speedy coming of an era of calmer judgment, of real and healthy patriotism, when every American citizen will claim our whole land as his country. When the civil war began, my home was with the family of Mr. John Dunn, in Butler County, Pennsylvania. The old gentleman was a Democrat, and at first had little to say about the war. One evening he returned from the village in a state of intense excitement. He had heard of the disastrous battle at Bull Run. It is no exaggeration to say that he "pranced" around the room, chewing his tobacco with great vigor, telling how many of our "poor boys" had been slaughtered by the rebels. His apathy was at an end. He could see where the line lay between treason and patriotism, when once that line was traced in blood.

At this time two Butler County companies, C and D, of the Eleventh Pennsylvania Reserve Volunteer Corps, were in camp near Pittsburg. The corps was sent forward to Washington at once, and from that time till the close of their term of service, they gallantly represented the Keystone State in every battle fought by the Army of the Potomac. My brother, Wm. A., was a private in Company C. He enlisted June 10, 1861, and fell, with many other brave men, at the battle of Gaines' Mill, June 27, 1862.

In this quiet village [Prospect, Butler County] one chilly morning in December, 1863, the writer mounted the stage-coach and went rattling over the frozen ground toward Pittsburg, to enlist in the volunteer service. Just seventeen years ago that very morning I had begun the business of life on rather limited capital; and although it had been improved with considerable success, yet the kindly prophecies, particularly of my copperhead friends, did not portend a very lengthy nor brilliant military career. The next day I made my way to the provost-marshal's office, and, after due examination, was pronounced all right, and sworn into the service. If I lied about my age, obliging memory has written it over with something else, and it is gone from me.

I selected Company D, of the Eleventh Pennsylvania Regular Volunteer Corps, and was assigned accordingly. The recruits were retained for some time at Camp Copeland, then about the dreariest, most uncomfortable place I ever saw; shelter and provisions insufficient, bad whisky and blacklegs abundant. Joe Stewart, John Alexander, and myself tented together here. They had enlisted for the One Hundredth Pennsylvania, the "Roundheads." Joe was an old acquaintance. He served gallantly till the close of the war.

John was a noble boy and found a soldier's death at Cold Harbor. After one of the fruitless charges made there, when the Roundheads came back foiled of their purpose, John was not with them. In the darkness of night which quickly closed around, Joe went out to search for him. As he was picking his way stealthily among the dead and dying, he heard a well known voice calling softly near by, "Joe, Joe, is that you?" It was John, lying there, shot through the breast. He warned his rescuer to be very cautious, as the rebel videttes were near. With much difficulty he got him back to our lines. This was the night of June 2d, and he died on the 4th.

I left the latter part of January to join the regiment, then camped at Bristoe Station, on the Orange and Alexandria Railroad. With me were two recruits for Company E, Abe Eshelman and Mike Coleman. The former was killed at Petersburg; the latter, a live Irishman, was mustered out at the close of the war, after a year and a half of valiant service for his adopted country. We went by Harrisburg, Baltimore, and Washington, thence by the Orange and Alexandria road, every mile historic ground, past Bull Run, where, the soldiers say, the dead would not stay buried, and finally we alight at Bristoe Station. On the right over there are the Bucktails; a little further toward the west the Second is camped. Over the hill toward Brentsville, past the artillery camp, is the Eleventh.

Here I found John Elliot, who had served with the regiment since its organization. He, brother William, and myself had been boy companions before the war, although I was younger than they. I went into the mess with him, S. L. Parker, and Benjamin Mushrush. After being with them but a short time, I was taken with that scourge of the army, measles, and was removed to the surgeon's tent. I was on picket when the disease made itself felt. The day and night on which I was on duty were stormy, rain and snow. As a result, I had a lively time of it. The disease left my voice so impaired that, for a long time, I was unable to speak above a whisper. During my stay at the surgeon's tent, I employed myself studying his books on surgery, and acquired a knowledge on the subject which was utilized at a later period.

John Elliot had enlisted April 25, 1861, although not mustered into the United States service until July 5th of the same year. He felt that he should be mustered out at the former date of 1864. As the time drew near, we conversed frequently on the subject, and he was in some perplexity as to duty in the case. The morning of the 25th found him on picket. I prepared the morning meal for the mess and then relieved him until he should breakfast. Soon he returned in a more than usually cheerful spirit. After chatting pleasantly for a time, he spoke of his term of enlistment. "I have that matter all arranged now," he said, "as far as I am concerned. I am not certain whether the government has a right to hold me any longer or not; but I will stay till it sees fit to discharge me. The country needs soldiers this Spring. I would like to visit home. It's been three years since I saw mother and the boys; but it's all right. God has kept me safely through all these battles, and I can trust him for time to come."

This was the substance of his language, his exact words, as near as I can remember. They are noble words; as grand as ever fell from the lips of Christian hero. Many a time afterward they were an inspiration to me. His face was bright that beautiful Spring morning with a joy that was not of earth. The night watches had been spent communing with God,—yes, face to face. Had he known that the midsummer sun would look down upon his grave, would his decision have been different? I think not. He knew too much of war and battles not to count the cost. From a Southern prison-pen his brave spirit went up to God.

⁓

April 29th we broke camp and proceeded to near Culpepper Court-house. Before leaving camp we sent our extra baggage, clothing, etc., to Washington, and, of course, never saw them again. During the night of May 3d we marched for the Rapidan, crossing at Germania Ford. The next evening we camped in order of battle near the Wilderness Tavern. The following morning the division moved out on a country road toward Robertson's Tavern. Passing through woods, we came to an open field, where line of battle was formed. The Bucktails were in front, skirmishing. We could see them on the ridge, and their occasional shouts and rapid firing showed that the battle had begun. For the first time I heard the whistle of the rifle ball, as a stray one now and then whistled over the line of battle.

After waiting thus for some time, we moved back some distance, in the direction from which we had come. Here I spoke a few words with John Elliot, the last we ever exchanged. In the confusion which followed he was made prisoner, and died at Andersonville.

Soon the noise of battle began to deepen in our front and at the right. Hurried orders were received; the line moved by the right flank, double-quick. The Seventh Regiment deployed and vanished into the woods, forward, and the Eleventh followed in line of battle. Moving on through the thick underbrush, the enemy was quickly encountered. Their first volley was deadly. A ball struck Boss M'Cullough in the forehead. He fell dead, a portion of his shattered brain lodging on the arm of John Stanley, a boy of seventeen, who had come to us during the Spring.

John shuddered, shook it from the sleeve of his blouse, raised his gun and began firing. Captain Jones, of Company A, White, of Company C, and many others, fell dead before this first volley. Soon it was discovered that the division was flanked. Our line was at right angles with the position in which the subsequent fighting took place. To crown all, the woods took fire, and soon the only problem that remained was to withdraw as quickly and safely as possible.

While this turmoil was progressing, to me so strange and bewildering, the surgeon, Dr. Lyon, came across me, and directed me to go to a certain point at the edge of the woods, east of the Wilderness Tavern, to help care for the wounded. Thither I made my way. As I passed on through the woods, I was soon out of reach of the bullets, which had been flying thick and fast. When I came to the open ground, I saw more clearly than ever the results of the battle, still going on in the woods beyond. The multitude of wounded and dying men crowded the road. Some were limping painfully along; others were being carried on stretchers, or helped along by comrades.

Reaching the designated place, I found the field tents erected, and all full of suffering men. I took charge of one in which were twenty-seven wounded, several amputations, and other bad cases. They lay with their heads toward the canvas, a narrow path being left between their feet. All that could be done for them was to give them food and water, bathe their wounds, and render any little service by which their sufferings might be mitigated. Their heroic patience astonished me. Men, torn and mangled, would utter no groan, nor give any vocal expression to the agonies which racked them, except sometimes when sleep or delirium found the overmastering will off guard.

Toward evening I learned that the regiment was just beyond the Wilderness Tavern; and, getting relieved for a short time, I started to go to them, as I had the extra coffee of the mess. As I came in sight, they moved hurriedly away toward the right, where the battle was raging fiercely. It was useless to follow, and I began to retrace my steps. Pausing a moment on an elevated knoll, I gazed on the strange scene that spread out before me.

From the right on the turnpike, a line, somewhat curved, extended a distance of three or four miles to the left. On the right the line was enveloped in woods, in which a terrific conflict was going on. Sedgwick's corps was standing between the army and disaster. In the center, on elevated ground, beyond some low woods, I could see a rebel line of battle, while the sharp fire of skirmishers in front showed that here the lines of blue and gray would soon smite together. Further toward the left, a line of blue extended along the edge of a narrow field, facing the woods just beyond, into which it poured incessant volleys, while the smoke that rose up from the woods showed that an active foe was there. Behind our line, flat on the ground, lay a second one. A tragedy, grandly, awfully sublime, was enacting before me.

A hundred thousand men were grappling in deadly conflict. While I gazed the line of battle slackened its fire; the second one rose from the ground; then both swept forward across the field and into the woods beyond, bearing the enemy before them. For a few moments there was silence, and then the struggle was renewed as fiercely as ever. I returned to the field-tents to go on with my work of mercy among the suffering.

As night drew on, the battle ceased, and the men lay down to sleep where they had fought, ready to renew the strife at the return of light. In the tents there, while the army beyond was resting, part of our nation's heroes continued the contest through the solemn hours of night. They fought with the giant Pain, and some of them went down into the dark valley, and close by the chill waters they faced the King of Terrors.

I slept none that night. As morning approached, I went to the edge of the little opening which had been cleared in the woods for the tents. While I stood here looking off toward the scene of yesterday's battle, the sound of a single rifle shot rang out on the air, then another and another, and then a deafening roar of musketry burst forth and raged along the whole line, continuing almost without interruption all day.

In the afternoon Lieutenant Boggs and David Steen were brought in wounded, the former by a rifle ball in the thigh, the latter severely bruised by a fragment of shell. He had been wounded at Gaines' Mill and Fredericksburg. After his return this time, I heard him say that he had come to have more dread of going into battle since he had been wounded so often. Still he never shrank from duty. He was killed the following August at Welden Railroad.

Here I saw the only instance of impatience on the part of a wounded man of which I have any recollection. A young fellow lay about the middle of the tent, wounded in the knee, a ball having cut the skin on one side without injuring the bone. His long legs were extended almost across the narrow path along which I was compelled to walk in passing from one to another. He was grumbling and complaining, demanding and receiving attentions in a gruff and uncivil manner. He would also mutter threatenings of what he would do should I hurt him in stepping over his crooked legs outstretched in my way. To all of this I paid no attention and signs of ill-nature continued. Finally, a bright young man opposite, whose leg was amputated at the thigh, raised himself on his elbow and proceeded to express his opinion of such conduct in language much more forcible than pious.

From this place we moved some distance to the left, where the tents were erected in an open field. Here an incident occurred which illustrates the false estimate placed upon the civilization of the North by the masses of the South. A wounded rebel, an intelligent-looking young man, was brought in from the field in an ambulance. We came with a stretcher to carry him into the tent. He looked at us with a frightened, helpless look, and asked:

"You won't hurt me, will you?"

I assured him we would be just as careful as possible. He seemed surprised to be treated with kindness, having been taught, evidently, that the Yankee invader was a barbarian. Removed to the tent, I examined his wound. A bullet had passed through the ankle joint, and the only remedy was amputation. He inquired how it was. It seemed hard to tell him that he must go through life maimed.

"That is a bad foot; but the surgeons will do the best they can for it. You may lose it." Some time after he was removed, I suppose to have his foot amputated, and I saw him no more.

The next move was to Spotsylvania. Grant had grappled with his enemy, intending to hold on "all Summer." The same spirit seemed to animate his army, from General Meade down to the latest recruit in the ranks. The lines of blue came out from the smoking underbrush of the Wilderness, their ranks torn and decimated, and closed in around the bristling batteries and rifle-pits of Spotsylvania with a relentless courage that was sublime.

Here the tents were pitched in a little, open lot, a house to the right as you faced the position where the fighting was in progress. The tents were not sufficient to contain the wounded, and they lay on the ground on the outside by thousands. Those long rows of suffering forms, gashed and mangled in every conceivable manner, told a dreadful tale of human wrath. That gallant division, the Reserves, had preserved their well-earned reputation for stubborn valor at a terrible cost. Their greatest loss was sustained in a single onset against the rebel position. The enemy was posted in strong rifle-pits, beyond a narrow strip of swamp. Orders were given to charge these works. The division moved forward. They had never failed in such an undertaking. Their charge had always pierced the enemy's line. This had been their record during three years of warfare. But men can not accomplish impossibilities. Baffled by the swamp, cut by the merciless fire that blazed out from the pits, they are driven back, rally, re-form and charge the second and third time, and then retire to the position from which they had come out.

The field-tents here were nearer the front than before. Bullets and an occasional shell whistled over us. My work was still the same, caring for the wounded, assisting the surgeon, or occasionally binding up a wound myself.

During the second day, while engaged at the farther end of the tent, I heard at the front a familiar voice. As soon as I was disengaged I went to the front end of the tent, eager to learn from whom the well-known voice proceeded. There lay a large, noble-looking young man, severely wounded in the thigh. He was conversing quietly with a wounded comrade by his side. Voice and face were as familiar as if heard and seen but yesterday. Puzzled and deeply interested, I did not speak, but proceeded to bathe his wound. While thus engaged, his eyes fell upon my face. Looking at me intently a moment, his face brightened, and he exclaimed:

"You are Rob M'Bride, aren't you?"

"Yes; and you are Billy Craig," was the immediate reply.

As soon as he pronounced my name, it all came to me in a moment. We had been school-mates at Courtney's School-house. He was then one of the "big boys," and I a lad of nine or ten. I had not seen him since. He was one of those large-hearted, royal souls that could find pleasure in little acts of kindness, that bound me to him very closely. He bore his sufferings with heroic fortitude. When the time came to remove the wounded, and they were being hurried away in ambulances and rough army wagons, I went to Dr. Lyon and told him of the case. He went with me to an ambulance and ordered room reserved in it for him. I then had him carried to it, made him as comfortable as possible, bade him good-bye and God speed, and saw him no more on earth. He died from his wound some time in June.

—◦—

May 11th, Lewis Grossman, of Company C, was brought in, terribly wounded by a shell. One arm and leg were crushed, and he was otherwise bruised. I did not see him until after the arm and leg were amputated. He was a young man of great physical endurance, or he would never have rallied from the shock. He was as pale as a corpse when first brought into the tent, but rallied in a little while, and was able to take some refreshment. When left to himself his mind wandered, and he would talk as if he were engaged in the quiet pursuits of peace. Unless prevented, he would remove the bandages from the stumps of his amputated limbs. When spoken to, however, he would refrain from this, and talk rationally of the present circumstances. Dr. Lyon finally told me to give my attention entirely to him. This I did until he was sent away. He told me how his wound was received. He was in front, skirmishing. He was in the road in front of a rebel battery, and in the act of loading his gun. Perceiving they were about to fire, he still delayed a moment, thinking to get in another shot before leaping to the shelter of a large tree that stood near. It was a costly delay.

The shell came screaming toward him, burst, and dashed him stunned and mangled to the ground. As he concluded this narrative, he added, with the utmost seriousness: "But they haven't made much off me, after all. I've peppered them in almost every battle the Potomac army has fought since the war began."

He got along finely, and there seemed every prospect of recovery. When some of the boys called on him at Washington, on their way home in June, he requested them to say nothing to his friends about the extent of his wounds. But from some cause—perhaps gangrene—he died August 3d, and is buried in the National Cemetery at Arlington.

Nearly opposite Lewis lay a young man of very fine face and attractive appearance. He was mortally wounded. Most of the time his sufferings were very great, but no earthly skill could bring any relief. As death drew on, his mind wandered. He was fighting his battles over again. He was not the poor, crushed mortality that lay here. His spirit was over yonder, where the cannon's sullen roar and the awful din of musketry, the cheers of the struggling combatants, told of a deadly strife.

Sometimes he was distressed and troubled, sometimes exultant. Anon his face would light up with the strange fire of battle, and he would raise his arm and cheer. Once he said quite distinctly: "Here is a chance for a brave man." Later he became calm, and quietly fell asleep, to wake no more on earth till the great day of God.

One of the Bucktail Regiment lay on the ground in front of the tent, shot through the chest. He was, perhaps, twenty-five years of age, large and well-formed, his face stamped with the marks of intelligence. While engaged near him, I saw another of that band of heroes coming toward him with great strides, an expression of anguish on his face which I can not forget. He threw himself on his knees by the wounded man, kissed him, then covered his face with his hands, and his great manly form shook with convulsive sobbings. Tears trickled down the cheeks of the other. Not a word was spoken until, after a while, the storm of emotion had passed. Then they conversed calmly for a while, and parted with the quiet dignity of brave men who say farewell while the shadow of death lies dark around them.

A man was brought in shot through both thighs. I did not know his name, but had heard his voice among the worshipers in the church-tent at Bristoe Station, and knew that he was a man of God. After a brief examination, the surgeon announced that amputation would be necessary.

"Very well, doctor; get around to it as quick as you can. I suffer terribly."

Another was shot in the thigh, the bone shattered to the hip. When told that the limb must be amputated he objected.

"But you will die if it is not done."

"I can't help that; it shall not be amputated with my consent."

Within twenty-four hours he was dead. Whether wise in his decision or not, he met the result without flinching or complaint.

A boy with his arm torn off by a shell expressed his only complaint in the words, "I never can fight any more."

One evening, worn out by constant labor and watching, I lay down in a vacant place in the tent, from which a dead soldier had been removed, to find rest for mind and body in sleep. As I lay there thinking of the dreadful scenes around me, of the wounded and dying here, the dead just over yonder, I began to wonder what would be the sensations of a man shot in the brain. Suddenly there came a shock, as if the whole machinery of life had stopped at once. How long a time elapsed before consciousness was resumed I do not know; the interval may have been momentary; but as a dim sense of being stole over me again, I was quite convinced that a stray shot had struck me in the head. Rousing myself, I deliberately felt my head, to learn the exact state of things. To my surprise and gratification, I found every thing in due order. I leave it to those who are skilled in the mysteries of the nervous system to explain the phenomenon; but you must allow me to believe that I know something of what it is to be shot in the head.

The time arrived, at length, when the field hospitals must be moved because of the changed position of the army. A heavy rain began on the 11th, and continued for some days, making the roads almost impassable. The wounded that remained were removed as speedily and as mercifully as possible. Some had to be left behind. Nurses were detailed to remain with them. As night came on, every thing was in readiness, and the rest of us were directed to take our departure without delay. Two of us started together after dark. We made our way through the mud and intense darkness about twenty rods, to the edge of a wood. We resolved to go no further, come what might. Doubling myself up at the root of an old stump, I was soon oblivious to both rain and danger. Just as day was breaking, I awoke, and arousing my companion, we hastened away.

This closed my experience in the hospital.

Chapter 2

A Confederate Soldier Speaks His Mind
By Carlton McCarthy

The fortitude and bravery of Confederate soldiers—from officers to privates—has been well documented in many accounts. Less often seen in print are stories that reveal the mind-set of the men in gray. What were they thinking? What motivated them and sustained them through years of desperate struggles. Some of the answers to those questions are provided by the book Detailed Minutiae of Soldier Life in the Army of Northern Virginia, 1861–1865, *by Carlton McCarthy. This excerpt, and others in some chapters that follow, provide a rare insight into the thinking of the rebel soldiers who defied a nation.*

—Lamar Underwood

We are familiar with the names and deeds of the "generals," from the commander-in-chief down to the almost innumerable brigadiers, and we are all more or less ignorant of the habits and characteristics of the individuals who composed the rank and file of the "grand armies" of 1861–65.

As time rolls on, the historian, condensing matters, mentions "the men" by brigades, divisions, and corps. But here let us look at the individual soldier separated from the huge masses of men composing the armies, and doing his own work and duty.

The fame of Lee and Jackson, world-wide, and as the years increase ever brighter, is but condensed and personified admiration of the Confederate soldier, wrung from an unwilling world by his matchless courage, endurance, and devotion. Their fame is an everlasting monument to the mighty deeds of the nameless host who followed them through so much toil and blood to glorious victories.

The weak, as a rule, are borne down by the strong; but that does not prove that the strong are also the right. The weak suffer wrong, learn the bitterness of it, and finally, by resisting it, become the defenders of right and justice. When the mighty nations of the earth oppress the feeble, they nerve the arms and fire the hearts of God's instruments for the restoration of justice; and when one section of a country oppresses and insults another, the result is the pervasive malady—war! which will work out the health of the nation, or leave it a bloody corpse.

The principles for which the Confederate soldier fought, and in defense of which he died, are to-day the harmony of this country. So long as they were held in abeyance, the country was in turmoil and on the verge of ruin.

It is not fair to demand a reason for actions above reason. The heart is greater than the mind. No man can exactly define the cause for which the Confederate soldier fought. He was above human reason and above human law, secure in his own rectitude of purpose, accountable to God only, having assumed for himself a "nationality," which he was minded to defend with his life and his property, and thereto pledged his sacred honor.

In the honesty and simplicity of his heart, the Confederate soldier had neglected his own interests and rights, until his accumulated wrongs and indignities forced him to one grand, prolonged effort to free himself from the pain of them. He dared not refuse to hear the call to arms, so plain was the duty and so urgent the call. His brethren and friends were answering the bugle-call and the roll of the drum. To stay was dishonor and shame!

He would not obey the dictates of tyranny. To disobey was death. He disobeyed and fought for his life. The romance of war charmed him, and he hurried from the embrace of his mother to the embrace of death. His playmates, his friends, and his associates were gone; he was lonesome, and he sought a reunion "in camp." He would not receive as gospel the dogmas of fanatics, and so he became a "rebel." Being a rebel, he must be punished. Being punished, he resisted. Resisting, he died.

The Confederate soldier opposed immense odds. If the Confederate soldier had then had only this disparity of numbers to contend with, he would have driven every invader from the soil of Virginia.

But the Confederate soldier fought, in addition to these odds, the facilities for the transportation and concentration of troops and supplies afforded by the network of railways in the country north of him, all of which were subject to the control of the government, and backed by a treasury which was turning out money by the ton, one dollar of which was equal to sixty Confederate dollars.

It should be remembered also that, while the South was restricted to its own territory for supplies, and its own people for men, the North drew on the world for material, and on every nation of the earth for men.

The arms and ammunition of the Federal soldiers were abundant and good—so abundant and so good that they supplied *both* armies, and were greatly preferred by Confederate officers. The equipment of the Federal armies was well-nigh perfect. The facilities for manufacture were simply unlimited, and the nation thought no expenditure of treasure too great, if only the country, the *Union!* could be saved. The factory and the foundry chimneys made a pillar of smoke by day and of fire by night. The latest improvements were hurried to the front, and adopted by both armies almost simultaneously; for hardly had the Federal bought, when the Confederate captured, and used, the *very latest*.

Commissary stores were piled up all over Virginia, for the use of the invading armies. They had more than they could protect, and their loss was gain to the hungry defenders of the soil.

The Confederate soldier fought a host of ills occasioned by the deprivation of chloroform and morphia, which were excluded from the Confederacy, by the blockade, as contraband of war. The man who has submitted to amputation without chloroform, or tossed on a couch of agony for a night and a day without sleep for the want of a dose of morphia, may possibly be able to estimate the advantages which resulted from the possession by the Federal surgeons of an unlimited supply of these.

The Confederate soldier fought bounties and regular monthly pay; the "Stars and Stripes," the "Star Spangled Banner," "Hail Columbia," "Tramp, Tramp, Tramp," "John Brown's Body," "Rally 'round the Flag," and all the fury and fanaticism which skilled minds could create—opposing this grand array with the modest and homely refrain of "Dixie," supported by a mild solution of "Maryland, My Maryland." He fought good wagons, fat horses, and tons of quartermaster's stores; pontoon trains, of splendid material and construction, by the mile; gunboats, wooden and iron, and men-of-war; illustrated papers, to cheer the "Boys in Blue" with sketches of the glorious deeds they did not do; Bibles by the car load, and tracts by the million—the first to prepare them for death, and the second to urge upon them the duty of dying.

The Confederate soldier fought the "Sanitary Commission," whose members, armed with every facility and convenience, quickly carried the sick and wounded of the Federal army to comfortable quarters, removed the bloody garments, laid the sufferer on a clean and dry couch, clothed him in clean things, and fed him on the best the world could afford and money buy.

He fought the well-built, thoroughly equipped ambulances, the countless surgeons, nurses, and hospital stewards, and the best surgical appliances known to the medical world. He fought the commerce of the United States and all the facilities for war which Europe could supply, while his own ports were closed to all the world. He fought the trained army officers and the regular troops of the United States Army, assisted by splendid native volunteer soldiers, besides swarms of men, the refuse of the earth—Portuguese, Spanish, Italian, German, Irish, Scotch, English, French, Chinese, Japanese—white, black, olive, and brown. He laid down life for life with this hireling host, who died for pay, mourned by no one, missed by no one, loved by no one; who were better fed and clothed, fatter, happier, and more contented in the army than ever they were at home, and whose graves strew the earth in lonesome places, where none go to weep. When one of these fell, two could be bought to fill the gap. The Confederate soldier killed these without compunction, and their comrades buried them without a tear.

The Confederate soldier fought the cries of distress which came from his home—tales of woe, want, insult, and robbery. He fought men who knew that *their* homes (when they had any) were safe, their wives and children, their parents and sisters, sheltered, and their business affairs more than usually prosperous; who could draw sight drafts, have them honored, and make the camp table as bountiful and luxurious as that of a New York hotel. He fought a government founded by the genius of his fathers, which derived its strength from principles they formulated, and which persuaded its soldiers that they were the champions of the constitutional liberty which they were marching to invade, and eventually to destroy.

The relative strength of armies becomes a matter of secondary importance when these facts are considered. The disparity of numbers only would never have produced the result which the combination of these various forces did—the surrender of the Army of Northern Virginia.

The Confederate soldier was purely patriotic. He foresaw clearly, and deliberately chose, the trials which he endured. He was an individual who could not become the indefinite portion of a mass, but fought for himself, on his own account. He was a self-sacrificing hero, but did not claim that distinction or any merit, feeling only that he was in the line of duty to self, country, and God. He fought for a principle, and needed neither driving nor urging, but was eager and determined to fight. He was not a politic man, but a man under fervent feeling, forgetful of the possibilities and calamities of war, pressing his claims to the rights of humanity.

The Confederate soldier was a monomaniac for four years. His mania was the independence of the Confederates States of America, secured by force of arms.

The Confederate soldier was a venerable old man, a youth, a child, a preacher, a farmer, merchant, student, statesman, orator, father, brother, husband, son—the wonder of the world, the terror of his foes!

If the peace of this country can only be preserved by forgetting the Confederate soldier's deeds and his claims upon the South, the blessing is too dearly bought. We have sworn to be grateful to him. Dying, his head pillowed on the bosom of his mother, Virginia, he heard that his name would be honored.

When we fill up, hurriedly, the bloody chasm opened by war, we should be careful that we do not bury therein many noble deeds, some tender memories, some grand examples, and some hearty promises washed with tears.

CHAPTER 3

America's Deadliest Day: One Officer's Story

By Frederick L. Hitchcock

"The air was full of whizzing, singing, buzzing bullets. Once down on the ground under cover of the hill, it required very strong resolution to get up where these missiles of death were flying so thickly, yet that was the duty of us officers, especially us of the field and staff." That vivid description from Frederick L. Hitchcock's book War from the Inside *is but a glimpse of the horrors of battle that took place in the single bloodiest day in American history. Unlike Gettysburg, which lasted three days, Antietam—or "Sharpsburg" as the Confederates called it—took place in a single day. On September 17, 1862, Union forces under General George McClellan had the opportunity to surround and destroy the army of Robert E. Lee at this small Maryland town and nearby Antietam Creek. Although fighting hard, with a horrific loss of life, the Union forces on the field held too much strength in reserve, with the result that Lee's Army of Northern Virginia escaped. As with the Union army, Lee's forces sustained massive dead and wounded, but escaped to fight again. Later, General McClellan was relived of command by President Abraham Lincoln.*

—LAMAR UNDERWOOD

I WAS APPOINTED ADJUTANT OF THE ONE HUNDRED AND THIRTY-SECOND REGIMENT, Pennsylvania Volunteers, by our great war Governor, Andrew G. Curtin, at the solicitation of Colonel Richard A. Oakford, commanding the regiment, my commission dating the 22d day of August, 1862. I reported for duty to Colonel Oakford at Camp Whipple, where the regiment was then encamped, on the 3d day of September, 1862. This was immediately following the disasters of "Chantilly" and "Second Bull Run," and as I passed through Washington to Camp Whipple, I found the greatest excitement prevailing because of these reverses, and a general apprehension for the safety of the capital in consequence. The wildest rumors were abroad concerning the approach of the victorious rebel troops, and an alarm amounting almost to a panic existed. Being without a horse or other means of transportation, I was obliged to make my way, valise in hand, on foot from Washington over the "long bridge" across the Potomac, to Camp Whipple, some two miles up the river nearly opposite Georgetown. From the wild rumors floating about Washington, I did not know but I should be captured bag and baggage before reaching camp. Undertaking this trip under those circumstances, I think, required almost as much nerve as "real work" did later on.

Getting beyond the long bridge there were abundant evidences of the reported disasters. Straggling troops, army wagons, etc., were pouring in from the "front" in great disorder.

I was assigned quarters, and a copy of the daily routine orders of camp was placed in my hands, and my attention specially called to the fact that the next "order of business" was "dress parade" at six o'clock. I inquired the cause of this special notice to me, and was informed that I was expected to officiate as adjutant of the regiment at that ceremony. I pleaded with the colonel to be allowed a day or so in camp to see how things were done before undertaking such difficult and important duties; that I knew absolutely nothing about any part of military service; had never served a day in any kind of military work, except in a country fire company; had never seen a dress parade of a full regiment in my life, and knew nothing whatever about the duties of an adjutant.

My pleadings were all in vain. The only reply I received was a copy of the "Army Regulations," with the remark that I had two hours in which to study up and master the details of dress parade, and that I could not learn my duties any easier nor better than by actual practice; that my condition was no different from that of my fellow officers; that we were all there in a camp of instruction learning our duties, and there was not a moment to lose. I then began to realize something of the magnitude of the task which lay before me. To do difficult things, without knowing how; that is, to learn how in the doing, was the universal task of the Union volunteer officer.

I took up my "Army Regulations" and attacked the ceremony of dress parade as a life and death matter. Before my two hours were ended, I could repeat every sentence of the ceremony verbatim, and felt that I had mastered the thing, and was not going to my execution in undertaking my duties as adjutant. Alas for the frailty of memory; it failed me at the crucial moment, and I made a miserable spectacle of myself before a thousand officers and men, many of them old friends and acquaintances, all of whom, it seemed to me, were specially assembled on that occasion to witness my début, and see me get "balled up." They were not disappointed. Things tactically impossible were freely done during that ceremony.

Looking back now upon that scene, from the long distance of forty years, I see a green country boy undertaking to handle one thousand men in the always difficult ceremony of a dress parade. (I once heard Governor Hartranft, who attained the rank of a major-general during the war, remark, as he witnessed this ceremony, that he had seen thousands of such parades, and among them all, only one that he considered absolutely faultless.) I wonder now that we got through it at all. Think of standing to give your first command at the right of a line of men five hundred abreast, that is, nearly one thousand feet in length, and trying to make the men farthest away hear your small, unused, and untrained voice. I now can fully forgive my failure. The officers and men were considerate of me, however, and, knowing what was to be done, went through with it after a fashion in spite of my blunders.

Another feature is the utter change in one's individual liberty. To be no longer the arbiter of your own time and movements, but to have it rubbed into you at every turn that you are a very small part of an immense machine, whose business is to march and fight; that your every movement is under the control of your superior officers; that, in fact, you have no will of your own that can be exercised; that your individuality is for the time sunk, is a trial to an American freeman which patriotism alone can overcome. Not the least feature of this transition is the practical obliteration of the Lord's day. This is a great shock to a Christian who has learned to love the Lord's day and its hallowed associations. Routine duty, the march, the fighting, all go right on, nothing stops for Sunday.

On Saturday, September 6, we received orders to join the Army of the Potomac— again under the command of "Little Mac"—at Rockville, Md., distant about eighteen miles. [Reference to General George McCellan] This was our first march. The day was excessively hot, and Colonel Oakford received permission to march in the evening. We broke camp about six o'clock P.M. It was a lovely moonlight night, the road was excellent, and for the first six miles the march was a delight. We marched quite leisurely, not making over two miles an hour, including rests, nevertheless the last half of the distance was very tiresome, owing to the raw and unseasoned condition of our men, and the heavy load they were carrying. We reached the bivouac of the grand Army of the Potomac, of which we were henceforth to be a part, at about three o'clock the next morning. Three miles out from the main camp we encountered the outpost of the picket line and were duly halted. The picket officer had been informed of our coming, and so detained us only long enough to satisfy himself that we were all right.

Here we encountered actual conditions of war with all its paraphernalia for the first time. Up to this time we had been playing at war, so to speak, in a camp of instruction. Now we were entering upon the thing itself, with all its gruesome accessories. Everything here was business, and awful business, too. Here were parks of artillery quiet enough just now, but their throats will speak soon enough, and when they do it will not be the harmless booming of Fourth of July celebrations. Here we pass a bivouac of cavalry, and yonder on either side the road, in long lines of masses, spread out like wide swaths of grain, lie the infantry behind long rows of stacked guns. Here were upward of seventy-five thousand men, all, except the cordon of pickets, sound asleep. In the midst of this mighty host the stillness was that of a graveyard; it seemed almost oppressive.

Halting the regiment, Colonel Oakford and I made our way to the head-quarters of Major-General Sumner, commanding the Second Army Corps, to whom the colonel was ordered to report. We finally found him asleep in his head-quarters wagon. A tap on the canvas top of the wagon quickly brought the response, "Hello! Who's there? What's wanted?"

Colonel Oakford replied, giving his name and rank, and that his regiment was here to report to him, according to orders.

"Oh, yes, colonel, that is right," replied the general. "How many men have you?"

Receiving the colonel's answer, General Sumner said: "I wish you had ten times as many, for we need you badly. Glad you are here, colonel. Make yourselves as comfortable as you can for the rest of the night, and I will assign you to your brigade in the morning."

Here was a cordial reception and hospitality galore. "Make yourselves comfortable"—in Hotel "Dame Nature!" Well, we were all weary enough to accept the hospitality. We turned into the adjacent field, "stacked arms," and in a jiffy were rolled up in our blankets and sound asleep. The mattresses supplied by Madame Nature were rather hard, but her rooms were fresh and airy, and the ceilings studded with the stars of glory. My last waking vision that night was a knowing wink from Jupiter and Mars, as much as to say, "sleep sweetly, we are here."

An interesting feature of the issue of rations was the method of supplying the fresh beef. Live cattle were driven to the army and issued alive to the several corps, from which details were made of men who had been butchers, who killed and dressed the beef. The animals were driven into an enclosure and expert marksmen shot them down as wanted. This seemed cruel work, but it was well done; the animal being hit usually at the base of its horns, death was instantaneous. This fresh meat, which we got but seldom after the march began, was cooked and eaten the day it was issued. Enough for one day was all that was issued at a time, and this, after the non-eatable portions had been eliminated, did not overburden the men.

The hard bread was a square cracker about the size of an ordinary soda cracker, only thicker, and very hard and dry. It was supposed to be of the same quality as sea biscuit or pilot bread, but I never saw any equal to that article. The salt pork was usually good for pork, but it was a great trial to us all to come down to camp fare, "hardtack and pork." Sometimes the "hardtack" was very old and poor. I have seen many a one placed in the palm of the hand, a smart blow, a puff of breath . . . a handful of "squirmers"—the boys' illustration of a "full hand." It came to be the rule to eat in daylight for protection against the unknown quantity in the hardtack. If we had to eat in the dark, after a prolonged march, our protection then lay in breaking our cracker into a cup of boiling coffee, stir it well and then flow enough of the coffee over to carry off most of the strangers and take the balance on faith.

On the march each man carried his own rations in haversacks. These were made of canvas and contained pockets for salt, sugar and coffee, besides room for about two days' rations of hard bread and pork. Sometimes five, six, and seven days' rations were issued, then the balance had to be stowed away in knapsacks and pockets of the clothing. When, as was usual in the latter cases, there was also issued sixty to one hundred rounds of ammunition, the man became a veritable pack-mule.

For the first month many of our men went hungry. Having enormous appetites consequent upon this new and most strenuous mode of life, they would eat their five days' supply in two or three, and then have to "skirmish" or go hungry until the next supply was issued. Most, however, soon learned the necessity as well as the benefit of restricting their appetites to the supply. But there were always some improvident ones, who never had a supply ahead, but were always in straights for grub. They were ready to black boots, clean guns, in fact, do any sort of menial work for their comrades for a snack to eat. Their improvidence made them the drudges of the company.

Whatever may be said about other portions of the rations, the coffee was always good. I never saw any poor coffee, and it was a blessing it was so, for it became the soldiers' solace and stay, in camp, on picket and on the march. Tired, footsore, and dusty from the march, or wet and cold on picket, or homesick and shivering in camp, there were rest and comfort and new life in a cup of hot coffee. We could not always have it on picket nor on the march. To make a cup of coffee two things were necessary besides the coffee, namely, water and fire, both frequently very difficult to obtain. On picket, water was generally plentiful, but in the immediate presence of the enemy, fire was forbidden, for obvious reasons. On the march both were usually scarce, as I shall show later on.

How was our coffee made? Each man was provided with a pint tin cup. As much coffee as could comfortably be lifted from the haversack by the thumb and two fingers—depending somewhat on the supply—was placed in the cup, which was filled about three-fourths full of water, to leave room for boiling. It was then placed upon some live coals and brought to a boil, being well stirred in the meantime to get the strength of the coffee. A little cold water was then added to settle it. Eggs, gelatin, or other notions of civilization, for settling, were studiously omitted. Sometimes sugar was added, but most of the men, especially the old vets, took it straight. It was astonishing how many of the "wrinkles of grim visaged war" were temporarily smoothed out by a cup of coffee. This was the mainstay of our meals on the march, a cup of coffee and a thin slice of raw pork between two hardtacks frequently constituting a meal. Extras fell in the way once in a while. Chickens have been known to stray into camp, the result of a night's foraging.

The army mule has been much caricatured, satirized, and abused, but the soldier had no more faithful or indispensable servant than this same patient, plodding, hard-pulling, long-eared fellow of the roomy voice and nimble heels. The "boys" told a story which may illustrate the mule's education. A "tenderfoot" driver had gotten his team stalled in a mud hole, and by no amount of persuasion could he get them to budge an inch. Helpers at the wheels and new hands on the lines were all to no purpose. A typical army bummer had been eying the scene with contemptuous silence. Finally he cut loose:

"Say! You 'uns dunno the mule language. Ye dunno the dilec. Let a perfesser in there."

He was promptly given the job. He doffed cap and blouse, marched up to those mules as if he weighed a ton and commanded the army. Clearing away the crowd, he seized the leader's line, and distending his lungs, he shot out in a voice that could have been heard a mile a series of whoops, oaths, adjectives, and billingsgate that would have silenced the proverbial London fish vender. The mules recognized the "dilec" at once, pricked up their ears and took the load out in a jiffy.

"Ye see, gents, them ar mules is used to workin' with a perfesser."

We are bound northward through Maryland, the vets tell us, on a chase after the rebs. The army marches in three and four parallel columns, usually each corps in a column by itself, and distant from the other columns equal to about its length in line of battle, say a half to three-fourths of a mile. Roads were utilized as far as practicable, but generally were left to the artillery and the wagon trains, whilst the infantry made roads for themselves directly through the fields.

The whole army marches surrounded by "advance and rear guards," and "flankers," to prevent surprise. Each column is headed by a corps of pioneers who, in addition to their arms, are provided with axes, picks and shovels, with the latter stone walls and fences are levelled sufficiently to permit the troops to pass, and ditches and other obstructions covered and removed. It is interesting to see how quickly this corps will dispose of an ordinary stone wall or rail fence. They go down so quickly that they hardly seem to pause in their march.

We learn that the Johnnies are only a couple of days ahead of us. That they marched rapidly and were on their good behavior, all marauding being forbidden, and they were singing a new song, entitled "My Maryland," thus trying to woo this loyal border State over to the Confederacy. We were told that Lee hung two soldiers for stealing chickens and fruit just before they entered Frederick City.

Much could be written about the discomforts of these marches, the chief of which was the dust more than the heat and the fatigue. No rain had fallen for some time, and the roads and the fields through which we passed were powdered into fine dust, which arose in almost suffocating clouds, so that mouth, lungs, eyes, and ears were filled with it. Sometimes it became so dense that men could not be seen a dozen yards away. The different regiments took turns in heading the columns. There was comparative comfort at the head, but there were so many regiments that during the whole campaign our regiment enjoyed this privilege but once.

Another feature of the march was the inability to satisfy thirst. The dust and heat no doubt produced an abnormal thirst which water did not seem to satisfy. The water we could get was always warm, and generally muddy and filthy. The latter was caused by the multitude of men using the little streams, springs, or wells. Either of these, ordinarily abundant for many more than ever used them, were hardly a cup full apiece for a great army. Hence many a scrimmage took place for the first dash at a cool well or spring.

On our second or third day's march, such a scrap took place between the advanced columns for a well, and in the melee one man was accidentally pushed down into it, head first, and killed. He belonged to one of the Connecticut regiments, I was told. We passed by the well, and were unable to get water, because a dead soldier lay at the bottom of it. His regiment probably got his body out, but we had to march on without stopping to learn whether they did or not.

The problem of water for our army we found to be a troublesome one. Immediately we halted, much of our rest would be taken up in efforts to get water. We lost no opportunity to fill our canteens. Arriving in bivouac for the night, the first thing was a detail to fill canteens and camp kettles for supper coffee. We always bivouacked near a stream, if possible. But, then, so many men wanting it soon roiled it for miles, so that our details often had to follow the stream up three and four miles before they could get clean water. This may seem a strong statement, but if one will stop a moment and think of the effect upon even a good-sized stream, of a hundred thousand men, besides horses and mules, all wanting it for drinking, cooking, washing, and bathing (both the latter as peremptory needs as the former), he will see that the statement is no exaggeration.

The officers at this time experienced difficulty in getting food to eat. The men were supplied with rations and forced to carry them, but rations were not issued to officers—though they might purchase of the commissary such as the men had, when there was a supply. The latter were supposed to provide their own mess, for which purpose their mess-kits were transported in a wagon supplied to each regiment. The field and staff usually made one mess, and the line or company officers another. Sometimes the latter messed with their own men, carrying their rations along on the march the same as the men. This was discouraged by the government, but it proved the only way to be sure of food when needed, and was later on generally adopted.

We had plenty of food with our mess-kit and cook, but on the march, and especially in the presence of the enemy, our wagons could never get within reach of us. Indeed, when we bivouacked, they were generally from eight to ten miles away. The result was we often went hungry, unless we were able to pick up a meal at a farm-house—which seldom occurred, for the reason that most of these farmers were rebel sympathizers and would not feed us "Yanks," or they would be either sold out, or stolen out, of food. The tale generally told was, "You 'uns has stolen all we 'uns had." This accounts for the entry in my diary that the next morning I marched without breakfast, but got a good bath in the Monocacy—near which we encamped—in place of it. I got a "hardtack" and bit of raw pork about 10 A.M.

An interesting feature of our first two days' march was the clearing out of knapsacks to reduce the load. Naturally each man was loaded with extras of various sorts, knicknacks of all varieties, but mostly supposed necessaries of camp life, put in by loving hands at home, a salve for this, a medicine for that, a keepsake from one and another, some the dearest of earth's treasures, each insignificant in itself, yet all taking room and adding weight to over-burdened shoulders. At the mid-day halt, on the first day knapsacks being off for rest, they came open and the sorting began. It was sad, yet comical withal, to notice the things that went out. The most bulky and least treasured went first.

At the second halting, an hour later, still another sorting was made. The sun was hot and the knapsack was heavy. After the second day's march, those knapsacks contained little but what the soldier was compelled to carry, his rations, extra ammunition, and clothing. Were these home treasures lost? Oh, no! Not one. Our friends, the vets, gathered them all in as a rich harvest. They had been there themselves, and knowing what was coming, were on hand to gather the plums as they fell. The only difference was that another mother's or sweetheart's "boy" got the treasures.

On our third day's march we were halted for rest, when an orderly rode through the lines saying to the different colonels, "General McClellan will pass this way in ten minutes." This meant that we were to be ready to cheer "Little Mac" when he came along, which, of course, we all did.

Many of the old vets, who had been with him on the Peninsula, and now greeted him again after his reinstatement, were very enthusiastic. But notwithstanding their demonstrations, they rather negatived their praises by the remark, "No fight to-day; Little Mac has gone to the front." "Look out for a fight when he goes to the rear." On the other hand, they said when "Old Man Sumner"—our corps commander—"goes to the front, look out for a fight."

Never did day open more beautiful. We were astir at the first streak of dawn. We had slept, and soundly too, just where nightfall found us under the shelter of the hill near Keedysville. No reveille call this morning. Too close to the enemy. Nor was this needed to arouse us. A simple call of a sergeant or corporal and every man was instantly awake and alert. All realized that there was ugly business and plenty of it just ahead. This was plainly visible in the faces as well as in the nervous, subdued demeanor of all. The absence of all joking and play and the almost painful sobriety of action, where jollity had been the rule, was particularly noticeable.

Before proceeding with the events of the battle, I should speak of the "night before the battle," of which so much has been said and written. My diary says that Lieutenant-Colonel Wilcox, Captain James Archbald, Co. I, and I slept together, sharing our blankets; that it rained during the night; this fact, with the other, that we were close friends at home, accounts for our sharing blankets. Three of us with our gum blankets could so arrange as to keep fairly dry, notwithstanding the rain.

The camp was ominously still this night. We were not allowed to sing or make any noise, nor have any fires—except just enough to make coffee—for fear of attracting the fire of the enemies' batteries. But there was no need of such an inhibition as to singing or frolicking, for there was no disposition to indulge in either. Unquestionably, the problems of the morrow were occupying all breasts. Letters were written home—many of them "last words"—and quiet talks were had, and promises made between comrades. Promises providing against the dreaded possibilities of the morrow. "If the worst happens, Jack." "Yes, Ned, send word to mother and to, and these; she will prize them," and so directions were interchanged that meant so much.

I can never forget the quiet words of Colonel Oakford, as he inquired very particularly if my roster of the officers and men of the regiment was complete, for, said he, with a smile, "We shall not all be here to-morrow night."

Now to resume the story of the battle. We were on the march about six o'clock and moved, as I thought, rather leisurely for upwards of two miles, crossing Antietam creek, which our men waded nearly waist deep, emerging, of course, soaked through, our first experience of this kind. It was a hot morning and, therefore, the only ill effects of this wading was the discomfort to the men of marching with soaked feet. It was now quite evident that a great battle was in progress. A deafening pandemonium of cannonading, with shrieking and bursting shells, filled the air beyond us, towards which we were marching. An occasional shell whizzed by or over, reminding us that we were rapidly approaching the "debatable ground."

Soon we began to hear a most ominous sound which we had never before heard, except in the far distance at South Mountain, namely, the rattle of musketry. It had none of the deafening bluster of the cannonading so terrifying to new troops, but to those who had once experienced its effect, it was infinitely more to be dreaded. The fatalities by musketry at close quarters, as the two armies fought at Antietam and all through the Civil War, as compared with those by artillery, are at least as 100 to 1, probably much more than that.

These volleys of musketry we were approaching sounded in the distance like the rapid pouring of shot upon a tinpan, or the tearing of heavy canvas, with slight pauses interspersed with single shots, or desultory shooting. All this presaged fearful work in store for us, with what results to each personally the future, measured probably by moments, would reveal.

How does one feel under such conditions? To tell the truth, I realized the situation most keenly and felt very uncomfortable. Lest there might be some undue manifestation of this feeling in my conduct, I said to myself, this is the duty I undertook to perform for my country, and now I'll do it, and leave the results with God. My greater fear was not that I might be killed, but that I might be grievously wounded and left a victim of suffering on the field.

The nervous strain was plainly visible upon all of us. All moved doggedly forward in obedience to orders, in absolute silence so far as talking was concerned. The compressed lip and set teeth showed that nerve and resolution had been summoned to the discharge of duty. A few temporarily fell out, unable to endure the nervous strain, which was simply awful. There were a few others, it must be said, who skulked, took counsel of their cowardly legs, and, despite all efforts of "file closers" and officers, left the ranks. Of these two classes most of the first rejoined us later on, and their dropping out was no reflection on their bravery. The nervous strain produced by the excitement and danger gave them the malady called by the vets, the "cannon quickstep."

On our way into "position" we passed the "Meyer Spring," a magnificent fountain of sweet spring water. It was walled in, and must have been ten or twelve feet square and at least three feet deep, and a stream was flowing from it large enough to make a respectable brook. Many of us succeeded in filling our canteens from this glorious spring, now surrounded by hundreds of wounded soldiers. What a Godsend it was to those poor fellows.

About eight o'clock we were formed into line of battle and moved forward through a grove of trees but before actually coming under musketry fire of the enemy we were moved back again, and swung around nearly a mile to the left to the base of a circular knoll to the left of the Roulette farm-house and the road which leads up to the Sharpsburg pike, near the Dunkard church. The famous "sunken road"—a road which had been cut through the other side of this knoll—extended from the Roulette Lane directly in front of our line towards Sharpsburg. I had ridden by the side of Colonel Oakford, except when on duty, up and down the column, and as the line was formed by the colonel and ordered forward, we dismounted and sent our horses to the rear by a servant. I was immediately sent by the colonel to the left of the line to assist in getting that into position. A rail fence separated us from the top of the knoll. Bullets were whizzing and singing by our ears, but so far hitting none where I was. Over the fence and up the knoll in an excellent line we went. In the center of the knoll, perhaps a third of the way up, was a large tree, and under and around this tree lay a body of troops doing nothing. They were in our way, but our orders were forward, and through and over them we went.

Reaching the top of the knoll we were met by a terrific volley from the rebels in the sunken road down the other side, not more than one hundred yards away, and also from another rebel line in a corn-field just beyond. Some of our men were killed and wounded by this volley. We were ordered to lie down just under the top of the hill and crawl forward and fire over, each man crawling back, reloading his piece in this prone position and again crawling forward and firing. These tactics undoubtedly saved us many lives, for the fire of the two lines in front of us was terrific. The air was full of whizzing, singing, buzzing bullets. Once down on the ground under cover of the hill, it required very strong resolution to get up where these missiles of death were flying so thickly, yet that was the duty of us officers, especially us of the field and staff. My duty kept me constantly moving up and down that whole line.

On my way back to the right of the line, where I had left Colonel Oakford, I met Lieutenant-Colonel Wilcox, who told me the terrible news that Colonel Oakford was killed. Of the details of his death, I had no time then to inquire. We were then in the very maelstrom of the battle. Men were falling every moment. The horrible noise of the battle was incessant and almost deafening. Except that my mind was so absorbed in my duties, I do not know how I could have endured the strain.

Yet out of this pandemonium memory brings several remarkable incidents. They came and went with the rapidity of a quickly revolving kaleidoscope. You caught stupendous incidents on the instant, and in an instant they had passed. One was the brave death of the major of this regiment that was lying idle under the tree. The commanding officer evidently was not doing his duty, and this major was endeavoring to rally his men and get them at work. He was swinging his hat and cheering his men forward, when a solid shot decapitated him. His poor body went down as though some giant had picked it up and furiously slammed it on the ground, and I was so near him that I could almost have touched him with my sword.

The inaction of this regiment lying behind us under that tree was very demoralizing to our men, setting them a bad example. General Kimball, who commanded our brigade, was seated on his horse just under the knoll in the rear of our regiment, evidently watching our work, and he signalled me to come to him, and then gave me orders to present his compliments to the commanding officer of that regiment and direct him to get his men up and at work. I communicated this order as directed. The colonel was hugging the ground, and merely turned his face towards me without replying or attempting to obey the order. General Kimball saw the whole thing, and again called me to him and, with an oath, commanded me to repeat the order to him at the muzzle of my revolver, and shoot him if he did not immediately obey.

Said General Kimball: "Get those cowards out of there or shoot them." My task was a most disagreeable one, but I must deliver my orders, and did so, but was saved the duty of shooting by the other officers of the regiment bravely rallying their men and pushing them forward to the firing-line, where they did good work. What became of that skulking colonel, I do not know.

The air was now thick with smoke from the muskets, which not only obscured our vision of the enemy, but made breathing difficult and most uncomfortable. The day was excessively hot, and no air stirring, we were forced to breathe this powder smoke, impregnated with saltpeter, which burned the coating of nose, throat, and eyes almost like fire.

Captain Abbott, commanding Company G, from Mauch Chunk, a brave and splendid officer, was early carried to the rear, a ball having nearly carried away his under jaw. He afterwards told me that his first sensation of this awful wound was his mouth full of blood, teeth, and splintered bones, which he spat out on the ground, and then found that unless he got immediate help he would bleed to death in a few minutes.

Fortunately he found Assistant Surgeon Hoover, who had been assigned to us just from his college graduation, who, under the shelter of a hay-stack, with no anæsthetic, performed an operation which Dr. Gross, of Philadelphia, afterwards said had been but once before successfully performed in the history of surgery, and saved his life. Lieutenant Anson C. Cranmer, Company C, was killed, and the ground was soon strewn with the dead and wounded. Soon our men began to call for more ammunition, and we officers were kept busy taking from the dead and wounded and distributing to the living. Each man had eighty rounds when we began the fight. One man near me rose a moment, when a missile struck his gun about midway, and actually capsized him. He pulled himself together, and, finding he was only a little bruised, picked up another gun, with which the ground was now strewn, and went at it again.

Directly, a lull in the enemy's firing occurred, and we had an opportunity to look over the hill a little more carefully at their lines. Their first line in the sunken road seemed to be all dead or wounded, and several of our men ran down there, to find that literally true. They brought back the lieutenant-colonel, a fine-looking man, who was mortally wounded. I shook his hand, and he said, "God bless you, boys, you are very kind." He asked to be laid down in some sheltered place, for, said he, "I have but a few moments to live."

I well remember his refined, gentlemanly appearance, and how profoundly sorry I felt for him. He was young, lithely built, of sandy complexion, and wore a comparatively new uniform of Confederate gray, on which was embroidered the insignia of the "5th Ga., C. S. A." He said, "You have killed all my brave boys; they are there in the road." And they were, I saw them next day lying four deep in places as they fell, a most awful picture of battle carnage. This lull was of very short duration, and like the lull of a storm presaged a renewal of the firing with greater fury, for a fresh line of rebel troops had been brought up. This occurred three times before we were relieved.

During the fiercest of the firing, another remarkable incident occurred, which well illustrated the fortunes of war. I heard a man shouting, "Come over here men, you can see 'em better," and there, over the brow of the knoll, absolutely exposed, was Private George Coursen, of Company K, sitting on a boulder, loading and firing as calmly as though there wasn't a rebel in the country. I yelled to him to come back under the cover of the hill-top, but he said he could see the rebels better there, and refused to leave his vantage-ground. I think he remained there until we were ordered back and did not receive a scratch. His escape was nothing less than a miracle. He seemed to have no idea of fear.

A remarkable fact about our experience during this fight was that we took no note of time. When we were out of ammunition and about to move back I looked at my watch and found it was 12.30 P.M. We had been under fire since eight o'clock. I couldn't believe my eyes; was sure my watch had gone wrong. I would have sworn that we had not been there more than twenty minutes, when we had actually been in that very hell of fire for four and a half hours.

Just as we were moving back, the Irish brigade came up, under command of General Thomas Francis Meagher. They had been ordered to complete our work by a charge, and right gallantly they did it. Many of our men, not understanding the order, joined in that charge. General Meagher rode a beautiful white horse, but made a show of himself by tumbling off just as he reached our line. The boys said he was drunk, and he certainly looked and acted like a drunken man. He regained his feet and floundered about, swearing like a crazy man. The brigade, however, made a magnificent charge and swept everything before it.

Another incident occurred during the time we were under fire. My attention was arrested by a heavily built general officer passing to the rear on foot. He came close by me and as he passed he shouted: "You will have to get back. Don't you see yonder line of rebels is flanking you?" I looked in the direction he pointed, and, sure enough, on our right and now well to our rear was an extended line of rebel infantry with their colors flying, moving forward almost with the precision of a parade. They had thrown forward a beautiful skirmish line and seemed to be practically masters of the situation. My heart was in my mouth for a couple of moments, until suddenly the picture changed, and their beautiful line collapsed and went back as if the d——l was after them. They had run up against an obstruction in a line of the "boys in blue," and many of them never went back. This general officer who spoke to me, I learned, was Major-General Richardson, commanding the First Division, then badly wounded, and who died a few hours after.

Our regiment now moved back and to the right some three-quarters of a mile, where we were supplied with ammunition, and the men were allowed to make themselves a cup of coffee and eat a "hardtack." I was faint for want of food, for I had only a cup of coffee in the early morning, and was favored with a hardtack by one of the men, who were always ready and willing to share their rations with us. We now learned that our brigade had borne the brunt of a long and persistent effort by Lee to break our line at this point, and that we were actually the third line which had been thrown into this breach, the other two having been wiped out before we advanced; that as a matter of fact our brigade, being composed so largely of raw troops—our regiment being really more than half the brigade in actual number—was designed to be held in reserve.

But the onslaught of the enemy had been so terrific, that by eight o'clock A.M. our reserve line was all there was left and we had to be sent in. The other three regiments were veterans, old and tried. They had an established reputation of having never once been forced back or whipped, but the One Hundred and Thirty-second was new and, except as to numbers, an unknown quantity. We had been unmercifully guyed during the two preceding weeks, as I have said before, as a lot of "greenhorns," "pretty boys" in "pretty new clothes," "mamma's darlings," etc., etc., to the end of the vets' slang calendar. Now that we had proved our metal under fire, the atmosphere was completely changed.

Not the semblance of another jibe against the One Hundred and Thirty-second Penn-sylvania Volunteers.

We did not know how well we had done, only that we had tried to do our duty under trying circumstances, until officers and men from other regiments came flocking over to congratulate and praise us. I didn't even know we had passed through the fire of a great battle until the colonel of the Fourteenth Indiana came over to condole with us on the loss of Colonel Oakford, and incidentally told us that this was undoubtedly the greatest battle of the war thus far, and that we probably would never have such another.

After getting into our new position, I at once began to look up our losses. I learned that Colonel Oakford was killed by one of the rebel sharp-shooters just as the regiment scaled the fence in its advance up the knoll, and before we had fired a shot. It must have occurred almost instantly after I left him with orders for the left of the line. I was probably the last to whom he spoke. He was hit by a minie-ball in the left shoulder, just below the collar-bone. The doctor said the ball had severed one of the large arteries, and he died in a very few minutes. He had been in command of the regiment a little more than a month, but during that brief time his work as a disciplinarian and drill-master had made it pos-sible for us to acquit ourselves as creditably as they all said we had done. General Kimball was loud in our praise and greatly lamented Colonel Oakford's death, whom he admired very much. He was a brave, able, and accomplished officer and gentleman, and his loss to the regiment was irreparable.

Had Colonel Oakford lived his record must have been brilliant and his promotion rapid, for very few volunteer officers had so quickly mastered the details of military tactics and routine. He was a thorough disciplinarian, an able tactician, and the interests and welfare of his men were constantly upon his heart.

My diary records the fact that I saw Captain Willard, of the Fourteenth Connecticut, fall as we passed their line on our way to the rear; that he appeared to have been hit by a grape-shot or piece of shell. I did not know him, only heard that he was a brother of E. N. Willard, of Scranton. The Fourteenth Connecticut men said he was a fine man and splendid officer.

Among the wounded—reported mortally—was Sergeant Martin Hower, of Com-pany K, one of our very best non-commissioned officers. I saw him at the hospital, and it was very hard to be able to do nothing for him. It seemed our loss must reach upward of two hundred killed, wounded and missing. Out of seven hundred and ninety-eight who answered to roll-call in the morning, we had with us less than three hundred at the close of the fight.

Of the missing, many of them were of those who joined the Irish brigade in their charge, and who did not find us again for a day or so. It may seem strange that a man should not be able to find his regiment for so long a time, when really it is so close at hand. But when one remembers that our army of about seventy-five thousand men had upward of two hundred regiments massed within say two square miles, and that they were constantly changing position, it will be seen that looking for any one regiment is almost like looking for a needle in a hay-mow.

During the afternoon of this day we were again moved further to the right and placed as supports of a battery. We were posted about two hundred yards directly in front of the guns on low ground. The battery was evidently engaged in another artillery duel. We were in a comparatively safe position, so long as the rebel guns directed their firing at our battery; but after a time they began "feeling for the supports," first dropping their shells beyond our guns, then in front of them, until they finally got a pretty good range on our line and filled the air with bursting shells over our heads. One and another was carried to the rear, wounded, and the line became very restive. We were required to lie perfectly quiet. We found this very much more trying than being at work, and the line began to show symptoms of wavering, when General Kimball, who with his staff had dismounted and was resting near us, immediately mounted his horse and, riding up and down the line, shouted: "Stand firm, trust in God, and do your duty."

It was an exceedingly brave act, and its effect was electric upon the men. There was no more wavering, and the rebel battery, evidently thinking they had not found the "supports," soon ceased firing upon us. It was now near night and the firing very perceptibly slackened in our vicinity, though a mile or more to the left it still continued very heavy. This, we afterwards learned, was the work at what has passed into history as "Burnside's" bridge—the effort of Burnside's corps to capture the stone bridge over Antietam creek, near the village of Sharpsburg, and the heights beyond. These were gallantly carried after a terrific fight quite late in the afternoon.

Our work, so far as this battle was concerned, was done. We rested "on our arms" where we were for the next forty-eight hours, expecting all the next day a renewal of the fighting; but nothing was done in our neighborhood beyond a few shots from the battery we were supporting. On the second day it became known that Lee had hauled off, and there was no immediate prospect of further fighting. Our companies were permitted to gather up their dead, and burying parties were organized.

We were allowed to go over the field freely. It was a gruesome sight. Our own dead had been cared for, but the rebel dead remained as they had fallen. In the hot sun the bodies had swollen and turned black. Nearly all lay with faces up and eyes wide open, presenting a spectacle to make one shudder. The distended nostrils and thickened lips made them look like negroes, except for their straight hair. Their limbs and bodies were so enlarged that their clothing seemed ready to burst. Some ghouls had been among them, whether from their own lines or from ours, could not be known, but every man's pockets had been ripped out and the contents taken.

In company with Captain Archbald I went over the position occupied by our regiment and brigade, the famous "sunken road," that is, the lane or road extending from near the "Roulette house" towards Sharpsburg. For some distance it had been cut through the opposite side of the knoll upon which we fought, and had the appearance of a sunken road. It was literally filled with rebel dead, which in some places lay three and four bodies deep. We afterwards saw pictures of this road in the illustrated papers, which partially portrayed the horrible scene. Those poor fellows were the Fifth Georgia regiment. This terrible work was mostly that of our regiment, and bore testimony to the effectiveness of the fire of our men.

The position was an alluring one: the road was cut into the hill about waist high, and seemed to offer secure protection to a line of infantry, and so no doubt this line was posted there to hold the knoll and this Sharpsburg road. It proved, however, nothing but a death-trap, for once our line got into position on the top of this crescent-shaped ridge we could reach them by a direct fire on the center and a double flanking fire at the right and left of the line, and only about one hundred yards away. With nothing but an open field behind them there was absolutely no escape, nothing but death or surrender, and they evidently chose the former, for we saw no white flag displayed. We could now understand the remark of their lieutenant-colonel, whom our boys brought in, as already mentioned: "You have killed all my poor boys. They lie there in the road." I learned later that the few survivors of this regiment were sent South to guard rebel prisoners.

The lines of battle of both armies were not only marked by the presence of the dead, but by a vast variety of army equipage, such as blankets, canteens, haversacks, guns, gun-slings, bayonets, ramrods, some whole, others broken—verily, a besom of destruction had done its work faithfully here. Dead horses were everywhere, and the stench from them and the human dead was horrible. "Uncle" Billy Sherman has said, "War is hell!" yet this definition, with all that imagination can picture, fails to reveal all its bloody horrors.

The positions of some of the dead were very striking. One poor fellow lay face down on a partially fallen stone wall, with one arm and one foot extended, as if in the act of crawling over. His position attracted our attention, and we found his body literally riddled with bullets—there must have been hundreds—and most of them shot into him after he was dead, for they showed no marks of blood. Probably the poor fellow had been wounded in trying to reach shelter behind that wall, was spotted in the act by our men, and killed right there, and became thereafter a target for every new man that saw him. Another man lay, still clasping his musket, which he was evidently in the act of loading when a bullet pierced his heart, literally flooding his gun with his life's blood, a ghastly testimonial to his heroic sacrifice.

We witnessed the burying details gathering up and burying the dead. The work was rough and heartless, but only comporting with the character of war. The natural reverence for the dead was wholly absent. The poor bodies, all of them heroes in their death, even though in a mistaken cause, were "planted" with as little feeling as though they had been so many logs. A trench was dug, where the digging was easiest, about seven feet wide and long enough to accommodate all the bodies gathered within a certain radius; these were then placed side by side, cross-wise of the trench, and buried without anything to keep the earth from them. In the case of the Union dead, the trenches were usually two or three feet deep, and the bodies were wrapped in blankets before being covered, but with the rebels no blankets were used, and the trenches were sometimes so shallow as to leave the toes exposed after a shower.

No ceremony whatever attended this gruesome service, but it was generally accompanied by ribald jokes, at the expense of the poor "Johnny" they were "planting." This was not the fruit of debased natures or degenerate hearts on the part of the boys, who well knew it might be their turn next, under the fortunes of war, to be buried in like manner, but it was recklessness and thoughtlessness, born of the hardening influences of war.

Having now given some account of the scenes in which I participated during the battle and the day after, let us look at another feature of the battle, and probably the most heart-breaking of all, the field hospital. There was one established for our division some three hundred yards in our rear, under the shelter of a hill. Here were gathered as rapidly as possible the wounded, and a corps of surgeons were busily engaged in amputating limbs and dressing wounds. It should be understood that the accommodations were of the rudest character. A hospital tent had been hurriedly erected and an old house and barn utilized. Of course, I saw nothing of it or its work until the evening after the battle, when I went to see the body of our dead colonel and some of our Scranton boys who were wounded.

Outside the hospital were piles of amputated arms, legs, and feet, thrown out with as little care as so many pieces of wood. There were also many dead soldiers—those who had died after reaching the hospital—lying outside, there being inside scant room only for the living. Here, on bunches of hay and straw, the poor fellows were lying so thickly that there was scarce room for the surgeon and attendants to move about among them. Others were not allowed inside, except officers and an occasional friend who might be helping. Our chaplain spent his time here and did yeoman service helping the wounded. Yet all that could be done with the limited means at hand seemed only to accentuate the appalling need. The pallid, appealing faces were patient with a heroism born only of the truest metal. I was told by the surgeons that such expressions as this were not infrequent as they approached a man in his "turn": "Please, doctor, attend to this poor fellow next; he's worse than I," and this when his own life's blood was fast oozing away.

Most of the wounded had to wait hours before having their wounds dressed, owing to insufficient force and inadequate facilities. I was told that not a surgeon had his eyes closed for three days after this battle. The doctors of neighboring towns within reach came and voluntarily gave their services, yet it is doubtless true that hundreds of the wounded perished for want of prompt and proper care. This is one of the unavoidable incidents of a great battle—a part of the horrors of war. The rebel wounded necessarily were second to our own in receiving care from the surgeons, yet they, too, received all the attention that was possible under the circumstances. Some of their surgeons remained with their wounded, and I am told they and our own surgeons worked together most energetically and heroically in their efforts to relieve the sufferings of all, whether they wore the blue or the gray. Suffering, it has been said, makes all the world akin. So here, in our lines, the wounded rebel was lost sight of in the suffering brother.

We remained on the battle-field until September 21, four days after the fight.

My notes of this day say that I was feeling so miserable as to be scarcely able to crawl about, yet was obliged to remain on duty; that Lieutenant-Colonel Wilcox, now in command, and Major Shreve were in the same condition. This was due to the nervous strain through which we had passed, and to insufficient and unwholesome food. As stated before, we had been obliged to eat whatever we could get, which for the past four days had been mostly green field corn roasted as best we could. The wonder is that we were not utterly prostrated. Nevertheless, I not only performed all my duties, but went a mile down the Antietam creek, took a bath, and washed my underclothing, my first experience in the laundry business.

We had been now for two weeks and more steadily on the march, our baggage in wagons somewhere en route, without the possibility of a change of clothing or of having any washing done. Most of this time marching in a cloud of dust so thick that one could almost cut it, and perspiring freely, one can imagine our condition. Bathing as frequently as opportunity offered, yet our condition was almost unendurable. For with the accumulation of dirt upon our body, there was added the ever-present scourge of the army, body lice. These vermin, called by the boys "graybacks," were nearly the size of a grain of wheat, and derived their name from their bluish-gray color. They seemed to infest the ground wherever there had been a bivouac of the rebels, and following them as we had, during all of this campaign, sleeping frequently on the ground just vacated by them, no one was exempt from this plague. They secreted themselves in the seams of the clothing and in the armpits chiefly. A good bath, with a change of underclothing, would usually rid one of them, but only to acquire a new crop in the first camp. The clothing could be freed of them by boiling in salt water or by going carefully over the seams and picking them off. The latter operation was a frequent occupation with the men on any day which was warm enough to permit them to disrobe for the purpose. One of the most laughable sights I ever beheld was the whole brigade, halted for a couple of hours' rest one hot day, with clothing off, "skirmishing," as the boys called it, for "graybacks." This was one of the many unpoetical features of army life which accentuated the sacrifices one made to serve his country.

How did we ordinarily get our laundrying done? The enlisted men as a rule always did it themselves. Occasionally in camp a number of them would club together and hire some "camp follower" or some other soldier to do it. Officers of sufficient rank to have a servant, of course, readily solved the question. Those of us of lesser rank could generally hire it done, except on the march. Then we had to be our own laundrymen. Having, as in the above instance, no change of clothing at hand, the washing followed a bath, and consisted in standing in the running water and rubbing as much of the dirt out of the underwear as could be done without soap, for that could not be had for love or money; then hanging them on the limb of a tree and sitting in the sun, as comfortable as possible, whilst wind and sun did the drying. A "snap-shot" of such a scene would no doubt be interesting. But "snap-shots" unfortunately were not then in vogue, and so a picture of high art must perish. We could not be over particular about having our clothes dry. The finishing touches were added as we wore them back to camp.

My diary notes that there were nine hundred and ninety-eight rebel dead gathered and buried from in front of the lines of our division. This line was about a quarter of a mile long, and this was mostly our work (our division), although Richardson's division had occupied part of this ground before us, but had been so quickly broken that they had not made much impression upon the enemy. Our division had engaged them continuously and under a terrific fire from eight o'clock A.M. until 12.30 P.M. It may be asked why during that length of time and under such a fire all were not annihilated. The answer is, that inaccuracy and unsteadiness in firing on both sides greatly reduce its effectiveness, and taking all possible advantage of shelter by lying prone upon the ground also prevents losses; but the above number of rebel dead, it should be remembered, represents, probably, not more than twenty to twenty-five per cent of their casualties in that area of their lines; the balance were wounded and were removed. So that with nine hundred and ninety-eight dead it can be safely estimated that their losses exceeded four thousand killed and wounded in that area. This would indicate what was undoubtedly true, that we were in the very heart of that great battle.

Here I wish to say that some chroniclers of battles have undertaken to measure the effectiveness and bravery of the different regiments, batteries, etc., by the numbers they have lost in certain battles; for example, one historian has made a book grading the regiments by the number of men they lost in action, assuming that the more men killed and wounded, the more brilliant and brave had been its work. This assumption is absolutely fallacious. Heavy losses may be the result of great bravery with splendid work. On the other hand, they may be the result of cowardice or inefficiency. Suppose, under trying circumstances, officers lose their heads and fail to properly handle their men, or if the latter prove cowardly and incapable of being moved with promptness to meet the exigency, great loss usually ensues, and this would be chargeable to cowardice or inefficiency. According to the loss way of estimating fighting regiments, the least deserving are liable to be credited with the best work. The rule is, the better drilled, disciplined, and the better officered, the less the losses in any position on the firing-line.

This fixing up of quarters had been done in contemplation of remaining here through the winter, and we had taken our cue from like actions of our brigade officers, who were supposed to know something about the movements of the army. When we got orders on the 29th of October to prepare for the march, I was assured by the adjutant-general of our brigade that it was nothing more than a day's reconnoissance, and that we were certainly not going to move our quarters. He knew as much about it as I did. Within an hour after this order another came directing us to move in heavy marching order, with three days' rations and sixty rounds of ammunition. And so we moved out of Harper's Ferry on the

31st of October, leaving our fixed-up quarters, with my four-dollar stove, to Geary's division, which succeeded to our camp.

We crossed the Shenandoah on a pontoon bridge and skirted the mountain under Loudon Heights over the same route south that we had taken on our way in from the Leesburg raid. We marched very leisurely, making during the first four days only about twenty-five miles, to a village bearing the serious name of Snickersville. Here we had the first evidence of the presence of the enemy. We were hurried through this village and up through the gap in the mountain called "Snicker's Gap" to head off the rebels. We soon came on to their scouts and pickets, who fled precipitately without firing a gun. Part of our division halted on the top of the gap, while a couple of regiments skirmished through the woods both sides of the road down to the foot of the mountain on the other side. The enemy had taken "French leave," and so our men returned and our division bivouacked here for the night.

We now learned that these giant armies were moving south in parallel columns, the mountain separating them. At every gap or pass in the mountain a bristling head or a clinched fist, so to speak, of one would be thrust through and the other would try to hit it. This was our mission, as we double-quicked it through this gap. When we got there the "fist" had been withdrawn, and our work for the time was over. But our bivouac here—how beautiful it was! The fields were clean and green, with plenty of shade, for right in the gap were some good farms. Then the cavalry had not cleaned the country of everything eatable, as was usual, they being always in the advance. There was milk and bread to be had, and somehow—I never dared to inquire too closely about it—some good mutton came into camp that night, so that we had a splendid breakfast next morning. Some fine honey was added to the bill of fare. The man who brought in the latter claimed that a rebel hive of bees attacked him whilst on picket duty, and he confiscated the honey as a measure of retaliation.

But the special feature that makes that camp linger in my memory was the extraordinary beauty of the scene in the valley below us when the evening camp-fires were lighted. We were on a sort of table-land two or three hundred feet above the broad valley, which widened out at this point and made a most charming landscape. As the darkness drew on the camp-fires were lighted, and the scene became one of weird, bewitching beauty. Almost as far as the eye could reach, covering three and possibly four square miles, were spread out the blazing camp-fires of that mighty host of our "Boys in Blue."

No drums were beaten and the usual retreat call was not sounded, but the thousands of camp-fires told of the presence of our men. A martial city was cooking its evening coffee and resting its weary limbs in the genial camp-fire glow, whilst weary hearts were refreshed with the accompanying chat about friends and dearer ones at home. The scouting "Johnny Rebs" (and there were no doubt plenty of them viewing the scene) could have gotten from it no comforting information to impart as to our numbers. Most of the Army of the Potomac, now largely augmented by new regiments, was there, probably not less than one hundred thousand men. It was a picture not of a lifetime, but of the centuries. It made my blood leap as I realized that I was looking down upon the grandest army, all things considered, of any age or time. Its mission was to save to liberty and freedom the life of the best government the world ever saw. In its ranks was the best blood of a free people.

In intelligence it was far superior to any other army that ever existed. Scholars of all professions, tradesmen and farmers, were there, fighting side by side, animated by the same patriotic impulse. I said to myself, it is impossible that that army should be beaten. It is the strong right arm of the Union, and under God it shall assuredly deal the death-blow to the rebellion.

This it certainly did, though at a fearful cost, for it was fighting the same blood.

The inspiration of that scene made me glad from the bottom of my heart that I had the privilege of being just one in that glorious army. After forty years, what would I take for that association with all its dangers and hardships? What for these pictures and memories? They are simply priceless. I only wish I could so paint the pictures and reproduce the scenes that they might be an inspiration to the same patriotism that moved this mighty host.

CHAPTER 4

Lincoln at War: Prominent Letters and Papers
By Abraham Lincoln

The president was not only a man of clear thinking; he had a sharp wit to deliver his thoughts with great force. The tough going for the Union army in the early stages of the war sometimes moved Abraham Lincoln to tears, and sometimes to anger.

—LAMAR UNDERWOOD

TELEGRAM TO GENERAL G. B. McCLELLAN.
WAR DEPARTMENT, WASHINGTON, D.C.
September 15, 1862. 2.45 P.M.
MAJOR-GENERAL McCLELLAN:

Your despatch of to-day received. God bless you, and all with you. Destroy the rebel army if possible.

A. LINCOLN.

TELEGRAM TO J. K. DUBOIS.
WASHINGTON, D.C.,
September 15, 1862. 3 P.M.
HON. K. DUBOIS, Springfield, Illinois:

I now consider it safe to say that General McClellan has gained a great victory over the great rebel army in Maryland, between Fredericktown and Hagerstown. He is now pursuing the flying foe.

RECORD EXPLAINING THE DISMISSAL OF MAJOR JOHN J. KEY FROM THE MILITARY SERVICE OF THE UNITED STATES. EXECUTIVE MANSION, WASHINGTON,

September 26, 1862.

MAJOR JOHN J. KEY:

I am informed that, in answer to the question, "Why was not the rebel army bagged immediately after the battle near Sharpsburg?" propounded to you by Major Levi C. Turner, Judge Advocate, etc., you said: "That is not the game. The object is, that neither army shall get much advantage of the other; that both shall be kept in the field till they are exhausted, when we will make a compromise and save slavery."

I shall be very happy if you will, within twenty-four hours from the receipt of this, prove to me by Major Turner that you did not, either literally or in substance, make the answer stated.

[Above delivered to Major Key at 10.25 A.M. September 27th.]

At about 11 o'clock A.M., September 27, 1862, Major Key and Major Turner appeared before me. Major Turner says:

"As I remember it, the conversation was: 'Why did we not bag them after the battle of Sharpsburg?' Major Key's reply was: 'That was not the game; that we should tire the rebels out and ourselves; that that was the only way the Union could be preserved, we come together fraternally, and slavery be saved.'"

On cross-examination, Major Turner says he has frequently heard Major Key converse in regard to the present troubles, and never heard him utter a sentiment unfavorable to the maintenance of the Union. He has never uttered anything which he, Major T., would call disloyalty. The particular conversation detailed was a private one.

In my view, it is wholly inadmissible for any gentleman holding a military commission from the United States to utter such sentiments as Major Key is within proved to have done. Therefore, let Major John J. Key be forthwith dismissed from the military service of the United States.

A. LINCOLN.

TO GENERAL G. B. McCLELLAN.

EXECUTIVE MANSION, WASHINGTON, October 13, 1862.

MY DEAR SIR—You remember my speaking to you of what I called your over-cautiousness. Are you not over-cautious when you assume that you cannot do what the enemy is constantly doing? Should you not claim to be at least his equal in prowess, and act upon the claim?

As I understand, you telegraphed General Halleck that you cannot subsist your army at Winchester unless the railroad from Harper's Ferry to that point be put in working order. But the enemy does now subsist his army at Winchester, at a distance nearly twice as great from railroad transportation as you would have to do, without the railroad last named. He now wagons from Culpepper Court-House, which is just about twice as far as you would have to do from Harper's Ferry. He is certainly not more than half as well provided with wagons as you are. I certainly should be pleased for you to have the advantage of the railroad from Harper's Perry to Winchester; but it wastes the remainder of autumn to give it to you, and, in fact, ignores the question of time, which cannot and must not be ignored.

Again, one of the standard maxims of war, as you know, is "to operate upon the enemy's communications as much as possible, without exposing your own." You seem to act as if this applies against you, but cannot apply in your favor. Change positions with the enemy, and think you not he would break your communication with Richmond within the next twenty-four hours? You dread his going into Pennsylvania. But if he does so in full force, he gives up his communications to you absolutely, and you have nothing to do but to follow and ruin him; if he does so with less than full force, fall upon and beat what is left behind all the easier.

Exclusive of the water line, you are now nearer to Richmond than the enemy is, by the route that you can and he must take. Why can you not reach there before him, unless you admit that he is more than your equal on a march? His route is the arc of a circle, while yours is the chord. The roads are as good on yours as on his.

You know I desired, but did not order, you to cross the Potomac below instead of above the Shenandoah and Blue Ridge. My idea was that this would at once menace the enemy's communications, which I would seize if he would permit. If he should move northward, I would follow him closely, holding his communications. If he should prevent our seizing his communications, and move toward Richmond, I would press closely to him, fight him if a favorable opportunity should present, and at least try to beat him to Richmond on the inside track. I say "try;" if we never try, we shall never succeed. If he makes a stand at Winchester, moving neither north or south, I would fight him there, on the idea that if we cannot beat him when he bears the wastage of coming to us, we never can when we bear the wastage of going to him. This proposition is a simple truth, and is too important to be lost sight of for a moment. In coming to us he tenders us an advantage which we should not waive. We should not so operate as to merely drive him away. As we must beat him somewhere or fail finally, we can do it, if at all, easier near to us than far away. If we cannot beat the enemy where he now is, we never can, he again being within the entrenchments of Richmond.

Recurring to the idea of going to Richmond on the inside track, the facility of supplying from the side away from the enemy is remarkable, as it were, by the different spokes of a wheel extending from the hub toward the rim, and this whether you move directly by the chord or on the inside arc, hugging the Blue Ridge more closely. The chord line, as you see, carries you by Aldie, Hay Market, and Fredericksburg; and you see how turnpikes, railroads, and finally the Potomac, by Aquia Creek, meet you at all points from WASHINGTON; the same, only the lines lengthened a little, if you press closer to the Blue Ridge part of the way.

The gaps through the Blue Ridge I understand to be about the following distances from Harper's Ferry, to wit: Vestal's, 5 miles; Gregory's, 13; Snicker's, 18; Ashby's, 28; Manassas, 38; Chester, 45; and Thornton's, 53. I should think it preferable to take the route nearest the enemy, disabling him to make an important move without your knowledge, and compelling him to keep his forces together for dread of you. The gaps would enable you to attack if you should wish. For a great part of the way you would be practically between the enemy and both WASHINGTON and Richmond, enabling us to spare you the greatest number of troops from here. When at length running for Richmond ahead of him enables him to move this way, if he does so, turn and attack him in rear. But I think he should be engaged long before such a point is reached. It is all easy if our troops march as well as the enemy, and it is unmanly to say they cannot do it. This letter is in no sense an order.

Yours truly,

A. LINCOLN.

GENERAL McCLELLAN'S TIRED HORSES
TELEGRAM TO GENERAL G. B. McCLELLAN.
WAR DEPARTMENT, WASHINGTON CITY, October 24 [25?], 1862.
MAJOR-GENERAL McCLELLAN:

I have just read your despatch about sore-tongued and fatigued horses. Will you pardon me for asking what the horses of your army have done since the battle of Antietam that fatigues anything?

A. LINCOLN.

TELEGRAM TO GENERAL G. B. McCLELLAN.
EXECUTIVE MANSION WASHINGTON, October 26, 1862. 11.30 A.M.
MAJOR-GENERAL McCLELLAN:

Yours, in reply to mine about horses, received. Of course you know the facts better than I; still two considerations remain: Stuart's cavalry outmarched ours, having certainly done more marked service on the Peninsula and everywhere since. Secondly, will not a movement of our army be a relief to the cavalry, compelling the enemy to concentrate instead of foraging in squads everywhere? But I am so rejoiced to learn from your despatch to General Halleck that you begin crossing the river this morning.

A. LINCOLN.

TELEGRAM TO GENERAL G. B. McCLELLAN.
EXECUTIVE MANSION, WASHINGTON, October 27, 1862. 3.25 P.M.
MAJOR-GENERAL McCLELLAN:

Your despatch of 3 P.M. to-day, in regard to filling up old regiments with drafted men, is received, and the request therein shall be complied with as far as practicable.

And now I ask a distinct answer to the question, Is it your purpose not to go into action again until the men now being drafted in the States are incorporated into the old regiments?

A. LINCOLN.

TELEGRAM TO GENERAL G. B. McCLELLAN.
EXECUTIVE MANSION, WASHINGTON D.C., October 29, 1863.
MAJOR-GENERAL McCLELLAN:

Your despatches of night before last, yesterday, and last night all received. I am much pleased with the movement of the army. When you get entirely across the river let me know. What do you know of the enemy?

A. LINCOLN.

ORDER RELIEVING GENERAL G. B. McCLELLAN
AND MAKING OTHER CHANGES.
EXECUTIVE MANSION, WASHINGTON, D.C., November 5, 1862.

By direction of the President, it is ordered that Major-General McClellan be relieved from the command of the Army of the Potomac, and that Major-General Burnside take the command of that army. Also that Major-General Hunter take command of the corps in said army which is now commanded by General Burnside. That Major-General Fitz. John Porter be relieved from command of the corps he now commands in said army, and that Major-General Hooker take command of said corps.

The general-in-chief is authorized, in [his] discretion, to issue an order substantially as the above forthwith, or so soon as he may deem proper.

A. LINCOLN.

DELAYING TACTICS OF GENERALS
TO GENERAL N. P. BANKS.
EXECUTIVE MANSION, WASHINGTON, November 22, 1862.
MY DEAR GENERAL BANKS:—Early last week you left me in high hope with your assurance that you would be off with your expedition at the end of that week, or early in this. It is now the end of this, and I have just been overwhelmed

and confounded with the sight of a requisition made by you which, I am assured, cannot be filled and got off within an hour short of two months. I enclose you a copy of the requisition, in some hope that it is not genuine—that you have never seen it. My dear General, this expanding and piling up of impedimenta has been, so far, almost our ruin, and will be our final ruin if it is not abandoned. If you had the articles of this requisition upon the wharf, with the necessary animals to make them of any use, and forage for the animals, you could not get vessels together in two weeks to carry the whole, to say nothing of your twenty thousand men; and, having the vessels, you could not put the cargoes aboard in two weeks more. And, after all, where you are going you have no use for them. When you parted with me you had no such ideas in your mind. I know you had not, or you could not have expected to be off so soon as you said. You must get back to something like the plan you had then, or your expedition is a failure before you start. You must be off before Congress meets. You would be better off anywhere, and especially where you are going, for not having a thousand wagons doing nothing but hauling forage to feed the animals that draw them, and taking at least two thousand men to care for the wagons and animals, who otherwise might be two thousand good soldiers. Now, dear General, do not think this is an ill-natured letter; it is the very reverse. The simple publication of this requisition would ruin you.

Very truly your friend,

A. LINCOLN.

CONGRATULATIONS TO THE ARMY OF THE POTOMAC
EXECUTIVE MANSION, WASHINGTON,
December 22, 1862.
TO THE ARMY OF THE POTOMAC:

I have just read your general's report of the battle of Fredericksburg. Although you were not successful, the attempt was not an error, nor the failure other than accident. The courage with which you, in an open field, maintained the contest against an intrenched foe, and the consummate skill and success with which you crossed and recrossed the river in the face of the enemy, show that you possess all the qualities of a great army, which will yet give victory to the cause of the country and of popular government.

Condoling with the mourners for the dead, and sympathizing with the severely wounded, I congratulate you that the number of both is comparatively so small.

I tender to you, officers and soldiers, the thanks of the nation.

A. LINCOLN.

LETTER OF CONDOLENCE
TO MISS FANNY McCULLOUGH.
EXECUTIVE MANSION, WASHINGTON, December, 23, 1862.
DEAR FANNY:—It is with deep regret that I learn of the death of your kind
and brave father, and especially that it is affecting your young heart beyond what
is common in such cases. In this sad world of ours sorrow comes to all, and to the
young it comes with bittered agony because it takes them unawares.

The older have learned ever to expect it. I am anxious to afford some allevi-
ation of your present distress, perfect relief is not possible, except with time. You
cannot now realize that you will ever feel better. Is not this so? And yet it is a
mistake. You are sure to be happy again. To know this, which is certainly true, will
make you some less miserable now. I have had experience enough to know what
I say, and you need only to believe it to feel better at once. The memory of your
dear father, instead of an agony, will yet be a sad, sweet feeling in your heart, of a
purer and holier sort than you have known before.

Please present my kind regards to your afflicted mother.

Your sincere friend,

A. LINCOLN.

ORDER RELIEVING GENERAL A. E. BURNSIDE AND MAKING
OTHER CHANGES.
(General Orders No.20.)
WAR DEPARTMENT, ADJUTANT-GENERAL'S OFFICE,
WASHINGTON, D.C. JANUARY 25, 1863.
I. The President of the United States has directed:

1st. That Major-General A. E. Burnside, at his own request, be relieved from
the command of the Army of the Potomac.

2d. That Major-General E. V. Sumner, at his own request, be relieved from
duty in the Army of the Potomac.

3d. That Major-General W. B. Franklin be relieved from duty in the Army
of the Potomac.

4th. That Major-General J. Hooker be assigned to the command of the Army
of the Potomac.

II. The officers relieved as above will report in person to the adjutant-general
of the army.

By order of the Secretary of War: D. TOWNSEND, Assistant Adjutant-
General

TO GENERAL J. HOOKER.
EXECUTIVE MANSION, WASHINGTON, D.C., January 26, 1863.
MAJOR-GENERAL HOOKER.

GENERAL:—I have placed you at the head of the Army of the Potomac. Of course I have done this upon what appear to me to be sufficient reasons, and yet I think it best for you to know that there are some things in regard to which I am not quite satisfied with you. I believe you to be a brave and skillful soldier, which of course I like. I also believe you do not mix politics with your profession, in which you are right. You have confidence in yourself, which is a valuable if not an indispensable quality. You are ambitious, which within reasonable bounds does good rather than harm; but I think that during General Burnside's command of the army you have taken counsel of your ambition and thwarted him as much as you could, in which you did a great wrong to the country and to a most meritorious and honorable brother officer. I have heard, in such a way as to believe it, of your recently saying that both the army and the government needed a dictator. Of course it was not for this, but in spite of it, that I have given you the command. Only those generals who gain successes can set up dictators. What I now ask of you is military success, and I will risk the dictatorship. The government will support you to the utmost of its ability, which is neither more nor less than it has done and will do for all commanders. I much fear that the spirit that you have aided to infuse into the army, of criticizing their commander and withholding confidence from him, will now turn upon you. I shall assist you as far as I can to put it down. Neither you nor Napoleon, if he were alive again, could get any good out of an army while such a spirit prevails in it. And now beware of rashness. Beware of rashness, but with energy and sleepless vigilance go forward and give us victories.

Yours very truly,
A. LINCOLN.

TELEGRAM TO GENERAL S. HOOKER.
WASHINGTON, D.C., April 15, 1863. 10.15 P.M.
MAJOR-GENERAL HOOKER:

It is now 10.15 P.M. An hour ago I received your letter of this morning, and a few moments later your despatch of this evening. The latter gives me considerable uneasiness. The rain and mud of course were to be calculated upon. General S. is not moving rapidly enough to make the expedition come to anything. He has now been out three days, two of which were unusually fair weather, and all three without hindrance from the enemy, and yet he is not twenty-five miles from where he started. To reach his point he still has sixty to go, another river (the Rapidan) to cross, and will be hindered by the enemy. By arithmetic, how many days will it take him to do it? I do not know that any better can be done, but I greatly fear it is another failure already. Write me often. I am very anxious.

Yours truly,
A. LINCOLN.

TELEGRAM TO GENERAL HOOKER.
WASHINGTON, D.C., May 6, 1863. 2.25 P.M.
MAJOR-GENERAL HOOKER:

We have through General Dix the contents of Richmond papers of the 5th. General Dix's despatch in full is going to you by Captain Fox of the navy. The substance is General Lee's despatch of the 3d (Sunday), claiming that he had beaten you and that you were then retreating across the Rappahannock, distinctly stating that two of Longstreet's divisions fought you on Saturday, and that General [E. F.] Paxton was killed, Stonewall Jackson severely wounded, and Generals Heth and A. P. Hill slightly wounded. The Richmond papers also stated, upon what authority not mentioned, that our cavalry have been at Ashland, Hanover Court-House, and other points, destroying several locomotives and a good deal of other property, and all the railroad bridges to within five miles of Richmond.

A. LINCOLN.

TELEGRAM TO GENERAL HOOKER
WASHINGTON, D.C., May 6, 1863. 12.30 P.M.

Just as I telegraphed you contents of Richmond papers showing that our cavalry has not failed, I received General Butterfield's of 11 A.M. yesterday. This, with the great rain of yesterday and last night securing your right flank, I think puts a new face upon your case; but you must be the judge.

A. LINCOLN.

TELEGRAM TO COLONEL R. INGALLS.
WASHINGTON, D.C., May 6, 1863. 1.45 P.M.
COLONEL INGALLS:

News has gone to General Hooker which may change his plans. Act in view of such contingency.

A. LINCOLN.

TO GENERAL J. HOOKER.
HEADQUARTERS ARMY OF THE POTOMAC, May 7, 1863.
MAJOR-GENERAL HOOKER.
MY DEAR SIR:—The recent movement of your army is ended without effecting its object, except, perhaps, some important breakings of the enemy's com-

munications. What next? If possible, I would be very glad of another movement early enough to give us some benefit from the fact of the enemy's communication being broken; but neither for this reason nor any other do I wish anything done in desperation or rashness. An early movement would also help to supersede the bad moral effect of there certain, which is said to be considerably injurious. Have you already in your mind a plan wholly or partially formed? If you have, prosecute it without interference from me. If you have not, please inform me, so that I, incompetent as I may be, can try and assist in the formation of some plan for the army.

Yours as ever,
A. LINCOLN.

TELEGRAM TO GENERAL J. HOOKER.
WASHINGTON, D.C. May 8, 1863. 4 P.M.
MAJOR-GENERAL HOOKER:

The news is here of the capture by our forces of Grand Gulf—a large and very important thing. General Willich, an exchanged prisoner just from Richmond, has talked with me this morning. He was there when our cavalry cut the roads in that vicinity. He says there was not a sound pair of legs in Richmond, and that our men, had they known it, could have safely gone in and burned everything and brought in Jeff Davis. We captured and paroled 300 or 400 men. He says as he came to City Point there was an army three miles long (Longstreet's, he thought) moving toward Richmond.

Muroy has captured a despatch of General Lee, in which he says his loss was fearful in his last battle with you.

A. LINCOLN.

TO GENERAL J. HOOKER.
EXECUTIVE MANSION, WASHINGTON, D.C. May 14, 1863.
MAJOR-GENERAL HOOKER, Commanding.

MY DEAR SIR:—When I wrote on the 7th, I had an impression that possibly by an early movement you could get some advantage from the supposed facts that the enemy's communications were disturbed and that he was somewhat deranged in position. That idea has now passed away, the enemy having re-established his communications, regained his positions, and actually received reinforcements. It does not now appear probable to me that you can gain anything by an early renewal of the attempt to cross the Rappahannock. I therefore shall not complain if you do no more for a time than to keep the enemy at bay and out of other mischief by menaces and occasional cavalry raids, if practicable, and to put your own army in good condition again. Still, if in your own clear judgment you can renew the attack successfully, I do not mean to restrain you. Bearing upon this last point, I must tell you that I have some painful intimations that some of your corps and division commanders are not giving you their entire confidence. This would be ruinous, if true, and you should therefore, first of all, ascertain the real facts beyond all possibility of doubt.

Yours truly,

A. LINCOLN.

TELEGRAM TO GENERAL HOOKER.
WASHINGTON, D.C. JUNE 5, 1863
MAJOR-GENERAL HOOKER:

Yours of to-day was received an hour ago. So much of professional military skill is requisite to answer it that I have turned the task over to General Halleck. He promises to perform it with his utmost care. I have but one idea which I think worth suggesting to you, and that is, in case you find Lee coming to the north of the Rappahannock, I would by no means cross to the south of it. If he should leave a rear force at Fredericksburg, tempting you to fall upon it, it would fight in entrenchments and have you at advantage, and so, man for man, worst you at that point, While his main force would in some way be getting an advantage of you northward. In one word, I would not take any risk of being entangled up on the river like an ox jumped half over a fence and liable to be torn by dogs front and rear without a fair chance to gore one way or to kick the other.

If Lee would come to my side of the river I would keep on the same side and fight him, or act on the defensive, according as might be my estimate of his strength relatively to my own. But these are mere suggestions, which I desire to be controlled by the judgment of yourself and General Halleck.

A. LINCOLN.

TELEGRAM TO GENERAL HOOKER.
WASHINGTON, D.C. June 10, 1863
MAJOR-GENERAL HOOKER:

Your long despatch of to-day is just received. If left to me, I would not go south of the Rappahannock upon Lee's moving north of it. If you had Richmond invested to-day you would not be able to take it in twenty days; meanwhile your communications, and with them your army, would be ruined. I think Lee's army, and not Richmond, is your true objective point. If he comes towards the upper Potomac, follow on his flank, and on the inside track, shortening your lines while he lengthens his. Fight him, too, when opportunity offers. If he stay where he is, fret him and fret him.

A. LINCOLN.

RESPONSE TO A "BESIEGED" GENERAL
TELEGRAM TO GENERAL TYLER.
WAR DEPARTMENT, June 14, 1863.
GENERAL TYLER, Martinsburg:

If you are besieged, how do you despatch me? Why did you not leave before being besieged?

A. LINCOLN.

TELEGRAM TO GENERAL HOOKER.
WASHINGTON, D.C., June 14, 1863. 3.50 P.M.
MAJOR-GENERAL HOOKER:

So far as we can make out here, the enemy have Muroy surrounded at Winchester, and Tyler at Martinsburg. If they could hold out a few days, could you help them? If the head of Lee's army is at Martinsburg and the tail of it on the plank-road between Fredericksburg and Chancellorsville, the animal must be very slim somewhere; could you not break him?

A. LINCOLN.

TELEGRAM TO GENERAL HOOKER.
WASHINGTON, June 16, 1863. 10 P.M.
MAJOR-GENERAL HOOKER:

To remove all misunderstanding, I now place you in the strict military relation to General Halleck of a commander of one of the armies to the general-in-chief of all the armies. I have not intended differently, but as it seems to be differently understood I shall direct him to give you orders and you to obey them.

A. LINCOLN.

TELEGRAM TO GENERAL COUCH.
WAR DEPARTMENT, June 24, 1863.
MAJOR-GENERAL COUCH, Harrisburg, Pa.:

Have you any reports of the enemy moving into Pennsylvania? And if any, what?
A. LINCOLN.

ANNOUNCEMENT OF NEWS FROM GETTYSBURG.
WASHINGTON, D.C.
July 4, 10.30 A.M.

The President announces to the country that news from the Army of the Potomac, up to 10 P.M. of the 3d, is such as to cover that army with the highest honor, to promise a great success to the cause of the Union, and to claim the condolence of all for the many gallant fallen; and that for this he especially desires that on this day He whose will, not ours, should ever be done be everywhere remembered and reverenced with profoundest gratitude.

A. LINCOLN.

TELEGRAM TO GENERAL FRENCH. [Cipher] WAR DEPARTMENT, WASHINGTON, D.C.,
July 5, 1863.
MAJOR-GENERAL FRENCH, Fredericktown, Md.:

I see your despatch about destruction of pontoons. Cannot the enemy ford the river?

A. LINCOLN.

CONTINUED FAILURE TO PURSUE ENEMY
TELEGRAM TO GENERAL H. W. HALLECK.
SOLDIERS' HOME, WASHINGTON, JULY 6 1863. 7 P.M.
MAJOR-GENERAL HALLECK:

I left the telegraph office a good deal dissatisfied. You know I did not like the phrase—in Orders, No. 68, I believe—"Drive the invaders from our soil." Since that, I see a despatch from General French, saying the enemy is crossing his wounded over the river in flats, without saying why he does not stop it, or even intimating a thought that it ought to be stopped. Still later, another despatch from General Pleasonton, by direction of General Meade, to General French, stating that the main army is halted because it is believed the rebels are concentrating "on the road towards Hagerstown, beyond Fairfield," and is not to move until it is ascertained that the rebels intend to evacuate Cumberland Valley.

These things appear to me to be connected with a purpose to cover Baltimore and Washington and to get the enemy across the river again without a further collision, and they do not appear connected with a purpose to prevent his crossing and to destroy him. I do fear the former purpose is acted upon and the latter rejected.

If you are satisfied the latter purpose is entertained, and is judiciously pursued, I am content. If you are not so satisfied, please look to it.

Yours truly,
A. LINCOLN.

TELEGRAM FROM GENERAL HALLECK TO GENERAL G. C. MEADE.
WASHINGTON, D.C., July 8, 1863.
MAJOR-GENERAL MEADE, Frederick, Md.:

There is reliable information that the enemy is crossing at Williamsport. The opportunity to attack his divided forces should not be lost. The President is urgent and anxious that your army should move against him by forced marches.

H. W. HALLECK, General-in-Chief

TELEGRAM TO F. F. LOWE.
WAR DEPARTMENT, WASHINGTON, D.C., July 8, 1863.
HON. F. F. LOWE, San Francisco, Cal.:

There is no doubt that General Meade, now commanding the Army of the Potomac, beat Lee at Gettysburg, Pa., at the end of a three days' battle, and that the latter is now crossing the Potomac at Williamsport over the swollen stream and with poor means of crossing, and closely pressed by Meade. We also have despatches rendering it entirely certain that Vicksburg surrendered to General Grant on the glorious old 4th.

A. LINCOLN.

TO GENERAL GRANT.
EXECUTIVE MANSION, WASHINGTON, July 13, 1863.
MAJOR-GENERAL GRANT:

MY DEAR GENERAL:—I do not remember that you and I ever met personally. I write this now as a grateful acknowledgment of the almost inestimable service you have done the Country. I write to say a word further. When you first reached the vicinity of Vicksburg, I thought you should do what you finally did—march the troops across the neck, run the batteries with the transports, and thus go below; and I never had any faith except a general hope that you knew better than I, that the Yazoo Pass expedition and the like could succeed. When you dropped below, and took Port Gibson, Grand Gulf, and vicinity, I thought you should go down the river and join General Banks; and when you turned northward, east of the Big Black, I feared it was a mistake. I now wish to make the personal acknowledgment that you were right and I was wrong.

Yours very truly,
A. LINCOLN.

TO GENERAL H. W. HALLECK.
EXECUTIVE MANSION, July 29, 1863.
MAJOR-GENERAL HALLECK:

Seeing General Meade's despatch of yesterday to yourself causes me to fear that he supposes the Government here is demanding of him to bring on a general engagement with Lee as soon as possible. I am claiming no such thing of him. In fact, my judgment is against it; which judgment, of course, I will yield if yours and his are the contrary. If he could not safely engage Lee at Williamsport, it seems absurd to suppose he can safely engage him now, when he has scarcely more than two thirds of the force he had at Williamsport, while it must be that Lee has been reinforced. True, I desired General Meade to pursue Lee across the Potomac, hoping, as has proved true, that he would thereby clear the Baltimore and Ohio Railroad, and get some advantages by harassing him on his retreat.

These being past, I am unwilling he should now get into a general engagement on the impression that we here are pressing him, and I shall be glad for you to so inform him, unless your own judgment is against it.

Yours truly,
A. LINCOLN.

H. W. HALLECK, General-in-Chief.
MILITARY STRATEGY
TO GENERAL H. W. HALLECK
EXECUTIVE MANSION, WASHINGTON, D.C., September 19, 1863.
MAJOR-GENERAL HALLECK:

By General Meade's despatch to you of yesterday it appears that he desires your views and those of the government as to whether he shall advance upon the enemy. I am not prepared to order, or even advise, an advance in this case, wherein I know so little of particulars, and wherein he, in the field, thinks the risk is so great and the promise of advantage so small.

And yet the case presents matter for very serious consideration in another aspect. These two armies confront each other across a small river, substantially midway between the two capitals, each defending its own capital, and menacing the other. General Meade estimates the enemy's infantry in front of him at not less than 40,000. Suppose we add fifty per cent to this for cavalry, artillery, and extra-duty men stretching as far as Richmond, making the whole force of the enemy 60,000.

General Meade, as shown by the returns, has with him, and between him and Washington, of the same classes, of well men, over 90,000. Neither can bring the whole of his men into a battle; but each can bring as large a percentage in as the other. For a battle, then, General Meade has three men to General Lee's two. Yet, it having been determined that choosing ground and standing on the defensive gives so great advantage that the three cannot safely attack the two, the three are left simply standing on the defensive also.

If the enemy's 60,000 are sufficient to keep our 90,000 away from Richmond, why, by the same rule, may not 40,000 of ours keep their 60,000 away from Washington, leaving us 50,000 to put to some other use? Having practically come to the mere defensive, it seems to be no economy at all to employ twice as many men for that object as are needed. With no object, certainly, to mislead myself, I can perceive no fault in this statement, unless we admit we are not the equal of the enemy, man for man. I hope you will consider it.

To avoid misunderstanding, let me say that to attempt to fight the enemy slowly back into his entrenchments at Richmond, and then to capture him, is an idea I have been trying to repudiate for quite a year.

My judgment is so clear against it that I would scarcely allow the attempt to be made if the general in command should desire to make it. My last attempt upon Richmond was to get McClellan, when he was nearer there than the enemy was, to run in ahead of him. Since then I have constantly desired the Army of the Potomac to make Lee's army, and not Richmond, its objective point. If our army cannot fall upon the enemy and hurt him where he is, it is plain to me it can gain nothing by attempting to follow him over a succession of intrenched lines into a fortified city.

Yours truly,

A. LINCOLN.

CHAPTER 5

A Common Soldier
By Leander Stillwell

In a book published in 1920, many interesting and important details of life in the ranks of the Union army are shared in the memoir of Leander Stillwell, who served with Company D, 61st Illinois Infantry. Back then, as now, the life of the soldier was often one of drudgery.

—Lamar Underwood

ONE IMPORTANT FEATURE IN THE LIFE OF A SOLDIER WAS THE MATTER OF HIS PAY, AND a few words on that subject may not be out of place. When I enlisted in January, 1862, the monthly pay of the enlisted men of a regiment of infantry was as follows: First sergeant, $20; duty sergeants, $17; corporals and privates, $13. By act of Congress of May 1st, 1864, the monthly pay of the enlisted men was increased, and from that date was as follows: First sergeant, $24; duty sergeants, $20; corporals, $18; privates, $16. That rate existed as long, at least, as we remained in the service. The first payment made to our regiment was on May 1st, 1862, while we were in camp at Owl Creek, Tennessee. The amount I received was $49.40, and of this I sent $45 home to my father at the first opportunity. For a poor man, he was heavily in debt at the time of my enlistment, and was left without any boys to help him do the work upon the farm, so I regarded it as my duty to send him every dollar of my pay that possibly could be spared, and did so as long as I was in the service. But he finally got out of debt during the war. He had good crops, and all manner of farm products brought high prices, so the war period was financially a prosperous one for him. And, to be fair about it, I will say that he later repaid me, when I was pursuing my law studies at the Albany, New York, Law School, almost all the money I had sent him while in the army. So the result really was that the money received by me, as a soldier, was what later enabled me to qualify as a lawyer.

I have heretofore said in these reminiscences that the great "stand-bys" in the way of the food of the soldiers of the western armies were coffee, sow-belly, Yankee beans, and hardtack. But other articles of diet were also issued to us, some of which we liked, while others were flat failures. I have previously said something about the antipathy I had for rice. The French General, Baron Gourgaud, in his "Talks of Napoleon at St. Helena" (p. 240), records Napoleon as having said, "Rice is the best food for the soldier." Napoleon, in my opinion, was the greatest soldier that mankind ever produced, but all the same, I emphatically dissent from his rice proposition. His remark may have been correct when applied to European soldiers of his time and place, but I know it wouldn't fit western American boys of 1861–65.

There were a few occasions when an article of diet was issued called "desiccated potatoes." For "desiccated" the boys promptly substituted "desecrated," and "desecrated potatoes" was its name among the rank and file from start to finish. It consisted of Irish potatoes cut up fine and thoroughly dried. In appearance it much resembled the modern preparation called "grape nuts." We would mix it in water, grease, and salt, and make it up into little cakes, which we would fry, and they were first rate.

There was a while when we were at Bolivar, Tennessee, that some stuff called "compressed vegetables" was issued to us, which the boys, almost unanimously, considered an awful fraud. It was composed of all sorts of vegetables, pressed into small bales, in a solid mass, and as dry as threshed straw. The conglomeration contained turnip-tops, cabbage leaves, string-beans (pod and all), onion blades, and possibly some of every other kind of a vegetable that ever grew in a garden. It came to the army in small boxes, about the size of the Chinese tea-boxes that were frequently seen in this country about fifty years ago. In the process of cooking, it would swell up prodigiously, a great deal more so than rice.

The Germans in the regiment would make big dishes of soup out of this "baled hay," as we called it, and they liked it, but the native Americans, after one trial, wouldn't touch it. I think about the last box of it that was issued to our company was pitched into a ditch in the rear of the camp, and it soon got thoroughly soaked and loomed up about as big as a fair-sized hay-cock.

"Split-peas" were issued to us, more or less, during all the time we were in the service. My understanding was that they were the ordinary garden peas. They were split in two, dried, and about as hard as gravel. But they yielded to cooking, made excellent food, and we were all fond of them. In our opinion, when properly cooked, they were almost as good as Yankee beans.

When our forces captured Little Rock in September, 1863, we obtained possession, among other plunder, of quite a quantity of Confederate commissary stores. Among these was a copious supply of "jerked beef." It consisted of narrow, thin strips of beef, which had been dried on scaffolds in the sun, and it is no exaggeration to say that it was almost as hard and dry as a cottonwood chip. Our manner of eating it was simply to cut off a chunk about as big as one of our elongated musket balls, and proceed to "chaw." It was rather a comical sight to see us in our cabins of a cold winter night, sitting by the fire, and all solemnly "chawing" away, in profound silence, on the Johnnies' jerked beef. But, if sufficiently masticated, it was nutritious and healthful, and we all liked it. I often thought it would have been a good thing if the government had made this kind of beef a permanent and regular addition to our rations. As long as kept in the dry, it would apparently keep indefinitely, and a piece big enough to last a soldier two or three days would take up but little space in a haversack.

Passing from the topic of army rations, I will now take leave to say here, with sincerity and emphasis, that the best school to fit me for the practical affairs of life that I ever attended was in the old 61st Illinois during the Civil War. It would be too long a story to undertake to tell all the benefits derived from that experience, but a few will be alluded to. In the first place, when I was a boy at home, I was, to some extent, a "spoiled child." I was exceedingly particular and "finicky" about my food. Fat meat I abhorred, and wouldn't touch it, and on the other hand, when we had chicken to eat, the gizzard was claimed by me as my sole and exclusive tid-bit, and "Leander" always got it.

Let it be known that in the regiment those habits were gotten over so soon that I was astonished myself. The army in time of war is no place for a "sissy-boy;" it will make a man of him quicker, in my opinion, than any other sort of experience he could undergo. And suffice it to say, on the food question, that my life as a soldier forever cured me of being fastidious or fault-finding about what I had to eat. I have gone hungry too many times to give way to such weakness when sitting down in a comfortable room to a table provided with plenty that was good enough for any reasonable man. I have no patience with a person who is addicted to complaining or growling about his food.

Some years ago there was an occasion when I took breakfast at a decent little hotel at a country way-station on a railroad out in Kansas. It was an early breakfast, for the accommodation of guests who would leave on an early morning train, and there were only two at the table, a young traveling commercial man and myself. The drummer ordered (with other things) a couple of fried eggs, and that fellow sent the poor little dining room girl back with those eggs three times before he got them fitted to the exact shade of taste to suit his exquisite palate. And he did this, too, in a manner and words that were offensive and almost brutal. It was none of my business, so I kept my mouth shut and said nothing, but I would have given a reasonable sum to have been the proprietor of that hotel about five minutes. That fool would then have been ordered to get his grip and leave the house, and he would have left, too.

I do not know how it may have been with other regiments in the matter now to be mentioned, but I presume it was substantially the same as in ours. And the course pursued with us had a direct tendency to make one indifferent as to the precise cut of his clothes. It is true that attention was paid to shoes, to that extent, at least, that the quartermaster tried to give each man a pair that approximated to the number he wore. But coats, trousers, and the other clothes were piled up in separate heaps, and each man was just thrown the first garment on the top of the heap; he took it and walked away. If it was an outrageous fit, he would swap with some one if possible, otherwise he got along as best he could.

Now, in civil life, I have frequently been amused in noting some dudish young fellow in a little country store trying to fit himself out with a light summer coat, or something similar. He would put on the garment, stand in front of a big looking glass, twist himself into all sorts of shapes so as to get a view from every possible angle, then remove that one, and call for another. Finally, after trying on about every coat in the house, he would leave without making a purchase, having found nothing that suited the exact contour of his delicately moulded form. A very brief experience in a regiment that had a gruff old quartermaster would take that tuck out of that Beau Brummell, in short order.

Sometimes I have been, at a late hour on a stormy night, at a way-station on some "jerk-water" railroad, waiting for a belated train, with others in the same predicament. And it was comical to note the irritation of some of these fellows and the fuss they made about the train being late. The railroad, and all the officers, would be condemned and abused in the most savage terms on account of this little delay. And yet we were in a warm room, with benches to sit on, with full stomachs, and physically just as comfortable as we possibly could be. The thought would always occur to me, on such episodes, that if those kickers had to sit down in a dirt road, in the mud, with a cold rain pelting down on them, and just endure all this until a broken bridge in front was fixed up so that the artillery and wagon train could get along, then a few incidents of that kind would be a benefit to them. And instances like the foregoing might be multiplied indefinitely. On the whole, life in the army in a time of war tended to develop patience, contentment with the surroundings, and equanimity of temper and mind in general. And, from the highest to the lowest, differing only in degree, it would bring out energy, prompt decision, intelligent action, and all the latent force of character a man possessed.

I suppose, in reminiscences of this nature, one should give his impressions, or views, in relation to that much talked about subject, "Courage in battle." Now, in what I have to say on that head, I can speak advisedly mainly for myself only. I think that the principal thing that held me to the work was simply pride; and am of the opinion that it was the same thing with most of the common soldiers.

A prominent American functionary some years ago said something about our people being "too proud to fight." With the soldiers of the Civil War it was exactly the reverse— they were "too proud to run"—unless it was manifest that the situation was hopeless, and that for the time being nothing else could be done. And, in the latter case, when the whole line goes back, there is no personal odium attaching to any one individual; they are all in the same boat.

The idea of the influence of pride is well illustrated by an old-time war story, as follows: A soldier on the firing line happened to notice a terribly affrighted rabbit running to the rear at the top of its speed. "Go it, cotton-tail!" yelled the soldier. "I'd run too if I had no more reputation to lose than you have."

It is true that in the first stages of the war the fighting qualities of American soldiers did not appear in altogether a favorable light. But at that time the fact is that the volunteer armies on both sides were not much better than mere armed mobs, and without discipline or cohesion. But those conditions didn't last long—and there was never but one Bull Run.

Enoch Wallace was home on recruiting service some weeks in the fall of 1862, and when he rejoined the regiment he told me something my father said in a conversation that occurred between the two. They were talking about the war, battles, and topics of that sort, and in the course of their talk Enoch told me that my father said that while he hoped his boy would come through the war all right, yet he would rather "Leander should be killed dead, while standing up and fighting like a man, than that he should run, and disgrace the family."

I have no thought from the nature of the conversation as told to me by Enoch that my father made this remark with any intention of its being repeated to me. It was sudden and spontaneous, and just the way the old backwoodsman felt. But I never forgot it, and it helped me several times. For, to be perfectly frank about it, and tell the plain truth, I will set it down here that, so far as I was concerned, away down in the bottom of my heart I just secretly dreaded a battle. But we were soldiers, and it was our business to fight when the time came, so the only thing to then do was to summon up our pride and resolution, and face the ordeal with all the fortitude we could command. And while I admit the existence of this feeling of dread before the fight, yet it is also true that when it was on, and one was in the thick of it, with the smell of gun-powder permeating his whole system, then a signal change comes over a man. He is seized with a furious desire to kill. There are his foes, right in plain view, give it to 'em, d——'em!—and for the time being he becomes almost oblivious to the sense of danger.

And while it was only human nature to dread a battle—and I think it would be mere affectation to deny it, yet I also know that we common soldiers strongly felt that when fighting did break loose close at hand, or within the general scope of our operations, then we ought to be in it, with the others, and doing our part. That was what we were there for, and somehow a soldier didn't feel just right for fighting to be going on all round him, or in his vicinity, and he doing nothing but lying back somewhere, eating government rations.

But, all things considered, the best definition of true courage I have ever read is that given by Gen. Sherman in his Memoirs, as follows:

"I would define true courage," (he says) "to be a perfect sensibility of the measure of danger, and a mental willingness to endure it." (*Sherman's Memoirs*, revised edition, Vol. 2, p. 395.) But, I will further say, in this connection, that, in my opinion, much depends, sometimes, especially at a critical moment, on the commander of the men who is right on the ground, or close at hand. This is shown by the result attained by Gen. Milroy in the incident I have previously mentioned. And, on a larger scale, the inspiring conduct of Gen. Sheridan at the battle of Cedar Creek, Virginia, is probably the most striking example in modern history of what a brave and resolute leader of men can accomplish under circumstances when apparently all is lost. And, on the other hand, I think there is no doubt that the battle of Wilson's Creek, Missouri, on August 10, 1861, was a Union victory up to the time of the death of Gen. Lyon, and would have remained such if the officer who succeeded Lyon had possessed the nerve of his fallen chief. But he didn't, and so he marched our troops off the field, retreated from a beaten enemy, and hence Wilson's Creek figures in history as a Confederate victory. (See *The Lyon Campaign in Missouri*, by Eugene F. Ware, pp. 324–339.) I have read somewhere this saying of Bonaparte's: "An army of deer commanded by a lion is better than an army of lions commanded by a deer." While that statement is only figurative in its nature, it is, however, a strong epigrammatic expression of the fact that the commander of soldiers in battle should be, above all other things, a forcible, determined, and brave man.

CHAPTER 6

The Soldier's Life: A Confederate View
By Carlton McCarthy

Returning to a book we introduced back in chapter 2, Detailed Minutiae of Soldier Life in the Army of Northern Virginia, 1861–1865, *you'll find a portrait of daily life in the Confederate army with vivid details that bring a "felt life" to the printed page.*
—LAMAR UNDERWOOD

WHO DOES NOT KNOW ALL ABOUT THE MARCHING OF SOLDIERS? THOSE WHO HAVE never marched with them and some who have. The varied experience of thousands would not tell the whole story of the march. Every man must be heard before the story is told, and even then the part of those who fell by the way is wanting.

Orders to move! Where? when? what for?—are the eager questions of the men as they begin their preparations to march. Generally nobody can answer, and the journey is commenced in utter ignorance of where it is to end. But shrewd guesses are made, and scraps of information will be picked up on the way. The main thought must be to "get ready to move." The orderly sergeant is shouting "Fall in!" and there is no time to lose. The probability is that before you get your blanket rolled up, find your frying pan, haversack, axe, etc., and "fall in," the roll-call will be over, and some "extra duty" provided.

No wonder there is bustle in the camp. Rapid decisions are to be made between the various conveniences which have accumulated, for some must be left. One fellow picks up the skillet, holds it awhile, mentally determining how much it weighs, and what will be the weight of it after carrying it five miles, and reluctantly, with a half-ashamed, sly look, drops it and takes his place in ranks. Another having added to his store of blankets too freely, now has to decide which of the two or three he will leave. The old water-bucket looks large and heavy, but one stout-hearted, strong-armed man has taken it affectionately to his care.

This is the time to say farewell to the breadtray, farewell to the little piles of clean straw laid between two logs, where it was so easy to sleep; farewell to those piles of wood, cut with so much labor; farewell to the girls in the neighborhood; farewell to the spring, farewell to "our tree" and "our fire," good-by to the fellows who are not going, and a general good-by to the very hills and valleys.

Soldiers commonly threw away the most valuable articles they possessed. Blankets, overcoats, shoes, bread and meat—all gave way to the necessities of the march; and what one man threw away would frequently be the very article that another wanted and would immediately pick up; so there was not much lost after all.

The first hour or so of the march was generally quite orderly, the men preserving their places in ranks and marching in solid column; but soon some lively fellow whistles an air, somebody else starts a song, the whole column breaks out with roars of laughter; "route step" takes the place of order, and the jolly singing, laughing, talking, and joking that follows no one could describe.

Now let any young officer who sports a new hat, coat, saddle, or anything odd, or fine, dare to pass along, and how nicely he is attended to. The expressions of good-natured fun, or contempt, which one regiment of infantry was capable of uttering in a day for the benefit of such passers-by, would fill a volume. As one thing or another in the dress of the "subject" of their remarks attracted attention, they would shout, "Come out of that hat!—you can't hide in thar!" "Come out of that coat, come out—there's a man in it!" "Come out of them boots!" The infantry seemed to know exactly what to say to torment cavalry and artillery, and generally said it. If any one on the roadside was simple enough to recognize and address by name a man in the ranks, the whole column would kindly respond, and add all sorts of pleasant remarks, such as, "Halloa, John, here's your brother!" "Bill! oh, Bill! here's your ma!" "Glad to see you! How's your grandma?" "How d'ye do!" "Come out of that 'biled shirt'!"

Troops on the march were generally so cheerful and gay that an outsider, looking on them as they marched, would hardly imagine how they suffered. In summer time, the dust, combined with the heat, caused great suffering. The nostrils of the men, filled with dust, became dry and feverish, and even the throat did not escape. The "grit" was felt between the teeth, and the eyes were rendered almost useless. There was dust in eyes, mouth, ears, and hair. The shoes were full of sand, and the dust, penetrating the clothes, and getting in at the neck, wrists, and ankles, mixed with perspiration, produced an irritant almost as active as cantharides. The heat was at times terrific, but the men became greatly accustomed to it, and endured it with wonderful ease. Their heavy woolen clothes were a great annoyance; tough linen or cotton clothes would have been a great relief; indeed, there are many objections to woolen clothing for soldiers, even in winter. The sun produced great changes in the appearance of the men: their skins, tanned to a dark brown or red, their hands black almost, and long uncut beard and hair, burned to a strange color, made them barely recognizable to the home folks.

If the dust and the heat were not on hand to annoy, their very able substitutes were: mud, cold, rain, snow, hail and wind took their places. Rain was the greatest discomfort a soldier could have; it was more uncomfortable than the severest cold with clear weather. Wet clothes, shoes, and blankets; wet meat and bread; wet feet and wet ground; wet wood to burn, or rather not to burn; wet arms and ammunition; wet ground to sleep on, mud to wade through, swollen creeks to ford, muddy springs, and a thousand other discomforts attended the rain. There was no comfort on a rainy day or night except in "bed"—that is, under your blanket and oil-cloth. Cold winds, blowing the rain in the faces of the men, increased the discomfort. Mud was often so deep as to submerge the horses and mules, and at times it was necessary for one man or more to extricate another from the mud holes in the road. Night marching was attended with additional discomforts and dangers, such as falling off bridges, stumbling into ditches, tearing the face and injuring the eyes against the bushes and projecting limbs of trees, and getting separated from your own company and hopelessly lost in the multitude. Of course, a man lost had no sympathy. If he dared to ask a question, every man in hearing would answer, each differently, and then the whole multitude would roar with laughter at the lost man, and ask him "if his mother knew he was out?"

Very few men had comfortable or fitting shoes, and fewer had socks, and, as a consequence, the suffering from bruised and inflamed feet was terrible. It was a common practice, on long marches, for the men to take off their shoes and carry them in their hands or swung over the shoulder. Bloody footprints in the snow were not unknown to the soldiers of the Army of Northern Virginia!

When large bodies of troops were moving on the same road, the alternate "halt" and "forward" was very harassing. Every obstacle produced a halt, and caused the men at once to sit and lie down on the roadside where shade or grass tempted them; about the time they got fixed they would hear the word "forward!" and then have to move at increased speed to close up the gap in the column. Sitting down for a few minutes on a long march is pleasant, but it does not always pay; when the march is resumed the limbs are stiff and sore, and the man rather worsted by the halt.

About noon on a hot day, some fellow with the water instinct would determine in his own mind that a well was not far ahead, and start off in a trot to reach it before the column. Of course another and another followed, till a stream of men were hurrying to the well, which was soon completely surrounded by a thirsty mob, yelling and pushing and pulling to get to the bucket as the windlass brought it again and again to the surface. But their impatience and haste would soon overturn the windlass, and spatter the water all around the well till the whole crowd were wading in mud, the rope would break, and the bucket fall to the bottom. But there was a substitute for rope and bucket. The men would hasten away and get long, slim poles, and on them tie, by the straps a number of canteens, which they lowered into the well and filled; and unless, as was frequently the case, the whole lot slipped off and fell to the bottom, drew them to the top and distributed them to their owners, who at once threw their heads back, inserted the nozzles in their mouths and drank the last drop, hastening at once to rejoin the marching column, leaving behind them a dismantled and dry well. It was in vain that the officers tried to stop the stream of men making for the water, and equally vain to attempt to move the crowd while a drop remained accessible. Many, who were thoughtful, carried full canteens to comrades in the column, who had not been able to get to the well; and no one who has not had experience of it knows the thrill of gratification and delight which those fellows felt when the cool stream gurgled from the battered canteen down their parched throats.

In very hot weather, when the necessities of the service permitted, there was a halt about noon, of an hour or so, to rest the men and give them a chance to cool off and get the sand and gravel out of their shoes. This time was spent by some in absolute repose; but the lively boys told many a yarn, cracked many a joke, and sung many a song between "Halt" and "Column forward!" Some took the opportunity, if water was near, to bathe their feet, hands, and face, and nothing could be more enjoyable.

The passage of a cider cart (a barrel on wheels) was a rare and exciting occurrence. The rapidity with which a barrel of sweet cider was consumed would astonish any one who saw it for the first time, and generally the owner had cause to wonder at the small return in cash. Sometimes a desperately enterprising darkey would approach the column with a cartload of pies, "so-called." It would be impossible to describe accurately the taste or appearance of those pies. They were generally similar in appearance, size, and thickness to a pale specimen of "Old Virginia" buckwheat cakes, and had a taste which resembled a combination of rancid lard and crab apples. It was generally supposed that they contained dried apples, and the sellers were careful to state that they had "sugar in 'em" and were "mighty nice." It was rarely the case that any "trace" of sugar was found, but they filled up a hungry man wonderfully.

Men of sense, and there were many such in the ranks, were necessarily desirous of knowing where or how far they were to march, and suffered greatly from a feeling of helpless ignorance of where they were and whither bound—whether to battle or camp. Frequently, when anticipating the quiet and rest of an ideal camp, they were thrown, weary and exhausted, into the face of a waiting enemy, and at times, after anticipating a sharp fight, having formed line of battle and braced themselves for the coming danger, suffered all the apprehension and got themselves in good fighting trim, they were marched off in the driest and prosiest sort of style and ordered into camp, where, in all probability, they had to "wait for the wagon," and for the bread and meat therein, until the proverb, "Patient waiting is no loss," lost all its force and beauty.

Occasionally, when the column extended for a mile or more, and the road was one dense moving mass of men, a cheer would be heard away ahead—increasing in volume as it approached, until there was one universal shout. Then some favorite general officer, dashing by, followed by his staff, would explain the cause. At other times, the same cheering and enthusiasm would result from the passage down the column of some obscure and despised officer, who knew it was all a joke, and looked mean and sheepish accordingly. But no *man* could produce more prolonged or hearty cheers than the "old hare" which jumped the fence and invited the column to a chase; and often it was said, when the rolling shout arose: "There goes old General Lee or a Molly Cotton Tail!"

The men would help each other when in real distress, but their delight was to torment any one who was unfortunate in a ridiculous way. If, for instance, a piece of artillery was fast in the mud, the infantry and cavalry passing around the obstruction would rack their brains for words and phrases applicable to the situation, and most calculated to worry the cannoniers, who, waist deep in the mud, were tugging at the wheels.

Brass bands, at first quite numerous and good, became very rare and their music very poor in the latter years of the war. It was a fine thing to see the fellows trying to keep the music going as they waded through the mud. But poor as the music was, it helped the footsore and weary to make another mile, and encouraged a cheer and a brisker step from the lagging and tired column.

As the men tired, there was less and less talking, until the whole mass became quiet and serious. Each man was occupied with his own thoughts. For miles nothing could be heard but the steady tramp of the men, the rattling and jingling of canteens and accoutrements, and the occasional "Close up, men—close up!" of the officers.

The most refreshing incidents of the march occurred when the column entered some clean and cozy village where the people loved the troops. Matron and maid vied with each other in their efforts to express their devotion to the defenders of their cause. Remembering with tearful eyes the absent soldier brother or husband, they yet smiled through their tears, and with hearts and voices welcomed the coming of the road-stained troops. Their scanty larders poured out the last morsel, and their bravest words were spoken, as the column moved by. But who will tell the bitterness of the lot of the man who thus passed by his own sweet home, or the anguish of the mother as she renewed her farewell to her darling boy? Then it was that men and women learned to long for the country where partings are no more.

As evening came on, questioning of the officers was in order, and for an hour it would be, "Captain, when are we going into camp?" "I say, lieutenant, are we going to —— or to ——?" "Seen anything of our wagon?" "How long are we to stay here?" "Where's the spring?" Sometimes these questions were meant simply to tease, but generally they betrayed anxiety of some sort, and a close observer would easily detect the seriousness of the man who asked after "our wagon," because he spoke feelingly, as one who wanted his supper and was in doubt as to whether or not he would get it. People who live on country roads rarely know how far it is from anywhere to anywhere else. This is a distinguishing peculiarity of that class of people. If they do know, then they are a malicious crew. "Just over the hill there," "Just beyond those woods," "'Bout a mile," "Round the bend," and other such encouraging replies, mean anything from a mile to a day's march!

An accomplished straggler could assume more misery, look more horribly emaciated, tell more dismal stories of distress, eat more and march further (to the rear), than any ten ordinary men. Most stragglers were real sufferers, but many of them were ingenious liars, energetic foragers, plunder hunters and gormandizers. Thousands who kept their place in ranks to the very end were equally as tired, as sick, as hungry, and as hopeless, as these scamps, but too proud to tell it or use it as a means of escape from hardship. But many a poor fellow dropped in the road and breathed his last in the corner of a fence, with no one to hear his last fond mention of his loved ones. And many whose ambition it was to share every danger and discomfort with their comrades, overcome by the heat, or worn out with disease, were compelled to leave the ranks, and while friend and brother marched to battle, drag their weak and staggering frames to the rear, perhaps to die pitiably alone, in some hospital.

After all, the march had more pleasure than pain. Chosen friends walked and talked and smoked together; the hills and valleys made themselves a panorama for the feasting of the soldiers' eyes; a turnip patch here and an onion patch there invited him to occasional refreshment; and it was sweet to think that "camp" was near at hand, and rest, and the journey almost ended.

⌒

Rations in the Army of Northern Virginia were alternately superabundant and altogether wanting. The quality, quantity, and frequency of them depended upon the amount of stores in the hands of the commissaries, the relative position of the troops and the wagon trains, and the many accidents and mishaps of the campaign. During the latter years and months of the war, so uncertain was the issue as to time, quantity, and composition, that the men became in large measure independent of this seeming absolute necessity, and by some mysterious means, known only to purely patriotic soldiers, learned to fight without pay and to find subsistence in the field, the stream, or the forest, and a shelter on the bleak mountain side.

Sometimes there was an abundant issue of bread, and no meat; then meat in any quantity, and no flour or meal; sugar in abundance, and no coffee to be had for "love or money"; and then coffee in plenty, without a grain of sugar; for months nothing but flour for bread, and then nothing but meal (till all hands longed for a biscuit); or fresh meat until it was nauseating, and then salt-pork without intermission.

To be one day without anything to eat was common. Two days' fasting, marching and fighting was not uncommon, and there were times when no rations were issued for three or four days. On one march, from Petersburg to Appomattox, no rations were issued to Cutshaw's battalion of artillery for one entire week, and the men subsisted on the corn intended for the battery horses, raw bacon captured from the enemy, and the water of springs, creeks, and rivers.

A soldier in the Army of Northern Virginia was fortunate when he had his flour, meat, sugar, and coffee all at the same time and in proper quantity. Having these, the most skillful axeman of the mess hewed down a fine hickory or oak, and cut it into "lengths." All hands helped to "tote" it to the fire. When wood was convenient, the fire was large, the red coals abundant, and the meal soon prepared.

The man most gifted in the use of the skillet was the one most highly appreciated about the fire, and as tyrannical as a Turk; but when he raised the lid of the oven and exposed the brown-crusted tops of the biscuit, animosity subsided. The frying-pan, full of "grease," then became the center of attraction. As the hollow-cheeked boy "sopped" his biscuit, his poor, pinched countenance wrinkled into a smile, and his sunken eyes glistened with delight. And the coffee, too—how delicious the aroma of it, and how readily each man disposed of a quart! The strong men gathered round, chuckling at their good luck, and "cooing" like a child with a big piece of cake. Ah, this was a sight which but few of those who live and die are permitted to see!

And now the last biscuit is gone, the last drop of coffee, and the frying-pan is "wiped" clean. The tobacco-bag is pulled wide open, pipes are scraped, knocked out, and filled, the red coal is applied, and the blue smoke rises in wreaths and curls from the mouths of the no longer hungry, but happy and contented soldiers. Songs rise on the still night air, the merry laugh resounds, the woods are bright with the rising flame of the fire, story after story is told, song after song is sung, and at midnight the soldiers steal away one by one to their blankets on the ground, and sleep till reveille. Such was a meal when the mess was fortunate.

How different when the wagons have not been heard from for forty-eight hours. Now the question is, how to do the largest amount of good to the largest number with the smallest amount of material? The most experienced men discuss the situation and decide that "somebody" must go foraging. Though the stock on hand is small, no one seems anxious to leave the small certainty and go in search of the large uncertainty of supper from some farmer's well-filled table; but at last several comrades start out, and as they disappear the preparations for immediate consumption commence. The meat is too little to cook alone, and the flour will scarcely make six biscuits. The result is that "slosh" or "coosh" must do. So the bacon is fried out till the pan is half full of boiling grease. The flour is mixed with water until it flows like milk, poured into the grease and rapidly stirred till the whole is a dirty brown mixture. It is now ready to be served. Perhaps some dainty fellow prefers the more imposing "slapjack." If so, the flour is mixed with less water, the grease reduced, and the paste poured in till it covers the bottom of the pan, and, when brown on the underside, is, by a nimble twist of the pan, turned and browned again. If there is any sugar in camp it makes a delicious addition.

About the time the last scrap of "slapjack" and the last spoonful of "slosh" are disposed of, the unhappy foragers return. They take in the situation at a glance, realize with painful distinctness that they have sacrificed the homely slosh for the vain expectancy of apple butter, shortcake, and milk, and, with woeful countenance and mournful voice, narrate their adventure and disappointment thus: "Well, boys, we have done the best we could. We have walked about nine miles over the mountain, and haven't found a mouthful to eat. Sorry, but it's a fact. Give us our biscuits." Of course there are none, and, as it is not contrary to army etiquette to do so, the whole mess professes to be very sorry. Sometimes, however, the foragers returned well laden with good things, and as good comrades should, shared the fruits of their toilsome hunt with their comrades.

Foragers thought it not indelicate to linger about the house of the unsuspecting farmer till the lamp revealed the family at supper, and then modestly approach and knock at the door. As the good-hearted man knew that his guests were "posted" about the meal in progress in the next room, the invitation to supper was given, and, shall I say it, accepted with an unbecoming lack of reluctance.

The following illustrates the ingenuity of the average forager. There was great scarcity of meat, and no prospect of a supply from the wagons. Two experienced foragers were sent out, and as a farmer about ten miles from the camp was killing hogs, guided by soldier instinct, they went directly to his house, and found the meat nicely cut up, the various pieces of each hog making a separate pile on the floor of an outhouse. The proposition to buy met with a surprisingly ready response on the part of the farmer. He offered one entire pile of meat, being one whole hog, for such a small sum that the foragers instantly closed the bargain, and as promptly opened their eyes to the danger which menaced them. They gave the old gentleman a ten-dollar bill and requested change. Pleased with their honest method he hastened away to his house to obtain it. The two honest foragers hastily examined the particular pile of pork which the simple-hearted farmer designated as theirs, found it very rank and totally unfit for food, transferred half of it to another pile, from which they took half and added to theirs, and awaited the return of the farmer. On giving them their change, he assured them that they had a bargain. They agreed that they had, tossed good and bad together in a bag, said good-by, and departed as rapidly as artillerymen on foot can. The result of the trip was a "pot-pie" of large dimensions; and some six or eight men gorged with fat pork declared that they had never cared for and would not again wish to eat pork—especially pork-pies.

A large proportion of the eating of the army was done in the houses and at the tables of the people, not by the use of force, but by the wish and invitation of the people. It was at times necessary that whole towns should help to sustain the army of defense, and when this was the case, it was done voluntarily and cheerfully. The soldiers—all who conducted themselves properly—were received as honored guests and given the best in the house. There was a wonderful absence of stealing or plundering, and even when the people suffered from depredation they attributed the cause to terrible necessity rather than to wanton disregard of the rights of property. And when armed guards were placed over the smoke-houses and barns, it was not so much because the commanding general doubted the honesty as that he knew the necessities of his troops. But even pinching hunger was not held to be an excuse for marauding expeditions.

The inability of the government to furnish supplies forced the men to depend largely upon their own energy and ingenuity to obtain them. The officers, knowing this, relaxed discipline to an extent which would seem, to a European officer, for instance, ruinous. It was no uncommon sight to see a brigade or division, which was but a moment before marching in solid column along the road, scattered over an immense field searching for the luscious blackberries. And it was wonderful to see how promptly and cheerfully all returned to the ranks when the field was gleaned. In the fall of the year a persimmon tree on the roadside would halt a column and detain it till the last persimmon disappeared.

The sutler's wagon, loaded with luxuries, which was so common in the Federal army, was unknown in the Army of Northern Virginia, for two reasons: the men had no money to buy sutlers' stores, and the country no men to spare for sutlers. The nearest approach to the sutler's wagon was the "cider cart" of some old darkey, or a basket of pies and cakes displayed on the roadside for sale.

The Confederate soldier relied greatly upon the abundant supplies of eatables which the enemy was kind enough to bring him, and he cheerfully risked his life for the accomplishment of the twofold purpose of whipping the enemy and getting what he called "a square meal." After a battle there was general feasting on the Confederate side. Good things, scarcely ever seen at other times, filled the haversacks and the stomachs of the "Boys in Gray." Imagine the feelings of men half famished when they rush into a camp at one side, while the enemy flees from the other, and find the coffee on the fire, sugar at hand ready to be dropped into the coffee, bread in the oven, crackers by the box, fine beef ready cooked, desiccated vegetables by the bushel, canned peaches, lobsters, tomatoes, milk, barrels of ground and roasted coffee, soda, salt, and in short everything a hungry soldier craves. Then add the liquors, wines, cigars, and tobacco found in the tents of the officers and the wagons of the sutlers, and, remembering the condition of the victorious party, hungry, thirsty, and weary, say if it did not require wonderful devotion to duty, and great self-denial to push on, trampling under foot the plunder of the camp, and pursue the enemy till the sun went down.

When it was allowable to halt, what a glorious time it was! Men, who a moment before would have been delighted with a pone of corn bread and a piece of fat meat, discuss the comparative merits of peaches and milk and fresh tomatoes, lobster and roast beef, and, forgetting the briar-root pipe, faithful companion of the vicissitudes of the soldier's life, snuff the aroma of imported Havanas.

In sharp contrast with the mess-cooking at the big fire was the serious and diligent work of the man separated from his comrades, out of reach of the woods, but bent on cooking and eating. He has found a coal of fire, and having placed over it, in an ingenious manner, the few leaves and twigs near his post, he fans the little pile with his hat. It soon blazes. Fearing the utter consumption of his fuel, he hastens to balance on the little fire his tin cup of water. When it boils, from some secure place in his clothes he takes a little coffee and drops it in the cup, and almost instantly the cup is removed and set aside; then a slice of fat meat is laid on the coals, and when brown and crisp, completes the meal—for the "crackers," or biscuit, are ready. No one but a soldier would have undertaken to cook with such a fire, as frequently it was no bigger than a quart cup.

Crackers, or "hard tack" as they were called, are notoriously poor eating, but in the hands of the Confederate soldier were made to do good duty. When on the march and pressed for time, a piece of solid fat pork and a dry cracker was passable or luscious, as the time was long or short since the last meal. When there was leisure to do it, hardtack was soaked well and then fried in bacon grease. Prepared thus, it was a dish which no Confederate had the weakness or the strength to refuse.

Sorghum, in the absence of the better molasses of peace times, was greatly prized and eagerly sought after. A "Union" man living near the Confederate lines was one day busy boiling his crop. Naturally enough, some of "our boys" smelt out the place and determined to have some of the sweet fluid. They had found a yearling dead in the field hard by, and in thinking over the matter determined to sell the Union man if possible. So they cut from the dead animal a choice piece of beef, carried it to the old fellow and offered to trade. He accepted the offer, and the whole party walked off with canteens full.

Artillerymen, having tender consciences and no muskets, seldom, if ever, shot stray pigs; but they did sometimes, as an act of friendship, wholly disinterested, point out to the infantry a pig which seemed to need shooting, and by way of dividing the danger and responsibility of the act, accept privately a choice part of the deceased.

On one occasion, when a civilian was dining with the mess, there was a fine pig for dinner. This circumstance caused the civilian to remark on the good fare. The "forager" replied that pig was an uncommon dish, this one having been kicked by one of the battery horses while stealing corn, and instantly killed. The civilian seemed to doubt the statement after his teeth had come down hard on a pistol bullet, and continued to doubt, though assured that it was the head of a horse-shoe nail.

The most melancholy eating a soldier was ever forced to do, was, when pinched with hunger, cold, wet, and dejected, he wandered over the deserted field of battle and satisfied his cravings with the contents of the haversacks of the dead. If there is anything which will overcome the natural abhorrence which a man feels for the enemy, the loathing of the bloated dead, and the awe engendered by the presence of death, solitude, and silence, it is hunger. Impelled by its clamoring, men of high principle and tenderest humanity become for the time void of sensibility, and condescend to acts which, though justified by their extremity, seem afterwards, even to the doers, too shameless to mention.

When rations became so very small that it was absolutely necessary to supplement them, and the camp was permanently established, those men who had the physical ability worked for the neighborhood farmers at cutting cord-wood, harvesting the crops, killing hogs, or any other farm-work. A stout man would cut a cord of wood a day and receive fifty cents in money, or its equivalent in something eatable. Hogs were slaughtered for the "fifth quarter." When the corn became large enough to eat, the roasting ears, thrown in the ashes with the shucks on, and nicely roasted, made a grateful meal. Turnip and onion patches also furnished delightful and much-needed food, good raw or cooked.

Occasionally, when a mess was hard pushed for eatables, it became necessary to resort to some ingenious method of disgusting a part of the mess, that the others might eat their fill. The "pepper treatment" was a common method practiced with the soup. A shrewd fellow, who loved things "hot," decided to have plenty of soup, and to accomplish his purpose, as he passed and repassed the boiling pot, dropped in a pod of red pepper. But, alas! for him, there was another man like minded who adopted the same plan, and the result was that all the mess waited in vain for that pot of soup to cool.

The individual coffee-boiler of one man in the Army of Northern Virginia was always kept at the boiling point. The owner of it was an enigma to his comrades. They could not understand his strange fondness for "red-hot" coffee. Since the war he has explained that he found the heat of the coffee prevented its use by others, and adopted the plan of placing his cup on the fire after every sip. This same character never troubled himself to carry a canteen, though a great water drinker. When he found a good canteen he would kindly give it to a comrade, reserving the privilege of an occasional drink when in need. He soon had an interest in thirty or forty canteens and their contents, and could always get a drink of water if it was to be found in any of them. He pursued the same plan with blankets, and always had plenty in that line. His entire outfit was the clothes on his back and a haversack accurately shaped to hold one half pone of corn bread.

Roasting-ear time was a trying time for the hungry private. Having been fed during the whole of the winter on salt meat and coarse bread, his system craved the fresh, luscious juice of the corn, and at times his honesty gave way under the pressure. How could he resist? He didn't—he took some roasting ears! Sometimes the farmer grumbled, sometimes he quarreled, and sometimes he complained to the officers of the depredations of "the men." The officers apologized, ate what corn they had on hand, and sent their "boy" for some more. One old farmer conceived the happy plan of inviting some privates to his house, stating his grievances, and securing their coöperation in the effort to protect his corn. He told them that of course *they* were not the *gentlemen* who took his corn! Oh no! of course *they* would not do such a thing; but wouldn't they please speak to the others and ask them please not to take his corn? Of course! certainly! oh, yes! they would remonstrate with their comrades. How they burned, though, as they thought of the past and contemplated the near future. As they returned to camp through the field they filled their haversacks with the silky ears, and were met on the other side of the field by the kind farmer and a file of men, who were only too eager to secure the plucked corn "in the line of duty."

A faithful officer, worn out with the long, weary march, sick, hungry, and dejected, leaned his back against a tree and groaned to think of his inability to join in the chase of an old hare, which, he knew, from the wild yells in the wood, his men were pursuing. But the uproar approached him—nearer, nearer, and nearer, until he saw the hare bounding towards him with a regiment at her heels. She spied an opening made by the folds of the officer's cloak and jumped in, and he embraced his first meal for forty-eight hours.

An artilleryman, camped for a day where no water was to be found easily, awakened during the night by thirst, went stumbling about in search of water; and to his great delight found a large bucketful. He drank his fill, and in the morning found that what he drank had washed a bullock's head, and was crimson with its blood.

Some stragglers came up one night and found the camp silent. All hands asleep. Being hungry they sought and to their great delight found a large pot of soup. It had a peculiar taste, but they "worried" it down, and in the morning bragged of their good fortune. The soup had defied the stomachs of the whole battery, being strongly impregnated with the peculiar flavor of defunct cockroaches.

Shortly before the evacuation of Petersburg, a country boy went hunting. He killed and brought to camp a muskrat. It was skinned, cleaned, buried a day or two, disinterred, cooked, and eaten with great relish. It was splendid. During the seven days' battles around Richmond, a studious private observed the rats as they entered and emerged from a corn-crib. He killed one, cooked it privately, and invited a friend to join him in eating a fine squirrel. The comrade consented, ate heartily, and when told what he had eaten, forthwith disgorged. But he confesses that up to the time when he was enlightened he had greatly enjoyed the meal. It was at this time, when rats were a delicacy, that the troops around Richmond agreed to divide their rations with the poor of the city, and they were actually hauled in and distributed. Comment here would be like complimenting the sun on its brilliancy.

Orators dwell on the genius and skill of the general officers; historians tell of the movements of divisions and army corps, and the student of the art of war studies the geography and topography of the country and the returns of the various corps: they all seek to find and to tell the secret of success or failure. The Confederate soldier knows the elements of his success—courage, endurance, and devotion. He knows also by whom he was defeated—sickness, starvation, death. He fought not men only, but food, raiment, pay, glory, fame, and fanaticism. He endured privation, toil, and contempt. He won, and despite the cold indifference of all and the hearty hatred of some, he will have for all time, in all places where generosity is, a fame untarnished.

CHAPTER 7

Robert E. Lee in Command
By Captain Robert E. Lee (General Lee's son)

Because Robert E. Lee never published a memoir or autobiography, revisiting the actual words of one of the most famous generals in history requires the works of others and General Lee's own letters and dispatches. Captain Robert E. Lee, General Lee's son, provides an illuminating treasury of General Lee's words in the book Recollections and Letters of General Robert E. Lee. *From turning down Lincoln's offer for him to command the Union army to glimpses of Lee's personal life, the book provides an intimate portrait and great insight into the life of the Virginian who inspired the entire Confederate army, even though he officially only led the Army of Northern Virginia.*

—LAMAR UNDERWOOD

GENERAL LEE'S UNION ARMY RESIGNATION IN FEBRUARY, 1861, AFTER THE SECESSION of Texas, my father was ordered to report to General Scott, the Commander-in-Chief of the United States Army. He immediately relinquished the command of his regiment, and departed from Fort Mason, Texas, for Washington. He reached Arlington March 1st. April 17th, Virginia seceded. On the 18th Colonel Lee had a long interview with General Scott. On April 20th he tendered his resignation of his commission in the United States Army. The same day he wrote to General Scott the following letter:

"Arlington, Virginia, April 20, 1861.
"General: Since my interview with you on the 18th inst. I have felt that I ought no longer to retain my commission in the Army. I therefore tender my resignation, which I request you will recommend for acceptance. It would have been presented at once but for the struggle it has cost me to separate myself from a service to which I have devoted the best years of my life, and all the ability I possessed.

"During the whole of that time—more than a quarter of a century—I have experienced nothing but kindness from my superiors and a most cordial friendship from my comrades. To no one, General, have I been as much indebted as to yourself for uniform kindness and consideration, and it has always been my ardent desire to merit your approbation. I shall carry to the grave the most grateful recollections of your kind consideration, and your name and fame shall always be dear to me.

"Save in the defense of my native State, I never desire again to draw my sword.

"Be pleased to accept my most earnest wishes for the continuance of your happiness and prosperity, and believe me most truly yours,

"(Signed)

"R. E. Lee"

His resignation was written the same day.

"Arlington, Washington City P.O., April 20, 1861.

"Honourable Simon Cameron, Secretary of War.

"Sir: I have the honour to tender the resignation of my command as Colonel of the First Regiment of Cavalry.

"Very respectfully your obedient servant,

"R. E. Lee,

"Colonel First Cavalry"

To show further his great feeling in thus having to leave the army with which he had been associated for so long, I give two more letters, one to his sister, Mrs. Anne Marshall, of Baltimore, the other to his brother, Captain Sydney Smith Lee, of the United States Navy:

"Arlington, Virginia, April 20, 1861.

"My Dear Sister: I am grieved at my inability to see you. . . . I have been waiting for a 'more convenient season,' which has brought to many before me deep and lasting regret. Now we are in a state of war which will yield to nothing. The whole South is in a state of revolution, into which Virginia, after a long struggle, has been drawn; and though I recognise no necessity for this state of things, and would have forborne and pleaded to the end for redress of grievances, real or supposed, yet in my own person I had to meet the question whether I should take part against my native State.

"With all my devotion to the Union and the feeling of loyalty and duty of an American citizen, I have not been able to make up my mind to raise my hand against my relatives, my children, my home. I have therefore resigned my commission in the Army, and save in defense of my native State, with the sincere hope that my poor services may never be needed, I hope I may never be called on to draw my sword. I know you will blame me; but you must think as kindly of me as you can, and believe that I have endeavoured to do what I thought right.

"To show you the feeling and struggle it has cost me, I send you a copy of my letter of resignation. I have no time for more. May God guard and protect you and yours, and shower upon you everlasting blessings, is the prayer of your devoted brother, R. E. Lee."

"Arlington, Virginia, April 20, 1860.
"My Dear Brother Smith: The question which was the subject of my earnest consultation with you on the 18th inst. has in my own mind been decided. After the most anxious inquiry as to the correct course for me to pursue, I concluded to resign, and sent in my resignation this morning. I wished to wait till the Ordinance of secession should be acted on by the people of Virginia; but war seems to have commenced, and I am liable at any time to be ordered on duty which I could not conscientiously perform. To save me from such a position, and to prevent the necessity of resigning under orders, I had to act at once, and before I could see you again on the subject, as I had wished. I am now a private citizen, and have no other ambition than to remain at home. Save in defense of my native State, I have no desire ever again to draw my sword. I send you my warmest love.
    "Your affectionate brother,
    "R. E. Lee."

PRESIDENT LINCOLN'S OFFER

I will give here one of my father's letters, written after the war, in which is his account of his resignation from the United States Army:

"Lexington, Virginia, February 25, 1868.
"Honourable Reverdy Johnson,
"United States Senate, Washington, D.C.
"My Dear Sir: My attention has been called to the official report of the debate in the Senate of the United States, on the 19th instant, in which you did my the kindness to doubt the correctness of the statement made by the Honourable Simon Cameron, in regard to myself. I desire that you may feel certain of my conduct on the occasion referred to, so far as my individual statement can make you. I never intimated to any one that I desired the command of the United States Army; nor did I ever have a conversation with but one gentleman, Mr. Francis Preston Blair, on the subject, which was at his invitation, and, as I understood, at the instance of President Lincoln. After listening to his remarks, I declined the offer that he made me, to take command of the army that was to be brought into

the field; stating, as candidly and courteously as I could, that, though opposed to secession and deprecating war, I could take no part in an invasion of the Southern States. I went directly from the interview with Mr. Blair to the office of General Scott; told him of the proposition that had been made to me, and my decision. Upon reflection after returning to my home, I concluded that I ought no longer to retain the commission I held in the United States Army, and on the second morning thereafter I forwarded my resignation to General Scott. At the time, I hoped that peace would have been preserved; that some way would have been found to save the country from the calamities of war; and I then had no other intention than to pass the remainder of my life as a private citizen. Two days afterward, upon the invitation of the Governor of Virginia, I repaired to Richmond; found that the Convention then in session had passed the ordinance withdrawing the State from the Union; and accepted the commission of commander of its forces, which was tendered me.

"These are the ample facts of the case, and they show that Mr. Cameron has been misinformed.

"I am with great respect,

"Your obedient servant,

"R. E. Lee."

ON TO RICHMOND

My father reached Richmond April 22, 1861. The next day he was introduced to the Virginia Convention, and offered by them the command of the military forces of his State. In his reply to Mr. John Janney, the President, who spoke for the Convention, he said:

"Mr. President and Gentlemen of the Convention: Deeply impressed with the solemnity of the occasion on which I appear before you, and profoundly grateful for the honour conferred upon me, I accept the position your partiality has assigned me, though I would greatly have preferred your choice should have fallen on one more capable.

"Trusting to Almighty God, an approving conscience, and the aid of my fellow citizens, I will devote myself to the defense and service of my native State, in whose behalf alone would I have ever drawn my sword."

On April 26th, from Richmond, he wrote to his wife:

"I am very anxious about you. You have to move and make arrangements to go to some point of safety, which you must select. The Mount Vernon plate and pictures ought to be secured. Keep quiet while you remain and in your preparation. War is inevitable, and there is no telling when it will burst around you.

Virginia, yesterday, I understand, joined the Confederate States. What policy they may adopt I cannot conjecture. May God bless and preserve you, and have mercy upon all our people, is the constant prayer of your affectionate husband,

"R. E. Lee."

On April 30th:

"On going to my room last night I found my trunk and sword there, and opening them this morning discovered the package of letters and was very glad to learn you were all well and as yet peaceful. I fear the latter state will not continue long. . . . I think therefore you had better prepare all things for removal, that is, the plate, pictures, etc., and be prepared at any moment. Where to go is the difficulty. When the war commences no place will be exempt, in my opinion, and indeed all the avenues into the State will be the scenes of military operations.

"There is no prospect or intention of the Government to propose a truce. Do not be deceived by it. . . . May God preserve you all and bring peace to our distracted country."

Again to my mother at Arlington:

"Richmond, May 2, 1861.

"My dear Mary: I received last night your letter of the 1st, with contents. It gave me great pleasure to learn that you are all well and in peace. You know how pleased I should be to have you and my dear daughters with me. That I fear can not be. There is no place that I can expect to be but in the field, and there is no rest for me to look to, but I want you to be in a place of safety. . . . We have only to be resigned to God's will and pleasure, and do all we can for our protection. . . . I have just received Custis's letter of the 30th, inclosing the acceptance of my resignation. It is stated that it will take effect April 25th. I resigned on the 20th, and wished it to take effect that day. I cannot consent to its running on further, and he must receive no pay, if they tender it, beyond that day, but return the whole, if need be."

From another letter to my mother, dated May 8th:

"I grieve at the necessity that drives you from your home. I can appreciate your feelings on the occasion, and pray that you may receive comfort and strength in the difficulties that surround you. When I reflect upon the calamity impending over the country, my own sorrows sink into insignificance. . . . Be content and resigned to God's will. I shall be able to write seldom. Write to me, as you letters will be my greatest comfort. I send a check for $500; it is all I have in bank. Pay the children's school expenses."

To my mother, still at Arlington:

"Richmond, May 11, 1861.

"I have received your letter of the 9th from Arlington. I had supposed you were at Ravensworth. . . . I am glad to hear that you are at peace, and enjoying the sweet weather and beautiful flowers. You had better complete your arrangements and retire further from the scene of war. It may burst upon you at any time. It is sad to think of the devastation, if not ruin, it may bring upon a spot so endeared to us. But God's will be done. We must be resigned. May He guard and keep you all, is my constant prayer."

HANDLING PERSONAL AFFAIRS

All this time my father was very hard at work organizing and equipping the volunteers who were pouring into Richmond from the Southern States, but he was in constant correspondence with my mother, helping her all he could in her arrangements for leaving her home. His letters show that he thought of everything, even the least, and he gave the most particular directions about his family, their effects, the servants, the horses, the farm, pictures, plate, and furniture. Being called to Norfolk suddenly, before going he wrote to my mother:

"Richmond, May 16, 1861.

"My Dear Mary: I am called down to Norfolk and leave this afternoon. I expect to return Friday, but may be delayed. I write to advise you of my absence, in case you should not receive answers to any letters that may arrive. I have not heard from you since I last wrote; nor have I anything to relate. I heard from my dear little Rob, who had an attack of chills and fever. He hoped to escape the next paroxysm. . . . I witnessed the opening of the convention [The Episcopal Convention of the Diocese of Virginia] yesterday, and heard the good Bishop's [Bishop Meade, of Virginia] sermon, being the 50th anniversary of his ministry. It was a most impressive scene, and more than once I felt the tears coming down my cheek. It was from the text, 'and Pharoh said unto Jacob, how old art thou?' It was full of humility and self-reproach. I saw Mr. Walker, Bishop Johns, Bishop Atkinson, etc. I have not been able to attend any other services, and presume the session will not be prolonged. I suppose it may be considered a small attendance. Should Custis arrive during my absence, I will leave word for him to take my room at the Spotswood till my return. Smith [his brother, S. S. Lee, C. S. N.] is well and enjoys a ride in the afternoon with Mrs. Stannard. The charming women, you know, always find him out. Give much love to Cousin Anna, Nannie, and dear daughters. When Rob leaves the University take him with you.

"Truly and affectionately, R. E. Lee."

By this time my mother and all the family had left Arlington. My brother, Custis, had joined my father in Richmond, the girls had gone to Fauquier county, to visit relatives, and my mother to Ravensworth, about ten miles from Arlington towards Fairfax Court House, where her aunt, Mrs. A. M. Fitzhugh, lived. Always considerate of the happiness and comfort of others, my father feared that his wife's presence at Ravensworth might possibly bring annoyance to "Cousin Anna," as he called our aunt, and he wrote to my mother, urging her not to remain there. He sympathised with her in having to leave her home, which she never saw again.

"Richmond, May 25, 1861.
"I have been trying, dearest Mary, ever since the receipt of your letter by Custis, to write to you. I sympathise deeply in your feelings at leaving your dear home. I have experienced them myself, and they are constantly revived. I fear we have not been grateful enough for the happiness there within our reach, and our Heavenly Father has found it necessary to deprive us of what He has given us. I acknowledge my ingratitude, my transgressions, and my unworthiness, and submit with resignation to what he thinks proper to inflict upon me. We must trust all then to him, and I do not think it prudent or right for you to return there, while the United States troops occupy that country. I have gone over all this ground before, and have just written Cousin Anna on the subject.

"While writing, I received a telegram from Cousin John Goldsborough [a cousin of Mrs. Fitzhugh], urging your departure 'South.' I suppose he is impressed with the risk of your present position, and in addition to the possibility, or probability, of personal annoyance to yourself, I fear your presence may provoke annoyance in Cousin Anna. But unless Cousin Anna goes with you, I shall be distressed about her being there alone. If the girls went to 'Kinloch' or 'Eastern View,' you and Cousin Anna might take care of yourselves, because you could get in the carriage and go off in an emergency. But I really am afraid that you may prove more harm than comfort to her. Mr. Wm. C. Rives has just been in to say that if you and Cousin Anna will go to his house, he will be very glad for you to stay as long as you please. That his son has a commodious house just opposite his, unoccupied, partially furnished; that you could, if you prefer, take that, bring up servants and what you desire, and remain there as independent as at home. . . . I must now leave the matter to you, and pray that God may guard you. I have no time for more. I know and feel the discomfort of your position, but it cannot be helped, and we must bear our trials like Christians. . . . If you and Cousin Anna choose to come here, you know how happy we shall be to see you. I shall take the field as soon now as I can.

"Ever yours truly and devotedly,
"R. E. Lee."

Three days later he was at Manassas, only a short distance from Ravensworth, and he sent her this short note:

"Manassas, May 28, 1861.

"I reached here, dearest Mary, this afternoon. I am very much occupied in examining matters, and have to go out to look over the ground. Cousin John tempts me strongly to go down, but I never visit for many reasons. If for no other, to prevent compromising the house, for my visit would certainly be known.

"I have written to you fully and to Cousin Anna. I am decidedly of the opinion that it would be better for you to leave, on your account and Cousin Anna's. My only objection is the leaving of Cousin Anna alone, if she will not go with you. If you prefer Richmond, go with Nannie. Otherwise, go to the upper country, as John indicates. I fear I cannot be with you anywhere. I do not think Richmond will be permanent.

"Truly, R."

I may as well say here, that "Cousin Anna" never did leave "Ravensworth" during the war. She remained there, with only a few faithful servants, and managed to escape any serious molestation. "Nannie" was Mrs. S. S. Lee, who shortly after this time went to Richmond.

On May 25th, my father was transferred, with all the Virginia troops, to the Confederate States Army. He ceased to be a Major-General, and became a Brigadier, no higher rank having been created as yet in the Confederate service. Later, when the rank was created, he was made a full general. By the end of May, to quote from General Long, "Lee had organized, equipped, and sent to the field more than thirty thousand men, and various regiments were in a forward state of preparation."

When the Confederate government moved from Montgomery to Richmond, and President Davis took charge of all military movements, my father was kept near him as his constant and trusted adviser. His experience as an engineer was of great service to the young Confederacy, and he was called upon often for advice for the location of batteries and troops on our different defensive lines. In a letter to my mother he speaks of one of these trips to the waters east of Richmond.

"Richmond, June 9, 1861.

"I have just returned from a visit to the batteries and troops on James and York rivers, etc., where I was some days. I called a few hours at the White House. Saw Charlotte and Annie. Fitzhugh was away, but got out of the cars as I got in. Our little boy looked very sweet and seemed glad to kiss me good-bye. Charlotte said she was going to prepare to leave for the summer, but had not determined where to go. I could only see some of the servants about the house and the stables. They were all well. . . . You may be aware that the Confederate Government is established here. Yesterday I turned over to it the command of the military and naval forces of the State, in accordance with the proclamation of the Government and the agreement between the State and the Confederate States. I do not know what my position will be. I should like to retire to private life, if I could be with you and the children, but if I can be of any service to the State or her cause I must continue. Mr. Davis and all his Cabinet are here. . . . Good-bye. Give much love to kind friends. May God guard and bless you, them, and our suffering country, and enable me to perform my duty. I think of you constantly. Write me what you will do. Direct here.

"Always yours,
"R. E. Lee."

To my mother, who was now in Fauquier county, staying at "Kinloch," Mr. Edward Turner's home, he writes on June 24th, from Richmond:

"Your future arrangements are the source of much anxiety to me. No one can say what is in the future, nor is it wise to anticipate evil. But it is well to prepare for what may reasonably happen and be provided for the worst. There is no saying when you can return to your home or what may be its condition when you do return. What, then, can you do in the meantime? To remain with friends may be incumbent, and where can you go? . . . My movements are very uncertain, and I wish to take the field as soon as certain arrangements can be made. I may go at any moment, and to any point where it may be necessary. . . . Many of our old friends are dropping in. E. P. Alexander is here, Jimmy Hill, Alston, Jenifer, etc., and I hear that my old colonel, A. S. Johnston, is crossing the plains from California.

"As ever, R. E. Lee."

I again quote from a letter to my mother, dated Richmond, July 12, 1861:

"I am very anxious to get into the field, but am detained by matters beyond my control. I have never heard of the appointment, to which you allude, of Commander-in-Chief of the Confederate States Army, nor have I any expectation or wish for it. President Davis holds that position. Since the transfer of the military operations in Virginia to the authorities of the Confederate States, I have only occupied the position of a general in that service, with the duties devolved on me by the President. I have been labouring to prepare and get into the field the Virginia troops, and to strengthen, by those from the other States, the threatened commands of Johnston, Beauregard, Huger, Garnett, etc. Where I shall go I do not know, as that will depend upon President Davis. As usual in getting through with a thing, I have broken down a little and had to take my bed last evening, but am at my office this morning and hope will soon be right again. . . . My young friend Mr. Vest has just returned from a search in the city for 'Dixie,' and says he has visited every place in Richmond without finding it. I suppose it is exhausted.

"Always yours,

"R. E. Lee.

"The booksellers say 'Dixie' is not to be had in Virginia. R. E. L."

VICTORY AT MANASSAS

On July 21st occurred the battle of Manassas. In a letter to my mother written on the 27th, my father says:

"That indeed was a glorious victory and has lightened the pressure upon our front amazingly. Do not grieve for the brave dead. Sorrow for those they left behind—friends, relatives, and families. The former are at rest. The latter must suffer. The battle will be repeated there in greater force. I hope God will again smile on us and strengthen our hearts and arms. I wished to partake in the former struggle, and am mortified at my absence, but the President thought it more important I should be here. I could not have done as well as has been done, but I could have helped, and taken part in the struggle for my home and neighbourhood. So the work is done I care not by whom it is done. I leave to-morrow for the Northwest Army. I wished to go before, as I wrote you, and was all prepared, but the indications were so evident of the coming battle, and in the uncertainty of the result, the President forbade my departure. Now it is necessary and he consents. I cannot say for how long, but will write you. . . . I enclose you a letter from Markie [Miss Martha Custis Williams—second cousin of my mother, afterward Mrs. Admiral Carter, U.S.N.]. Write to her if you can and thank her for her letter to me. I have not time. My whole time is occupied, and all my thoughts and strength are given to the cause to which my life, be it long or short, will be devoted. Tell her not to mind the reports she sees in the papers. They are made to injure and occasion distrust. Those that know me will not believe them. Those that do not will not care for them. I laugh at them. Give love to all, and for yourself accept the constant prayers and love of truly yours,

"R. E. Lee."

CHAPTER 8

Slaughterhouse at Fredericksburg
By Frederick L. Hitchcock

From his book War from the Inside, *concerning the 132nd Regiment, Pennsylvania Volunteer Infantry, Frederick Hitchcock has already given us a chapter on America's deadliest single day of battle in our chapter 3, the story of Antietam. Now he turns to another of the Union army's most costly battles, at Fredericksburg, Virginia. Here the casualties of dead and wounded among Union soldiers charging fixed positions of Confederates were like suicide attacks. The slaughter of the engagement so impressed Confederate General James Longstreet that he could never shake off the obvious waste of having soldiers charging into the deadly fire of modern weapons. Such memories no doubt played a large part in his actions at Gettysburg, urging Lee to take up defensive positions againt Meade's Union army instead of attacking fixed positions.*

—Lamar Underwood

Just at the time I was taken sick, on the 9th of November, whilst the army was approaching Warrenton, the order relieving General McClellan from the command of the Army of the Potomac was issued. He was ordered to report to his home in Trenton, N. J., on waiting orders. Great was the consternation among the veterans of that army on his retirement, for they really had a strong attachment for "Little Mac," as they fondly called him. He took his leave in an affectionate order, recounting the heroic deeds of this noble army. This was followed by a grand review, accompanied by battery salutes, and the military career of General George B. McClellan passed into history.

———

I picked up an old "crow-bait" of a horse, the only four-footed transportation possibly obtainable, and started for Fredericksburg to find my regiment. The only directions I had about disposing of this frame of a horse was to "turn the bones loose when you get through with him." He could go only at a snail's pace, and when I reached Fredericksburg it must have been nine o'clock. I crossed the pontoon bridge, which had been laid the morning before under circumstances of the greatest gallantry by Howard's division of our corps.

The "ball" was now well opened. Marye's Heights (pronounced Marie, with the accent on the last letter, as if spelled Maree), circling the city from the river above to a point below the city, was literally crowded with batteries of rebel artillery. These guns were firing at our batteries on the heights on the other side of the river, and also upon our troops occupying the city. The air was filled with screeching, bursting shells, and a deafening pandemonium was in progress. It was not a very inviting place to enter under these circumstances, but it was as safe for me as for my regiment, and my duty was to be with them. The trouble was to find it in that multitude of troops filling all the streets of the city. Our corps alone numbered probably twelve thousand men at that time, and the Ninth Corps was there besides. However, I soon found Kimball's brigade to my great delight, supposing our regiment was in it, as it was when I went away. General Kimball greeted me with great cordiality; but when I asked where my regiment was, he said he was sorry he could not inform me; that they had that morning been transferred, much against his will, to General Max Weber's brigade, and where that was he did not know. It was probably somewhere in the city. Said he:

"You cannot possibly find it now, and it is a waste of time to try. I can give you plenty of work to-day. Stay with me and serve as an aide on my staff."

The officers of his staff, all of whom were personal friends, urgently joined in the general's invitation. But I felt that I must be with the regiment if it were possible to find it, and so declined what would have been a distinguishing service. Some distance down the main street I ran on to the regiment just when I had abandoned all hope of finding it. My reception was exceedingly cordial, accompanied with the remark: "Just in time, adjutant, just in time." I found Lieutenant-Colonel Albright in command and with no help from our field and staff. Colonel Wilcox was still on sick leave. Major Shreve had returned to camp during the heavy cannonading of the day before, and Colonel Albright had lost his voice from a severe cold, so that I had to supply voice for him in the issuing of orders, in addition to my other duties.

The situation was most portentous. We lay in the main street under the shelter of the houses, which were being bombarded by the rebel batteries in their efforts to reach our troops. The houses were all vacant; the people had fled on the approach of our army. Not a soul did we see of the inhabitants of the city during the two days we occupied it. They had evidently left in great haste, taking but few things with them. I was told that in some houses the boys found and ate meals that had been prepared and left in their flight, and in all there was more or less food, which was appropriated. Flour was plentiful, and the night after the battle there were army flapjacks galore. In some cases it might have been said these were fearfully and wonderfully made, but they went just the same.

An incident connected with this occupation of Fredericksburg comes to light after forty years. If General Howard should see it the mystery of the sudden disappearance of his breakfast on that morning might be cleared up. Our regiment happened to be quartered in the morning near his head-quarters. Rations were scarce. General Howard's servant had prepared him a most tempting breakfast from supplies found and confiscated from one of the houses. The sight of this repast and its savory fumes were too much for the empty stomachs of two of our men, who shall be nameless here. The trick was a neat one. One of them got the attention of the cook and held it until the other reached into the tent and dumped the contents of the main dish, hot and steaming, into his haversack and quietly sauntered away. When the cook discovered his loss the other fellow was gone. These rascals said it was the best dish of ham and eggs they ever ate.

Many houses had fine pianos and other musical instruments, and in some instances impromptu dances were on whilst Confederate shells whanged through the house above their heads. It is safe to say that there was little left of valuable bric-à-brac to greet the fugitive people on their return. And it is highly probable that pianos and handsome furniture needed considerable repairing after the exodus of the "Yank." This was not due to pure vandalism, although war creates the latter, but to the feeling of hatred for the miserable rebels who had brought on the war and were the cause of our being there. And it must be admitted there were some who pocketed all they could for the commercialism there might be in it, the argument again being, "somebody will take it, and I might as well have it as the other fellow." The first part of the argument was doubtless as true as the latter part was false.

Many trinkets were hawked about among the men after the fight as souvenirs. Among them was a silver-plated communion flagon. Some scamp had filched it from one of the churches and was trying to sell it. Fortunately, he did not belong to our regiment. Our chaplain took it from him and had it strapped to his saddle-bag. His purpose was to preserve it for its owner if the time should come that it could be returned. But in the meantime its presence attached to his saddle made him the butt of any amount of raillery from both officers and men.

When I joined the regiment it was lying in front of the Court-House, from the steeple of which some sixty or seventy feet high, the flags of our signal-corps were most actively wagging. It occurred to me that those signal-men were mighty nervy fellows. They were a beautiful mark for the rebel batteries, which were evidently doing their best to knock them out. The steeple was a plain, old-fashioned affair, having an open belfry, which seemed to be supported by four upright posts or timbers. I saw one of those uprights knocked out by a rebel shell. A couple more equally good shots and our signal-fellows would come ignominiously—no, gloriously—down, for there could be no ignominy with such pluck. But the wig-wagging went on, I fancied, with a little more snap and audacity than before, and they maintained their station there in the very teeth of the rebel batteries until the army was withdrawn. So much for "Yankee nerve."

I afterwards learned that the signal-officer there was none other than Lieutenant Frederick Fuller, of Scranton, one of my most intimate personal friends. Lieutenant Fuller told me that he was on duty at Burnside's head-quarters on that morning; that a station was ordered opened in the belfry of that Court-House, and another officer was despatched thither for that duty; that after waiting some time for the flags to appear he was ordered over to see what the trouble was. He found the other officer sitting under shelter, afraid to mount the belfry, nor could any persuasion induce him to face that storm of shell. Lieutenant Fuller thereupon climbed up into the belfry, opened the station himself, and ran it during the whole battle.

About ten o'clock the command "Forward" was sounded, and our brigade moved out towards Marye's Heights. Some idea of the topography of Fredericksburg and its rear I find is necessary to an understanding of what follows. Marye's Heights, which encircle the city back some five hundred yards, are the termination of a plateau which rises from one hundred and fifty to two hundred feet in an abrupt terrace from the plain upon which the city stands. These heights form a half-circle from the river above to a point below the city some little distance from the river, and are from a mile to a mile and a half long and are most admirably adapted for defensive purposes. The rebel batteries, numbering at least one hundred guns, were massed on these heights, and covered not only every street leading out from the city, but every square foot of ground of the plain below. A third of the way down the terrace was an earthwork filled with infantry, whilst at its foot ran the famous stone wall extending southward from the cemetery above the city, and was continued by an earthwork around the whole circle. Behind this stone wall was massed a double line of Confederate infantry. To enter either street leading out to those heights was to face the concentrated fire of that mass of artillery and the deadly work of those three lines of infantry. Yet that was just what we had before us.

Our division (French's) led the assault. Our regiment brought up the rear of our brigade column. As each regiment turned into the street leading out, it took up the run to cover this exposed ground as quickly as possible. Lieutenant-Colonel Albright was leading our regiment and I was by his side. We passed rapidly up the street, already covered with the dead and wounded which had fallen from the regiments that had preceded us, until we reached the embankment of a railroad, which was nearly parallel with the enemy's works. A temporary halt was made here preparatory to moving forward in line of battle.

Turning to see that our men were in position, I was amazed to find that we had but one company with us. It was my duty as adjutant to go back and find and bring up the balance of the regiment. The distance was about four hundred yards. I can truthfully say that in that moment I gave my life up. I do not expect ever again to face death more certainly than I thought I did then. It did not seem possible that I could go through that fire again and return alive. The grass did not grow under my feet going back. My sprinting record was probably made then. It may be possible to see the humorous side at this distance, but it was verily a life and death matter then. One may ask how such dangers can be faced. The answer is, there are many things more to be feared than death. Cowardice and failure of duty with me were some of them. I can fully appreciate the story of the soldier's soliloquy as he saw a rabbit sprinting back from the line of fire:

"Go it, cotton tail; if I hadn't a reputation at stake, I'd go to."

Reputation and duty were the holding forces. I said to myself, "This is duty. I'll trust in God and do it. If I fall, I cannot die better." Without the help and stimulus of that trust I could not have done it, for I doubt if any man was ever more keenly susceptible to danger than I, and the experience of Antietam had taught me the full force of this danger. The nervous strain was simply awful. It can be appreciated only by those who have experienced it. The atmosphere seemed surcharged with the most startling and frightful things. Deaths, wounds, and appalling destruction everywhere. As fast as I was running back over that street, my eyes caught an incident that I can see now, which excited my pity, though I had no time to offer help. A fine-looking fellow had been struck by a shot, which had severed one leg and left it hanging by one of the tendons, the bone protruding, and he was bleeding profusely. Some men were apparently trying to get him off the street. They had hold of his arms and the other leg, but were jumping and dodging at every shell that exploded, jerking and twisting this dangling leg to his horrible torture. I remember hearing him beseeching them to lay him down and let him die. They were probably a trio of cowards trying to get back from the front, and were using this wounded man to get away with, a not infrequent occurrence with that class of bummers.

I found the balance of the regiment had passed our street and were in confusion further down the main street. As the second company was about turning to follow the column a shell had exploded in their faces, killing and wounding some ten men and throwing it into disorder. Before it could be rallied the advancing column was out of sight. It was the work of but a few moments to straighten out the tangle and head them again for the front. No body of men could have more quickly and bravely responded, though they told me afterwards that they read in my pallid face the character of the work before them. Back we went up that street on the run, having to pick our way to avoid stepping on the dead and wounded, for the ground was now blue with our fallen heroes.

Reaching the place in the rear of that railroad embankment, where I had left the brigade, I found it had just gone forward in line of battle, and a staff officer directed me to bring the rest of the regiment forward under fire, which I did, fortunately getting them into their proper position.

The line was lying prone upon the ground in that open field and trying to maintain a fire against the rebel infantry not more than one hundred and fifty yards in our front behind that stone wall. We were now exposed to the fire of their three lines of infantry, having no shelter whatever. It was like standing upon a raised platform to be shot down by those sheltered behind it. Had we been ordered to fix bayonets and charge those heights we could have understood the movement, though that would have been an impossible undertaking, defended as they were. But to be sent close up to those lines to maintain a firing-line without any intrenchments or other shelter, if that was its purpose, was simply to invite wholesale slaughter without the least compensation. It was to attempt the impossible, and invite certain destruction in the effort. On this interesting subject I have very decided convictions, which I will give later on.

Proceeding now with my narrative, we were evidently in a fearful slaughter-pen. Our men were being swept away as by a terrific whirlwind. The ground was soft and spongy from recent rains, and our faces and clothes were bespattered with mud from bullets and fragments of shells striking the ground about us, whilst men were every moment being hit by the storm of projectiles that filled the air. In the midst of that frightful carnage a man rushing by grasped my hand and spoke. I turned and looked into the face of a friend from a distant city. There was a glance of recognition and he was swept away. What his fate was I do not know.

That same moment I received what was supposed to be my death wound. Whilst the men were lying down, my duties kept me on my feet. Lieutenant Charles McDougal, commanding the color company, called to me that the color-guard were all either killed or wounded. We had two stands of colors, the national and State flags. These colors were carried by two color-sergeants, protected by six color-corporals, which made up the color-guard. If either sergeant became disabled the nearest corporal took the colors, and so on until the color-guard were down. This was the condition when this officer called to me to replace these disabled men, so that the colors should be kept flying.

He had one flag in his hand as I approached him, and he was in the act of handing it to me when a bullet crashed through his arm and wrist, spattering my face with his warm blood. I seized the staff as it fell from his shattered arm. The next instant a bullet cut the staff away just below my hand. An instant later I was struck on the head by the fragment of a shell and fell unconscious with the colors in my hand.

How long I remained unconscious I do not know, possibly twenty minutes or more. What were my sensations when hit? I felt a terrific blow, but without pain, and the thought flashed through my mind, "This is the end," and then everything was black. I do not remember falling. It takes time to write this, but events moved then with startling rapidity. From the time we went forward from the embankment until the line was swept back could have been but a few minutes, otherwise all must have been killed.

When I revived I was alone with the dead and wounded. The line of battle had been swept away. The field about me was literally covered with the blue uniforms of our dead and wounded men. The firing had very perceptibly decreased. I had worn into the battle my overcoat, with my sword buckled on the outside. I had been hit on the left side of my head, and that side of my body was covered with blood down to my feet, which was still flowing.

My first thought was as to my condition, whether mortally wounded or not. I was perceptibly weakened from loss of blood, but lying there I could not tell how much strength I had left. I did not dare move, for that would make me a target for the guns that covered that terrible wall, the muzzles of which I could plainly see. Many of them were still spitting out their fire with a venom that made my position exceedingly uncomfortable. What should I do? What could I do? To remain there was either to bleed to death or be taken prisoner and sent to Libby, which I felt would mean for me a sure lingering death. To make a move to get off the field would draw the fire of those guns, which would surely finish me. These were the alternatives.

I carefully stretched my legs to test my strength, and I made up my mind I had enough left to carry me off the field, and I resolved to take my chances in the effort. I determined that I would zigzag my course to the rear so as not to give them a line shot at me. So getting myself together I made a supreme effort and sprang up and off in jumps, first to the right, then to the left. As I expected, they opened on me, and the bullets flew thick and fast about me. The first turn I got a bullet through my right leg just above the ankle. It felt like the stinging cut of a whip and rather accelerated my speed.

About fifty yards back was an old slab fence to my right, and I plunged headlong behind that, hoping to find shelter from those bullets. I fell directly behind several other wounded men, two of whom rolled over dead from bullets that came through the slabs and which were probably aimed at me. This flushed me again, and by the same zigzag tactics I succeeded in getting back to the railroad embankment, where, to my great joy, I found Colonel Albright with what remained of the regiment. Colonel Albright grasped me in his arms as I came over, with the exclamation, "We thought you were killed." Sergeant-Major Clapp told me that he had rolled me over and satisfied himself that I was dead before they went back.

As I reached cover under this embankment I remember noticing a field-officer rallying his men very near us on our right, and that instant his head was literally carried away by a shell. So intense was the situation that even this tragic death received only a passing thought. Then came the Irish brigade, charging over our line as they did at Antietam. They came up and went forward in fine form, but they got but a few yards beyond the embankment, when they broke and came back, what was left of them, in great confusion.

No troops could stand that fire. Our division and the whole Second Corps, in fact, were now completely disorganized, and the men were making their way back to the city and the cover of the river-bank as best they could, whilst the splendid old Ninth Corps was advancing to take its place. Profiting by our experience, they did not advance by those streets through which we came, but made their way through houses and yards and so escaped that concentrated fire on the streets. Their advancing lines, covering the whole city front, looked magnificent, and it was dreadful to think that such a splendid body of men must march into such a slaughter-pen.

Their movement was a repetition of ours. With bayonets unfixed they moved forward and attempted to maintain a firing-line under Marye's Heights on the ground from which we had been driven, only to be hurled mercilessly back as we had been. Our line had been the first to make this effort, and for some reason we had approached to within about one hundred yards of their main line of infantry, much closer than any of the troops that followed. The others had barely got beyond the embankment, when they were swept away. We, having approached nearer their line, were, of course, longer exposed to their fire and lost more heavily.

I was always curious to know why we of the first line of that fateful movement succeeded in getting so much nearer their works than the equally brave and determined men who followed us. Some years afterwards on revisiting this location I met an ex-Confederate who commanded one of the rebel batteries on those heights that day. In answer to my questions, he said the first "Yankee" line was permitted to approach much nearer than those that followed, for, said he, "we knew they were our meat, and when we finally opened on them with our full force, the slaughter was so awful it made me heart sick. But you kept coming with such persistency that we did not dare repeat those tactics."

This may have been partially true so far as concerned their infantry fire, but a more potent reason, in my judgment, was that we had developed the utter hopelessness of the attempt, and men could not put heart into the effort.

Recurring to myself again, Colonel Albright stanched the flowing of blood from my wound in the head by making a strong compress of my large bandana handkerchief. The other wound in my leg did not give me much trouble then. In that condition, accompanied by another wounded man, I made my way back into the city. We found it one vast hospital. Every house was literally crowded with wounded men. We were fortunate enough to run against our brigade surgeon, who had taken possession of a brick building on the main street for hospital purposes. The only thing he could give me to lie down upon was a wooden bench. We had dismounted and left our horses with a servant when we went forward, and our blankets, etc., were with them, and where they were now there was no means of knowing. I was therefore without those comforts. Everything of that nature left by the rebels had long before been appropriated.

The doctor hastily examined my wounds, pronounced them not dangerous, ordered the hospital steward to dress them, and was away. He, however, appropriated my red handkerchief. I had been presented by a friend on leaving Scranton with two large old-fashioned red silk bandana handkerchiefs, and they were exceedingly useful. The doctor, seeing them, said, "I must have these to nail up over the outside door to show that this is a hospital," and, without so much as saying by your leave, carried them off.

The effort was to secure as much protection as possible from the fire of the enemy, and to do this the red flag of the hospital must be displayed. It is against the rules of civilized warfare to fire upon a hospital. The doctor said my red silk handkerchiefs were the first red stuff of any kind he had been able to get hold of. Of course I was glad to part with them for that purpose, though they were worth at that time $2 each in gold. The wound in my head was fortunately a glancing blow from a fragment of a shell. It tore the scalp from the bone about three inches in length in the form of a V. It has never given me serious trouble, more than to be a barometer of changing weather. The wound in my leg nearly severed the big tendon. They both quickly healed, and I was off duty with them but the one day I took to get back to camp.

After my wounds had been dressed I tried to sleep, being not only very weak from loss of blood, but almost in a condition of nervous exhaustion. I laid down on my bench, but shells were continually crashing through the building, and sleep was impossible. I went out on the street. It was crowded with wounded and straggling soldiers. The stragglers were hunting for their regiments, the wounded for hospital room. It seemed as if the army must have disintegrated. This was practically true of the Second and Ninth Corps, which had made the assault.

Towards night General French rode down the street, accompanied by his staff. Seeing me, he stopped his horse and exclaimed, "Adjutant, where is my division? Tell me where my men are. My God, I am without a command!" and the tears were flowing down his red, weather-beaten face. He was beside himself over the awful losses of his division. Well he might be, for a great number of them were lying on yonder field in front of Marye's Heights, and the balance were scattered through the houses and on the river-bank practically disorganized.

I was greatly alarmed for our safety that night. It seemed to me highly probable that General Lee would come down upon us and capture all that were in the city, as he could easily have done. Possibly he was satisfied with the damage already inflicted, and did not care to assume the care of our wounded, which that would have involved. I remained on my bench in that hospital through that long night without food or covering. I had eaten nothing since early morning. With the constant whanging of shells through ours and adjacent buildings and the moaning of the wounded lying all about me, sleep or rest was impossible. It was a night too dreadful to think of, and makes me shudder again as I write.

We remained in the city the next day, Sunday, and I rejoined our regiment, which, with other troops, was lying under the shelter of the river-bank. Officers were getting their men together as far as possible and bringing order out of chaos. We had Sunday about two hundred for duty out of three hundred and fifty taken into the battle. On Monday, the 15th, we who were wounded were told to make our way across the river back to our old camps as best we could. I was now very weak, and my head and leg were very sore. The latter gave me much trouble in walking, nevertheless there was a three-mile tramp before us. Lieutenant Musselman, also wounded, went with me on this weary tramp.

We did not reach camp that night, and so had to find shelter at a farm-house, already full of straggling and wounded soldiers. The owner was a widow, living with a grown-up daughter, and was a bitter rebel, although professing Union sentiments whilst our army was there. She was, of course, greatly annoyed by the presence of these soldiers, most of whom were eating up her provisions without paying for them. Some of them were "bummers," who had run away from the battle and had persuaded her to feed and shelter them for the protection they professed to afford her.

She was in great wrath when we reached there and peremptorily forbade us entering. But I told her firmly that we were wounded men and must have shelter; that I would willingly pay for accommodations, but, permission or not, the latter we must have. This argument seemed to be convincing, and the daughter led us up to the garret, which, she said, was the only unoccupied room in the house. Here she spread a blanket on the floor for us to sleep on. I suppose this was the best she could do. Then, at our solicitation, she got us some supper, an exceedingly frugal meal, but we were glad to get that.

The daughter did not seem to share her mother's bitterness, but as often as she could would interject a word in our favor, and really did all she could for us. I sincerely hope she was ultimately made a permanent prisoner by some good "boy in blue." Here would have been an excellent opportunity to have woven into this narrative the golden thread of romance. This pretty secesh girl, with flashing blue eyes and golden hair, rebel to the core, yet befriending a wounded Union soldier, etc. How readily it lends itself, but the truth must be told. The little arrow god had already driven home his shaft, and so the romance could not mature.

During the evening General Franz Sigel and staff came to the house and demanded supper. Our lady was very polite, assured him that it was impossible. "Very well," said General Sigel, "I think I shall want this place to-morrow for a hospital. Madam, your kindness will be reciprocated." He spoke very emphatically, whereat the pretty daughter began to cry, and the mother to stammer apologies, and said she would do the best she could for them, but she really had nothing to cook. The general retired very indignant. Whether or not his threat was carried out I do not know, for the next morning we were off without trying to get breakfast.

On asking for her bill we were surprised to find her charges were evidently based on the highest war-time hotel rates. We had so poor a supper that we had no desire for breakfast there, and had slept on the garret floor. For this she demanded one dollar. We paid her fifty cents, which was more than double its worth, and left amidst a great volley of her choicest anathemas.

We reached camp towards noon, and found we had tramped about five miles out of our way. The regiment was there ahead of us, the troops having evacuated Fredericksburg on Monday, two days after the battle, without opposition. We were actually under fire in this battle, that is, from the time the assault began until we were swept back, probably not more than thirty minutes as against four and one-half hours at Antietam. Yet our losses were proportionately much heavier. During my absence on sick leave, our regiment, after leaving Warrenton, had been detailed on heavy "fatigue" duty, loading and unloading vessels and various kinds of laborer's work at Belle-plain, and in consequence many were on the sick list, others were on various details, so that when we went into this battle we had only three hundred and fifty men for duty, against seven hundred and fifty at Antietam. Of this number my diary, written the 15th, says we lost: Killed, 7; wounded, 80; missing, 20; total, 107.

Lieutenant Hoagland, Company H, was killed. Of the wounded, four were officers—Captain Richard Stillwell and First Lieutenant John B. Floyd, Company K; First Lieutenant Musselman, Company E, and First Lieutenant McDougal, commanding Company C. Lieutenant McDougal's arm was shattered by a minie-ball whilst handing me the colors, detailed above.

Captain Stillwell received a very singular wound. A bullet struck the side of his neck near the big artery and appeared to have gouged out a bit of flesh and glanced off. It bled more than this circumstance would have seemed to warrant, but the captain was sure he was not hurt and made light of it. Swelling and pain speedily developed in his shoulder, and it was found that the missile, instead of glancing off, had taken a downward course and finally lodged near his shoulder-joint, a distance of ten or twelve inches from where it entered. He was given leave of absence on account of wounds, and the ball was cut out after his return home, and ultimately the whole channel made by the ball had to be opened, when it was found lined with whiskers which the ball had carried in with it.

Most of those computed above as missing were undoubtedly killed, but had not been so reported at that time. Our loss in that half-hour was nearly one-third. One stand of our colors, the one whose staff was shot away in my hand, was missing, and the other was badly torn by shells and bullets.

CHAPTER 9

Among the Wounded
By Walt Whitman

One of America's greatest writers describes what he saw during his frequent visits to hospitals during the Civil War.

—Lamar Underwood

As this tremendous war goes on, the public interest becomes more general and gathers more and more closely about the wounded, the sick, and the Government hospitals, the surgeons, and all appertaining to the medical department of the army. Up to the date of this writing (December 9, 1864) there have been, as I estimate, near four hundred thousand cases under treatment, and there are to-day, probably, taking the whole service of the United States, two hundred thousand, or an approximation to that number, on the doctors' list. Half of these are comparatively slight ailments or hurts. Every family has directly or indirectly some representative among this vast army of the wounded and sick.

The following sketch is made to gratify the general interest in this field of the war, and also for a few special persons through whose means alone I have aided the men. It extends over a period of two years, coming down to the present hour, and exhibits the army hospitals at Washington, the camp hospitals in the field, etc. A very few cases are given as specimens of thousands. The account may be relied upon as faithful, though rapidly thrown together. It will put the reader in as direct contact as may be with scenes, sights, and cases of these immense hospitals. As will be seen, it begins back two years since, at a very gloomy period of the contest.

Began my visits (December 21, 1862) among the camp hospitals in the Army of the Potomac, under General Burnside. Spent a good part of the day in a large brick mansion on the banks of the Rappahannock, immediately opposite Fredericksburg. It is used as a hospital since the battle, and seems to have received only the worst cases. Outdoors, at the foot of a tree, within ten yards of the front of the house, I notice a heap of amputated feet, legs, arms, hands, etc.—about a load for a one-horse cart. Several dead bodies lie near, each covered with its brown woollen blanket. In the dooryard, toward the river, are fresh graves, mostly of officers, their names on pieces of barrel staves or broken board, stuck in the dirt. (Most of these bodies were subsequently taken up and transported North to their friends.)

The house is quite crowded, everything impromptu, no system, all bad enough, but I have no doubt the best that can be done; all the wounds pretty bad, some frightful, the men in their old clothes, unclean and bloody. Some of the wounded are rebel officers, prisoners. One, a Mississippian—a captain—hit badly in the leg, I talked with some time; he asked me for papers, which I gave him. (I saw him three months afterward in Washington, with leg amputated, doing well.)

I went through the rooms, down stairs and up. Some of the men were dying. I had nothing to give at that visit, but wrote a few letters to folks home, mothers, etc. Also talked to three or four who seemed most susceptible to it, and needing it.

December 22 to 31.—Am among the regimental brigade and division hospitals somewhat. Few at home realize that these are merely tents, and sometimes very poor ones, the wounded lying on the ground, lucky if their blanket is spread on a layer of pine or hemlock twigs, or some leaves. No cots; seldom even a mattress on the ground. It is pretty cold. I go around from one case to another. I do not see that I can do any good, but I cannot leave them. Once in a while some youngster holds on to me convulsively, and I do what I can for him; at any rate stop with him, and sit near him for hours, if he wishes it.

Besides the hospitals, I also go occasionally on long tours through the camps, talking with the men, etc.; sometimes at night among the groups around the fires, in their she-bang enclosures of bushes. I soon get acquainted anywhere in camp with officers or men, and am always well used. Sometimes I go down on picket with the regiments I know best.

As to rations, the army here at present seems to be tolerably well supplied, and the men have enough, such as it is. Most of the regiments lodge in the flimsy little shelter tents. A few have built themselves huts of logs and mud, with fireplaces.

I might give a long list of special cases, interesting items of the wounded men here, but have not space.

Left Falmouth, January, 1863, by Aquia creek railroad, and so on Government steamer up the Potomac. Many wounded were with us on cars and boat. The cars were just common platform ones. The railroad journey of ten or twelve miles was made mostly before sunrise. The soldiers guarding the road came out from their tents or shebangs of bushes with rumpled hair and half-awake look. Those on duty were walking their posts, some on banks over us, others down far below the level of the track. I saw large cavalry camps off the road. At Aquia Creek Landing were numbers of wounded going North. While I waited some three hours, I went around among them. Several wanted word sent home to parents, brothers, wives, etc., which I did for them (by mail the next day from Washington). On the boat I had my hands full. One poor fellow died going up.

Am now (January, February, etc., 1863) in and around Washington, daily visiting the hospitals. Am much in Campbell, Patent-office, Eighth-street, H-street, Armory-square, and others. Am now able to do a little good, having money (as almoner of others home), and getting experience. I would like to give lists of cases, for there is no end to the interesting ones; but it is impossible without making a large volume, or rather several volumes. I must, therefore, let one or two days' visits at this time suffice as specimens of scores and hundreds of subsequent ones, through the ensuing spring, summer, and fall, and, indeed, down to the present week.

Sunday, January 25.—Afternoon and till 9 in the evening, visited Campbell hospital. Attended specially to one case in Ward I, very sick with pleurisy and typhoid fever, young man, farmer's son—D. F. Russell, Company E, Sixtieth New York—down-hearted and feeble; a long time before he would take any interest; soothed and cheered him gently; wrote a letter home to his mother, in Malone, Franklin county, N.Y., at his request; gave him some fruit and one or two other gifts; enveloped and directed his letter, etc. Then went thoroughly through Ward 6; observed every case in the ward (without, I think, missing one); found some cases I thought needed little sums of money; supplied them (sums of perhaps thirty, twenty-five, twenty, or fifteen cents); distributed a pretty bountiful supply of cheerful reading matter, and gave perhaps some twenty to thirty persons, each one some little gift, such as oranges, apples, sweet crackers, figs, etc., etc., etc.

Thursday, January 29.—Devoted the main part of the day, from 11 to 3.30 o'clock, to Armory-square hospital; went pretty thoroughly through Wards F, G, H, and I—some fifty cases in each ward. In Ward H supplied the men throughout with writing paper and a stamped envelope each, also some cheerful reading matter; distributed in small portions, about half of it in this ward, to proper subjects, a large jar of first-rate preserved berries; also other small gifts. In Wards G, H, and I, found several cases I thought good subjects for small sums of money, which I furnished in each case. The poor wounded men often come up "dead broke," and it helps their spirits to have even the small sum I give them.

My paper and envelopes all gone, but distributed a good lot of amusing reading matter; also, as I thought judicious, tobacco, oranges, apples, etc. Some very interesting cases in Ward I: Charles Miller, Bed No. 19, Company D, Fifty-third Pennsylvania, is only sixteen years of age, very bright, courageous boy, left leg amputated below the knee; next bed below him, young lad very sick—gave the two each appropriate gifts; in the bed above also amputation of the left leg—gave him a part of a jar of raspberries; Bed No. 1, this ward, gave a small sum also; also to a soldier on crutches, sitting on his bed near.

Evening, same day.—Went to see D. F. R., Campbell hospital, before alluded to; found him remarkably changed for the better—up and dressed (quite a triumph; he afterwards got well and went back to his regiment). Distributed in the wards a quantity of note-paper and forty or fifty, mostly paid, envelopes, of which the men were much in need; also a four-pound bag of gingersnaps I bought at a baker's in Seventh street.

Here is a case of a soldier I found among the crowded cots in the Patent hospital—(they have removed most of the men of late and broken up that hospital). He likes to have some one to talk to, and we will listen to him. He got badly wounded in the leg and side at Fredericksburg that eventful Saturday, 13th December. He lay the succeeding two days and nights helpless on the field, between the city and those grim batteries, for his company and his regiment had been compelled to leave him to his fate. To make matters worse, he lay with his head slightly down hill, and could not help himself. At the end of some fifty hours he was brought off, with other wounded, under a flag of truce.

We ask him how the Rebels treated him during those two days and nights within reach of them—whether they came to him—whether they abused him? He answers that several of the Rebels, soldiers and others, came to him, at one time and another. A couple of them, who were together, spoke roughly and sarcastically, but did not act. One middle-aged man, however, who seemed to be moving around the field among the dead and wounded for benevolent purposes, came to him in a way he will never forget. This man treated our soldier kindly, bound up his wounds, cheered him, gave him a couple of biscuits, gave him a drink of whiskey and water, asked him if he could eat some beef. This good Secesh, however, did not change our soldier's position, for it might have caused the blood to burst from the wounds where they were clotted and stagnated. Our soldier is from Pennsylvania; has had a pretty severe time; the wounds proved to be bad ones. But he retains a good heart, and is at present on the gain. It is not uncommon for the men to remain on the field this way, one, two, or even four or five days.

I continue among the hospitals during March, April, etc., without intermission. My custom is to go through a ward, or a collection of wards, endeavoring to give some trifle to each, without missing any. Even a sweet biscuit, a sheet of paper, or a passing word of friendliness, or but a look or nod, if no more. In this way I go through large numbers without delaying, yet do not hurry. I find out the general mood of the ward at the time; sometimes see that there is a heavy weight of listlessness prevailing, and the whole ward wants cheering up. I perhaps read to the men, to break the spell, calling them around me, careful to sit away from the cot of any one who is very bad with sickness or wounds. Also I find out, by going through in this way, the cases that need special attention, and can then devote proper time to them. Of course I am very cautious, among the patients, in giving them food. I always confer with the doctor, or find out from the nurse or ward-master about a new case. But I soon get sufficiently familiar with what is to be avoided, and learn also to judge almost intuitively what is best.

I do a good deal of writing letters by the bedside, of course—writing all kinds, including love letters. Many sick and wounded soldiers have not written home to parents, brothers, sisters, and even wives, for one reason or another, for a long, long time. Some are poor writers; some cannot get paper and envelopes; many have an aversion to writing, because they dread to worry the folks at home—the facts about them are so sad to tell. I always encourage the men to write, and promptly write for them.

As I write this, in May, 1863, the wounded have begun to arrive from Hooker's command, from bloody Chancellorsville. I was down among the first arrivals. The men in charge of them told me the bad cases were yet to come. If that is so, I pity them, for these are bad enough. You ought to see the scene of the wounded arriving at the landing here, foot of Sixth street, at night. Two boat-loads came about half-past seven last night. A little after eight it rained, a long and violent shower. The poor, pale, helpless soldiers had been debarked, and lay around on the wharf and neighborhood, anywhere. The rain was, probably, grateful to them; at any rate they were exposed to it.

The few torches light up the spectacle. All around on the wharf, on the ground, out on side places, etc., the men are lying on blankets, old quilts, etc., with the bloody rags bound around their heads, arms, legs, etc. The attendants are few, and at night few outsiders also—only a few hard-worked transportation men and drivers. (The wounded are getting to be common, and people grow callous.) The men, whatever their condition, lie there and patiently wait till their turn comes to be taken up. Near by the ambulances are now arriving in clusters, and one after another is called to back up and take its load. Extreme cases are sent off on stretchers. The men generally make little or no ado, whatever their sufferings—a few groans that cannot be repressed, and occasionally a scream of pain as they lift a man into the ambulance.

To-day, as I write, hundreds more are expected; and to-morrow and the next day more, and so on for many days.

The soldiers are nearly all young men, and far more Americans than is generally supposed—I should say nine tenths are native born. Among the arrivals from Chancellorsville I find a large proportion of Ohio, Indiana, and Illinois men. As usual there are all sorts of wounds. Some of the men are fearfully burnt from the explosion of artillery caissons. One ward has a long row of officers, some with ugly hurts. Yesterday was perhaps worse than usual: amputations are going on; the attendants are dressing wounds. As you pass by you must be on your guard where you look. I saw, the other day, a gentleman, a visitor, apparently from curiosity, in one of the wards, stop and turn a moment to look at an awful wound they were probing, etc.; he turned pale, and in a moment more he had fainted away and fallen on the floor.

I buy, during the hot weather, boxes of oranges from time to time, and distribute them among the men; also preserved peaches and other fruits; also lemons and sugar for lemonade. Tobacco is also much in demand. Large numbers of the men come up, as usual, without a cent of money. Through the assistance of friends in Brooklyn and Boston, I am again able to help many of those that fall in my way. It is only a small sum in each case, but it is much to them. As before, I go around daily and talk with the men, to cheer them up.

My note-books are full of memoranda of the cases of this summer, and the wounded from Chancellorsville, but space forbids my transcribing them.

As I sit writing this paragraph (sundown, Thursday, June 25) I see a train of about thirty huge four-horse wagons, used as ambulances, filled with wounded, passing up

Fourteenth street, on their way, probably, to Columbian, Carver, and Mount Pleasant hospitals. This is the way the men come in now, seldom in small numbers, but almost always in these long, sad processions. Through the past winter, while our army lay opposite Fredericksburg, the like strings of ambulances were of frequent occurrence along Seventh street, passing slowly up from the steam-boat wharf, from Aquia creek.

This afternoon, July 22, 1863, I spent a long time with a young man I have been with considerable, named Oscar F. Wilber, Company G, One Hundred Fifty-fourth New York, low with chronic diarrhoea and a bad wound also. He asked me to read him a chapter in the New Testament. I complied and asked him what I should read. He said, "Make your own choice." I opened at the close of one of the first books of the Evangelists, and read the chapters describing the latter hours of Christ and the scenes at the crucifixion. The poor wasted young man asked me to read the following chapter also, how Christ rose again. I read very slowly, for Oscar was feeble. It pleased him very much, yet the tears were in his eyes. He asked me if I enjoyed religion. I said, "Perhaps not, my dear, in the way you mean, and yet may-be it is the same thing." He said, "It is my chief reliance." He talked of death, and said he did not fear it. I said, "Why, Oscar, don't you think you will get well?" He said, "I may, but it is not probable." He spoke calmly of his condition. The wound was very bad; it discharged much. Then the diarrhoea had prostrated him, and I felt that he was even then the same as dying. He behaved very manly and affectionate. The kiss I gave him as I was about leaving, he returned fourfold. He gave me his mother's address, Mrs. Sally D. Wilber, Alleghany post-office, Cattaraugus county, N.Y. I had several such interviews with him. He died a few days after the one just described.

August, September, October, etc.—I continue among the hospitals in the same manner, getting still more experience, and daily and nightly meeting with most interesting cases. Through the winter of 1863–4, the same. The work of the army hospital visitor is indeed a trade, an art, requiring both experience and natural gifts, and the greatest judgment. A large number of the visitors to the hospitals do no good at all, while many do harm. The surgeons have great trouble from them. Some visitors go from curiosity—as to a show of animals. Others give the men improper things. Then there are always some poor fellows, in the crises of sickness or wounds, that imperatively need perfect quiet—not to be talked to by strangers. Few realize that it is not the mere giving of gifts that does good; it is the proper adaption. Nothing is of any avail among the soldiers except conscientious personal investigation of cases, each for itself; with sharp, critical faculties, but in the fullest spirit of human sympathy and boundless love. The men feel such love more than anything else. I have met very few persons who realize the importance of humoring the yearnings for love and friendship of these American young men, prostrated by sickness and wounds.

February, 1864.—I am down at Culpepper and Brandy station, among the camp of First, Second, and Third Corps, and going through the division hospitals. The condition of the camps here this winter is immensely improved from last winter near Falmouth. All the army is now in huts of logs and mud, with fireplaces; and the food is plentiful and tolerably good. In the camp hospitals I find diarrhoea more and more prevalent, and in chronic form. It is at present the great disease of the army. I think the doctors generally give too much medicine, oftener making things worse. Then they hold on to the cases in camp too long. When the disease is almost fixed beyond remedy, they send it up to Washington. Alas! how many such wrecks have I seen landed from boat and railroad and deposited in the Washington hospitals, mostly but to linger awhile and die, after being kept at the front too long.

The hospitals in front, this winter, are also much improved. The men have cots, and often wooden floors, and the tents are well warmed.

March and April, 1864.—Back again in Washington. They are breaking up the camp hospitals in Meade's army, preparing for a move. As I write this, in March, there are all the signs. Yesterday and last night the sick were arriving here in long trains, all day and night. I was among the new-comers most of the night. One train of a thousand came into the depot, and others followed. The ambulances were going all night, distributing them to the various hospitals here. When they come in, some literally in a dying condition, you may well imagine it is a lamentable sight. I hardly know which is worse, to see the wounded after a battle, or these wasted wrecks.

I remain in capital health and strength, and go every day, as before, among the men, in my own way, enjoying my life and occupation more than I can tell.

Of the army hospitals now in and around Washington, there are thirty or forty. I am in the habit of going to all, and to Fairfax seminary, Alexandria, and over Long Bridge to the convalescent camp, etc. As a specimen of almost any one of these hospitals, fancy to yourself a space of three to twenty acres of ground, on which are grouped ten or twelve very large wooden barracks, with, perhaps, a dozen or twenty, and sometimes more than that number, of small buildings, capable all together of accommodating from five hundred to a thousand or fifteen hundred persons. Sometimes these large wooden barracks, or wards, each of them, perhaps, from a hundred to a hundred and fifty feet long, are arranged in a straight row, evenly fronting the street; others are planned so as to form an immense V; and others again arranged around a hollow square. They make all together a huge cluster, with the additional tents, extra wards for contagious diseases, guard-houses, sutler's stores, chaplain's house, etc. In the middle will probably be an edifice devoted to the offices of the surgeon in charge and the ward surgeons, principal attachés, clerks, etc. Then around this center radiate or are gathered the wards for the wounded and sick.

These wards are either lettered alphabetically, Ward G, Ward K, or else numerically, 1, 2, 3, etc. Each has its ward surgeon and corps of nurses. Of course there is, in the aggregate, quite a muster of employees, and over all the surgeon in charge. Any one of these hospitals is a little city in itself. Take, for instance, the Carver hospital, out a couple of miles, on a hill, northern part of Fourteenth street. It has more inmates than an ordinary country town. The same with the Lincoln hospital, east of the Capitol, or the Finley hospital, on high grounds northeast of the city; both large establishments. Armory-square hospital, under Dr. Bliss, in Seventh street (one of the best anywhere), is also temporarily enlarged this summer, with additional tents, sheds, etc. It must have nearly a hundred tents, wards, sheds, and structures of one kind and another. The worst cases are always to be found here.

A wanderer like me about Washington pauses on some high land which commands the sweep of the city (one never tires of the noble and ample views presented here, in the generally fine, soft, peculiar air and light), and has his eyes attracted by these white clusters of barracks in almost every direction. They make a great show in the landscape, and I often use them as landmarks. Some of these clusters are very full of inmates. Counting the whole, with the convalescent camps (whose inmates are often worse off than the sick in the hospitals), they have numbered, in this quarter and just down the Potomac, as high as fifty thousand invalid, disabled, or sick and dying men.

My sketch has already filled up so much room that I shall have to omit any detailed account of the wounded of May and June, 1864, from the battles of the Wilderness, Spottsylvania, etc. That would be a long history in itself. The arrivals, the numbers, and the severity of the wounds, out-viewed anything that we have seen before. For days and weeks a melancholy tide set in upon us. The weather was very hot. The wounded had been delayed in coming, and much neglected. Very many of the wounds had worms in them. An unusual proportion mortified. It was among these that, for the first time in my life, I began to be prostrated with real sickness, and was, before the close of the summer, imperatively ordered North by the physician to recuperate and have an entire change of air.

What I know of first Fredericksburg, Chancellorsville, Wilderness, etc., makes clear to me that there has been, and is yet, a total lack of science in elastic adaptation to the needs of the wounded after a battle. The hospitals are long afterward filled with proofs of this.

I have seen many battles, their results, but never one where there was not, during the first few days, an unaccountable and almost total deficiency of everything for the wounded—appropriate sustenance, nursing, cleaning, medicines, stores, etc. (I do not say surgical attendance, because the surgeons cannot do more than human endurance permits.)

Whatever pleasant accounts there may be in the papers of the North, this is the actual fact. No thorough previous preparation, no system, no foresight, no genius. Always plenty of stores, no doubt, but always miles away; never where they are needed, and never the proper application. Of all harrowing experiences, none is greater than that of the days following a heavy battle. Scores, hundreds, of the noblest young men on earth, uncomplaining, lie helpless, mangled, faint, alone, and so bleed to death, or die from exhaustion, either actually untouched at all, or with merely the laying of them down and leaving them, when there ought to be means provided to save them.

The reader has doubtless inferred the fact that my visits among the wounded and sick have been as an independent missionary, in my own style, and not as an agent of any commission. Several noble women and men of Brooklyn, Boston, Salem, and Providence, have voluntarily supplied funds at times. I only wish they could see a tithe of the actual work performed by their generous and benevolent assistance among the suffering men.

He who goes among the soldiers with gifts, etc., must beware how he proceeds. It is much more of an art than one would imagine. They are not charity-patients, but American young men, of pride and independence. The spirit in which you treat them, and bestow your donations, is just as important as the gifts themselves; sometimes more so. Then there is continual discrimination necessary. Each case requires some peculiar adaptation to itself. It is very important to slight nobody—not a single case. Some hospital visitors, especially the women, pick out the handsomest looking soldiers, or have a few for their pets. Of course some will attract you more than others, and some will need more attention than others; but be careful not to ignore any patient. A word, a friendly turn of the eye or touch of the hand in passing, if nothing more.

One hot day toward the middle of June I gave the inmates of Carver hospital a general ice-cream treat, purchasing a large quantity, and going around personally through the wards to see to its distribution.

Here is a characteristic scene in a ward: It is Sunday afternoon (middle of summer, 1864), hot and oppressive, and very silent through the ward. I am taking care of a critical case, now lying in a half lethargy. Near where I sit is a suffering Rebel from the Eighth Louisiana; his name is Irving. He has been here a long time, badly wounded, and lately had his leg amputated. It is not doing very well. Right opposite me is a sick soldier boy laid down with his clothes on, sleeping, looking much wasted, his pallid face on his arm. I see by the yellow trimming on his jacket that he is a cavalry boy. He looks so handsome as he sleeps, one must needs go nearer to him. I step softly over, and find by his card that he is named William Cone, of the First Maine Cavalry, and his folks live in Skowhegan.

Well, poor John Mahay is dead. He died yesterday. His was a painful and lingering case. I have been with him at times for the past fifteen months. He belonged to Company A, One Hundred and First New York, and was shot through the lower region of the abdomen at second Bull Run, August, 1862. One scene at his bedside will suffice for the agonies of nearly two years. The bladder had been perforated by a bullet going entirely through him. Not long since I sat a good part of the morning by his bedside, Ward E, Armory-square; the water ran out of his eyes from the intense pain, and the muscles of his face were distorted, but he utters nothing except a low groan now and then. Hot moist cloths were applied, and relieved him somewhat.

Poor Mahay, a mere boy in age, but old in misfortune, he never knew the love of parents, was placed in his infancy in one of the New York charitable institutions, and subsequently bound out to a tyrannical master in Sullivan county (the scars of whose cowhide and club remained yet on his back). His wound here was a most disagreeable one, for he was a gentle, cleanly, and affectionate boy. He found friends in his hospital life, and, indeed, was a universal favorite. He had quite a funeral ceremony.

Through Fourteenth street to the river, and then over the long bridge and some three miles beyond, is the huge collection called the convalescent camp. It is a respectable sized army in itself, for these hospitals, tents, sheds, etc., at times contain from five to ten thousand men. Of course there are continual changes. Large squads are sent off to their regiments or elsewhere, and new men received. Sometimes I found large numbers of paroled returned prisoners here. During October, November, and December, 1864, I have visited the military hospitals about New York City, but have not room in this article to describe these visits.

I have lately been (November 25) in the Central-park hospital, near One Hundred and Fourth street; it seems to be a well-managed institution. During September, and previously, went many times to the Brooklyn city hospital, in Raymond street, where I found (taken in by contract) a number of wounded and sick from the army. Most of the men were badly off, and without a cent of money, many wanting tobacco. I supplied them, and a few special cases with delicacies; also repeatedly with letter-paper, stamps, envelopes, etc., writing the addresses myself plainly—(a pleased crowd gathering around me as I directed for each one in turn.) This Brooklyn hospital is a bad place for soldiers, or anybody else. Cleanliness, proper nursing, watching, etc., are more deficient than in any hospital I know. For dinner on Sundays I invariably found nothing but rice and molasses. The men all speak well of Drs. Yale and Kissam for kindness, patience, etc., and I think, from what I saw, there are also young medical men. In its management otherwise, this is the poorest hospital I have been in, out of many hundreds.

Among places, apart from soldiers', visited lately (December 7) I must specially mention the great Brooklyn general hospital and other public institutions at Flatbush, including the extensive lunatic asylum, under charge of Drs. Chapin and Reynolds. Of the latter (and I presume I might include these county establishments generally) I have deliberately to put on record about the profoundest satisfaction with professional capacity, completeness of house arrangements to ends required, and the right vital spirit animating all, that I have yet found in any public curative institution among civilians.

In Washington, in camp and everywhere, I was in the habit of reading to the men. They were very fond of it, and liked declamatory, poetical pieces. Miles O'Reilly's pieces were also great favorites. I have had many happy evenings with the men. We would gather in a large group by ourselves, after supper, and spend the time in such readings, or in talking, and occasionally by an amusing game called the game of Twenty Questions.

For nurses, middle-aged women and mothers of families are best. I am compelled to say young ladies, however refined, educated, and benevolent, do not succeed as army nurses, though their motives are noble; neither do the Catholic nuns, among these home-born American young men. Mothers full of motherly feeling, and however illiterate, but bringing reminiscences of home, and with the magnetic touch of hands, are the true women nurses. Many of the wounded are between fifteen and twenty years of age.

I should say that the Government, from my observation, is always full of anxiety and liberality toward the sick and wounded. The system in operation in the permanent hospitals is good, and the money flows without stint. But the details have to be left to hundreds and thousands of subordinates and officials. Among these, laziness, heartlessness, gouging, and incompetency are more or less prevalent. Still, I consider the permanent hospitals, generally, well conducted.

A very large proportion of the wounded come up from the front without a cent of money in their pockets. I soon discovered that it was about the best thing I could do to raise their spirits and show them that somebody cared for them, and practically felt a fatherly or brotherly interest in them, to give them small sums, in such cases, using tact and discretion about it.

A large majority of the wounds are in the arms and legs. But there is every kind of wound in every part of the body. I should say of the sick, from my experience in the hospitals, that the prevailing maladies are typhoid fever and the camp fevers generally, diarrhoea, catarrhal affections and bronchitis, rheumatism and pneumonia. These forms of sickness lead, all the rest follow. There are twice as many sick as there are wounded. The deaths range from six to ten per cent of those under treatment.

I must bear my most emphatic testimony to the zeal, manliness, and professional spirit and capacity generally prevailing among the surgeons, many of them young men, in the hospitals and the army. I will not say much about the exceptions, for they are few (but I have met some of those few, and very foolish and airish they were). I never ceased to find the best young men, and the hardest and most disinterested workers, among these surgeons, in the hospitals. They are full of genius, too. I have seen many hundreds of them, and this is my testimony.

During my two years in the hospitals and upon the field, I have made over six hundred visits, and have been, as I estimate, among from eighty thousand to one hundred thousand of the wounded and sick, as sustainer of spirit and body in some slight degree, in their time of need. These visits varied from an hour or two, to all day or night; for with dear or critical cases I watched all night. Sometimes I took up my quarters in the hospital, and slept or watched there several nights in succession. I may add that I am now just resuming my occupation in the hospitals and camps for the winter of 1864–5, and probably to continue the seasons ensuing.

To many of the wounded and sick, especially the youngsters, there is something in personal love, caresses, and the magnetic flood of sympathy and friendship, that does, in its way, more good than all the medicine in the world. I have spoken of my regular gifts of delicacies, money, tobacco, special articles of food, knick-knacks, etc., etc. But I steadily found more and more that I could help, and turn the balance in favor of cure, by the means here alluded to, in a curiously large proportion of cases. The American soldier is full of affection and the yearning for affection. And it comes wonderfully grateful to him to have this yearning gratified when he is laid up with painful wounds or illness, far away from home, among strangers. Many will think this merely sentimentalism, but I know it is the most solid of facts. I believe that even the moving around among the men, or through the ward, of a hearty, healthy, clean, strong, generous-souled person, man or woman, full of humanity and love, sending out invisible, constant currents thereof, does immense good to the sick and wounded.

To those who might be interested in knowing it, I must add, in conclusion, that I have tried to do justice to all the suffering that fell in my way. While I have been with wounded and sick in thousands of cases from the New England States, and from New York, New Jersey, and Pennsylvania, and from Michigan, Wisconsin, Indiana, Illinois, and the Western States, I have been with more or less from all the States North and South, without exception. I have been with many from the border States, especially from Maryland and Virginia, and found far more Union Southerners than is supposed. I have been with many Rebel officers and men among our wounded, and given them always what I had, and tried to cheer them the same as any. I have been among the army teamsters considerably, and indeed always find myself drawn to them. Among the black soldiers, wounded or sick, and in the contraband camps, I also took my way whenever in their neighborhood, and I did what I could for them.

W. W.

From the *New York Times*, December 11, 1864.

CHAPTER 10

On Confederate Battlefields
By Carlton McCarthy

In vivid prose, personal and in great detail, a Confederate soldier describes the marches, the battles, and the agony that followed.

—LAMAR UNDERWOOD

A BATTLE-FIELD, WHEN ONLY A FEW THOUSANDS OF MEN ARE ENGAGED, IS A MORE extensive area than most persons would suppose. When large bodies of men—twenty to fifty thousand on each side—are engaged, a mounted man, at liberty to gallop from place to place, could scarcely travel the field over during the continuance of the battle; and a private soldier, in the smallest affair, sees very little indeed of the field. What occurs in his own regiment, or probably in his own company, is about all, and is sometimes more than he actually sees or knows. Thus it is that, while the field is extensive, it is to each individual limited to the narrow space of which he is cognizant.

The dense woods of Virginia, often choked with heavy undergrowth, added greatly to the difficulty of observing the movements of large bodies of troops extended in line of battle. The commanders were compelled to rely almost entirely upon the information gained from their staff officers and the couriers of those in immediate command on the lines.

The beasts of burden which travel the Great Desert scent the oasis and the well miles away, and, cheered by the prospect of rest and refreshment, press on with renewed vigor; and in the book of Job it is said of the horse, "He saith among the trumpets, Ha! ha! and he smelleth the battle afar off, the thunder of the captains, and the shoutings." So a soldier, weary and worn, recognizing the signs of approaching battle, did quicken his lagging steps and cry out for joy at the prospect.

The column, hitherto moving forward with the steadiness of a mighty river, hesitates, halts, steps back, then forward, hesitates again, halts. The colonels talk to the brigadier, the brigadiers talk to the major-general, some officers hurry forward and others hurry to the rear. Infantry stands to one side of the road while cavalry trots by to the front. Now some old wagons marked "Ord. Dept." go creaking and rumbling by. One or two light ambulances, with a gay and careless air, seem to trip along with the ease of a dancing-girl. They and the surgeons seem cheerful. Some, not many, ask "What is the matter?" Most of the men there know exactly: they are on the edge of battle.

Presently a very quiet, almost sleepy looking man on horseback, says, "Forward, 19th!" and away goes the leading regiment. A little way ahead the regiment jumps a fence, and— pop! bang! whiz! thud! is all that can be heard, until the rebel yell reverberates through the woods. Battle? No! skirmishers advancing.

Step into the woods now and watch these skirmishers. See how cheerfully they go in. How rapidly they load, fire, and re-load. They stand six and twelve feet apart, calling to each other, laughing, shouting and cheering, but advancing. There: one fellow has dropped his musket like something red hot. His finger is shot away. His friends congratulate him, and he walks sadly away to the rear. Another staggers and falls with a ball through his neck, mortally wounded. Two comrades raise him to his feet and try to lead him away, but one of them receives a ball in his thigh which crushes the bone, and he falls groaning to the ground.

The other advises his poor dying friend to lie down, helps him to do so, and runs to join his advancing comrades. When he overtakes them he finds every man securely posted behind a tree, loading, firing, and conducting himself generally with great delib- eration and prudence. They have at last driven the enemy's skirmishers in upon the line of battle, and are waiting. A score of men have fallen here, some killed outright, some slightly, some sorely, and some mortally wounded. The elements now add to the horrors of the hour. Dense clouds hovering near the tree tops add deeper shadows to the woods. Thunder, deep and ominous, rolls in prolonged peals across the sky, and lurid lightning darts among the trees and glistens on the gun barrels. But still they stand.

Now a battery has been hurried into position, the heavy trails have fallen to the ground, and at the command "Commence firing!" the cannoniers have stepped in briskly and loaded. The first gun blazes at the muzzle and away goes a shell. The poor fellows in the woods rejoice as it crashes through the trees over their heads, and cheer when it explodes over the enemy's line. Now, what a chorus! Thunder, gun after gun, shell after shell, musketry, pelting rain, shouts, groans, cheers, and commands!

But help is coming. At the edge of the woods, where the skirmishers entered, the brigade is in line. Somebody has ordered, "Load!"

The ramrods glisten and rattle down the barrels of a thousand muskets. "F-o-o-o-o- r-r-r-r-w-a-a-a-r-r-r-d!" is the next command, and the brigade disappears in the woods, the canteens rattling, the bushes crackling, and the officers never ceasing to say, "Close up, men; close up! guide c-e-n-t-e-r-r-r-r!"

The men on that skirmish line have at last found it advisable to lie down at full length on the ground, though it is so wet, and place their heads against the trees in front. They cannot advance and they cannot retire without, in either case, exposing themselves to almost certain death. They are waiting for the line of battle to come to their relief.

At last, before they see, they hear the line advancing through the pines. The snapping of the twigs, the neighing of horses, and hoarse commands, inspire a husky cheer, and when the line of the old brigade breaks through the trees in full view, they fairly yell! Every man jumps to his feet, the brigade presses firmly forward, and soon the roll of musketry tells all who are waiting to hear that serious work is progressing away down in the woods. All honor to the devoted infantry. The hour of glory has arrived for couriers, aides-de-camp, and staff officers generally. They dash about from place to place like spirits of unrest. Brigade after brigade and division after division is hurried into line, and pressed forward into action. Battalions of artillery open fire from the crests of many hills, and the battle is begun.

Ammunition trains climb impassable places, cross ditches without bridges, and manage somehow to place themselves in reach of the troops. Ambulances, which an hour before went gayly forward, now slowly and solemnly return loaded. Shells and musket balls which must have lost their way, go flitting about here and there, wounding and killing men who deem themselves far away from danger. The negro cooks turn pale as these unexpected visitors enter the camps at the rear, and the rear is "extended" at once.

But our place now is at the front, on the field. We are to watch the details of a small part of the great expanse. As we approach, a ludicrous scene presents itself. A strong-armed artilleryman is energetically thrashing a dejected looking individual with a hickory bush, and urging him to the front. He has managed to keep out of many a fight, but now he *must* go in. The captain has detailed a man to *whip* him in, and the man is doing it. With every blow the poor fellow yells and begs to be spared, but his determined guardian will not cease. They press on, the one screaming and the other lashing, till they reach the battery in position and firing on the retiring enemy. A battery of the enemy is replying, and shells are bursting overhead, or ploughing huge furrows in the ground. Musket balls are "rapping" on the rims of the wheels and sinking with a deep "thud" into the bodies of the poor horses. Smoke obscures the scene, but the cannoniers in faint outline can be seen cheerfully serving the guns.

As the opposing battery ceases firing, and having limbered up, scampers away, and the last of the enemy's infantry slowly sinks into the woods out of sight and out of reach, a wild cheer breaks from the cannoniers, who toss their caps in the air and shout, shake hands and shout again, while the curtain of smoke is raised by the breeze and borne away.

The cavalry is gone. With jingle and clatter they have passed through the lines and down the hill, and are already demanding surrender from many a belated man. There will be no rest for that retreating column. Stuart, with a twinkle in his eye, his lips puckered as if to whistle a merry lay, is on their flanks, in their rear, and in their front. The enemy will send their cavalry after him, of course, but he will stay with them, nevertheless.

Add now the stream of wounded men slowly making their way to the rear; the groups of dejected prisoners plodding along under guard, and you have about as much of a battle as one private soldier ever sees.

But after the battle, man will tell to man what each has seen and felt, until every man will feel that he has seen the whole. Hear, then, the stories of battle.

An artilleryman—he must have been a driver—says: when the firing had ceased an old battery horse, his lower jaw carried away by a shot, with blood streaming from his wound, staggered up to him, gazed beseechingly at him, and, groaning piteously, laid his bloody jaws on his shoulder, and so made his appeal for sympathy. He was beyond help.

The pathetic nature of this story reminds a comrade that a new man in the battery, desiring to save the labor incident to running up the gun after the rebound, determined to hold on to the handspike, press the trail into the ground, and hold her fast. He did try, but the rebound proceeded as usual, and the labor-saving man was "shocked" at the failure of his effort. Nothing daunted, the same individual soon after applied his lips to the vent of the gun, which was choked, and endeavored to clear it by an energetic blast from his lungs. The vent was not cleared but the lips of the recruit were nicely browned, and the detachment greatly amused.

At another gun it has happened that No. 1 and No. 3 have had a difficulty. No. 3 having failed to serve the vent, there was a premature explosion, and No. 1, being about to withdraw the rammer, fell heavily to the ground, apparently dead. No. 3, seeing what a calamity he had caused, hung over the dead man and begged him to speak and exonerate him from blame. After No. 3 had exhausted all his eloquence and pathos, No. 1 suddenly rose to his feet and informed him that the premature explosion was a fact, but the death of No. 1 was a joke intended to warn him that if he ever failed again to serve that vent, he would have his head broken by a blow from a rammer-head. This joke having been completed in all its details, the firing was continued.

Another man tells how Eggleston had his arm torn away by a solid shot, and, as he walked away, held up the bleeding, quivering stump, exclaiming, "Never mind, boys; I'll come back soon and try 'em with this other one." Alas! poor fellow, he had fought his last fight.

Poor Tom, he who was always, as he said, "willing to give 'em half a leg, or so," was struck about the waist by a shot which almost cut him in two. He fell heavily to the ground, and, though in awful agony, managed to say: "Tell mother I died doing my duty."

While the fight lasted, several of the best and bravest received wounds apparently mortal, and were laid aside covered by an old army blanket. They refused to die, however, and remain to this day to tell their own stories of the war and of their marvelous recovery.

At the battle of the Wilderness, May, 1864, a man from North Carolina precipitated a severe fight by asking a very simple and reasonable question. The line of battle had been pressed forward and was in close proximity to the enemy. The thick and tangled undergrowth prevented a sight of the enemy, but every man felt he was near. Everything was hushed and still. No one dared to speak above a whisper. It was evening, and growing dark. As the men lay on the ground, keenly sensible to every sound, and anxiously waiting, they heard the firm tread of a man walking along the line. As he walked they heard also the jingle-jangle of a pile of canteens hung around his neck. He advanced with deliberate mien to within a few yards of the line and opened a terrific fight by quietly saying, "Can any you fellows tell a man whar he can git some water?" Instantly the thicket was illumined by the flash of a thousand muskets, the men leaped to their feet, the officers shouted, and the battle was begun. Neither side would yield, and there they fought till many died.

Soon, however, the reserve brigade began to make its way through the thicket. The first man to appear was the brigadier, thirty yards ahead of his brigade, his sword between his teeth, and parting the bushes with both hands as he spurred his horse through the tangled growth. Eager for the fight, his eyes glaring and his countenance lit up with fury, his first word was "Forward!" and forward went the line.

On the march from Petersburg to Appomattox, after a sharp engagement, some men of Cutshaw's artillery battalion, acting as infantry, made a stand for a while on a piece of high ground. They noticed, hanging around in a lonely, distracted way, a tall, lean, shaggy fellow holding, or rather leaning on, a long staff, around which hung a faded battle-flag. Thinking him out of his place and skulking, they suggested to him that it would be well for him to join his regiment. He replied that his regiment had all run away, and he was merely waiting a chance to be useful. Just then the enemy's advancing skirmishers poured a hot fire into the group, and the artillerymen began to discuss the propriety of leaving. The color-bearer, remembering their insinuations, saw an opportunity for retaliation. Standing, as he was, in the midst of a shower of musket balls, he seemed almost ready to fall asleep. But suddenly his face was illumined with a singularly pleased and childish smile. Quietly walking up close to the group, he said, "Any you boys want to *charge?*" The boys answered, "Yes." "Well," said the imperturbable, "I'm the man to carry this here old flag for you. Just follow me." So saying he led the squad full into the face of the advancing enemy, and never once seemed to think of stopping until he was urged to retire with the squad. He came back smiling from head to foot, and suffered no more insinuations.

At Gettysburg, when the artillery fire was at its height, a brawny fellow, who seemed happy at the prospect for a hot time, broke out singing:

> Backward, roll backward, O Time in thy flight:
> Make me a child again, just for this fight!

Another fellow near him replied, "Yes; and a *gal* child at that."

At Fredericksburg a good soldier, now a farmer in Chesterfield County, Virginia, was desperately wounded and lay on the field all night. In the morning a surgeon approached him and inquired the nature of his wound. Finding a wound which is always considered fatal, he advised the man to remain quietly where he was and die. The man insisted on being removed to a hospital, saying in the most emphatic manner, that though every man ever wounded as he was (his bowels were punctured by the ball) had died, he was determined not to die. The surgeon, struck by the man's courage and nerve, consented to remove him, advising him, however, not to cherish the hope of recovery. After a hard struggle he did recover, and is to-day a living example of the power of a determined will.

At the Wilderness, when the fight was raging in the tangled woods and a man could scarcely trust himself to move in any direction for fear of going astray or running into the hands of the enemy, a mere boy was wounded. Rushing out of the woods, his eyes staring and his face pale with fright, he shouted, "Where's the rear. Mister! I say, Mister! where's the rear?" Of course he was laughed at. The very grim fact that there was no "rear," in the sense of safety, made the question irresistibly ludicrous. The conduct of this boy was not exceptional. It was no uncommon thing to see the best men badly demoralized and eager to go to the rear because of a wound scarcely worthy of the name. On the other hand, it sometimes happened that men seriously wounded could not be convinced of their danger, and remained on the field.

The day General Stuart fell, mortally wounded, there was a severe fight in the woods not far from the old Brook Church, a few miles from Richmond; the enemy was making a determined stand, in order to gain time to repair a bridge which they were compelled to use, and the Confederate infantry skirmishers were pushing them hard. The fighting was stubborn and the casualties on the Confederate side very numerous. In the midst of the fight a voice was heard shouting, "Where's my boy? I'm looking for my boy!" Soon the owner of the voice appeared, tall, slim, aged, with silver gray hair, dressed in a full suit of broadcloth. A tall silk hat and a clerical collar and cravat completed his attire. His voice, familiar to the people of Virginia, was deep and powerful. As he continued to shout, the men replied, "Go back, old gentleman; you'll get hurt here. Go back; go back!"

"No, no," said he. "I can go anywhere my boy has to go, and the Lord is here. I want to see my boy, and I will see him!" Then the order, "Forward!" was given and the men made once more for the enemy. The old gentleman, his beaver in one hand, a big stick in the other, his long hair flying, shouting, "Come on, boys!" disappeared in the depths of the woods, well in front. He was a Methodist minister, an old member of the Virginia Conference, but his carriage that day was soldierly and grand. One thought—that his boy was there—made the old man feel that he might brave the danger, too. No man who saw him there will ever forget the parson who led the charge at Brook Church.

At the battle of Spottsylvania Court House, a gun in position somewhat in advance of the line was so much exposed to the enemy's fire that it was abandoned. Later in the day the battery being ordered to move, the captain directed the sergeant to take his detachment and bring in the gun. The sergeant and his gunner, with a number of men, went out to bring in the gun by hand. Two men lifted the trail and the sergeant ordered, "All together!" The gun moved, but moved *in a circle*. The fire was hot, and *all hands were on the same side*—the side farthest from the enemy! After some persuasion the corporal and the sergeant managed to induce a man or two to get on the other side, with them, and they were moving along very comfortably when a shrapnel whacked the sergeant on his breast, breaking his ribs and tearing away the muscle of one arm. He fell into the arms of the corporal. Seeing that their only hope of escaping from this fire was work, the cannoniers bent to the wheels, and the gun rolled slowly to shelter.

It was at Spottsylvania Court House that the Federal infantry rushed over the works, and, engaging in a hand-to-hand fight, drove out the Confederate infantry. On one part of the line the artillerymen stood to their posts, and when the Federal troops passing the works had massed themselves inside, fired to the right and left, up and down the lines, cutting roadways through the compact masses of men, and holding their positions until the Confederate infantry reformed, drove out the enemy and re-occupied the line. Several batteries were completely overrun, and the cannoniers sought and found safety in front of the works, whence the enemy had made their charge.

At another point on the lines, where there was no infantry support, the enemy charged repeatedly and made every effort to carry the works, but were handsomely repulsed by artillery alone. An examination of the ground in front of the works after the fight, disclosed the fact that all the dead and wounded were victims of artillery fire. The dead were literally torn to pieces, and the wounded dreadfully mangled. Scarcely a man was hurt on the Confederate side.

At Fort Harrison, a few miles below Richmond, in 1864, a ludicrous scene resulted from the firing of a salute with shotted guns. Federal artillery occupied the fort, and the lines immediately in front of it were held by the "Department Battalion," composed of the clerks in the various government offices in Richmond, who had been ordered out to meet an emergency. Just before sundown the detail for picket duty was formed, and about to march out to the picket line, the clerks presenting quite a soldierly appearance. Suddenly bang! went a gun in the fort, and a shell came tearing over. Bang! again, and bang! bang! and more shells exploding. Pow! pow! what consternation! In an instant the beautiful line melted away as by magic. Every man took to shelter, and the place was desolate. The firing was rapid, regular, and apparently aimed to strike the Confederate lines, but ceased as suddenly as it had begun.

General Custis Lee, whose tent was near by, observing the panic, stepped quietly up to the parapet of the works, folded his arms, and walked back and forth without uttering a word or looking to the right or to the left. His cool behavior, coupled with the silence of the guns, soon reassured the trembling clerks, and one by one they dropped into line again. General Butler had heard some news that pleased him, and ordered a salute with shotted guns. That was all.

Two boys who had volunteered for service with the militia in the same neighborhood, were detailed for picket duty. It was the custom to put three men on each post, two militia boys and one veteran. The boys and an old soldier of Johnston's division were marched to their post, where they found, ready dug, a pit about five feet deep and three feet wide. It was quite dark, and the boys, realizing fully their exposed position, at once occupied the pit. The old soldier saw he had an opportunity to have a good time, knowing that those boys would keep wide awake. Giving them a short lecture about the importance of great watchfulness, he warned them to be ready to leave there very rapidly at any moment, and, above all, to keep very quiet. His words were wasted, as the boys would not have closed their eyes or uttered a word for the world. These little details arranged, the cunning old soldier prepared to make himself comfortable. First he gathered a few small twigs and made a *very small* fire. On the fire he put a battered old tin cup. Into this he poured some coffee from his canteen. From some mysterious place in his clothes he drew forth sugar and dropped it into the cup. Next, from an old worn haversack, he took a "chunk" of raw bacon and a "pone" of corn bread. Then, drawing a large pocket knife, in a dexterous manner he sliced and ate his bread and meat, occasionally sipping his coffee.

His evening meal leisurely completed, he filled his pipe, smoked, and stirred up the imaginations of the boys by telling how dangerous a duty they were performing; told them how easy it would be for the Yankees to creep up and shoot them or capture and carry them off. Having finished his smoke, he knocked out the ashes and dropped the pipe in his pocket. Then he actually unrolled his blanket and oil-cloth. It made the perspiration start on the brows of the boys to see the man's folly. Then taking off his shoes, he laid down on one edge, took hold of the blanket and oil-cloth, rolled himself over to the other side, and with a kind "good night" to the boys, began to snore. The poor boys stood like statues in the pit till broad day. In the morning the old soldier thanked them for not disturbing him, and quietly proceeded to prepare his breakfast.

After the fight at Fisher's Hill, in 1864, Early's army, in full retreat and greatly demoralized, was strung out along the valley pike. The Federal cavalry was darting around picking up prisoners, shooting drivers, and making themselves generally disagreeable. It happened that an artilleryman, who was separated from his gun, was making pretty good time on foot, getting to the rear, and had the appearance of a demoralized infantryman who had thrown away his musket. So one of these lively cavalrymen trotted up, and, waving his sabre, told the artilleryman to "surrender!" But he didn't stop. He merely glanced over his shoulder, and kept on. Then the cavalryman became indignant and shouted, "Halt, d—n you; halt!" And still he would not. "Halt," said the cavalryman, "halt, you d—n s— of a ——; halt!" Then the artilleryman halted, and remarking that he didn't allow any man to speak to him that way, seized a huge stick, turned on the cavalryman, knocked him out of his saddle, and proceeded on his journey to the rear.

This artilleryman fought with a musket at Sailor's Creek. He found himself surrounded by the enemy, who demanded surrender. He refused; said they must take him; and laid about him with the butt of his musket till he had damaged some of the party considerably. He was, however, overpowered and made a prisoner.

Experienced men, in battle, always availed themselves of any shelter within reach. A tree, a fence, a mound of earth, a ditch, anything. Sometimes their efforts to find shelter were very amusing and even silly. Men lying on the ground have been seen to put an old canteen before their heads as a shelter from musket balls; and during a heavy fire of artillery, seemed to feel safer under a tent. Only recruits and fools neglected the smallest shelter.

The more experienced troops knew better when to give up than green ones, and never fought well after they were satisfied that they could not accomplish their purpose. Consequently it often happened that the best troops failed where the raw ones did well. The old Confederate soldier would decide some questions for himself. To the last he maintained the right of private judgment, and especially on the field of battle.

CHAPTER 11

How Private George W. Peck
Put Down the Rebellion
(Or Funny Experiences of a Raw Recruit)
By George W. Peck

Humor in uniform, aka service comedy, became a great staple in American life in World War II and afterward—Korea, for instance. But even during the Civil War, certain writers turned talented pens toward putting smiles on readers' faces. George W. Peck was the leader in that department.

—LAMAR UNDERWOOD

FOR THE LAST YEAR OR MORE I HAVE BEEN READING THE ARTICLES IN THE *CENTURY* MAGazine, written by generals and things who served on both the Union and Confederate sides, and have been struck by the number of "decisive battles" that were fought, and the great number of generals who fought them and saved the country. It seems that each general on the Union side, who fought a battle, and writes an article for the aforesaid magazine, admits that his battle was the one which did the business. On the Confederate side, the generals who write articles invariably demonstrate that they everlastingly whipped their opponents, and drove them on in disorder.

To read those articles it seems strange that the Union generals who won so many decisive battles should not have ended the war much sooner than they did, and to read the accounts of battles won by the Confederates, and the demoralization that ensued in the ranks of their opponents, it seems marvellous that the Union army was victorious. Any man who has followed these generals of both sides, in the pages of that magazine, must conclude that the war was a draw game, and that both sides were whipped. Thus far no general has lost a battle on either side, and all of them tacitly admit that the whole thing depended on them, and that other commanders were mere ciphers. This is a kind of history that is going to mix up generations yet unborn in the most hopeless manner.

It has seemed to me as though the people of this country had got so mixed up about the matter that it was the duty of some private soldier to write a description of *the* decisive battle of the war, and as I was the private soldier who fought that battle on the Union side, against fearful odds, *viz*: against a Confederate soldier who was braver than I was, a better horseback rider, and a better poker player, I feel it my duty to tell about it. I have already mentioned it to a few veterans, and they have advised me to write an article for the *Century*, but I have felt a delicacy about entering the lists, a plain, unvarnished private soldier, against those generals. While I am something of a liar myself, and can do fairly well in my own class, I should feel that in the *Century* I was entered in too fast a class of liars, and the result would be that I should not only lose my entrance fee, but be distanced. So I have decided to contribute this piece of history solely for the benefit of the readers of my own paper, as they will believe me.

It was in 1864 that I joined a cavalry regiment in the department of the Gulf, a raw recruit in a veteran regiment. It may be asked why I waited so long before enlisting, and why I enlisted at all, when the war was so near over. I know that the most of the soldiers enlisted from patriotic motives, and because they wanted to help shed blood, and wind up the war. I did not. I enlisted for the bounty. I thought the war was nearly over, and that the probabilities were that the regiment I had enlisted in would be ordered home before I could get to it. In fact the recruiting officer told me as much, and he said I would get my bounty, and a few months' pay, and it would be just like finding money. He said at that late day I would never see a rebel, and if I did have to join the regiment, there would be no fighting, and it would just be one continued picnic for two or three months, and there would be no more danger than to go off camping for a duck shoot. At my time of life, now that I have become gray, and bald, and my eyesight is failing, and I have become a grandfather, I do not want to open the sores of twenty-two years ago. I want a quiet life. So I would not assert that the recruiting officer deliberately lied to me, but I was the worst deceived man that ever enlisted, and if I ever meet that man, on this earth, it will go hard with him. Of course, if he is dead, that settles it, as I shall not follow any man after death, where I am in doubt as to which road he has taken, but if he is alive, and reads these lines, he can hear of something to his advantage by communicating with me. I would probably kill him. As far as the bounty was concerned, I got that all right, but it was only three-hundred dollars.

Within twenty-four hours after I had been credited to the town from which I enlisted, I heard of a town that was paying as high as twelve-hundred dollars for recruits. I have met with many reverses of fortune in the course of a short, but brilliant career, have loaned money and never got it back, have been taken in by designing persons on three card monte, and have been beaten trading horses, but I never suffered much more than I did when I found that I had got to go to war for a beggarly three-hundred dollars bounty, when I could have had twelve hundred dollars by being credited to another town. I think that during two years and a half of service nothing tended more to dampen my ardor, make me despondent, and hate myself, than the loss of that nine-hundred dollars bounty. There was not an hour of the day, in all of my service, that I did not think of what might have been. It was a long time before I brought to my aid that passage of scripture, "There is no use crying for spilled bounty," but when I did it helped me some. I thought of the hundreds who didn't get any bounty.

I joined my regiment, and had a cavalry horse issued to me, and was assigned to a company. I went up to the captain of the company, whom I had known as a farmer before the war commenced, and told him I had come to help him put down the rebellion. I never saw a man so changed as he was. I thought he would ask me to bring my things into his tent, and stay with him, but he seemed to have forgotten that he had known me, when he worked on the farm. He was dressed up nicely, and I thought he put on style, and I could only think of him at home, with his overalls tucked in his boots, driving a yoke of oxen to plow a field. He seemed to feel that I had known him under unfavorable circumstances before the war, and acted as though he wanted to shun me. I had drawn an infantry knapsack, at Madison, before I left for the front, and had it full of things, besides a small trunk. The captain called a soldier and told him to find quarters for me, and I went out of his presence.

At my quarters, which consisted of what was called a pup-tent, I found no conveniences, and it soon dawned on me that war was no picnic, as that lying recruiting officers had told me it was. I found that I had got to throw away my trunk and knapsack, and all the articles that I couldn't strap on a saddle, and when I asked for a mattress the men laughed at me. I had always slept on a mattress, or a feather bed, and when I was told that I would have to sleep on the ground, under that little tent, I felt hurt. I had known the colonel when he used to teach school at home, and I went to him and told him what kind of a way they were treating me, but he only laughed. He had two nice cots in his tent, and I told him I thought I ought to have a cot, too. He laughed some more. Finally I asked him who slept in his extra cot, and intimated that I had rather sleep in his tent than mine, but he sent me away, and said he would see what could be done. I laid on the ground that night, but I didn't sleep. If I ever get a pension it will be for rheumatism caught by sleeping on the ground. The rheumatism has not got hold of me yet, though twenty-two years have passed, but it may be lurking about my system, for all I know.

I had never rode a horse, before enlisting. The only thing I had ever got straddle of was a stool in a country printing office, and when I was first ordered to saddle up my horse, I could not tell which way the saddle and bridle went, and I got a colored man to help me, for which I paid him some of the remains of my bounty. I hired him permanently, to take care of my horse, but I soon learned that each soldier had to take care of his own horse. That seemed pretty hard. I had been raised a pet, and had edited a newspaper, which had been one of the most outspoken advocates of crushing the rebellion, and it seemed to me, as much as I had done for the government, in urging enlistments, I was entitled to more consideration then to become my own hostler. However, I curbed my proud spirit, and after the nigger cook had saddled my horse, I led the animal up to a fence to climb on. From the remarks of the soldiers, and the general laugh all around, it was easy to see that mounting a cavalry horse from off the top of a rail fence was not according to tactics, but it was the only way I could see to get on, in the absence of step-ladders. They let me ride into the ranks, after mounting, and then they laughed. It was hard for me to be obliged to throw away all the articles I had brought with me, so I strapped them on the saddle in front and behind, and only my head stuck out over them. There was one thing, it would be a practicable impossibility to fall off.

The regiment started on a raid. The colonel came along by my company during the afternoon, and I asked him where we were going. He gave me an evasive answer, which hurt my feelings. I asked his pardon, but told him I would like to know where we were going, so as to have my letters sent to me, but he went off laughing, and never told me, while the old soldiers laughed, though I couldn't see what they were laughing at. I did not suppose there was so much difference between officers and privates, and wondered if it was the policy of this government to have a cavalry regiment to start off on a long raid and not let the soldiers know where they were going, and during the afternoon I decided to write home to the paper I formerly edited and give my opinion of such a fool way of running a war. Suppose anybody at home was sick, they wouldn't know where to write for me to come back. There is nothing that will give a man such an appetite as riding on a galloping horse, and along about the middle of the afternoon I began to get hungry, and asked the orderly sergeant when we were going to get any dinner. He said there was a hotel a short distance ahead, and the colonel had gone forward to order dinner for the regiment. I believed him, because I had known the orderly before the war, when he drove a horse in a brickyard, grinding clay. But he was a liar, too, as I found out afterwards. There was not a hotel within fifty miles, and soldiers did not stop at hotels, anyway. Finally the orderly sergeant came along and announced that dinner was ready, and I looked for the hotel, but the only dinner I saw was some raw pork that soldiers took out of their saddle bags, with hard tack. We stopped in the woods, dismounted, and the boys would cut off a slice of fat pork and spread it on the hard tack and eat it. I had never supposed the government would subject its soldiers to such fare as that, and I wouldn't eat. I did not dare dismount, as there was no fence near that I could use to climb on to my horse, so I sat in the saddle and let the horse eat some grass, while I thought of home, and pie and cake, and what a condemned fool a man was to leave a comfortable home to go and put down anybody's rebellion.

The way I felt then I wouldn't have touched a rebellion if one lay right in the road. What business was it of mine if some people in the South wanted to dissolve partnership and go set up business for themselves? How was I going to prevent them from having a Southern Confederacy, by riding an old rack of bones of a horse, that would reach his nose around every little while and chew my legs? If the recruiting officer who inveigled me into the army had come along then, his widow would now be drawing a pension. While I was thinking, dreaming of home, and the horse was eating grass, the fool animal suddenly took it into his head to lay down and roll, and before I could kick any of his ribs in, he was down, and I was rolling off, with one leg under him.

The soldiers quit eating and pulled the horse off me, and hoisted me up into the space between my baggage, and then they laughed, lit their pipes and smoked, as happy as could be. I couldn't see how they could be happy, and wondered if they were not sick of war. Then they mounted, and on we went. My legs and body became chafed, and it seemed as though I couldn't ride another minute, and when the captain came along I told him about it, and asked him if I couldn't be relieved some way. He said the only way was for me to stand on my head and ride, and he winked at a soldier near me, and, do you know, that soldier actually changed ends with himself and stood on his head and hands in the saddle and rode quite a distance, and the captain said that was the way a cavalry soldier rested himself. Gracious, I wouldn't have tried that for the world, and I found out afterwards that the soldier who stood on his head formerly belonged with a circus.

I suppose it was wrong to complain, but the horse they gave me was the meanest horse in the regiment. He would bite and kick the other horses, and they would kick back, and about half the time I was dodging the heels of horses, and a good deal of the time I was wondering if a man would get any pension if he was wounded that way. It would seem pretty tough to go home on a stretcher, as a wounded soldier, and have people find out a horse kicked you. I never had been a man of blood, and didn't enlist to kill anybody, as I could prove by that recruiting officer, and I didn't want to fight, but from what I could gather from the conversation of the soldiers, fighting and killing people was about all they thought about.

They talked about this one and that one who had been killed, and the hundreds of Confederates they had all shot or killed with sabres, until my hair just stood right up. It seems that twelve or fifteen men, more or less, had been shot off the horse I was riding, and one fellow who rode next to me said no man who ever rode that old yellow horse had escaped alive. This was cheering to me, and I would have given my three-hundred dollars bounty, and all I could borrow, if I could get out of the army. However, I found out afterwards that the soldier lied. In fact they all lied, and they lied for my benefit. We struck into the woods, and traveled until after dark, with no road, and the march was enlivened by remarks of the soldiers near me to the effect that we would probably never get out of the woods alive. They said we were trying to surround an army of rebels, and cut them off from the main army, and the chances were that when tomorrow's sun rose it would rise on the ghostly corpses of the whole regiment, with jackals and buzzards eating us.

One of the soldiers took something from his pocket, about the size of a testament, pressed it to his heart, and then kissed it, and I felt as though I was about to faint, but by the light of a match which another soldier had scratched on his pants to light his pipe, I saw that what I supposed to be a testament, was a box of sardines the soldier had bought of the sutler. I was just about to die of hunger, exhaustion, and fright at the fearful stories the veterans had been telling, when there was a shout at the head of the regiment, which was taken up all along the line, my horse run under the limb of a tree and raked me out of the saddle, and I hung to the limb, my legs hanging down.

— ⁓ —

The careful readers of this history have no doubt been worried about the manner in which the first chapter closed, leaving me hanging to a limb of a tree, like Absalom weeping for her children, my horse having gone out from under me. But I have not been hanging there all this time. The soldiers took me down, and caught my horse, and the regiment dismounted and a council of war was held. I suppose it was a council of war, as I noticed the officers were all in a group under a tree, with a candle, examining a map, and drinking out of a canteen. I had read of councils of war, but I had never seen one, and so I walked over to the crowd of officers and asked the colonel if there was anything particular the matter. I never saw a crowd of men who seemed so astonished as those officers were, and suddenly I felt myself going away from where they were consulting, with somebody's strong hand on my collar, and an unmistakable cavalry boot, with a man in it, in the vicinity of my pantaloons. I do not know to this day, which officer it was that kicked me, but I went away and sat under a tree in the dark, so hungry that I was near dead, and I wished I *was* dead.

I guess the officers wished that I was, too. The soldiers tried to console me by telling me I was too fresh, but I couldn't see why a private soldier, right from home, who knew all about the public sentiment at the north in regard to the way the war was conducted, should not have a voice in the consultations of officers. I had written many editorials before I left home, criticizing the manner in which many generals had handled their commands, and pointed out to my readers how defeat could have been turned into victory, if the generals had done as I would have done in their places. It seemed to me the officers of my regiment were taking a suicidal course in barring me out of their consultations. A soldier had told me that we were lost in the woods, and as I had studied geography when at school, and was well posted about Alabama, it seemed as though a little advice from me would be worth a good deal. But I concluded to let them stay lost forever before I would volunteer any information.

It was crawling along towards midnight, of my first day in the army, and I had eaten nothing since morning. As I sat there under the tree I fell asleep, and was dreaming of home, and warm biscuit, with honey, and a feather bed, when I was rudely awakened by a corporal who told me to mount. I asked him what for, and told him that I didn't want to ride any more that night. What I wanted was to be let alone, to sleep. He said to get on the horse too quick, and I found there was no use arguing with a common corporal, so the boys hoisted me on to the horse, and about nine of us started off through the woods in the moonlight, looking for a main road.

The corporal was kind enough to say that as soon as we found a road we would put out a picket, and send a courier back to the regiment to inform the colonel that we had got out of the woods, and the rest of us would lay down and sleep till morning. I don't think I was ever so anxious to see a road in all my life, because I *did* want to lay down and sleep, and die. Oh, if I could have telegraphed home, how I would have warned the youth of the land to beware of the allurements held out by recruiting officers, and to let war alone.

In an hour or so we came to a clearing, and presently to a road, and we stopped. The corporal detailed me to go up the road a short distance and stand picket on my horse. That was not what I had expected of the corporal. I used to know him before the war when he worked in a paint shop in a wagon factory, and I had always treated him well, and it seemed as though he ought to favor me by letting somebody else go on picket. I told him that the other boys were more accustomed to such work than I was, and that I would resign in their favor, because what I wanted was rest, but he said I would have to go, and he called me "Camp and Garrison Equipage," because I carried so much luggage on my horse, a name that held to me for months. I found that there was no use kicking against going on picket duty that night, though I tried to argue with the corporal that it would be just as well to all lay down and sleep till morning, and put out a picket when it got light enough to see.

I was willing to work during the day time for the government, but it seemed as though it was rushing things a little to make a man work day and night for thirteen dollars a month. So the corporal went out on the road with me about a quarter of a mile, and placed me in position and gave me my instructions. The instructions were to keep a sharp lookout up and down the road for Confederate cavalry, and if I saw anybody approaching to sing out "halt!" and if the party did not halt to shoot him, and then call for the corporal of the guard, who would come out to see what was the matter. I asked him what I should do if anybody came along and shot me, and he said that would be all right, that the boys would come out and bury me. He said I must keep awake, for if I got to sleep on my post I would be court-martialed and shot, and then he rode away and left me alone, on a horse that kept whinnying, and calling the attention of possible Confederates to my position.

I do not think any reader of these papers will envy me the position I was in at that time. If I remained awake, I was liable to be killed by the enemy, and if I fell asleep on my post I would be shot anyway. And if I was not killed, it was probable I would be a murderer before morning. Hunger was gnawing at my stomach, and the horse was gnawing at my legs, and I was gnawing at a hard tack which I had found in the saddle-bag. Every little while I would hear a noise, and my hair would raise my hat up, and it would seem to me as though the next minute a volley would be fired at me, and I shrunk down between the piles of baggage on my saddle to be protected from bullets.

Suddenly the moon came out from behind a cloud and around a turn in the road a solitary horseman might have been seen coming towards me. I never have seen a horse that looked as high as that horse did. He seemed at least eighteen feet high, and the man on him was certainly twelve feet high. My heart pounded against a tin canteen that I had strung around my shoulder, so I could hear the beating perfectly plain. The man was approaching, and I was trying to think whether I had been instructed to shoot and then call for the corporal of the guard, or call for the corporal and then ask him to halt. I knew there was a halt in my instructions, and wondered if it would not conciliate the enemy to a certain extent if I would say "Please Halt."

The fact was, I didn't want to have any fuss. If I could have backed my horse up into the woods, and let the man go by, it seemed as though it would save precipitating a conflict. It is probable that no military man was ever in so tight a place as I was that minute. The enemy was advancing, and I wondered if, when he got near enough, I could say "halt," in a commanding tone of voice. I knew enough, then, to feel that to ask the stranger to halt in a trembling and husky voice would give the whole thing away, that I was a recruit and a coward. Ye gods, how I suffered! I wondered if I could hit a man with a bullet. Before the war I was quite a good shot with a shotgun, shooting into flocks of pigeons and ducks, and I thought what a good idea it would be if I could get that approaching rebel into a flock.

The idea seemed so ridiculous that I laughed right out loud. It was not a hearty, happy laugh, but it was a laugh all the same, and I was proud that I could laugh in the face of danger, when I might be a corpse any minute. The man on the horse stopped. Whether he heard me laugh it is impossible to say, but he stopped. That relieved me a great deal. As he had stopped it was unnecessary for me to invite him to halt. He was welcome to stay there if he wanted to. I argued that it was not my place to go howling around the Southern Confederacy, ordering people to halt, when they had already halted. If he would let me alone and stay where he was, what sense was there in picking a quarrel with him?

Why should I want to shoot a total stranger, who might have a family at home, somewhere in the South, who would mourn for him. He might be a dead shot, as many Southern gentlemen were, and if I went to advising him about halting, it would, very likely cause his hot Southern blood to boil, and he would say he had just as much right to that road as I had. If it come right down to the justice of the thing, I should have to admit that Alabama was not my state. Wisconsin was my home, and if I was up there, and a man should trespass on my property, it would be reasonable enough for me to ask him to go away from there, and enforce my request by calling a constable and having him put off the premises. But how did I know but he owned property there, and was a tax-payer.

I had it all figured out that I was right in not disturbing that rebel, and I knew that I could argue with my colonel for a week, if necessary, on the law points in the case, and the courtesy that I deemed proper between gentlemen, if any complaint was made for not doing my duty. But, lordy, how I *did* sweat while I was deciding to let him alone if he would let me alone. The war might have been going on now, and that rebel and myself might have been standing there today, looking at each other, if it hadn't been for the action of the fool horse that I rode.

My horse had been evidently asleep for some time, but suddenly he woke up, pricked up his ears, and began to prance, and jump sideways like a race horse that is on the track, and wants to run. The horse reared up and plunged, and kept working up nearer to my Southern friend, and I tried to hold him, and keep him still, but suddenly he got the best of me and started towards the other man and horse, and the other horse started, as though some one had said "go."*

I do not suppose any man on this earth, or any other earth, ever tried to stop a fool horse quite as hard as I did that one. I pulled until my arms ached, but he went for all that was out, and the horse ahead of me was buckling in as fast as he could. I could not help wondering what would happen if I should overtake that Southern man. I was gaining on him, when suddenly eight or nine men who were sleeping beside the road, got up and began to shoot at us. They were the friends of the rebel, who believed that the whole Union army was making a charge on them.

We got by the shooters alive, and then, as we passed the rickety old judge's stand, I realized that we were on a race track, and for a moment I forgot that I was a soldier, and only thought of myself as a rider of a race horse, and I gave the horse his head, and kicked him, and yelled like a Comanche Indian, and I had the satisfaction of seeing my horse go by the rebel, and I yelled some more.

I got a glimpse of my rebel's face as I went by him, and he didn't look much more like a fighting man than I did, but he was, for as soon as I had got ahead of him he drew a revolver and began firing at me on the run. I thought that was a mean trick, and spoke to him about it afterwards, but he said he only wanted me to stop so he could get acquainted with me.

Well, I never could find any bullets in any of the clothes strapped on the back of my saddle, but it did seem to me as though every bullet from his revolver hit very near my vital parts. But a new danger presented itself. We were rapidly approaching the corporal and his men, with whose command I belonged, and they would wake up and think the whole Confederate army was charging them, and if I was not killed by the confounded rebel behind me, I should probably be shot all to pieces by our own men.

As we passed our men they fired a few sleepy shots towards us, and took to the woods. On went the two night riders, and when the rebel had exhausted his revolver he began to urge his horse, and passed me, and I drew my revolver and began to fire at him. As we passed the judge's stand the second time a couple of shots from quite a distance in the

*Before I get any further on this history of the war, it is necessary to explain. The facts proved to be that my regiment had got lost in the woods, and the scouting party, under the corporal, who had been sent out to find a road, had come upon the three-quarter stretch of an old private race track on a deserted Southern plantation, instead of a main road, and I had been placed on picket near the last turn before striking the quarter stretch. A small party of Confederates, who had been out on a scout, and got lost, had come on the track further down, near the judges' stand, and they had put a man, on picket up near where I was, supposing they had struck the road, and intending to wait until morning so as to find out where they were. My horse was an old race horse, and as soon as he saw the other horse, he was in for a race and the other horse was willing. This will show the situation as well as though I had a race track engraved, showing the positions of the two armies. The Confederates, except the man on picket, were asleep beside the track near the quarter stretch, and our fellows, except myself, were asleep over by the three-quarter pole.

woods showed that his rebel friends had taken alarm at the frequent charges of cavalry, and had skipped to the woods and were getting away as fast as possible. We went around the track once more, and when near the judge's stand I was right behind him, and his horse fell down and my horse stumbled over him, and I guess we were both stunned.

Finally I crawled out from under my horse, and the rebel was trying to raise up, when I said, "What in thunder you want to chase a man all around the Southern Confederacy for, on a dark night, trying to shoot him?"

He asked me to help him up, which I did, when he said, "Who commenced this here chasing? If you had kept whar you was, I wouldn't a had no truck with you." Then I said, "You are my prisoner," and he said, "No, you are my prisoner." I told him I was no hand to argue, but it seemed to me it was about a stand off, as to which was 'tother's prisoner.

I told him that was my first day's service as a soldier, and I was not posted as to the customs of civilized warfare, but I was willing to wait till daylight, leaving matters just as they were, each of us on the defensive, giving up none of our rights, and after daylight we would play a game of seven-up to see which was the prisoner. That seemed fair to him, and he accepted the situation, remarking that he had only been conscripted a few days and didn't know any more about war than a cow. He said he was a newspaper man from Georgia, and had been taken right from the case in his office before his paper could be got out. I told him I was only a few days out of a country printing office my-self, the sheriff having closed out my business on an old paper bill. A bond of sympathy was inaugurated at once between us, and when he limped along the track to the fence, and found that his ankle was hurt by the fall, I brought a bottle of horse liniment out of my saddle-bags, and a rag, and bound some liniment on his ankle.

He said he had never seen a Yankee soldier before, and he was glad he had met me. I told him he was the first rebel I had ever met, and I hoped he would be the last, until the war was over. By this time our horses had gone to nibbling grass, as though there were no such thing as war. We could hear occasional bugle calls off in the woods in two directions, and knew that our respective commands had gone off and got lost again, so we concluded to camp there till morning. After the excitement was over I began to get hungry, and I asked him if he had anything to eat. He said he had some corn bread and bacon, and he could get some sweet potatoes over in a field.

So I built a fire there on the track, and he hobbled off after potatoes. Just about daylight breakfast was served, consisting of coffee, which I carried in a sack, made in a pot he carried, bacon fried in a half of a tin canteen, sweet potatoes roasted in the ashes, and Confederate corn bread, warmed by holding it over the fire on a sharp stick. My friend, the rebel, sat on my saddle, which I had removed from my horse, after he had promised me on his honor to help me to put it on when it was time to mount. He knew how to put on saddles, and I didn't, and as his ankle was lame I gave him the best seat, he being my guest, that is, he was my guest if I beat him in the coming game of seven-up, which we were to play to see if he was my prisoner, or I was his.

It being daylight, I could see him, and study his character, and honestly he was a mighty fine-looking fellow. As we eat our early breakfast I began to think that the recruiting officer was more than half right about war being a picnic. He talked about the newspaper business in the South, and before breakfast was over we had formed a partnership to publish a paper at Montgomery, Ala., after the war should be over.

I have eaten a great many first-class meals in my time, have feasted at Delmonico's, and lived at the best hotels in the land, besides partaking pretty fair food camping out, where an appetite was worked up by exercise and sporting, but in all my life I have never had anything taste as good as that combination Union-Confederate breakfast on the Alabama race track, beside the judges stand. After the last potato peeling, and the last crumb of corn bread had been "sopped" in the bacon gravy and eaten, we whittled some tobacco off a plug, filled our pipes and leaned up against the fence and smoked the most enjoyable smoke that ever was smoked.

After smoking in silence a few minutes my rebel friend said, as he blew the smoke from his handsome mouth, "War is not so unpleasant, after all." Then we fell to talking about the manner in which the different generals on each side had conducted things. He went on to show that if Lee had taken his advice, the Yankees would then be on the run for the North, and I showed him, by a few well-chosen remarks that if I could have been close to Grant, and given him some pointers, that the Confederates would be hunting their holes. We were both convinced that it was a great mistake that we were nothing but private soldiers, but felt that it would not be long before we were called to occupy high places. It seemed to stand to reason that true merit would find its reward.

Then he knocked the ashes out of his pipe and said if I had a pack of cards we would go up in the judges stand and play seven-up to see whether I was his prisoner, or he was mine. I wanted to take a prisoner back to the regiment, at I thought it would make me solid with the colonel, and I played a strong game of seven-up, but before we got started to playing he suggested that we call it a stand-off, and agree that neither of us should be a prisoner, but that when we got ready to part each should go hunt up his own command, and tell the biggest lie we could think of as to the fight we had had.

That was right into my hand, and I agreed, and then my friend suggested that we play poker for money. I consented and he put up Confederate money, against my greenbacks, ten to one. We played about an hour, and at the close he had won the balance of my bounty, except what I had given to the chaplain for safe keeping, and a pair of pants, and a blouse, and a flannel shirt, and a pair of shoes, which I had on my saddle. I was rather glad to get rid of some of my extra baggage, and when he put on the clothes he had won from me, blessed if I wasn't rather proud of him. A man could wear any kind of clothes in the Confederate army, and my rebel looked real comfortable in my clothes, and I felt that it was a real kind act to allow him to win a blue suit that I did not need.

If the men of both the armies, and the people of both sections of the distracted country could have seen us two soldiers together, there in the judges stand, peacefully playing poker, while the battles were raging in the East and in the West, that would have felt that an era of good feeling was about to dawn on the country. After we had played enough poker, and I had lost everything I had that was loose, I suggested that he sing a song, so he sung the "Bonnie Blue Flag." I did not think it was right for him to work in a rebel song on me, but it did sound splendid, and I forgot that there was any war, in listening to the rich voice of my new friend. When he got through he asked me to sing something.

I never could sing, anyway. My folks had always told me that my voice sounded like a corn sheller, but he urged me at his own peril, and I sung, or tried to, "We'll Hang Jeff Davis to a Sour Apple Tree." I had no designs on Mr. Davis, honestly I hadn't, and it was the farthest thing from my thoughts to hurt the feelings of that young man, but before I had finished the first verse he took his handkerchief out and placed it to his eyes. I stopped and apologized, but he said not to mind him, as he was better now. He told me, afterwards, in the strictest confidence, that my singing was the worst he ever heard, and gave it as his opinion that if Jeff Davis could hear me sing he would be willing, even anxious, to be hung.

If I had been sensitive about my musical talents, probably there would have been hard feelings, and possibly bloodshed, right there, but I told him I always knew I couldn't sing, and he said that I was in luck. Well, we fooled around there till about ten o'clock in the morning, and decided that we would part, and each seek our respective commands, so I put some more horse liniment on his sprained ankle, and he saddled my horse for me, and after expressions of mutual pleasure at meeting each other, and promises that after the war we would seek each other out, we mounted, he gave three cheers for the Yanks, and I gave three cheers for the Johnnies, he divided his plug of tobacco with me, and I gave him the bottle of horse liniment, he turned his horse towards the direction his gray coats had taken the night before, while I turned my horse towards the hole in the woods our fellows had made, and we left the race track where we had fought so gamely, eat so heartily, and played poker so disastrously, to me. As we were each about going into the woods, half a mile apart, he waved his handkerchief at me, and I waved mine at him, and we plunged into the forest.

After riding for an hour or so, alone in the woods, thinking up a good lie to tell about where I had been, and what I had been doing, I heard horses neighing, and presently I came upon my regiment, just starting out to hunt me up. The colonel looked at me and said, "Kill the fat prodigal, the calf has got back."

The last chapter of this history left me facing my regiment, which had started out to hunt me up, after my terrible fight with that Confederate. The colonel rode up to me and shook me by the hand, and congratulated me, and the major and adjutant said they had never expected to see me alive, and the soldiers looked at me as one returned from the grave, and from what I could gather by the looks of the boys, I was something of a hero, even before I had told my story.

The colonel asked me what had become of all the baggage I had on my saddle when I went away, and I told him that I had thrown ballast over-board all over the Southern Confederacy, when I was charging the enemy, because I found my horse drew too much water for a long run. He said something about my being a Horse-Marine, and sent me back to my company, telling me that when we got into camp that night he would send for me and I could tell the story of my capture and escape. I rode back into my company, and you never saw such a change of sentiment towards a raw recruit, as there was towards me, and they asked me questions about my first fight. The corporal who had placed me on picket, and stampeded at the first fire, was unusually gracious to me, and said when he saw a hundred and fifty rebels come charging down the road, yelling and firing, he knew it was no place for his small command, so he lit out. He said he supposed of course I was shot all to pieces.

I didn't tell him that it was me that did all the yelling, and that there was only one rebel, and that he was perfectly harmless, but I told him that he miscalculated the number of the enemy, as there were, all told, at least five hundred, and that I had killed fourteen that I knew of, besides a number had been taken away in ambulances, wounded. The boys opened their eyes, and nothing was too good for me during that march. We went into camp in the pine woods late in the afternoon, and after supper the colonel sent for me, and I went to his tent.

All the officers were there, and as many soldiers as dared crowd around. The colonel said the corporal had reported where he left me, and how the enemy had charged in force, and he supposed that I had been promptly killed. That he felt that he could not hold his position against such immense odds, so he had fallen back slowly, firing as he did so, until the place was too hot for him, and now he wanted to hear my story. I told the colonel that I was new at the business, and may be I did not use the best judgment in the world, by remaining to fight against such odds, but I meant well. I told him I did not wish to complain of the corporal, who no doubt was an able fighter, but it did seem to me that he ought at least to have waited till the battle had actually commenced.

I said that the first charge, which stampeded the corporal and his men, was not a marker to what took place afterwards. I said when the enemy first appeared, I dismounted, got behind a tree, and poured a murderous fire into the ranks of the rebels, and that they fell all around. I could not tell how many were killed, but probably ten, as I fired eleven shots from my carbine, and I usually calculated on missing one out of ten, when shooting at a mark.

Then they fell back and I mounted my horse and rode to their right flank and poured it into them red hot from my revolver, and that I saw several fall from their horses, when they stampeded, and I drew my saber and charged them, and after cutting down several, I was surrounded by the whole rebel army and captured. They tied me to the wheel of a gun carriage, and after trying to pump me as to the number of men I had fighting against them, they left me to hold a council of war, when I untied myself, mounted my horse, and cut my way out, and took to the woods. I apologized to the colonel for running away from the enemy, but told him it seemed to me, after the number I had killed, and the length of time I had held them at bay, it was no more than right to save my own life, as I had use for it in my business.

During my recital of the lie I had made up, the officers and soldiers stood around with mouths open, and when I had concluded my story, there was silence for a moment, when the colonel stepped forward and took me by the hand, and in a few well chosen remarks congratulated me on my escape, and thanked me for so valiantly standing my ground against such fearful odds, and he said I had reflected credit upon my regiment, and that hereafter I would be classed as a veteran instead of a recruit.

He said he had never known a man to come right from the paths of peace, and develop into a warrior with a big "W" so short a time. The other officers congratulated me, and the soldiers said I was a bully boy. The colonel treated to some commissary whisky, and then the business of the evening commenced, which I found to be draw poker. I sat around for some time watching the officers play poker, when the chaplain, who was a nice little pious man, asked me to step outside the tent, as he wished to converse with me. I went out into the moonlight with him, and he took me away from the tents, under a tree, and told me he had been much interested in my story. I thanked him, and said I had been as brief as possible.

He said, "I was interested, because I used to be something of a liar myself, before I reformed, and studied for the ministry." It occurred to me that possibly the chaplain did not believe my simple tale, and I asked him if he doubted my story. "That is about the size of it," says he.

I told him I was sorry I had not told the story in such a manner that he would believe it, because I valued the opinion of the chaplain above all others. He said he had known a good many star liars in his time, some that had national reputations, but he had never seen one that could hold a candle to me in telling a colossal lie, or aggregation of lies, and tell them so easy. I thanked him for his good opinion, and told him that I flattered myself that for a recruit, right fresh from the people, who had never had any experience as a military liar, I had done pretty well. He said I certainly had, and he was glad to make my acquaintance.

I asked him to promise not to give it away to the other officers, which he did, and then I told him the whole story, as it was, and that I was probably the biggest coward that ever lived, and that I was only afraid that my story of blood-letting would encourage the officers to be constantly putting me into places of danger, which I did not want to be in. I told him I believed this war could be ended without killing any more men, and cited the fact that I had been a soldier nearly forty-eight hours, and nobody had been killed, and the enemy was on the run.

I had now been fighting the battles of my country for two weeks, and felt that I needed rest, and one day I became so homesick that it *did* seem as though it would kill me.

Including the week it had taken me to get from home to my regiment, three weeks had elapsed since I bid good-bye to my friends, and I wanted to go home. I would lay awake nights and think of people at home and wonder what they were doing, and if they were laying awake nights thinking of me, or caring whether I was alive, or buried in the swamps of the South. It was about the time of year when at home we always went off shooting, and I thought how much better it was to go off shooting ducks and geese, and chickens, that could not shoot back, than to be hunting bloodthirsty Confederates that were just as liable to hunt us, and who could kill, with great ease. I thought of a pup I had at home that was just the right age to train, and that he would be spoiled if he was not trained that season. Oh, how I did want to train that pup.

The news that one of my comrades had been granted a furlough, after three years' service, and that he was going home, made me desperate, and I dreamed that I had waylaid and murdered the fortunate soldier, and gone home on his furlough. The idea of getting a furlough was the one idea in my mind, and the next morning as I took my horse to the veterinary surgeon for treatment,* I had a talk with the horse doctor about the possibilities of getting a furlough. I had known him before the war, when he kept a livery stable, and as I owed him a small livery bill, I thought he would give it to me straight.

The horse doctor had his sleeves rolled up, and was holding a horse's tongue in one hand while he poured some medicine down the animal's throat out of a bottle with the other hand, which made me sorry for the horse, as I remembered my experience at surgeon's call, in drinking a dose of castor oil out of a bottle, and I was mean-enough to be glad they played it on horses as well as the soldiers. The horse doctor returned the horse's tongue to its mouth, kicked the animal in the ribs, turned and wiped his hands on a bale of hay, and said:

"Well, George, to get a furlough a man has got to have plenty of gall, especially a man who has only been to the front a couple of weeks. There is no use making an application in the regular way, to your captain, have him endorse it and send it to regimental headquarters, and so on to brigade headquarters, because you would never hear of it again. My idea would be for you to go right to the general commanding the division, and tell him you have got to go home. But you mustn't go crawling to him, and whining. He is a quick-tempered man, and he hates a coward. Go to him and talk familiar with him, and act as though you had always associated with him, and slap him on the shoulder, and make yourself at home. Just make up a good, plausible story, and give it to him, and if he seems irritated, give him to understand that he can't frighten you, and just as likely as not he

---

*I neglected to say, in my account of the battle at the race track, that when firing with my revolver, at my friend the rebel, I put one bullet-hole through the right ear of my horse. I was so excited at the time that I did not know it, and only discovered it a week later when currying off my horse, which I made a practice of doing once a week, with a piece of barrel-stave, when I noticed the horse's ear was swelled up about as big as a canvas ham. I took him to the horse doctor, who reduced the swelling so we could find the hole through the horse's ear, and the horse doctor tied a blue ribbon in the hole. He said the blue ribbon would help heal the sore, but later I found that he had put the ribbon in the ear to call attention to my poor marksmanship, and the boys got so they made comments and laughed at me every time I appeared with the horse.

will give you a furlough. I don't say he will, mind you, but it would be just like him. But he does like to be treated familiar like, by the boys."

I thanked the horse doctor and went away with my horse, resolved to have a furlough or know the reason why. The general's headquarters were about half a mile from our camp, and after drill that morning I went to see him. I had seen him several times, at the colonel's headquarters, and he always seemed mad about something, and I had thought he was about the crossest looking man I ever saw, but if there was any truth in what the horse doctor had told me, he was easily reached if a man went at him right, and I resolved that if pure, unadulterated cheek and monumental gall would accomplish anything, I would have a furlough before night, for a homesicker man never lived than I was. I went up to the general's tent and a guard halted me and asked me what I wanted, and I said I wanted to see "his nibs," and I walked right by the guard, who seemed stunned by my cheek. I saw the general in his tent, with his coat off, writing, and he *did* look savage. Without taking off my hat, or saluting him, I went right up to him and sat down on the end of a trunk that was in the tent, and with a tremendous effort to look familiar, I said:

"Hello, Boss, writing to your girl?"

I have seen a good many men in my time who were pretty mad, but I have never seen a man who appeared to be as mad as the general did. He was a regular army officer, I found afterwards, and hated a volunteer as he did poison. He turned red in the face and pale, and I thought he frothed at the mouth, but may be he didn't. He seemed to try to control himself, and said through his clenched teeth, in a sarcastic manner, I thought, in imitation of a ring master in a circus:

"What will the little lady have next?"

I had been in circuses myself, and when the general said that I answered the same as a clown always does, and I said:

"The banners, my lord."

I thought he would be pleased at my joking with him, but he looked around as though he was seeking a revolver or a saber with which to kill me finally he said:

"What do you want, man?"

It was a little tough to be called plain "man," but I swallowed it. I made up my mind it was time to act, so I stood up, put my hand on the shoulder of the general familiarly, and said:

"The fact is, old man, I want a furlough to go home. I have got business that demands my attention; I am sick of this inactivity in camp, and besides the shooting season is just coming on at home, and I have got a setter pup that will be spoiled if he is not trained this season. I came down here two weeks ago, to help put down the rebellion; but all we have done since I got here is to monkey around drilling and cleaning off horses, while the officers play poker for red chips. Let me go home till the poker season is over, and I will be back in time for the fall fighting. What do you say, old apoplexy. Can I go?"

I do not now, and never did know, how I got out of the general's tent, whether he kicked me out, or threw his trunk at me, or whether there was an explosion, but when I got outside there were two soldiers trying to untangle me from the guy ropes of the general's tent, his wash basin and pail of water were tipped over, and a cord that was strung outside with a lot of uniforms, shirts, sabers, etc., had fallen down, and the general was walking up and down his tent in an excited manner, calling me an escaped lunatic, and telling the guards to tie me up by the thumbs, and buck and gag me. They led me away, and from their conversation I concluded I had committed an unpardonable offense, and would probably be hung, though I couldn't see as I had done much more than the horse doctor told me to.

Finally the officer of the day came along and told the guards to get a rail and make me carry it. So they got a rail and put it on my shoulder, and I carried it up and down the camp, as a punishment for insulting the general. I thought they picked out a pretty heavy rail, but I carried it the best I could for an hour, when I threw it down and told the guards I didn't enlist to carry rails. If the putting down of this rebellion depended on carrying fence rails around the Southern Confederacy, and I had to carry the rails, the aforesaid rebellion never would be put down. I said I would fight if I had to, and be a hostler, and cook my own food, and sleep on the ground, and try to earn my thirteen dollars a month, but there must be a line drawn somewhere, and I drew it at transporting fences around the sunny South. The guards were inclined to laugh at my determination, but they said I could carry the rail or be tied up by the thumbs; and I said they could go ahead, but if they hurt me I would bring suit against the government.

They were fixing to tie me up when the colonel of my regiment rode up to see the general, and he got the guards to let up on me till he could see the general. The general sent for me after the colonel had talked with him, and they called me in and asked me how I happened to be so fresh with the general; and I told them about the horse doctor's advice as to how to get a furlough; and then they both laughed, and said I owed the horse doctor one, and I must get even with him. The colonel told the general who I was, that he had known me before the war, and that I was all right only a little green, and that the boys were having fun with me. The colonel told the general about my first fight the first day of my service, and how I had, single-handed, put to flight a large number of rebels, and the general got up and shook hands with me, and said he forgave me for my impertinence, and gave me some advice about letting the boys play it on me, and said I might go back to my company. He was all smiles, and insisted on my taking a drink with himself and the colonel. When I was about leaving his tent, I turned to him and said: "Then I don't get any furlough?" "Not till the cruel war is over," said the general, with a laugh, and I went away.

The guards treated me like a gentleman when they saw me taking a drink with the general, and I went back to my regiment, resolved not to go home, and to get even with the horse doctor for causing me to make a fool of myself. However, I was glad I visited the general, for, after getting acquainted with him, he seemed a real nice man, and he kept a better article of liquor than the chaplain.

For several days nothing occurred that was worthy of note, except that the chaplain took a liking to my horse, and wanted to trade a mule for him. I never did like a mule, and didn't really want to trade, but the chaplain argued his case so eloquently that I was half persuaded. He said the horse I rode, from its friskiness, and natural desire to "get there, Eli!" would eventually get me killed, for if I ever got in sight of the enemy the horse would rush to the front, and I couldn't hold him. He said he didn't want to have me killed, and with the mule there would be no danger, as the mule knew enough to keep away from a fight. The chaplain said he had always rode a mule, because he thought the natural solemnity of a mule was in better keeping with a pious man, but lately he had begun to go into society some, in the town near where we were camped, and sometimes had to preach to different regiments, so he thought he ought to have a horse that put on a little more style, and as he knew I wanted an animal that would keep as far from the foe as possible, and not lose its head and go chasing around after rebels, and running me into danger, as my spiritual adviser he would recommend the mule to me. He warranted the mule sound in every particular, and as a mule was worth more than a horse he would trade with me for ten dollars to boot. He said there was not another man in the regiment he would trade with on such terms, but he had taken a liking to me, and would part with his mule to me, though it broke his heart.

At home there was a sentiment against trading horses with a minister, as men who did so always got beat, but I thought it would be an insult to the chaplain to refuse to trade, when he seemed to be working for my interests, to prevent me from being killed in a fight by the actions of my horse, so I concluded to trade, though it seemed to me that if I couldn't shoot off a horse without hitting its ears, I would fill a mule's ears full of bullets. I spoke to the chaplain about that, and he said there was no danger, because whenever fighting commenced the mule always wore his ears lopped down below the line of fire. He said the mule had been trained to that, and I would find him a great comfort in time of trial, and a sympathizing companion always, one that I would become attached to. I told him there was one thing I wanted to know, and that was if the mule would kick. I had always been prejudiced against mules because they kicked. He said he knew mules had been traduced, and that their reputations were not good, but he believed this mule was as free from the habit of kicking as any mule he had ever met. He said he would not deny that this mule could kick, and in fact he had kicked a little, but he would warrant the mule not to kick unless something unusual happened. He said I wouldn't want a mule that had no individuality at all, one that hadn't sand enough to protect itself. What I wanted, the chaplain said, was a mule that would treat everybody right, but that would, if imposed upon, stand up for its rights and kick. I told the chaplain that was about the kind of mule I wanted, if I had any mule at all, and we traded.

The chaplain rode off to town on my horse, on a canter, as proud as a peacock, while I climbed on to the solemn, lop-eared mule and went out to drill with my company. I do not know what it was that went wrong with the mule while we were drilling, but as we were wheeling in company front, the mule began to "assert his individuality," as the chaplain said he probably would, and he whirled around sideways and kicked three soldiers off their horses; then he backed up the other way and broke up the second platoon, kicked four horses in the ribs, stampeded the company, and stood there alone kicking at the air. The major rode down to where I was and began to swear at me, but I told him I couldn't help it. He told me to dismount and lead the mule away, but I couldn't dismount until the mule stopped kicking, and he seemed to be wound up for all day. The major got too near and the mule kicked him on the shin, and then started for the company again, which had got into ranks, kicking all the way, and the company broke ranks and started for camp, the mule following, kicking and braying all the way. I never was so helpless in all my life. The more I spurred the mule, the more it kicked, and if I stopped spurring it, it kicked worse. When we got to camp, I fell off some way, and rushed into the chaplain's tent, and the mule kicked the tent down, and some boys drove the mule away, and while I was fixing up the tent the chaplain came back looking happy, and asked me how I liked the mule. I never was a hypocrite, anyway, and I was mad, so I said: "Oh, damn that mule!"

Of course it is wrong to use such language, especially in the presence of a minister, but I couldn't help it. I could see it hurt the chaplain, for he sighed and said he was sorry to hear such words from me, inasmuch as he had just got me detailed as his clerk, where I would have a soft thing, and no drilling or fighting. He said he had wanted a clerk, one who was a good-hearted, true man, and he had picked me out, but if I used such language, that settled it. He said he didn't expect to find a private soldier that was as pious as he was, but he did think I would be the best man he could find.

I wanted a soft job, with no fighting, as bad as any man ever did, and I told the chaplain that he need not fear as to my swearing again, as it was foreign to my nature, but I told him if he had been on the hurricane deck of a kicking mule for an hour, and seen comrades fall one by one, and bite the dust, and be carried on with marks of mule shoes all over their persons, he would swear, and I would bet on it. So it was arranged that I was to be the chaplain's clerk, and I moved my outfit over to his tent, and for the first time since I had been a soldier, I was perfectly happy. There was no danger of being detached for guard duty, police duty, drilling, or fighting, and the only boss I had was the chaplain. The chaplain and myself sat that evening in his tent, and ate sanitary stores, drank wine for sickess, and smoked pipes, and didn't care whether school kept or not, and that night I slept on a cot, and had the first good night's rest, and in the morning I awoke refreshed, and with no fear of orderly sergeants, or anybody. I had a soft snap.

CHAPTER 12

What I Saw of Shiloh
By *Ambrose Bierce*

Like no other war, the Civil War has captured the American imagination. This is not surprising: It had great leaders, such as Abraham Lincoln, Robert E. Lee, Ulysses S. Grant, Stonewall Jackson, and William T. Sherman. It had great battles, too, such as Shiloh, Chickamauga, Antietam, and Gettysburg. This war—the only war fought on American soil, between Americans—was surely one of the most heroic and the most horrific. During the four years of this brutal, bloody conflict, Americans killed each other in greater numbers than in any war before or since. The Civil War left the Southern Confederacy defeated and the Union intact, and it ended slavery, all at the cost of nearly 1,100,000 casualties and more than 620,000 lives.

Between the first shots fired at Fort Sumter on April 12, 1861, and Lee's surrender to Grant at Appomattox on April 9, 1865, the nation was irrevocably changed. Homes were transformed into headquarters; churches and schools into makeshift hospitals. Marauding armies decimated the once-peaceful landscape, pillaging farms, burning towns, and killing each other wherever they met. And whether soldier or civilian, the lives of those who lived through the war were irrevocably changed, too.

Newspaper columnist, satirist, essayist, short-story writer, and novelist Ambrose Bierce was a veteran of the war, fighting for the Union at several major battles, including Shiloh and Chickamauga, before he was severely wounded in the head at Kennesaw Mountain.

In contrast to the romanticism of most turn-of-the-century writers, the work of Ambrose Bierce is far more realistic, whether he was writing short stories or nonfiction pieces. Bierce wrote gritty, often disturbing tales of wartime experience. His "What I Saw of Shiloh" is an idiosyncratic account of this famous battle, which in two days claimed a greater number of American lives than all previous wars combined.

—Lisa Purcell

I

THIS IS A SIMPLE STORY OF A BATTLE; SUCH A TALE AS MAY BE TOLD BY A SOLDIER WHO is no writer to a reader who is no soldier.

The morning of Sunday, the sixth day of April, 1862, was bright and warm. Reveille had been sounded rather late, for the troops, wearied with long marching, were to have a day of rest. The men were idling about the embers of their bivouac fires; some preparing breakfast, others looking carelessly to the condition of their arms and accoutrements, against the inevitable inspection; still others were chatting with indolent dogmatism on that never-failing theme, the end and object of the campaign. Sentinels paced up and down the confused front with a lounging freedom of mien and stride that would not have been tolerated at another time. A few of them limped unsoldierly in deference to blistered feet. At a little distance in rear of the stacked arms were a few tents out of which frowsy-headed officers occasionally peered, languidly calling to their servants to fetch a basin of water, dust a coat or polish a scabbard. Trim young mounted orderlies, bearing dispatches obviously unimportant, urged their lazy nags by devious ways amongst the men, enduring with unconcern their good-humored raillery, the penalty of superior station. Little negroes of not very clearly defined status and function lolled on their stomachs, kicking their long, bare heels in the sunshine, or slumbered peacefully, unaware of the practical waggery prepared by white hands for their undoing.

Presently the flag hanging limp and lifeless at headquarters was seen to lift itself spiritedly from the staff. At the same instant was heard a dull, distant sound like the heavy breathing of some great animal below the horizon. The flag had lifted its head to listen. There was a momentary lull in the hum of the human swarm; then, as the flag drooped the hush passed away. But there were some hundreds more men on their feet than before; some thousands of hearts beating with a quicker pulse.

Again the flag made a warning sign, and again the breeze bore to our ears the long, deep sighing of iron lungs. The division, as if it had received the sharp word of command, sprang to its feet, and stood in groups at "attention." Even the little blacks got up. I have since seen similar effects produced by earthquakes; I am not sure but the ground was trembling then. The mess-cooks, wise in their generation, lifted the steaming camp-kettles off the fire and stood by to cast out. The mounted orderlies had somehow disappeared. Officers came ducking from beneath their tents and gathered in groups. Headquarters had become a swarming hive.

The sound of the great guns now came in regular throbbings—the strong, full pulse of the fever of battle. The flag flapped excitedly, shaking out its blazonry of stars and stripes with a sort of fierce delight. Toward the knot of officers in its shadow dashed from somewhere—he seemed to have burst out of the ground in a cloud of dust—a mounted aide-de-camp, and on the instant rose the sharp, clear notes of a bugle, caught up and repeated, and passed on by other bugles, until the level reaches of brown fields, the line of woods trending away to far hills, and the unseen valleys beyond were "telling of the sound," the farther, fainter strains half drowned in ringing cheers as the men ran to range themselves behind the stacks of arms. For this call was not the wearisome "general" before which the tents go down; it was the exhilarating "assembly," which goes to the heart as wine and stirs the blood like the kisses of a beautiful woman. Who that has heard it calling to him above the grumble of great guns can forget the wild intoxication of its music?

II

The Confederate forces in Kentucky and Tennessee had suffered a series of reverses, culminating in the loss of Nashville. The blow was severe: immense quantities of war material had fallen to the victor, together with all the important strategic points. General Johnston withdrew Beauregard's army to Corinth, in northern Mississippi, where he hoped so to recruit and equip it as to enable it to assume the offensive and retake the lost territory.

The town of Corinth was a wretched place—the capital of a swamp. It is two days' march west of the Tennessee River, which here and for a hundred and fifty miles farther, to where it falls into the Ohio at Paducah, runs nearly north. It is navigable to this point— that is to say, to Pittsburg Landing, where Corinth got to it by a road worn through a thickly wooded country seamed with ravines and bayous, rising nobody knows where and running into the river under sylvan arches heavily draped with Spanish moss. In some places they were obstructed by fallen trees. The Corinth road was at certain seasons a branch of the Tennessee River. Its mouth was Pittsburg Landing. Here in 1862 were some fields and a house or two; now there are a national cemetery and other improvements.

It was at Pittsburg Landing that Grant established his army, with a river in his rear and two toy steamboats as a means of communication with the east side, whither General Buell with thirty thousand men was moving from Nashville to join him. The question has been asked, Why did General Grant occupy the enemy's side of the river in the face of a superior force before the arrival of Buell? Buell had a long way to come; perhaps Grant was weary of waiting. Certainly Johnston was, for in the gray of the morning of April 6th, when Buell's leading division was en bivouac near the little town of Savannah, eight or ten miles below, the Confederate forces, having moved out of Corinth two days before, fell upon Grant's advance brigades and destroyed them. Grant was at Savannah, but hastened to the Landing in time to find his camps in the hands of the enemy and the remnants of his beaten army cooped up with an impassable river at their backs for moral support. I have related how the news of this affair came to us at Savannah. It came on the wind—a messenger that does not bear copious details.

III

On the side of the Tennessee River, over against Pittsburg Landing, are some low bare hills, partly inclosed by a forest. In the dusk of the evening of April 6 this open space, as seen from the other side of the stream—whence, indeed, it was anxiously watched by thousands of eyes, to many of which it grew dark long before the sun went down—would have appeared to have been ruled in long, dark lines, with new lines being constantly drawn across. These lines were the regiments of Buell's leading division, which having moved from Savannah through a country presenting nothing but interminable swamps and pathless "bottom lands," with rank overgrowths of jungle, was arriving at the scene of action breathless, footsore and faint with hunger. It had been a terrible race; some regiments had lost a third of their number from fatigue, the men dropping from the ranks as if shot, and left to recover or die at their leisure. Nor was the scene to which they had been invited likely to inspire the moral confidence that medicines physical fatigue. True, the air was full of thunder and the earth was trembling beneath their feet; and if there is truth in the theory of the conversion of force, these men were storing up energy from every shock that burst its waves upon their bodies. Perhaps this theory may better than another explain the tremendous endurance of men in battle. But the eyes reported only matter for despair.

Before us ran the turbulent river, vexed with plunging shells and obscured in spots by blue sheets of low-lying smoke. The two little steamers were doing their duty well. They came over to us empty and went back crowded, sitting very low in the water, apparently on the point of capsizing. The farther edge of the water could not be seen; the boats came out of the obscurity, took on their passengers and vanished in the darkness. But on the heights above, the battle was burning brightly enough; a thousand lights kindled and expired in every second of time. There were broad flushings in the sky, against which the branches of the trees showed black. Sudden flames burst out here and there, singly and in dozens. Fleeting streaks of fire crossed over to us by way of welcome. These expired in blinding flashes and fierce little rolls of smoke, attended with the peculiar metallic ring of bursting shells, and followed by the musical humming of the fragments as they struck into the ground on every side, making us wince, but doing little harm. The air was full of noises. To the right and the left the musketry rattled smartly and petulantly; directly in front it sighed and growled. To the experienced ear this meant that the death-line was an arc of which the river was the chord. There were deep, shaking explosions and smart shocks; the whisper of stray bullets and the hurtle of conical shells; the rush of round shot. There were faint, desultory cheers, such as announce a momentary or partial triumph. Occasionally, against the glare behind the trees, could be seen moving black figures, singularly distinct but apparently no longer than a thumb. They seemed to me ludicrously like the figures of demons in old allegorical prints of hell. To destroy these and all their belongings the enemy needed but another hour of daylight; the steamers in that case would have been doing him fine service by bringing more fish to his net. Those of us who had the good fortune to arrive late could then have eaten our teeth in important rage. Nay, to make his victory sure it did not need that the sun should pause in the heavens; one of many random shots falling into the river would have done the business had chance directed it into the engine-room of a steamer. You can perhaps fancy the anxiety with which we watched them leaping down.

But we had two other allies besides the night. Just where the enemy had pushed his right flank to the river was the mouth of a wide bayou, and here two gunboats had taken station. They too were of the toy sort, plated perhaps with railway metals, perhaps with boiler-iron. They staggered under a heavy gun or two each. The bayou made an opening in the high bank of the river. The bank was a parapet, behind which the gunboats crouched, firing up the bayou as through an embrasure. The enemy was at this disadvantage: he could not get at the gunboats, and he could advance only by exposing his flank to their ponderous missiles, one of which would have broken a half-mile of his bones and made nothing of it. Very annoying this must have been—these twenty gunners beating back an army because a sluggish creek had been pleased to fall into a river at one point rather than another. Such is the part that accident may play in the game of war.

As a spectacle this was rather fine. We could just discern the black bodies of these boats, looking very much like turtles. But when they let off their big guns there was a conflagration. The river shuddered in its banks, and hurried on, bloody, wounded, terrified! Objects a mile away sprang toward our eyes as a snake strikes at the face of its victim. The report stung us to the brain, but we blessed it audibly. Then we could hear the great shell tearing away through the air until the sound died out in the distance; then, a surprisingly long time afterward, a dull, distant explosion and a sudden silence of small-arms told their own tale.

IV

There was, I remember, no elephant on the boat that passed us across that evening, nor, I think, any hippopotamus. These would have been out of place. We had, however, a woman. Whether the baby was somewhere on board I did not learn. She was a fine creature, this woman; somebody's wife. Her mission, as she understood it, was to inspire the failing heart with courage; and when she selected mine I felt less flattered by her preference than astonished by her penetration. How did she learn? She stood on the upper deck with the red blaze of battle bathing her beautiful face, the twinkle of a thousand rifles mirrored in her eyes; and displaying a small ivory-handled pistol, she told me in a sentence punctuated by the thunder of great guns that if it came to the worst she would do her duty like a man! I am proud to remember that I took off my hat to this little fool.

V

Along the sheltered strip of beach between the river bank and the water was a confused mass of humanity—several thousands of men. They were mostly unarmed; many were wounded; some dead. All the camp-following tribes were there; all the cowards; a few officers. Not one of them knew where his regiment was, nor if he had a regiment. Many had not. These men were defeated, beaten, cowed. They were deaf to duty and dead to shame. A more demented crew never drifted to the rear of broken battalions. They would have stood in their tracks and been shot down to a man by a provost-marshal's guard, but they could not have been urged up that bank. An army's bravest men are its cowards. The death which they would not meet at the hands of the enemy they will meet at the hands of their officers, with never a flinching.

Whenever a steamboat would land, this abominable mob had to be kept off her with bayonets; when she pulled away, they sprang on her and were pushed by scores into the water, where they were suffered to drown one another in their own way. The men disembarking insulted them, shoved them, struck them. In return they expressed their unholy delight in the certainty of our destruction by the enemy.

By the time my regiment had reached the plateau night had put an end to the struggle. A sputter of rifles would break out now and then, followed perhaps by a spiritless hurrah. Occasionally a shell from a far-away battery would come pitching down somewhere near, with a whir crescendo, or flit above our heads with a whisper like that made by the wings of a night bird, to smother itself in the river. But there was no more fighting. The gunboats, however, blazed away at set intervals all night long, just to make the enemy uncomfortable and break him of his rest.

For us there was no rest. Foot by foot we moved through the dusky fields, we knew not whither. There were men all about us, but no camp-fires; to have made a blaze would have been madness. The men were of strange regiments; they mentioned the names of unknown generals. They gathered in groups by the wayside, asking eagerly our numbers. They recounted the depressing incidents of the day. A thoughtful officer shut their mouths with a sharp word as he passed; a wise one coming after encouraged them to repeat their doleful tale all along the line.

Hidden in hollows and behind clumps of rank brambles were large tents, dimly lighted with candles, but looking comfortable. The kind of comfort they supplied was indicated by pairs of men entering and reappearing, bearing litters; by low moans from within and by long rows of dead with covered faces outside. These tents were constantly receiving the wounded, yet were never full; they were continually ejecting the dead, yet were never empty. It was as if the helpless had been carried in and murdered, that they might not hamper those whose business it was to fall to-morrow.

The night was now black-dark; as is usual after a battle, it had begun to rain. Still we moved; we were being put into position by somebody. Inch by inch we crept along, treading on one another's heels by way of keeping together. Commands were passed along the line in whispers; more commonly none were given. When the men had pressed so closely together that they could advance no farther they stood stock-still, sheltering the locks of their rifles with their ponchos. In this position many fell asleep. When those in front suddenly stepped away those in the rear, roused by the tramping, hastened after with such zeal that the line was soon choked again. Evidently the head of the division was being piloted at a snail's pace by someone who did not feel sure of his ground. Very often we struck our feet against the dead; more frequently against those who still had spirit enough to resent it with a moan. These were lifted carefully to one side and abandoned. Some had sense enough to ask in their weak way for water. Absurd! Their clothes were soaked, their hair dank; their white faces, dimly discernible, were clammy and cold. Besides, none of us had any water. There was plenty coming, though, for before midnight a thunderstorm broke upon us with great violence. The rain, which had for hours been a dull drizzle, fell with a copiousness that stifled us; we moved in running water up to our ankles. Happily, we were in a forest of great trees heavily "decorated" with Spanish moss, or with an enemy standing to his guns the disclosures of the lightning might have been inconvenient. As it was, the incessant blaze enabled us to consult our watches and encouraged us by displaying our numbers; our black, sinuous line, creeping like a giant serpent beneath the trees, was apparently interminable. I am almost ashamed to say how sweet I found the companionship of those coarse men.

So the long night wore away, and as the glimmer of morning crept in through the forest we found ourselves in a more open country. But where? Not a sign of battle was here. The trees were neither splintered nor scarred, the underbrush was unmown, the ground had no footprints but our own. It was as if we had broken into glades sacred to eternal silence. I should not have been surprised to see sleek leopards come fawning about our feet, and milk-white deer confront us with human eyes.

A few inaudible commands from an invisible leader had placed us in order of battle. But where was the enemy? Where, too, were the riddled regiments that we had come to save? Had our other divisions arrived during the night and passed the river to assist us? Or were we to oppose our paltry five thousand breasts to an army flushed with victory? What protected our right? Who lay upon our left? Was there really anything in our front?

There came, borne to us on the raw morning air, the long weird note of a bugle. It was directly before us. It rose with a low clear, deliberate warble, and seemed to float in the gray sky like the note of a lark. The bugle calls of the Federal and the Confederate armies were the same: it was the "assembly"! As it died away I observed that the atmosphere had suffered a change; despite the equilibrium established by the storm, it was electric. Wings were growing on blistered feet. Bruised muscles and jolted bones, shoulders pounded by the cruel knapsack, eyelids leaden from lack of sleep—all were pervaded by the subtle fluid, all were unconscious of their clay. The men thrust forward their heads, expanded their eyes and clenched their teeth. They breathed hard, as if throttled by tugging at the leash. If you had laid your hand in the beard or hair of one of these men it would have crackled and shot sparks.

VI

I suppose the country lying between Corinth and Pittsburg Landing could boast a few inhabitants other than alligators. What manner of people they were it is impossible to say, inasmuch as the fighting dispersed, or possibly exterminated them; perhaps in merely classing them as non-saurian I shall describe them with sufficient particularity and at the same time avert from myself the natural suspicion attaching to a writer who points out to persons who do not know him the peculiarities of persons whom he does not know. One thing, however, I hope I may without offense affirm of these swamp-dwellers—they were pious. To what deity their veneration was given—whether, like the Egyptians, they worshiped the crocodile, or, like other Americans, adored themselves, I do not presume to guess. But whoever, or whatever, may have been the divinity whose ends they shaped, unto Him, or It, they had built a temple. This humble edifice, centrally situated in the heart of a solitude, and conveniently accessible to the supersylvan crow, had been christened Shiloh Chapel, whence the name of the battle. The fact of a Christian church—assuming it to have been a Christian church—giving name to a wholesale cutting of Christian throats by Christian hands need not be dwelt on here; the frequency of its recurrence in the history of our species has somewhat abated the moral interest that would otherwise attach to it.

VII

Owing to the darkness, the storm and the absence of a road, it had been impossible to move the artillery from the open ground about the Landing. The privation was much greater in a moral than in a material sense. The infantry soldier feels a confidence in his cumbrous arm quite unwarranted by its actual achievements in thinning out the opposition. There is something that inspires confidence in the way a gun dashes up to the front, shoving fifty or a hundred men to one side as if it said, "Permit me!" Then it squares its shoulders, calmly dislocates a joint in its back, sends away its twenty-four legs and settles down with a quiet rattle which says as plainly as possible, "I've come to stay." There is a superb scorn in its grimly defiant attitude, with its nose in the air; it appears not so much to threaten the enemy as deride him.

Our batteries were probably toiling after us somewhere; we could only hope the enemy might delay his attack until they should arrive. "He may delay his defense if he likes," said a sententious young officer to whom I had imparted this natural wish. He had read the signs aright; the words were hardly spoken when a group of staff officers about the brigade commander shot away in divergent lines as if scattered by a whirlwind, and galloping each to the commander of a regiment gave the word. There was a momentary confusion of tongues, a thin line of skirmishers detached itself from the compact front and pushed forward, followed by its diminutive reserves of half a company each—one of which platoons it was my fortune to command. When the straggling line of skirmishers had swept four or five hundred yards ahead, "See," said one of my comrades, "she moves!" She did indeed, and in fine style, her front as straight as a string, her reserve regiments in columns doubled on the center, following in true subordination; no braying of brass to apprise the enemy, no fifing and drumming to amuse him; no ostentation of gaudy flags; no nonsense. This was a matter of business.

In a few moments we had passed out of the singular oasis that had so marvelously escaped the desolation of battle, and now the evidences of the previous day's struggle were present in profusion. The ground was tolerably level here, the forest less dense, mostly clear of undergrowth, and occasionally opening out into small natural meadows. Here and there were small pools—mere discs of rainwater with a tinge of blood. Riven and torn with cannon-shot, the trunks of the trees protruded bunches of splinters like hands, the fingers above the wound interlacing with those below. Large branches had been lopped, and hung their green heads to the ground, or swung critically in their netting of vines, as in a hammock. Many had been cut clean off and their masses of foliage seriously impeded the progress of the troops. The bark of these trees, from the root upward to a height of ten or twenty feet, was so thickly pierced with bullets and grape that one could not have laid a hand on it without covering several punctures. None had escaped. How the human body survives a storm like this must be explained by the fact that it is exposed to it but a few moments at a time, whereas these grand old trees had had no one to take their places, from the rising to the going down of the sun. Angular bits of iron, concavo-convex, sticking in the sides of muddy depressions, showed where shells had exploded in their furrows. Knapsacks, canteens, haversacks distended with soaken and swollen biscuits, gaping to disgorge, blankets beaten into the soil by the rain, rifles with bent barrels or splintered stocks, waist-belts, hats and the omnipresent sardine-box—all the wretched debris of the battle still littered the spongy earth as far as one could see, in every direction. Dead horses were everywhere; a few disabled caissons, or limbers, reclining on one elbow, as it were; ammunition wagons standing disconsolate behind four or six sprawling mules. Men? There were men enough; all dead apparently, except one, who lay near where I had halted my platoon to await the slower movement of the line—a Federal sergeant, variously hurt, who had been a fine giant in his time. He lay face upward, taking in his breath in convulsive, rattling snorts, and blowing it out in sputters of froth which crawled creamily down his cheeks, piling itself alongside his neck and ears. A bullet had clipped a groove in his skull, above the temple; from this the brain protruded in bosses, dropping off in flakes and strings. I had not previously known one could get on, even in this unsatisfactory fashion, with so little brain. One of my men whom I knew for a womanish fellow, asked if he should put his bayonet through him. Inexpressibly shocked by the cold-blooded proposal, I told him I thought not; it was unusual, and too many were looking.

VIII

It was plain that the enemy had retreated to Corinth. The arrival of our fresh troops and their successful passage of the river had disheartened him. Three or four of his gray cavalry videttes moving amongst the trees on the crest of a hill in our front, and galloping out of sight at the crack of our skirmishers' rifles, confirmed us in the belief; an army face to face with its enemy does not employ cavalry to watch its front. True, they might be a general and his staff. Crowning this rise we found a level field, a quarter of a mile in width; beyond it a gentle acclivity, covered with an undergrowth of young oaks, impervious to sight. We pushed on into the open, but the division halted at the edge. Having orders to conform to its movements, we halted too; but that did not suit; we received an intimation to proceed. I had performed this sort of service before, and in the exercise of my discretion deployed my platoon, pushing it forward at a run, with trailed arms, to strengthen the skirmish line, which I overtook some thirty or forty yards from the wood. Then—I can't describe it—the forest seemed all at once to flame up and disappear with a crash like that of a great wave upon the beach—a crash that expired in hot hissings, and the sickening "spat" of lead against flesh. A dozen of my brave fellows tumbled over like ten-pins. Some struggled to their feet only to go down again, and yet again. Those who stood fired into the smoking brush and doggedly retired. We had expected to find, at most, a line of skirmishers similar to our own; it was with a view to overcoming them by a sudden coup at the moment of collision that I had thrown forward my little reserve. What we had found was a line of battle, coolly holding its fire till it could count our teeth. There was no more to be done but get back across the open ground, every superficial yard of which was throwing up its little jet of mud provoked by an impinging bullet. We got back, most of us, and I shall never forget the ludicrous incident of a young officer who had taken part in the affair walking up to his colonel, who had been a calm and apparently impartial spectator, and gravely reporting: "The enemy is in force just beyond this field, sir."

IX

In subordination to the design of this narrative, as defined by its title, the incidents related necessarily group themselves about my own personality as a center; and, as this center, during the few terrible hours of the engagement, maintained a variably constant relation to the open field already mentioned, it is important that the reader should bear in mind the topographical and tactical features of the local situation. The hither side of the field was occupied by the front of my brigade—a length of two regiments in line, with proper intervals for field batteries. During the entire fight the enemy held the slight wooded acclivity beyond. The debatable ground to the right and left of the open was broken and thickly wooded for miles, in some places quite inaccessible to artillery and at very few points offering opportunities for its successful employment. As a consequence of this the two sides of the field were soon studded thickly with confronting guns, which flamed away at one another with amazing zeal and rather startling effect. Of course, an infantry attack delivered from either side was not to be thought of when the covered flanks offered inducements so unquestionably superior; and I believe the riddled bodies of my poor skirmishers were the only ones left on this "neutral ground" that day. But there was a very pretty line of dead continually growing in our rear, and doubtless the enemy had at his back a similar encouragement.

The configuration of the ground offered us no protection. By lying flat on our faces between the guns we were screened from view by a straggling row of brambles, which marked the course of an obsolete fence; but the enemy's grape was sharper than his eyes, and it was poor consolation to know that his gunners could not see what they were doing, so long as they did it. The shock of our own pieces nearly deafened us, but in the brief intervals we could hear the battle roaring and stammering in the dark reaches of the forest to the right and left, where our other divisions were dashing themselves again and again into the smoking jungle. What would we not have given to join them in their brave, hopeless task! But to lie inglorious beneath showers of shrapnel darting divergent from the unassailable sky—meekly to be blown out of life by level gusts of grape—to clench our teeth and shrink helpless before big shot pushing noisily through the consenting air—this was horrible! "Lie down, there!" a captain would shout, and then get up himself to see that his order was obeyed. "Captain, take cover, sir!" the lieutenant-colonel would shriek, pacing up and down in the most exposed position that he could find.

O those cursed guns!—not the enemy's, but our own. Had it not been for them, we might have died like men. They must be supported, forsooth, the feeble, boasting bullies! It was impossible to conceive that these pieces were doing the enemy as excellent a mischief as his were doing us; they seemed to raise their "cloud by day" solely to direct aright the streaming procession of Confederate missiles. They no longer inspired confidence, but begot apprehension; and it was with grim satisfaction that I saw the carriage of one and another smashed into matchwood by a whooping shot and bundled out of the line.

X

The dense forests wholly or partly in which were fought so many battles of the Civil War, lay upon the earth in each autumn a thick deposit of dead leaves and stems, the decay of which forms a soil of surprising depth and richness. In dry weather the upper stratum is as inflammable as tinder. A fire once kindled in it will spread with a slow, persistent advance as far as local conditions permit, leaving a bed of light ashes beneath which the less combustible accretions of previous years will smolder until extinguished by rains. In many of the engagements of the war the fallen leaves took fire and roasted the fallen men. At Shiloh, during the first day's fighting, wide tracts of woodland were burned over in this way and scores of wounded who might have recovered perished in slow torture. I remember a deep ravine a little to the left and rear of the field I have described, in which, by some mad freak of heroic incompetence, a part of an Illinois regiment had been surrounded, and refusing to surrender was destroyed, as it very well deserved. My regiment having at last been relieved at the guns and moved over to the heights above this ravine for no obvious purpose, I obtained leave to go down into the valley of death and gratify a reprehensible curiosity.

Forbidding enough it was in every way. The fire had swept every superficial foot of it, and at every step I sank into ashes to the ankle. It had contained a thick undergrowth of young saplings, every one of which had been severed by a bullet, the foliage of the prostrate tops being afterward burnt and the stumps charred. Death had put his sickle into this thicket and fire had gleaned the field. Along a line which was not that of extreme depression, but was at every point significantly equidistant from the heights on either hand, lay the bodies half buried in ashes; some in the unlovely looseness of attitude denoting sudden death by the bullet, but by far the greater number in postures of agony that told of the tormenting flame. Their clothing was half burnt away—their hair and beard entirely; the rain had come too late to save their nails. Some were swollen to double girth; others shriveled to manikins. According to degree of exposure, their faces were bloated and black or yellow and shrunken. The contraction of muscles which had given them claws for hands had cursed each countenance with a hideous grin. Faugh! I cannot catalogue the charms of these gallant gentlemen who had got what they enlisted for.

XI

It was now three o'clock in the afternoon, and raining. For fifteen hours we had been wet to the skin. Chilled, sleepy, hungry and disappointed—profoundly disgusted with the inglorious part to which they had been condemned—the men of my regiment did everything doggedly. The spirit had gone quite out of them. Blue sheets of powder smoke, drifting amongst the trees, settling against the hillsides and beaten into nothingness by the falling rain, filled the air with their peculiar pungent odor, but it no longer stimulated. For miles on either hand could be heard the hoarse murmur of the battle, breaking out nearby with frightful distinctness, or sinking to a murmur in the distance; and the one sound aroused no more attention than the other.

We had been placed again in rear of those guns, but even they and their iron antagonists seemed to have tired of their feud, pounding away at one another with amiable infrequency. The right of the regiment extended a little beyond the field. On the prolongation of the line in that direction were some regiments of another division, with one in reserve. A third of a mile back lay the remnant of somebody's brigade looking to its wounds. The line of forest bounding this end of the field stretched as straight as a wall from the right of my regiment to Heaven knows what regiment of the enemy. There suddenly appeared, marching down along this wall, not more than two hundred yards in our front, a dozen files of gray-clad men with rifles on the right shoulder. At an interval of fifty yards they were followed by perhaps half as many more; and in fair supporting distance of these stalked with confident mien a single man! There seemed to me something indescribably ludicrous in the advance of this handful of men upon an army, albeit with their left flank protected by a forest. It does not so impress me now. They were the exposed flanks of three lines of infantry, each half a mile in length. In a moment our gunners had grappled with the nearest pieces, swung them half round, and were pouring streams of canister into the invaded wood. The infantry rose in masses, springing into line. Our threatened regiments stood like a wall, their loaded rifles at "ready," their bayonets hanging quietly in the scabbards. The right wing of my own regiment was thrown slightly backward to threaten the flank of the assault. The battered brigade away to the rear pulled itself together.

Then the storm burst. A great gray cloud seemed to spring out of the forest into the faces of the waiting battalions. It was received with a crash that made the very trees turn up their leaves. For one instant the assailants paused above their dead, then struggled forward, their bayonets glittering in the eyes that shone behind the smoke. One moment, and those unmoved men in blue would be impaled. What were they about? Why did they not fix bayonets? Were they stunned by their own volley? Their inaction was maddening! Another tremendous crash!—the rear rank had fired! Humanity, thank Heaven! is not made for this, and the shattered gray mass drew back a score of paces, opening a feeble fire. Lead had scored its old-time victory over steel; the heroic had broken its great heart against the commonplace. There are those who say that it is sometimes otherwise.

All this had taken but a minute of time, and now the second Confederate line swept down and poured in its fire. The line of blue staggered and gave way; in those two terrific volleys it seemed to have quite poured out its spirit. To this deadly work our reserve regiment now came up with a run. It was surprising to see it spitting fire with never a sound, for such was the infernal din that the ear could take in no more. This fearful scene was enacted within fifty paces of our toes, but we were rooted to the ground as if we had grown there. But now our commanding officer rode from behind us to the front, waved his hand with the courteous gesture that says apres vous, and with a barely audible cheer we sprang into the fight. Again the smoking front of gray receded, and again, as the enemy's third line emerged from its leafy covert, it pushed forward across the piles of dead and wounded to threaten with protruded steel. Never was seen so striking a proof of the paramount importance of numbers. Within an area of three hundred yards by fifty there struggled for front places no fewer than six regiments; and the accession of each, after the first collision, had it not been immediately counterpoised, would have turned the scale.

As matters stood, we were now very evenly matched, and how long we might have held out God only knows. But all at once something appeared to have gone wrong with the enemy's left; our men had somewhere pierced his line. A moment later his whole front gave way, and springing forward with fixed bayonets we pushed him in utter confusion back to his original line. Here, among the tents from which Grant's people had been expelled the day before, our broken and disordered regiments inextricably intermingled, and drunken with the wine of triumph, dashed confidently against a pair of trim battalions, provoking a tempest of hissing lead that made us stagger under its very weight. The sharp onset of another against our flank sent us whirling back with fire at our heels and fresh foes in merciless pursuit—who in their turn were broken upon the front of the invalided brigade previously mentioned, which had moved up from the rear to assist in this lively work.

As we rallied to reform behind our beloved guns and noted the ridiculous brevity of our line—as we sank from sheer fatigue, and tried to moderate the terrific thumping of our hearts—as we caught our breath to ask who had seen such-and-such a comrade, and laughed hysterically at the reply—there swept past us and over us into the open field a long regiment with fixed bayonets and rifles on the right shoulder. Another followed, and another; two—three—four! Heavens! Where do all these men come from, and why did they not come before? How grandly and confidently they go sweeping on like long blue waves of ocean chasing one another to the cruel rocks! Involuntarily we draw in our weary feet beneath us as we sit, ready to spring up and interpose our breasts when these gallant lines shall come back to us across the terrible field, and sift brokenly through among the trees with spouting fires at their backs. We still our breathing to catch the full grandeur of the volleys that are to tear them to shreds. Minute after minute passes and the sound does not come. Then for the first time we note that the silence of the whole region is not comparative, but absolute. Have we become stone deaf? See; here comes a stretcher-bearer, and there a surgeon! Good heavens! a chaplain!

The battle was indeed at an end.

XII

And this was, O so long ago! How they come back to me—dimly and brokenly, but with what a magic spell—those years of youth when I was soldiering! Again I hear the far warble of blown bugles. Again I see the tall, blue smoke of camp-fires ascending from the dim valleys of Wonderland. There steals upon my sense the ghost of an odor from pines that canopy the ambuscade. I feel upon my cheek the morning mist that shrouds the hostile camp unaware of its doom, and my blood stirs at the ringing rifle-shot of the solitary sentinel. Unfamiliar landscapes, glittering with sunshine or sullen with rain, come to me demanding recognition, pass, vanish and give place to others. Here in the night stretches a wide and blasted field studded with half-extinct fires burning redly with I know not what presage of evil. Again I shudder as I note its desolation and its awful silence. Where was it? To what monstrous inharmony of death was it the visible prelude?

O days when all the world was beautiful and strange; when unfamiliar constellations burned in the Southern midnights, and the mocking-bird poured out his heart in the moon-gilded magnolia; when there was something new under a new sun; will your fine, far memories ever cease to lay contrasting pictures athwart the harsher features of this later world, accentuating the ugliness of the longer and tamer life? Is it not strange that the phantoms of a blood-stained period have so airy a grace and look with so tender eyes?—that I recall with difficulty the danger and death and horrors of the time, and without effort all that was gracious and picturesque? Ah, Youth, there is no such wizard as thou! Give me but one touch of thine artist hand upon the dull canvas of the Present; gild for but one moment the drear and somber scenes of to-day, and I will willingly surrender another life than the one that I should have thrown away at Shiloh.

CHAPTER 13

Gettysburg: The Decisive Second Day
By Abner Doubleday

The debates have raged for decades: Was this the day the South lost the war? Was Confederate General Longstreet to blame, because of his delays in getting an attack started that afternoon? General Abner Doubleday's account is one of the most detailed and clearest ever written on what happened that day, Thursday, July 2, 1863. On the previous day, Lee's forces had more or less groped toward Gettysburg from the northwest without word on the Union movements for days from Jeb Stuart's cavalry, the "eyes and ears of the army." Stuart had allowed his raids to separate himself from contact with Lee's army as it moved into Pennsylvania. As the first day's battle developed and deepend in intensity, the Confederates made strong advances against fierce resistance, but in the end they failed to take the heights called Cemetery Hill adjacent to the town. Lee had ordered General Richard Ewell to take the hill late in the day, but included the words, "if practicable." That "if" was enough for Ewell to stand his exhausted men down from the attack. The hill was not taken, and the Union forces under General George Meade began gathering there in great numbers in troop movements that went on all night. They occupied the height of the land and were ready for Lee on the morning of the second day.

*—*Lamar Underwood

THE RIDGE UPON WHICH THE UNION FORCES WERE NOW ASSEMBLING HAS ALREADY been partially described. In two places it sunk away into intervening valleys. One between Culp's Hill and Cemetery Hill; the other lay for several hundred yards north of Little Round Top, as the lesser of the two eminences on the left was called to distinguish it from the higher peak called Round Top.

At 1 A.M. Meade arrived from Taneytown. When I saw him, soon after daylight, he seemed utterly worn out and hollow-eyed. Anxiety and want of sleep were evidently telling upon him. At dawn he commenced forming his line by concentrating his forces on the right with a view to descend into the plain and attack Lee's left, and the Twelfth Corps were sent to Wadsworth's right to take part in the movement.

It seems to me that this would have been a very hazardous enterprise, and I am not surprised that both Slocum and Warren reported against it. The Fifth and Sixth Corps would necessarily be very much fatigued after making a forced march. To put them in at once, and direct them to drive a superior force of Lee's veterans out of a town where every house would have been loop-holed, and every street barricaded, would hardly have been judicious. If we had succeeded in doing so, it would simply have reversed the battle of Gettysburg, for the Confederate army would have fought behind Seminary Ridge, and we would have been exposed in the plain below.

Nor do I think it would have been wise strategy to turn their left, and drive them between us and Washington, for it would have enabled them to threaten the capital, strengthen and shorten their line of retreat, and endanger our communications at the same time. It is an open secret that Meade at that time disapproved of the battle-ground Hancock had selected.

Warren and Slocum having reported an attack against Lee's left as unadvisable, Meade began to post troops on our left, with a view to attack the enemy's right. This, in my opinion, would have been much more sensible. Lee, however, solved the problem for him, and, fortunately for us, forced him to remain on the defensive, by ordering an assault against each extremity of the Union line.

There has been much discussion and a good deal of crimination and recrimination among the rebel generals engaged as to which of them lost the battle of Gettysburg.

I have already alluded to the fact that universal experience demonstrates that columns converging on a central force almost invariably fail in their object and are beaten in detail. Gettysburg seems to me a striking exemplification of this; repeated columns of assault launched by Lee against our lines came up in succession and were defeated before the other parts of his army could arrive in time to sustain the attack. He realized the old fable. The peasant could not break the bundle of fagots, but he could break one at a time until all were gone.

Lee's concave form of battle was a great disadvantage, for it took him three times as long as it did us to communicate with different parts of his line, and concentrate troops. His couriers who carried orders and the reinforcements he sent moved on the circumference and ours on the chord of the arc.

The two armies were about a mile apart. The Confederates—Longstreet and Hill—occupied Seminary Ridge, which runs parallel to Cemetery Ridge, upon which our forces were posted. Ewell's corps, on the rebel left, held the town, Hill the center, and Longstreet the right.

Lee could easily have maneuvered Meade out of his strong position on the heights, and should have done so. When he determined to attack, he should have commenced at daybreak, for all his force was up except Pickett's division; while two corps of the Union army, the Fifth and Sixth, were still far away, and two brigades of the Third Corps were also absent.

The latter were marching on the Emmetsburg road, and as that was controlled by the enemy, Sickles felt anxious for the safety of his men and trains, and requested that the cavalry be sent to escort them in. This was not done, however. The trains were warned off the road, and the two brigades were, fortunately, not molested.

There has been a great deal of bitter discussion between Longstreet, Fitz Lee, Early, Wilcox, and others as to whether Lee did or did not order an attack to take place at 9 A.M., and as to whether Longstreet was dilatory, and to blame for not making it. When a battle is lost there is always an inquest, and a natural desire on the part of each general to lay the blame on somebody else's shoulders. Longstreet waited until noon for Law's brigade to come up, and afterward there was a good deal of marching and countermarching to avoid being seen by our troops. There was undoubtedly too much delay. The fact is, Longstreet saw we had a strong position and was not well pleased at the duty assigned him, for he thought it more than probable his attempt would fail. He had urged Lee to take up a position where Meade would be forced to attack him, and was not in very good humor to find his advice disregarded. The rebel commander, however, finding the Army of the Potomac in front of him, having unbounded confidence in his troops, and elated by the success of the first day's fight, believed he could gain a great victory then and there, and end the war, and determined to attempt it. He was sick of these endless delays and constant sacrifices, and hoped one strong sword-thrust would slay his opponent, and enable the South to crown herself queen of the North American continent.

By 9 A.M. our skirmish line, in front of the Peach Orchard, was actively engaged with that of the enemy, who were making a reconnaissance toward the Emmetsburg road. No serious affair, however, occurred for some hours. Meade, as stated, was forming his lines on the right of the position he afterward occupied. The Fifth Corps, which came up about 1 P.M., was posted, as a reserve, south of the Twelfth Corps, with a view to the attack which has already been referred to. About 3 P.M. the Sixth Corps began to arrive from its long and toilsome march of thirty-four miles, and its tired troops were placed on the Taneytown road in the rear of Round Top, to reinforce the other corps in case our troops made an attack on the left. Lee, however, did not wait for Meade to advance against him, but boldly directed that each flank of the Union army should be assailed at the same time, while constant demonstrations against our center were to be kept up, to prevent either wing from being reinforced. It was another attempt to converge columns with an interval of several miles between them upon a central force, and, like almost all such enterprises, failed from want of proper co-operation in the different fractions of his line.

Longstreet's attack was over before Ewell came into action, and although Ewell succeeded in temporarily establishing himself on our extreme right, it was due to an unfortunate order given by General Meade, by which the force in that part of the field was withdrawn just as Ewell advanced against it. But we are anticipating our narrative.

Hood, who commanded the division on the right of Longstreet's corps, complains that he was not allowed to go past Round Top and flank us on the south, as he might have done, but was required by his orders to break in at the Peach Orchard and drive Sickles' line along the Emmetsburg road toward Cemetery Hill; but it seems to me, as he started late in the afternoon, if he had made the detour which would have been necessary in order to attack us on the south, he would have met Sedgwick in front, while Sickles and Sykes might have interposed to cut him off from the main body.

Before describing Longstreet's attack we will give the final disposition made by General Meade when it became necessary to fight a defensive battle. The ridge was nearly in the shape of a horseshoe. The Twelfth Corps was on the extreme right; next came one division of the First Corps on Culp's Hill, then the Eleventh Corps on Cemetery Hill, with two divisions of the First Corps at the base; next the Second Corps; then the Third, and the Fifth Corps on the extreme left, the Sixth Corps being posted in rear of Round Top as a general reserve to the army. Sickles, however, denies that any position was ever marked out for him. He was expected to prolong Hancock's line to the left, but did not do so for the following reasons: *First*, because the ground was low, and *second*, on account of the commanding position of the Emmetsburg road, which ran along a cross ridge oblique to the front of the line assigned him, and which afforded the enemy an excellent position for their artillery; *third*, because the ground between the valley he was expected to occupy, and the Emmetsburg road constituted a minor ridge, very much broken and full of rocks and trees, which afforded excellent cover for an enemy operating in his immediate front. He had previously held an interview with General Meade and asked that an experienced staff officer be sent with him to assist in locating a suitable position for his corps. At his request, General Hunt, the Chief of Artillery, was sent for that purpose.

They rode out to the ridge and Sickles directed that his troops should be posted along that road, with his center at the Peach Orchard, which was about a mile from and nearly opposite to Little Round Top; his right wing, under Humphreys, extending along the road, while his left wing, under Birney, made a right angle at the Peach Orchard with the other part of the line, and bent around, so as to cover the front of Little Round Top at the base.

The disadvantages of this position are obvious enough. It is impossible for any force to hold its ground when attacked at once on both sides which constitute the right angle. When that is the case, and it was so in the present instance—each side constituting the angle is taken in flank, and the position is no longer tenable.

Sickles claimed that he acted with the implied sanction of General Meade, who, however, censured the movement afterward. As soon as Sickles took position, General Buford's division of cavalry was sent to the rear at Westminster, to guard the trains there; and Kilpatrick's division was ordered to Hunterstown to attack the rebel left.

Sykes' corps—the Fifth—came up from the right about 5 P.M., soon after Longstreet's attack on Sickles was fairly under way, and formed along the outer base of Little Round Top, with Crawford's Pennsylvania Reserves at their right and front.

There had been a council of war, or conference of corps commanders, called at Meade's headquarters, and it was universally agreed to remain and hold the position. As the Third Corps, in answer to the guns of Clark's battery, was suddenly assailed by a terrible concentrated artillery fire, General Sickles rode back to his command and General Meade went with him. The latter objected to Sickles' line, but thought it was then too late to change it.

The severe artillery fire which opened against the two sides of the angle at the Peach Orchard was a prelude to a furious attack against Ward's brigade on the left. This attack soon extended to the Peach Orchard. The fight became very hot against Birney's division from the left to the center, but the troops on the right of the center—Humphreys' division—were not at first actively engaged, and Humphreys reinforced Birney with one of his brigades, and subsequently with a regiment.

The battle which now raged among these trees, rocks, and ravines was so complicated that it is hard to follow and difficult to describe the movements of the contestants.

About 3.30 P.M. the rebels commenced the movement against our left, by sending a flanking force from Hood's division, formed in two lines, around to attack Sickles' left, held by General J. Hobart Ward's brigade, which occupied the open ground covering the approaches to Little Round Top; Ward's line passing in front of the mountain, and his flank resting on a rocky depression in the ground called the Devil's Den. The right extended to the minor spur or wooded ridge beyond the wheat-field. The engagement was furious; commencing on the rebel right, it extended to the left, until it reached the Peach Orchard, where it became especially violent. This central point of Sickles' line was held by eleven regiments of Birney's and Humphreys' divisions. Birney's two brigades, commanded by Graham and De Trobriand, held on bravely, for the men who fought with Kearney in the Peninsula were not easily driven; but the line was too attenuated to resist the shock very long, and reinforcements became absolutely necessary to sustain that unlucky angle at the Peach Orchard.

Sickles had authority to call on Sykes, whose corps was resting from a long and fatiguing march, but the latter wished his men to get their coffee and be refreshed before sending them in; and as those who are fighting almost always exaggerate the necessity for immediate reinforcements, Sykes thought Sickles could hold on a while longer, and did not respond to the call for three-quarters of an hour.

It would seem that Lee supposed that Meade's main line of battle was on the Emmetsburg pike, and that the flank rested on the Peach Orchard, for he ordered Longstreet to form Hood's division perpendicular to that road, whereas Sickles occupied an advanced line, and Sykes the main line in rear. McLaws says that Lee thought turning the Peach Orchard was turning the Union left. With this idea, he directed Longstreet to form across the Emmetsburg road, and push our troops toward Cemetery Hill. Kershaw, after the minor ridge was taken, reported to Longstreet that he could not carry out these orders without exposing his right flank to an attack from Sykes' corps.

Ward fought bravely against Benning's and Anderson's brigades on the left, driving back two attacks of the latter, but his line was long and weak, and the enemy overlapped it by the front of nearly two brigades. Being concealed from view, from the nature of the ground they could concentrate against any point with impunity. He attempted to strengthen his forces at the Devil's Den by detaching the 99th Pennsylvania from his right, and, although De Trobriand had no troops to spare, he was directed by General Birney to send the 40th New York, under Colonel Egan, to reinforce that flank. Egan arrived too late to perform the duty assigned to him, as Ward had been already driven back, but not too late to make a gallant charge upon the rebel advance.

The fighting soon extended to the Peach Orchard, but as it commenced on the left, we will describe that part of the engagement first.

General Warren, who was on Meade's staff as Chief Engineer, had ridden about this time to the signal station on Little Round Top, to get a better view of the field. He saw the long line of the enemy approaching, and about to overlap Ward's left, and perceived that unless prompt succor arrived Little Round Top would fall into their hands. Once in their possession they would flank our whole line and post guns there to drive our troops from the ridge; so that this eminence was in reality the key of the battle-field, and must be held at all hazards. He saw Barnes' division, which Sykes had ordered forward, formed for a charge, and about to go to the relief of De Trobriand, who held the center of Birney's line, and who was sorely beset. Without losing a moment he rode down the slope, over to Barnes, took the responsibility of detaching Vincent's brigade, and hurried it back to take post on Little Round Top. He then sent a staff officer to inform General Meade of what he had done and to represent the immense importance of holding this commanding point.

The victorious column of the enemy was subjected to the fire of a battery on Little Round Top, and to another farther to the right; but it kept on, went around Ward's brigade and rushed eagerly up the ravine between the two Round Tops to seize Little Round Top which seemed to be defenseless. Vincent's brigade rapidly formed on the crest of a small spur which juts out from the hill, and not having time to load, advanced with the bayonet, in time to save the height. The contest soon became furious and the rocks were alive with musketry. General Vincent sent word to Barnes that the enemy were on him in overwhelming numbers, and Hazlett's regular battery, supported by the 140th New York under Colonel O'Rorke of Weed's brigade, was sent as a reinforcement.

The battery was dragged with great labor to the crest of Little Round Top, and the 140th were posted on the slope on Vincent's right. They came upon the field just as the rebels, after failing to penetrate the center, had driven back the right. In advancing to this exposed position, Colonel O'Rorke, a brilliant young officer who had just graduated at the head of his class at West Point, was killed and his men thrown into some confusion, but Vincent rallied the line and repulsed the assault. In doing so he exposed himself very much and was soon killed by a rebel sharpshooter.

General Weed, who was on the crest with the battery, was mortally wounded in the same way; and as Hazlett leaned over to hear his last message, a fatal bullet struck him also and he dropped dead on the body of his chief. Colonel Rice of the 44th New York now took command in place of Vincent.

The enemy having been foiled at the center and right, stole around through the woods and turned the left of the line; but Chamberlain's regiment—the 20th Maine—was folded back by him, around the rear of the mountain, to resist the attack. The rebels came on like wolves, with deafening yells, and forced Chamberlain's men over the crest; but they rallied and drove their assailants back in their turn. This was twice repeated and then a brigade of the Pennsylvania Reserves and one of the Fifth Corps dashed over the hill. The 20th Maine made a grand final charge and drove the rebels from the valley between the Round Tops, capturing a large number of prisoners. Not a moment too soon, for Chamberlain had lost a third of his command and was entirely out of ammunition. Vincent's men in this affair took two colonels, fifteen officers, and five hundred men prisoners, and a thousand stand of arms. Hill in his official report says "Hood's right was held as in a vise."

We will now return to the Peach Orchard. In answer to a shot from Clark's battery a long line of guns opened from the eleven batteries opposite. Graham's infantry were partially sheltered from this iron hail, but the three batteries with him in the beginning, which were soon reinforced by four more from the reserve artillery, under Major McGilvery, were very much cut up; and at last it became necessary to sacrifice one of them—that of Bigelow—to enable the others to retire to a new line in the rear.

Graham still held the Peach Orchard, although he was assailed on two fronts, by Barksdale's brigade on the north and Kershaw's brigade on the west. A battery was brought forward to enfilade Sickles' line on the Emmetsburg road, and under cover of its fire Barksdale* carried the position, but was mortally wounded in doing so. Sickles lost a leg about this time (5.30 P.M.), and Graham, who was also badly wounded, fell into the enemy's hands. The command of the Third Corps now devolved upon General Birney.

The batteries under Major McGilvery, which lined the cross road below the Peach Orchard, were very effective, but were very much shattered. Kershaw captured them at one time but was driven off temporarily by a gallant charge of the 141st Pennsylvania of Graham's brigade, who retook the guns, which were then brought off by hand.

---

*Barksdale soon after was brought into my lines and died like a brave man, with dignity and resignation. I had known him as an officer of volunteers in the Mexican war. As a member of Congress he was very influential in bringing on the Rebellion.

Bigelow was ordered by Major McGilvery to sacrifice his battery to give the others time to form a new line. He fought until the enemy were within six feet of him, and then retired with the loss of three officers and twenty-eight men. Phillips' battery, which adjoined his, had a similar experience. McLaws bears testimony to the admirable manner with which this artillery was served. He says one shell killed and wounded thirty men, out of a company of thirty-seven.

The capture of the Peach Orchard necessarily brought the enemy directly on Humphreys' left flank and De Trobriand's right. The disaster then became irremediable, because every force thrown in after this period, had to contend with a direct fire in front, and an enfilading fire from the right.

While the Peach Orchard was assailed, several combats took place in the vicinity, which had a general relation to the defence of Sickles' line. A little stream runs through a ravine parallel to the cross road, and about five hundred yards south of it, and then turns abruptly to the south at the corner of a wheat-field, passing through a rocky wooded country, to empty in Plum Run. De Trobriand held the north bank of this stream with a very insufficient force—a front of two regiments—and his contest with Semmes' brigade in front and Kershaw's brigade, which was trying to penetrate into the Peach Orchard, on his right, was at very close range and very destructive. At the same time as Ward's left was turned and driven back the enemy came in on the left and rear of De Trobriand, and occupied the wheat-field. Barnes' division of the Fifth Corps, composed of Sweitzer's and Tilton's brigades, soon came to his assistance. The former, by wheeling to the left and retaining several lines, kept up the fight successfully against the enemy who came up the ravine, but the latter was flanked and obliged to give way. De Trobriand's two regiments in front had a most determined fight, and would not yield the ground. When relieved by Zook's force they fell back across the wheat-field. There Birney used them as a basis of a new line, brought up two fresh regiments, charged through the field, and drove the enemy back to the stone fence which bounded it.

Caldwell's division of Hancock's corps now came on to renew the contest. Caldwell formed his men with the brigades of Cross and Kelly in front, and those of Zook and Brooke in rear. In the advance Colonel Cross was killed, and the front line being enfiladed in both directions, was soon so cut up that the rear line came forward in its place. Zook was killed, but Brooke made a splendid charge, turning Kershaw's right and driving Semmes back through the supporting batteries. Sweitzer's brigade then came up a second time to aid Brooke, but it was useless, for there was still another line of batteries beyond, and as the Peach Orchard by this time was in possession of the enemy, Brooke's advanced position was really a disadvantage, for both his flanks were turned. Semmes' brigade, together with parts of Benning's and Anderson's brigades, rallied behind a stone wall, again came forward, and succeeded in retaking the knoll and the batteries they had lost. Caldwell, under cover of our artillery, extricated his division with heavy loss, for both Zook's and Kelly's brigades were completely surrounded.

Then Ayres,* who had been at the turning-point of so many battles, went in with his fine division of regulars, commanded by Day and Burbank, officers of courage and long experience in warfare. He struck the enemy in flank who were pursuing Caldwell, and who would have renewed the attack on Little Round Top, doubled them up, and drove them back to the position Caldwell had left; but his line, from the nature of things, was untenable, for a whole brigade with ample supports had formed on his right rear, so that nothing remained but to face about and fight his way home again. This was accomplished with the tremendous loss of fifty per cent. of his command in killed and wounded. His return was aided by the artillery on Little Round Top, and by the advance of part of the Sixth Corps. When the troops were all gone, Winslow's battery still held the field for a time, and withdrew by piece.

The enemy, Wofford's, Kershaw's, and Anderson's brigades, now swarmed in the front of our main line between the wheat-field and Little Round Top. General S. Wiley Crawford, who commanded a division composed of two brigades of the Pennsylvania Reserve Corps, was ordered to drive them farther back. This organization, which at one time I had the honor to command, were veterans of the Peninsula, and were among the most dauntless men in the army.

Crawford called upon them to defend the soil of their native State, and headed a charge made by McCandless' brigade, with the colors of one of the regiments in his hand. The men went forward with an impetus nothing could withstand. The enemy took shelter behind a stone fence on the hither side of the wheat-field, but McCandless stormed the position, drove them beyond the field, and then, as it was getting dark, both sides rested on their arms. The other brigade of Crawford's division—that of Fisher—had previously been sent to reinforce Vincent in his desperate struggle on the slope of Little Round Top. The enemy retired before it, so that it was not engaged, and it then took possession of the main Round Top on the left of Little Round Top and fortified it.

As Crawford charged, two brigades of Sedgwick's corps, those of Nevin and Eustis, formed under Wheaton on the right and below Little Round Top. The sight of the firm front presented by these fresh troops thoroughly discouraged Longstreet, who went forward to reconnoitre, and he gave up all attempts at making any farther advance.

The enemy at night took post at the western base of the ridge, and held a fortified line as far south as the Devil's Den, in which rocky cavern they took shelter.

It remains now to describe the effect of the loss of the Peach Orchard and the wounding of Sickles and Graham—which took place soon after—upon the fate of Humphreys' division, posted on the right along the Emmetsburg road. When Sickles lost his leg, Birney assumed command of the corps, and ordered Humphreys to move his left wing back to form a new oblique line to the ridge, in connection with Birney's division. Humphreys, up to the loss of the Peach Orchard, had not been actively engaged, as the enemy had

---

*General Ayres, whose service in the war commenced with the first Bull Run and ended at Appomattox, may almost be called an impersonation of the Army of the Potomac, as he took part in nearly all its battles and minor engagements.

merely demonstrated along his front; but now he was obliged, while executing the difficult maneuver of a change of front to rear, to contend with Barksdale's brigade of McLaws' division on his left at the Peach Orchard, and enfilading batteries there also, while his entire front was called upon to repel a most determined assault from Anderson's division, which hitherto had not been engaged, and which now pressed with great force on his right, which still clung to the road.

Four regiments were thrown in by Hancock to support that part of the line, but the attack was so sudden and violent that they only had time to fire a few volleys before Humphreys received orders to give up his advanced position and fall back to the ridge itself. There he turned at bay. Hancock, who had been placed in command of the First, Second, and Third Corps, was indefatigable in his vigilance and personal supervision, "patching the line" wherever the enemy was likely to break through. His activity and foresight probably preserved the ridge from capture. Toward the last Meade brought forward Lockwood's Maryland brigade from the right and sent them in to cover Sickles' retreat. Humphreys was followed up by the brigades of Wilcox, Perry, and Wright—about the best fighting material in the rebel army. Perry was driven back by the fire of our main line, and as his brigade was between the other two, his retreat left each of them in a measure unsupported on the flanks. Posey's and Mahone's brigades were to advance as soon as the others became actively engaged, but failed to do so, and therefore Pender, who was to follow after them, did not move forward.

Hence the great effort of Wilcox and Wright, which would have been ruinous to us if followed up, was fruitless of results. Both were repulsed for lack of support, but Wright actually reached the crest with his Georgians and turned a gun, whose cannoneers had been shot, upon Webb's brigade of the Second Corps. Webb gave him two staggering volleys from behind a fence, and went forward with two regiments. He charged, regained the lost piece, and turned it upon them. Wright, finding himself entirely isolated in this advanced position, went back again to the main line, and Wilcox did the same.

On this occasion Wright did what Lee failed to accomplish the next day at such a heavy expense of life, for he pierced our center, and held it for a short time, and had the movement been properly supported and energetically followed up, it might have been fatal to our army, and would most certainly have resulted in a disastrous retreat. It was but another illustration of the difficulty of successfully converging columns against a central force. Lee's divisions seemed never to strike at the hour appointed. Each came forward separately, and was beaten for lack of support.

Wright attained the crest and Wilcox was almost on a line with him. The latter was closely followed up and nearly surrounded, for troops rushed in on him from all sides. He lost very heavily in extricating himself from his advanced position. Wilcox claims to have captured temporarily twenty guns and Wright eight.

As they approached the ridge a Union battery limbered up and galloped off. The last gun was delayed and the cannoneer, with a long line of muskets pointing at him within a few feet, deliberately drove off the field. The Georgians manifested their admiration for his bravery by crying out "Don't shoot," and not a musket was fired at him.* I regret that I have not been able to ascertain the man's name.

In the morning General Tidball, who was attached to the cavalry as Chief of Artillery, rode along the entire crest from Little Round Top to Culp's Hill to make himself familiar with the line. As he passed by headquarters he noticed some new troops, the Second Vermont brigade under General Stannard, which formed part of my command. They were a fine-looking body of men, and were drawn up in close column by division, ready to go to any part of the field at a moment's notice. After inquiring to what corps they belonged he passed over to the right. On his return late in the day he saw Sickles' whole line driven in and found Wright's rebel brigade established on the crest barring his way back.

He rode rapidly over to Meade's headquarters and found the general walking up and down the room, apparently quite unconscious of the movements which might have been discerned by riding to the top of the hill, and which should have been reported to him by some one of his staff. Tidball said, "General, I am very sorry to see that the enemy have pierced our center." Meade expressed surprise at the information and said, "Why, where is Sedgwick?" Tidball replied, "I do not know, but if you need troops, I saw a fine body of Vermonters a short distance from here, belonging to the First Corps, who are available."

Meade then directed him to take an order to Newton and put the men in at once; the order was communicated to me and I went with my division at double quick to the point indicated. There we pursued Wright's force as it retired, and retook, at Hancock's instigation, four guns taken by Wright earlier in the action. When these were brought in I sent out two regiments, who followed the enemy up nearly to their lines and retook two more guns. I have been thus particular in narrating this incident as Stannard's Vermont brigade contributed greatly to the victory of the next day and it is worthy of record to state how they came to be located in that part of the field.

It is claimed that unless Sickles had taken up this advanced position Hood's division would have turned our left, have forced us from the shelter of the ridge, and probably have intervened between us and Washington. The movement, disastrous in some respects, was propitious as regards its general results, for the enemy had wasted all their strength and valor in gaining the Emmetsburg road, which after all was of no particular benefit to them. They were still outside our main line. They pierced the latter it is true, but the gallant men who at such heavy expense of life and limb stood triumphantly on that crest were obliged to retire because the divisions which should have supported them remained inactive. I must be excused for thinking that the damaging resistance these supports encountered on the first day from the men of my command exerted a benumbing influence on the second day.

---

*As it is well to verify these incidents, I desire to state that this is a reminiscence of Dr. J. Robie Wood, of New York, a Georgian, a relative of Wendell Phillips, who was in the charge with Wright. Wood fell struck by six bullets, but recovered.

It is said, that Hood being wounded, Longstreet led the last advance against Little Round Top in person, but when he saw Sedgwick's corps coming into line he gave up the idea of capturing the heights as impracticable. This eminence should have been the first point held and fortified by us early in the day, as it was the key of the field, but no special orders were given concerning it and nothing but Warren's activity and foresight saved it from falling into the hands of the enemy.

Meade was considerably startled by the fact that the enemy had pierced our center. He at once sent for Pleasonton and gave him orders to collect his cavalry with a view to cover the retreat of the army. Indeed, in an article on the "Secret History of Gettysburg," published in the "Southern Historical Papers," by Colonel Palfrey, of the Confederate army, he states that the movement to the rear actually commenced, and that Ewell's pickets heard and reported that artillery was passing in that direction. After a short time the noise of the wheels ceased. He also says that in a conversation he had with Colonel Ulric Dahlgren of our cavalry, who had lost a leg, and was a prisoner in Richmond, he was told that while the battle of Gettysburg was going on he (Dahlgren) captured a Confederate scout with a dispatch from Jefferson Davis to General Lee, in which the former wrote of the exposed condition of Richmond owing to the presence of a large Union force at City Point.

Dahlgren said a retreat had been ordered, but when Meade read this dispatch, he looked upon it as a sign indicating the weakness of the enemy, and perhaps thinking it would not do to supplement the probable capture of Richmond by a retreat of the Army of the Potomac, countermanded the order. Sedgwick, who was high in the confidence of General Meade, told one of his division commanders that the army would probably fall back on Westminster. General Pleasonton testifies that he was engaged, by order of General Meade, until 11 P.M. in occupying prominent points with his cavalry, to cover the retreat of the army. Nevertheless it has been indignantly denied that such a movement was contemplated.

Although it was General Lee's intention that both flanks of the Union army should be assailed at the same time, while the intermediate forces made demonstrations against the center, Ewell did not move to attack the right of our line at Culp's Hill until Longstreet's assault on the left had failed. Longstreet attributes it to the fact that Ewell had broken his line of battle by detaching two brigades up the York road. There is always some reason why columns never converge in time. Johnson's division, which was on the extreme left of the rebel army, and had not been engaged, made their way, sheltered by the ravine of Rock Creek, to assail the right at Culp's Hill, held by Wadsworth's division of the First Corps, and that part of the line still farther to the right where Geary's division of the Twelfth Corps was posted.

In his desire to reinforce the Fifth Corps at the close of the conflict with Longstreet, General Meade made the sad mistake of ordering the Twelfth Corps to abandon its position on the right and report to General Sykes for duty on the left. General Slocum, sensible that this would be a suicidal movement, reported that the enemy were advancing on his front, and begged permission to keep Geary's division there to defend the position. General Meade finally allowed him to retain Greene's brigade, and no more, and thus it happened that Ewell's troops, finding the works on the extreme right of our line defenseless, had nothing to do but walk in and occupy them. If Meade was determined to detach this large force, there seems no good reason why two of Sedgwick's brigades should not have been sent to take its place, but nothing was done.

Johnson's division, as it came on, deployed and crossed Rock Creek about half an hour before sunset. It suffered so severely from our artillery, that one brigade, that of Jones, fell back in disorder, its commander being wounded. The other, however, advanced against Wadsworth, and Greene on his right; but as these generals had their fronts well fortified, the attack was easily repulsed. Nevertheless, the left of Johnson's line, not being opposed, took possession of Geary's works about 9 P.M. and thus endangered our communications.

Gregg's division of cavalry which was posted east of Slocum's position saw this movement of Johnson. Gregg opened fire on the column with his artillery and sent out his men dismounted to skirmish on the flank of the enemy. Johnson detached Walker's brigade to meet him, and the contest continued until after dark. Greene, in the meantime, swung his right around on the edge of a ravine, perpendicular to the main line and fortified it, to avoid being flanked. He was an accomplished soldier and engineer, having graduated second in his class at West Point, and knew exactly what ought to be done and how to do it. He held on strongly, and as it was dark, and the enemy did not exactly know where they were, or where our troops were posted, they waited until daylight before taking any further action. Yet they were now but a short distance from General Meade's headquarters, and within easy reach of our reserve artillery. A night attack on the rear of our army, in conjunction with an advance from the opposite side on Hancock's front, would have thrown us into great confusion and must have succeeded.

During the night Ewell sent Smith's brigade to reinforce Johnson. Geary, after all, did not reach Little Round Top or report to Sykes, and if he had done so, his troops would have been of no use, as the battle was over in that part of the field. There was a mystery about his movements which needs to be cleared up.

To supplement this attack on the extreme right, and prevent reinforcements from being sent there, Early's division was directed to carry Cemetery Hill by storm. Before it advanced, a vigorous artillery fire was opened from four rebel batteries on Benner's Hill, to prepare the way for the assault, but our batteries on Cemetery Hill, which were partially sheltered by earthworks, replied and soon silenced those of the enemy. Then Early's infantry moved forth, Hays' brigade on the right, Hoke's brigade on the left, under Colonel Avery, and Gordon's brigade in reserve. It was supposed Johnson's division would protect Early's left flank, while Rodes' and Pender's divisions would come forward in time to prevent any attack against his right. The enemy first struck Von Gilsa's brigade, which was posted behind a stone fence at the foot of the hill. Still farther to its left, at the base of the hill, was Ames' brigade, both enclosing Rickett's and Weidrick's and Stevens' batteries, which had been a good deal cut up on the first day, were now brought to bear on the approaching enemy. Colonel Wainwright, Chief of Artillery of the First Corps, gave them orders not to attempt to retreat if attacked, but to fight the guns to the last.

The enemy advanced up the ravine which was specially commanded by Stevens' battery. Weidrick, Ricketts, and Stevens played upon the approaching line energetically. The rebel left and center fell back, but the right managed to obtain shelter from houses and undulating ground, and came on impetuously, charging over Von Gilsa's brigade, and driving it up the hill, through the batteries. In doing so Hays says the darkness and smoke saved his men from a terrible slaughter. Weidrick's battery was captured, and two of Ricketts' guns were spiked. The enemy, in making this movement, exposed their left flank to Stevens' battery, which poured a terrible fire of double canister into their ranks. The 33d Massachusetts also opened a most effective oblique fire. The batteries were penetrated but would not surrender.

Dearer than life itself to the cannoneer is the gun he serves, and these brave men fought hand to hand with hand spikes, rammers, staves, and even stones. They shouted, *"Death on the soil of our native State rather than lose our guns."* Hancock all this time should have been kept busy on his own front repelling an attack from Rodes and Pender, but as they did not come forward, and as he felt that there was great danger that Howard would lose Cemetery Hill and his own right be turned, he sent Carroll's brigade to the rescue. Carroll was joined by the 106th Pennsylvania and some reinforcements from Schurz's division. For a few minutes, Hays says, there was an ominous silence and then the tramp of our infantry was heard. They came over the hill and went in with a cheer. The enemy, finding they were about to be overwhelmed, retreated, as no one came to their assistance. When they fell back our guns opened a very destructive fire. It is said that out of 1,750 men of the organization known as "The Louisiana Tigers," only 150 returned. Hays attributes his defeat to the fact that Gordon was not up in time to support him.

The failure to carry the hill isolated Johnson's division on our extreme right. As it could only be reached by a long circuit it was not easy for Lee to maintain it there, without unduly weakening other parts of his line. That Rodes' division did not reach Cemetery Hill in time to co-operate with Early's attack was not owing to any lack of zeal or activity on the part of that energetic officer. He was obliged to move out of Gettysburg by the flank, then change front and advance double the distance Early had to traverse, and by the time he had done so Early had made the attack and had been repulsed.

The day closed with the rebels defeated on our left, but victorious on our right. Fortunately for us, this incited Lee to continue his efforts. He could not bear to retreat after his heavy losses, and acknowledge that he was beaten. He resolved to reinforce Johnson's division, now in rear of our right, and fling Pickett's troops, the élite of his army, who had not been engaged, against our center. He hoped a simultaneous attack made by Pickett in front and Johnson in rear, would yet win those heights and scatter the Union army to the winds. Kilpatrick, who had been resting the tired men and horses of his cavalry division at Abbotsford after the conflict at Hanover, went on the afternoon of the 2d to circle around and attack the left and rear of the enemy by way of Hunterstown. This plan was foiled, however, by the sudden arrival of Stuart's cavalry from its long march. They reached that part of the field about 4 P.M. After a fierce combat, in which Farnsworth's and Custer's brigades and Estes' squadron were principally engaged against Hampton's brigade supported by the main body, darkness put an end to the fight. Kilpatrick then turned back and bivouacked at Two Taverns for the night.

Gregg's division of cavalry left Hanover at noon and took post opposite and about three miles east of Slocum's corps on the right. There, as stated, he saw Johnson's division moving to the attack and after throwing some shells into their ranks deployed his own skirmish line and advanced against the one they threw out to meet him. At 10 P.M. he withdrew and took post on the Baltimore pike where it crosses Cress Run, near Rock Creek. By so doing he guarded the right and rear of the army from any demonstration by Stuart's cavalry.

At night a council of war was held, in which it was unanimously voted to stay and fight it out. Meade was displeased with the result, and although he acquiesced in the decision, he said angrily, "Have it your own way, gentlemen, but Gettysburg is no place to fight a battle in." The fact that a portion of the enemy actually prolonged our line on the right and that our center had been pierced during the day, made him feel far from confident. He thought it better to retreat with what he had, than run the risk of losing all.*

---

*Since the above was written, the discussion has been renewed in the public prints as to whether General Meade did or did not intend to leave the field. So far as the drawing up of an order of retreat is concerned, it was undoubtedly right and proper to do so, for it is the duty of a general to be prepared for every emergency. It is easy to criticize, and say what should have been done, after a battle has been fought, after the position of troops is all laid down on the maps, and the plans of every commander explained in official reports; but amid the doubt and confusion of actual combat, where there has been great loss of men and material, it is not always so easy to decide. On the night of the 2d the state of affairs was disheartening. In the combats of the preceding days, the First, Third, and Eleventh Corps had been almost annihilated; the Fifth Corps and a great part of the Second were shattered, and only the Sixth Corps and Twelfth Corps were comparatively fresh. It was possible therefore that the enemy might gain some great success the next day, which would stimulate them to extra exertions, and diminish the spirit of our men in the same proportion.

In such a case it was not improbable that the army might be destroyed as an organization, and there is a vast difference between a destroyed army and a defeated army. By retiring while it was yet in his power to do so, General Meade felt that he would assure the safety of our principal cities, for the enemy were too exhausted to pursue; and being out of ammunition, and far from their base of supplies, were not in a condition to do much further damage, or act very energetically. Whereas our troops could soon be largely reinforced from the draft which had just been established, and, being in the center of their resources, could be supplied with all that was necessary for renewed effort.

There is no question in my mind that, at the council referred to, General Meade did desire to retreat, and expressed fears that his communications with Taneytown might be endangered by remaining at Gettysburg.

It has also been stated that both General Gibbon and General Newton objected to our position at Gettysburg, but this is an error. They merely recommended some additional precautions to prevent the enemy from turning our left at Round Top, and thus intervening between us and Washington. Hancock, in giving his vote, said the Army of the Potomac had retreated too often, and he was in favor of remaining now to fight it out.

CHAPTER 14

Gettysburg: Pickett's Charge
By Abner Doubleday

After the second day of battle ended in a stalemate, General Robert E. Lee's blood was still up and running hot. He was still thinking one more decisive attack on the middle of the Union line on Cemetery Hill could bring a rout and victory. His army had not broken the position with attacks on the left on the first day, Wednesday, July 1. On the second day, Longstreet's attacks on the right had reached the crest but had not broken through. Now, on Friday, July 3, he wanted Longstreet to attack the center of the line, using Pickett's fresh division to lead the attack. Here is exactly what Longstreet told him, as reported from several sources, including Longstreet's own memoir: "General, I have been a soldier all my life. I have been with soldiers engaged in fights by couples, by squads, companies, regiments, divisions, and armies, and should know as well as any one what soldiers can do. It is my opinion that no fifteen thousand men ever arrayed for battle can take that position." He was pointing at Cemetery Hill as he spoke. Lee went ahead with the attack. The rest is history, and it is not pretty for the Confederate army.
—LAMAR UNDERWOOD

OUR LINE WAS ONCE MORE INTACT. ALL THAT THE ENEMY HAD GAINED BY DOGGED determination and desperate bravery was lost from a lack of co-ordination, caused perhaps by the great difficulty of communicating orders over this long concave line where every route was swept by our fire.

Lee had now attacked both flanks of the Army of the Potomac without having been able to establish himself permanently on either. Notwithstanding the repulse of the previous day he was very desirous of turning the left, for once well posted there he could secure his own retreat while interposing between Meade and Washington. He rode over with Longstreet to that end of the line to see what could be done. General Wofford, who commanded a brigade of McLaws' division, writes in a recent letter to General

Crawford, United States Army, as follows: "Lee and Longstreet came to my brigade Friday morning before the artillery opened fire. I told him that the afternoon before, I nearly reached the crest. He asked if I could not go there now. I replied, 'No, General, I think not.' He said quickly, 'Why not?' 'Because,' I said, 'General, the enemy have had all night to intrench and reinforce. I had been pursuing a broken enemy and the situation was now very different.'"

Having failed at each extremity, it only remained to Lee to retreat, or attack the center. Such high expectations had been formed in the Southern States in regard to his conquest of the North that he determined to make another effort. He still had Pickett's division, the flower of Virginia, which had not been engaged, and which was full of enthusiasm. He resolved to launch them against our center, supported on either flank by the advance of the main portion of the army. He had hoped that Johnson's division would have been able to maintain its position on the right, so that the Union center could be assailed in front and rear at the same time, but Johnson having been driven out, it was necessary to trust to Pickett alone, or abandon the whole enterprise and return to Virginia.

Everything was quiet up to 1 P.M., as the enemy were massing their batteries and concentrating their forces preparatory to the grand charge—the supreme effort—which was to determine the fate of the campaign, and to settle the point whether freedom or slavery was to rule the Northern States.

It seems to me there was some lack of judgment in the preparations. Heth's division, now under Pettigrew, which had been so severely handled on the first day, and which was composed in a great measure of new troops, was designated to support Pickett's left and join in the attack at close quarters. Wilcox, too, who one would think had been pretty well fought out the day before, in his desperate enterprise of attempting to crown the crest, was directed to support the right flank of the attack. Wright's brigade was formed in rear, and Pender's division on the left of Pettigrew, but there was a long distance between Wilcox and Longstreet's forces on the right.

At 1 P.M. a signal gun was fired and one hundred and fifteen guns opened against Hancock's command, consisting of the First Corps under Newton, the Second Corps under Gibbon, the Third Corps under Birney, and against the Eleventh Corps under Howard. The object of this heavy artillery fire was to break up our lines and prepare the way for Pickett's charge. The exigencies of the battle had caused the First Corps to be divided, Wadsworth's division being on the right at Culp's Hill, Robinson on Gibbon's right, and my own division intervening between Caldwell on the left and Gibbon on the right. The convex shape of our line did not give us as much space as that of the enemy, but General Hunt, Chief of Artillery, promptly posted eighty guns along the crest—as many as it would hold—to answer the fire, and the batteries on both sides suffered severely in the two hours' cannonade. Not less than eleven caissons were blown up and destroyed; one quite near me. When the smoke went up from these explosions rebel yells of exultation could be heard along a line of several miles. At 3 P.M. General Hunt ordered our artillery fire to cease, in order to cool the guns, and to preserve some rounds for the contest at close quarters, which he foresaw would soon take place.

My own men did not suffer a great deal from this cannonade, as I sheltered them as much as possible under the crest of the hill, and behind rocks, trees, and stone fences.

The cessation of our fire gave the enemy the idea they had silenced our batteries, and Pickett at once moved forward, to break the left center of the Union line and occupy the crest of the ridge.* The other forces on his right and left were expected to move up and enlarge the opening thus made, so that finally, the two wings of the Union army would be permanently separated, and flung off by this entering wedge in eccentric directions.

This great column of attack, it was supposed, numbered about seventeen thousand men, but Southern writers have a peculiar arithmetic by which they always cipher down their forces to nothing. Even on the left, on the preceding day, when our troops in front of Little Round Top were assailed by a line a mile and a half long, they figure it almost out of existence. The force that now advanced would have been larger still had it not been for a spirited attack by Kilpatrick against the left of Longstreet's corps, detaining some troops there which otherwise might have co-operated in the grand assault against our center.

It necessarily took the rebels some time to form and cross the intervening space, and Hunt took advantage of the opportunity to withdraw the batteries that had been most injured, sending others in their place from the reserve artillery, which had not been engaged. He also replenished the ammunition boxes, and stood ready to receive the foe as he came forward—first with solid shot, next with shell, and lastly, when he came to close quarters, with canister.

General Meade's headquarters was in the center of this cannonade, and as the balls were flying very thickly there, and killing the horses of his staff, he found it necessary temporarily to abandon the place. Where nothing is to be gained by exposure it is sound sense to shelter men and officers as much as possible. He rode over to Power's Hill, made his headquarters with General Slocum, and when the firing ceased rode back again. During his absence the charge took place. He has stated that it was his intention to throw the Fifth and Sixth Corps on the flanks of the attacking force, but no orders to this effect were issued, and it is questionable whether such an arrangement would have been a good one. It would have disgarnished the left, where Longstreet was still strong in numbers, and in forming perpendicular to our line of battle the two corps would necessarily have exposed their own outer flanks to attack. Indeed, the rebels had provided for just such a contingency, by posting Wilcox's brigade and Perry's brigade under Colonel Lang on the left, both in rear of the charging column under Pickett and Pettigrew. Owing to a mistake or misunderstanding, this disposition, however, did not turn out well for the enemy. It was not intended by Providence that the Northern States should pass under the iron rule of

---

*The attack was so important, so momentous, and so contrary to Longstreet's judgment, that when Pickett asked for orders to advance he gave no reply, and Pickett said proudly, "I shall go forward, sir!"

the slave power, and on this occasion every plan made by Lee was thwarted in the most unexpected manner.

The distance to be traversed by Pickett's column was about a mile and a half from the woods where they started, to the crest of the ridge they desired to attain. They suffered severely from our artillery, which opened on them with solid shot as soon as they came in sight; when half way across the plain they were vigorously shelled; double canisters were reserved for their nearer approach.

At first the direction of their march appeared to be directly toward my division. When within five hundred yards of us, however, Pickett halted and changed direction obliquely about forty-five degrees, so that the attack passed me and struck Gibbon's division on my right. Just here one of those providential circumstances occurred which favored us so much, for Wilcox and Lang, who guarded Pickett's right flank, did not follow his oblique movement, but kept on straight to the front, so that soon there was a wide interval between their troops and the main body, leaving Pickett's right fully uncovered.

The rebels came on magnificently. As fast as the shot and shell tore through their lines they closed up the gaps and pressed forward. When they reached the Emmetsburg road the canister began to make fearful chasms in their ranks. They also suffered severely from a battery on Little Round Top, which enfiladed their line. One shell killed and wounded ten men. Gibbon had directed his command to reserve their fire until the enemy were near enough to make it very effective. Pickett's advance dashed up to the fence occupied by the skirmishers of the Second Corps, near the Emmetsburg road, and drove them back; then the musketry blazed forth with deadly effect, and Pettigrew's men began to waver on the left and fall behind; for the nature of the ground was such that they were more exposed than other portions of the line. They were much shaken by the artillery fire, and that of Hays' division sent them back in masses.*

Before the first line of rebels reached a second fence and stone wall, behind which our main body was posted, it was obliged to pass a demi-brigade under Colonel Theodore B. Gates, of the 20th New York State Militia, and a Vermont brigade under General Stannard, both belonging to my command. When Pickett's right became exposed in consequence of the divergence of Wilcox's command, Stannard seized the opportunity to make a flank attack, and while his left regiment, the 14th, poured in a heavy oblique fire, he changed front with his two right regiments, the 13th and 16th, which brought them perpendicular to the rebel line of march. In cases of this kind, when struck directly on the flank, troops are more or less unable to defend themselves, and Kemper's brigade crowded in toward the center in order to avoid Stannard's energetic and deadly attack. They were closely followed up by Gates' command, who continued to fire into them at close range. This caused many to surrender, others to retreat outright, and others simply to crowd together. Simultaneously with Stannard's attack, the 8th Ohio, which was on

---

*The front line of Hays' division, which received this charge, was composed of the 12th New Jersey, 14th Connecticut, and 1st Delaware. The second line was composed of the 111th, 125th, 126th, and 39th New York.

picket, overlapping the rebel left, closed in on that flank with great effect. Nevertheless, the next brigade—that of Armistead—united to Garnett's brigade, pressed on, and in spite of death-dealing bolts on all sides, Pickett determined to break Gibbon's line and capture his guns.

Although Webb's front was the focus of the concentrated artillery fire, and he had already lost fifty men and some valuable officers, his line remained firm and unshaken. It devolved upon him now to meet the great charge which was to decide the fate of the day. It would have been difficult to find a man better fitted for such an emergency. He was nerved to great deeds by the memory of his ancestors, who in former days had rendered distinguished services to the Republic, and felt that the results of the whole war might depend upon his holding of the position. His men were equally resolute. Cushing's battery, A, 4th United States Artillery, which had been posted on the crest, and Brown's Rhode Island Battery on his left, were both practically destroyed by the cannonade. The horses were prostrated, every officer but one was struck, and Cushing had but one serviceable gun left.

As Pickett's advance came very close to the first line, young Cushing, mortally wounded in both thighs, ran his last serviceable gun down to the fence, and said: "Webb, I will give them one more shot!" At the moment of the last discharge he called out, "Goodby!" and fell dead at the post of duty.

Webb sent for fresh batteries to replace the two that were disabled, and Wheeler's 1st New York Independent Battery came up just before the attack, and took the place of Cushing's battery on the left.

Armistead pressed forward, leaped the stone wall, waving his sword with his hat on it, followed by about a hundred of his men, several of whom carried battle-flags. He shouted, "Give them the cold steel, boys!" and laid his hands upon a gun. The battery for a few minutes was in his possession, and the rebel flag flew triumphantly over our line. But Webb was at the front, very near Armistead, animating and encouraging his men. He led the 72d Pennsylvania regiment against the enemy, and posted a line of wounded men in rear to drive back or shoot every man that deserted his duty. A portion of the 71st Pennsylvania, behind a stone wall on the right, threw in a deadly flanking fire, while a great part of the 69th Pennsylvania and the remainder of the 71st made stern resistance from a copse of trees on the left, near where the enemy had broken the line, and where our men were shot with the rebel muskets touching their breasts.

Then came a splendid charge of two regiments, led by Colonel Hall, which passed completely through Webb's line, and engaged the enemy in a hand-to-hand conflict.*Armistead was shot down by the side of the gun he had taken. It is said he had fought on our side in the first battle at Bull Run, but had been seduced by Southern affiliations to join in the rebellion; and now, dying in the effort to extend the area of slavery over the

---

*Colonel Norman J. Hall, commanding a brigade in Hancock's corps, who rendered this great service, was one of the garrison who defended Fort Sumter at the beginning of the war. At that time he was the Second Lieutenant of my company.

free States, he saw with a clearer vision that he had been engaged in an unholy cause, and said to one of our officers who leaned over him: "Tell Hancock I have wronged him and have wronged my country."

Both Gibbon and Webb were wounded, and the loss in officers and men was very heavy; two rebel brigadier-generals were killed, and more prisoners were taken than twice Webb's brigade; 6 battle-flags, and 1,463 muskets were also gathered in.

My command being a little to the left, I witnessed this scene, and, after it was over, sent out stretcher-bearers attached to the ambulance train, and had numbers of wounded Confederates brought in and cared for. I was told that there was one man among these whose conversation seemed to indicate that he was a general officer. I sent to ascertain his rank, but he replied: "Tell General Doubleday in a few minutes I shall be where there is no rank." He expired soon after, and I never learned his name.

The rebels did not seem to appreciate my humanity in sending out to bring in their wounded, for they opened a savage fire against the stretcher-bearers. One shell burst among us, a piece of it knocked me over on my horse's neck, and wounded Lieutenant Cowdry of my staff.

When Pickett—the great leader—looked around the top of the ridge he had temporarily gained, he saw it was impossible to hold the position. Troops were rushing in on him from all sides. The Second Corps were engaged in a furious assault on his front. His men were fighting with clubbed muskets, and even banner staves were intertwined in a fierce and hopeless struggle. My division of the First Corps were on his right flank, giving deadly blows there, and the Third Corps were closing up to attack. Pettigrew's forces on his left had given way, and a heavy skirmish line began to accumulate on that flank. He saw his men surrendering in masses, and, with a heart full of anguish, ordered a retreat. Death had been busy on all sides, and few indeed now remained of that magnificent column which had advanced so proudly, led by the Ney of the rebel army, and those few fell back in disorder, and without organization, behind Wright's brigade, which had been sent forward to cover the retreat. At first, however, when struck by Stannard on the flank, and when Pickett's charge was spent, they rallied in a little slashing, where a grove had been cut down by our troops to leave an opening for our artillery. There two regiments of Rowley's brigade of my division, the 151st Pennsylvania and the 20th New York State Militia, under Colonel Theodore R. Gates, of the latter regiment, made a gallant charge, and drove them out. Pettigrew's division, it is said, lost 2,000 prisoners and 15 battle-flags on the left.

While this severe contest was going on in front of Webb, Wilcox deployed his command and opened a feeble fire against Caldwell's division on my left. Stannard repeated the maneuver which had been so successful against Kemper's brigade by detaching the 14th and 16th Vermont to take Wilcox in flank. Wilcox thus attacked on his right, while a long row of batteries tore the front of his line to pieces with canister, could gain no foothold. He found himself exposed to a tremendous cross fire, and was obliged to retreat, but a great portion of his command were brought in as prisoners by Stannard* and battle-flags were gathered in sheaves.

A portion of Longstreet's corps, Benning's, Robertson's, and Law's brigades, advanced against the two Round Tops to prevent reinforcements from being sent from that vicinity to meet Pickett's charge. Kilpatrick interfered with this program, however, for about 2 P.M. he made his appearance on our left with Farnsworth's brigade and Merritt's brigade of regulars, accompanied by Graham's and Elder's batteries of the regular army, to attack the rebel right, with a view to reach their ammunition trains, which were in the vicinity. The rebels say his men came on yelling like demons. Having driven back the skirmishers who guarded that flank, Merritt deployed on the left and soon became engaged there with Anderson's Georgia brigade, which was supported by two batteries. On the right Farnsworth, with the 1st Vermont regiment of his brigade, leaped a fence, and advanced until he came to a second stone fence, where he was checked by an attack on his right flank from the 4th Alabama regiment of Law's brigade, which came back for that purpose from a demonstration it was making against Round Top. Farnsworth then turned and leaping another fence in a storm of shot and shell, made a gallant attempt to capture Backman's battery, but was unable to do so, as it was promptly supported by the 9th Georgia regiment of Anderson's brigade. Farnsworth was killed in this charge, and the 1st Vermont found itself enclosed in a field, with high fences on all sides, behind which masses of infantry were constantly rising up and firing. The regiment was all broken up and forced to retire in detachments. Kilpatrick, after fighting some time longer without making much progress, fell back on account of the constant reinforcements that were augmenting the force opposed to him. Although he had not succeeded in capturing the ammunition train, he had made a valuable diversion on the left, which doubtless prevented the enemy from assailing Round Top with vigor, or detaching a force to aid Pickett.

The Confederate General Benning states that the prompt action of General Law in posting the artillery in the road and the 7th and 9th Georgia regiments on each side, was all that saved the train from capture. "There was nothing else to save it." He also says that two-thirds of Pickett's command were killed, wounded, or captured. Every brigade commander and every field officer except one fell. Lee and Longstreet had seen from the edge of the woods, with great exultation, the blue flag of Virginia waving over the crest occupied by the Union troops. It seemed the harbinger of great success to Lee. He thought the Union army was conquered at last. The long struggle was over, and peace would soon come, accompanied by the acknowledgment of the independence of the Southern Confederacy. It was but a passing dream; the flag receded, and soon the plain was covered with fugitives making their way to the rear. Then, anticipating an immediate

---

*As Stannard's brigade were new troops, and had been stationed near Washington, the men had dubbed them *The Paper Collar Brigade*, because some of them were seen wearing paper collars, but after this fight the term was never again applied to them.

pursuit, he used every effort to rally men and officers, and made strenuous efforts to get his artillery in position to be effective.

The Confederate General A. R. Wright criticizes this attack and very justly says, "The difficulty was not so much in reaching Cemetery Ridge or taking it. My brigade did so on the afternoon of the 2d, but the trouble was to hold it, for the whole Federal army was massed in a sort of horse shoe, and could rapidly reinforce the point to any extent; while the long enveloping Confederate line could not support promptly enough." This agrees with what I have said in relation to the convex and concave orders of battle.

General Gibbon had sent Lieutenant Haskell of his staff to Power's Hill to notify General Meade that the charge was coming. As Meade approached his old headquarters he heard firing on the crest above, and went up to ascertain the cause. He found the charge had been repulsed and ejaculated "Thank God!"

When Lee learned that Johnson had yielded his position on the right, and therefore could not co-operate with Pickett's advance, he sent Stuart's cavalry around to accomplish the same object by attacking the right and rear of our army. Howard saw the rebel cavalry moving off in that direction, and David McM. Gregg, whose division was near White's Creek where it crosses the Baltimore pike, received orders about noon to guard Slocum's right and rear.

Custer had already been contending with his brigade against portions of the enemy's force in that direction, when Gregg sent forward McIntosh's brigade to relieve him, and followed soon after with J. Irvin Gregg's brigade. Custer was under orders to join Kilpatrick's command, to which he belonged, but the exigencies of the battle soon forced Gregg to detain him. McIntosh, having taken the place of Custer, pushed forward to develop the enemy's line, which he found very strongly posted, the artillery being on a commanding ridge which overlooked the whole country, and covered by dismounted cavalry in woods, buildings, and behind fences below. McIntosh became warmly engaged and send back for Randol's battery to act against the rebel guns on the crest, and drive the enemy out of the buildings. The guns above were silenced by Pennington's and Randol's batteries, and the force below driven out of the houses by Lieutenant Chester's section of the latter. The buildings and fences were then occupied by our troops. The enemy attempted to regain them by a charge against McIntosh's right flank, but were repulsed. In the meantime Gregg came up with the other brigade, and assumed command of the field.

The battle now became warm, for W. H. F. Lee's brigade, under Chambliss, advanced to support the skirmish line, and the 1st New Jersey, being out of ammunition, was charged and routed by the 1st Virginia. The 7th Michigan, a new regiment which came up to support it, was also driven in; for the enemy's dismounted line reinforced the 1st Virginia. The latter regiment, which had held on with desperate tenacity, although attacked on both flanks, was at last compelled to fall back by an attack made by part of the 5th Michigan. The contending forces were now pretty well exhausted when, to the dismay of our men, a fresh brigade under Wade Hampton, which Stuart had kept in reserve, made its appearance, and new and desperate exertions were required to stem its progress. There was little time to act, but every sabre that could be brought forward was used. As Hampton came on, our artillery under Pennington and Randol made terrible gaps in his ranks.

Chester's section kept firing canister until the rebels were within fifty yards of him. The enemy were temporarily stopped by a desperate charge on their flank, made by only sixteen men of the 3d Pennsylvania Cavalry, under Captains Triechel and Rogers, accompanied by Captain Newhall of McIntosh's staff. This little band of heroes were nearly all disabled or killed, but they succeeded in delaying the enemy, already shattered by the canister from Chester's guns, until Custer was able to bring up the 1st Michigan and lead them to the charge, shouting "Come on, you wolverines!"

Every available sabre was thrown in. General McIntosh and his staff and orderlies charged into the mélée as individuals. Hampton and Fitz Lee headed the enemy, and Custer our troops. Lieutenant Colonel W. Brooke-Rawle, the historian of the conflict, who was present, says, "For minutes, which seemed like hours, amid the clashing of the sabres, the rattle of the small arms, the frenzied imprecations, the demands to surrender, the undaunted replies, and the appeals for mercy, the Confederate column stood its ground." A fresh squadron was brought up under Captain Hart of the 1st New Jersey, and the enemy at last gave way and retired. Both sides still confronted each other, but the battle was over, for Pickett's charge had failed, and there was no longer any object in continuing the contest. Stuart was undoubtedly baffled and the object of his expedition frustrated; yet he stated in his official report that he was in a position to intercept the Union retreat in case Pickett had been successful. At night he retreated to regain his communications with Ewell's left.

This battle being off of the official maps has hardly been alluded to in the various histories which have been written; but its results were important and deserve to be commemorated.

When Pickett's charge was repulsed, and the whole plain covered with fugitives, we all expected that Wellington's command at Waterloo, of "Up, guards, and at them!" would be repeated, and that a grand counter-charge would be made. But General Meade had made no arrangements to give a return thrust. It seems to me he should have posted the Sixth and part of the Twelfth Corps in rear of Gibbon's division the moment Pickett's infantry were seen emerging from the woods, a mile and a half off. If they broke through our center these corps would have been there to receive them, and if they failed to pierce our line and retreated, the two corps could have followed them up promptly before they had time to rally and reorganize. An advance by Sykes would have kept Longstreet in position. In all probability we would have cut the enemy's army in two, and captured the long line of batteries opposite us, which were but slightly guarded. Hancock, lying wounded in an ambulance, wrote to Meade, recommending that this be done.

Meade, it is true, recognized in some sort the good effects of a counter-blow; but to be effective the movement should have been prepared beforehand. It was too late to commence making preparations for an advance when some time had elapsed and when

Lee had rallied his troops and had made all his arrangements to resist an assault. It was ascertained afterward that he had twenty rounds of ammunition left per gun, but it was not evenly distributed and some batteries in front had fired away all their cartridges. A counter-charge under such circumstances is considered almost imperative in war; for the beaten army, running and dismayed, cannot, in the nature of things, resist with much spirit; whereas the pursuers, highly elated by their success, and with the prospect of ending the contest, fight with more energy and bravery. Rodes says the Union forces were so long in occupying the town and in coming forward after the repulse of the enemy that it was generally thought they had retreated. Meade rode leisurely over to the Fifth Corps on the left, and told Sykes to send out and see if the enemy in his front was firm and holding on to their position. A brigade preceded by skirmishers was accordingly sent forward, but as Longstreet's troops were well fortified, they resisted the advance, and Meade—finding some hours had elapsed and that Lee had closed up his lines and was fortifying against him—gave up all idea of a counter-attack.

CHAPTER 15

Gettysburg: Lee's Escape
By *Abner Doubleday*

General Doubleday continues his account of the most important battle in American history. On Saturday, July 4, 1863, soundly defeated after three days of battle, Robert E. Lee began withdrawing his exhausted forces back to the Potomac and the safety of Virginia. They were low on ammunition and food, and burdened by wounded and prisoners. Union Commander George Meade did not pursue with forces that could have ended the war—which was destined to go on for two more years of bloodshed.
—LAMAR UNDERWOOD

LEE WAS GREATLY DISPIRITED AT PICKETT'S FAILURE, BUT WORKED WITH UNTIRING energy to repair the disaster.

There was an interval of a full mile between Hill and Longstreet, and the plain was swarming with fugitives making their way back in disorder. He hastened to get ready to resist the counter-charge, which he thought was inevitable, and to plant batteries behind which the fugitives could rally. He also made great personal exertions to reassure and reassemble the detachments that came in. He did not for a moment imagine that Meade would fail to take advantage of this golden opportunity to crush the Army of Virginia and end the war.

The most distinguished rebel officers admit the great danger they were in at this time, and express their surprise that they were not followed up.

The fact is, Meade had no idea of leaving the ridge. I conversed the next morning with a corps commander who had just left him. He said: "Meade says he thinks he can hold out for part of another day here, if they attack him."

This language satisfied me that Meade would not go forward if he could avoid it, and would not impede in any way the rebel retreat across the Potomac. Lee began to make preparations at once and started his trains on the morning of the 4th. By night Rodes' division, which followed them, was in bivouac two miles west of Fairfield. It was a difficult task to retreat burdened with 4,000 prisoners, and a train fifteen miles long, in the presence of a victorious enemy, but it was successfully accomplished as regards his main body. The roads, too, were bad and much cut up by the rain.

While standing on Little Round Top Meade was annoyed at the fire of a rebel battery posted on an eminence beyond the wheat-field, about a thousand yards distant. He inquired what troops those were stationed along the stone fence which bounded the hither side of the wheat-field. Upon ascertaining that it was Crawford's division of the Fifth Corps, he directed that they be sent forward to clear the woods in front of the rebel skirmishers, who were very annoying, and to drive away the battery, but not to get into a fight that could bring on a general engagement.

As Crawford unmasked from the stone fence the battery opened fire on his right. He sent Colonel Ent's regiment, deployed as skirmishers, against the guns, which retired as Ent approached. McCandless, who went forward with his brigade, moved too far to the right, and Crawford ordered him to change front and advance toward Round Top. He did so and struck a rebel brigade in flank which was behind a temporary breastwork of rails, sods, etc. When this brigade saw a Union force apparently approaching from their own lines to attack them in flank, they retreated in confusion, after a short resistance, and this disorder extended during the retreat to a reserve brigade posted on the low ground in their rear. Their flight did not cease until they reached Horner's woods, half a mile distant, where they immediately intrenched themselves. These brigades belonged to Hood's division, then under Law.

Longstreet says, "When this (Pickett's) charge failed, I expected that, of course, the enemy would throw himself against our shattered ranks and try to crush us. I sent my staff officers to the rear to assist in rallying the troops, and hurried to our line of batteries as the only support that I could given them. . . . I knew if the army was to be saved these batteries must check the enemy. . . . For unaccountable reasons the enemy did not pursue his advantage."

Longstreet always spoke of his own men as invincible, and stated that on the 2d they did the best three hours' fighting that ever was done, but Crawford's* attack seemed to show that they too were shaken by the defeat of Pickett's grand charge.

In regard to the great benefit we would have derived from a pursuit, it may not be out of place to give the opinion of a few more prominent Confederate officers.

Colonel Alexander, Chief of Longstreet's artillery, says in a communication to the "Southern Historical Papers":

*Crawford was also one of those who took a prominent part in the defense of Fort Sumter, at the beginning of the war. We each commanded detachments of artillery on that occasion.

"I have always believed that the enemy here lost the greatest opportunity they ever had of routing Lee's army by a prompt offensive. They occupied a line shaped somewhat like a horseshoe. I suppose the greatest diameter of this horseshoe was not more than one mile, and the ground within was entirely sheltered from our observation and fire, with communications by signals all over it, and they could concentrate their whole force at any point and in a very short time without our knowledge. Our line was an enveloping semi-circle, over four miles in development, and communication from flank to flank, even by courier, was difficult, the country being well cleared and exposed to the enemy's view and fire, the roads all running at right angles to our lines, and, some of them at least, broad turnpikes where the enemy's guns could rake for two miles. Is it necessary now to add any statement as to the superiority of the Federal force, or the exhausted and shattered condition of the Confederates for a space of at least a mile in their very center, to show that a great opportunity was thrown away? I think General Lee himself was quite apprehensive the enemy would riposte, and that it was that apprehension which brought him alone out to my guns, where he could observe all the indications."

General Trimble, who commanded a division of Hill's corps, which supported Pickett in his advance, says, "By all the rules of warfare the Federal troops should (as I expected they would) have marched against our shattered columns and sought to cover our army with an overwhelming defeat."

Colonel Simms, who commanded Semmes' Georgia brigade in the fight with Crawford just referred to, writes to the latter, "There was much confusion in our army so far as my observation extended, and I think we would have made but feeble resistance, if you had pressed on, on the evening of the 3d."

General Meade, however, overcome by the great responsibilities of his position, still clung to the ridge, and fearful of a possible disaster would not take the risk of making an advance. And yet if he could have succeeded in crushing Lee's army then and there, he would have saved two years of war with its immense loss of life and countless evils. He might at least have thrown in Sedgwick's corps, which had not been actively engaged in the battle, for even if it was repulsed the blows it gave would leave the enemy little inclination to again assail the heights.

At 6.30 P.M. the firing ceased on the part of the enemy, and although they retained their position the next day, the battle of Gettysburg was virtually at an end.

The town was still full of our wounded, and many of our surgeons, with rare courage, remained there to take charge of them, for it required some nerve to run the risk of being sent to Libby prison when the fight was over, a catastrophe which has often happened to our medical officers. Among the rest, the chief surgeons of the First Corps, Doctor Theodore Heard and Doctor Thomas H. Bache, refused to leave their patients, and in consequence of the hasty retreat of the enemy were fortunately not carried off.

After the battle Meade had not the slightest desire to recommence the struggle. It is a military maxim that to a flying enemy must be given a wall of steel or a bridge of gold. In the present instance it was unmistakably the bridge of gold that was presented. It was hard to convince him that Lee was actually gone, and at first he thought it might be a device to draw the Union army from its strong position on the heights.

Our cavalry were sent out on the 4th to ascertain where the enemy were, and what they were doing. General Birney threw forward a reconnoitering party and opened fire with a battery on a column making their way toward Fairfield, but he was checked at once and directed *on no account to bring on a battle.* On the 5th, as it was certain the enemy were retreating, Sedgwick received orders to follow up the rear of the rebel column. He marched eight miles to Fairfield Pass. There Early, who was in command of the rear guard, was endeavoring to save the trains, which were heaped up in great confusion. Sedgwick, after a distant cannonade, reported the position too strong to be forced. It was a plain, two miles wide, surrounded by hills, and it would not have been difficult to take it, but Sedgwick knew Meade favored the "bridge of gold" policy, and was not disposed to thwart the wishes of his chief.

In my opinion Sedgwick should have made an energetic attack, and Meade should have supported it with his whole army, for our cavalry were making great havoc in the enemy's train in rear; and if Lee, instead of turning on Kilpatrick, had been forced to form line against Meade, the cavalry, which was between him and his convoys of ammunition, in all probability might have captured the latter and ended the war. Stuart, it is true, was following up Kilpatrick, but he took an indirect route and was nearly a day behind. I do not see why the force which was now promptly detached from the garrisons of Washington and Baltimore and sent to Harper's Ferry could not have formed on the Virginia side of the Potomac opposite Williamsport, and with the co-operation of General Meade have cut off the ammunition of which Lee stood so much in need.

As the river had risen and an expedition sent out by General French from Frederick had destroyed the bridge at Falling Waters, everything seemed to favor such a plan. The moment it was ascertained that Lee was cut off from Richmond and short of ammunition the whole North would have turned out and made a second Saratoga of it. As it was, he had but few roads for his cannon, and our artillery could have opened a destructive fire on him from a distance without exposing our infantry. It was worth the effort and there was little or no danger in attempting it. Meade had Sedgwick's fresh corps and was reinforced by a division of 11,000 men under General W. F. Smith (Baldy Smith). French's division of 4,000 at Frederick, and troops from Washington and Baltimore were also available to assist in striking the final blow. The Twelfth Corps was also available, as Slocum volunteered to join in the pursuit. Meade, however, delayed moving at all until Lee had reached Hagerstown and then took a route that was almost twice as long as that adopted by the enemy. Lee marched day and night to avoid pursuit, and when the river rose and his bridge was gone, so that he was unable to cross, he gained six days in which to choose a position, fortify it, and renew his supply of ammunition before Meade made his appearance.

In consequence of repeated orders from President Lincoln to attack the enemy, Meade went forward and confronted Lee on the 12th. He spent that day and the next in making reconnoissances and resolved to attack on the 14th; but Lee left during the night, and by 8 A.M. the entire army of the enemy were once more on Virginia soil.

The Union loss in this campaign is estimated by the Count of Paris, who is an impartial observer, at 2,834 killed, 13,700 wounded, and 6,643 missing; total, 23,186.

The rebel loss he puts at 2,665 killed, 12,599 wounded, 7,464 missing; total, 22,728.

Among the killed in the battle on the rebel side were Generals Armistead, Barksdale, Garnett, Pender, and Semmes; and Pettigrew during the retreat.

Among the wounded were Generals G. T. Anderson, Hampton, Jenkins, J. M. Jones, Kemper, and Scales.

Archer was captured on the first day.

Among the killed on the Union side were Major-General Reynolds and Brigadier-Generals Vincent, Weed, and Zook.

Among the wounded were Major-Generals Sickles (losing a leg), Hancock, Doubleday, Gibbon, Barlow, Warren, and Butterfield, and Brigadier-Generals Graham, Stannard, Paul (losing both eyes), Barnes, Brooke, and Webb.

CHAPTER 16

The Truth about Gettysburg

By Helen D. Longstreet

The Gettysburg battle was so important that it remained a subject of great debate for years after the war. In her book, Lee and Longstreet at High Tide: Gettysburg in the Light of the Official Records, *1904, the wife of Confederate General James Longstreet picked up the torch in defense of her much-maligned husband. Her book is a treasure for students of the Civil War, including your editor. The three days of battle at Gettysburg are like a three-act play, each day with heroes and villlians. Longstreet played a key role on the second and third days, and his performance on both days has been scrutinized endlessly. The controversies have been made even more lively by the fact that Robert E. Lee did not write a memoir or autobiography. We know his words only through letters, official army reports, or quotes remembered by other people. Mrs. Longstreet takes on the critics with her own barrage of facts she has learned from her husband and others. She includes excerpts from speeches, newspaper articles, official army reports, and General Longstreet's memoir,* From Manassas to Appomattox: Memoirs of the Civil War in America. *To introduce her book, Mrs. Longstreet asked Union General Daniel Sickles to write an article. It was Sickles' troops who had opposed Longstreet on the second day. After the war ended, General Sickles came to be friends with Longstreet, and his Introduction to Mrs. Longstreet's book provides a close look at the opening of the battle of the second day, in which Sickles was wounded (and lost a leg) in the fighting at the now-legendary Wheat Field and Peach Orchard. His Introduction gives us a candid and personal view of the great esteem he felt for the Confederate general. Although General Sickles' Introduction was in the opening pages of Mrs. Longstreet's book, I have chosen to use excerpts from her text first, followed by Sickles' Introduction.*

—LAMAR UNDERWOOD

BACK OF THE DAY THAT OPENED SO AUSPICIOUSLY FOR THE CONFEDERATE CAUSE AT THE first Manassas, and of the four years that followed, lies Longstreet's record of a quarter of a century in the Union army, completing one of the most lustrous pages in the world's war history. That page cannot be dimmed or darkened; it rests secure in its own white splendor, above the touch of detractors.

The detractors of General Longstreet's military integrity assert that, being opposed to fighting an offensive battle at Gettysburg, he was "balky and stubborn" in executing Lee's orders; that he disobeyed the commanding general's orders to attack at sunrise on the morning of July 2; that, again ordered to attack with half the army on the morning of July 3, his culpably slow attack with only Pickett's division, supported by some of Hill's troops, caused the fatal Confederate defeat in that encounter.

General Gordon has seen fit, in a recent publication, to revive this cruel aspersion.

When General Longstreet surrendered his sword at Appomattox his war record was made up. It stands unassailable—needing no defenders. Back of the day that opened so auspiciously for the Confederate cause at the first Manassas, and of the four years that followed, lies the record of a quarter of a century in the Union army.

In those times General Longstreet, at Cerro Gordo, Molino del Rey, and Chapultepec, was aiding to win the great empire of the West; in subsequent hard Indian campaigns lighting the fagots of a splendid western civilization, adding new glory to American arms and, in the struggles of a nation that fell, a new star of the first magnitude to the galaxy of American valor, completing one of the most lustrous pages in the world's war history. That page cannot be dimmed or darkened; it rests secure in its own white splendor, above the touch of detractors. General Longstreet has of late years deemed it unnecessary to make defense of his military integrity, save such as may be found in his memoirs, "Manassas to Appomattox," published nearly ten years since. He has held that his deeds stand on the impartial pages of the nation's records—their own defender.

The cold historian of our Civil War of a hundred years hence will not go for truth to the picturesque reminiscences of General John B. Gordon, nor to the pyrotechnics of General Fitzhugh Lee, nor yet to the somewhat hysterical ravings of Rev. Mr. Pendleton and scores of other modern essayists who have sought to fix the failure of Gettysburg upon General Longstreet. The coming chronicler will cast aside the rubbish of passion and hate that followed the war, and have recourse to the nation's official war records, and in the cool, calm lights of the letters and reports of the participants, written at the time, will place the blunder of Gettysburg where it belongs. Longstreet's fame has nothing to fear in that hour.

But for the benefit of the present—of the young, the busy, who have neither time nor inclination to study the records, and for that sentiment that is increasingly shaped by the public press—for these and other reasons it appears fitting that in this hour historical truth should have a spokesman on the Gettysburg contentions. In the absence of one more able to speak, this little story of the truth is written. The writer belongs to a generation that has come up since the gloom of Appomattox closed the drama of the great "Lost

Cause" of American history—a generation that seeks the truth, unwarped and undistorted by passion, and can face the truth.

In the prosecution of my researches for the origin of the extraordinary calumnies aimed at General Longstreet's honor as a soldier, two most significant facts have continually pressed upon my attention.

First, not one word appears to have been published openly accusing him of disobedience at Gettysburg until the man who could forever have silenced all criticism was in his grave—until the knightly soul of Robert Edward Lee had passed into eternity.

Second, General Longstreet's operations on the field of Gettysburg were above the suspicion of reproach until he came under the political ban in the South, for meeting in the proper spirit, as he saw it, the requirements of good citizenship in the observance of his Appomattox parole, and, after the removal of his political disabilities, for having accepted office at the hands of a Republican President who happened to be his old West Point comrade—Grant.

Then the storm broke. He was heralded as traitor, deserter of his people, deserter of Democracy, etc. In the fury of this onslaught originated the cruel slander that he had disobeyed Lee's most vital orders, causing the loss of the Gettysburg battle and the ultimate fall of the Confederate cause. Most singularly, this strange discovery was not made until some years after the battle and General Lee's death. Thereafter for two decades the South was sedulously taught to believe that the Federal victory was wholly the fortuitous outcome of the culpable disobedience of General Longstreet.

The sectional complaint that he deserted "Democracy" is about as relevant and truthful as the assertion that he lost Gettysburg. He was a West Pointer, a professional soldier. He had never cast a ballot before the Civil War; he had no politics. Its passions and prejudices had no dwelling-place in his mind. The war was over, and he quietly accepted the result, fraternizing with all Americans. It was no great crime.

But the peculiar circumstances favored an opportunity to make Longstreet the long-desired scape-goat for Gettysburg. There was an ulterior and deeper purpose, however, than merely besmirching his military record. Short-sighted partisans seemingly argued that the disparagement of Longstreet was necessary to save the military reputation of Lee. But Lee's great fame needed no such sacrifice.

The outrageous charges against Longstreet have been wholly disproved. Much of the partisan rancor that once pursued him has died out. Many of the more intelligent Southerners have been long convinced that he was the victim of a great wrong.

It was unworthy of Major-General John B. Gordon, once of the Army of Northern Virginia, to revive this dead controversy. He simply reiterates the old charges in full, produces no evidence in their support, and gratuitously endorses a false and cruel verdict. His contribution is of no historical value. It carries inherent evidence that General Gordon made no critical examination of the documentary history of Gettysburg. He assumes to render a verdict on the say-so of others.

Gordon's unsupported assertions would require no attention but for one fact. Both South and North there is a widespread impression that Gordon was a conspicuous figure at Gettysburg. This is erroneous. He was merely a brigade commander there, stationed five miles from Longstreet. It is not certain that he personally saw either Lee or Longstreet while the army was in Pennsylvania.

In his official report Gordon uses this language regarding the operations of his own small command at Gettysburg when the heaviest fighting was going on, finely showing the scope of his opportunities for observation:

> *"The movements during the succeeding days of the battle, July 2 and 3, I do not consider of sufficient importance to mention."*

It is but just to Gordon, however, to say that in his subordinate capacity at the head of one of the thirty-seven brigades of infantry comprising Lee's army, he performed excellent service on the first day's battle. But in estimating his value as a personal witness, the foregoing undisputed facts must be taken into consideration. His testimony is obviously of the hearsay kind. In fact, as will be observed from his own admission, it is no more than his own personal conclusions, wholly deduced from the assertions of others, based on an assumed state of facts which did not exist.

In his recent publication, "Reminiscences of the Civil War," Gordon says,

> *"It now seems certain that impartial military critics, after thorough investigation, will consider the following facts established:*
> *"First, that General Lee distinctly ordered Longstreet to attack early on the morning of the second day, and if Longstreet had done so two of the largest corps of Meade's army would not have been in the fight; but Longstreet delayed the fight until four o'clock in the afternoon, and thus lost his opportunity of occupying Little Round Top, the key of the position, which he might have done in the morning without firing a shot or losing a man."*

It is competent to point out that Longstreet's orders from General Lee were "to move around to gain the Emmitsburg road, on the enemy's left." In short, he was "to attack up the Emmitsburg road," as all the authorities agree. He therefore could not well "occupy" Little Round Top up the Emmitsburg road, because it was but a fraction less than a mile to the east of that road. It is as clear as noonday that Lee had no thought at first, if ever, that Little Round Top was the "key to the position." Lee merely contemplated driving the enemy from some high ground on the Emmitsburg road from which the "more elevated ground" of Cemetery Hill in its rear, more than a mile to the northward of Little Round Top, could be subsequently assailed.

Lee's luminous report of the battle, dated July 31, 1863, only four weeks after, has escaped Gordon's notice, or has been conveniently ignored by him. It is found at page 305 *et seq.*, of Part II., Vol. XXVII., of the printed War Records, easily accessible to everybody. At page 308, Lee's report:

> *"In front of General Longstreet the enemy held a position from which, if he could be driven, it was thought our artillery could be used to advantage in assailing the more elevated ground beyond, and thus enable us to reach the crest of the ridge. That officer was directed to carry this position. . . . After a severe struggle, Longstreet succeeded in getting possession of and holding the desired ground. . . . The battle ceased at dark."*

The "desired ground" captured was that held by Sickles's Federal Third Corps—the celebrated peach-orchard, wheat-field, and adjacent high ground, from which Cemetery Hill was next day assailed by the Confederate artillery as a prelude to Pickett's infantry assault.

It was the "crest of the ridge," not the Round Top, that Lee wished to assail. His eye from the first appears to have been steadily fixed upon the Federal center. That is why he ordered the "attack up the Emmitsburg road."

Longstreet's official report is very explicit on this point. It was written July 27, 1863. On page 358 of the same book he says,

> *"I received instructions from the commanding general to move, with the portion of my command that was up, around to gain the Emmitsburg road, on the enemy's left."*

Lieutenant-General R. H. Anderson, then of Hill's corps, also makes this definite statement:

> *"Shortly after the line had been formed, I received notice that Lieutenant-General Longstreet would occupy the ground on my right, and that his line would be in a direction nearly at right angles with mine, and that he would assault the extreme left of the enemy and drive him towards Gettysburg."*

Just here it is pertinent to say that General Longstreet had the afternoon previous, and again that morning, suggested to General Lee the more promising plan of a movement by the Confederate right to interpose between the Federals and their capital, and thus compel General Meade to give battle at a disadvantage. On this point General Longstreet uses the following language in a newspaper publication more than a quarter of a century ago:

> *"When I overtook General Lee at five o'clock that afternoon [July 1], he said, to my surprise, that he thought of attacking General Meade upon the heights the next day. I suggested that this course seemed to be at variance with the plan of the campaign that had been agreed upon before leaving Fredericksburg.*
>
> *"He said, 'If the enemy is there to-morrow, we must attack him.'*
>
> *"I replied: 'If he is there, it will be because he is anxious that we should attack him—a good reason in my judgment for not doing so.'*

"I urged that we should move around by our right to the left of Meade and put our army between him and Washington, threatening his left and rear, and thus force him to attack us in such position as we might select. . . . I called his attention to the fact that the country was admirably adapted for a defensive battle, and that we should surely repulse Meade with crushing loss if we would take position so as to force him to attack us, and suggested that even if we carried the heights in front of us, and drove Meade out, we should be so badly crippled that we could not reap the fruits of victory; and that the heights of Gettysburg were in themselves of no more importance to us than the ground we then occupied, and that the mere possession of the ground was not worth a hundred men to us. That Meade's army, not its position, was our objective. General Lee was impressed with the idea that by attacking the Federals he could whip them in detail. I reminded him that if the Federals were there in the morning it would be proof that they had their forces well in hand, and that with Pickett in Chambersburg, and Stuart out of reach, we should be somewhat in detail. He, however, did not seem to abandon the idea of attack on the next day. He seemed under a subdued excitement which occasionally took possession of him when 'the hunt was up,' and threatened his superb equipoise. . . . When I left General Lee on the night of the 1st, I believed that he had made up his mind to attack, but was confident that he had not yet determined as to when the attack should be made."

But General Lee persisted in the direct attack "up the Emmitsburg road." Hood, deployed on Longstreet's extreme right, at once perceived that the true direction was by flank against the southern slopes of Big Round Top. He delayed the advance to advise of the discovery he had made. Soon the positive order came back: "General Lee's orders are to attack up the Emmitsburg road." He still hesitated and repeated the suggestion. Again it was reiterated: "General Lee's orders are to attack up the Emmitsburg road."

Then the troops moved to the attack. There was no alternative. Lee's orders were imperative, and made after he had personally examined the enemy's position. Longstreet was ordered to attack a specific position "up the Emmitsburg road," which was not Little Round Top, as assumed by Gordon. This point is particularly elaborated because in it lies the "milk in the coconut" of the charges against Longstreet. Without consulting the records Gordon has merely followed the lead of some of General Lee's biographers, notably Fitzhugh Lee, who asserts that his illustrious uncle "expected Longstreet to seize Little Round Top on the 2d of July." The records clearly show that nothing was farther from General Lee's thoughts.

After the war it was discovered that a very early attack on Little Round Top would perhaps have found it undefended, hence the afterthought that General Longstreet was ordered to attack at sunrise. But whatever the hour Longstreet was ordered to attack, it was most certainly not Little Round Top that was made his objective.

General Longstreet's personal account of this magnificent battle "up the Emmitsburg road" will not be out of place here. In the newspaper article previously quoted from, he very graphically describes the advance of the two divisions of McLaws and Hood, for when he went into battle it must be understood that even yet one of his divisions, that of Pickett, was still absent. He states his total force at thirteen thousand men. An account of this clash of arms must send a thrill of pride through every Southern heart:

"At half-past three o'clock the order was given General Hood to advance upon the enemy, and, hurrying to the head of McLaws's division, I moved with his line. Then was fairly commenced what I do not hesitate to pronounce the best three hours' fighting ever done by any troops on any battle-field. Directly in front of us, occupying the peach-orchard, on a piece of elevated ground that General Lee desired me to take and hold for his artillery, was the Third Corps of the Federals, commanded by General Sickles.

"Prompt to the order the combat opened, followed by artillery of the other corps, and our artillerists measured up to the better metal of the enemy by vigilant work. . . .

"In his usual gallant style Hood led his troops through the rocky fastnesses against the strong lines of his earnest adversary, and encountered battle that called for all of his power and skill. The enemy was tenacious of his strong ground; his skilfully handled batteries swept through the passes between the rocks; the more deadly fire of infantry concentrated as our men bore upon the angle of the enemy's line and stemmed the fiercest onset until it became necessary to shorten their work by a desperate charge. This pressing struggle and the cross-fire of our batteries broke in the salient angle, but the thickening fire, as the angle was pressed back, hurt Hood's left and held him in steady fight. His right brigade was drawn towards Round Top by the heavy fire pouring from that quarter, Benning's brigade was pressed to the thickening line at the angle, and G. T. Anderson's was put in support of the battle growing against Hood's right.

"I rode to McLaws, found him ready for his opportunity, and Barksdale chafing in his wait for the order to seize the battery in his front. Kershaw's brigade of his right first advanced and struck near the angle of the enemy's line where his forces were gathering strength. After additional caution to hold his ranks closed, McLaws ordered Barksdale in. With glorious bearing he sprang to his work, overriding obstacles and dangers. Without a pause to deliver a shot, he had the battery. Kershaw, joined by Semmes's brigade, responded, and Hood's men, feeling the impulsion of relief, resumed their bold fight, and presently the enemy's line was broken through its length. But his well-seasoned troops knew how to utilize the advantage of their ground and put back their dreadful fires from rocks, depressions, and stone fences, as they went for shelter about Little Round Top. . . . The fighting had become tremendous, and brave men and officers were stricken by hundreds. Posey and Wilcox dislodged the forces about the Brick House.

"General Sickles was desperately wounded!

"General Willard was dead!

"General Semmes, of McLaws's division, was mortally wounded! . . .

"I had one brigade—Wofford's—that had not been engaged in the hottest battle. To urge the troops to their reserve power in the precious moments, I rode with Wofford. The *rugged field, the rough plunge of artillery fire, and the piercing musket-shots delayed somewhat the march, but Alexander dashed up with his batteries and gave new spirit to the worn infantry ranks. . . . While Meade's lines were growing my men were dropping; we had no others to call to their aid, and the weight against us was too heavy to carry. . . . Nothing was heard or felt but the clear ring of the enemy's fresh metal as he came against us. No other part of the army had engaged! My seventeen thousand against the Army of the Potomac! The sun was down, and with it went down the severe battle."*

Surely these are not the utterances of one who had been slow, balky, and obstructive on that field. The ring of these sentences tells no tale of apathy or backwardness because his advice to pursue a different line of operations had been ignored by Lee.

General Gordon, continuing, very complacently assumes that "two of the largest corps of Meade's army would not have been in the fight" of the 2d had Longstreet attacked early in the morning. He refers to the Union Fifth and Sixth Corps. That statement is correct only as regards the Sixth Corps, which, it is true, did not arrive on the field until late in the afternoon. But it took only a slight part at dark on the 2d, when the battle was over. Indeed, as it was so slightly engaged, the hour of its arrival at Gettysburg is unimportant. The losses of the different corps conclusively show what part the Sixth, which was the largest in the army, took in the battle of the 2d of July; as given in the Rebellion Records:

Killed and wounded: First Corps, 3980; Second Corps, 3991; Third Corps, 3662; Fifth Corps, 1976; Sixth Corps, 212; Eleventh Corps, 2353; Twelfth Corps, 1016.

Its non-participation strongly militates against the spirit of Gordon's argument, in that Meade entirely frustrated Lee's plans and defeated the Confederate army, scarcely using the Sixth Corps, some fifteen thousand men, at all. This is a significant commentary on the anti-Longstreet assumption of how easy it was to win at Gettysburg if only Longstreet had obeyed orders!

At sunrise on the 2d, the hour at which Longstreet's critics would have had this attack delivered, the Federal Fifth Corps was as near the battle-ground of that day as Longstreet's troops. Longstreet's troops were bivouacked the night previous at Marsh Creek, four miles west of Gettysburg. They began to arrive near Lee's head-quarters on Seminary Ridge not earlier than 7 A.M. of the 2d, and the last of the column did not get in until near noon. Then they were still five miles by the route pursued from the chosen point of attack.

The Union Fifth Corps was bivouacked five miles east of Gettysburg about the same hour on the 1st that Longstreet's tired infantry reached Marsh Creek. At four o'clock A.M. of the 2d they marched on Gettysburg, arriving about the same hour that Longstreet's troops were being massed near Lee's head-quarters, and were thereupon posted upon the extreme Federal right.

Upon the first manifestation of Confederate movements on the right and left, we know that the Fifth Corps was immediately drawn in closer, and about nine o'clock massed at the bridge over Rock Creek on the Baltimore pike, ready for developments. Meade thought Lee intended to attack his right. That Lee contemplated it is quite certain. Colonel Venable, of his staff, was sent about sunrise to consult with Lieutenant-General Ewell upon the feasibility of a general attack from his front. Lee wanted Ewell's views as to the advisability of moving all the available troops around to that front for such a purpose. Venable and Ewell rode from point to point to determine if this should be done. Finally, Venable says, Lee himself came to Ewell's lines, and eventually the design for an attack on the Union right was abandoned.

Where the Fifth Corps was finally massed, it was only one and a half miles in the rear of General Sickles's position. Moreover, it had an almost direct road to that point. This facility for reinforcing incidentally illustrates the advantages of the Union position. At the same hour General Longstreet's troops were still massed near the Chambersburg pike, three miles on a straight line from the point of attack. That is to say, Longstreet had twice as far to march on an air-line to strike Sickles "up the Emmitsburg road" as Sykes had to reinforce the threatened point. But, in fact, Sykes's advantage was far greater in point of time, because, by order of Lee, Longstreet was compelled to move by back roads and lanes, out of sight of the enemy's signal officers on Round Top. His troops actually marched six or seven miles to reach the point of deployment.

Longstreet eventually attacked about 4 P.M., and the Fifth Corps was used very effectively against him. But no historian who esteems the truth, with the undisputed records before him, will deny that it could and would have been used just as effectively at seven or eight o'clock in the morning. The moment Longstreet's movement was detected it was immediately hurried over to the left and occupied Round Top. If Longstreet had moved earlier, the Fifth Corps also would have moved earlier. It could have been on Sickles's left and rear as early as seven o'clock A.M., had it been necessary. If Ewell and not Longstreet had delivered the general attack it would have been found in his front.

It is mathematically correct to say that the troops which met Longstreet on the afternoon of the 2d could have been brought against him in the morning. The reports of General Meade, General Sykes, the commander of the Fifth Corps of Sykes's brigade, and regimental commanders, and various other documentary history bearing on the subject, are convincing upon this point.

General Sickles's advance was made in consequence of the Confederate threatening, and would have been sooner or later according as that threatening was made. The critics ignore this fact.

General Longstreet says on this point:

"General Meade was with General Sickles discussing the feasibility of moving the Third Corps back to the line originally assigned for it; the discussion was cut short by the opening of the Confederate battle. If that opening had been delayed thirty or forty minutes, Sickles's corps would have been drawn back to the general line, and my first deployment would have enveloped Little Round Top and carried it before it could have been strongly manned. The point should have been that the battle was opened too soon."

So much for one part of Gordon's assumption, based upon other assumptions founded upon an erroneous presumption, that if Longstreet had taken wings and flown on an airline from his bivouac at Marsh Creek to the Federal left and attacked at sunrise he would have found no enemy near the Round Tops.

In another equally unwarranted assumption of what the "impartial" military critic will consider an "established fact," Gordon declares:

"Secondly, that General Lee ordered Longstreet to attack at daylight on the morning of the third day, and that the latter did not attack until two or three o'clock in the afternoon, the artillery opening at one."

Lee himself mentions no such order. In his final report, penned six months afterwards, he merely mentions that the "general plan was unchanged," and Longstreet, reinforced, ordered to attack "next morning," no definite hour being fixed. It is significant, however, that in his letter to Jefferson Davis from the field, dated July 4, Lee uses this language:

"Next day (July 3), the third division of General Longstreet's corps having come up, a more extensive attack was made," etc.

The "third division" was Pickett's, which did not arrive from Chambersburg until 9 A.M. of the 3d. In the same report, Lee himself states that "Pickett, with three of his brigades, joined Longstreet the following morning." There is no dispute, however, about the hour of Pickett's arrival.

So that, as Pickett was selected by Lee to lead the charge, and as Lee knew exactly where Pickett was, it is morally impossible that it was fixed for daylight, five hours before Pickett's troops were up.

In one place Lee remarks in his report: "The morning was occupied in necessary preparations, and the battle recommenced in the afternoon of the 3d." Time was not an essential element in the problem of the 3d. The Federal army was then all up, whereas Pickett's Confederate division was still absent. The delay of a few hours was therefore a distinct gain for the Confederates, and not prejudicial, as Gordon would have the world believe.

But Longstreet's official report is decisive of the whole question. He says—

"On the following morning (that is, after the fight of the 2d) our arrangements were made for renewing the attack by my right, with a view to pass round the hill occupied by the enemy's left, and gain it by flank and reverse attack. A few moments after my orders for the execution of this plan were given, the commanding general joined me, and ordered a column of attack to be formed of Pickett's, Heth's, and part of Pender's divisions, the assault to be made directly at the enemy's main position, the Cemetery Hill."

Clearly this shows that Longstreet had no orders for the morning of July 3. As Longstreet's report passed through Lee's hands, the superior would most certainly have returned it to the subordinate for correction if there were errors in it. This he did not do, neither did Lee endorse upon the document itself any dissent from its tenor.

As Pickett did not come up until 9 A.M., and as General Lee says "the morning was occupied in necessary preparations," it was logistically and morally impossible to make an attack at daylight, and General Longstreet states that it could not have been delivered sooner than it was.

Finally, Longstreet emphatically denies that Lee ordered him to attack at daylight on the 3d. He says that he had no orders of any kind on that morning until Lee personally came over to his front and ordered the Pickett charge. No early attack was possible under the conditions imposed by Lee to use Pickett's, Pettigrew's, and Pender's troops, widely separated.

But without any orders from Lee, as is quite apparent, Longstreet had already given orders for a flank attack by the southern face of Big Round Top, as an alternative to directly attacking again the impregnable heights from which he had been repulsed the night before.

That would have been "simple madness," to quote the language of the Confederate General Law. But such an act of "simple madness" was the only daylight attack possible from Longstreet's front on the morning of the 3d. Lee substituted for the feasible early attack projected by Longstreet the Pickett movement straight on Cemetery Heights which it required hours of preparation to fulminate, and which proved the most disastrous and destructive in Confederate annals. It was, in fact, the death-knell of the Southern republic.

In his published memoirs, page 385, General Longstreet makes this concise statement in regard to Lee's alleged orders for the early morning operations on the 3d: "He [General Lee] did not give or send me orders for the morning of the third day, nor did he reinforce me by Pickett's brigades for morning attack. As his head-quarters were about four miles from the command, I did not ride over, but sent, to report the work of the second day. In the absence of orders, I had scouting parties out during the night in search of a way by which we might strike the enemy's left and push it down towards his center. I found a way that gave some promise of results, and was about to move the command when he [Lee] rode over after sunrise and gave his orders."

But in his paper of 1877, on Gettysburg, herein-before freely quoted from, General Longstreet goes more into detail with relation to Lee's plans and orders for the morning of the 3d, and more fully discloses the genesis of the Pickett charge. In this account his own opposition to a renewal of the attack on Cemetery Hill is developed and the obvious reasons therefor. As he is confirmed in nearly every particular by participants and by the records, his account is here reprinted:

"On the next morning he came to see me, and, fearing that he was still in his disposition to attack, I tried to anticipate him by saying, 'General, I have had my scouts out

all night, and I find that you still have an excellent opportunity to move around to the right of Meade's army and maneuver him into attacking us.'

"*He replied, pointing with his fist at Cemetery Hill, 'The enemy is there, and I am going to strike him.' I felt then that it was my duty to express my convictions. I said, 'General, I have been a soldier all my life. I have been with soldiers engaged in fights by couples, by squads, companies, regiments, divisions, and armies, and should know as well as any one what soldiers can do. It is my opinion that no fifteen thousand men ever arrayed for battle can take that position,' pointing to Cemetery Hill.*

"*General Lee, in reply to this, ordered me to prepare Pickett's division for the attack. I should not have been so urgent had I not foreseen the hopelessness of the proposed assault. I felt that I must say a word against the sacrifice of my men; and then I felt that my record was such that General Lee would or could not misconstrue my motives. I said no more, however, but turned away. The most of the morning was consumed in waiting for Pickett's men and getting into position.*"

To make the attitude of the superior and his subordinate more clear in relation to the proposed desperate throw of General Lee for victory, and to further explain the foregoing protest of General Longstreet, quotations from a second paper of the series printed in 1877 are here given, in which he says,

"*In my first article I declared that the invasion of Pennsylvania was a movement that General Lee and his council agreed should be defensive in tactics, while of course it was offensive in strategy; that the campaign was conducted on this plan until we had left Chambersburg, when, owing to the absence of our cavalry and our consequent ignorance of the enemy's whereabouts, we collided with them unexpectedly, and that General Lee had lost the matchless equipoise that usually characterized him, and through excitement and the doubt that enveloped the enemy's movements, changed the whole plan of the campaign and delivered a battle under ominous circumstances.*

"*Pickett swept past our artillery in splendid style, and the men marched steadily and compactly down the slope. As they started up the ridge over one hundred cannon from the breastworks of the Federals hurled a rain of canister, grape, and shell down upon them; still they pressed on until half-way up the slope, when the crest of the hill was lit with a solid sheet of flame as the masses of infantry rose and fired. When the smoke cleared away Pickett's division was gone. Nearly two-thirds of his men lay dead on the field.*"LONGSTREET ON PICKETT'S CHARGE.

General Longstreet's description of the Pickett charge itself also throws much light on these old controversies. It is confirmed in all essential particulars by General Alexander and others who have written on the subject since the war, and also by the reports:

"The plan of assault was as follows: Our artillery was to be massed in a wood from which Pickett was to charge, and it was to pour a continuous fire upon the cemetery. Under cover of this fire, and supported by it, Pickett was to charge. General E. P. Alexander, a brave and gifted officer, being at the head of the column, and being first in position, and being besides an officer of unusual promptness, sagacity, and intelligence, was given charge of the artillery. The arrangements were completed about one o'clock. General Alexander had arranged that a battery of seven 11-pound howitzers, with fresh horses and full caissons, were to charge with Pickett, at the head of his line, but General Pendleton, from whom the guns had been borrowed, recalled them just before the charge was made, and thus deranged this wise plan.

"Never was I so depressed as upon that day. I felt that my men were to be sacrificed, and that I should have to order them to make a hopeless charge. I had instructed General Alexander, being unwilling to trust myself with the entire responsibility, to carefully observe the effect of the fire upon the enemy, and when it began to tell to notify Pickett to begin the assault. I was so much impressed with the hopelessness of the charge that I wrote the following note to General Alexander:

"If the artillery fire does not have the effect to drive off the enemy or greatly demoralize him, so as to make our efforts pretty certain, I would prefer that you should not advise General Pickett to make the charge. I shall rely a great deal on your judgment to determine the matter, and shall expect you to let Pickett know when the moment offers.'

"To my note the general replied as follows:

"I will only be able to judge the effect of our fire upon the enemy by his return fire, for his infantry is but little exposed to view, and the smoke will obscure the whole field. If, as I infer from your note, there is an alternative to this attack, it should be carefully considered before opening our fire, for it will take all of the artillery ammunition we have left to test this one thoroughly, and if the result is unfavorable, we will have none left for another effort, and even if this is entirely successful it can only be so at a very bloody cost.'

"I still desired to save my men, and felt that if the artillery did not produce the desired effect I would be justified in holding Pickett off. I wrote this note to Colonel Walton at exactly 1.30 P.M.:

"Let the batteries open. Order great precision in firing. If the batteries at the peach-orchard cannot be used against the point we intend attacking, let them open on the enemy at Rocky Hill.'

"The cannonading which opened along both lines was grand. In a few moments a courier brought a note to General Pickett (who was standing near me) from Alexander, which, after reading, he handed to me. It was as follows:

"If you are coming at all you must come at once, or I cannot give you proper support; but the enemy's fire has not slackened at all; at least eighteen guns are still firing from the cemetery itself.'

"After I had read the note Pickett said to me, 'General, shall I advance?' My feelings had so overcome me that I would not speak for fear of betraying my want of confidence to him. I bowed affirmation and turned to mount my horse. Pickett immediately said, 'I shall lead my division forward, sir.' I spurred my horse to the wood where Alexander was stationed with artillery. When I reached him he told me of the disappearance of the seven guns which were to have led the charge with Pickett, and that his ammunition was so low that he could not properly support the charge. I at once ordered him to stop Pickett until the ammunition had been replenished. He informed me that he had no ammunition with which to replenish. I then saw that there was no help for it, and that Pickett must advance under his orders. He swept past our artillery in splendid style, and the men marched steadily and compactly down the slope. As they started up the ridge over one hundred cannon from the breastworks of the Federals hurled a rain of canister, grape, and shell down upon them; still they pressed on until half-way up the slope, when the crest of the hill was lit with a solid sheet of flame as the masses of infantry rose and fired. When the smoke cleared away Pickett's division was gone. Nearly two-thirds of his men lay dead on the field, and the survivors were sullenly retreating down the hill. Mortal man could not have stood that fire. In half an hour the contested field was cleared and the battle of Gettysburg was over.

"When this charge had failed I expected that of course the enemy would throw himself against our shattered ranks and try to crush us. I sent my staff-officers to the rear to assist in rallying the troops, and hurried to our line of batteries as the only support that I could give them, knowing that my presence would impress upon every one of them the necessity of holding the ground to the last extremity. I knew if the army was to be saved those batteries must check the enemy."

Continuing on the subject of Longstreet's alleged disobedience, Gordon considers the following as another of the "facts established:"

"That General Lee, according to the testimony of Colonel Walter Taylor, Colonel C. S. Venable, and General A. L. Long, who were present when the order was given, ordered Longstreet to make the attack on the last day with the three divisions of his own corps and two divisions of A. P. Hill's corps, and that instead of doing so Longstreet sent only fourteen thousand men to assail Meade's army in the latter's strong and heavily intrenched position."

This is the old story that Longstreet was culpable in not sending McLaws and Hood to the attack with Pickett.

But, in fact, Lee's own utterances show that McLaws and Hood were not to join in the Pickett attack, but, on the contrary, were excluded for other vital service by Lee's specific directions. It is true this was done upon Longstreet's strenuous representations that twenty thousand Federals were massed behind the Round Top to swoop down on the Confederate flank if Hood and McLaws were withdrawn. After viewing the ground himself Lee acquiesced. The eye-witnesses quoted by Gordon heard only the original order; they evidently did not know of its necessary modification, after Lee was made aware by his own personal observations and by Longstreet's explanations that it was impossible to withdraw Hood and McLaws.

The official reports of both Lee and Longstreet are conclusive on this point, and they substantially agree. In the paragraph quoted in the preceding chapter, Longstreet states explicitly that "the commanding general joined me" (on the far right on the morning of the 3d) "and ordered a column of attack to be formed of Pickett's, Heth's, and part of Pender's divisions," etc. If this was a misstatement, why did not Lee correct it before sending the report to the War Department? He did not; on the contrary, Lee corroborates Longstreet in these paragraphs of his own official report, in which he also explains in detail why McLaws and Hood were not ordered forward with Pickett:

> "General Longstreet was delayed by a force occupying the high rocky hills on the enemy's extreme left, from which his troops could be attacked in reverse as they advanced. His operations had been embarrassed the day previous by the same cause, and he now deemed it necessary to defend his flank and rear with the divisions of Hood and McLaws. He was therefore reinforced by Heth's division and two brigades of Pender's. . . . General Longstreet ordered forward the column of attack, consisting of Pickett's and Heth's divisions in two lines, Pickett on the right."

Now, one of Lee's favorite officers, General Pickett, had personal supervision of the formation of the attacking column. General Lee was for a time personally present while this work was going on, conversing with Pickett concerning the proper dispositions and making various suggestions. He therefore knew by personal observation, before the charge was made, exactly what troops were included and what were not. He knew that the extreme right of Hood's division was at that moment fully three miles away, holding a difficult position in face of an overwhelming force of Federals, and McLaws almost equally distant. With these documents before him, how can Gordon believe it an "established fact" that Lee expected McLaws and Hood to take part in the Pickett charge?

It is admitted by almost if not quite all authority on the subject that Pickett's charge was hopeless. The addition of McLaws and Hood would not have increased the chances of success. The Confederates under Longstreet and R. H. Anderson had tested the enemy's position on that front thoroughly in the battle of the 2d, and with a much larger force, including these same divisions of McLaws and Hood, who had been repulsed. There was every reason to believe that the position was much stronger on the final day than when Longstreet attacked it on the 2d. The troops of Hood and McLaws, in view of their enormous losses, were in no condition to support Pickett effectively, even had they been free for that purpose. But it has been shown above by the testimony of both Lee and Longstreet that they were required to maintain the position they had won in the desperate struggle of the evening previous to prevent the twenty-two thousand men of the Union Fifth and Sixth Corps from falling *en masse* upon Pickett's right flank, or their own flank and rear had they moved in unison with Pickett.

Having proved from Lee's own official written utterances that the three foregoing points set up by Gordon cannot possibly be accepted as "established facts," we now come to his "fourthly," which is really a summing up of the whole case against Longstreet—viz., that he was disobedient, slow, "balky," and obstructive at Gettysburg. He says—

> *"Fourthly, that the great mistake of the halt on the first day would have been repaired on the second, and even on the third day, if Lee's orders had been vigorously executed, and that General Lee died believing that he lost Gettysburg at last by Longstreet's disobedience of orders."*

The first positive utterance holding General Longstreet responsible for the defeat at Gettysburg, through failure to obey Lee's orders, came from Rev. Dr. William N. Pendleton, an Episcopal clergyman of Virginia (and a prominent figure in the Getttysburg battle) on the 17th of January, 1873. General Lee had then been dead more than two years. In view of what follows it is well to bear in mind these two distinct dates. There had been some vague hints, particularly among some of the higher ex-Confederates from Virginia prior to Pendleton's categorical story, but Pendleton was the first person to distinctly formulate the indictment against Longstreet for disobedience of orders. In an address delivered in the town of Lexington, Virginia, on the date mentioned, in behalf of a memorial church to General Lee, Pendleton uses this language, referring to the battle of Gettysburg:

> *"The ground southwest of the town [Gettysburg] was carefully examined by me after the engagement of July 1. . . . Its practicable character was reported to our commanding general. He informed me that he had ordered Longstreet to attack on that front at sunrise next morning. And he added to myself: 'I want you to be out long before sunrise, so as to re-examine and save time.' He also desired me to communicate with General Longstreet, as well as himself. The reconnoissance was accordingly made as soon as it was light enough on the 2d. . . . All this, as it occurred under my personal observation, it is nothing short of imperative duty that I thus fairly state."*

EDITOR'S NOTE: In his Introduction to Mrs. Longstreet's book, Union General Daniel Sickles not only provides important facts about the second day at Gettysburg, his tribute to General Longstreet's character is moving and revealing. Here are two generals, enjoying life together, the battles long ended, but the memories everlasting.

Introduction
By Major General Daniel Sickles

I am glad to write an introduction to a memoir of Lieutenant-General Longstreet.

If it be thought strange that I should write a preface to a memoir of a conspicuous adversary, I reply that the Civil War is only a memory, its asperities are forgotten, both armies were American, old army friendships have been renewed and new army friendships have been formed among the combatants, the truth of history is dear to all of us, and the amenities of chivalrous manhood are cherished alike by the North and the South, when justice to either is involved. Longstreet's splendid record as a soldier needs neither apologies nor eulogium. And if I venture, further along in this introduction, to defend him from unfair criticism, it is because my personal knowledge of the battle of July 2, 1863, qualifies me to testify in his behalf. It was the fortune of my corps to meet Longstreet on many great fields. It is now my privilege to offer a tribute to his memory. As Colonel Damas says in "The Lady of Lyons," after his duel with Melnotte, "It's astonishing how much I like a man after I've fought with him."

Often adversaries on the field of battle, we became good friends after peace was restored. He supported President Grant and his successors in their wise policy of restoration. Longstreet's example was the rainbow of reconciliation that foreshadowed real peace between the North and South. He drew the fire of the irreconcilable South. His statesmanlike forecast blazed the path of progress and prosperity for his people, impoverished by war and discouraged by adversity. He was the first of the illustrious Southern war leaders to accept the result of the great conflict as final. He folded up forever the Confederate flag he had followed with supreme devotion, and thenceforth saluted the Stars and Stripes of the Union with unfaltering homage. He was the trusted servant of the republic in peace, as he had been its relentless foe in war. The friends of the Union became his friends, the enemies of the Union his enemies.

I trust I may be pardoned for relating an incident that reveals the sunny side of Longstreet's genial nature. When I visited Georgia, in March, 1892, I was touched by a call from the General, who came from Gainesville to Atlanta to welcome me to his State. On St. Patrick's Day we supped together as guests of the Irish Societies of Atlanta, at their banquet. We entered the hall arm in arm, about nine o'clock in the evening, and were received by some three hundred gentlemen, with the wildest and loudest "rebel yell" I had ever heard. When I rose to respond to a toast in honor of the Empire State of the North, Longstreet stood also and leaned with one arm on my shoulder, the better to hear what I had to say, and this was a signal for another outburst. I concluded my remarks by proposing—

"Health and long life to my old adversary, Lieutenant-General Longstreet,"

assuring the audience that, although the General did not often make speeches, he would sing the "Star-Spangled Banner." This was, indeed, a risky promise, as I had never heard the General sing. I was greatly relieved by his exclamation:

"Yes, I will sing it!"

And he did sing the song admirably, the company joining with much enthusiasm.

As the hour was late, and we had enjoyed quite a number of potations of hot Irish whiskey punch, we decided to go to our lodgings long before the end of the revel, which appeared likely to last until daybreak. When we descended to the street we were unable to find a carriage, but Longstreet proposed to be my guide; and, although the streets were dark and the walk a long one, we reached my hotel in fairly good form. Not wishing to be outdone in courtesy, I said—

"Longstreet, the streets of Atlanta are very dark and it is very late, and you are somewhat deaf and rather infirm; now I must escort you to your head-quarters."

"All right," said Longstreet; "come on and we'll have another handshake over the bloody chasm."

When we arrived at his stopping-place and were about to separate, as I supposed, he turned to me and said—

"Sickles, the streets of Atlanta are very dark and you are lame, and a stranger here, and do not know the way back to your hotel; I must escort you home."

"Come along, Longstreet," was my answer.

On our way to the hotel, I said to him—

"Old fellow, I hope you are sorry for shooting off my leg at Gettysburg. I suppose I will have to forgive you for it some day."

"Forgive me?" Longstreet exclaimed. "You ought to thank me for leaving you one leg to stand on, after the mean way you behaved to me at Gettysburg."

How often we performed escort duty for each other on that eventful night I have never been able to recall with precision; but I am quite sure that I shall never forget St. Patrick's Day in 1892, at Atlanta, Georgia, when Longstreet and I enjoyed the good Irish whiskey punch at the banquet of the Knights of St. Patrick.

Afterwards Longstreet and I met again, at Gettysburg, this time as the guests of John Russell Young, who had invited a number of his literary and journalistic friends to join us on the old battle-field. We rode in the same carriage. When I assisted the General in climbing up the rocky face of Round Top, he turned to me and said—

"Sickles, you can well afford to help me up here now, for if you had not kept me away so long from Round Top on the 2d of July, 1863, the war would have lasted longer than it did, and might have had a different ending."

As he said this, his stern, leonine face softened with a smile as sweet as a brother's.

We met in March, 1901, at the reception given to President McKinley on his second inauguration. In the midst of the great throng assembled on that occasion Longstreet and I had quite a reception of our own. He was accompanied on this occasion by Mrs.

Longstreet. Every one admired the blended courtliness and gallantry of the veteran hero towards the ladies who were presented to him and his charming wife.

At the West Point Centennial Longstreet and I sat together on the dais, near President Roosevelt, the Secretary of War, Mr. Root, and the commander of the army, Lieutenant-General Miles. Here among his fellow-graduates of the Military Academy, he received a great ovation from the vast audience that filled Cullum Hall. Again and again he was cheered, when he turned to me, exclaiming—

"Sickles, what are they all cheering about?"

"They are cheering you, General," was my reply.

Joy lighted up his countenance, the war was forgotten, and Longstreet was at home once more at West Point.

Again we stood upon the same platform, in Washington, on May 30—Memorial Day—1902. Together we reviewed, with President Roosevelt, the magnificent column of Union veterans that marched past the President's reviewing-stand. That evening Longstreet joined me in a visit to a thousand or more soldiers of the Third Army Corps, assembled in a tent near the White House. These veterans, with a multitude of their comrades, had come to Washington to commemorate another Memorial Day in the Capitol of the Nation. The welcome given him by this crowd of old soldiers, who had fought him with all their might again and again, on many battle-fields, could hardly have been more cordial if he had found himself in the midst of an equal number of his own command. His speech to the men was felicitous, and enthusiastically cheered. In an eloquent peroration he said, "I hope to live long enough to see my surviving comrades march side by side with the Union veterans along Pennsylvania Avenue, and then I will die happy." This was the last time I met Longstreet.

Longstreet was unjustly blamed for not attacking earlier in the day, on July 2, 1863, at Gettysburg. I can answer that criticism, as I know more about the matter than the critics. If he had attacked in the morning, as it is said he should have done, he would have encountered Buford's division of cavalry, five thousand sabres, on his flank, and my corps would have been in his front, as it was in the afternoon. In a word, all the troops that opposed Longstreet in the afternoon, including the Fifth Army Corps and Caldwell's division of the Second Corps, would have been available on the left flank of the Union army in the morning. Every regiment and every battery that fired a shot in the afternoon was on the field in the morning, and would have resisted an assault in the morning as stubbornly as in the afternoon. Moreover, if the assault had been made in the morning, Law's strong brigade of Alabamians could not have assisted in the attack, as they did not arrive on the field until noon. On the other hand, if Lee had waited an hour later, I would have been on Cemetery Ridge, in compliance with General Meade's orders, and Longstreet could have marched, unresisted, from Seminary Ridge to the foot of Round Top, and might, perhaps, have unlimbered his guns on the summit.

General Meade's telegram to Halleck, dated 3 P.M., July 2, does not indicate that Lee was then about to attack him. At the time that despatch was sent, a council of corps commanders was assembled at General Meade's head-quarters. It was broken up by the sound of Longstreet's artillery. The probability is that Longstreet's attack held the Union army at Gettysburg. If Longstreet had waited until a later hour, the Union army might have been moving towards Pipe Creek, the position chosen by General Meade on June 30.

The best proof that Lee was not dissatisfied with Longstreet's movements on July 2 is the fact that Longstreet was intrusted with the command of the column of attack on July 3—Lee's last hope at Gettysburg. Of the eleven brigades that assaulted the Union left center on July 3, only three of them—Pickett's division—belonged to Longstreet's corps, the other eight brigades belonged to Hill's corps. If Longstreet had disappointed Lee on July 2, why would Lee, on the next day, give Longstreet a command of supreme importance, of which more than two-thirds of the troops were taken from another corps commander?

Longstreet did not look for success on July 3. He told General Lee that "the fifteen thousand men who could make a successful assault over that field had never been arrayed for battle," and yet the command was given to Longstreet. Why? Because the confidence of Lee in Longstreet was unshaken; because he regarded Longstreet as his most capable lieutenant.

Longstreet was never censured for the failure of the assault on July 3, although General Lee intimates, in his official report, that it was not made as early in the day as was expected. Why, then, is Longstreet blamed by them for the failure on July 2, when no fault was found by General Lee with Longstreet's dispositions on that day? The failure of both assaults must be attributed to insurmountable obstacles, which no commander could have overcome with the force at Longstreet's disposal—seventeen thousand men on July 2, and fifteen thousand men on July 3, against thirty thousand adversaries!

In General Lee's official report not a word appears about any delay in Longstreet's movements on July 2, although, referring to the assault of July 3, General Lee says, "General Longstreet's dispositions were not completed as early as was expected." If General Lee did not hesitate to point out unlooked for delay on July 3, why was he silent about delay on July 2? His silence about delay on July 2 implies that there was none on July 2. *Expresio unius exclusio alterius.*

General Lee says, in his report, referring to July 3—

"General Longstreet was delayed by a force occupying the high, rocky hills on the enemy's extreme left, from which his troops could be attacked in reverse as they advanced. His operations had been embarrassed the day previous by the same cause, and he now deemed it necessary to defend his flank and rear with the divisions of Hood and McLaws."

Another embarrassment prevented an earlier attack on July 2. It was the plan of General Lee to surprise the left flank of the Union army. General Lee ordered Captain Johnson, the engineer officer of his staff, to conduct Longstreet's column by a route concealed from the enemy. But the formation and movements of the attacking column had been discovered by my reconnoissance; this exposure put an end to any chance of surprise. Other dispositions became necessary; fresh orders from head-quarters were asked for; another line of advance had to be found, less exposed to view. All this took time. These circumstances were, of course, known to General Lee; hence he saw no reason to reproach Longstreet for delay.

The situation on the left flank of the Union army was entirely changed by my advance to the Emmitsburg road. Fitzhugh Lee says, "Lee was deceived by it and gave orders to attack up the Emmitsburg road, partially enveloping the enemy's left; there was much behind Sickles." The obvious purpose of my advance was to hold Lee's force in check until General Meade could bring his reserves from his right flank, at Rock Creek, to the Round Tops, on the left. Fortunately for me, General Lee believed that my line from the Peach-Orchard north—about a division front—was all Longstreet would have to deal with. Longstreet soon discovered that my left rested beyond Devil's Den, about twelve hundred yards easterly from the Emmitsburg road, and at a right angle to it. Of course, Longstreet could not push forward to Lee's objective—the Emmitsburg road ridge— leaving this force on his flank and rear, to take him in reverse. An obstinate conflict followed, which detained Longstreet until the Fifth Corps, which had been in reserve on the Union right, moved to the left and got into position on the Round Tops. Thus it happened that my salient at the Peach-Orchard, on the Emmitsburg road, was not attacked until six o'clock, the troops on my line, from the Emmitsburg road to the Devil's Den, having held their positions until that hour. The surprise Lee had planned was turned upon himself. The same thing would have happened if Longstreet had attacked in the morning; all the troops that resisted Longstreet in the afternoon—say thirty thousand—would have opposed him in the forenoon.

The alignment of the Union forces on the left flank at 11 A.M., when Lee gave his preliminary orders to Longstreet for the attack, was altogether different from the dispositions made by me at 3 P.M., when the attack was begun. At eleven in the morning my command was on Cemetery Ridge, to the left of Hancock. At two o'clock in the afternoon, anticipating General Lee's attack, I changed front, deploying my left division (Birney's) from Plum Run, near the base of Little Round Top, to the Peach-Orchard, at the intersection of Millerstown and Emmitsburg roads. My right division (Humphrey's) was moved forward to the Emmitsburg road, its left connecting with Birney at the Orchard, and its right *en echelon* with Hancock, parallel with the Codori House.

Longstreet was ordered to conceal his column of attack, for which the ground on Lee's right afforded excellent opportunities. Lee's plan was a repetition of Jackson's attack on the right flank of the Union army at Chancellorsville. In the afternoon, however, in view of the advance of my corps, General Lee was obliged to form a new plan of battle. As he believed that both of my flanks rested on the Emmitsburg road, Lee directed Longstreet to envelop my left at the Peach-Orchard, and press the attack northward "up the Emmitsburg road."

Colonel Fairfax, of Longstreet's staff, says that Lee and Longstreet were together at three o'clock, when the attack began. Lieutenant-General Hill, commanding the First Corps of Lee's army, says in his report—

> *"The corps of General Longstreet (McLaws's and Hood's divisions) was on my right, and in a line very nearly at right angles to mine. General Longstreet was to attack the left flank of the enemy, and sweep down his line, and I was ordered to co-operate with him with such of my brigades from the right as could join in with his troops in the attack. On the extreme right, Hood commenced the attack about two o'clock, McLaws about 5.30 o'clock."*

Longstreet was not long in discovering, by his artillery practice, that my position at the Peach-Orchard was a salient, and that my left flank really rested twelve hundred yards eastward, at Plum Run, in the valley between Little Round Top and the Devil's Den, concealed from observation by woods; my line extended to the high ground along the Emmitsburg road, from which Lee says, "It was thought our artillery could be used to advantage in assailing the more elevated ground beyond."

General J. B. Hood's story of his part in the battle of July 2, taken from a communication addressed to General Longstreet, which appears in Hood's "Advance and Retreat," pages 57–59, is a clear narrative of the movements of Longstreet's assaulting column. It emphasizes the firm adherence of Longstreet to the orders of General Lee. Again and again, as Hood plainly points out, Longstreet refused to listen to Hood's appeal for leave to turn Round Top and assail the Union rear, always replying, "General Lee's orders are to attack up the Emmitsburg road."

These often repeated orders of General Lee to "attack up the Emmitsburg road" could not have been given until near three in the afternoon of July 2, because before that hour there was no Union line of battle on the Emmitsburg road. There had been only a few of my pickets there in the morning, thrown forward by the First Massachusetts Infantry. It distinctly appears that Lee rejected Longstreet's plan to turn the Federal left on Cemetery Ridge. And Hood makes it plain enough that Longstreet refused to listen to Hood's appeal for permission to turn Round Top, on the main Federal line, always replying, "No; General Lee's orders are to attack up the Emmitsburg road." Of course, that plan of battle was not formed until troops had been placed in positions commanding that road. This, we have seen, was not done until towards three in the afternoon.

The only order of battle announced by General Lee on July 2 of which there is any record was to assail my position on the Emmitsburg road, turn my left flank (which he erroneously supposed to rest on the Peach-Orchard), and sweep the attack "up the Emmitsburg road." This was impossible until I occupied that road, and it was then that Longstreet's artillery began its practice on my advanced line.

I am unable to see how any just person can charge Longstreet with deviation from the orders of General Lee on July 2. It is true enough that Longstreet had advised different tactics; but he was a soldier—a West Pointer—and once he had indicated his own views, he obeyed the orders of the general commanding—he did not even exercise the discretion allowed to the chief of a *corps d'armée*, which permits him to modify instructions when an unforeseen emergency imposes fresh responsibilities, or when an unlooked-for opportunity offers tempting advantages.

We have seen that many circumstances required General Lee to modify his plans and orders on July 2 between daybreak, when his first reconnoissance was made, and three o'clock in the afternoon, when my advanced position was defined. We have seen that if a morning attack had been made the column would have encountered Buford's strong division of cavalry on its flank, and that it would have been weakened by the absence of Law's brigade of Hood's division. We have seen that Longstreet, even in the afternoon, when Law had come up and Buford had been sent to Westminster, was still too weak to contend against the reinforcements sent against him. We have seen that Lee was present all day on July 2, and that his own staff-officer led the column of attack. We have seen that General Lee, in his official report, gives no hint of dissatisfaction with Longstreet's conduct of the battle of July 2, nor does it appear that Longstreet was ever afterwards criticized by Lee. On the contrary, Lee points out that the same danger to Longstreet's flank, which required the protection of two divisions on July 3, existed on July 2, when his flank was unsupported. We have seen that again and again, when Hood appealed to Longstreet for leave to swing his column to the right and turn the Round Tops, Longstreet as often refused, always saying, "No; General Lee's orders are to attack up the Emmitsburg road." The conclusion is irrefutable, that whilst the operations were directed with signal ability and sustained by heroic courage, the failure of both assaults, that of July 2 and the other of July 3, must be attributed to the lack of strength in the columns of attack on both days, for which the commanding general alone was responsible.

It was Longstreet's good fortune to live until he saw his country hold a high place among the great powers of the world. He saw the new South advancing in prosperity, hand in hand with the North, East, and West. He saw his people in the ranks of our army, in Cuba, Puerto Rico, the Philippines, China, and Panama; he saw the Union stars and the blue uniform worn by Fitzhugh Lee, and Butler, and Wheeler. He witnessed the fulfilment of his prediction—that the hearty reunion of the North and South would advance the welfare of both. He lived long enough to rejoice with all of us in a reunited nation, and to know that his name was honored wherever the old flag was unfurled. His fame as a soldier belongs to all Americans.

Farewell, Longstreet! I shall follow you very soon. May we meet in the happy realm where strife is unknown and friendship is eternal!

CHAPTER 17

The Clash of Ironclad Titans:

Merrimac vs. *Monitor*

By H. Ashton Ramsay, Major, C.S.A., Chief Engineer of the Merrimac

They were behemoths afloat—weird fortresses doing battle on the waters off Virginia. This is the story of the fateful day they met.

—LAMAR UNDERWOOD

THE *MERRIMAC* WAS BUILT IN 1856 AS A FULL-RIGGED WAR-FRIGATE, OF THIRTY-ONE hundred tons' burden, with auxiliary steam power to be used only in case of head winds. She was a hybrid from her birth, marking the transition from sails to steam as well as from wooden ships to ironclads. I became her second assistant engineer in Panama Bay in 1859, cruising in her around the Horn and back to Norfolk. Her chief engineer was Alban C. Stimers. Little did we dream that he was to be the right-hand man of Ericsson in the construction of the *Monitor*, while I was to hold a similar post in the conversion of our own ship into an ironclad, or that, in less than a year and a half, we would be seeking to destroy each other, he as chief engineer of the *Monitor* and I in the corresponding position on the *Merrimac*.

In the harbor of Rio on our return voyage we met the *Congress* and as we sailed away after coaling she fired a friendly salute and cheered us, and we responded with a will. When the two ships next met it was in one of the deadliest combats of naval history.

The machinery of the *Merrimac* was condemned, and she went out of commission on our return. She was still at Norfolk when the war broke out, and was set on fire by the Federals when Norfolk was evacuated. Some of the workmen in the navy-yard scuttled and sank her, thus putting out the flames. When she was raised by the Confederates she was nothing but a burned and blackened hulk.

Her charred upper works were cut away, and in the center a casement shield one hundred and eighty feet long was built of pitch-pine and oak, two feet thick. This was covered with iron plates, one to two inches thick and eight inches wide, bolted over each other and through and through the woodwork, giving a protective armor four inches in thickness. The shield sloped at an angle of about thirty-six degrees, and was covered with an iron grating that served as an upper deck. For fifty feet forward and aft her decks were submerged below the water, and the prow was shod with an iron beak to receive the impact when ramming.

Even naval officers were skeptical as to the result. The plates were rolled at the Tredegar mills at Richmond, and arrived so slowly that we were nearly a year in finishing her. We could have rolled them at Norfolk and built four *Merrimacs* in that time, had the South understood the importance of a navy at the outbreak of the war.

I remember that my old friend and comrade, Captain Charles MacIntosh, while awaiting orders, used to come over and stand on the granite curbing of the dock to watch the work as it crawled along.

"Good-by, Ramsay," he said, sadly, on the eve of starting to command a ram at New Orleans. "I shall never see you again. She will prove your coffin." A short time afterward the poor fellow had both legs shot from under him and died almost immediately.

Rifled guns were just coming into use, and Lieutenant Brooke, who designed the *Merrimac*, considered the question of having some of her guns rifled. How to procure such cannon was not easily discovered, as we had no foundries in the South. There were many cast-iron cannon that had fallen into our hands at Norfolk, and he conceived the idea of turning some of this ordnance into rifles. In order to enable them to stand the additional bursting strain we forged wrought-iron bands and shrank them over the chambers, and we devised a special tool for rifling the bore of the guns. They gave effective service.

Many details remained uncompleted when we were at last floated out of dry-dock, but there was great pressure for us to make some demonstration that might serve to check McClellan in his advance up the Peninsula.

The ship was still full of workmen hurrying her to completion when Commodore Franklin Buchanan arrived from Richmond one March morning and ordered every one out of the ship, except her crew of three hundred and fifty men which had been hastily drilled on shore in the management of the big guns, and directed Executive Officer Jones to prepare to sail at once.

At that time nothing was known of our destination. All we knew was that we were off at last. Buchanan sent for me. The veteran sailor, the beau ideal of a naval officer of the old school, with his tall form, harsh features, and clear, piercing eyes, was pacing the deck with a stride I found it difficult to match, although he was then over sixty and I but twenty-four.

"Ramsay," he asked, "what would happen to your engines and boilers if there should be a collision?"

"They are braced tight," I assured him. "Though the boilers stand fourteen feet, they are so securely fastened that no collision could budge them."

"I am going to ram the *Cumberland*," said my commander. "I'm told she has the new rifled guns, the only ones in their whole fleet we have cause to fear. The moment we are in the Roads I'm going to make right for her and ram her. How about your engines? They were in bad shape in the old ship, I understand. Can we rely on them? Should they be tested by a trial trip?"

"She will have to travel some ten miles down the river before we get to the Roads," I said. "If any trouble develops I'll report it. I think that will be sufficient trial trip."

I watched the machinery carefully as we sped down the Elizabeth River, and soon satisfied myself that all was well. Then I went on deck.

"How fast is she going do you think?" I asked one of the pilots.

"Eight or nine knots an hour," he replied, making a rapid calculation from objects ashore. The *Merrimac* as an ironclad was faster under steam than she had ever been before with her top hamper of masts and sails.

I presented myself to the commodore. "The machinery is all right, sir," I assured him.

Across the river at Newport News gleamed the batteries and white tents of the Federal camp and the vessels of the fleet blockading the mouth of the James, chief among them the *Congress* and the *Cumberland*, tall and stately, with every line and spar clearly defined against the blue March sky, their decks and ports bristling with guns, while the rigging of the *Cumberland* was gay with the red, white, and blue of sailors' garments hung out to dry.

As we rounded into view the white-winged sailing craft that sprinkled the bay and long lines of tugs and small boats scurried to the far shore like chickens on the approach of a hovering hawk. They had seen our black hulk which looked like the roof of a barn afloat. Suddenly huge volumes of smoke began to pour from the funnels of the frigates *Minnesota* and *Roanoke* at Old Point. They had seen us, too, and were getting up steam. Bright-colored signal flags were run up and down the masts of all the ships of the Federal fleet. The *Congress* shook out her topsails. Down came the clothes-line on the *Cumberland*, and boats were lowered and dropped astern.

Our crew was summoned to the gun-deck, and Buchanan addressed us: "Sailors, in a few minutes you will have the long-looked-for opportunity of showing your devotion to our cause. Remember that you are about to strike for your country and your homes. The Confederacy expects every man to do his duty. Beat to quarters." Every terse, burning word is engraved on my memory, though fifty years have passed since they were spoken.

Just as he had finished, the mess caterer touched my elbow and whispered: "Better get your lunch now, Mr. Ramsay. It will be your last chance. The galley-fires must be put out when the magazines are opened."

On my way I saw Assistant-Surgeon Garnett at a table laying out lint and surgical implements. I had no appetite, and merely tasted some cold tongue and a cup of coffee.

Passing along the gun-deck, I saw the pale and determined countenances of the guns' crews, as they stood motionless at their posts, with set lips unsmiling, contrasting with the careless expression of sailors when practiced at "fighting quarters" on a man-of-war. This was the real thing.

As we approached the Federal ships we were met by a veritable storm of shells which must have sunk any ship then afloat—except the *Merrimac*. They struck our sloping sides, were deflected upward to burst harmlessly in the air, or rolled down and fell hissing into the water, dashing the spray up into our ports.

As we drew nearer the *Cumberland*, above the roar of battle rang the voice of Buchanan, "Do you surrender?"

"Never!" retorted the gallant Morris.

The crux of what followed was down in the engine-room. Two gongs, the signal to stop, were quickly followed by three, the signal to reverse.

There was an ominous pause, then a crash, shaking us all off our feet. The engines labored. The vessel was shaken in every fiber. Our bow was visibly depressed. We seemed to be bearing down with a weight on our prow. Thud, thud, thud, came the rain of shot on our shield from the double-decked battery of the *Congress*. There was a terrible crash in the fire-room. For a moment we thought one of the boilers had burst. No, it was the explosion of a shell in our stack. Was any one hit? No, thank God! The firemen had been warned to keep away from the up-take, so the fragments of shell fell harmlessly on the iron floor-plates.

We had rushed on the doomed ship, relentless as fate, crashing through her barricade of heavy spars and torpedo fenders, striking her below her starboard fore-chains, and crushing far into her. For a moment the whole weight of her hung on our prow and threatened to carry us down with her, the return wave of the collision curling up into our bow port.

The *Cumberland* began to sink slowly, bow first, but continued to fight desperately for the forty minutes that elapsed after her doom was sealed, while we were engaged with both the *Cumberland* and the *Congress* being right between them.

We had left our cast-iron beak in the side of the *Cumberland*. Like the wasp, we could sting but once, leaving it in the wound.

Our smoke-stack was riddled, our flag was shot down several times, and was finally secured to a rent in the stack. On our gun-deck the men were fighting like demons. There was no thought or time for the wounded and dying as they tugged away at their guns, training and sighting their pieces while the orders rang out, "Sponge, load, fire!"

"The muzzle of our gun has been shot away," cried one of the gunners.

"No matter, keep on loading and firing—do the best you can with it," replied Lieutenant Jones.

"Keep away from the side ports, don't lean against the shield, look out for the sharpshooters," rang the warnings. Some of our men who failed to heed them and leaned against the shield were stunned and carried below, bleeding at the ears. All were full of courage and worked with a will; they were so begrimed with powder that they looked like negroes.

"Pass along the cartridges."

"More powder."

"A shell for number six."

"A wet wad for the hot-shot gun."

"Put out that pipe and don't light it again on peril of your life."

Such were the directions and commands, issued like clockwork amid the confusion of battle. Our executive officer seemed to be in a dozen places at once.

This gives some faint notion of the scene passing behind our grim iron casement, which to the beholders without seemed a machine of destruction. Human hearts were beating and bleeding there. Human lives were being sacrificed. Pain, death, wounds, glory—that was the sum of it.

On the doomed ship *Cumberland* the battle raged with equal fury. The sanded deck was red and slippery with blood. Delirium seized the crew. They stripped to their trousers, kicked off their shoes, tied handkerchiefs about their heads, and fought and cheered as their ship sank beneath their feet. Then the order came, "All save who can." There was a scramble for the spar-deck and a rush overboard. The ship listed. The after pivot-gun broke loose and rushed down the decline like a furious animal, rolling over a man as it bounded overboard, leaving a mass of mangled flesh on deck.

We now turned to the *Congress*, which had tried to escape but had grounded, and the battle raged once more, broadside upon broadside, delivered at close range, the *Merrimac* working closer all the time with her bow pointed as if to ram the *Congress*. A shell from Lieutenant Wood's gun sped through their line of powder-passers, not only cutting down the men, but exploding the powder buckets in their hands, spreading death and destruction and setting fire to the ship.

At last came the order, "Cease firing."

"The *Congress* has surrendered," some one cried. "Look out of the port. See, she has run up white flags. The officers are waving their handkerchiefs."

At this several of the officers started to leave their posts and rush on deck, but Lieutenant Jones in his stentorian voice sang out: "Stand by your guns, and, lieutenants, be ready to resume firing at the word. See that your guns are well supplied with ammunition during the lull. Dr. Garnett, see how those poor fellows yonder are coming on. Mr. Littlepage, tell Paymaster Semple to have a care of the berth-deck and use every precaution against fire. Mr. Hasker, call away the cutter's crew and have them in readiness. Mr. Lindsay [to the carpenter], sound the well, examine the forehold, and report if you find anything wrong."

Such was Catesby Ap. R. Jones, the executive officer of the *Merrimac*.

When it was fully evident that there was to be a suspension of hostilities, and these details had all been attended to, several of the officers went to stand beside Buchanan on the upper grating.

The whole scene was changed. A pall of black smoke hung about the ships and obscured the clean-cut outlines of the shore. Down the river were the three frigates *St. Lawrence*, *Roanoke*, and *Minnesota*, also enveloped in the clouds of battle that now and then reflected the crimson lightnings of the god of war. The masts of the *Cumberland* were protruding above the water. The *Congress* presented a terrible scene of carnage.

The gunboats *Beaufort* and *Raleigh* were signaled to take off the wounded and fire the ship. They were driven away by sharpshooters on shore, who suddenly turned their fire on us, notwithstanding the white flag of the *Congress*. Buchanan fell, severely wounded in the groin.

As he was being carried below he said to Executive Officer Jones: "Plug hot shot into her and don't leave her until she's afire. They must look after their own wounded, since they won't let us"—a characteristic command when it is remembered that his own brother, McKean Buchanan, was paymaster of the *Congress* and might have been numbered among the wounded.

We had kept two furnaces for the purpose of heating shot. They were rolled into the flames on a grating, rolled out into iron buckets, hoisted to the gun-deck, and rolled into the guns, which had been prepared with wads of wet hemp. Then the gun would be touched off quickly and the shot sent on its errand of destruction.

Leaving the *Congress* wrapped in sheets of flame, we made for the three other frigates. The *St. Lawrence* and *Roanoke* had run aground, but were pulled off by tugs and made their escape. The *Minnesota* was not so fortunate, but we drew twenty-three feet of water and could not get near enough to destroy her, while our guns could not be elevated owing to the narrow embrasures, and their range was only a mile; so we made for our moorings at Sewall's Point.

All the evening we stood on deck watching the brilliant display of the burning ship. Every part of her was on fire at the same time, the red-tongued flames running up shrouds, masts, and stays, and extending out to the yard-arms. She stood in bold relief against the black background, lighting up the Roads and reflecting her lurid lights on the bosom of the now placid and hushed waters. Every now and then the flames would reach one of the loaded cannon and a shell would hiss at random through the darkness. About midnight came the grand finale. The magazines exploded, shooting up a huge column of firebrands hundreds of feet in the air, and then the burning hulk burst asunder and melted into the waters, while the calm night spread her sable mantle over Hampton Roads.

The *Monitor* arrived during the evening and anchored under the stern of the *Minnesota*, her lighter draught enabling her to do so without danger. To us the ensuing engagement was in the nature of a surprise. If we had known we were to meet her we would have at least been supplied with solid shot for our rifled guns. We might even have thought best to wait until our iron beak, lost in the side of the *Cumberland*, could be replaced. Buchanan was incapacitated by his wound, and the command devolved upon Lieutenant Jones.

We left our anchorage shortly before eight o'clock next morning and steamed across and up stream toward the *Minnesota*, thinking to make short work of her and soon return with her colors trailing under ours. We approached her slowly, feeling our way cautiously along the edge of the channel, when suddenly, to our astonishment, a black object that looked like the historic description, "a barrel-head afloat with a cheese-box on top of it," moved slowly out from under the *Minnesota* and boldly confronted us. It must be confessed that both ships were queer-looking craft, as grotesque to the eyes of the men of '62 as they would appear to those of the present generation.

And now the great fight was on, a fight the like of which the world had never seen. With the battle of yesterday old methods had passed away, and with them the experience of a thousand years "of battle and of breeze" was brought to naught.

We hovered about each other in spirals, gradually contracting the circuits until we were within point-blank range, but our shell glanced from the *Monitor's* turret just as hers did from our sloping sides. For two hours the cannonade continued without perceptible damage to either of the combatants.

On our gun-deck all was bustle, smoke, grimy figures, and stern commands, while down in the engine and boiler rooms the sixteen furnaces were belching out fire and smoke, and the firemen standing in front of them, like so many gladiators, tugged away with devil's-claw and slice-bar, inducing by their exertions more and more intense combustion and heat. The noise of the cracking, roaring fires, escaping steam, and the loud and labored pulsations of the engines, together with the roar of battle above and the thud and vibration of the huge masses of iron which were hurled against us produced a scene and sound to be compared only with the poet's picture of the lower regions.

And then an accident occurred that threatened our utter destruction. We stuck fast aground on a sand-bar.

Our situation was critical. The *Monitor* could, at her leisure, come close up to us and yet be out of our reach, owing to our inability to deflect our guns. In she came and began to sound every chink in our armor—every one but that which was actually vulnerable, had she known it.

The coal consumption of the two days' fight had lightened our prow until our unprotected submerged deck was almost awash. The armor on our sides below the water-line had been extended but about three feet, owing to our hasty departure before the work was finished. Lightened as we were, these exposed portions rendered us no longer an ironclad, and the *Monitor* might have pierced us between wind and water had she depressed her guns.

Fearing that she might discover our vulnerable "heel of Achilles" we had to take all chances. We lashed down the safety valves, heaped quick-burning combustibles into the already raging fires, and brought the boilers to a pressure that would have been unsafe under ordinary circumstances. The propeller churned the mud and water furiously, but the ship did not stir. We piled on oiled cotton waste, splints of wood, anything that would burn faster than coal. It seemed impossible that the boilers could stand the pressure we were crowding upon them. Just as we were beginning to despair there was a perceptible movement, and the *Merrimac* slowly dragged herself off the shoal by main strength. We were saved.

Before our adversary saw that we were again afloat we made a dash for her, catching her quite unprepared, and tried to ram her, but our commander was dubious about the result of a collision without our iron-shod beak, and gave the signal to reverse the engines long before we reached the *Monitor*. As a result I did not feel the slightest shock down in the engine-room, though we struck her fairly enough.

The carpenter reported that the effect was to spring a leak forward. Lieutenant Jones sent for me and asked me about it.

"It is impossible we can be making much water," I replied, "for the skin of the vessel is plainly visible in the crank-pits."

A second time he sent for me and asked if we were making any water in the engine-room.

"With the two large Worthington pumps, besides the bilge injections, we could keep her afloat for hours, even with a ten-inch shell in her hull," I assured him, repeating that there was no water in the engine and boiler rooms.

We glided past, leaving the *Monitor* unscathed, but got between her and the *Minnesota* and opened fire on the latter. The *Monitor* gallantly rushed to her rescue, passing so close under our submerged stern that she almost snapped off our propeller. As she was passing, so near that we could have leaped aboard her, Lieutenant Wood trained the stern-gun on her when she was only twenty yards from its muzzle and delivered a rifle-pointed shell which dislodged the iron logs sheltering the *Monitor*'s conning-tower, carrying away the steering-gear and signal apparatus, and blinding Captain Worden. It was a mistake to place the conning-tower so far from the turret and the vitals of the ship. Since that time it has been located over the turret. The *Monitor*'s turret was a death-trap. It was only twenty feet in diameter, and every shot knocked off bolt-heads and sent them flying against the gunners. If one of them barely touched the side of the turret he would be stunned and momentarily paralyzed. Lieutenant Greene had been taken below in a dazed condition and never fully recovered from the effects. One of the port shutters had been jammed, putting a gun out of commission, and there was nothing for the *Monitor* to do but to retreat and leave the *Minnesota* to her fate.

Captain Van Brunt, of the latter vessel, thought he was now doomed and was preparing to fire his ship when he saw the *Merrimac* also withdrawing toward Norfolk.

It was at this juncture that Lieutenant Jones had sent for me and said: "The pilots will not place us nearer to the *Minnesota*, and we cannot afford to run the risk of getting aground again. I'm going to haul off under the guns of Sewall's Point and renew the attack on the rise of the tide. Bank your fires and make any necessary adjustments to the machinery, but be prepared to start up again later in the afternoon."

I went below to comply with his instructions, and later was astonished to hear cheering. Rushing on deck, I found we were passing Craney Island on our way to Norfolk, and were being cheered by the soldiers of the battery.

Our captain had consulted with some of his lieutenants. He explained afterward that as the *Monitor* had proved herself so formidable an adversary he had thought best to get a supply of solid shot, have the prow replaced, the port shutters put on, the armor belt extended below water, and the guns whose muzzles had been shot away replaced, and then renew the engagement with every chance of victory. I remember feeling as though a wet blanket had been thrown over me. His reasoning was doubtless good, but it ignored the moral effect of leaving the Roads without forcing the *Minnesota* to surrender.

As the *Merrimac* passed up the river, trailing the ensign of the *Congress* under the stars and bars, she received a tremendous ovation from the crowds that lined the shores, while hundreds of small boats, gay with flags and bunting, converted our course into a triumphal procession.

We went into dry-dock that very afternoon, and in about three weeks were ready to renew the battle upon more advantageous terms, but the *Monitor*, though reinforced by two other ironclads, the *Galena* and the *Naugatuck*, and every available vessel of the United States Navy, was under orders from Washington to refuse our challenge and bottle us up in the Roads. This strategy filled us with rage and dismay, but it proved very effective.

Our new commander, Commodore Josiah Tatnall, was burning to distinguish himself, but he was under orders not to risk the destruction or capture of the *Merrimac* by leaving the Roads, as General Huger's division at Norfolk would then be at the mercy of the Federal fleet. Week after week was passing and with it his golden opportunity. At last we went to Richmond and pressed a plan for a sortie upon the President. He returned one afternoon and ordered every one aboard. That night we slipped down the Roads and were soon passing Fort Monroe on our way out into the Chesapeake.

Presently our army signal officer began waving his lantern communicating with our distant batteries, and then told the result to Officer Jones, who reported to Tatnall. "We have been ordered to return, sir," he said.

Tatnall was viewing the dim outlines of the fort through his glass and pretended not to hear.

"The order is peremptory," repeated Jones.

Tatnall hesitated. He was of half a mind to disobey. "Old Huger has outwitted me," he muttered. "Do what you please. I leave you in command. I'm going to bed," and he went below in a high dudgeon. Tatnall was a striking-looking man, standing over six feet, with florid complexion, deep-sunken blue eyes, and a protruding under lip. That he did not have a chance to fight was no fault of his.

Our life on board for the weeks that followed was far from comfortable. We were within sight of the enemy, and at every movement of the opposing fleet it was "clear away for action." Steam was kept up continually. Our cabins were without air ports and no ray of light even penetrated the ward-rooms. There was nowhere to walk but on the upper grating—a modern prison is far more comfortable. Sometimes the sailors waded on the submerged deck, giving rise to the superstition among the darkies that they were the crew of the "debble ship" with power to walk on the water.

Norfolk was now being evacuated and we were covering Huger's retreat. When this was effected we were to receive the signal and to make our own way up the James. Norfolk was in Federal hands, and Huger had disappeared without signaling us, when our pilots informed us that Harrison's Bar, which we must cross, drew only eighteen feet of water. Under their advice, on the night of May 11th we lightened ship by throwing overboard all our coal and ballast, thus raising our unprotected decks above water. At last all was ready—and then we found that the wind which had been blowing down-stream all day had swept the water off the bar. When morning dawned the Federal fleet must discover our defenseless condition, and defeat and capture were certain, for we were now no longer an ironclad.

It was decided to abandon the vessel and set her on fire. We took the *Merrimac* to the bight of Craney Island, and about midnight the work of disembarking the crew began. We had but two boats, and it was sunrise before our three hundred and fifty men were all ashore. Cotton waste and trains of powder were strewn about the deck, and Executive Officer Jones, who was the last to leave the ship, applied the slow match. Then we marched silently through the woods to join Huger, fifteen miles away at Suffolk.

Still unconquered, we hauled down our drooping colors, their laurels all fresh and green, with mingled pride and grief, gave her to the flames, and set the lambent fires roaring about the shotted guns. The slow match, the magazine, and that last, deep, low, sullen, mournful boom told our people, now far away on the march, that their gallant ship was no more.

CHAPTER 18

The Flag Bearer

By Theodore Roosevelt

Politician, hunter, naturalist, explorer, soldier—all these words describe our twenty-sixth president. He was also a prodigious writer, producing scores of volumes. This gem is from the book Hero Tales from American History, *which he coauthored with the distinguished senator and historian Henry Cabot Lodge.*

—LAMAR UNDERWOOD

Mine eyes have seen the glory of the coming of the Lord;
He is trampling out the vintage where the grapes of wrath are stored;
He hath loosed the fateful lightning of His terrible swift sword;
His truth is marching on.

I have seen Him in the watch-fires of a hundred circling camps;
They have builded Him an altar in the evening dews and damps;
I can read his righteous sentence by the dim and flaring lamps;
His day is marching on.

He has sounded forth the trumpet that shall never beat retreat;
He is sifting out the hearts of men before his judgment seat;
Oh! be swift, my soul, to answer him! be jubilant, my feet!
Our God is marching on.
—Julia Ward Howe

IN NO WAR SINCE THE CLOSE OF THE GREAT NAPOLEONIC STRUGGLES HAS THE FIGHTING been so obstinate and bloody as in the Civil War. Much has been said in song and story of the resolute courage of the Guards at Inkerman, of the charge of the Light Brigade, and of the terrible fighting and loss of the German armies at Mars La Tour and Gravelotte.

The praise bestowed, upon the British and Germans for their valor, and for the loss that proved their valor, was well deserved; but there were over one hundred and twenty regiments, Union and Confederate, each of which, in some one battle of the Civil War, suffered a greater loss than any English regiment at Inkerman or at any other battle in the Crimea, a greater loss than was suffered by any German regiment at Gravelotte or at any other battle of the Franco-Prussian war. No European regiment in any recent struggle has suffered such losses as at Gettysburg befell the 1st Minnesota, when 82 per cent. of the officers and men were killed and wounded; or the 141st Pennsylvania, which lost 76 per cent.; or the 26th North Carolina, which lost 72 per cent.; such as at the second battle of Manassas befell the 101st New York, which lost 74 per cent., and the 21st Georgia, which lost 76 per cent. At Cold Harbor the 25th Massachusetts lost 70 per cent., and the 10th Tennessee at Chickamauga 68 per cent.; while at Shiloh the 9th Illinois lost 63 per cent., and the 6th Mississippi 70 per cent.; and at Antietam the 1st Texas lost 82 percent. The loss of the Light Brigade in killed and wounded in its famous charge at Balaklava was but 37 per cent.

These figures show the terrible punishment endured by these regiments, chosen at random from the head of the list which shows the slaughter-roll of the Civil War. Yet the shattered remnants of each regiment preserved their organization, and many of the severest losses were incurred in the hour of triumph, and not of disaster. Thus, the 1st Minnesota, at Gettysburg, suffered its appalling loss while charging a greatly superior force, which it drove before it; and the little huddle of wounded and unwounded men who survived their victorious charge actually kept both the flag they had captured and the ground from which they had driven their foes.

A number of the Continental regiments under Washington, Greene, and Wayne did valiant fighting and endured heavy punishment. Several of the regiments raised on the northern frontier in 1814 showed, under Brown and Scott, that they were able to meet the best troops of Britain on equal terms in the open, and even to overmatch them in fair fight with the bayonet. The regiments which, in the Mexican war, under the lead of Taylor, captured Monterey, and beat back Santa Anna at Buena Vista, or which, with Scott as commander, stormed Molino Del Rey and Chapultepec, proved their ability to bear terrible loss, to wrest victory from overwhelming numbers, and to carry by open assault positions of formidable strength held by a veteran army. But in none of these three wars was the fighting so resolute and bloody as in the Civil War.

Countless deeds of heroism were performed by Northerner and by Southerner, by officer and by private, in every year of the great struggle. The immense majority of these deeds went unrecorded, and were known to few beyond the immediate participants. Of those that were noticed it would be impossible even to make a dry catalogue in ten such volumes as this. All that can be done is to choose out two or three acts of heroism, not as exceptions, but as examples of hundreds of others. The times of war are iron times, and bring out all that is best as well as all that is basest in the human heart. In a full recital of the civil war, as of every other great conflict, there would stand out in naked relief feats of wonderful daring and self-devotion, and, mixed among them, deeds of cowardice, of treachery, of barbarous brutality. Sadder still, such a recital would show strange contrasts in the careers of individual men, men who at one time acted well and nobly, and at another time ill and basely. The ugly truths must not be blinked, and the lessons they teach should be set forth by every historian, and learned by every statesman and soldier; but, for our good fortune, the lessons best worth learning in the nation's past are lessons of heroism.

From immemorial time the armies of every warlike people have set the highest value upon the standards they bore to battle. To guard one's own flag against capture is the pride, to capture the flag of one's enemy the ambition, of every valiant soldier. In consequence, in every war between peoples of good military record, feats of daring performed by color-bearers are honorably common. The Civil War was full of such incidents. Out of very many two or three may be mentioned as noteworthy.

One occurred at Fredericksburg on the day when half the brigades of Meagher and Caldwell lay on the bloody slope leading up to the Confederate entrenchments. Among the assaulting regiments was the 5th New Hampshire, and it lost one hundred and eighty-six out of three hundred men who made the charge. The survivors fell sullenly back behind a fence, within easy range of the Confederate rifle-pits. Just before reaching it the last of the color guard was shot, and the flag fell in the open. A Captain Perry instantly ran out to rescue it, and as he reached it was shot through the heart; another, Captain Murray, made the same attempt and was also killed; and so was a third, Moore. Several private soldiers met a like fate. They were all killed close to the flag, and their dead bodies fell across one another. Taking advantage of this breastwork, Lieutenant Nettleton crawled from behind the fence to the colors, seized them, and bore back the blood-won trophy.

Another took place at Gaines' Mill, where Gregg's 1st South Carolina formed part of the attacking force. The resistance was desperate, and the fury of the assault unsurpassed. At one point it fell to the lot of this regiment to bear the brunt of carrying a certain strong position. Moving forward at a run, the South Carolinians were swept by a fierce and searching fire. Young James Taylor, a lad of sixteen, was carrying the flag, and was killed after being shot down three times, twice rising and struggling onward with the colors. The third time he fell the flag was seized by George Cotchet, and when he, in turn, fell, by Shubrick Hayne. Hayne was also struck down almost immediately, and the fourth lad, for none of them were over twenty years old, grasped the colors, and fell mortally wounded across the body of his friend. The fifth, Gadsden Holmes, was pierced with no less than seven balls. The sixth man, Dominick Spellman, more fortunate, but not less brave, bore the flag throughout the rest of the battle.

Yet another occurred at Antietam. The 7th Maine, then under the command of Major T. W. Hyde, was one of the hundreds of regiments that on many hard-fought fields established a reputation for dash and unyielding endurance. Toward the early part of the day at Antietam it merely took its share in the charging and long-range firing, together with the New York and Vermont regiments which were its immediate neighbors in the line. The fighting was very heavy. In one of the charges, the Maine men passed over what had been a Confederate regiment. The gray-clad soldiers were lying, both ranks, privates and officers, as they fell, for so many had been killed or disabled that it seemed as if the whole regiment was prone in death.

Much of the time the Maine men lay on the battle-field, hugging the ground, under a heavy artillery fire, but beyond the reach of ordinary musketry. One of the privates, named Knox, was a wonderful shot, and had received permission to use his own special rifle, a weapon accurately sighted for very long range. While the regiment thus lay under the storm of shot and shell, he asked leave to go to the front; and for an hour afterward his companions heard his rifle crack every few minutes. Major Hyde finally, from curiosity, crept forward to see what he was doing, and found that he had driven every man away from one section of a Confederate battery, tumbling over gunner after gunner as they came forward to fire. One of his victims was a general officer, whose horse he killed. At the end of an hour or so, a piece of shell took off the breech of his pet rifle, and he returned disconsolate; but after a few minutes he gathered three rifles that were left by wounded men, and went back again to his work.

At five o'clock in the afternoon the regiment was suddenly called upon to undertake a hopeless charge, owing to the blunder of the brigade commander, who was a gallant veteran of the Mexican war, but who was also given to drink. Opposite the Union lines at this point were some haystacks, near a group of farm buildings. They were right in the center of the Confederate position, and sharpshooters stationed among them were picking off the Union gunners. The brigadier, thinking that they were held by but a few skirmishers, rode to where the 7th Maine was lying on the ground, and said: "Major Hyde, take your regiment and drive the enemy from those trees and buildings." Hyde saluted, and said that he had seen a large force of rebels go in among the buildings, probably two brigades in all. The brigadier answered, "Are you afraid to go, sir?" and repeated the order emphatically. "Give the order, so the regiment can hear it, and we are ready, sir," said Hyde. This was done, and "Attention" brought every man to his feet. With the regiment were two young boys who carried the marking guidons, and Hyde ordered these to the rear. They pretended to go, but as soon as the regiment charged came along with it. One of them lost his arm, and the other was killed on the field. The colors were carried by the color corporal, Harry Campbell.

Hyde gave the orders to left face and forward and the Maine men marched out in front of a Vermont regiment which lay beside them; then, facing to the front, they crossed a sunken road, which was so filled with dead and wounded Confederates that Hyde's horse had to step on them to get over.

Once across, they stopped for a moment in the trampled corn to straighten the line, and then charged toward the right of the barns. On they went at the double-quick, fifteen skirmishers ahead under Lieutenant Butler, Major Hyde on the right on his Virginia thoroughbred, and Adjutant Haskell to the left on a big white horse. The latter was shot down at once, as was his horse, and Hyde rode round in front of the regiment just in time to see a long line of men in gray rise from behind the stone wall of the Hagerstown pike, which was to their right, and pour in a volley; but it mostly went too high. He then ordered his men to left oblique.

Just as they were abreast a hill to the right of the barns, Hyde, being some twenty feet ahead, looked over its top and saw several regiments of Confederates, jammed close together and waiting at the ready; so he gave the order left flank, and, still at the double quick, took his column past the barns and buildings toward an orchard on the hither side, hoping that he could get them back before they were cut off, for they were faced by ten times their number. By going through the orchard he expected to be able to take advantage of a hollow, and partially escape the destructive flank fire on his return.

To hope to keep the barns from which they had driven the sharpshooters was vain, for the single Maine regiment found itself opposed to portions of no less than four Confederate brigades, at least a dozen regiments all told. When the men got to the orchard fence, Sergeant Benson wrenched apart the tall pickets to let through Hyde's horse. While he was doing this, a shot struck his haversack, and the men all laughed at the sight of the flying hardtack.

Going into the orchard there was a rise of ground, and the Confederates fired several volleys at the Maine men, and then charged them. Hyde's horse was twice wounded, but was still able to go on.

No sooner were the men in blue beyond the fence than they got into line and met the Confederates, as they came crowding behind, with a slaughtering fire, and then charged, driving them back. The color corporal was still carrying the colors, though one of his arms had been broken; but when half way through the orchard, Hyde heard him call out as he fell, and turned back to save the colors, if possible.

The apple-trees were short and thick, and he could not see much, and the Confederates speedily got between him and his men. Immediately, with the cry of "Rally, boys, to save the Major," back surged the regiment, and a volley at arm's length again destroyed all the foremost of their pursuers; so they rescued both their commander and the flag, which was carried off by Corporal Ring.

Hyde then formed the regiment on the colors, sixty-eight men all told, out of two hundred and forty who had begun the charge, and they slowly marched back toward their place in the Union line, while the New Yorkers and Vermonters rose from the ground cheering and waving their hats. Next day, when the Confederates had retired a little from the field, the color corporal, Campbell, was found in the orchard, dead, propped up against a tree, with his half-smoked pipe beside him.

CHAPTER 19

Love, Loss, and Army Life of the Common Soldier

By Leander Stillwell

In the ranks of the Union army, pain and drama sometimes went beyond the battlefields.
—LAMAR UNDERWOOD

SOON AFTER OUR OCCUPATION OF CORINTH A CHANGE IN THE POSITION OF OUR FORCES took place, and all the command at Owl creek was transferred to Bethel, a small station on the Mobile and Ohio railroad, some twenty or twenty-five miles to the northwest. We left Owl creek on the morning of June 6th, and arrived at Bethel about dark the same evening. Thanks to my repeated long walks in the woods outside of our lines, I was in pretty fair health at this time, but still somewhat weak and shaky.

On the morning we took up the line of march, while waiting for the "fall in" call, I was seated at the foot of a big tree in camp, with my knapsack, packed, at my side. Enoch Wallace came to me and said: "Stillwell, are you going to try to carry your knapsack?" I answered that I reckoned I had to, that I had asked Hen. King (our company teamster) to let me put it in his wagon, and he wouldn't—said he already had too big a load. Enoch said nothing more, but stood silently looking down at me a few seconds, then picked up my knapsack and threw it into our wagon, which was close by, saying to King, as he did so, "Haul that knapsack"—and it was hauled.

I shall never forget this act of kindness on the part of Enoch. It would have been impossible for me to have made the march carrying the knapsack. The day was hot, and much of the road was over sandy land, and through long stretches of black-jack barrens, that excluded every breath of a breeze. The men suffered much on the march, and fell out by scores. When we stacked arms at Bethel that evening, there were only four men of Co. D in line, just enough to make one stack of guns, but my gun was in the stack.

There was no earthly necessity for making this march in one day. We were simply "changing stations;" the Confederate army of that region was down in Mississippi, a hundred miles or so away, and there were no armed foes in our vicinity excepting some skulking bands of guerrillas. Prior to this our regiment had made no marches, except little short movements during the siege of Corinth, none of which exceeded two or three miles. And nearly all the men were weak and debilitated by reason of the prevailing type of illness, and in no condition whatever to be cracked through twenty miles or more on a hot day.

We should have marched only about ten miles the first day, with a halt of about ten minutes every hour, to let the men rest a little, and get their wind. Had that course been pursued, we would have reached our destination in good shape, with the ranks full, and the men would have been benefited by the march. As it was, it probably caused the death of some, and the permanent disabling of more. The trouble at that time was the total want of experience on the part of the most of our officers of all grades, combined with an amazing lack of common sense by some of high authority. I am not blaming any of our regimental officers for this foolish "forced march"—for it amounted to that—the responsibility rested higher up.

Our stay at Bethel was brief and uneventful. However, I shall always remember the place on account of a piece of news that came to me while we were there, and which for a time nearly broke me all up. It will be necessary to go back some years in order to explain it. I began attending the old Stone school house at Otter creek when I was about eight years old. One of my schoolmates was a remarkably pretty little girl, with blue eyes and auburn hair, nearly my own age. We kept about the same place in our studies, and were generally in the same classes. I always liked her, and by the time I was about fifteen years old was head over heels in love. She was far above me in the social scale of the neighborhood.

Her folks lived in a frame house on "the other side of the creek," and were well-to-do, for that time and locality. My people lived in a log cabin, on a little farm in the broken country that extended from the south bank of Otter creek to the Mississippi and Illinois rivers. But notwithstanding the difference in our respective social and financial positions, I knew that she had a liking for me, and our mutual relations became quite "tender" and interesting. Then the war came along, I enlisted and went South.

We had no correspondence after I left home; I was just too deplorably bashful to attempt it, and, on general principles, didn't have sense enough to properly carry on a proceeding of that nature. It may be that here was where I fell down. But I thought about her every day, and had many boyish day dreams of the future, in which she was the prominent figure. Soon after our arrival at Bethel I received a letter from home. I hurriedly opened it, anxious, as usual, to hear from the folks, and sitting down at the foot of a tree, began reading it. All went well to nearly the close, when I read these fatal words:

"Billy Crane and Lucy Archer got married last week."

The above names are fictitious, but the bride was my girl.

I can't explain my feelings—if you ever have had such an experience, you will under-stand. I stole a hurried glance around to see if anybody was observing my demeanor, then thrust the letter into my jacket pocket, and walked away. Not far from our camp was a stretch of swampy land, thickly set with big cypress trees, and I bent my steps in that direction. Entering the forest, I sought a secluded spot, sat down on an old log, and read and re-read that heart-breaking piece of intelligence. There was no mistaking the words; they were plain, laconic, and nothing ambiguous about them. And, to intensify the bit-terness of the draught, it may be set down here that the groom was a dudish young squirt, a clerk in a country store, who lacked the pluck to go for a soldier, but had stayed at home to count eggs and measure calico. In my opinion, he was not worthy of the girl, and I was amazed that she had taken him for a husband.

I remember well some of my thoughts as I sat with bitterness in my heart, alone among those gloomy cypresses. I wanted a great big battle to come off at once, with the 61st Illinois right in front, that we might run out of cartridges, and the order would be given to fix bayonets and charge! Like Major Simon Suggs, in depicting the horrors of an apprehended Indian war, I wanted to see blood flow in a "great gulgin' torrent, like the Tallapoosa river." Well, it was simply a case of pure, intensely ardent boy-love, and I was hit, hard, but survived. And I now heartily congratulate myself on the fact that this youthful shipwreck ultimately resulted in my obtaining for a wife the very best woman (excepting only my mother) that I ever knew in my life.

I never again met my youthful flame, to speak to her, and saw her only once, and then at a distance, some years after the close of the war when I was back in Illinois on a visit to my parents. Several years ago her husband died, and in course of time she married again, this time a man I never knew, and the last I heard of or concerning her, she and her second husband were living somewhere in one of the Rocky Mountain States.

~

On this march I was a participant in an incident which was somewhat amusing, and also a little bit irritating. Shortly before noon of the first day, Jack Medford, of my company, and myself, concluded we would "straggle," and try to get a country dinner. Availing ourselves of the first favorable opportunity, we slipped from the ranks, and struck out. We followed an old country road that ran substantially parallel to the main road on which the column was marching, and soon came to a nice looking old log house standing in a grove of big native trees. The only people at the house were two middle-aged women and some chil-dren. We asked the women if we could have some dinner, saying that we would pay for it. They gave an affirmative answer, but their tone was not cordial and they looked "daggers." Dinner was just about prepared, and when all was ready, we were invited, with evident coolness, to take seats at the table. We had a splendid meal, consisting of corn bread, new Irish potatoes, boiled bacon and greens, butter and buttermilk. Compared with sow-belly and hardtack, it was a feast. Dinner over, we essayed to pay therefor. Their charge was something less than a dollar for both of us, but we had not the exact change. The smallest denomination of money either of us had was a dollar greenback, and the women said that they had no money at all to make change. Thereupon we proffered them the entire dollar.

They looked at it askance, and asked if we had any "Southern" or Confederate money. We said we had not, that this was the only kind of money we had. They continued to look exceedingly sour, and finally remarked that they were unwilling to accept any kind of money except "Southern." We urged them to accept the bill, told them it was United States money, and that it would pass readily in any place in the South occupied by our soldiers; but no, they were obdurate, and declined the greenback with unmistakable scorn. Of course we kept our temper; it never would have done to be saucy or rude after getting such a good dinner, but, for my part, I felt considerably vexed. But there was nothing left to do except thank them heartily for their kindness and depart.

From their standpoint their course in the matter was actuated by the highest and most unselfish patriotism, but naturally we couldn't look at it in that light. I will say here, "with malice towards none, and with charity for all," that in my entire sojourn in the South during the war, the women were found to be more intensely bitter and malignant against the old government of the United States, and the national cause in general, than were the men. Their attitude is probably another illustration of the truth of Kipling's saying, "The female of the species is more deadly than the male."

This probably is a fitting place for something to be said about our method of traveling by rail during the Civil War, as compared with the conditions of the present day in that regard. At the time I am now writing, about fifteen thousand United States soldiers have recently been transported on the cars from different places in the interior of the country, to various points adjacent to the Mexican border, for the purpose of protecting American interests. And it seems that in some cases the soldiers were carried in ordinary passenger coaches. Thereupon bitter complaints were made on behalf of such soldiers because Pullman sleepers were not used! And these complaints were effective, too, for, according to the press reports of the time, the use of passenger coaches for such purposes was summarily stopped and Pullmans were hurriedly concentrated at the places needed, and the soldiers went to war in them. Well, in our time, the old regiment was hauled over the country many times on trains, the extent of our travels in that manner aggregating hundreds and hundreds of miles. And such a thing as even ordinary passenger coaches for the use of the enlisted men was never heard of. And I have no recollection now that (during the war) any were provided for the use of the commissioned officers, either, unless they were of pretty high rank.

The cars that we rode in were the box or freight cars in use in those days. Among them were cattle cars, flat or platform cars, and in general every other kind of freight car that could be procured. We would fill the box cars, and in addition clamber upon the roofs thereof and avail ourselves of every foot of space. And usually there was a bunch on the cow-catchers. The engines used wood for fuel; the screens of the smoke-stacks must have been very coarse, or maybe they had none at all, and the big cinders would patter down on us like hail. So, when we came to the journey's end, by reason of the cinders and soot we were about as dirty and black as any regiment of sure-enough colored troops that fought under the Union flag in the last years of the war.

When the regiment was sent home in September, 1865, some months after the war was over, the enlisted men made even that trip in our old friends, the box cars. It is true that on this occasion there was a passenger coach for the use of the commissioned officers, and that is the only time that I ever saw such a coach attached to a train on which the regiment was taken anywhere. Now, don't misunderstand me. I am not kicking because, more than half a century after the close of the Civil War, Uncle Sam sent his soldier boys to the front in Pullmans. The force so sent was small and the government could well afford to do it, and it was right. I just want you to know that in my time, when we rode, it was in any kind of an old freight car, and we were awful glad to get that. And now on this matter, "The words of Job are ended."

On the afternoon of December 18th, suddenly, without any previous warning or notification, the bugle sounded "Fall in!" and all the regiment fit for duty and not on guard at once formed on the regimental parade ground. From there we marched to the depot, and with the 43rd Illinois of our brigade got on the cars, and were soon being whirled over the road in a northerly direction. It was a warm, sunshiny day, and we common soldiers supposed we were going on just some little temporary scout, so we encumbered ourselves with nothing but our arms, and haversacks, and canteens. Neglecting to take our blankets was a grievous mistake, as later we found out to our sorrow. We arrived at Jackson a little before sundown, there left the cars, and, with the 43rd, forthwith marched out about two miles east of town.

A little after dark we halted in an old field on the left of the road, in front of a little old country graveyard called Salem Cemetery, and there bivouacked for the night. Along in the evening the weather turned intensely cold. It was a clear, star-lit night, and the stars glittered in the heavens like little icicles. We were strictly forbidden to build any fires, for the reason, as our officers truly said, the Confederates were not more than half a mile away, right in our front. As before stated, we had no blankets, and how we suffered with the cold! I shall never forget that night of December 18th, 1862. We would form little columns of twenty or thirty men, in two ranks, and would just trot round and round in the tall weeds and broom sedge to keep from chilling to death. Sometimes we would pile down on the ground in great bunches, and curl up close together like hogs, in our efforts to keep warm. But some part of our bodies would be exposed, which soon would be stinging with cold, then up we would get and renew the trotting process.

At one time in the night some of the boys, rendered almost desperate by their suffering, started to build a fire with some fence rails. The red flames began to curl around the wood, and I started for the fire, intending to absorb some of that glowing heat, if, as

Uncle Remus says, "it wuz de las' ack." But right then a mounted officer dashed up to the spot, and sprang from his horse. He was wearing big cavalry boots, and jumped on that fire with both feet and stamped it out in less time than I am taking to tell about it. I heard afterwards that he was Col. Engelmann, of the 43rd Illinois, then the commander of our brigade.

Having put out the fire, he turned on the men standing around, and swore at them furiously. He said that the rebels were right out in our front, and in less than five minutes after we had betrayed our presence by fires, they would open on us with artillery, and "shell hell out of us"—and more to the same effect. The boys listened in silence, meek as lambs, and no more fires were started by us that night. But the hours seemed interminably long, and it looked like the night would never come to an end.

At last some little woods birds were heard, faintly chirping in the weeds and underbrush near by, then some owls set up a hooting in the woods behind us, and I knew that dawn was approaching. When it became light enough to distinguish one another, we saw that we presented a doleful appearance—all hollow-eyed, with blue noses, pinched faces, and shivering as if we would shake to pieces. Permission was then given to build small fires to cook our breakfast, and we didn't wait for the order to be repeated. I made a quart canful of strong, hot coffee, toasted some bacon on a stick, and then, with some hardtack, had a good breakfast and felt better.

Christmas Day in the year eighteen hundred and sixty-two was a gloomy one, in every respect, for the soldiers of the Union army in West Tennessee. Five days before, the Confederate General Van Dorn had captured Grant's depot of supplies at Holly Springs, and government stores of the value of a million and a half of dollars had gone up in smoke and flame. About the same time Forrest had struck the Mobile and Ohio railroad, on which we depended to bring us from the north our supplies of hardtack and bacon, and had made a wreck of the road from about Jackson, Tennessee, nearly to Columbus, Kentucky.

For some months previous to these disasters the regiment to which I belonged, the 61st Illinois Infantry, had been stationed at Bolivar, Tennessee, engaged in guarding the railroad from that place to Toone's Station, a few miles north of Bolivar. On December 18, with another regiment of our brigade, we were sent by rail to Jackson to assist in repelling Forrest, who was threatening that place. On the following day the two regiments, numbering in the aggregate about 500 men, in connection with a small detachment of our cavalry, had a lively and spirited little brush with the Confederate forces about two miles east of Jackson, near a country burying ground called Salem Cemetery, which resulted in our having the good fortune to give them a salutary check.

Reinforcements were sent out from Jackson, and Forrest disappeared. The next day our entire command marched about fifteen miles eastwardly in the direction of the Tennessee river. It was doubtless supposed by our commanding general that the Confederates had retreated in that direction, but he was mistaken. Forrest had simply whipped around

Jackson, struck the railroad a few miles north thereof, and then had continued north up the road, capturing and destroying as he went. On the succeeding day, December 21st, we all marched back to Jackson, and my regiment went into camp on a bleak, muddy hillside in the suburbs of the town, and there we remained until December 29th, when we were sent to Carroll Station, about eight miles north of Jackson.

I well remember how gloomy I felt on the morning of that Christmas Day at Jackson, Tennessee. I was then only a little over nineteen years of age. I had been in the army nearly a year, lacking just a few days, and every day of that time, except a furlough of two days granted at our camp of instruction before we left Illinois for the front, had been passed with the regiment in camp and field.

Christmas morning my thoughts naturally turned to the little old log cabin in the backwoods of western Illinois, and I couldn't help thinking about the nice Christmas dinner that I knew the folks at home would sit down to on that day.

There would be a great chicken pot pie, with its savory crust and a superabundance of light, puffy dumplings; delicious light, hot biscuits; a big ball of our own home-made butter, yellow as gold; broad slices of juicy ham, the product of hogs of our own fattening, and home cured with hickory-wood smoke; fresh eggs from the barn in reckless profusion, fried in the ham gravy; mealy Irish potatoes, baked in their jackets; coffee with cream about half an inch thick; apple butter and crab apple preserves; a big plate of wild honey in the comb; and winding up with a thick wedge of mince pie that mother knew so well how to make—such mince pie, in fact, as was made only in those days, and is now as extinct as the dodo.

And when I turned from these musings upon the bill of fare they would have at home to contemplate the dreary realities of my own possible dinner for the day—my oyster can full of coffee and a quarter ration of hardtack and sow-belly comprised the menu. If the eyes of some old soldier should light upon these lines, and he should thereupon feel disposed to curl his lip with unutterable scorn and say: "This fellow was a milksop and ought to have been fed on Christian Commission and Sanitary goods, and put to sleep at night with a warm rock at his feet"—I can only say in extenuation that the soldier whose feelings I have been trying to describe was only a boy—and, boys, you probably know how it was yourselves during the first year of your army life. But, after all, the soldier had a Christmas dinner that day, and it is of that I have started out to speak.

CHAPTER 20

A Night Ride of the Wounded
By Randall Parrish

The chances of a wounded soldier surviving, even after treatment, were slight. "A Night Ride of the Wounded," by Randall Parrish, vividly captures the trauma of being transported from the battlefield to one of the makeshift hospitals, where facilities were primitive at best, medical treatments still crude, and conditions unsanitary.

—LISA PURCELL

IT WAS A WILD, RUDE SCENE WITHOUT, YET IN ITS WAY TYPICAL OF A LITTLE-UNDERSTOOD chapter of the Civil War. Moreover it was one with which I was not entirely unacquainted. Years of cavalry scouting, bearing me beyond the patrol lines of the two great armies, had frequently brought me into contact with those various independent, irregular forces which, co-operating with us, often rendered most efficient service by preying on the scattered Federal camps and piercing their lines of communication. Seldom risking an engagement in the open, their policy was rather to dash down upon some outpost or poorly guarded wagon train, and retreat with a rapidity rendering pursuit hopeless. It was partisan warfare, and appealed to many ill-adapted to abide the stricter discipline of regular service. These border rangers would rendezvous under some chosen leader, strike an unexpected blow where weakness had been discovered, then disappear as quickly as they came, oftentimes scattering widely until the call went forth for some fresh assault. It was service not dissimilar to that performed during the Revolutionary struggle by Sumter and Marion in the Carolinas, and added in the aggregate many a day to the contest of the Confederacy.

Among these wild, rough riders between the lines no leader was more favorably known of our army, nor more dreaded by the enemy, than Mosby. Daring to the point of recklessness, yet wary as a fox, counting opposing numbers nothing when weighed against the advantage of surprise, tireless in saddle, audacious in resource, quick to plan and equally quick to execute, he was always where least expected, and it was seldom he failed to win reward for those who rode at his back. Possessing regular rank in the Confederate army, making report of his operations to the commander-in-chief, his peculiar talent as a partisan leader had won him what was practically an independent command. Knowing him as I did, I was not surprised that he should now have swept suddenly out of the black night upon the very verge of the battle to drive his irritating sting into the hard-earned Federal victory.

An empty army wagon, the "U. S. A." yet conspicuous upon its canvas cover, had been overturned and fired in front of the hospital tent to give light to the raiders. Grouped about beneath the trees, and within the glow of the flames, was a picturesque squad of horsemen, hardy, tough-looking fellows the most of them, their clothing an odd mixture of uniforms, but every man heavily armed and admirably equipped for service. Some remained mounted, lounging carelessly in their saddles, but far the larger number were on foot, their bridle-reins wound about their wrists. All alike appeared alert and ready for any emergency. How many composed the party I was unable to judge with accuracy, as they constantly came and went from out the shadows beyond the circumference of the fire. As all sounds of firing had ceased, I concluded that the work planned had been already accomplished. Undoubtedly, surprised as they were, the small Federal force left to guard this point had been quickly overwhelmed and scattered.

The excitement attendant upon my release had left me for the time being utterly forgetful as to the pain of my wounds, so that weakness alone held me to the blanket upon which I had been left. The night was decidedly chilly, yet I had scarcely begun to feel its discomfort, when a man strode forward from out the nearer group and stood looking down upon me. He was a young fellow, wearing a gray artillery jacket, with high cavalry boots coming above the knees. I noticed his firm-set jaw, and a pearl-handled revolver stuck carelessly in his belt, but observed no symbol of rank about him.

"Is this Captain Wayne?" he asked, not unpleasantly. I answered by an inclination of the head, and he turned at once toward the others.

"Cass, bring three men over here, and carry this officer to the same wagon you did the others," he commanded briefly. "Fix him comfortably, but be in a hurry about it."

They lifted me in the blanket, one holding tightly at either corner, and bore me tenderly out into the night. Once one of them tripped over a projecting root, and the sudden jar of his stumble shot a spasm of pain through me, which caused me to cry out even through my clinched teeth.

"Pardon me, lads," I panted, ashamed of the weakness, "but it slipped out before I could help it."

"Don't be after a mentionin' av it, yer honor," returned a rich brogue. "Sure an me feet got so mixed oup that I wondher I didn't drap ye entoirely."

"If ye had, Clancy," said the man named Cass, grimly, "I reckon as how the Colonel would have drapped you."

At the foot of a narrow ravine, leading forth into the broader valley, we came to a covered army wagon, to which four mules had been already attached. The canvas was drawn aside, and I was lifted up and carefully deposited in the hay that thickly covered the bottom. It was so intensely dark within I could see nothing of my immediate surroundings, but a low moan told me there must be at least one other wounded man present. Outside I heard the tread of horses' hoofs, and then the sound of Mosby's voice.

"Jake," he said, "drive rapidly, but with as much care as possible. Take the lower road after you cross the bridge, and you will meet with no patrols. We will ride beside you for a couple of miles."

Then a hand thrust aside the canvas, and a face peered in. I caught a faint glimmer of stars, but could distinguish little else.

"Boys," said the leader, kindly, "I wish I might give you better transportation, but this is the only form of vehicle we can find. I reckon you'll get pretty badly bumped over the road you are going, but I'm furnishing you all the chance to get away in my power."

"For one I am grateful enough," I answered, after waiting for someone else to speak. "A little pain is preferable to imprisonment."

"After you pass the bridge you will be perfectly safe on that score," he said heartily. "Anything more I can do for any of you?"

"How many of us are there?" asked someone faintly from out the darkness.

"Oh, yes," returned Mosby, with a laugh, "I forgot; you will want to know each other. There are three of you—Colonel Colby of North Carolina, Major Wilkins of Thome's Battery, and Captain Wayne, —th Virginia. Let that answer for an introduction, gentlemen, and now good-night. We shall guard you as long as necessary, and then must leave you to the kindly ministrations of the driver."

He reached in, leaning down from his saddle to do so, drew the blanket somewhat closer about me, and was gone. I caught the words of a sharp, short order, and the heavy wagon lurched forward, its wheels bumping over the irregularities in the road, each jolt sending a fresh spasm of pain through my tortured body.

May the merciful God ever protect me from such a ride again! It seemed interminable, while each long mile we travelled brought with it new and greater agony of mind and body. That I did not suffer alone was early evident from the low moans borne to me from out the darkness. Once a weak, trembling voice prayed for release—a short, fervent prayer, which so impressed me in the weakness of my own anguish that I added to it "Amen," spoken unconsciously aloud.

"Who spoke?" asked the same voice, faintly.

"I am Captain Wayne," I answered, almost glad to break the terrible silence by speech of any kind, "and I merely echoed your prayer. Death would indeed prove a welcome relief from such intensity of suffering."

"Yes," he acquiesced gently. "I fear I have not sufficient strength to bear mine for long; yet I am a Christian, and there are wife and child waiting for me at home. God knows I am ready when He calls, but my duty is to live, if possible, for their sake. They will have nothing left if I pass on."

"The road must grow smoother as we come down into the valley. Are your wounds serious?"

"I was struck by fragments of a shell," he answered, and I could tell he spoke the words through his clinched teeth, "and am wounded in the head as well as the body—oh, my God!" The cry was wrung from him by a sudden tilting of the wagon, and for a moment my own pain prevented utterance.

"I hear nothing from the other man," I managed to say at last. "Colonel Mosby said there were three of us; surely the third man cannot be already dead?"

"Mercifully unconscious, I think; at least he has made no sound since I was placed in here."

"No, friends," spoke another and deeper voice from farther back within the jolting wagon, "I am not unconscious, but less noticeably in pain. I have lost a leg, yet the stump seems seared and dead, hurting me little unless I touch it."

We lapsed into solemn silence, it was such an effort to talk, and we had so little to say. Each man, no doubt, was struggling, as I know I was, to withhold expression of his agony for the sake of the others. I lay racked in every nerve, my teeth tightly clinched, my temples beaded with perspiration. I could hear the troopers riding without, the jingling of their accoutrements, and the steady beat of their horses' feet being easily distinguishable above the deeper rumble of the wheels. Then there came a quick order in Mosby's familiar voice, a calling aloud of some further directions to the driver, and afterwards nothing was distinguishable excepting the noise of our own rapid progress.

Jake drove, it seemed to me, most recklessly. I could hear the almost constant crack of his lash and the rough words of goading hurled at the straining mules. The road appeared to be filled with roots, while occasionally the wheels would strike a stone, coming down again with a jar that nearly drove me frantic. The chill night air swept in through the open front of the hood, and made me feel as if my veins were filled with ice, even while the inflammation of my wounds burned and throbbed as with fire. The pitiful moaning of the man who lay next me grew gradually fainter, and finally ceased altogether. Tortured as I was, yet I could not but think of the wife and child far away praying for his safe return. For their sake I forced back the intensity of my own sufferings and spoke into the darkness.

"The man who prayed," I said, not knowing which of my two companions it might be. "Are you suffering less, that you have ceased to moan?"

There was no answer. Then the loose hay rustled, as though someone was slowly dragging his helpless body through it. A moment later the deep voice spoke:

"He is dead," solemnly. "God has answered his prayer. His hand already begins to feel cold."

"Dead?" I echoed, inexpressibly shocked. "Do you know his name?"

"As I am Major Wilkins, it must be Colonel Colby who has died. May God be merciful to the widow and the orphan."

The hours that followed were all but endless. I knew we had reached the lower valley, for the road became more level, yet the slightest jolting now was sufficient to render me crazed with pain, and I had lost all power of restraint. My tortured nerves throbbed; the fever gripped me, and my mind began to wander. Visions of delirium came, and I dreamed dreams too terrible for record: demons danced on the drifting clouds before me, while whirling savages chanting in horrid discord stuck my frenzied body full of blazing brands. At times I was awake, calling in vain for water to quench a thirst which grew maddening, then I lapsed into a semi-consciousness that drove me wild with its delirious fancies. I knew vaguely that the Major had crept back through the darkness and passed his strong arm gently beneath my head. I heard him shouting in his deep voice to the driver for something to drink, but was unaware of any response. All became blurred, confused, bewildering. I thought it was my mother comforting me. The faint gray daylight stole in at last through the cracks of the wagon cover; I could dimly distinguish a dark face bending over me, framed by a heavy gray beard, and then, merciful unconsciousness came, and I rested as one dead beside the corpse of the Colonel.

CHAPTER 21

The Unforgettable Private Peck:
Further Adventures of a Raw Recruit
By George W. Peck

He's back, and funnier than ever, continuing the hilarious escapades begun in chapter 11.
—LAMAR UNDERWOOD

I TOLD THE CHAPLAIN THAT IF THERE WAS ONE THING I DIDN'T WANT TO SEE, IT WAS blood. Others might have an insatiable appetite for gore, but I didn't want any at all. I was willing to do anything for this government but fight; and if he could recommend to me any line of action by which I could pull through without being sent out to do battle with strangers who could shoot well, I should consider it a favor. What I wanted was a soft job, where there was no danger. The chaplain looked thoughtful a moment, and then took me over to his tent, where he opened a bottle of blackberry brandy. He took a small dose, after placing his hand on his stomach and groaning a little.

He asked me if I did not sometimes have a pain under my vest. I told him I never had a pain anywhere. Then he said I couldn't have any brandy. He said the brandy came from the sanitary commission, and was controlled entirely by the chaplains of the different regiments, and the instructions were to only use it in case of sickness. He said a great many of the boys had pains regularly, and came to him for relief. He smacked his lips and said if I felt any pain coming on, to help myself to the brandy. It is singular how a pain will sometimes come on when you least expect it. It was not a minute before I began to feel a small pain, not bigger than a man's hand, and as I looked at the bottle the pain increased, and I had to tell the chaplain that I must have relief before it was everlastingly too late, so he poured out a dose of brandy for me. I could see that I was becoming a veteran very fast, as I could work the chaplain for sanitary stores pretty early in the game.

Well, the chaplain and me had pains off and on, for an hour or two, and became good friends. He told me of quite a number of methods of shirking active duty, such as being detailed to take care of baggage, acting as orderly, and going to surgeon's call. He said if a man went to surgeon's call, the doctor would report him sick, and he could not be sent out on duty.

The next day we went back to our post, where the regiment was stationed, and where they had barracks, that they wintered in, and remained there several weeks, drilling.

I was drilled in mounting and dismounting, and soon got so I could mount a horse without climbing on to him from a fence. But the drill became irksome, and I decided to try the chaplain's suggestion about going to surgeon's call. I got in line with about twenty other soldiers, and we marched over to the surgeon's quarters. I supposed the doctor would take each soldier into a private room, feel of his pulse, look at his tongue, and say that what he needed was rest, and give him some powders to be taken in wafers, or in sugar.

But all he did was to say "What's the matter?" and the sick man would tell him, when the doctor would tell his assistant to give the man something, and pass on to the next. I was the last one to be served, and the interview was about as follows:

Doc.—What's the matter?

Me—Bilious.

Doc.—Run out your tongue. Take a swallow out of the black bottle.

That seems very simple, indeed, but it nearly killed me. When he told me to run out my tongue, I run out perhaps six inches of the lower end of it, the doctor glanced at it as though it was nothing to him anyway, and then he told me to take a swallow out of the bottle. In all my life I had never taken four doses of medicine, and when I did the medicine was disguised in preserves or something. The hospital steward handed me the bottle that a dozen other sick soldiers had drank out of, and it was sticky all around the top, and contained something that looked like castor oil, for greasing a buggy. He told me to take a good big swallow, and I tried to do so.

Talk about the suffering brought on by the war, it seems to me nobody ever suffered as I did, trying to drink a swallow of that castor oil out of a two quart bottle, that was dirty. It run so slow that it seemed, an age before I got enough to swallow, and then it seemed another age before the oil could pass a given point in my neck.

And great Caesar's ghost how it did taste. I think it went down my neck, and I just had strength enough to ask the steward to give me something to take the taste out of my mouth. He handed me a blue pill. O, I could have killed him. I rushed to the chaplain's tent and took a drink of blackberry brandy, and my life was saved, but for three years after that I was never sick enough to get farther than the chaplain's quarters.

The true historian has got to get in all the particulars. I think I never felt quite as downhearted as I did the day or two after the skirmish, when our boys were killed. It had seemed as though there was no danger of anybody getting hurt, as long as they looked out for themselves, but now there was a feeling that anybody was liable to be killed, any time, and why not me? Of course the old veterans of the regiment were the ones who would naturally be expected to take the brunt of the battle, but there was a habit of sending raw recruits into places of danger that struck me as being mighty careless, as well as very bad judgment. Then there were great preparations being made for an advance movement, or a retreat, or something, and my mind was constantly occupied in trying to find out whether it was to be an advance or a retreat. If it was an advance, I wanted to arrange to be in the rear, and if it was a retreat, it seemed to me as as though the proper place for a man who wanted to live to go home, was in front. And yet what chance was there for a common private soldier to find out whether it was an advance or a retreat. Finally I decided that when the regiment *did* start out, I would manage to be about the middle, so it wouldn't make much difference which way we went.

When that idea occurred to me I pondered over it a good deal and told the chaplain, and he said it was a piece of as brilliant strategy as he had ever heard of, and he was willing to adopt it, only being a staff officer it was necessary for him and me to ride with the colonel, and the colonel most always rode at the head, though his place was about the middle. He said he would speak to the colonel about it. It made my hair stand to see the preparations that were being made for carnage. Ammunition enough was issued to kill a million men, and the doctors were packing bandages and plasters, and physic, and splints and probes, until it made me sick to look at them. When I thought of actual war, my mind reverted to my mule, the kicking brute that was no good, and I decided to get a horse. I had got so, actually, that I could hear bullets whistle without turning pale and having cold chills run over me, and it seemed as though a horse was none too good for me, so I went to the colonel and told him that a soldier couldn't make no show on a kicking mule and I wanted a horse. I told him I supposed, as chaplain's clerk. I should have to ride with him and his staff on the march, and he didn't want to see as nice a looking fellow as I was riding a kicking mule that would kick the ribs of the officers horses, and break the officers legs.

The colonel said he had not thought of that contingency. He had enjoyed seeing me ride the mule, because I was so patient when the mule kicked. He said they used that mule in the regiment to teach recruits to ride. A man who could stay on that mule could ride any horse in the regiment, and as I had been successful, and had displayed splendid mulemanship, I should be promoted to ride a horse, and he told the quartermaster to exchange with me and give me the chestnut-sorrel horse that the Confederate was shot off of. I went with the quartermaster to the corral, turned out my mule, and cornered the beautiful horse that had been rode so proudly a few days before by my friend, the rebel. It took six of us to catch the horse, and bridle and saddle him, and the men about the corral said the horse was no good. He hadn't eaten anything since being captured, and his eyes looked bad, and he wanted to kick and bite everybody.

I told them the poor horse was homesick, that was all that ailed him. The horse was a Confederate at heart, and he naturally had no particular love for Yankees. I remembered that once or twice when I was riding with the rebels, after they captured me, the young fellow on this horse patted him on the neck and called him "Jeff," so I knew that was his name, so I led him out of the corral away from the other fellows, where there was some grass growing, and made up my mind I would "mash" him. After he had eaten grass a little while, looking at me out of the corner of his eyes as though he didn't know whether to kick my head on, or walk on me, as I sat under a tree, I got up and patted him on the neck and said, "Well, Jeff, old boy, how does the grass fit your stomach?"

You may talk about brute intelligence, but that horse was human. He stopped eating, with his mouth full of grass, looked astonished at being addressed by a stranger without an introduction, and turned a pair of eyes as beautiful and soft as a woman's upon me, and then began to chew slowly, as though thinking. I rubbed his sleek coat with my bare hands and did not say much, desiring to have Jeff make the first advances. He looked me over, and finally put his nose on my sleeve, and rubbed me, and looked in my face, and acted as though he would say, "Well, of course this red-headed fellow is no comparison to my dead master, but evidently he's no slouch, and if I have got to be bossed around by a Yankee, as he is the only one that has spoken a kind word to me since I was captured, and he seems to know my name, I guess I will tie to him," and the intelligent animal rubbed his nose all over me, and licked my hand. I rubbed the horse all over, petted him, took up his feet and looked at them, and spoke his name, and pretty soon we were the best of friends. I mounted him and rode around and it was just like a rocking chair.

That poor, dead Confederate had probably rode Jeff since he was a kid and Jeff was a colt, and had broken him well, and I was awfully sorry that the original owner was not alive, riding his horse home safe and sound, to be greeted by his family with loving embraces. But he was dead and buried, and his horse belonged to me, by all the laws of war. And yet I had not become a hardened warrior to such an extent that I could forget the hearts that would ache at his home, and I made up mind that horse would be treated as tenderly as though he was one of my family. I rode Jeff around for an hour or two, found that he was trained to jump fences, stand on his hind feet, trot, pace, rack, and that he could run like a scared wolf, and everything the horse did he would sort of look around at me with one eye as much as to say, "Boss, you will find I have got all the modern improvements, and you needn't be afraid that I will disgrace you in any society." I was fairly in love with my new horse, and, except for a feeling that I was an interloper with the horse, and sorry for the poor boy that had been shot off him, I should have been perfectly happy.

Everybody knew I had been recommended for a commission, and they all called me "Lieutenant," but all the same I was doing duty as a private. For two or three days I was detailed to drive mules for the quartermaster, and that was the worst service I ever did perform. It seemed as though the colonel wanted to prepare me for any service that in the nature of things I was liable to be called upon to perform. I kicked some at being detailed to drive a six-mule team, but the colonel said I might see the time when I could save the government a million dollars by being able to jump on to a wheel mule and drive a wagon loaded with ammunition, or paymaster's cash, out of danger of being captured by the enemy.

So I went to work and learned to gee-haw a six-mule team of the stubbornest mules in the world, hauling bacon, but there was no romance in taking care of six mules that would kick so you had to put the harness on them with a pitchfork, for fear of having your head kicked off. If I ever get a pension it will be for my loss of character and temper in driving those mules. I have been in some dangerous places, but I was never in so dangerous a place, in battle, as I was one day while driving those mules. One of the lead mules got his forward foot over the bridle some way, and I went to fix it, and the team started and "straddled" me.

As soon as I saw that I was between the two lead mules, and that the team had started, I knew my only safety was in laying down and taking the chances of the three pairs of mules and wagon going straight over me. To attempt to get out would mix them all up, so I fell right down in the mud, which was about a foot deep, and just like soft mortar. As the mules passed on each side of me, every last one of them kicked at me, and I was under the impression that each wheel of the wagon kicked at me, but I escaped everything except the mud, and when I got up on my feet behind the wagon, the quartermaster, who was ahead on horseback, had stopped the team. He called a colored man to drive, and told me I could go back to the regiment.

I tried to sneak in the back way, and not see anybody, but when I passed the chaplain's tent a lot of officers, who had been sampling his sanitary stores, come out, and one of them recognized me, and they insisted on my stopping and talking something with them. Honestly, there was not an inch of my clothing but was covered with red mud, that every soldier remembers who has been through Alabama. They had fun with me for half an hour and then let me go. I have never been able to look at a mule since, without a desire to kill it.

⚊⚊

When I went away from the party of officers, where we had been playing draw-poker, with a hundred dollars in my pocket, which I had won from men who thought they were pretty good poker players, I felt as though I owned the earth. I had my hand in my pocket, hold of the roll of greenbacks, and in that way constantly realized that I was no common pauper. I had never thought that I was an expert at cards, but this triumph convinced me that there was more money to be made playing poker than in any other way. I figured up in my mind that if I could win a hundred dollars a night, and only played five nights a week, I could lay up two thousand dollars a month. To keep it up a year would make me rich, and if the war lasted a couple of years I could go home with money enough to buy out the best newspaper in Wisconsin.

It is wonderful what a train of thought a young man's first success in gambling, or speculation, brings to him. I went to bed with my hundred dollars buttoned inside my flannel shirt, and dreamed all night about holding four aces, full hands, and three of a kind. All that night, in my sleep, I never failed to "fill" when I drew to a hand. I made up my mind to break every officer in the regiment, at poker, and then turn my attention to other regiments, and win all the money the paymaster should bring to the brigade. I got up in the morning with a headache, and thought how long it would be before night, when we could play poker again, and I wondered why we couldn't play during the day, as there was nothing else going on.

It got rumored around the regiment that I had cleaned the officers out at poker the night before, and the boys seemed glad that a private had made them pay attention. I had not yet got my commission, and so any victory I might achieve was considered a victory for a private soldier. Several of the boys congratulated me. The nearest I ever come to quarreling with my old partner, Jim, was over this poker business. I showed him my roll, and told him how I had cleaned the officers out, and instead of feeling good over it, Jim said I was a confounded fool. I tried to argue the matter with Jim, but he couldn't be convinced, and insisted that they had made a fool of me, and had let me win on purpose, and that they would win it all back, and all I had besides. He said I had better let the chaplain take the hundred dollars to keep for me, and stay away from that poker game, and I would be a hundred ahead, but I didn't want any second-class chaplain to be a guardian over me, and I told Jim I was of age, and could take care of myself.

Jim said he thought I had some sense before I was commissioned, but it had spoiled me. He said in less than a week I would be borrowing money of him. I knew better, and went around camp with my thumbs stuck in my armholes, and felt big. It was an awful long day, but I put in the time thinking how I would draw cards, and bet judiciously, and finally night came, and I went over to the major's tent, where the officers usually congregated. I was early, and had to wait half an hour before the crowd showed up. As they came in each had something to say to me. "Here's the man who walked off with our wealth last night," said one. "Here's our victim," said another. "We will send him to his tent tonight without a dollar."

They chaffed me a good deal, but I made up my mind that I could play as well as they could, and some of them were old fellows that had played poker before I was born. Well, we went to work, and the first hand I got I lost ten dollars. It was the history of all smart Alecks, and there is no use of going into details. In less than an hour they had won the hundred dollars, and fifty that I had sewed inside my shirt to keep for a rainy day, and they had joked me every time I bet until I was exasperated to such an extent that I could have killed them.

Winning or losing money with them was a mere pastime, and they seemed to enjoy losing about as much as winning. I was too proud, or too big a fool to leave the game when I had lost all I had, and I borrowed a little of each of them, and lost it, and then I said I was tired and I guessed I would go to bed, and I went out, dizzy and sick at heart, and the officers laughed so I could hear them clear to my tent.

On the way to my tent, and as I walked around for half an hour before going there, I thought over what a fool I was, how I had forgotten all the good advice ever given me by my friends. Knowing that I was not intended by nature for a gambler, I had gone in with my eyes open, made a temporary success, got the big head, as all boys do, and gone back and laid down my bundle, and become the laughing stock of the whole crowd. I figured up that I was just an even hundred dollars out of pocket, and decided that I would never try to get it back. I would simply swear off gambling right there, forget that I knew one card from another, pay up my gambling debts when I got my first pay, and never touch a card again.

———

When I enlisted in the cavalry I bought a pair of top boots, of the Wellington pattern, stitched with silk up and down the legs, which were of shiny morocco. They came clear above my knees, and from the pictures I had seen of cavalry soldiers, it struck me those boots would be a pass-port to any society in the army. The first few months of my service, it seemed to me, the boots gave me more tone than any one thing. I learned afterwards that all new recruits came to the regiment with such boots, and that they were the laughing stock of all the old veterans. I did not know that I was being guyed by the boys, and I loved those boots above all things I had. To be sure, when we struck an unusually muddy country, some idiot of an officer seemed to be inspired to order us to dismount. The boys who had common army boots would dismount anywhere, in mud or water, but it seemed to me cruel for officers to order a dismount, when they knew I would have to step in the mud half way up to my knees, with those morocco boots on.

Several times when ordered to dismount in the mud, I have ridden out of the road, where it was not muddy, to dismount, but the boys would laugh so loud, and the officers would swear so wickedly, that I got so I would dismount wherever they told me, suppress my emotions, as I felt my beautiful, shiny boots sink into the red clay, and when we got into camp I would spend half the night cleaning my boots. The captain said if I would spend half the time cleaning my carbine and saber that I did cleaning my boots, I would have been a model soldier.

I think that for the first year of my service I had as elegant a pair of boots as could be found in the army. But it was the hardest work to keep track of them. The first three months it was all I could do to keep the chaplain from trading me a pair of old army shoes for my boots. The arguments he used to convince me that morocco boots were far above my station, and that they were intended for a chaplain, were labored. If he had used the same number of words in the right direction, he could have converted the whole army.

I had to sleep with my boots under my head every night, to prevent them from being stolen and twice they were stolen from my tent, but in each case recovered at the sutler's, where they had been pawned for a bottle of brandy peaches, which I had to pay for to redeem the boots. The boots had become almost a burden to me, in keeping them, but I enjoyed them so much that money could not have bought them. When we were in a town for a few days, and I rode around, it did not make any difference whether I had any other clothes on, of any account, the morocco boots captured the town. The natives could not see how a man who wore such boots could be anything but a high-up thoroughbred.

The last time I lost my boots will always be remembered by those who were in the same command. We were on the march with a Michigan and a New Jersey regiment, through the dustiest country that ever was. The dust was eight inches deep in the road, and just like fine ashes. Every time a horse put his foot down the dust would raise above the trees, and as there were two thousand horses, with four feet apiece, and each foot in constant motion, it can be imagined that the troops were dusty. And it was so hot that the perspiration oozed out of us, but the dust covered it.

The three regiments took turns in acting as rear guard, to pick up stragglers, and on this hot and dusty day the New Jersey regiment was in the rear. It was composed of Germans entirely, with a German colonel, a man who had seen service in Europe, and he looked upon a soldier as a machine, with no soul, fit only to obey orders. That was not the kind of a soldier I was.

During the day's march the boys stripped off everything they could. I know all I had on was a shirt and pants, and a handkerchief around my head. I took off my boots and coat and let the colored cook of the company strap them on to his saddle with the camp kettles. He usually rode right behind the company, and I thought I could get my things any time if I wanted to dress up. It was the hardest day's march that I ever experienced, lungs full of dust, and every man so covered with dust that you could not recognize your nearest neighbor. Afternoon the command halted beside a stream, and it was announced that we would go into camp for the night. The colored cook came along soon after, and he was perfectly pale, whether from dust or fright I could not tell, but he announced to me, in a manner that showed that he appreciated the calamity which had befallen the command, that he had lost my boots. I was going to kill him, but my carbine was full of dust, and I made it a point never to kill a man with a dirty gun, so I let him explain. He said:

"I fell back to de rear, by dat plantation where de cotton gin was burning, to see if I couldn't get a canteen of buttermilk to wash de dust outen my froat, when dat Dutch Noo Jersey gang come along, and de boss he said, 'nicker, you got back ahead fere you pelong, or I gick you in de pack mit a saber, aind't it,' and when I get on my mule to come along he grab de boots and he say, 'nicker, dot boots is better for me,' and when I was going to take dem away from him he stick me in de pants wid a saber. Den I come away."

I could have stood up under having an arm shot off, but to lose my boots was more than I could bear. It never did take me long to decide on any important matter, and in a moment I decided to invade the camp of that New Jersey regiment, recapture my boots or annihilate every last foreigner on our soil, so I started off, barefooted, without a coat, and covered with dust, for the headquarters of the New Jersey fellows. They had been in camp but a few minutes, but every last one of them had taken a bath in the river, brushed the dust off his clothes, and looked ready for dress parade. That was one fault of those foreigners, they were always clean, if they had half a chance.

I went right to the colonel's tent, and he was surrounded with officers, and they were opening bottles of beer, and how cool it looked. There was something peculiar about those foreigners, no matter if they were doing duty in the most inaccessible place in the South, and were short of transportation, you could always find beer at their headquarters. I walked right in, and the colonel was just blowing the foam off a glass of beer. He looked at me in astonishment, and I said in a voice husky from dust down my neck:

"Colonel this is an important epoch in the history of our beloved country. Events have transpired within the past hour, which leaves it an open question whether, as a nation, we are afoot or on horseback."

"Great hefens," said the colonel, stopping with his glass of beer half drank, "you vrighten me. Vot has habbened. But vait, und dake a glass of beer, as you seem exhausted, und proke up. Captain Ouskaspiel, hand the shendleman some peer. Mine Gott, bud you look hard, strancher."

I do not believe that I ever drank anything that seemed to go right to the spot, the way that beer did. It seemed to start a freshet of dust down my neck, clear my throat, and brace me up. While I was drinking it I noticed that the German colonel and his officers eyed me closely, my bare feet, my flannel shirt full of dust, and my hair that looked as though I had stood on my head in the road. They waited for me to continue, and after draining the last drop in the glass, I said:

> *"Colonel, it was no ordinary circumstance that induced you brave foreigners, holding allegiance to European sovereigns, to fly to arms to defend this new nation from an internecine foe. While we natives, and to the manor born, left our plows in the furrow, to spring to-arms, you left your shoemaker shops, the spigots of your beer saloons, the marts of commerce in which you were engaged, and stood shoulder to shoulder. Where the bullets of the enemy whistled, there could be found the brave Dutchmen of New Jersey. It brings tears to eyes unused to weeping, to think of the German fathers and mothers of our land, who are waiting and watching for the return of sons who will never come back, and this is, indeed, harder for them to bear, when we reflect that these boys were not obliged to fight for our country, holding allegiance, as I said before to——"*

"Waid a minute, of you blease," said the colonel. "Dake von more drink, and dell me, of you please, vot de hell you vos drying to get at. Capt. Hemrech, gif der shendleman a glass of beer."

A second glass of beer was given me, and I drank it. There was evidently a suspicion on the part of the New Jersey officers that the importance of my visit had been over-rated by them, and they seemed anxious to have me come to the point.

"On the march today," said I, wiping the foam off my moustache on my shirt-sleeve, "one of your thieving soldiers stole my boots from our nigger cook, who was conveying them for me. A cavalry soldier without boots, is no good. I came after my boots, and I will have them or blood. Return my boots, or by the eternal, the Wisconsin cavalry regiment will come over here and everlastingly gallop over your fellows. The Constitution of the United States and the Declaration of Independence, are on my side. In civil life a man's house is his castle. In the army a man's boots is his castle. Give me my boots, sir, or the blood of the slain will rest on your heads."

The colonel was half mad and half pleased. He tapped his forehead with his fore-finger, and looked at his officers in a manner that showed he believed my head was wrong, but he said kindly:

"My man, you go oud and sit under a tree, in the shade, and I vill hafe your poots found if they are in my rechiment," and I went out. I heard the colonel say to one of his officers, "It vas too pad dot two good glasses of beer should be spoiled, giving them to dot grazy solcher. Ve must be more careful mit de beer."

Pretty soon an officer came out and asked me how the boots were taken, and I gave him all the information I had, and he sent men all around the regiment, and in an hour or so the boots were brought to me, the man who stole them was arrested, the officers apologized to me, and I went back to my regiment in triumph, with my boots under my arms.

CHAPTER 22

Bull Run

By Joseph A. Altsheler

By the late 1800s and early 1900s, with the war a respectable distance in the past, it had become easy to romanticize soldiers' lives—especially those from the South. Joseph A. Altsheler was one of many turn-of-the-century authors who set his tales in the midst of the war. Altsheler, a prolific writer, turned out several novels featuring a company of Southern soldiers, the "Invincibles," who, in the selection here from The Guns of Bull Run, *face the first decisive battle of the war.*

—LISA PURCELL

HARRY ROSE TO HIS FEET AND SHOOK ST. CLAIR AND LANGDON. "UP, BOYS!" HE SAID. "The enemy will soon be here. I can see their bayonets glittering on the hills."

The Invincibles sprang to their feet almost as one man, and soon all the troops of Evans were up and humming like bees. Food and coffee were served to them hastily, but, before the last cup was thrown down, a heavy crash came from one of the hills beyond Bull Run, and a shell, screaming over their heads, burst beyond them. It was quickly followed by another, and then the round shot and shells came in dozens from batteries which had been posted well in the night.

The Southern batteries replied with all their might and the riflemen supported them, sending the bullets in sheets across Bull Run. The battle flamed in fifteen minutes into extraordinary violence. Harry had never before heard such a continuous and terrific thunder. It seemed that the drums of his ears would be smashed in, but over his head he heard the continuous hissing and whirring of steel and lead. The Northern riflemen were at work, too, and it was fortunate for the Invincibles that they were able to lie down, as they poured their fire into the bushes and woods on the opposite bank.

The volume of smoke was so great that they could no longer see the position of the enemy, but Harry believed that so much metal must do great damage. Although he was a lieutenant he had snatched up a rifle dropped by some fallen soldier, and he loaded and fired it so often that the barrel grew hot to his hand. Lying so near the river, most of the hostile fire went over the heads of the Invincibles, but now and then a shell or a cluster of bullets struck among them, and Harry heard groans. But he quickly forgot these sounds as he watched the clouds of smoke and the blaze of fire on the other side of Bull Run.

"They are not trying to force the passage of the bridge! Everything is for the best!" shouted Langdon.

"No, they dare not," shouted St. Clair in reply. "No column could live on that bridge in face of our fire."

It seemed strange to Harry that the Northern troops made no attempt to cross. Why did all this tremendous fire go on so long, and yet not a foe set foot upon the bridge? It seemed to him that it had endured for hours. The sun was rising higher and higher and the day was growing hotter and hotter. It lay with the North to make the first movement to cross Bull Run, and yet no attempt was made.

Colonel Talbot came repeatedly along the line of the Invincibles, and Harry saw that he was growing uneasy. Such a great volume of fire, without any effort to take advantage of it, made the veteran suspicious. He knew that those old comrades of his on the other side of Bull Run would not waste their metal in a mere cannonade and long range rifle fire. There must be something behind it. Presently, with the consent of the commander, he drew the Invincibles back from the river, where they were permitted to cease firing, and to rest for a while on their arms.

But as they drew long breaths and tried to clear the smoke from their throats, a rumor ran down the lines. The attack at the bridge was but a feint. Only a minor portion of the hostile army was there. The greater mass had gone on and had already crossed the river in face of the weak left flank of the Southern army. Beauregard had been outwitted. The Yankees were now in great force on his own side of Bull Run, and it would be a pitched battle, face to face.

The whole line of the Invincibles quivered with excitement, and then Harry saw that the rumor was true, or that their commander at least believed it to be so. The firing stopped entirely and the bugles blew the retreat. All the brigades gathered themselves up and, wild with anger and chagrin, slowly withdrew.

"Why are we retreating?" exclaimed Langdon, angrily. "Not a Yankee set his foot on the bridge! We're not whipped!"

"No," said Harry, "we're not whipped, but if we don't retreat we will be. If fifteen or twenty thousand Yankees struck us on the flank while those fellows are still in front everything would go."

These were young troops, who considered a retreat equivalent to a beating, and fierce murmurs ran along the line. But the officers paid no attention, marching them steadily on, while the artillery rumbled by their side. Both to right and left they heard the sound of firing, and they saw the smoke floating against both horizons, but they paid little attention to it. They were wondering what was in store for them.

"Cheer up, you lads!" cried Colonel Talbot. "You'll get all the fighting you can stand, and it won't be long in coming, either."

They marched only half an hour and then the troops were drawn up on a hill, where the officers rapidly formed them into position. It was none too soon. A long blue line, bristling with cannon on either flank, appeared across the fields. It was Burnside with the bulk of the Northern army moving down upon them. Harry was standing beside Colonel Talbot, ready to carry his orders, and he heard the veteran say, between his teeth:

"The Yankees have fooled us, and this is the great battle at last."

The two forces looked at each other for a few moments. Elsewhere great guns and rifles were already at work, but the sounds came distantly. On the hill and in the fields there was silence, save for the steady tramp of the advancing Northern troops. Then from the rear of the marching lines suddenly came a burst of martial music. The Northern bands, by a queer inversion, were playing Dixie:

"In Dixie's land
I'll take my stand,
To live and die for Dixie.
Look away! Look away!
Down South in Dixie."

Harry's feet beat to the tune, the wild and thrilling air played for the first time to troops going into battle.

"We must answer that," he said to St. Clair.

"Here comes the answer," said St. Clair, and the Southern bands began to play "The Girl I Left Behind Me." The music entered Harry's veins. He could not look without a quiver upon the great mass of men bearing down upon them, but the strains of fife and drum put courage in him and told him to stand fast. He saw the face of Colonel Talbot grow darker and darker, and he had enough experience himself to know that the odds were heavily against them.

The intense burning sun poured down a flood of light, lighting up the opposing ranks of blue and gray, and gleaming along swords and bayonets. Nearer and nearer came the piercing notes of Dixie.

"They march well," murmured Colonel Talbot, "and they will fight well, too."

He did not know that McDowell himself, the Northern commander, was now before them, driving on his men, but he did know that the courage and skill of his old comrades were for the present in the ascendant. Burnside was at the head of the division and it seemed long enough to wrap the whole Southern command in its folds and crush it.

Scattered rifle shots were heard on either flank, and the young Invincibles began to breathe heavily. Millions of black specks danced before them in the hot sunshine, and their nervous ears magnified every sound tenfold.

"I wish that tune the Yankees are playing was ours," said Tom Langdon. "I think I could fight battles by it."

"Then we'll have to capture it," said Harry.

Now the time for talking ceased. The rifle fire on the flanks was rising to a steady rattle, and then came the heavy boom of the cannon on either side. Once more the air was filled with the shriek of shells and the whistling of rifle bullets. Men were falling fast, and through the rising clouds of smoke Harry saw the blue lines still coming on. It seemed to him that they would be overwhelmed, trampled under foot, routed, but he heard Colonel Talbot shouting:

"Steady, Invincibles! Steady!"

And Lieutenant-Colonel St. Hilaire, walking up and down the lines, also uttered the same shout. But the blue line never ceased coming. Harry could see the faces dark with sweat and dust and powder still pressing on. It was well for the Southerners that nearly all of them had been trained in the use of the rifle, and it was well for them, too, that most of their officers were men of skill and experience. Recruits, they stood fast nevertheless and their rifles sent the bullets in an unceasing bitter hail straight into the advancing ranks of blue. There was no sound from the bands now. If they were playing somewhere in the rear no one heard. The fire of the cannon and rifles was a steady roll, louder than thunder and more awful.

The Northern troops hesitated at last in face of such a resolute stand and such accurate firing. Then they retreated a little and a shout of triumph came from the Southern lines, but the respite was only for a moment. The men in blue came on again, walking over their dead and past their wounded.

"If they keep pressing in, and it looks as if they would, they will crush us," murmured Colonel Talbot, but he did not let the Invincibles hear him say it. He encouraged them with voice and example, and they bent forward somewhat to meet the second charge of the Northern army, which was now coming. The smoke lifted a little and Harry saw the green fields and the white house of the Widow Henry standing almost in the middle of the battlefield, but unharmed. Then his eyes came back to the hostile line, which, torn by shot and shell, had closed up, nevertheless, and was advancing again in overwhelming force.

Harry now had a sudden horrible fear that they would be trodden under foot. He looked at St. Clair and saw that his face was ghastly. Langdon had long since ceased to smile or utter words of happy philosophy.

"Open up and let the guns through!" someone suddenly cried, and a wild cheer of relief burst from the Invincibles as they made a path. The valiant Bee and Bartow, rushing to the sound of the great firing, had come with nearly three thousand men and a whole battery. Never were men more welcome. They formed instantly along the Southern front, and the battery opened at once with all its guns, while the three thousand men sent a new fire into the Northern ranks. Yet the Northern charge still came. McDowell, Burnside, and the others were pressing it home, seeking to drive the Southern army from its hill, while they were yet able to bring forces largely superior to bear upon it.

The thunder and crash of the terrible conflict rolled over all the hills and fields for miles. It told the other forces of either army that here was the center of the battle, and here was its crisis. The sounds reached an extraordinary young-old man, bearded and awkward, often laughed at, but never to be laughed at again, one of the most wonderful soldiers the world has ever produced, and instantly gathering up his troops he rushed them toward the very heart of the combat. Stonewall Jackson was about to receive his famous nickname.

Jackson's burning eyes swept proudly over the ranks of his tall Virginians, who mourned every second they lost from the battle. An officer retreating with his battery glanced at him, opened his mouth to speak, but closed it again without saying a word, and infused with new hope, turned his guns afresh toward the enemy. Already men were feeling the magnetic current of energy and resolution that flowed from Jackson like water from a fountain.

A message from Colonel Talbot, which he was to deliver to Jackson himself, sent Harry to the rear. He rode a borrowed horse and he galloped rapidly until he saw a long line of men marching forward at a swift but steady pace. At their head rode a man on a sorrel horse. His shoulders were stooped a little, and he leaned forward in the saddle, gazing intently at the vast bank of smoke and flame before him. Harry noticed that the hands upon the bridle reins did not twitch nor did the horseman seem at all excited. Only his burning eyes showed that every faculty was concentrated upon the task. Harry was conscious even then that he was in the presence of General Jackson.

The boy delivered his message. Jackson received it without comment, never taking his eyes from the battle, which was now raging so fiercely in front of them. Behind came his great brigade of Virginians, the smoke and flame of the battle entering their blood and making their hearts pound fast as they moved forward with increasing speed.

Harry rode back with the young officers of his staff, and now they saw men dash out of the smoke and run toward them. They cried that everything was lost. The lip of Jackson curled in contempt. The long line of his Virginians stopped the fugitives and drove them back to the battle. It was evident to Harry, young as he was, that Jackson would be just in time.

Then they saw a battery galloping from that bank of smoke and flame, and, its officer swearing violently, exclaimed that he had been left without support. The stern face and somber eyes of Jackson were turned upon him.

"Unlimber your guns at once," he said. "Here is your support."

Then the valiant Bee himself came, covered with dust, his clothes torn by bullets, his horse in a white lather. He, too, turned to that stern brown figure, as unflinching as death itself, and he cried that the enemy in overwhelming numbers were beating them back.

"Then," said Jackson, "we'll close up and give them the bayonet."

His teeth shut down like a vise. Again the electric current leaped forth and sparkled through the veins of Bee, who turned and rode back into the Southern throng, the Virginians following swiftly. Then Jackson looked over the field with the eye and mind of genius, the eye that is able to see and the mind that is able to understand amid all the thunder and confusion and excitement of battle.

He saw a stretch of pines on the edge of the hill near the Henry house. He quickly marched his troops among the trees, covering their front with six cannon, while the great horseman, Stuart, plumed and eager, formed his cavalry upon the left. Harry felt instinctively that the battle was about to be restored for the time at least, and he turned back to Colonel Talbot and the Invincibles. A shell burst near him. A piece struck his horse in the chest, and Harry felt the animal quiver under him. Then the horse uttered a terrible neighing cry, but Harry, alert and agile, sprang clear, and ran back to his own command.

On the other side of Bull Run was the Northern command of Tyler, which had been rebuffed so fiercely three days before. It, too, heard the roar and crash of the battle, and sought a way across Bull Run, but for a time could find none. An officer named Sherman, also destined for a mighty fame, saw a Confederate trooper riding across the river further down, and instantly the whole command charged at the ford. It was defended by only two hundred Southern skirmishers whom they brushed out of the way. They were across in a few minutes, and then they advanced on a run to swell McDowell's army. The forces on both sides were increasing and the battle was rising rapidly in volume. But in the face of repeated and furious attacks the Southern troops held fast to the little plateau. Young's Branch flowed on one side of it and protected them in a measure; but only the indomitable spirit of Jackson and Evans, of Bee and Bartow, and others kept them in line against those charges which threatened to shiver them to pieces.

"Look!" cried Bee to some of his men who were wavering. "Look at Jackson, standing there like a stone wall!"

The men ceased to waver and settled themselves anew for a fresh attack.

But in spite of everything the Northern army was gaining ground. Sherman at the very head of the fresh forces that had crossed Bull Run hurled himself upon the Southern army, his main attack falling directly upon the Invincibles. The young recruits reeled, but Colonel Talbot and Lieutenant-Colonel St. Hilaire still ran up and down the lines begging them to stand. They took fresh breath and planted their feet deep once more. Harry raised his rifle and took aim at a flitting figure in the smoke. Then he dropped the muzzle. Either it was reality or a powerful trick of the fancy. It was his own cousin, Dick Mason, but the smoke closed in again, and he did not see the face.

The rush of Sherman was met and repelled. He drew back only to come again, and along the whole line the battle closed in once more, fiercer and more deadly than ever. Upon all the combatants beat the fierce sun of July, and clouds of dust rose to mingle with the smoke of cannon and rifles.

The advantage now lay distinctly with the Northern army, won by its clever passage of Bull Run and surprise. But the courage and tenacity of the Southern troops averted defeat and rout in detail. Jackson, in his strong position near the Henry house, in the cellars of which women were hiding, refused to give an inch of ground. Beauregard, called by the cannon, arrived upon the field only an hour before noon, meeting on the way many fugitives, whom he and his officers drove back into the battle. Hampton's South Carolina

Legion, which reached Richmond only that morning, came by train and landed directly upon the battlefield about noon. In five minutes it was in the thick of the battle, and it alone stemmed a terrific rush of Sherman, when all others gave way.

Noon had passed and the heart of McDowell swelled with exultation. The Northern troops were still gaining ground, and at many points the Southern line was crushed. Some of the recruits in gray, their nerves shaken horribly, were beginning to run. But fresh troops coming up met them and turned them back to the field. Beauregard and Johnston, the two senior generals, both experienced and calm, were reforming their ranks, seizing new and strong positions, and hurrying up every portion of their force. Johnston himself, after the first rally, hurried back for fresh regiments, while Jackson's men not only held their ground but began to drive the Northern troops before them.

The Invincibles had fallen back somewhat, leaving many dead behind them. Many more were wounded. Harry had received two bullets through his clothing, and St. Clair was nicked on the wrist. Colonel Talbot and Lieutenant-Colonel St. Hilaire were still unharmed, but a deep gloom had settled over the Invincibles. They had not been beaten, but certainly they were not winning. Their ranks were seamed and rent. From the place where they now stood they could see the place where they formerly stood, but Northern troops occupied it now. Tears ran down the faces of some of the youngest, streaking the dust and powder into hideous, grinning masks.

Harry threw himself upon the ground and lay there for a few moments, panting. He choked with heat and thirst, and his heart seemed to have swollen so much within him that it would be a relief to have it burst. His eyes burned with the dust and smoke, and all about him was a fearful reek. He could see from where he lay most of the battlefield. He saw the Northern batteries fire, move forward, and then fire again. He saw the Northern infantry creeping up, ever creeping, and far behind he beheld the flags of fresh regiments coming to their aid. The tears sprang to his eyes. It seemed in very truth that all was lost. In another part of the field the men in blue had seized the Robinson house, and from points near it their artillery was searching the Southern ranks. A sudden grim humor seized the boy.

"Tom," he shouted to Langdon, "what was that you said about sleeping in the White House at Washington with your boots on?"

"I said it," Langdon shouted back, "but I guess it's all off! For God's sake, Harry, give me a drink of water! I'll give anybody a million dollars and a half dozen states for a single drink!"

A soldier handed him a canteen, and he drank from it. The water was warm, but it was nectar, and when he handed it back, he said:

"I don't know you and you don't know me, but if I could I'd give you a whole lake in return for this. Harry, what are our chances?"

"I don't know. We've lost one battle, but we may have time to win another. Jackson and those Virginians of his seem able to stand anything. Up, boys, the battle is on us again!"

The charge swept almost to their feet, but it was driven back, and then came a momentary lull, not a cessation of the battle, but merely a sinking, as if the combatants were gathering themselves afresh for a new and greater effort. It was two o'clock in the afternoon, and the fierce July sun was at its zenith, pouring its burning rays upon both armies, alike upon the living and upon the dead who were now so numerous.

The lull was most welcome to the men in gray. Some fresh regiments sent by Johnston had come already, and they hoped for more, but whether they came or not, the army must stand. The brigades were massed heavily around the Henry house with that of Jackson standing stern and indomitable, the strongest wall against the foe. His fame and his spirit were spreading fast over the field.

The lull was brief, the whole Northern army, its lines reformed, swept forward in a half curve, and the Southern army sent forth a stream of shells and bullets to meet it. The brigades of Jackson and Sherman, indomitable foes, met face to face and swept back and forth over the ground, which was littered with their fallen. Everywhere the battle assumed a closer and fiercer phase. Hampton, who had come just in time with his guns, went down wounded badly. Beauregard himself was wounded slightly, and so was Jackson, hit in the hand. Many distinguished officers were killed.

The whole Northern army was driven back four times, and it came a fifth time to be repulsed once more. In the very height of the struggle Harry caught a glimpse in front of them of a long horizontal line of red, like a gleaming ribbon.

"It's those Zouaves!" cried Langdon. "Shoot their pants!"

He did not mean it as a jest. The words just jumped out, and true to their meaning the Invincibles fired straight at that long line of red, and then reloading fired again. The Zouaves were cut to pieces, the field was strewed with their brilliant uniforms. A few officers tried to bring on the scattered remnants, but two regiments of regulars, sweeping in between and bearing down on the Invincibles, saved them from extermination.

The Invincibles would have suffered the fate they had dealt out to the Zouaves, but fresh regiments came to their help and the regulars were driven back. Sherman and Jackson were still fighting face to face, and Sherman was unable to advance. Howard hurled a fresh force on the men in gray. Bee and Bartow, who had done such great deeds earlier in the day, were both killed. A Northern force under Heintzelman, converging for a flank attack, was set upon and routed by the Southerners, who put them all to flight, captured three guns and took the Robinson house.

Fortune, nevertheless, still seemed to favor the North. The Southerners had barely held their positions around the Henry house. Most of their cannon were dismounted. Hundreds had dropped from exhaustion. Some had died from heat and excessive exertion. The mortality among the officers was frightful. There were few hopeful hearts in the Southern army.

It was now three o'clock in the afternoon and Beauregard, through his glasses, saw a great column of dust rising above the tops of the trees. His experience told him that it must be made by marching troops, but what troops were they, Northern or Southern? In an agony of suspense he appealed to the generals around him, but they could tell nothing.

He sent off aides at a gallop to see, but meanwhile he and his generals could only wait, while the column of dust grew broader and broader and higher and higher. His heart sank like a plummet in a pool. The cloud was on the Federal flank and everything indicated that it was the army of Patterson, marching from the Valley of Virginia.

Harry and his comrades had also seen the dust, and they regarded it anxiously. They knew as well as any general present that their fate lay within that cloud.

"It's coming fast, and it's growing faster," said Harry. "I've got so used to the roar of this battle that it seems to me alien sounds are detached from it, and are heard easily. I can hear the rumble of cannon wheels in that cloud."

"Then tell us, Harry," said Langdon, "is it a Northern rumble or a Southern rumble that you hear?"

Harry laughed.

"I'll admit it's a good deal of a fancy," he said.

Arthur St. Clair suddenly leaped high in the air, and uttered at the very top of his voice the wild note of the famous rebel yell.

"Look at the flags aloft in that cloud of dust! It's the Stars and Bars! God bless the Bonnie Blue Flag! They are our own men coming, and coming in time!"

Now the battle flags appeared clearly through the dust, and the great rebel yell, swelling and triumphant, swept the whole Southern line. It was the remainder of Johnston's Army of the Shenandoah. It had slipped away from Patterson, and all through the burning day it had been marching steadily toward the battlefield, drummed on by the thudding guns. Johnston, the silent and alert, was himself with them now, and aflame with zeal they were advancing on the run straight for the heart of the Northern army.

Kirby Smith, one of Harry's own Kentucky generals, was in the very van of the relieving force. A man after Stonewall Jackson's own soul, he rushed forward with the leading regiments and they hurled themselves bodily upon the Northern flank.

The impact was terrible. Smith fell wounded, but his men rushed on and the men behind also threw themselves into the battle. Almost at the same instant Jubal Early, who had made a circuit with a strong force, hurled it upon the side of the Northern army. The brave troops in blue were exhausted by so many hours of fierce fighting and fierce heat. Their whole line broke and began to fall back. The Southern generals around the Henry house saw it and exulted. Swift orders were sent and the bugles blew the charge for the men who had stood so many long and bitter hours on the defense.

"Now, Invincibles, now!" cried Colonel Leonidas Talbot. "Charge home, just once, my boys, and the victory is ours!"

Covered with dust and grime, worn and bleeding with many wounds, but every heart beating triumphantly, what was left of the Invincibles rose up and followed their leader. Harry was conscious of a flame almost in his face and of whirling clouds of smoke and dust. Then the entire Southern army burst upon the confused Northern force and shattered it so completely that it fell to pieces.

The bravest battle ever fought by men, who, with few exceptions, had not smelled the powder of war before, was lost and won.

As the Southern cannon and rifles beat upon them, the Northern army, save for the regulars and the cavalry, dissolved. The generals could not stem the flood. They rushed forward in confused masses, seeking only to save themselves. Whole regiments dashed into the fords of Bull Run and emerged dripping on the other side. A bridge was covered with spectators come out from Washington to see the victory, many of them bringing with them baskets of lunch. Some were members of Congress, but all joined in the panic and flight, carrying to the capital many untrue stories of disaster.

A huge mass of fleeing men emerged upon the Warrenton turnpike, throwing away their weapons and ammunition that they might run the faster. It was panic pure and simple, but panic for the day only. For hours they had fought as bravely as the veterans of twenty battles, but now, with weakened nerves, they thought that an overwhelming force was upon them. Every shell that the Southern guns sent among them urged them to greater speed. The cavalry and little force of regulars covered the rear, and with firm and unbroken ranks retreated slowly, ready to face the enemy if he tried pursuit.

But the men in gray made no real pursuit. They were so worn that they could not follow, and they yet scarcely believed in the magnitude of their own victory, snatched from the very jaws of defeat. Twenty-eight Northern cannon and ten flags were in their hands, but thousands of dead and wounded lay upon the field, and night was at hand again, close and hot.

Harry turned back to the little plateau where those that were left of the Invincibles were already kindling their cooking fires. He looked for his two comrades and recognized them both under their masks of dust and powder.

"Are you hurt, Tom?" he said to Langdon.

"No, and I'm going to sleep in the White House at Washington after all."

"And you, Arthur?"

"There's a red line across my wrist, where a bullet passed, but it's nothing. Listen, what do you think of that, boys?"

A Southern band had gathered in the edge of the wood and was playing a wild thrilling air, the words of which meant nothing, but the tune everything:

"In Dixie's land
I'll take my stand,
To live and die for Dixie.
Look away! Look away!
Look away down South in Dixie."

"So we have taken their tune from them and made it ours!" St. Clair exclaimed jubilantly. "After all, it really belonged to us! We'll play it through the streets of Washington."

But Colonel Leonidas Talbot, who stood close by, raised his hand warningly.

"Boys," he said, "this is only the beginning."

CHAPTER 23

Andersonville: Confederate Prison Horrors
By John L. Maile

Hell on earth existed for Union army prisoners in the peaceful Georgia countryside. This account of the horror is from a survivor who was there and saw it happen. For an in-depth account in fiction, don't miss looking up the novel Andersonville *by MacKinlay Kantor.*

—LAMAR UNDERWOOD

AT THE TIME OF OUR INCARCERATION IN ANDERSONVILLE, THE CRISIS OF THE WAR OF the rebellion was reached. General Grant was fighting the great battles of the Wilderness in Virginia; the investment of Petersburg was about to begin, and General Lee was resisting the impact of the Federal forces with unsurpassed skill and heroism. General Sherman was also hastening his preparations to penetrate the vitals of the Confederacy by his famous "March to the Sea."

Skirmishes by the contending forces were of daily occurrence, and frequently battles were fought that now loom large in history. To bury the dead was not difficult; but the care of the wounded was a grave concern to both armies. An affair of still greater magnitude was the gathering up of the captured officers and soldiers, the transporting of them hundreds of miles, and the placing of them in prisons for safe keeping.

The Confederate authorities adopted a simple and logical plan. Foodstuffs for their armies could not be gathered in war-swept Virginia, nor to any great extent from the border States. In Georgia and Alabama, in parts of the Carolinas, Mississippi and Louisiana faithful slave labor produced an abundant supply of rice, corn and bacon, sweet potatoes and beans.

To transport these bulky materials to the armies of Lee, Hood and Johnson required every locomotive and freight car that could be mustered on Southern railroads. Hence the northward-bound trains were heavily laden. Those going southward were empty, and were available to carry away the thousands of Union prisoners. At several points in the South Atlantic and Gulf States, stockade prisons were set up, notably that in southwestern Georgia, named after an adjacent hamlet, "Andersonville."

This celebrated place of confinement for Federal prisoners below the rank of commissioned officer was located about sixty-two miles from Macon. It consisted of a stockade made of pine logs twenty-five feet long, set upright in a trench five feet deep, inclosing some sixteen acres, afterwards enlarged to twenty-six acres.

This inclosure was oblong in form, with its longest dimension in a general north and south direction, and had two gates in its western side, near the north and south ends respectively. It was commanded by several stands of artillery, comprising sixteen guns, located at a distance on rising ground. From four directions the guns could sweep the prison interior with grapeshot or shells.

A line of poles was planted along the lengthwise center of the pen. We were informed that if the men gathered in unusual crowds between the range of the poles and the north and south gates, the cannon would open upon us.

A report was circulated among us to the effect that General Sherman had started an expedition to release us; and we were informed that if his troops approached within seven miles of the stockade the prisoners would be mowed down by grapeshot. The fact is that one of his generals proposed a sortie that never was made. "About July 20, 1864, General Stoneman was authorized at his own desire to march (with cavalry) on Macon and Andersonville in an effort to rescue the National prisoners of war in the military prisons there."

Outside and against the stockade platforms for guards were placed two or three rods apart, and were so constructed that the sentinel climbed a ladder and stood waist high above the top of the wall and under a board roof, which sheltered him from the sun and rain.

Each of the guards faced the vast mass of prisoners and was ordered to closely watch the dead line before and below him half way to his comrade on his right and left.

The "dead line" formed a complete circuit parallel to the inside of the stockade and about twenty feet therefrom. It consisted of a narrow strip of board nailed to a row of stakes, which were about four feet high. "Shoot any prisoner who touches the dead line" was the standing order to the guards. Several companies from Georgia regiments were detailed for the duty, and their muskets were loaded with "buck and ball" (i.e., a large bullet and two buckshot). The day guard at the stockade consisted of one hundred and eighty-six men; the day reserve of eighty-six men. The night reserve consisted of one hundred and ten men; the outlay pickets of thirty-eight men.

A sick prisoner inadvertently placing his hand on the dead line for support, or one who was "moon blind" running against it, or anyone touching it with suicidal intent, would be instantly shot at, the scattering balls usually striking others than the one aimed at.

The intervening space between the wall and the dead line was overgrown with weeds, and was occasionally tested by workmen with long drills to ascertain the existence of tunnels. In attempting to escape by this means the prisoners endeavored to emerge at night some distance from the stockade and take to the woods. To frustrate such attempts, which would inevitably be discovered at roll-call the following morning, man-tracking hounds were led by mounted men on a wide circuit around the prison, with the well-nigh universal result that the trail was struck and the fugitive taken.

Later a stockade was erected parallel to the first, and some ten or twelve rods beyond. Tunnels could not be carried so far with the means available. They were dug with knives and the dirt was taken out in haversacks or bags drawn in and out by a cord. The work of digging was usually carried on at night. During the day a sick man lay over the tunnel's mouth in a tent or under a blanket. That the roll-call sergeant might not discover the fresh earth, it was sifted early in the morning from the pocket and down the trouser leg of a comrade, who walked unconcernedly about. The little grains of earth which he dropped were soon trodden under foot.

To increase the difficulty of tunnel escape, slaves and teams were employed to build piles of pitch-pine along the cleared space beyond the outer stockade. At night, when these were lighted, a line of fires was made which illuminated a wide area. From these fires arose columns of dense smoke, which in the sultry air of a midsummer night hung like a pall over the silent city of disease and starvation. Yet the city was not wholly quiet, for undertones of thousands of voices that murmured during the day at night died away into the low moans of the sick and the expiring, or rose into the overtones of the outcry of distressful dreams. In the edge of the gloom beyond the fires, patrols paced to and fro until the dawn. Every evening the watch-call sounded, "Post number one, nine o'clock and all is well." This cry was repeated by each sentinel until it had traveled around the stockade back to the place of starting. "Nine and a half o'clock and all is well," was next spoken, and likewise repeated. Thus every half hour from dark to daylight the time was called off, and this grim challenge greeted our ears every night until the survivors bade the Confederacy good-bye. Not that our captors benevolently wished to increase the sense of the shortness of the time until our release, but to be assured that the guards were keeping awake.

——

The least that can be said of the prison sustenance is that it was exceedingly slim. But while the per diem rations dealt out to an Andersonville prisoner were too small for proper maintenance, and much of the time inferior in quality, yet the thirty-two thousand to thirty-five thousand men who had to be fed were as a rule promptly served.

To secure this result effective organization was necessary. It was accomplished as follows: Groups of two hundred and seventy men were named detachments and duly numbered. Every detachment was divided into the first, second and third nineties, each of which was in charge of one of our own sergeants. The nineties, in turn, were divided into the first, second and third thirties, which also were in charge of a sergeant or corporal.

At ten o'clock every forenoon a drum call was beaten from the platform at the south gate. At this signal the prisoners fell into line by detachments, forming as best they could in the narrow paths that separated the small tents, blanket shanties or dug-outs. At the same moment a company of Confederate sergeants entered the two gates for the purpose of counting and recording the number of the prisoners. To each of these officers a certain number of detachments were assigned. The men, unsheltered from the fierce sun-heat, had perforce to remain standing during the entire count. If a number less than that of yesterday was in evidence, the Federal sergeant had to account for the deficit. Sometimes a number of men were too ill to stand up, so the line was held the longer while the Confederate official viewed the sick where they lay.

The bodies of those who had died since the count of the previous day were early in the morning carried to the south street and laid in a row until the ration wagon could haul them to the burying trench. On a card attached to the wrist of the deceased was written by the detachment sergeant, his name, regiment and date of death. These names were taken by the enumerator, who verified the record as the bodies were carried through the gate. Such was the scarcity of clothing that garments of any value were taken by comrades from the dead before interment.

In the early summer prisoners were occasionally detailed under guard to carry the dead some distance from the gate. On the return they were allowed to gather up chips which had accumulated from the hewing of stockade timbers. The quantity a man, weakened by hunger and disease, could bring in would sell for five dollars, U.S. currency. Competition to get out on one of these details became so intense that the privilege was discontinued.

At four o'clock in the afternoon rations of corn bread and bacon were issued on the basis of the morning count of those who are able to stand up. Two army wagons drawn by mules entered the north and south gates simultaneously. They were piled high with bread, thin loaves of corn bread or Johnny cake, made of coarse meal and water by our men who had been paroled for that work. A blanket was spread upon the ground and the quantity for a detachment was placed thereon in three piles; one for every ninety, according to the number of men able to eat. In like manner the sergeants of nineties sub-divided the piles to the thirties.

The writer had charge of a division of thirty and distributed as follows:

His blanket was spread in front of his shelter tent and on it he spread the bread in as many pieces as there were men counted in the morning. Each man had his number and was intently watching the comparative size of the portions. "Sergeant," cries one, pointing to a cube of bread. "That piece is smaller than the one next to it." A crumb is taken from the one and placed upon the other. The relative size of any piece may be challenged by any member of the thirty, for his life is involved.

The equalization is finally completed to the satisfaction of all. The sergeant then takes up a piece in his hand and says, "Whose is this?" A designated comrade looking the other way calls a number. The owner steps up and takes his portion. This process is repeated until all are served. Some four or five pounds of bacon are then cut on a board into small pieces and issued in like manner.

The cube of bread and morsel of meat constitute the ration for twenty-four hours. One-half may be eaten at once; the remainder should be put in the haversack for breakfast. If any one yields to his insatiable hunger and eats the whole for supper he has to fast until the following evening and must then deny himself and put away the portion for the next morning's breakfast. Experiment proved that strength was better sustained by taking the scanty ration of food in two portions than by eating the whole at once.

When the number of prisoners exceeded fifteen thousand, the facilities of the cookhouse were inadequate. Therefore raw rations were issued alternately every two weeks to each side of the prison. In this form the amount per capita daily was a scant pint of corn meal and a scrap of uncooked bacon.

Occasionally boiled rice and cow beans were substituted for the meal, but these were very difficult to issue in accurate portions. Sometimes a quantity of this glutenous food was carried in a sleeve of a shirt or in the trouser's leg tied at the end.

The supply of fuel for cooking was wholly inadequate. Often the ration of wood was ironically called a "toothpick." It would be split into small short splinters and two men would sometimes combine their portions. Water in a quart tin cup setting on small blocks of clay could be brought to a boil before the wood under it was consumed. Into this water meal was stirred and, if the blaze could be yet further economized, partially cooked mush was the outcome. The sick could not, however, do this work for themselves. Many ate meal uncooked, but the experiment soon ended life.

It may be observed that many of the Andersonville prisoners were well supplied with money. The Federal armies were reclothed and paid off in the spring of 1864. The new recruits and re-enlisted veterans, in many instances, had with them bounty money when captured. Greenbacks could be pressed into the sole of a shoe, or placed inside a brass button. In various ways money was concealed about the person.

The authorities at Andersonville allowed supplies to be sold to the prisoners for Federal money. Numerous small restaurants flourished in the stockade. From small clay ovens they supplied fresh bread and baked meats. Irish and sweet potatoes, string beans, peas, tomatoes, melons, sweet corn, and other garden products were abundantly offered for sale. New arrivals were amazed to find these resources in the midst of utter destitution and starvation.

As this sketch is of the nature of personal experiences, the writer might tell how, in his case, the question of increasing the food supply was solved. A ration of fresh beef received by his thirty consisted of a shank bone on which a small amount of lean meat remained. This latter was cut into portions about the size of a little finger. These were easily issued, but what shall be done with the bone which towered on the meat board above the diminutive strips of beef? No tools were available by which it could be broken up. One and another cried out, "I don't want the bone for a ration." "Count it out for me." "I can't gnaw a bone." The writer knew that a wealth of nutriment was contained in the rich marrow and oil-filled joints, and in view of the unanimous rejection of the bone, said, "Well, boys, if none of you want it, I will take it as my portion." "Agreed," shouted the crowd, adding expressions like these, "Come, hurry up and call off that meat; I'm hungry." The strips were speedily issued, and, for the most part, eaten at once.

The fortunate possessor of what was a large soup bone borrowed from a comrade a kitchen knife with permission to cut on the back of the same teeth, which were made with a file procured from a tent-mate. The steel of the blade was exceedingly hard and by the time the teeth were finished the file was worn nearly smooth. However, this fact insured that the teeth would hold their edge. The bone was quickly cut in two and the marrow dug out with a splinter. What remained was melted out with boiling water and a marrow soup was prepared for six hungry patriots. Next, the joints were sawed into slices and the rich oil extracted therefrom with hot water. Thus for two meals a generous addition was made to our impoverished menu.

Soon after, while splitting wood by driving the knife into the end of a stick, the blade was snapped off about one and one-half inches from the handle. This disaster brought consternation, for the owner valued his knife at five dollars. However, a settlement was effected by which the user retained the broken parts and the worn-out file. The blade was set into a split stick to be used as a saw, as circumstances might require.

The broken end of the shank was scraped on a brick to form a beveled edge like a chisel. Later on, the fact was demonstrated that these tools were a providential preparation. The face of the writer became diseased with the much prevailing scurvy. A swollen cheek, inflamed and bleeding gums with loosening teeth, indicated the fact that a hard fight for life must be put up. How shall it be done? About this time a stockade was built on three sides of an enclosure attached to the north end of the prison, thus making more room for the thousands of additional prisoners who were constantly arriving from many battle fields. The intervening wall was taken up and most of the timber sold to the prisoners. From one who had purchased a log, the writer obtained the wood sufficient to make three water pails; working on a two-thirds share.

This material was delivered to the writer in split strips about three inches thick and four feet long. With the knife-blade saw these sticks of hard pine were slowly and laboriously cut into lengths for staves which were split on a curve by driving together several sharp-pointed wedges into a circular grain of the wood. Thus each stave was an arc of the circumference of the tree. A day's ration was traded for a board three inches wide and thirty inches long. A mortise was cut through this to receive the knife-chisel, which was held in place with a forked wedge after the manner of a carpenter's plane.

This was the jointer on which the edges of the staves were smoothed and its upper end was placed on the knee of the writer, who sat tailor fashion on the ground, and the lower end was placed in a hole in the earth. The pieces for the bottom of the pail were split flat across the circular grain of the tree, and the edges were also smoothed on the jointer. For the want of truss hoops, the problem of setting up the staves seemed insurmountable. A sleepless night was passed in thinking the matter through. At four o'clock in the morning the inspiration came, and the solution was: Dig a hole in the ground the form and slope of the prospective pail. This was speedily done, and the staves were successfully set half their length in this mold, and the last one driven home brought the whole into shape. Two knapsack straps were passed around the top of the pail and held it together. It was then carefully drawn out of the hole and hoops made of split saplings were put in place, and the handle of like material was made. Precious food was bartered for these split stems, and the resultant fasting added to prevailing starvation nearly cost the writer his life.

Pieces for the bottom were jointed, placed on the ground and on them the pail was set. A pencil was run round on this bottom and the end of each piece was cut with saw and chisel wherever the curved mark indicated.

Days of incessant labor with chisel and a borrowed jackknife sufficed to produce from hard pitch pine the staves for the sides and bottom of a water pail of the ordinary size.

When at last the pail was completed so imperfect were the joints that meal could be sifted through. Derisive laughter greeted the apparent failure of a pail to hold water, through the joints of which the light freely shone. However, the maker depended on the dry wood of the staves swelling tight if only the hoops proved strong enough to stand the immense pressure. Happily, this resulted and in triumph the first made pail was handed over to the owner of the log in payment for the wood from which three pails could be made.

The second pail was more speedily made and sold for $1.50 with which the proprietor bought vegetables which eaten raw cured the scurvy in his face.

During the following winter which was passed in the Confederate prison at Florence, South Carolina, the shoes worn by the most of our group, owing to defective machine stitching, peeled from the toe to the heel, causing almost constantly damp feet, to the serious detriment of health.

Again the writer was obliged to make a fight for life. Recalling the process of making his chisel, he scraped, on a brick, the shank of his worn-out file into a point like a pegging awl. A gum tree knot served as a handle. A two-inch nut from a car bolt was screwed to a handle for a shoe hammer. A piece of soft pine was whittled into a last. With the knife-saw maple chips were cut into right lengths for shoe pegs which were shaped one by one. With this equipment the loosened soles were tightly pegged to the uppers. The shoes thus made water tight contributed no little to our chances of survival.

The writer afterwards mended shoes for one of the wood-chopping party who secured, of field negroes, sweet potatoes which he brought with the working squad into the prison at evening, and with them paid for the mending. These were cooked by the writer and retailed to the prisoners with large profit in U.S. fractional currency.

Confederate money was secretly purchased forty dollars for one, and with this supplies could be lawfully bought of the prison sutler. Bread per small loaf, flour per pound, and a fair-sized cabbage could be bought each for ten dollars. We drove a flourishing trade in hot cabbage soup with men who possessed any money; especially to those who, without shelter, literally piled themselves together for mutual warmth during the piercing cold and rain of a southern winter night.

The soup was made in the following manner: A cabbage consisted of a stalk with a tuft of leaves on the upper end and a bunch of roots on the lower end. The whole was washed clean and chopped up fine with the knife-chisel. The sliced leaves, stem and roots were boiled in eight quarts of water until made as tender as heat could do it. Into the green colored liquid was stirred some flour thickening; the whole was salted and a minced red pepper was added for pungency, while a whole pepper floated on the surface as an advertisement.

For a soup dipper a piece of pail hoop was riveted to the side of a condensed milk can, the two rivets being cut from a copper cent with the chisel driven with the shoe hammer. For soup plates a canteen was melted apart and the two halves formed each a plate. On Market Square, down by the swamp, four slender stakes were driven and thereon was placed a pine shake, which formed the soup counter. The soup kettle was covered with a piece of woolen shirt, which kept in the heat. Very early each morning we opened up for business and a line of shivering men in rags and nearly perished from exposure formed as the soup brigade. The price per plate was a five-cent shinplaster of U.S. fractional currency. The poor fellow who had no money must needs go without. As new prisoners ceased to arrive the money supply was soon gathered up and the prison sutler went away and trade was brought to an end.

Our last plate of soup was sold to a Maine soldier who paid for it his last five cents. He was nearly naked and incessantly shivered from the cold. The writer found him the following morning, after a night of rain, to which he was exposed, with his knees drawn up to his chin in the instinctive effort to bring the surfaces of his body together for warmth. With difficulty his frame was straightened out for burial.

The profit of this business for several weeks gave to our group of six one fairly good meal each day and made possible the survival of those of our number who finally emerged from this awful prison life.

If the food supply of Andersonville was bad, the water supply was worse. To understand the situation and to see how little was done to overcome the difficulties involved, and to make the most of the existing facilities for the relief of the suffering, one has to consider the formation of this prison encampment.

The surface of the interior consisted of two hillsides, sloping respectively north and south towards the center which was occupied by a swamp of nearly four acres. This was traversed by a sluggish creek which was some five feet wide and six inches deep, and made its way along the foot of the south slope. Up the stream were located the headquarters of Capt. Wirtz, the camps of the Confederate artillery and infantry and the cook-house for the prisoners. The drainage of these localities entered the creek which flowed into the prison through spaces between the stockade timbers, and polluted the water which was the chief supply of the prison, and which, at midnight, in its clearest condition, was the color of amber. The intervening space at the foot of the north hill was a wide morass, and when overflowed by rains became a vast cesspool on which boundless swarms of flies settled down and laid their eggs; which were speedily hatched by the fervent heat of the nearly tropical sun, and became a horrible undulating mass. On a change of wind the odor could be detected miles away; indeed it was reported that the people of Macon petitioned General Howell Cobb, the military governor of Georgia, for a removal of the prison located sixty miles away, lest an awful pestilence sweep over their country!

The turkey buzzards, birds of ill omen, would come up against the wind, alight on the bare limbs of the tall pines overlooking the prison, and circle over the grizzled city as if waiting to descend for a carrion feast.

When we entered the prison on May 23rd, our detachment of two hundred and seventy men was scheduled fifty-five, indicating the presence of fourteen thousand eight hundred and fifty prisoners. The number steadily rose until a reported thirty-five thousand were present at one time. As the arrivals increased by hundreds and thousands, the daily mortality was counted by scores and hundreds, and many of the sick were without shelter from the heat of the pitiless sun.

As the killed and wounded are scattered over the fields of the sanguinary battle, so our dying sick lay around on every hand. In the early summer, Capt. Wirtz issued to the prisoners picks and shovels, with which to dig wells for increased water supply. From some of these wells the men started tunnels through which to escape. Discovering this, the commander withdrew the tools, and ordered the wells to be filled up. Permission to keep one of them open was purchased by a group of prisoners. It was sunk to a necessary depth, covered with a platform and trap door, and supplied about one thousand men.

Aside from this well, for the favored few, the only water supply was from about twelve feet of the length of the creek which reached between the dead-line and the bridge connecting the two divisions of the prison. A terrible water famine set in, with the result that many of the ailing ones became insane from thirst.

REPORTS ON ANDERSONVILLE: THE HORRORS REVEALED

"In November, 1863, an order was issued for the establishment of a prison in Georgia, the granary of the eastern part of the Confederacy, and for this purpose a tract of land was selected near the town of Andersonville. A stockade 15 feet high, inclosing 16-1/2 acres, was built, and this, in June, 1864, was enlarged to 26-1/2 acres, but 3-1/4 acres near the center were too marshy to be used. A small stream ran through the inclosure, which, it was thought, would furnish water sufficient for drinking and for bathing. The

trees within the stockade were cut down and no shelter was provided for the expected inmates, who began to arrive in February, 1864, before the rude prison was completed according to the design, and before an adequate supply of bacon for their use had been received. Prisoners continued to come until, on the 5th of May, there were about 12,000, which number went on increasing until in August it exceeded 32,000. Their condition was one of extreme wretchedness. Those who came first erected rude shelters from the debris of the stockade; later arrivals burrowed in the ground or protected themselves with any blankets or pieces of cloth of which they had not been deprived according to the practice of robbing men who were taken prisoners which prevailed on both sides. Through an unfortunate location of the baking and cooking houses on the creek above the stockade the water became polluted before it reached the prisoners, so that to obtain pure water they must dig wells. After a severe storm a spring broke out within the inclosure, and this became one of the main reliances for drinking water. The sinks were constructed over the lower part of the stream, but the current was not swift enough to carry away the ordure, and when the stream was swollen by rain and overflowed, the foecal matter was deposited over a wide area, producing a horrible stench. This was the famous prison of Andersonville."—From Rhodes' History of the United States, *Vol. V, pp. 483–515.*

"The history of Andersonville prison pen has shocked the world with its tales of horror, of woe, and of death, before unheard of and unknown to civilization. No pen can describe, no artist can paint, no imagination comprehend their fearful and unutterable sufferings.

"Into the narrow confines of this prison were herded more than thirty-five thousand enlisted men, whose only fault was they 'wore the Union blue,' many of them the bravest and best, the most devoted and heroic of those grand armies that carried the flag of the Union to final victory. For long and weary months they suffered and died for that flag. Here they suffered—unsheltered—from the burning rays of a southern sun, or were drenched by the rain and deadly dews of the night. All this while they were in every stage of physical disease—hungered, emaciated, starving.

"Is it a wonder that during the month of August, 1864, one man died in every eleven minutes, night and day, or that, for six months, beginning April, 1864, one died every twenty-two and one-half minutes night and day? This should forever silence the assertion that men would be taken prisoners rather than risk their lives on the firing line. The lack of water was the cause of much disease and suffering. Under the most favorable circumstances the water supply was insufficient for one-quarter of the number of men confined there. All the water obtainable was from a sluggish creek that ran through the grounds; and, in addition to this, there were thirty-six hundred men acting as guards camped on the bank of this stream before it reached the prison pen, and the water became so foul no words can describe it."—From "A Sketch of Andersonville," by Mrs. Lizabeth A. Turner, Chairman Andersonville Prison Board. *Journal of the Twenty-fifth National Convention of the Woman's Relief Corps, page 169.*

CHAPTER 24

Chickamauga
By James R. Carnahan

Blue and gray armies clash in a key battle in the Tennessee mountains. Described by a Union army officer, the action shows the difficulty of troop movements and the timing of attacks in rugged terrain.

—LAMAR UNDERWOOD

LEAVING MURFREESBORO IN JUNE, 1863, WE HAD MARCHED TO MCMINVILLE, TENN., and had there spent the summer as one of the out-posts of Gen. W. S. Rosecrans' army, while the remainder of his army advanced toward Chattanooga. Leaving McMinville when the time had fully come for the final advance, we marched to join the remainder of the army at Bridgeport. When we reached Bridgeport, however, we found the army had crossed the Tennessee River and was pushing on toward Chattanooga, and followed on.

Our first view of Chattanooga was had as our division, Van Cleve's, of Crittenden's Corps—the 21st—passed around the point of Lookout Mountain, where it touches the Tennessee River down below the town opposite Moccasin Point. There seemed nothing specially inviting to us in the little old town off to our left; in fact, the invitation came to us to go in another direction. Obeying the order we there received, we hastened away up the valley toward Rossville, and on toward Ringgold, in pursuit of Bragg, who was at the time reported to be retreating before Rosecrans' army. On we pushed, joining the remainder of our corps and the cavalry at Ringgold.

It was a delightful march; the roads were smooth, the weather was perfect, the enemy kept out of our way, and, in fact, we felt as though now there would be no more serious fighting. Had we not driven the Confederate army out of Kentucky, had whipped it at Stone River, and driven it all the way down from Murfreesboro, and out of their stronghold—Chattanooga—and were yet in pursuit? Certainly the war would soon be over. So the men thought and talked. When we reached Ringgold, we found, for some reason not clearly defined in words, that we would not advance any further in that particular direction. In fact, it was deemed advisable that our corps should advance over the same route by which we had come, back up into Lookout Mountain valley. Two weeks in that pleasant early autumn of 1863 we spent somewhat after the manner described in the old song, we

"Marched up the hill, and then marched down again."

We made a reconnoissance now here, now there, each time becoming more and more convinced that Gen. Bragg was in no very great hurry to get away, and speedily end the war; in fact, we became fully persuaded that he preferred to remain in our immediate front; nay, more, we were fast making the discovery that the enemy was for some reason becoming more and more aggressive.

The reconnoissance that was made by the Third Brigade of Van Cleve's Division on Sunday, September 13th, beyond Lee & Gordon's mills, developed the fact that the enemy's lines were stronger than ever before, and that all our efforts to dislodge him were in vain. That the Confederates were receiving reinforcements could not be longer doubted, and that a battle was imminent was now apparent to all; just where or when, whether our army would make the attack or be attacked, were the unsolved questions of the problem. Each day, as it came and passed, seemed to bring to all a more certain conviction that the conflict, when or wheresoever it should come, would be a most terrible one.

In this uncertainty, and with certain feverish restlessness that is always engendered in anticipation of a battle, the 21st Corps lay about Crawfish Springs and Lee & Gordon's mills. Extra ammunition had been issued to the troops as a precaution against any emergency that might arise. Each company officer had received orders to keep his men in camp; the horses of the artillery stood harnessed; everything seemed to be in readiness, come what might. Such was the condition of affairs with our portion of the army on Friday, the 18th of September, 1863. The forenoon of that day had been spent in general talk, both among officers and among men, on the now all-absorbing question as to the probabilities of a battle.

Our brigade, the Third, commanded by Col. Geo. F. Dick, of the 86th Indiana, lay near Crawfish Springs. We had just finished our noon-day meal and pipes were lighted, and we were preparing to spend the hours of the afternoon as best we might, when we caught the sound of a distant artillery shot off toward Ringgold. This proved to be the first shot of what was so soon to be the battle of Chickamauga.

The shots grew in number, and more and more distinct. It required but little time for each officer and soldier to take in the situation and realize the condition of affairs. We knew from the sounds that were borne to us that the army of Gen. Bragg had ceased to retreat and to act on the defensive, and was now advancing upon our army. This action was proof that the enemy had been largely reinforced, and now felt itself not only able to meet us in battle, but confident in its ability to defeat and put us to rout, and to recover all they had lost.

Not much time was given for thought or talk before our brigade was ordered to "fall in," and we were moved out down to the left, and past Lee & Gordon's mills, to the relief of our hard-pressed cavalry, now falling back onto our main army. How urgent the need of assistance to our cavalry we soon learned as we saw them coming in wounded and broken, riderless horses, ambulances filled with wounded and dying—all coming together told how fierce the onslaught that had been made on them, and they who were yet unwounded were contesting, with all the bravery and stubbornness that men could, every part of the distance that lay between us and the enemy. Our lines were formed, and we moved forward, checking the enemy's advance for the day. Our skirmish line and pickets were strengthened, and our brigade remained on duty through the night, and listened to the ominous sounds that came to us through the darkness, the distant rumbling of artillery wheels, the sound now and then of axes, all telling us of the preparations that were being made, and the perfecting of plans for the terrible contest of the morrow.

In the early morning of the 19th we were relieved from duty, and were sent back toward Lee & Gordon's mills, into an open field, there to prepare our breakfasts and get such sleep and rest as we could, until such time as our services would be demanded. The sun had scarcely appeared when a shot was heard over on the right of our line; in a short time another, as if one army or the other were feeling its way. Soon another shot, which brought an answering shot; then came the opening artillery duel that seemed to shake the very earth. From this, shots came from all along our lines, showing that the enemy had got well into position along our entire front during the night.

Now the firing increases on our right, and between the artillery shots we catch the sound of musketry; stronger and stronger the contest grows, and nearer, too, for now comes one continuous roar of artillery from the right, and volley after volley of musketry tells that the two armies have come together in the first charges of the battle. The contest gathers in strength, starting down from the right, on it comes to the lines in our front, and on past us toward the left, until at length it becomes one commingled roar of artillery and rattle of musketry from right to left. We see none of the lines engaged, but it must be that the Union army is holding its position against the furious charges that are being made upon it. A lull for a few moments comes in the contest, and you hear only scattering shots along the line; but looking off to our front, through an opening in the trees, could be seen, crossing the ridge, the marching columns of the enemy as they moved toward our left, preparatory to the terrible work of that Saturday afternoon.

Again the sound of the contest begins to gather and grow in strength. It comes on like the blasts of the tornado, sounding louder and louder, growing stronger and stronger until it comes in a great rush and roar of sound, before which those who hear and are not of it stand in awe and look each the other in the face, but dare not speak. Over on the right it again breaks forth, and with renewed strength rolls on down the lines, growing fiercer and fiercer, and louder and louder, as additional forces are brought into the contest, until it reaches the extreme left, when backward it would sweep again to the right, only again to go rolling, and jarring, and crashing in its fury as backward and forward it swept. It was as when the ocean is lashed to fury by the tempest, when great rolling waves come chasing one the other in their mighty rage, until they strike with a roar upon the mighty cliffs of stone, only to be broken and driven back upon other incoming waves as strong, or stronger, than they had been, so came to our ears the sound of that mighty tempest of war—volley after volley of musketry rolling in waves of dreadful sound, one upon the other, to which was added the deep sounding crash of the artillery, like mighty thunder peals through the roar of the tempest, making the ground under your feet tremble as it came and went, each wave more terrible than the former.

It was evident to those of us who listened that the enemy was making desperate efforts to overwhelm and break our lines.

Through that forenoon—and oh, how long it seemed—we waited outside the contest, and heard that mighty, that terrible tornado of war as it raged in our front and all about us, and saw the constantly moving columns of the enemy's infantry, with flying flags, and saw battery after battery as they moved before us like a great panorama unfolding in the opening to which I have referred. We had been sent back, as I have said, to rest after a night on duty, but rest there was none. The guns were stacked in line, and the battery attached to our brigade stood just in the rear of us, with horses hitched to guns and caissons, ready to move any instant. Now and then a stray shot or shell would fly over us, and strike in the ground or burst in the air, to our rear.

Our men grow restless, that restlessness that comes to men in that most trying of all times in the life of a soldier, when he hears the battle raging with all the might of the furies about him, when he can now and then catch the sound of the distant shouts that tell that the charge is being made, and can hear above the shouts the rattling, tearing, shrieking sound of the volleys of musketry, and the shot and shell and canister of the artillery that tells too well that the charge is met, and that great gaps are being made in the lines; that men and comrades are being maimed, and wounded, and killed. In such moments as these, when you see and hear, but are not a part of the battle, men grow pale and lose their firmness, their nerve; then it is they realize that war is terrible. They are hungry, but they cannot eat; they are tired but they cannot sit down; they lay prone upon the ground, but that is worse than standing, and they rise again; you speak to them, and they answer you as one who is half asleep; they laugh, but it is a laugh that has no joy in it.

The infantrymen stay close to their muskets; the artillerymen, drivers, and gunners stand close to their posts of duty in a terrible, fearful state of nervous unrest.

These men whom you thus see on that fearful September afternoon are not lacking in all true soldierly qualities; their bravery had been tested on other fields—at Donelson, at Shiloh, at Perryville, and at Stone River they met the enemy in the hottest of the battle with all the bravery and firmness of the Roman, and now when the time shall come for them to be ordered to the aid of their comrades, they will not be found wanting. Thus hour after hour has passed for us in this fearful state of anxiety and suspense. No tidings from the front; we only know that the battle is fearful, is terrible.

Noonday has passed, when suddenly from out the woods to our front and left onto the open field, dashes an officer, his horse urged to its greatest speed toward our command. The men see him coming, and in an instant they are aroused to the greatest interest. "There comes orders" are the words that pass from lip to lip along that line. Without commands the lines are formed behind the gun stacks; the cannoneers stand by their guns; the drivers stand with hand on rein and foot in stirrup, ready to mount. How quick, how great the change at the prospect of freedom from the suspense of the day. The eye lights up, the arm again grows strong, and the nerves are again growing steady; every head is bent forward to catch, if possible, the first news from the front, and to hear the orders that are to be given. All now are roused: there is to be no more suspense; it is to be action from now and on until the battle shall close.

Nearer and nearer comes the rider; now you catch his features, and can see the fearful earnestness that is written in every line of the face. He bends forward as he rides, in such haste he is. The horse he rides seems to have caught the spirit of the rider, and horse and rider tell to the experienced soldier that there is to be work for us; that the urgency is great, and that the peril is imminent.

How much there is of life, of the soldier's life, that cannot be painted on canvas or described in words; it is the inexpressible part—the face, the eye, the swaying of the body, the gesture of the hand, the movement of the head, as the officer, the soldier, feels that his comrades are in deepest peril, and that unless help comes, and comes quickly, all hope is gone. He speaks not a word, but his appearance speaks in thunder tones. Companions, you, and each of you, have seen just such times and such faces. Such was the face, and such the action of that staff officer that afternoon of September 19, 1863; and every soldier, as he saw him, read that face and form as though it were an open book—yes, and read it in all its awful, dreadful meaning—and, reading, realized their full duty. He reaches our line, and is met by our brigade commander, Col. Geo. F. Dick, as anxious to receive the orders as he is to give them. The command comes in quick, sharp words: "The General presents his compliments, and directs that you move your brigade at once to the support of Gen. Beard. Take the road, moving by the flank in 'double quick' to the left and into the woods, and go into line on the left of Gen. Beatty's brigade. I am to direct you. Our men are hard pressed." The last sentence was all that was said in words as to the condition of our troops, but it told that we had read aright before he had spoken.

Scarce had the order been delivered when the command to "take arms" is heard along the line, and to drivers and cannoneers to mount. It scarcely took the time required to tell it for our brigade to get in motion, moving off the field, the artillery taking the wagon road, the infantry alongside. It was a grand scene as we moved quickly into place, closing up the column and waiting but a moment for the command. The guns are at a right shoulder, and all have grown eager for the order, "Forward." The bugle sounds the first note of the command. Now look along that column; the men are leaning forward for the start; you see the drivers on the artillery teams tighten the rein in the left hand, and, with the whip in the uplifted right arm, rise in their stirrups; and as the last note of the bugle is sounded, the crack of the whips of thirty-six drivers over the backs of as many horses, and the stroke of the spurs, sends that battery of six guns and its caissons rattling and bounding over that road, while the infantry alongside are straining every nerve as they hasten to the relief of the comrades so hard pressed.

The spirits of the men grow higher and higher with each moment of the advance. The rattling of the artillery and the hoof beats of the horses add to the excitement of the onward rush, infantry and artillery thus side by side vying each with the other which shall best do his part. Now, as we come nearer, the storm of the battle seems to grow greater and greater. On and yet on we press, until reaching the designated point, the artillery is turned off to the left on to a ridge, and go into position along its crest, while the lines of the infantry are being formed to the right of the road over which we have just been hurrying. Our lines are scarcely formed, and the command to move forward given, when the lines which are in advance of us are broken by a terrific charge of the enemy, and are driven back in confusion onto our line—friend and foe so intermingled that we cannot fire a shot without inflicting as much injury on our men as upon the enemy.

Our artillery, on the crest of the ridge back of us, have unlimbered and gone into action, and their shell are now flying over our heads into the woods, where the enemy's lines had been. Confusion seems to have taken possession of our lines, and, to add to it, the lines to our right have been broken and the enemy are sweeping past our flank. The order is given to fall back on line with the artillery. Out of the wood, under the fire of our cannon, the men hasten.

Now on the crest of that ridge, without works of any kind to shelter them, our troops are again hastily formed, and none too soon. Down the gentle slope of that ridge, and away to our right and left and front stretches an open field, without tree or shrub to break the force of the balls. In our front, and at the edge of the field, two hundred yards away, runs the road parallel with our lines; beyond the road the heavy timber where the Confederate lines are formed, and well protected in their preparations for their charge. Scarce had our lines been formed when the sharp crack of the rifles along our front, and the whistling of the balls over our heads, give us warning that the advance of the enemy has begun, and in an instant the shots of the skirmishers are drowned by the shout that goes up from the charging column as it starts down in the woods.

Our men are ready. The 7th Indiana Battery—six guns—is on the right of my regiment; Battery M, 4th U.S. Artillery, is on our left. The gunners and every man of those two batteries are at their posts of duty, the tightly drawn lines in their faces showing their purpose there to stand for duty or die. Officers pass the familiar command of caution along the line—"Steady, men, steady." The shout of the charging foe comes rapidly on; now they burst out of the woods and onto the road. As if touched by an electric cord, so quick and so in unison was it, the rifles leap to the shoulder along the ridge where waves the stars and stripes.

Now the enemy are in plain view along the road covering our entire front; you can see them, as with cap visors drawn well down over their eyes, the gun at the charge, with short, shrill shout they come, and we see the colors of Longstreet's corps, flushed with victory, confronting us. Our men recognize the gallantry of their foe, and their pride is touched as well. All this is but the work of an instant, when, just as that long line of gray has crossed the road, quick and sharp rings out along our line the command "Ready," "Fire!"

It seems to come to infantry and artillery at the same instant, and out from the rifles of the men and the mouths of those cannons leap the death-dealing bullet and canister; again and again, with almost lightning rapidity, they pour in their deadly, merciless fire, until along that entire ridge it has become almost one continuous volley. Now that Corps that had known little of defeat begins to waver; their men had fallen thick and fast about them. Again and yet again the volleys are poured into them, and the artillery on our right and left have not ceased their deadly work. No troops can long withstand such fire; their lines waver, another volley and they are broken and now fall back in confusion. The charge was not long in point of time, but was terrible in its results to the foe.

Along the entire line to our right and left we can hear the battle raging with increased fury. We are now on the defensive; and all can judge that the lull in our front is only the stillness that forbodes the more terrible storm that is to come. A few logs and rails are hastily gathered together to form a slight breastwork. Soon the scattering shots that began to fall about us gave us warning that our foe was again moving on us.

Again we are ready, now laying behind our hastily-prepared works. Again we hear the shout as on they come with more determination than before; but with even greater courage do our men determine to hold their lines. The artillery is double shotted with canister. Again the command, "Fire!" and hotter, fiercer than before the battle rages along our front. Shout is answered with shout, shot by shots tenfold, until again our assailants break before our fire and are again forced back.

But why repeat further the story of that Saturday afternoon. Again and again were those charges repeated along our line, only to be hurled back—broken and shattered. It did seem as though our men were more than human. The artillerymen worked as never before. Their guns—double shotted—had scarce delivered their charges, and before the gun could complete its recoil, was caught by strong arms, made doubly strong in that fever heat of battle; was again in position, again double shotted, and again fired into the face of the foe.

The arms bared, the veins standing out in great strong lines, the hat or cap gone from the head, the eye starting almost from the socket, the teeth set, the face beaded with perspiration, balls falling all about them, those men of the 7th Indiana Battery and Battery M seemed to be supernaturally endowed with strength. Their comrades of the infantry vied with them in acts of heroism, and daring, and endurance. They shouted defiance at the foe with every shot; with face and hands begrimed in the smoke and dust and heat of the battle; with comrades falling about them, the survivors thought only of vengeance.

All the horses on two of the guns of the 7th Indiana Battery are shot down; another charge is beginning; those two guns might be lost; they must be gotten back. Quick as thought a company of infantry spring to the guns, one hand holding the rifle, the other on the cannon, and with the shot falling thick and fast in and about them, drag the guns over the brow of the ridge and down into the woods, just in the rear of our lines, and hasten back again to take their places in line, ready to meet the on-coming charge. An artilleryman is shot down; a man from the infantry takes his place and obeys orders as best he can.

When the charge begins our men are lying down. Now, in the midst of it, so great has become the excitement, so intense the anxiety, all fear and prudence vanishes, and the men leap to their feet, and fire and load, and fire and load, in the wildest frenzy of desperation. They have lost all ideas of danger, or the strength of the assailants. It was this absolute *desperation* of our men that held our lines. A soldier or officer is wounded; unless the wound was mortal or caused the fracture of a limb, they had the wound tied or bandaged as best they could, some tearing up their blouses for bandages, and again took their places in the lines beside their more fortunate comrades.

Each man feels the terrible weight of responsibility that rests on him personally for the results that shall be achieved that day. It is this thought, this decision, this purpose and grand courage that comes only to the American Citizen Soldier, who voluntarily and with unselfish patriotism stands in defense of principle and country, that makes such soldiers as those who fought in our ranks that day. On through the afternoon until nightfall did that furious storm beat against and rage about us.

Near night, Gen. J. J. Reynolds, who commanded that portion of the line immediately on our left, informed us that the lines to our right and left had been broken, and directed that we should fall back to the range of hills in our rear; and so, reluctantly, our men fell back after an afternoon in which they had helped to hold at bay the flower of the "Army of Northern Virginia" and of the Confederacy; and though suffering terribly in loss of men, our portion of the line had not lost a flag nor a gun.

A night of pinching cold with but little sleep illy fitted us for the duty that was to be ours after the Sabbath morning's sun should rise. With the morning and our hastily prepared breakfast came the question, everything then being so still, "Will there be fighting to-day? This is Sunday."

If there had been a faint hope that the army would rest on its arms that bright Sabbath morning, it was of short life, for soon the order came for an advance; and when it came there were no laggards found. Soldiers never obeyed more promptly, nor with more ready spirit than was that order obeyed. We had learned during the evening and night from various sources that the battle of Saturday had gone hard with some portions of our lines where the enemy had massed his troops most heavily, and our men joined in the desire to retrieve all that had been lost.

We moved out in line of battle with our skirmishers advanced, passing over a portion of the field that had been so hotly contested the day before. Soon the shots of the skirmishers warn us that work is before us; nor is it long until the skirmishers have pushed to their furtherest limit, and the line of battle joins them. The command for the charge is given, and, with a shout that might have come from ever-victorious troops, we dash upon their lines. Stubborn is the resistance, but impetuous and determined is the charge, comrade cheering comrade on—on with a fury that cannot be withstood; the air filled with leaden hail; men falling about us on every side; but on and on they push until at last the enemy's lines are broken, and we follow in hot pursuit, driving them back until they reach a line of reinforcements.

Again the battle rages; now with redoubled lines they charge upon us, and the very earth shakes under our feet from the terrible discharge that comes from artillery massed in our front. Shells are shrieking in the air and bursting over our heads; great limbs are torn from the trees and fall with the broken shells about us. Soon our lines are weighed down with the terrible onslaught, and we are driven back over the same ground over which we had just come.

Again our lines are rallied, and reformed, and strengthened; and again we charge to recover the lost ground. Four times that Sunday forenoon did our lines sweep down over that ground, and as many times were we driven back, until the ground was almost covered with friend and foe—the blue and the gray lying side by side, wounded, dying, and dead. Coming to us even in the heat and excitement of the battle, it was a terrible and sickening sight to see that battle field that day. As often as our lines were broken and driven back, so often did they rally and renew the attack, until again broken and forced back, turning and firing into the face of the foe as they went, until some soldier or officer would stop, and, with a brave and determined purpose, swear that there he would stand or die, as he turned his face once more to the enemy; and from that stand, so desperately and fearlessly made, calling on his comrades to "fall in," our lines would, almost as if by magic, be built out to right and left.

Those coming back would of their own volition halt and face about, and those who had passed beyond would, as soon as they found the line was reforming, hasten to rejoin it. But words would fail to tell of the many acts of heroism displayed on that field that day. How men fought singly from behind trees, in groups of from two to a dozen, desperately fighting, hoping against hope. The very desperation and fury with which these scattered few would fight—checking the enemy, detaining him, and giving us time to reform our broken lines—surpassed the stories of Napoleon's old guard. Flanked by the enemy, our lines would change front under the murderous fire of a foe greatly superior in numbers, and again confront him in the new direction. From hastily constructed breastworks we fought now on this side, now on that. No man was there who did not realize that we were greatly outnumbered; yet no one thought of ultimate defeat.

Chickamauga was a battle where officers and men were all and each alike—heroes of the noblest type. If never before, on that battle field of Chickamauga, men of the North and men of the South, Union and Confederate, learned that no imaginary lines separating North from South, or marking the boundary of States, make any difference in the spirit of courage, bravery, and daring of the American soldier, once he believes he is fighting for a principle, be that principle right or wrong. If one is more impetuous, the other will endure longer; if one is proud of his section, the other loves his whole country more.

The two, united as they should be and will be, combine the elements and qualities of an army on whose banners might be emblazoned the one word "Invincible." On and on through all the morning and late into the afternoon had the battle raged, now advancing, now retreating, so evenly did the honors rest, that now both armies seemed willing to rest on their arms. Gradually the firing began to die away, and soon almost ceased on our portion of the line. Late in the afternoon we commenced a movement by the flank, but so confused had we become in our bearings that we did not realize that it was to be anything more than a mere change of position for a renewal of the conflict, when after a short while we found ourselves out of the noise and din of the battle field on the road filled with our troops, and marching with them down past Rossville toward Chattanooga. Then it was that we learned that Chickamauga was, *not a defeat*, but what seemed at the time a great disaster to the Union army. And such it really was in point of munitions of war that were lost, and the great numbers of Union soldiers that fell wounded or dead. But a defeat it was not; and had the battle been fought at Chattanooga instead of Chickamauga, Chattanooga would have been lost to us, and disaster overwhelming and crushing would have been the fate of the Army of the Cumberland. Had we halted at Chattanooga instead of marching out to Chickamauga, even though McCook had been with us, we might have had Vicksburg reversed. I do not believe there was a man who remained in the front fighting on the Sunday of Chickamauga who thought of defeat, so little do they who are in the line know of the actual state of affairs in active army life.

We bivouacked around Rossville on Sunday night, and as we gathered in groups about our camp-fires that night, we talked of the scenes of the day or mourned the loss of the comrades who had fallen, and all discussed the probabilities of the morrow on another field, confident of ultimate success. The morning found our portion of the army moving back toward Chattanooga, our campanies and regiments intact, except for the actual losses of the battle field. Through the afternoon of that day we listened to the distant rumble and roar of the guns of the 14th Army Corps, sounding like the last mutterings of a great storm that had spent its strength, and was drawing to a close from sheer exhaustion. As proof of the fact that Chickamauga was not a defeat, we have the fact that Gen. Geo. H. Thomas, one of the grandest heroes and noblest men developed by the war, was able with a single corps to hold the entire army of Bragg at bay until our lines were established in and about Chattanooga. Nor was Bragg's army able to follow up the advantage gained at Chickamauga. He had been able only to check our further advance, but not to drive us back from Chattanooga. The bravery of our men at Chickamauga was fully equaled by their patience and endurance of the siege of Chattanooga—a siege for two long months that were full of all that goes to make the soldier's life something to be dreaded, except for a noble and holy cause.

CHAPTER 25

An Occurrence at Owl Creek Bridge
By Ambrose Bierce

Convicted as a spy, a Confederate prisoner faces hanging, and then . . .
—LAMAR UNDERWOOD

I

A MAN STOOD UPON A RAILROAD BRIDGE IN NORTHERN ALABAMA, LOOKING DOWN INTO the swift water twenty feet below. The man's hands were behind his back, the wrists bound with a cord. A rope closely encircled his neck. It was attached to a stout cross-timber above his head and the slack fell to the level of his knees. Some loose boards laid upon the sleepers supporting the metals of the railway supplied a footing for him and his executioners—two private soldiers of the Federal army, directed by a sergeant who in civil life may have been a deputy sheriff. At a short remove upon the same temporary platform was an officer in the uniform of his rank, armed. He was a captain. A sentinel at each end of the bridge stood with his rifle in the position known as "support," that is to say, vertical in front of the left shoulder, the hammer resting on the forearm thrown straight across the chest—a formal and unnatural position, enforcing an erect carriage of the body. It did not appear to be the duty of these two men to know what was occurring at the center of the bridge; they merely blockaded the two ends of the foot planking that traversed it.

Beyond one of the sentinels nobody was in sight; the railroad ran straight away into a forest for a hundred yards, then, curving, was lost to view. Doubtless there was an outpost farther along. The other bank of the stream was open ground—a gentle activity topped with a stockade of vertical tree trunks, loopholed for rifles, with a single embrasure through which protruded the muzzle of a brass cannon commanding the bridge. Midway of the slope between bridge and fort were the spectators—a single company of infantry in line, at "parade rest," the butts of the rifles on the ground, the barrels inclining slightly backward against the right shoulder, the hands crossed upon the stock. A lieutenant stood at the right of the line, the point of his sword upon the ground, his left hand resting upon his right. Excepting the group of four at the center of the bridge, not a man moved. The company faced the bridge, staring stonily, motionless. The sentinels, facing the banks of the stream, might have been statues to adorn the bridge. The captain stood with folded arms, silent, observing the work of his subordinates, but making no sign. Death is a dignitary who when he comes announced is to be received with formal manifestations of respect, even by those most familiar with him. In the code of military etiquette silence and fixity are forms of deference.

The man who was engaged in being hanged was apparently about thirty-five years of age. He was a civilian, if one might judge from his habit, which was that of a planter. His features were good—a straight nose, firm mouth, broad forehead, from which his long, dark hair was combed straight back, falling behind his ears to the collar of his well-fitting frock-coat. He wore a mustache and pointed beard, but no whiskers; his eyes were large and dark gray, and had a kindly expression which one would hardly have expected in one whose neck was in the hemp. Evidently this was no vulgar assassin. The liberal military code makes provision for hanging many kinds of persons, and gentlemen are not excluded.

The preparations being complete, the two private soldiers stepped aside and each drew away the plank upon which he had been standing. The sergeant turned to the captain, saluted and placed himself immediately behind that officer, who in turn moved apart one pace. These movements left the condemned man and the sergeant standing on the two ends of the same plank, which spanned three of the cross-ties of the bridge. The end upon which the civilian stood almost, but not quite, reached a fourth. This plank had been held in place by the weight of the captain; it was now held by that of the sergeant. At a signal from the former the latter would step aside, the plank would tilt and the condemned man go down between two ties. The arrangement commended itself to his judgment as simple and effective. His face had not been covered nor his eyes bandaged. He looked a moment at his "unsteadfast footing," then let his gaze wander to the swirling water of the stream racing madly beneath his feet. A piece of dancing driftwood caught his attention and his eyes followed it down the current. How slowly it appeared to move! What a sluggish stream!

He closed his eyes in order to fix his last thoughts upon his wife and children. The water, touched to gold by the early sun, the brooding mists under the banks at some distance down the stream, the fort, the soldiers, the piece of drift—all had distracted him. And now he became conscious of a new disturbance. Striking through the thought of his dear ones was a sound which he could neither ignore nor understand, a sharp, distinct, metallic percussion like the stroke of a blacksmith's hammer upon the anvil; it had the same ringing quality. He wondered what it was, and whether immeasurably distant or near by—it seemed both. Its recurrence was regular, but as slow as the tolling of a death knell. He awaited each stroke with impatience and—he knew not why—apprehension. The intervals of silence grew progressively longer; the delays became maddening. With their greater infrequency the sounds increased in strength and sharpness. They hurt his ear like the thrust of a knife; he feared he would shriek. What he heard was the ticking of his watch.

He unclosed his eyes and saw again the water below him. "If I could free my hands," he thought, "I might throw off the noose and spring into the stream. By diving I could evade the bullets and, swimming vigorously, reach the bank, take to the woods and get away home. My home, thank God, is as yet outside their lines; my wife and little ones are still beyond the invader's farthest advance."

As these thoughts, which have here to be set down in words, were flashed into the doomed man's brain rather than evolved from it the captain nodded to the sergeant. The sergeant stepped aside.

II

Peyton Farquhar was a well-to-do planter, of an old and highly respected Alabama family. Being a slave owner and like other slave owners a politician he was naturally an original secessionist and ardently devoted to the Southern cause. Circumstances of an imperious nature, which it is unnecessary to relate here, had prevented him from taking service with the gallant army that had fought the disastrous campaigns ending with the fall of Corinth, and he chafed under the inglorious restraint, longing for the release of his energies, the larger life of the soldier, the opportunity for distinction. That opportunity, he felt, would come, as it comes to all in war time. Meanwhile he did what he could. No service was too humble for him to perform in aid of the South, no adventure too perilous for him to undertake if consistent with the character of a civilian who was at heart a soldier, and who in good faith and without too much qualification assented to at least a part of the frankly villainous dictum that all is fair in love and war.

One evening while Farquhar and his wife were sitting on a rustic bench near the entrance to his grounds, a gray-clad soldier rode up to the gate and asked for a drink of water. Mrs. Farquhar was only too happy to serve him with her own white hands. While she was fetching the water her husband approached the dusty horseman and inquired eagerly for news from the front.

"The Yanks are repairing the railroads," said the man, "and are getting ready for another advance. They have reached the Owl Creek bridge, put it in order and built a stockade on the north bank. The commandant has issued an order, which is posted every-where, declaring that any civilian caught interfering with the railroad, its bridges, tunnels or trains will be summarily hanged. I saw the order."

"How far is it to the Owl Creek bridge?" Farquhar asked.

"About thirty miles."

"Is there no force on this side the creek?"

"Only a picket post half a mile out, on the railroad, and a single sentinel at this end of the bridge."

"Suppose a man—a civilian and student of hanging—should elude the picket post and perhaps get the better of the sentinel," said Farquhar, smiling, "what could he accomplish?"

The soldier reflected. "I was there a month ago," he replied. "I observed that the flood of last winter had lodged a great quantity of driftwood against the wooden pier at this end of the bridge. It is now dry and would burn like tow."

The lady had now brought the water, which the soldier drank. He thanked her ceremoniously, bowed to her husband and rode away. An hour later, after nightfall, he repassed the plantation, going northward in the direction from which he had come. He was a Federal scout.

III

As Peyton Farquhar fell straight downward through the bridge he lost consciousness and was as one already dead. From this state he was awakened—ages later, it seemed to him—by the pain of a sharp pressure upon his throat, followed by a sense of suffocation. Keen, poignant agonies seemed to shoot from his neck downward through every fiber of his body and limbs. These pains appeared to flash along well-defined lines of ramification and to beat with an inconceivably rapid periodicity. They seemed like streams of pulsating fire heating him to an intolerable temperature. As to his head, he was conscious of nothing but a feeling of fulness—of congestion. These sensations were unaccompanied by thought. The intellectual part of his nature was already effaced; he had power only to feel, and feeling was torment. He was conscious of motion. Encompassed in a luminous cloud, of which he was now merely the fiery heart, without material substance, he swung through unthinkable arcs of oscillation, like a vast pendulum. Then all at once, with terrible suddenness, the light about him shot upward with the noise of a loud plash; a frightful roaring was in his ears, and all was cold and dark. The power of thought was restored; he knew that the rope had broken and he had fallen into the stream. There was no additional strangulation; the noose about his neck was already suffocating him and kept the water from his lungs. To die of hanging at the bottom of a river!—the idea seemed to him ludicrous. He opened his eyes in the darkness and saw above him a gleam of light, but how distant, how inaccessible! He was still sinking, for the light became fainter and fainter until it was a mere glimmer. Then it began to grow and brighten, and he knew that he was rising toward the surface—knew it with reluctance, for he was now very comfortable. "To be hanged and drowned," he thought, "that is not so bad; but I do not wish to be shot. No; I will not be shot; that is not fair."

He was not conscious of an effort, but a sharp pain in his wrist apprised him that he was trying to free his hands. He gave the struggle his attention, as an idler might observe the feat of a juggler, without interest in the outcome. What splendid effort!—what magnificent, what superhuman strength! Ah, that was a fine endeavor! Bravo! The cord fell away; his arms parted and floated upward, the hands dimly seen on each side in the growing light. He watched them with a new interest as first one and then the other pounced upon the noose at his neck. They tore it away and thrust it fiercely aside, its undulations resembling those of a water-snake. "Put it back, put it back!" He thought he shouted these words to his hands, for the undoing of the noose had been succeeded by the direst pang that he had yet experienced. His neck ached horribly; his brain was on fire; his heart, which had been fluttering faintly, gave a great leap, trying to force itself out at his mouth. His whole body was racked and wrenched with an insupportable anguish! But his disobedient hands gave no heed to the command. They beat the water vigorously with quick, downward strokes, forcing him to the surface. He felt his head emerge; his eyes were blinded by the sunlight; his chest expanded convulsively, and with a supreme and crowning agony his lungs engulfed a great draught of air, which instantly he expelled in a shriek!

He was now in full possession of his physical senses. They were, indeed, preternaturally keen and alert. Something in the awful disturbance of his organic system had so exalted and refined them that they made record of things never before perceived. He felt the ripples upon his face and heard their separate sounds as they struck. He looked at the forest on the bank of the stream, saw the individual trees, the leaves and the veining of each leaf—saw the very insects upon them: the locusts, the brilliant-bodied flies, the gray spiders stretching their webs from twig to twig. He noted the prismatic colors in all the dewdrops upon a million blades of grass. The humming of the gnats that danced above the eddies of the stream, the beating of the dragon-flies' wings, the strokes of the water-spiders' legs, like oars which had lifted their boat—all these made audible music. A fish slid along beneath his eyes and he heard the rush of its body parting the water.

He had come to the surface facing down the stream; in a moment the visible world seemed to wheel slowly round, himself the pivotal point, and he saw the bridge, the fort, the soldiers upon the bridge, the captain, the sergeant, the two privates, his executioners. They were in silhouette against the blue sky. They shouted and gesticulated, pointing at him. The captain had drawn his pistol, but did not fire; the others were unarmed. Their movements were grotesque and horrible, their forms gigantic.

Suddenly he heard a sharp report and something struck the water smartly within a few inches of his head, spattering his face with spray. He heard a second report, and saw one of the sentinels with his rifle at his shoulder, a light cloud of blue smoke rising from the muzzle. The man in the water saw the eye of the man on the bridge gazing into his own through the sights of the rifle. He observed that it was a gray eye and remembered having read that gray eyes were keenest, and that all famous marksmen had them. Nevertheless, this one had missed.

A counter-swirl had caught Farquhar and turned him half round; he was again looking into the forest on the bank opposite the fort. The sound of a clear, high voice in a monotonous singsong now rang out behind him and came across the water with a distinctness that pierced and subdued all other sounds, even the beating of the ripples in his ears. Although no soldier, he had frequented camps enough to know the dread significance of that deliberate, drawling, aspirated chant; the lieutenant on shore was taking a part in the morning's work. How coldly and pitilessly—with what an even, calm into-nation, presaging, and enforcing tranquillity in the men—with what accurately measured intervals fell those cruel words:

"Attention, company! . . . Shoulder arms! . . . Ready! . . . Aim! . . . Fire!"

Farquhar dived—dived as deeply as he could. The water roared in his ears like the voice of Niagara, yet he heard the dulled thunder of the volley and, rising again toward the surface, met shining bits of metal, singularly flattened, oscillating slowly downward. Some of them touched him on the face and hands, then fell away, continuing their descent. One lodged between his collar and neck; it was uncomfortably warm and he snatched it out.

As he rose to the surface, gasping for breath, he saw that he had been a long time under water; he was perceptibly farther down stream—nearer to safety. The soldiers had almost finished reloading; the metal ramrods flashed all at once in the sunshine as they were drawn from the barrels, turned in the air, and thrust into their sockets. The two sen-tinels fired again, independently and ineffectually.

The hunted man saw all this over his shoulder; he was now swimming vigorously with the current. His brain was as energetic as his arms and legs; he thought with the rapidity of lightning.

"The officer," he reasoned, "will not make that martinet's error a second time. It is as easy to dodge a volley as a single shot. He has probably already given the command to fire at will. God help me, I cannot dodge them all!"

An appalling plash within two yards of him was followed by a loud, rushing sound, *diminuendo*, which seemed to travel back through the air to the fort and died in an explosion which stirred the very river to its deeps! A rising sheet of water curved over him, fell down upon him, blinded him, strangled him! The cannon had taken a hand in the game. As he shook his head free from the commotion of the smitten water he heard the deflected shot humming through the air ahead, and in an instant it was cracking and smashing the branches in the forest beyond.

"They will not do that again," he thought; "the next time they will use a charge of grape. I must keep my eye upon the gun; the smoke will apprise me—the report arrives too late; it lags behind the missile. That is a good gun."

Suddenly he felt himself whirled round and round—spinning like a top. The water, the banks, the forests, the now distant bridge, fort and men—all were commingled and blurred. Objects were represented by their colors only; circular horizontal streaks of color—that was all he saw. He had been caught in a vortex and was being whirled on with a velocity of advance and gyration that made him giddy and sick. In a few moments he was flung upon the gravel at the foot of the left bank of the stream—the southern bank—and behind a projecting point which concealed him from his enemies. The sudden arrest of his motion, the abrasion of one of his hands on the gravel, restored him, and he wept with delight. He dug his fingers into the sand, threw it over himself in handfuls and audibly blessed it. It looked like diamonds, rubies, emeralds; he could think of nothing beautiful which it did not resemble. The trees upon the bank were giant garden plants; he noted a definite order in their arrangement, inhaled the fragrance of their blooms. A strange, roseate light shone through the spaces among their trunks and the wind made in their branches the music of æolian harps. He had no wish to perfect his escape—was content to remain in that enchanting spot until retaken.

A whiz and rattle of grapeshot among the branches high above his head roused him from his dream. The baffled cannoneer had fired him a random farewell. He sprang to his feet, rushed up the sloping bank, and plunged into the forest.

All that day he traveled, laying his course by the rounding sun. The forest seemed interminable; nowhere did he discover a break in it, not even a woodman's road. He had not known that he lived in so wild a region. There was something uncanny in the revelation.

By night fall he was fatigued, footsore, famishing. The thought of his wife and children urged him on. At last he found a road which led him in what he knew to be the right direction. It was as wide and straight as a city street, yet it seemed untraveled. No fields bordered it, no dwelling anywhere. Not so much as the barking of a dog suggested human habitation. The black bodies of the trees formed a straight wall on both sides, terminating on the horizon in a point, like a diagram in a lesson in perspective. Overhead, as he looked up through this rift in the wood, shone great golden stars looking unfamiliar and grouped in strange constellations. He was sure they were arranged in some order which had a secret and malign significance. The wood on either side was full of singular noises, among which—once, twice, and again, he distinctly heard whispers in an unknown tongue.

His neck was in pain and lifting his hand to it he found it horribly swollen. He knew that it had a circle of black where the rope had bruised it. His eyes felt congested; he could no longer close them. His tongue was swollen with thirst; he relieved its fever by thrusting it forward from between his teeth into the cold air. How softly the turf had carpeted the untraveled avenue—he could no longer feel the roadway beneath his feet!

Doubtless, despite his suffering, he had fallen asleep while walking, for now he sees another scene—perhaps he has merely recovered from a delirium. He stands at the gate of his own home. All is as he left it, and all bright and beautiful in the morning sunshine. He must have traveled the entire night. As he pushes open the gate and passes up the wide white walk, he sees a flutter of female garments; his wife, looking fresh and cool and sweet, steps down from the veranda to meet him. At the bottom of the steps she stands waiting, with a smile of ineffable joy, an attitude of matchless grace and dignity. Ah, how beautiful she is! He springs forward with extended arms. As he is about to clasp her he feels a stunning blow upon the back of the neck; a blinding white light blazes all about him with a sound like the shock of a cannon—then all is darkness and silence!

Peyton Farquhar was dead; his body, with a broken neck, swung gently from side to side beneath the timbers of the Owl Creek bridge.

CHAPTER 26

Army Life in a Black Regiment
By *Thomas Wentworth Higginson*

Once they were slaves, now they are soldiers—armed and ready to fight.
—LAMAR UNDERWOOD

THE EDISTO EXPEDITION COST ME THE HEALTH AND STRENGTH OF SEVERAL YEARS. I could say, long after, in the words of one of the men, "I'se been a sickly person, eber since de expeditious." Justice to a strong constitution and good habits compels me, however, to say that, up to the time of my injury, I was almost the only officer in the regiment who had not once been off duty from illness. But at last I had to yield, and went North for a month.

We heard much said, during the war, of wounded officers who stayed unreasonably long at home. I think there were more instances of those who went back too soon. Such at least was my case. On returning to the regiment I found a great accumulation of unfinished business; every member of the field and staff was prostrated by illness or absent on detailed service; two companies had been sent to Hilton Head on fatigue duty, and kept there unexpectedly long: and there was a visible demoralization among the rest, especially from the fact that their pay had just been cut down, in violation of the express pledges of the government. A few weeks of steady sway made all right again; and during those weeks I felt a perfect exhilaration of health, followed by a month or two of complete prostration, when the work was done. This passing, I returned to duty, buoyed up by the fallacious hope that the winter months would set me right again.

We had a new camp on Port Royal Island, very pleasantly situated, just out of Beaufort. It stretched nearly to the edge of a shelving bluff, fringed with pines and overlooking the river; below the bluff was a hard, narrow beach, where one might gallop a mile and bathe at the farther end. We could look up and down the curving stream, and watch the few vessels that came and went. Our first encampment had been lower down that same river, and we felt at home.

The new camp was named Camp Shaw, in honor of the noble young officer who had lately fallen at Fort Wagner, under circumstances which had endeared him to all the men. As it happened, they had never seen him, nor was my regiment ever placed within immediate reach of the Fifty-Fourth Massachusetts. This I always regretted, feeling very desirous to compare the military qualities of the Northern and Southern blacks. As it was, the Southern regiments with which the Massachusetts troops were brigaded were hardly a fair specimen of their kind, having been raised chiefly by drafting, and, for this and other causes, being afflicted with perpetual discontent and desertion.

We had, of course, looked forward with great interest to the arrival of these new colored regiments, and I had ridden in from the picket-station to see the Fifty-Fourth. Apart from the peculiarity of its material, it was fresh from my own State, and I had relatives and acquaintances among its officers. Governor Andrew, who had formed it, was an old friend, and had begged me, on departure from Massachusetts, to keep him informed as to our experiment. I had good reason to believe that my reports had helped to prepare the way for this new battalion, and I had sent him, at his request, some hints as to its formation.

In the streets of Beaufort I had met Colonel Shaw, riding with his lieutenant-colonel and successor, Edward Hallowell, and had gone back with them to share their first meal in camp. I should have known Shaw anywhere by his resemblance to his kindred, nor did it take long to perceive that he shared their habitual truthfulness and courage. Moreover, he and Hallowell had already got beyond the commonplaces of inexperience, in regard to colored troops, and, for a wonder, asked only sensible questions. For instance, he admitted the mere matter of courage to be settled, as regarded the colored troops, and his whole solicitude bore on this point. Would they do as well in line-of-battle as they had already done in more irregular service, and on picket and guard duty? Of this I had, of course, no doubt, nor, I think, had he; though I remember his saying something about the possibility of putting them between two fires in case of need, and so cutting off their retreat. I should never have thought of such a project, but I could not have expected him to trust them as I did, until he had been actually under fire with them. That, doubtless, removed all his anxieties, if he really had any.

This interview had occurred on the 4th of June. Shaw and his regiment had very soon been ordered to Georgia, then to Morris Island; Fort Wagner had been assaulted, and he had been killed. Most of the men knew about the circumstances of his death, and many of them had subscribed towards a monument for him—a project which originated with General Saxton, and which was finally embodied in the "Shaw School-house" at Charleston. So it gave us all pleasure to name this camp for him, as its predecessor had been named for General Saxton.

The new camp was soon brought into good order. The men had great ingenuity in building screens and shelters of light poles, filled in with the gray moss from the live-oaks. The officers had vestibules built in this way, before all their tents; the cooking-places were walled round in the same fashion; and some of the wide company-streets had sheltered sidewalks down the whole line of tents. The sergeant on duty at the entrance of the camp had a similar bower, and the architecture culminated in a "Praise-House" for school and prayer-meetings, some thirty feet in diameter. As for chimneys and flooring, they were provided with that magic and invisible facility which marks the second year of a regiment's life.

Then the duties of inspection and drill, suspended during active service, resume their importance with a month or two of quiet. It really costs unceasing labor to keep a regiment in perfect condition and ready for service. The work is made up of minute and endless details, like a bird's pruning her feathers or a cat's licking her kittens into their proper toilet. Here are eight hundred men, every one of whom, every Sunday morning at farthest, must be perfectly *soigné* in all personal proprieties; he must exhibit himself provided with every article of clothing, buttons, shoe-strings, hooks and eyes, company letter, regimental number, rifle, bayonet, bayonet-scabbard, cap-pouch, cartridge-box, cartridge-box belt, cartridge-box belt-plate, gun-sling, canteen, haversack, knapsack, packed according to rule, forty cartridges, forty percussion caps; and every one of these articles polished to the highest brightness or blackness as the case may be, and moreover hung or slung or tied or carried in precisely the correct manner.

The men had that year a Christmas present which they enjoyed to the utmost—furnishing the detail, every other day, for provost-guard duty in Beaufort. It was the only military service which they had ever shared within the town, and it moreover gave a sense of self-respect to be keeping the peace of their own streets. I enjoyed seeing them put on duty those mornings; there was such a twinkle of delight in their eyes, though their features were immovable. As the "reliefs" went round, posting the guard, under charge of a corporal, one could watch the black sentinels successively dropped and the whites picked up—gradually changing the complexion, like Lord Somebody's black stockings which became white stockings—till at last there was only a squad of white soldiers obeying the "Support Arms! Forward, March!" of a black corporal.

Then, when once posted, they glorified their office, you may be sure. Discipline had grown rather free-and-easy in the town about that time, and it is said that the guard-house never was so full within human memory as after their first tour of duty. I remember hearing that one young reprobate, son of a leading Northern philanthropist in those parts, was much aggrieved at being taken to the lock-up merely because he was found drunk in the streets. "Why," said he, "the white corporals always showed me the way home." And I can testify that, after an evening party, some weeks later, I beard with pleasure the officers asking eagerly for the countersign.

One of the sergeants of the guard, on one of these occasions, made to one who questioned his authority an answer that could hardly have been improved. The questioner had just been arrested for some offense.

"Know what dat mean?" said the indignant sergeant, pointing to the chevrons on his own sleeve. "Dat mean *Guv'ment*." Volumes could not have said more, and the victim collapsed. The thing soon settled itself, and nobody remembered to notice whether the face beside the musket of a sentinel were white or black. It meant Government, all the same.

The men were also indulged with several raids on the mainland, under the direction of Captain J. E. Bryant, of the Eighth Maine, the most experienced scout in that region, who was endeavoring to raise by enlistment a regiment of colored troops. On one occasion Captains Whitney and Heasley, with their companies, penetrated nearly to Pocataligo, capturing some pickets and bringing away all the slaves of a plantation, the latter operation being entirely under the charge of Sergeant Harry Williams (Co. K), without the presence of any white man.

The whole command was attacked on the return by a rebel force, which turned out to be what was called in those regions a "dog-company," consisting of mounted riflemen with half a dozen trained bloodhounds. The men met these dogs with their bayonets, killed four or five of their old tormentors with great relish, and brought away the carcass of one. I had the creature skinned, and sent the skin to New York to be stuffed and mounted, meaning to exhibit it at the Sanitary Commission Fair in Boston; but it spoiled on the passage. These quadruped allies were not originally intended as "dogs of war," but simply to detect fugitive slaves, and the men were delighted at this confirmation of their tales of dog-companies, which some of the officers had always disbelieved.

Captain Bryant, during his scouting adventures, had learned to outwit these bloodhounds, and used his skill in eluding escape, during another expedition of the same kind. He was sent with Captain Metcalf's company far up the Combahee River to cut the telegraphic wires and intercept despatches. Our adventurous chaplain and a telegraphic operator went with the party. They ascended the river, cut the wires, and read the despatches for an hour or two. Unfortunately, the attached wire was too conspicuously hung, and was seen by a passenger on the railway train in passing.

The train was stopped and a swift stampede followed; a squad of cavalry was sent in pursuit, and our chaplain, with Lieutenant Osborn, of Bryant's projected regiment, were captured; also one private, the first of our men who had ever been taken prisoners. In spite of an agreement at Washington to the contrary, our chaplain was held as prisoner of war, the only spiritual adviser in uniform, so far as I know, who had that honor. I do not know but his reverence would have agreed with Scott's pirate-lieutenant, that it was better to live as plain Jack Bunce than die as Frederick Altamont; but I am very sure that he would rather have been kept prisoner to the close of the war, as a combatant, than have been released on parole as a non-resistant.

After his return, I remember, he gave the most animated accounts of the whole adventure, of which he had enjoyed every instant, from the first entrance on the enemy's soil to the final capture. I suppose we should all like to tap the telegraphic wires anywhere and read our neighbor's messages, if we could only throw round this process the dignity of a

Sacred Cause. This was what our good chaplain had done, with the same conscientious zest with which he had conducted his Sunday foraging in Florida. But he told me that nothing so impressed him on the whole trip as the sudden transformation in the black soldier who was taken prisoner with him. The chaplain at once adopted the policy, natural to him, of talking boldly and even defiantly to his captors, and commanding instead of beseeching. He pursued the same policy always and gained by it, he thought. But the negro adopted the diametrically opposite policy, also congenial to his crushed race, all the force seemed to go out of him, and he surrendered himself like a tortoise to be kicked and trodden upon at their will. This manly, well-trained soldier at once became a slave again, asked no questions, and, if any were asked, made meek and conciliatory answers. He did not know, nor did any of us know, whether he would be treated as a prisoner of war, or shot, or sent to a rice-plantation. He simply acted according to the traditions of his race, as did the chaplain on his side. In the end the soldier's cunning was vindicated by the result; he escaped, and rejoined us in six months, while the chaplain was imprisoned for a year.

The men came back very much exhausted from this expedition, and those who were in the chaplain's squad narrowly escaped with their lives. One brave fellow had actually not a morsel to eat for four days, and then could keep nothing on his stomach for two days more, so that his life was despaired of; and yet he brought all his equipments safe into camp. Some of these men had led such wandering lives, in woods and swamps, that to hunt them was like hunting an otter; shyness and concealment had grown to be their second nature.

After these little episodes came two months of peace. We were clean, comfortable, quiet, and consequently discontented. It was therefore with eagerness that we listened to a rumor of a new Florida expedition, in which we might possibly take a hand....

General Saxton, examining with some impatience a long list of questions from some philanthropic Commission at the North, respecting the traits and habits of the freedmen, bade some staff-officer answer them all in two words, "Intensely human." We all admitted that it was a striking and comprehensive description.

For instance, as to courage. So far as I have seen, the mass of men are naturally courageous up to a certain point. A man seldom runs away from danger which he ought to face, unless others run; each is apt to keep with the mass, and colored soldiers have more than usual of this gregariousness. In almost every regiment, black or white, there are a score or two of men who are naturally daring, who really hunger after dangerous adventures, and are happiest when allowed to seek them. Every commander gradually finds out who these men are, and habitually uses them; certainly I had such, and I remember with delight their bearing, their coolness, and their dash. Some of them were negroes, some mulattoes. One of them would have passed for white, with brown hair and blue eyes, while others were so black you could hardly see their features. These picked men varied in other respects too; some were neat and well-drilled soldiers, while others were slovenly, heedless fellows, the despair of their officers at inspection, their pride on a raid. They were the natural scouts and rangers of the regiment; they had the two-o'clock-in-the-morning courage, which Napoleon thought so rare. The mass of the regiment rose to the same level under excitement, and were more excitable, I think, than whites, but neither more nor less courageous.

Perhaps the best proof of a good average of courage among them was in the readiness they always showed for any special enterprise. I do not remember ever to have had the slightest difficulty in obtaining volunteers, but rather in keeping down the number. The previous pages include many illustrations of this, as well as of then: endurance of pain and discomfort. For instance, one of my lieutenants, a very daring Irishman, who had served for eight years as a sergeant of regular artillery in Texas, Utah, and South Carolina, said he had never been engaged in anything so risky as our raid up the St. Mary's. But in truth it seems to me a mere absurdity to deliberately argue the question of courage, as applied to men among whom I waked and slept, day and night, for so many months together. As well might he who has been wandering for years upon the desert, with a Bedouin escort, discuss the courage of the men whose tents have been his shelter and whose spears his guard. We, their officers, did not go there to teach lessons, but to receive them. There were more than a hundred men in the ranks who had voluntarily met more dangers in their escape from slavery than any of my young captains had incurred in all their lives. . . .

I used to think that I should not care to read "Uncle Tom's Cabin" in our camp; it would have seemed tame. Any group of men in a tent would have had more exciting tales to tell. I needed no fiction when I had Fanny Wright, for instance, daily passing to and fro before my tent, with her shy little girl clinging to her skirts. Fanny was a modest little mulatto woman, a soldier's wife, and a company laundress. She had escaped from the main-land in a boat, with that child and another. Her baby was shot dead in her arms, and she reached our lines with one child safe on earth and the other in heaven. I never found it needful to give any elementary instructions in courage to Fanny's husband, you may be sure.

I often asked myself why it was that, with this capacity of daring and endurance, they had not kept the land in a perpetual flame of insurrection; why, especially since the opening of the war, they had kept so still. The answer was to be found in the peculiar temperament of the races, in their religious faith, and in the habit of patience that centuries had fortified. The shrewder men all said substantially the same thing. What was the use of insurrection, where everything was against them? They had no knowledge, no money, no arms, no drill, no organization, above all, no mutual confidence. It was the tradition among them that all insurrections were always betrayed by somebody.

They had no mountain passes to defend like the Maroons (escaped slaves) of Jamaica— no unpenetrable swamps, like the Maroons of Surinam. Where they had these, even on a small scale, they had used them—as in certain swamps round Savannah and in the ever-glades of Florida, where they united with the Indians, and would stand fire—so I was told by General Saxton, who had fought them there—when the Indians would retreat.

It always seemed to me that, had I been a slave, my life would have been one long scheme of insurrection. But I learned to respect the patient self-control of those who had waited till the course of events should open a better way. When it came they accepted it. Insurrection on their part would at once have divided the Northern sentiment; and a large part of our army would have joined with the Southern army to hunt them down. By their waiting till we needed them, their freedom was secured.

Two things chiefly surprised me in their feeling toward their former masters—the absence of affection and the absence of revenge.

Certainly this indifference did not proceed from any want of personal affection, for they were the most affectionate people among whom I had ever lived. They attached themselves to every officer who deserved love, and to some who did not; and if they failed to show it to their masters, it proved the wrongfulness of the mastery.

But side by side with this faculty of patience, there was a certain tropical element in the men, a sort of fiery ecstasy when aroused, which seemed to link them by blood with the French Turcos, and made them really resemble their natural enemies, the Celts, far more than the Anglo-Saxon temperament. To balance this there were great individual resources when alone, a sort of Indian wiliness and subtlety of resource. Their gregariousness and love of drill made them more easy to keep in hand than white American troops, who rather like to straggle or go in little squads, looking out for themselves, without being bothered with officers. The blacks prefer organization.

The point of inferiority that I always feared, though I never had occasion to prove it, was that they might show less fiber, less tough and dogged resistance, than whites, during a prolonged trial—a long, disastrous march, for instance, or the hopeless defense of a besieged town. I should not be afraid of their mutinying or running away, but of their drooping and dying. It might not turn out so; but I mention it for the sake of fairness, and to avoid overstating the merits of these troops. As to the simple general fact of courage and reliability I think no officer in our camp ever thought of there being any difference between black and white. And certainly the opinions of these officers, who for years risked their lives every moment on the fidelity of their men, were worth more than those of all the world beside.

No doubt there were reasons why this particular war was an especially favorable test of the colored soldiers. They had more to fight for than the whites. Besides the flag and the Union, they had home and wife and child. They fought with ropes round their necks, and when orders were issued that the officers of colored troops should be put to death on capture, they took a grim satisfaction. It helped their esprit de corps immensely. With us, at least, there was to be no play-soldier. Though they had begun with a slight feeling of inferiority to the white troops, this compliment substituted a peculiar sense of self-respect. And even when the new colored regiments began to arrive from the North my men still pointed out this difference—that in case of ultimate defeat, the Northern troops, black or white, would go home, while the First South Carolina must fight it out or be re-enslaved. This was one thing that made the St. John's River so attractive to them and even to me—it was so much nearer the everglades. I used seriously to ponder, during the darker periods of the war, whether I might not end my days as an outlaw, a leader of Maroons.

It used to seem to me that never, since Cromwell's time, had there been soldiers in whom the religious element held such a place. "A religious army," "a gospel army," were their frequent phrases. In their prayer-meetings there was always a mingling, often quaint enough, of the warlike and the pious. "If each one of us was a praying man," said Corporal Thomas Long in a sermon, "it appears to me that we could fight as well with prayers as with bullets—for the Lord has said that if you have faith even as a grain of mustard-seed cut into four parts, you can say to the sycamore-tree, 'Arise,' and it will come up." And though Corporal Long may have got a little perplexed in his botany, his faith proved itself by works, for he volunteered and went many miles on a solitary scouting expedition into the enemy's country in Florida, and got back safe, after I had given him up for lost.

The extremes of religious enthusiasm I did not venture to encourage, for I could not do it honestly; neither did I discourage them, but simply treated them with respect, and let them have their way, so long as they did not interfere with discipline. In general they promoted it. The mischievous little drummer-boys, whose scrapes and quarrels were the torment of my existence, might be seen kneeling together in their tents to say their prayers at night, and I could hope that their slumbers were blessed by some spirit of peace, such as certainly did not rule over their waking. The most reckless and daring fellows in the regiment were perfect fatalists in their confidence that God would watch over them, and that if they died, it would be because their time had come. This almost excessive faith, and the love of freedom and of their families, all co-operated with their pride as soldiers to make them do their duty. I could not have spared any of these incentives. Those of our officers who were personally the least influenced by such considerations, still saw the need of encouraging them among the men.

The question was often asked, whether the Southern slaves or the Northern free blacks made the best soldiers. It was a compliment to both classes that each officer usually preferred those whom he had personally commanded. I preferred those who had been slaves, for their greater docility and affectionateness, for the powerful stimulus which their new freedom gave, and for the fact that they were fighting, in a manner, for their own homes and firesides. Every one of these considerations afforded a special aid to discipline, and cemented a peculiar tie of sympathy between them and their officers. They seemed like clansmen, and had a more confiding and filial relation to us than seemed to me to exist in the Northern colored regiments.

So far as the mere habits of slavery went, they were a poor preparation for military duty. Inexperienced officers often assumed that, because these men had been slaves before enlistment, they would bear to be treated as such afterwards. Experience proved the contrary. The more strongly we marked the difference between the slave and the soldier, the better for the regiment. One half of military duty lies in obedience, the other half in self-respect. A soldier without self-respect is worthless.

Consequently there were no regiments in which it was so important to observe the courtesies and proprieties of military life as in these. I had to caution the officers to be more than usually particular in returning the salutations of the men; to be very careful in their dealings with those on picket or guard-duty; and on no account to omit the titles of the non-commissioned officers. So, in dealing out punishments, we had carefully to avoid all that was brutal and arbitrary, all that savored of the overseer.

In all ways we had to educate their self-respect. For instance, at first they disliked to obey their own non-commissioned officers. "I don't want him to play de white man ober me," was a sincere objection. They had been so impressed with a sense of inferiority that the distinction extended to the very principles of honor. "I ain't got colored-man principles," said Corporal London Simmons, indignantly defending himself from some charge before me. "I'se got white-gemman principles. I'se do my best. If Cap'n tell me to take a man, s'pose de man be as big as a house, I'll clam hold on him till I die, inception [excepting] I'm sick."

But it was plain that this feeling was a bequest of slavery, which military life would wear off. We impressed it upon them that they did not obey their officers because they were white, but because they were their officers, just as the Captain must obey me, and I the General; that we were all subject to military law, and protected by it in turn. Then we taught them to take pride in having good material for non-commissioned officers among themselves, and in obeying them. On my arrival there was one white first sergeant, and it was a question whether to appoint others. This I prevented, but left that one, hoping the men themselves would at last petition for his removal, which at length they did. He was at once detailed on other duty. The picturesqueness of the regiment suffered, for he was very tall and fair, and I liked to see him step forward in the center when the line of first sergeants came together at dress-parade. But it was a help to discipline to eliminate the Saxon, for it recognized a principle.

Afterwards I had excellent battalion-drills without a single white officer, by way of experiment; putting each company under a sergeant, and going through the most difficult movements, such as division-columns and oblique-squares. And as to actual discipline, it is doing no injustice to the line-officers of the regiment to say that none of them received from the men more implicit obedience than Color-Sergeant Rivers. I should have tried to obtain commissions for him and several others before I left the regiment, had their literary education been sufficient; and such an attempt was finally made by Lieutenant-Colonel Trowbridge, my successor in immediate command, but it proved unsuccessful. It always seemed to me an insult to those brave men to have novices put over their heads, on the ground of color alone; and the men felt it the more keenly as they remained longer in service. There were more than seven hundred enlisted men in the regiment, when mustered out after more than three years' service. The ranks had been kept full by enlistment, but there were only fourteen line-officers instead of the full thirty. The men who should have filled those vacancies were doing duty as sergeants in the ranks.

In what respect were the colored troops a source of disappointment? To me in one respect only—that of health. Their health improved, indeed, as they grew more familiar with military life; but I think that neither their physical nor moral temperament gave them that toughness, that obstinate purpose of living, which sustains the more materialistic Anglo-Saxon. They had not, to be sure, the same predominant diseases, suffering in the pulmonary, not in the digestive organs; but they suffered a good deal. They felt malaria less, but they were more easily choked by dust and made ill by dampness. On the other hand, they submitted more readily to sanitary measures than whites, and, with efficient officers, were more easily kept clean. They were injured throughout the army by an undue share of fatigue duty, which is not only exhausting but demoralizing to a soldier; by the un-suitableness of the rations, which gave them salt meat instead of rice and hominy; and by the lack of good medical attendance. Their childlike constitutions peculiarly needed prompt and efficient surgical care; but almost all the colored troops were enlisted late in the war, when it was hard to get good surgeons for any regiments, and especially for these. In this respect I had nothing to complain of, since there were no surgeons in the army for whom I would have exchanged my own.

And this late arrival on the scene affected not only the medical supervision of the colored troops, but their opportunity for a career. It is not my province to write their history, nor to vindicate them, nor to follow them upon those larger fields compared with which the adventures of my regiment appear but a partisan warfare. Yet this, at least, may be said. The operations on the South Atlantic coast, which long seemed a merely subordinate and incidental part of the great contest, proved to be one of the final pivots on which it turned.

All now admit that the fate of the Confederacy was decided by Sherman's march to the sea. Port Royal was the objective point to which he marched, and he found the Department of the South, when he reached it, held almost exclusively by colored troops. Next to the merit of those who made the march was that of those who held open the door. That service will always remain among the laurels of the black regiments.

CHAPTER 27

Drummer Boy from Maine

By George T. Ulmer

He was so small that he often went unnoticed—even by the enemy.

—LAMAR UNDERWOOD

THE BOMBARDMENT OF FORT SUMTER.

This was the beginning and the first sound of actual war which inspired me, and kindled the fire of patriotism in my youthful breast. The little spark lay smoldering for two long years, till at last it burst forth into a full blaze. When Fort Sumter was bombarded, I was a midget of a boy; a barefooted, ragged newsboy in the city of New York. The bombardment was threatened for several weeks before it actually occurred; and many nights I would have been bankrupted, but that everyone was on the "qui vive" for the event, and I got myself into lots of trouble by shouting occasionally, "Fort Sumter Bombarded!" I needed money; it sold my papers, and I forgave myself. When the authentic news did come, I think it stirred up within me as big a piece of fighting desire as it did in larger and older people. I mourned the fact that I was then too small to fight, but lived in hopes that the war would last until I should grow. If I could have gone south, I felt that I could have conquered the rebellious faction alone, so confident was I of my fighting abilities.

In the fall of '61 my dear mother died, and my father who had a great desire to make possibilities out of improbabilities, and believing a farm the proper place to bring up a family of boys, bought one away in the interior of Maine. The farm was very hilly, covered with huge pines and liberally planted with granite ledges. I used to think God wanted to be generous to this state and gave it so much land it had to be stood up edgeways. Picture to yourself, dear reader, four boys taken from the busy life of a great city, place them in the wilderness of Maine, where they had to make a windrow of the forest to secure a garden spot for the house, pry out the stumps and blast the ledges to sow the seed, then ask yourself what should the harvest be?

Father's business required all of his time in New York City, and we were left with two hired men to develop the farm, our brains and muscles, but mine didn't seem to develop worth a cent. I didn't care for the farmer's life. The plow and scythe had no charms for me. My horny, hardened little hand itched and longed to beat the drums that would marshall men to arms.

After eight months of hard work we had cleared up quite a respectable little farm, an oasis in that forest of pines. A new house and barn had been built, also new fences and stone walls, but not much credit for this belonged to me. Soon after, we received a letter from father stating that he would be with us in a short time and bring us a new mother and a little step-sister. This was joyous news, the anticipation of a new mother, and above all a step-sister, inspired us with new ambition. The fences and barn received a coat of whitewash, the stones were picked out of the road in front of the house, the wood-pile was repiled and everything put into apple-pie order. We did not know what day they would arrive. So each day about the time the stage coach from Belfast should pass the corners, we would perch ourselves on the fence in front of the house to watch for it, and when it did come in sight, wonder if the folks were in it; if they were, it would turn at the corners and come toward our house. Day after day passed, and they did not come, and we had kind of forgotten about it.

Finally one day while we were all busy burning brush, brother Charlie came rushing towards us shouting, "The stage coach is coming! The stage is coming!" Well, such a scampering for the house! We didn't have time to wash or fix up, and our appearance would certainly not inspire our city visitors with much paternal pride or affection; we looked like charcoal burners. Our faces, hands and clothes were black and begrimed from the burning brush, but we couldn't help it; we were obliged to receive and welcome them as we were. I pulled up a handful of grass and tried to wipe my face, but the grass being wet, it left streaks all over it, and I looked more like a bogie man than anything else. We all struggled to brush up and smooth our hair, but it was no use, the stage coach was upon us, the door opened, father jumped out, and as we crowded around him, he looked at us in perfect amazement and with a kind of humiliated expression behind a pleasant fatherly smile he exclaimed, "Well, well, you are a nice dirty looking lot of boys. Lizzie," addressing his wife and helping her to alight, "this is our family, a little smoky; I can't tell which is which, so we'll have to wait till they get their faces washed to introduce them by their names." But our new mother was equal to the occasion for coming to each of us, and taking our dirty faces in her hands, kissed us, saying at the same time, "Philip, don't you mind, they are all nice, honest, hard-working boys, and I know I shall like them, even if this country air has turned their skins black." At this moment a tiny voice called, "Please help me out." All the boys started with a rush, each eager to embrace the little step-sister. I was there first, and in an instant, in spite of my dirty appearance, she sprang from the coach right into my arms; my brothers struggled to take her from me, but she tightened her little arms about my neck and clung to me as if I was her only protector. I started and ran with her, my brothers in full chase, down the road, over the stone walls, across the field, around the stumps with my prize, the brothers keeping up the chase till we were all completely tired out, and father compelled us to stop and bring the child to the house.

Afterward we took our turns at caressing and admiring her; finally we apologized for our behavior and dirty faces, listened to father's and mother's congratulations, concluded father's choice for a wife was a good one, and that our little step-sister was just exactly as we wanted her to be, and the prospect of a bright, new and happy home seemed to be already realized.

⌐⌐

The war grew more and more serious. Newspapers were eagerly sought; and every word about the struggle was read over and over again. A new call for troops was made, another and still another, and I was all the time fretting and chafing in the corn or potato field, because I was so young and small. I could not work; the fire of patriotism was burning me up. My eldest brother had arrived at the age and required size to fit him for the service; he enlisted and went to the front. This added new fuel to the flame already within me, and one day I threw down the hoe and declared that I would go to the war! I would join my brother at all hazards. My folks laughed at me and tried to dissuade me from so unwise a step, but my mind was made up, and I was bound to enlist. Enlist I did, when I was only fourteen years of age and extremely small for my years, but I thought I would answer for a drummer boy if nothing else. I found that up hill work, however, but I was bound to "get there," and—I did.

It was easy enough to enlist, but to get mustered into the service was a different thing. I tried for eight long weeks. I enlisted in my own town, but was rejected. I enlisted in an adjoining town—rejected, and so on for weeks and weeks. But I did not give up. . . .

The Yankee yearning for fight had possession of me, and I could neither eat, sleep nor work. I was bound to be a soldier. I prayed for it, and I sometimes thought, my prayers were answered; that the war should last till I was big enough to be one—for it did.

I had enlisted four times in different towns, and each time I went before a mustering officer, I was rejected. "Too small" I was every time pronounced, but I was not discouraged or dismayed—the indomitable pluck and energy of those downeast boys pervaded my system. I was bound to get there, for what I didn't know, I did not care or didn't stop to think. I only thought of the glory of being a soldier, little realizing what an absurd-looking one I would make; but the ambition was there, the pluck was there, and the patriotism of a man entered the breast of the wild dreamy boy. I wanted to go to the front—and I went.

After several unsuccessful attempts to be mustered into the service at Augusta, which was twenty-five miles from our little farm, I thought I would enlist from the town of Freedom and thereby get before a different mustering officer who was located in Belfast. I had grown, I thought, in the past six weeks, and before a new officer, I thought my chances of being accepted would improve; so on a bright morning in September I mounted my "gig," behind my little old gray horse, who seemed to say, as he turned his head to look at me when I jumped on to the seat, "What a fool you are, making me haul you all that distance, when you know they won't have you!" but kissing my little step-sister good-bye, with a wave of my hand to father and brothers who stood in the yard and door of the dear old home, I drove away, and as I did so I could see the expressions of ridicule and doubt on their faces, while underneath it all there was a tinge of sadness and fear. They did not think for a moment I would be mustered into the army, yet fear took possession of them when I drove off, for they knew my determined disposition.

Well, I arrived in Belfast. Instead of driving direct to the stable and hotel, and putting my horse up, I drove direct to the office of the mustering officer. I did not need to fasten my trusty horse, for he knew it would only be a few moments, and as I went to the office door, he turned his head and whinnied as if he were laughing at me. I entered that office like a young Napoleon. I had made up my mind to walk in before the officer very erect and dignified, even to raising myself on tiptoe. On telling the clerk my errand, he ushered me into an inner office, and imagine my surprise—my consternation—when, swinging around in his chair, I found myself in the presence of the very officer who had rejected me in Augusta so many times.

"Damn it," said he, "will you never let up? Go home to your mother, boy, don't pester me any more. I will not accept you, and let that end it."

I tremblingly told him I had grown since he saw me last, and that by the time I was mustered in I would grow some more, and that I would drum and fight, if it should prove actually necessary.

Thus I pleaded with him for fully one hour. Finally he said, "Well, damned if I don't muster you in, just to get rid of you. Sergeant, make out this young devil's papers and let him go and get killed." My heart leaped into my mouth. I tried to thank him, but he would not have it. He hurried me through, and at 5:30 P. M., September 15, 1863, I was a United States soldier. And when I donned that uniform, what a looking soldier! The smallest clothes they issued looked on me as if it would make a suit for my entire family, but in spite of the misfit, I took them and put them on, with the pants legs rolled up to the knees, and the overcoat dragging on the ground.

I went out of that office as proud as a peacock, but a laughing-stock for the boys, and all who gazed at me. I think even the old horse smiled and looked askance; he acted as if I was fooling him, and hungry as he was, when he turned towards the stable, he dragged along as if he either were sorry or ashamed to draw me among people; but I cared not for their jeers and laughs. I was now a soldier and anxious to get home. I pictured the feeling and joyous greetings of my brothers and sister as they would see me ride up in my uniform; how the boys would envy me, and how the sister would throw her arms about me and kiss me, and how her bosom would heave with pride as she gazed upon the uniform that covered her hero brother.

Oh! I pictured it all in my boyish fancy, and hastened all my arrangements, so full of joy that I could scarcely eat. I would not wait till morning, but started home about midnight, arriving there just at sunrise.

It was on the 17th of September, 1863, one of those bright, balmy days that we have in good old New England, seated in a "gig," might be seen the writer of this little sketch, dressed in soldiers' clothes, covered by one of those familiar cape overcoats that nearly covered the "gig" and poor old horse. I felt as proud as if I was the general in command of all the army.

Instead of giving the family a surprise, they had heard of my enlisting from the stage-driver, and I found them all in tears. But when I made my appearance tears changed to laughter, for the sight of me I think was enough to give them hope. They didn't believe our government would have such a little, ill-dressed soldier. And father said, after looking me all over: "Well, if they have mustered you in, after they see you in that uniform it will be muster out, my boy."

In about ten days I received orders to report in Augusta. Then the family realized there was more in it than they at first thought, but consoled themselves with the belief that when I reached headquarters, I would be found useless, and sent home. I went away, leaving them with that feeling of hope struggling behind their copious tears. And the lingering kiss of my little step-sister, and her soft sobbing, "Don't, don't, please don't go," as she hung around my neck, ran constantly in my mind from that time till now. All through the nights, on the long marches, in all my troubles, that soft, sweet voice was calling, "George, please, please, don't go." And I could see her little form, and her ever-thoughtful face, a guiding star and a compass that ever guided me away from the shoals and quicksands. She was an angel companion to me all through the trials and hardships of that awful war.

Well, I arrived in Portland, was sent to the barracks with three or four thousand others, was allotted a hard bunk, and then for the first time did I realize what I was doing, what I had committed myself to, and I think if I could have caught that mustering officer I should have appealed to him just as hard to muster me out, as I did to muster me in; but I was in it and must stay. I will never forget the first day of my soldier experience. With what feeling of awe and thumping of my cowardly, timid heart, I heard the different commands of the officers. The disciplining began; the routine of a soldier's life had really started right in Portland, far away from the front where I had only expected to find it. I was detained in those barracks only a few days, and the tap of the drum, and the sound of the bugle as they sounded their different calls, had grown monotonous to me; I no longer regarded them with awe, but with mockery. I wanted to go to the front where the real life of a soldier was known, where glory could be won. I wanted the reality, not boy's play.

I was glad when I was numbered among a squad of about 200 who had orders to go to Washington. That night we marched down to the depot and were crowded into cars. I did not care; I was overjoyed: I was delighted at the prospects of going to the seat of war, near the front, where I thought I might hear the booming of the cannon, and to a place where I would soon be forwarded to my regiment. We arrived in Boston and, to my disappointment, were laid over. We were marched to the barracks on Beach street, which in early days was the "Beach Street Theater." The seats, benches, gallery, stage and scenery were all there, and we were crowded into this old, unused temple of Thespis to select a place to sleep where best we could, on the floor, or anywhere. Here I began to grow sick of soldiering; we were in this old musty theater with a guard over us, not allowed to go on the street, and unable to find out how long we were to be incarcerated there, for we were treated more like prisoners than men who had volunteered to serve their country.

I thought it a great hardship at that time, and kicked at it loud and hard, without any result that benefited us; but since I have been through it all, I can see where it was absolutely necessary to use the rigid and seemingly ungrateful discipline. Well, we were kept in the old theater for about a week; we were allowed out for two hours each day on passes, and in the evening we sang songs and "acted" on the stage. Each one who could recite or do anything did it, and it was appreciated by a deadhead audience, something unusual nowadays. It was here in this old Beach Street Theater that my future life was undoubtedly mapped out; from that time I was impressed with a desire to become an actor, and there is no doubt that the seed was planted then and grew and increased in after years.

On the 11th of November, we were ordered to Washington, and embarked on the steamboat train via Fall River, and I shall never forget when we arrived in New York, the demonstration, the greeting, the cheers, the God-speeds that we received as we marched through the city to the ferry, and it seemed to me that I was the one all this was meant for; I thought I was a hero. It seemed that all eyes were on me, and perhaps they were, for among all those Maine giants I belied my state, for I was a dot only, a pigmy beside those mighty woodsmen.

We arrived in Washington without mishap. I was granted permission to go over the city, and then to report to the commanding officer of the camp at Alexandria. My first desire when I found myself with a privilege in the great capital was to visit President Lincoln, have a talk with him and also with Secretary Stanton. My admiration for those two men was almost love, and I fancied, now that I was a soldier, that I could easily meet them; that they would grasp me by the hand, compliment and shower me with congratulations and advice. It is needless to say that I found out that I had overestimated my importance; I did not discuss the war situation with either of those gentlemen. I was a little crestfallen at not meeting them, but contented myself by looking over the city; and wherever I went I noticed I was scrutinized by everybody; soldiers on guard would come to a halt, hesitate and then present arms; some officers would pass me by, then turn and look me over from head to foot; others would touch their caps and then turn and watch me with a kind of wondering gaze, as much as to say, "What is it?"

I forgot to mention that while in Portland I had a tailor make me a very handsome suit of military clothes. He was as ignorant of the regulation style as I was. He only knew the colors and knew that I wanted it nice and handsome. He made it and so covered it over with gold braid and ornaments, that you could not tell whether I was a drum-major or a brigadier-general; that accounted for the salutations and looks of astonishment I received.

The first night I was tired out and started for Alexandria; arrived at headquarters about midnight, and told the sentry I must see the colonel. He thought I had important messages, or was some officer, and escorted me to the colonel's quarters. I woke him up, told him I had reported and wanted a bed.

The colonel said, "Is that all you want? Corporal, put this man in the guard-house." He did!

That was my first experience, and I always after tried to avoid guard-houses. The next morning I was given a broom and put to sweeping around camp with about twenty tough-looking customers. The broom did not look well with my uniform, and as soon as an officer noticed me, I was summoned before the colonel in command. He asked, what I was? I told him I didn't know yet—would not know till I reached my regiment. He had a hearty laugh at my appearance; said I ought to be sent to some fair instead of the front. However, he detailed me as his orderly.

I held this position some time, until one day there was going to be a squad of recruits and returned furloughed men sent on a steam-barge to the front at City Point, where Butler was bottled up. I asked to be one of them. The colonel told me I was foolish, and better stay with him, but I insisted; and he allowed me to go. The barge was a kind of an open double-deck boat without cabin or shelter, and they crowded us on to her as thick as we could stand; we were like sardines. I secured a position against the smoke-stack, and before we reached Chesapeake bay I was glad of it, for it became bitterly cold, and I curled down around this smoke-stack, went to sleep, and when I awoke in the morning I was crisp, dirty, and nearly roasted alive. We crossed the bay in the afternoon. Oh, wasn't it rough! This old river barge would roll and pitch out of sight at times, and we were all wet from head to foot. Then I began to wish myself home on the farm again; but I was in for it, and could not back out. I had one thought that buoyed me up, the thought of meeting my brother.

That evening we passed by Fortress Monroe, up the James river. There was not much transpired to relieve the monotony or appease our hunger or thirst; in fact, it began to look dubious as to reaching City Point. The monotony, however, was somewhat relieved in the morning. About daylight a commotion was caused by the sound of distant cannonading. Everyone crowded to the front of the boat; everybody was asking questions of everybody. Each one had some idea to offer as to the cause. Some ventured to say it was a gunboat up the river practising. One old chap, who had evidently been to the front, facetiously claimed that it was the corks out of Butler's bottles.

The river was very crooked at this point, and you could not see very far; but presently we rounded a bend in the river, which revealed to us where the cannonading came from, but for what, we could not make out. About a mile ahead of us lay a United States

gunboat, and every few minutes a puff of smoke, and then a loud bang—erang—erang—
erang—with its long vibrations on that still morning, awoke a sense of fear in everyone
aboard that boat. No one could account for the situation. Even the captain of the barge
stood with pallid cheek, seemingly in doubt what to do as he rang the bell to slow down;
but on—on we kept moving—nearer and nearer this most formidable war-ship, and as we
did so the shots became more frequent. Then we noticed a man on the bank waving a flag
back and forth, up and down in a wild, excited sort of a way. I asked what that meant. An
old soldier said the man was signaling the boat to let them know they had hit the target.

Suddenly we were brought to an understanding of what it all meant, for we could
now hear the musketry very plain, and could even see the rebels on the banks of the river.
At this point a "gig" from the gunboat pulled alongside and gave orders to the captain
"to land those troops at once," telling him at the same time that this was Fort Powhatan
landing; that Fitzhugh Lee with his cavalry had swooped down upon the garrison, which
was only composed of two hundred negro troops, and that they must be re-enforced.

The captain protested, as the troops on board were all unarmed, being returned furloughed men and recruits; but it was no use, the order was imperative, and the captain
headed his barge toward the shore. There was no wharf. That had been burnt, so he was
obliged to run as far as he could onto the sand, then land us overboard. I tell you as that
boat neared toward the shore, my face felt as if it were marbleized; sharp twinges ran up
and down my whole body, and I'll bet that I was the picture of a coward. I was not the
only one. I looked them all over, every one looked just as I felt. One man who stood near
me, I know, was more frightened than I, for he was so frightened he smelt badly. But I
didn't blame any of those poor men; it was not the pleasantest thing in the world to be
placed before the enemy as we were. However, we all landed.

The firing above us on the bank became more intense. An officer who was on the boat
with us, returning from a leave of absence, assumed command. He ordered us to fall into
line, and marched us into a little ravine, halted, and told us the position and necessity of
the occasion. He said the fort was a very important position, and must be held at all hazards; that there were only two hundred colored troops there, and they could not hold it.

Now, he proposed, as we had no arms, to go in with a rush and a yell, and make
those rebels think that re-enforcements had arrived. All this time the musketry firing was
increasing. The whizz of bullets through the air and about our heads were becoming too
frequent. I was in the front rank, center of the line, and I tell you I think I had a little of
that frightened smell about me at this time. Whether it was that or my looks or what, the
officer probably took pity on me and told me to skirmish in the rear. I hardly knew where
the rear was, but I thought it would be safer under the bank of the river, and there I hastened, and none too soon, for the rebels had made a break through the lines and poured
several volleys into our poor, unarmed re-enforcements. The rebs became more cautious,
and that was what was wanted, as the only hope we had was to hold them at bay until
re-enforcements could arrive.

Well, I skirmished in the rear, and I found it hotter than the front, for the rebs would crawl to the bank at either end of the breastworks and kept a cross-fire up and down the river. Under and against the banking, there was a sort of old barn; this was filled with hay. The bullets were flying around so thickly that I squeezed myself behind this barn, and after I was well in, the bullets just rained against that old building; but I felt pretty secure till I looked up overhead—I saw that while I was in safety from bullets, a worse danger threatened me. The overhanging bank was liable to cave in and bury me alive.

The uncertainty of my position became more and more apparent. Each moment the increased storm of bullets on the barn prevented me from even looking out, and the constant rattling down of dirt and pebbles from above, told me plainly what a position I was in. I tell you I wished then I had never been mustered in. The uncertainty of my position was soon developed. I came to myself and found I was buried to my neck; my head and face were cut and bleeding, and a soldier was trying to wipe the sand from my eyes and ears. I found I had not been shot, but the banking had caved in and buried me. Gen. "Baldy" Smith, who was in command, happened to see me behind the barn just as the bank caved in. It was he who put the soldiers at work to rescue me. As soon as I was out, and the dust out of my eyes, the general rode down to the beach, leading an extra horse; he called to me. Ordered me to mount. I did so. He made me his orderly.

I was to carry dispatches across the field, but I did not now have the fear I did at first. I did not mind the sound of the bullets. I became accustomed to it, and I rode back and forth all day long without a scratch. I believe I was so small that I rode between those bullets, and from that time forth I had no fear. I felt as though I were bullet-proof. I felt as if it were ordained that I should go through the war unscathed and unscarred. It did seem so, for I would go through places where it rained bullets, and come out without a scratch. This was my experience all through, and was commented on by comrades, who said I had a charmed life.

Well, the day wore away the rebs making feints first at one point, then another. Finally they concentrated their forces against one point, and would have carried it, too, but just then a steamboat loaded with troops rounded the bend of the river. Well, the shouts that went up from the handful of brave soldiers at the sight of that boat I never can forget. The boys on the boat caught the sound. They took in the situation, and answered back the shout with three long, hearty cheers. It created consternation in the rebel lines. They knew the jig was up, but they drew up in line, like dare-devils that they were, and with a cool deliberation, poured volley after volley into the side of the steamer until her nose touched the shore.

Well, to see those soldiers leave that steamer was a sight never to be forgotten. They jumped overboard from every part of her. It did not seem five minutes from the time she touched shore until the banks were swarming with our boys in blue. The rebels had taken to flight—our boys followed some distance, and then returned, relieving us and allowing us to embark again for City Point. After the rebels had retreated, I went outside the breastworks, and the sight that met my eyes on every side would curdle the blood of stouter hearts than mine. It appeared that Lee, with his cavalry, had surprised the pickets, and being negroes, every one they captured they would hang up to a tree after they were mutilated. I saw several with fingers cut off in order to obtain a ring quickly, and many other sickening sights which tended to make me a hardened soldier. I was having lots of experience, even before I had really reached my regiment, and I tell you, the heroic ardor of my boyish dream was beginning to ooze out of me quite fast. I began to think I was not cut for a soldier.

Well, my first battle was over, my first experience before an enemy. The first sound of musketry had died away, and we were again steaming towards City Point to join our regiments. We arrived there the next night about ten o'clock. There didn't seem to be any one in command of us or any one to direct us. It was very dark on shore, but in the distance you could see a glaring light above the horizon, as if there was a long building on fire. But from the occasional sound of guns from that quarter, I made up my mind it was the advance line of our army. It was Butler's command, and our regiment, the Eighth Maine, must be there. The Eighth Maine, Company H, was the regiment and company to which my brother belonged, and in which I was enlisted.

I started out across the fields in the direction of the light—on, on I tramped, into ditches, through mires, over fences. The farther I went the faster I went. I was so impatient I could not hold myself to a walk; it was a dog-trot all the time. I was heedless of every obstacle, till I began to near the front. I realized the danger by the whizzing of shell, and the zip, zip of bullets. I found myself among lots of soldiers, and how ragged and dirty the poor fellows looked. I asked the first man I came to where the Eighth Maine was? He looked at me in perfect astonishment. "This is the Eighth, what's left of it." I asked him if he knew where my brother was—Charley Ulmer? "Oh, yes," he said, and pointing to a little group of men, who were round a wee bit of a fire; "there he is, don't you know him?"

I hesitated, for really I could hardly tell one from the other. He saw my bewilderment, and took me by the arm and led me over to the fire. They all started and stared at me, and to save my life I could not tell which was my brother; but one more ragged than the rest uttered a suppressed cry, rushed forward, and throwing his arm about my neck, sobbed and cried like a child. "My God! my brother! Oh George, George, why did you come here?" His grief seemed to touch them all, for they all began to wipe their eyes with their ragged coat-sleeves. This began to tell on me, and for the next ten minutes it was a kind of a blubbering camp. After awhile they reconciled themselves, and began to ply me with questions faster than I could answer.

My brother sat down with me and lectured me very soundly for coming, as there was no need of it. He gave a graphic description of the hardships they had endured, and I can never obliterate the picture he presented that night. His clothes were ragged and patched, begrimed with smoke, grease and dirt; his hat an old soft one, with part of the rim gone and the crown perforated with bullet holes; his beard scraggly and dirty; his big toes peeping out of a pair of old boots with the heels all run down, in fact, he was a sight—a strong contrast to my tailor-made suit. I will never forget the expression on my brother's face when about half an hour after my arrival he looked up to me with his eyes half full of tears glistening on that dirty face, and with a kind of cynical smile, asked, after looking me over and over: "What are you, anyhow?"

I told him I didn't know.

"Well, after you have been here awhile, those pretty clothes won't look as they do now, and you will probably find out what you are after you have dodged a few shells."

Our conversation was brought to a climax by orders to break camp and fall in. We learned we were going to embark somewhere on a boat; everything was hustle-bustle now; little sheltered tents were struck, tin cups, canteens, knapsacks were made ready, and in about fifteen minutes that begrimed, dirty, hungry family of Uncle Sam's was on the march to the river. We were marched on board an old ferry-boat, and crowded so thickly that we could scarcely stand.

My brother seemed now to feel that he had the responsibility of my comfort, even my life, on his hands—and being a favorite he elbowed me a place at the end of the boat, where we could sit down by letting our feet hang over the end of the boat. In that position we remained. We didn't have room to stand up and turn around. I was awful sleepy, but dared not go to sleep for fear I would fall overboard. Finally my brother fixed me so I could lay my head back, and he held on to me while I slept. The next morning we landed at a place called West Point, on the York river; why we landed there we didn't know.

Of course soldiers never did know anything of the whys and wherefores; they only obeyed orders, stood up or laid down and got killed—they had no choice in the matter. Well, we landed, and I tell you, we were stiff and hungry. While they were unloading the horses, which was done by lowering them into the water and letting them swim ashore, which took some time, they allowed us a chance to skirmish for food.

I had to resort to pork and hard tack for my breakfast. About noon that day we began our march. Where we were going, everybody guessed, but none knew. I didn't care. I was now a kind of a half-settled soldier, but from the first, I was a kind of privileged character. No one gave me orders. No one seemed to claim me. I had never been assigned to any company. I never had to answer roll-call. I could go and come as I pleased. Once in awhile a guard would halt me, but not often. They didn't know what I was, and they didn't care.

All the afternoon we marched. Our route was along the railroad, the rails of which had the appearance of being recently torn up by the rebels. About four o'clock I was becoming very tired. We came to a clearing, and some distance in the field was a darky plowing with a mule. I made a break for him, and the rest of that march I rode. No one objected, but the boys shouted as I made my appearance on the mule; a mile or two further along we sighted a farm-house. I drew reins on my mule and made for the house; I made the boys glad on my return, for I secured a demijohn of applejack, a big bundle of tobacco, and a box of eggs. That successful raid gave me courage, and I began to think that was what I was destined for, and I liked it first-rate, for it was a pleasure to me to see those poor, hungry boys have any delicacy, or even enough of ordinary food.

That night we had to halt, for the rebs had burned the bridge, and we had to wait for pontoons. The boys were tired and hungry. A guard was posted to prevent any foraging, but I was a privileged character, and I bolted through the lines. I had seen some pigs and calves scamper into the swamp about half a mile back from where we halted, and thinking a bit of fresh meat would be nice for the boys, I determined to have some. Cautiously I stole away, till I arrived at the edge of the swamp; and such a jungle! It was almost impossible to penetrate it, so I skirted the edge, hoping to see a pig emerge. After tramping an hour I was rewarded by seeing a calf. I drew my revolver, sneaked up and fired at poor bossy. It dropped—I was a good shot—but when I reached the poor beast I found it was as poor as a rail and covered with sores as big as my hand.

I was disappointed, but cut off as much as I could that was not sore, and took it to camp. We put the kettles on the fires in short order, and my brother's company had fresh meat broth—the first fresh meat in a month—and I tell you it was good, even if it had been sore. After that episode Company H claimed me and dubbed me their mascot. I accepted the position, and from that time forth I devoted my time to foraging, stealing anything I could for my company, and I doubt if there was a company in the whole army that fared better than ours, for I was always successful in my expeditions.

After a long, tedious march across pontoons, over corduroy roads, we confronted the Johnnies at "Cold Harbor." It was here that I found myself in a real, genuine battle. I got lost in the scuffle. I found myself amidst bursting shell and under heavy musketry fire. I was bewildered and frightened. I did not know which way to go. I ran this way and that, trying to find my brother and regiment. Every turn I made it seemed I encountered more bullets and shells. Soldiers were shouting and running in every direction, artillery was galloping here and there, on every side it seemed they were fighting for dear life.

On one side of me I saw horses and men fall and pile up on top of each other. Cannon and caissons with broken wheels were turned upside down, riderless horses were scampering here and there, officers were riding and running in all directions, the shells were whizzing through the air, and soldiers shouting at the top of their voices. Everything seemed upside down. I thought the world had come to an end. I tried to find shelter behind a tree, away from the bullets, but as soon as I found shelter on one side it seemed as though the bullets and shells came from all sides, and I lay down in utter despair and fright.

I don't know how long I was there, but when I awoke I thought the war was over, it was so still. I thought every one had been killed on both sides, excepting myself. I was just thinking I would try and find a live horse, ride back to Washington and tell them that the war was over, everybody was killed, when my brother tapped me on the shoulder and asked me where I had been. He had gone through it all, escaped with the loss of one toe, and had come to the rear to have it dressed and find me.

The next morning I was sent with the "Stretcher Corps" under a flag of truce to the battle field to help take the wounded to the rear and bury the dead, and when we reached the scene, how well could I imagine what the awful struggle had been. The worst of the great conflict had occurred in an orchard, and there the sight was most appalling; dead and dying heroes were lying about as thick as a slumbering camp would be, sleeping with their guns for pillows the night before a battle; to many of those poor fellows it was that sleep that knows no waking, while to others it was the awaking from unconsciousness by the twinges of a mortal gaping wound, awake just long enough to get a glimpse of the Gates Ajar, sink back and start on that journey from which no traveler returns.

Blue and the gray were mingled together on this awful field of slaughter, and both sides seemed to respect the solemnity by a cessation of hostilities, and the hushed silence was only broken by the painful cry of some helpless wounded, or dying groans of others. The little white cloth we wore around our arms to denote, we belonged to the stretcher corps, seemed to add to the sadness of the occasion, for to those poor wounded souls we were like ministering angels, and as I moved from one to the other with tear dimmed eyes offering water and assistance to those who needed it I saw many incidents of bravery and self-sacrifice that went far toward ameliorating the suffering and obliterating the bitterness of the blue and the gray. I noticed one poor fellow who had spread his rubber blanket to catch the dew of the night sharing the moisture thus gathered with an unfortunate Confederate who had lost a leg. Another, a Confederate was staying the life-blood of a Union officer by winding his suspenders around the mangled limb. Oh! the horror of such a picture can never be penned—or told, and contemplated only by soldiers who have been there.

One-half of our regiment had been killed or wounded. After this things settled down into a siege. I employed my time foraging for the company. One day I found an apple orchard, gathered as many apples as I could carry, took them to the company and made apple-sauce without sweetening. They ate very heartily of it, poor fellows. It was a treat for them; but it was a bad find, for the next day the whole lot of them were unfit for duty. That nearly put a stop to my reconnoitering. Our regiment lay here in the advance line of breastworks for thirteen days. The sappers and miners were constantly working our breastworks towards the enemy, and every time I wanted to reach my company I found it in a new place and more difficult to reach. The rebel sharpshooters, with their deadly aim, were waiting for such chaps as me. However, under cover of night, I always managed to find and reach the company with some palatable relish.

I will never forget one night; four men were detailed to go to the rear for rations. The commissary was located about two miles to the rear, and the wagon could only haul the rations within one mile of us on account of jungle and rebel sharpshooters. Therefore these men were detailed to pack the rations the rest of the way. I was one of the detail from my company.

We went back to the covered wagons that were waiting for us. The boys said I was too small to walk, and they threw me into the rear end of one of the wagons. We got to the commissary tent—a long tent open at both ends—and from both ends they weighed out the rations of coffee, sugar, etc. While the soldier who was doing the weighing on one end had his back turned, I managed to fill my haversack from a full barrel of coffee that stood at the end of the tent. I had two haversacks for that purpose, for I went there with that intent; but I came away with only one filled. I could not get a chance for the other; it was on the wrong side. Finally the rations were all aboard, and we started back. The boys repeated the operation of throwing me into the wagon again, and there was my opportunity. I would fill my other haversack from the bags in the wagon; that's what the boys expected I would do, and I did from the first bag I could get into. Each company had its own bag.

When we arrived at the breastworks my company crowded around me for plunder. I divided it up, and was looked upon as quite a hero, but when the rations were issued it was found our company's bag was short about thirty rations of sugar, but no one said a word. It was surmised that it got spilled.

Day after day our regiment lay there and our army did not seem to gain anything. I was becoming disgusted and discouraged.

One night the Johnnies made a charge on us. That was the only time I ever fired a gun in the whole war, and I honestly believe I killed a dozen men, for immediately after they stopped firing. It was only a few moments, however; on they came, only to be repulsed. They kept that up nearly all night, and I served my country by standing down in the trench, loading a gun and passing it up to my brother to fire. I did this all night, but I didn't see any less rebels in the morning.

Our next order was to fall back, under cover of darkness. We fell back about a mile and halted for some reason, I thought to get breakfast. Anyway I built a little fire behind a stone wall, put my coffee-pot on and the remnants of a pot of beans. They were getting nice and hot; my brother and I stood waiting, smacking our lips in the anticipation of a feast, when whizz came one of those nasty little "Cohorn" mortar shells and it dropped right into our coffee and beans. Then the bugle sounded, "fall in," and we started with downcast hearts and empty stomachs, and a longing good-bye to the debris of beans and coffee. It was a tiresome march. Of course, we didn't know where we were going, and that made it all the longer.

We eventually brought up at White-House landing on the York river, where we were put on board of a steam transport without being given time to draw rations. From there we steamed down the York and up the James river to the Appomattox, and up the river to Point of Rocks. We landed here on the Bermuda Hundred side, in the rear of Butler's works, obtained some bread and coffee, and then crossed the Appomattox on pontoons and pushed on towards Petersburg. Our regiment belonged at that time to the 2nd Brigade, 2nd Division of the 18th Corps, commanded by Major General "Baldy" Smith.

We soon met the enemy's pickets in front of Petersburg. They fled before that long, serpentine file of blue-coats like deer. On, on we went. We could see the rebels running in their shirt sleeves, throwing coats, guns and everything in their mad flight. I don't think there was a shot fired on either side till we reached a fort, Smith I think it was called. It was just at dusk. This fort was located on a mound or hill with a ravine in front of it. Our brigade was drawn up in line of battle in a wheat-field on the right. A colored brigade was ordered to charge the fort from the hill opposite, and across this ravine; then I beheld one of the grandest and most awful sights I ever saw; those colored troops started on a double quick, and as they descended the hill, the fort poured volley after volley into them. The men seemed to fall like blades of grass before a machine, but it did not stop them; they rallied and moved on; it was only the work of a few minutes. With a yell they were up and into that fort, and in less time than it takes to tell it, the guns were turned on the fleeing rebels.

Here was the greatest mistake of our greatest commander. All of our army was brought to a standstill by some one's foolish order. Not another move was made. We lay there waiting, and all night long we could hear the trains rumbling along on the other side of the Appomattox river. Lee had been outwitted. We had stolen a march on him. We had arrived in front of defenseless Petersburg, and could have gone right in and on to Richmond without a struggle. But that fatal order to halt gave him all night to hurry his forces from Cold Harbor, and in the morning we found plenty of determined rebels in front of us, and thereby the war was prolonged months and hundreds and thousands of lives lost. I swore all night. I kicked and condemned every general there was in the army for the blunder I saw they were making. I only wished I could be the general commanding for one hour. But it was no use; I couldn't be.

I was nothing but a boy. But I had my ideas. I thought, perhaps, more than some of the officers did. I kept myself posted on facts and the topography of the country. The dispositions of generals was a matter of grave importance to me. I believed generals should be selected to command, NOT for their qualifications in military tactics alone, NOT because they had graduated well-dressed from "West Point," but for their indomitable pluck, judgment and honesty of purpose. It did seem to me that some of our best officers were invariably placed in the most unimportant positions and commands.

Take, for instance, "Custer's" Brigade of daring men, headed by those intrepid officers, Alger and Towns, wasting their time and imperiling the lives of thousands of good soldiers around "Emettsburg," "Gordonsville," "Bottom Bridge," carrying out the foolish orders of superiors in command. Why could not these officers of cool judgment be with us at this critical moment?—they made THEIR victories, what would they have done had they the great opportunities that were presented to others who failed?

$\sim\!\!\sim$

All night about the camp-fire the boys would delight in nagging me—getting me into arguments and debates. They called me the "midget orator of the Army of the Potomac." I will never forget one night soon after the advance on Petersburg; we were clustered about with coffee cups and pipes; an argument waxed warm in regard to the possibilities of the war lasting two more years; finally I was called upon for my views. "Midget," said Col. McArthur, "if you had supreme command of our army, what would you do?"

What would I do? If Uncle Sam would give me one regiment from each State in the Union—give me Grant, Burnside, Sherman, Sheridan, Custer, Alger, Hooker, Hancock, Thomas and Siegel to command them, I would take Richmond and settle the rebellion before they had time to wire and ask Stanton if I should. This was received with cheering and applause. But my boyish fancies and ideas were never gratified; I never had the pleasure of seeing my ideal army together, and Richmond was not taken for many months afterward. A few days after our regiment was drawn up in line of battle in a wheatfield. It was just nightfall. I was lying down on the bank of a ditch waiting for the move-forward. Suddenly a shell came over my head and bust right in the center of my company. I thought I saw legs and arms flying in all directions.

I started on the dead run for the rear. I believed I was going right, but it seemed as if the shells were coming from our own guns in the rear. I thought they had mistaken us for the enemy. I could see the shells coming, and every time they would fire, I would fall on my stomach, and thought they all went just over my head. I was soon, however, out of range, and began to feel easy, when a new fear took possession of me. What if I had, in my bewilderment, run into the rebel lines?

I saw just ahead of me an old-fashioned Southern mansion, with a high board fence all around it, and in the inclosure several small cabins used for the slaves to live in. I could not remember seeing this before, so I made up my mind I was actually inside rebeldom. However, I decided to make the best of it, and if I were or were not I would see if I could find something to eat. With fear and faltering steps I moved toward the big gate, swung it open, and it gave an awful squeak as it swung on its old rusty hinges. There was not a sign of life in or about the place, and that gave me hope and courage. In the center of the yard was a large hen-house. Cautiously toward this I crawled, heard the cackle of fowl, went first on one side then on the other, looking for the door; and imagine my surprise, the fear that took possession of me—my hair stood on end; for sitting there on a bench back of this hen-house were two big Johnnies. I couldn't speak, I couldn't move, till one of them said, "Good evening, sar; got anything to eat?"

"Yes, yes," I stammered, "I have some hard tack." Finally, one of them seeing I was most scared to death, spoke up and said, "Don't be alarmed; we are only deserters and want to give ourselves up; show us to headquarters." I was brave now. I gave them what hard tack I had, and marched them ahead of me back to the rear, till we found headquarters.

Afterward, I was offered a furlough for capturing two of the enemy. I never told this before; I took the credit. But I was not satisfied; I'd rather have some of those chickens than live rebels. So back I went and I got five; started back to the rear, put a kettle on a fire and boiled them, kept them three days, till I found my brother and the remnant of the regiment.

This was on the day fixed for the great mine explosion; every soldier on the entire line was waiting with bated breath for the signal or prolonged rumble of that expected explosion. It did not come, however. The suspense was broken by the appearance nearly a half a mile away, of a soldier with something white on his back, that made a good target for the rebel sharpshooters. Down the railroad I came. I reached the first line of earthworks. For a short distance I would keep on top. In this way I kept on, on, first running one breast-work then another, till I reached the front line. On top of this I ran the whole length, heedless and unmindful of the rebel bullets that pelted about me. I almost flew along. The soldiers shouted to me to keep down, but I heeded them not. Finally I reached the place where my regiment was, jumped down as coolly as if I had run no risk, deposited my bag, received the congratulations of my company, who examined me all over to see if there were any wounds. They found none, however, but on opening the shirt every can of milk had a bullet hole through it, and condensed milk, extract of beef, and tobacco had to be eaten as a soufflee.

There was a desperate fight going on at the right of our line. I was pressed into the service of the stretcher corps, which is usually composed of drummer boys. I did duty at this all the forenoon. The onslaught was terrible, and many poor fellows did I help carry off that field; some to live for an hour, others to lose a limb that would prove their valor and courage for the balance of their lives.

This day our regiment was relieved from the front and supposing they were going to City Point to recruit, they came back about a half a mile, halted for orders; I heard of it and concluded I would go with them and so hastened to where they were, and soon after my arrival the order came to "fall in." They did so with alacrity and bright hopes of much needed rest. I took my drum and place at the head of the regiment and started with them.

The road to the left led to City Point. Imagine their surprise when nearing it, the order came, "FILE RIGHT, BY COMPANY INTO LINE, DOUBLE QUICK MARCH."

The entire regiment seemed paralyzed for a moment, but only for a moment, the whizzing of the shells and the zip zip of the rebel bullets plainly told them what caused the sudden change. I was dumbfounded, I didn't know what to do. My brother yelled to me to go to the rear quick, but I didn't; I kept on with them until it seemed to rain bullets, but on, on they went unmindful of the awful storm of leaden messengers of death—on, on and into one of the fiercest charges of the entire war. I saw men fall so thick and fast that there didn't seem as if there was any of my regiment left, and I made up my mind it was too hot for me, so started on the dead run to the rear for a place of safety, and I didn't stop until I was pretty sure I was out of harm's way.

I came to a place about one mile back where evidently there had been a battery located; here I sat down to rest and meditate. I examined myself all over to see if I was hit, found I was unhurt but my drum had received several bullet holes in it.

Finding a green spot I stretched myself out and listened to the awful sound of musketry firing which was going on at the front, around me on all sides was the debris of a deserted camp, empty tin cans, broken bayonets, pieces of guns, fragments of bursted shell, and occasionally a whole one that had failed to explode. I had only sat here a few moments thinking which was the best way to go when I was joined by another drummer boy from a Pennsylvania regiment. We sat down and talked over our exploits, and I thought he was the most profane lad I had ever met. Most every other word he uttered was an oath.

I asked him if he wasn't afraid to talk so.

"What the h—l should I be afraid of?" he asked, at the same time picking up an old tent stake and sticking it into the ground, trying to drive it in with the heel of his boot. Failing in this he reached over and got hold of an unexploded shell and used this on the stake, but it was heavy and unwieldy.

"I wonder if this was fired by those d—d rebs," he asked.

"I guess it was," I replied, "and you better look out, or it might go off."

"Off be d—d, their shells were never worth the powder to blow 'em to h—l, see the hole in the butt of it, it would make a G—d—d good mawl, wouldn't it?" and looking round at the same time he found an old broom. Stripping the brush and wire from the handle he said, "I'll make a mawl of it and drive that d—d rebel stake into the ground with one of their own d—d shells, be d—d if I don't." Inserting the broom handle into the end of the shell he walked over to a stump, and taking the shell in both hands commenced pounding onto the stick against the stump; "d—d tight fit," he hollored to me, and the next instant I was knocked down by a terrific explosion. I came to my senses in a minute and hastened to where he had been standing. There the poor fellow lay unconscious and completely covered with blood, there was hardly a shred of clothes on him, his hair was all burned and both hands taken completely off, as if done by a surgeon's saw.

I was excited and horror stricken for a moment. The sight was horrible, but I quickly regained my composure, knowing that something must be done, and done quickly. So taking the snares from my drum I wound them tightly around his wrists to stop the flow of blood, then I hailed an ambulance, and we took him to the held hospital about a mile to the rear.

On the way the poor fellow regained consciousness, and looking at his mutilated wrists, and then with a quick and bewildered glance at me,

"G—d—d tough, ain't it," then the tears started in his eyes, and he broke down and sobbed the rest of the way, "Oh, my God! What will my poor mother say? Oh, what will she do!"

We reached the field hospital, which is only a temporary place for the wounded where the wounds are hurriedly dressed, and then they are sent to regular hospitals, located in Baltimore, Philadelphia, Norfolk, Portsmouth, etc., where they have all the comforts possible.

We laid the little fellow down in one corner of the tent to wait his turn with the surgeon, and when I left him, he cried and begged for me to stay, but I couldn't stand his suffering longer, so I bade him good-bye with tears streaming down my own cheeks. I hurried out, and even after I reached the outside I could hear him cry, "Oh, my God! What will my poor mother say? Oh, what will she do!"

In the afternoon I was detailed to wait on the amputating tables at the field hospital.

It was a horrible task at first. My duty was to hold the sponge or "cone" of ether to the face of the soldier who was to be operated on, and to stand there and see the surgeons cut and saw legs and arms as if they were cutting up swine or sheep, was an ordeal I never wish to go through again. At intervals, when the pile became large, I was obliged to take a load of legs or arms and place them in a trench near by for burial. I could only stand this one day, and after that I shirked all guard duty. The monotony, the routine of life, in front of Petersburg, was becoming distasteful to me. I had stolen everything I could. My district or territory had given out, so the next day I started for the front to bid my brother good-bye.

Our regiment was sometimes relieved and ordered to the rear for rest; so it was on this occasion, they had fallen back and halted in a little ravine. I met my brother, who always expected me to bring him some stolen sweets or goodies of some kind, but unfortunately this time I came empty-handed. I had failed to find anything to steal. I was hungry myself, but when I looked at him I forgot my own hunger, for such a forlorn appearance as he presented almost broke my heart, and I determined to find him something to eat at all hazards. So off I started on an independent foraging expedition.

That night the regiment went into action, and my brother was slightly wounded several times. One shot would have proved fatal, but the watch received the bullet and the wound proved fatal only to the watch; it was smashed all to pieces. But my brother prizes the pieces now more than he ever did the whole watch.

The next day my regiment was ordered to the front again. I made up my mind I would not go with them. I concluded I needed rest in order to recuperate, so when the regiment started I bade my brother good-bye, gave him a parting kiss and God's blessings, so off I started.

About a half a mile from my regiment I came to one of those Virginia fences, got up on top of it, and sat thinking, and while sitting there the shells began to fly pretty thick. I thought I had better be moving, jumped down, and as I did so a shell struck one of the rails of the fence. A piece of the rail struck me and was harder than I was, for when I came to my senses I found I was in the hospital. I didn't think I was hurt very badly, but when I tried to get up, found I couldn't. From there they moved me to "Balfour Hospital" at Portsmouth, Virginia. I never will forget the shame and mortification I felt at the sight I must have presented when the boat that conveyed us to Portsmouth arrived.

An old negro came to my bunk and took me on his back, and with a boot in each hand dangling over his shoulder he carried me pickaback through the streets to the hospital, a large, fine building, formerly the "Balfour Hotel," and converted into a hospital after Portsmouth was captured. They took me up stairs into what was formerly the dining-room but now filled with over two hundred little iron beds, and each bed occupied by a wounded soldier. Everything in and about the place was as neat as wax. They carried me to a vacant bed near the center of the room, and I noticed the next bed to mine had several tin dishes hanging over it, suspended from the ceiling. These were filled with water, and from a small hole punctured in the bottom the water would slowly but constantly drip upon some poor fellow's wound to keep it moist. I had just sat down on the side of my bed, when I was startled by the sound of a familiar voice. "Hello, cully! What you been doin', playing with one of those d—d shells, too?"

No, I replied, the shells were playing with me. Then I recognized the occupant of the next bed as my drummer boy acquaintance who had his hands blown off a week ago. What a strange thing that we should be brought together side by side again, both wounded with a shell and nearly on the same spot.

He had changed wonderfully; his little white pinched face told too plainly the suffering he had endured. I asked him how he was getting along. "Oh I'm getting along pretty d—d fast. I guess I'll croak in a few days."

"Oh you musn't talk that way, you'll be all right in a little while."

"Oh, no, cully, I know better. I'm a goner; I know it. I don't want to live, anyhow. What in h—l is the good of a man without hands?" Then turning his bandaged head towards me, his eyes filling with tears. "I ain't afraid to die, cul., but I would like to see my old mother first. Do you think I will?"

Oh, yes, I said, no doubt of it; at the same time I felt that his days were numbered, but I wanted to make him feel as comfortable as possible. He was so much worse off than I, that I forgot my own injuries and was eager to assist him all I could. After a few minutes silence—

"Say, cully, reach under my pillow and find a little book there; it's a little Testament that my dear old mother gave me; read a little for me, will you please? You'll find a place mother marked for me, read that, please."

I turned the leaves over till I found a little white ribbon pinned to a leaf, marking the verse beginning, "Suffer little children to come unto me." I started to read for him, but the tears filled my eyes. I had to stop, and as I did so, I noticed he seemed very quiet. I glanced at him, and the open, staring eyes and the rigid drawn features told me too plainly that the little fellow was out of his sufferings—he was dead!

"Mother" was the countersign on his lips so thin, And the sentry in heaven must let him in.

I remained here three weeks, finally got up and around and began to think I had enough of soldier life. I had everything I wished for; some ladies in the town—God bless them, I never will forget them—visited the hospital occasionally, and they always took pains to bring me flowers or goodies of some kind. (Pardon me, but somehow I was always a favorite with ladies.) Well, after remaining there three or four weeks I concluded I didn't want to go to the front, so I sat down and wrote a personal letter to Secretary Stanton, told him who, how, and what I was, and asked him to advise me what to do; if I should go to the front or home. Soon after, a special order came back from him to have me transferred to the "2nd Battalion Veteran Reserve Corps." Let me here state to those who do not understand; all soldiers who were sick or wounded, unfit for field service were transferred to the Veteran Reserve Corps, for the purpose of doing light guard duty in camp, or at headquarters; they were divided into two battalions, 1st and 2nd. The 1st Battalion was supposed to be able to carry a musket for duty, while the 2nd Battalion was composed of one-armed men or totally disabled soldiers, and were supplied with a small sword; and thus I was condemned by special order; however I liked it. I had an easy time, nothing to do, and others to help me.

I continued here for about two months, until the hospital was ordered to be removed to Old Point Comfort. I had become a great favorite of Lieutenant Russell, the officer in charge of the hospital, and a nice man he was. When the order came to move, the fixtures, furniture, in fact everything in and about the building was ordered to be sold. I was detailed by Lieutenant Russell to remain behind and superintend the sale of the stuff, keep accounts, make a report when all was sold, and turn over the proceeds. That detained me there two weeks longer. I sold the beds, dishes, tables, everything. There remained about thirty tons of coal in the yard to be disposed of. I sold it in any quantity to poor people; took any price for it I could get, the same as everything else. Finally, everything was sold off, and I was ready to depart the next day for Old Point Comfort.

The next day I landed and reported to headquarters at Fortress Monroe. A day or two after, Lieutenant Russell sent for me; he wanted a foreman in the Government Printing Office. I was down for occupation on the pay-roll as a printer. He asked me if I understood the business. I said yes, I had some knowledge of it, so I was detailed with an extra eight dollars per month. I took charge of the office at once. The first day I had orders to print fifty thousand official envelopes. The press-boy brought me the proof, I looked it over, and marked it correct; they were printed and sent to headquarters.

A few days after Lieutenant Russell sent for me to report at his office. I didn't know what was up. Thought perhaps I was going to be sent to Washington to take charge of the Government Printing Office there. As I went in, the lieutenant turned to me with a quizzical smile on his face:

"Young man, you told me you were a printer?"

"Yes, sir."

"Did you 'O.K.' this job?" passing one of the envelopes he held in his hand.

"Yes sir," I answered.

"Umph! Is it correct?"

"Yes, sir."

"It is, eh?"

"Yes-s, sir."

"Umph! how do you spell business?"

"B-u-i-s-n-e-s-s," said I.

"You do, eh?"

"Yes, sir."

"Well," said he in an imperative manner, "our government sees fit to differ with you. You will go to your office and print fifty thousand more, but see that you spell business right, and bring me the proof. The lot you have printed we will send to Washington, and recommend that they be made into a paper mache statue of yourself, and label it 'Buisness' or the only government printer."

I was a little chagrined at the mistake, but did not take it to heart; but I was soon relieved by a man who was more careful in his spelling. A week or so after leaving the printing office, I was sent to the fort to act as a kind of a companion to the Confederate president, Jefferson Davis. I was instructed to walk and talk with him. I presume I was intended for a sort of guard. Perhaps our government wished to make him feel as if he were not under surveillance, and so placed one whose insignificant appearance would put him at his ease. However, I found it a very agreeable occupation.

One of the most pleasant weeks I ever passed was with Mr. Jefferson Davis. He was a most agreeable man to me. He gave me lots of good advice, and I learned more from conversation with him about national affairs than I ever expected to know; and if I ever become president I will avail myself of the advice and teaching of that great man. He pointed out the right and wrong paths for young men; urged me above all things to adhere strictly to honesty and integrity; to follow these two principles, and I would succeed in business and become great and respected.

I thanked him for his kind advice, and pressed his hand good-bye. "Good-bye, my boy," said he. "You have been a comfort to me in my loneliness and sorrow. God bless you, my boy, God bless you!"

A great, big something came up in my throat as I turned and left him, and I have regretted all my life that I was not fortunate enough to have the pleasure of meeting him again before he passed away; for I assure you, indulgent readers and comrades, that no matter what he had done, or what mistakes he had made, his memory will always find a warm spot in the heart of that little Drummer Boy from Maine.

CHAPTER 28

Suffering and Hatred
By Phoebe Yates Pember

Like Louisa May Alcott (see her chapter 33), many Northern and Southern women volunteered for duty in army hospitals as a way to serve their cause. Often inexperienced, many times from pampered backgrounds, they nonetheless rose to the challenge of this backbreaking—and heartbreaking—work. Phoebe Yates Levy Pember was a well-educated woman from a prosperous Jewish family in Charleston, South Carolina. A widow by 1861, she accepted the offer to serve as matron at the largest military hospital in the country at that time, Chimborazo Hospital in Richmond, Virginia. Even in this large and established facility, casualties were greatly compounded by severe shortages of personnel, food, medicine, and equipment. As did Alcott, Pember began her service in December 1862, but her stint lasted far longer. She remained at Chimborazo even after the fall of Richmond, until Union troops took it over. During that time, she did whatever she could to relieve her patients' miseries—from playing cards with recovering patients to holding the hands of dying young men. During her time at Chimborazo, she noticed the regard her Southern boys felt for their Northern counterparts. Yet, as the suffering in the South intensified, so did the hatred toward the foe. "Suffering and Hatred" is an excerpt from Pember's A Southern Woman's Story, *which takes place in 1864 as the war was grinding to a close.*

—LISA PURCELL

NOW DURING THE SUMMER OF 1864 BEGAN WHAT IS REALLY MEANT BY "WAR," FOR privations had to be endured which tried body and soul, and which temper and patience had to meet unflinchingly day and night. A growing want of confidence was forced upon the mind; and with doubts which though unexpressed were felt as to the ultimate success of our cause, there came into play the antagonistic qualities of human nature.

The money worthless, and a weak Congress and weaker financier failing to make it much more valuable than the paper it was printed on; the former refusing to the last to raise the hospital fund to meet the depreciation. Everything furnished through government contracts of the very poorest description, perhaps necessarily so from the difficulty of finding any supply.

The railroads were cut so constantly that what had been carefully collected in the country in the form of poultry and vegetables by hospital agents would be rendered unfit for use by the time the connection would be restored. The inducements for theft were great in this season of scarcity of food and clothing. The pathetic appeals made for the coarsest meal by starving men all wore upon the health and strength of those exposed to the strain, and made life weary and hopeless.

The rations became so small about this time that every ounce of flour was valuable, and there were days when it was necessary to refuse with aching heart and brimming eyes the request of decent, manly-looking fellows for a piece of dry corn-bread. If given it would have robbed the rightful owner of part of his scanty rations. After the flour or meal had been made into bread, it was almost ludicrous to see with what painful solicitude Miss G. and myself would count the rolls, or hold a council over the pans of corn-bread, measuring with a string how large we could afford to cut the squares, to be apportioned to a certain number.

Sometimes when from the causes above stated, the supplies were not issued as usual, invention had to be taxed to an extreme, and every available article in our pantry brought into requisition. We had constantly to fall back upon dried apples and rice for convalescing appetites, and herb-tea and arrowroot for the very ill. There was only one way of making the last at all palatable, and that was by drenching it with whiskey.

Long abstinence in the field from everything that could be considered, even then, a delicacy, had exaggerated the fancy of sick men for any particular article of food they wanted into a passion; and they begged for such peculiar dishes that surgeons and nurses might well be puzzled. The greatest difficulty in granting these desires was that tastes became contagious, and whatever one patient asked for, his neighbor and the one next to him, and so on throughout the wards, craved also, and it was impossible to decide upon whom to draw a check.

No one unacquainted with our domestic relations can appreciate the difficulties under which we labored. Stoves in any degree of newness or usefulness we did not have; they were rare and expensive luxuries. As may be supposed, they were not the most convenient articles in the world to pack away in blockade-running vessels; and the trouble and expense of land transportation also seriously affected the quality of the wood for fuel furnished us. Timber which had been condemned heretofore as unfit for use, light, soggy and decayed, became the only quality available. The bacon, too, cured the first two years of the war, when salt commanded an enormous price, in most cases was spoilt, from the economy used in preparing that article; and bacon was one of the sinews of war.

We kept up brave hearts, and said we could eat the simplest fare, and wear the coarsest clothing, but there was absolutely nothing to be bought that did not rank as a luxury. It was wasting time and brain to attempt to economize, so we bent to the full force of that wise precept, "Sufficient for the day is the evil thereof."

There really was a great deal of heroism displayed when looking back, at the calm courage with which I learned to count the number of mouths to be fed daily, and then contemplating the food, calculate not how much but how little each man could be satisfied with. War may be glorious in all its panoply and pride, when in the field opposing armies meet and strive for victory; but battles fought by starving the sick and wounded— by crushing in by main force day by day all the necessities of human nature, make victories hardly worth the name.

Another of my local troubles were the rats, who felt the times, and waxed strong and cunning, defying all attempts to entrap them, and skillfully levying blackmail upon us day by day, and night after night. Hunger had educated their minds and sharpened their reasoning faculties. Other vermin, the change of seasons would rid us of, but the coldest day in winter, and the hottest in summer, made no apparent difference in their vivacious strategy.

They examined traps with the air of connoisseurs, sometimes springing them from a safe position, and kicked over the bread spread with butter and strychnine to show their contempt for such underhand warfare. The men related wonderful rat-stories not well enough authenticated to put on record, but their gourmands ate all the poultices applied during the night to the sick, and dragged away the pads stuffed with bran from under the arms and legs of the wounded.

They even performed a surgical operation which would have entitled any of them to pass the board. A Virginian had been wounded in the very center of the instep of his left foot. The hole made was large, and the wound sloughed fearfully around a great lump of proud flesh which had formed in the center like an island. The surgeons feared to remove this mass, as it might be connected with the nerves of the foot, and lockjaw might ensue. Poor Patterson would sit on his bed all day gazing at his lame foot and bathing it with a rueful face, which had brightened amazingly one morning when I paid him a visit. He exhibited it with great glee, the little island gone, and a deep hollow left, but the wound washed clean and looking healthy. Some skillful rat surgeon had done him this good service while in the search for luxuries, and he only knew that on awaking in the morning he had found the operation performed.

I never had but one personal interview with any of them. An ancient gray gentleman, who looked a hundred years old, both in years and depravity, would eat nothing but butter, when that article was twenty dollars a pound; so finding all means of getting rid of him fail through his superior intelligence, I caught him with a fish-hook, well baited with a lump of his favorite butter, dropped into his domicile under the kitchen floor.

Epicures sometimes managed to entrap them and secure a nice broil for supper, declaring that their flesh was superior to squirrel meat; but never having tasted it, I cannot add my testimony to its merits. They staid with us to the last, nor did I ever observe any signs of a desire to change their politics. Perhaps some curious gourmet may wish a recipe for the best mode of cooking them. The rat must be skinned, cleaned, his head cut off and his body laid open upon a square board, the legs stretched to their full extent and secured upon it with small tacks, then baste with bacon fat and roast before a good fire quickly like canvas-back ducks.

One of the remarkable features of the war was the perfect good nature with which the rebels discussed their foes. In no instance up to a certain period did I hear of any remark that savored of personal hatred. They fought for a cause and against a power, and would speak in depreciation of a corps or brigade; but "they fit us, and we fit them," was the whole story generally, and till the blowing up of the mine at Petersburg there was a gay, insouciant style in their descriptions of the war scenes passing under their observation.

But after that time the sentiment changed from an innate feeling the Southern soldiers had that mining was "a mean trick," as they expressed it. They were not sufficiently versed in military tactics to recognize that stratagem is fair in war. . . . The men had heretofore been calm and restrained, particularly before a woman, never using oaths or improper language, but the wounded that were brought in from that fight emulated the talents of Uncle Toby's army in Flanders, and eyes gleamed, and teeth clenched as they showed me the locks of their muskets to which the blood and hair still clung, when after firing, without waiting to re-load, they had clenched the barrels and fought hand to hand. If their accounts could be relied upon, it was a gallant strife and a desperate one, and ghastly wounds bore testimony of the truth of many a tale then told.

Once again the bitter blood showed itself, when, after a skirmish, the foe cut the rail track, so that the wounded could not be brought to the city. Of all the monstrous crimes that war sanctions, this is surely the most sinful. Wounded soldiers without the shelter of a roof, or the comfort of a bed of straw, left exposed to sun, dew, and rain, with hardly the prospect of a warm drink or decent food for days, knowing that comfortable quarters awaited them, all ready prepared, but rendered useless by what seems an unnecessarily cruel act. Was it any wonder that their habitual indifference to suffering gave way, and the soldier cursed loud and deep at a causeless inhumanity, which, if practiced habitually, is worse than savage! When the sufferers at last reached the hospital, their wounds had not been attended to for three days, and the sight of them was shocking.

Busy in my kitchen, seeing that the supply of necessary food was in preparation, I was spared the sight of much of the suffering, but on passing among the ambulances going in and out of the wards I descried seated up on one of them a dilapidated figure, both hands holding his head which was tied up with rags of all descriptions. He appeared to be incapable of talking, but nodded and winked and made motions with head and feet. In the general confusion he had been forgotten, so I took him under my especial charge. He was taken into a ward, seated on a bed, while I stood on a bench to be able to unwind rag after rag from around his head. There was no sensitiveness on his part, for his eye was merry and bright, but when the last came off, what a sight!

Two balls had passed through his cheek and jaw within half an inch of each other, knocking out the teeth on both sides and cutting the tongue in half. The inflammation caused the swelling to be immense, and the absence of all previous attendance, in consequence of the detention of the wounded until the road could be mended, had aggravated the symptoms. There was nothing fatal to be apprehended, but fatal wounds are not always the most trying.

The sight of this was the most sickening my long experience had ever seen. The swollen lips turned out, and the mouth filled with blood, matter, fragments of teeth from amidst all of which the maggots in countless numbers swarmed and writhed, while the smell generated by this putridity was unbearable. Castile soap and soft sponges soon cleansed the offensive cavity, and he was able in an hour to swallow some nourishment he drew through a quill.

The following morning I found him reading the newspaper, and entertaining every one about him by his abortive attempts to make himself understood, and in a week he actually succeeded in doing so. The first request distinctly enunciated was that he wanted a looking-glass to see if his sweetheart would be willing to kiss him when she saw him. We all assured him that she would not be worthy of the name if she would not be delighted to do so.

An order came about this time to clear out the lower wards for the reception of improperly vaccinated patients, who soon after arrived in great numbers. They were dreadfully afflicted objects, many of them with sores so deep and thick upon arms and legs that amputation had to be resorted to, to preserve life. As fast as the eruption would be healed in one spot, it would break out in another, for the blood seemed entirely poisoned. The unfortunate victims bore the infliction as they had borne everything else painful—with calm patience and indifference to suffering. Sometimes a favorable comparison would be made between this and the greater loss of limbs.

No one who was a daily witness to their agonies from this cause, can help feeling indignant at charges made of inhumanity to Federal prisoners of war, who were vaccinated with the same virus; and while on this subject, though it may be outside of the recollections of hospital life, I cannot help stating that on no occasion was the question of rations and medicines to be issued for Federal prisoners discussed in my presence; and circumstances placed me where I had the best opportunity of hearing the truth (living with the wife of a cabinet officer); that good evidence was not given, that the Confederate commissary-general, by order of the government issued to them the same rations it gave its soldiers in the field, and only when reductions of food had to be made in our army, were they also made in the prisons. The question of supplies for them was an open and a vexed one among the people generally, and angry and cruel things were said; but every one cognizant of facts in Richmond knows that even when General Lee's army lived on corn-meal at times that the prisoners still received their usual rations.

At a cabinet meeting when the Commissary-General Northrop advocated putting the prisoners on the half rations which our soldiers had been obliged to content themselves with for some time, General Lee opposed him on the ground that men animated by companionship and active service could be satisfied with less than prisoners with no hope and leading an inactive life. Mr. Davis sided with him, and the question was settled that night, although in his anger Mr. Northrop accused General Lee of showing this consideration because his son was a prisoner in the enemy's lines.

CHAPTER 29

Vermont Sharp Shooters
By Wm. Y. W. Ripley

Unique rifles and special skills made them the forerunners of the elite Special Forces units so well-known in today's military.

—LAMAR UNDERWOOD

VERY SOON AFTER THE OUTBREAK OF THE WAR FOR THE UNION, IMMEDIATELY, IN FACT, upon the commencement of actual operations in the field, it became painfully apparent that, however inferior the rank and file of the Confederate armies were in point of education and general intelligence to the men who composed the armies of the Union, however imperfect and rude their equipment and material, man for man they were the superiors of their Northern antagonists in the use of arms.

Recruited mainly from the rural districts (for the South had but few large cities from which to draw its fighting strength), their armies were composed mainly of men who had been trained to the skillful use of the rifle in that most perfect school, the field and forest, in the pursuit of the game so abundant in those sparsely settled districts. These men, who came to the field armed at first, to a large extent, with their favorite sporting or target rifles, and with a training acquired in such a school, were individually more than the equals of the men of the North, who were, with comparatively few exceptions, drawn from the farm, the workshop, the office or the counter, and whose life-long occupations had been such as to debar them from those pursuits in which the men of the South had gained their skill. Indeed, there were in many regiments in the Northern armies men who had never even fired a gun of any description at the time of their enlistment.

On the other hand, there were known to be scattered throughout the loyal states, a great number of men who had made rifle shooting a study, and who, by practice on the target ground and at the country shooting matches, had gained a skill equal to that of the men of the South in any kind of shooting, and in long range practice a much greater degree of excellency.

There were many of these men in the ranks of the loyal army, but their skill was neutralized by the fact that the arms put into their hands, although the most perfect military weapons then known, were not of the description calculated to show the best results in the hands of expert marksmen.

Occasionally a musket would be found that was accurate in its shooting qualities, and occasionally such a gun would fall into the hands of a man competent to appreciate and utilize its best features. It was speedily found that such a gun, in the hands of such a man, was capable of results not possible to be obtained from a less accurate weapon in the hands of a less skillful man. To remedy this state of affairs, and to make certain that the best weapons procurable should be placed in the hands of the men best fitted to use them effectively, it was decided by the war department, early in the summer of 1861, that a regiment should be organized, to be called the First Regiment of United States Sharp Shooters, and to consist of the best and most expert rifle shots in the Northern States. The detail of the recruiting and organization of this regiment was entrusted to Hiram Berdan, then a resident of the city of New York, himself an enthusiastic lover of rifle shooting, and an expert marksman.

Col. Berdan set himself earnestly at work to recruit and organize such a body of men as should, in the most perfect manner, illustrate the capacity for warlike purposes of his favorite weapon.

It was required that a recruit should possess a good moral character, a sound physical development, and in other respects come within the usual requirements of the army regulations; but, as the men were designed for an especial service, it was required of them that before enlistment they should justify their claim to be called "sharp shooters" by such a public exhibition of their skill as should fairly entitle them to the name, and warrant a reasonable expectation of usefulness in the field. To insure this it was ordered that no recruit be enlisted who could not, in a public trial, make a string of ten shots at a distance of two hundred yards, the aggregate measurement of which should not exceed fifty inches. In other words, it was required that the recruit should, in effect, be able to place ten bullets in succession within a ten-inch ring at a distance of two hundred yards.

Any style of rifle was allowed—telescopic sights, however, being disallowed—and the applicant was allowed to shoot from any position he chose, only being required to shoot from the shoulder.

Circular letters setting forth these conditions, and Col. Berdan authority, were issued to the governors of the loyal states, and, as a first result from the state of Vermont, Capt. Edmund Weston of Randolph applied for and received of Gov. Holbrook authority to recruit one company of sharp shooters, which was mustered into the service as Co. F, First United States Sharp Shooters, and is the subject of this history.

Capt. Weston at once put himself in communication with well known riflemen in different parts of the state and appointed recruiting officers in various towns to receive applications and superintend the trials of skill, without which no person could be accepted.

The response was more hearty and more general than could have been expected, and many more recruits presented themselves than could be accepted—many of whom, however, failed to pass the ordeal of the public competition—and, as the event proved, more were accepted than could be legally mustered into the service.

All who were accepted, however, fully met the rigid requirements as to skill in the use of the rifle.

The company rendezvoused at Randolph early in September, 1861, and on the 13th of that month were mustered into the state service by Charles Dana.

Thus organized, the company, with one hundred and thirteen enlisted men, left the state on the same day on which they were mustered, and proceeded via New Haven and Long Island Sound to the rendezvous of the regiment at Weehawken Heights, near New York, where they went into camp with other companies of the regiment which had preceded them. On or about the 24th of September the regiment proceeded under orders from the war department to Washington, arriving at that city at a late hour on the night of the twenty-fifth, and were assigned quarters at the Soldiers' Rest, so well known to the troops who arrived at Washington at about that time. On the twenty-sixth they were ordered to a permanent camp of instruction well out in the country and near the residence and grounds of Mr. Corcoran, a wealthy resident of Washington of supposed secession proclivities, where they were for the first time in a regularly organized camp, and could begin to feel that they were fairly cut off at last from the customs and habits of civil life. Here they were regularly mustered into the service of the United States, thirteen enlisted men being rejected, however, to reduce the company to the regulation complement of one hundred enlisted men; so that of the one hundred and thirteen men charged to the company on the rolls of the Adjt. and Ins.-Gen. of Vermont, only one hundred took the field. Other companies from different states arrived at about the same time, and the regiment was at last complete, having its full complement of ten companies of one hundred men each.

Only one of the field officers had had a military education or military experience. Lieutenant-Colonel Mears was an officer of the regular army, a thorough drill master and a strict disciplinarian. Under his efficient command the regiment soon began to show a marked and daily improvement that augured well for its future usefulness. The officers of the regimental staff were, each in his own department, able and painstaking men. The chaplain alone was not quite popular among the rank and file, and they rather envied the Second Regiment of Sharp Shooters who were encamped near them, and whose chaplain, the Rev. Lorenzo Barber, was the beau ideal of an army chaplain. Tender hearted and kind, he was ever ready to help the weak and the suffering; now dressing a wound and now helping along a poor fellow, whose fingers were all thumbs and whose thoughts were too big for utterance (on paper), with his letter to the old mother at home; playing ball or running a foot race, beating the best marksmen at the targets, and finally preaching a rousing good sermon which was attentively listened to on Sunday. His *faith* was in the "Sword of the Lord and of Gideon," but his best *work* was put in with a twenty pound telescopic rifle which he used with wonderful effect. The original plan of armament contemplated the use exclusively of target or sporting rifles. The men had been encouraged to bring with them their favorite weapons, and had been told that the government would pay for such arms at the rate of sixty dollars each, while those who chose to rely upon the United States armories for their rifles were to be furnished with the best implements procurable. The guns to be so furnished were to be breach loaders, to have telescopic sights, hair triggers, and all the requisites for the most perfect shooting that the most skillful marksman could desire.

Many of the men had, with this understanding, brought with them their own rifles, and with them target shooting became a pastime, and many matches between individuals and companies were made and many very short strings were recorded.

Under the stimulus of competition and organized practice great improvement was noted in marksmanship, even among those who had been considered almost perfect marksmen before. On one occasion President Lincoln, accompanied by Gen. McClellan, paid a visit to the camp and asked to be allowed to witness some of the sharp shooting of which he had heard so much.

A detail of the best men was made and a display of skill took place which, perhaps, was never before equalled. President Lincoln himself, as did Gen. McClellan, Col. Hudson and others of the staff, took part in the firing, the President using a rifle belonging to Corporal H. J. Peck of the Vermont company.

At the close of the exhibition Col. Berdan, being asked to illustrate the accuracy of his favorite rifle, fired three shots at different portions of the six hundred yard target; when having satisfied himself that he had the proper range, and that both himself and rifle could be depended upon, announced that at the next shot he would strike the right eye of the gaily colored Zouave which, painted on the half of an A tent, did duty for a target at that range. Taking a long and careful aim, he fired, hitting the exact spot selected and announced beforehand. Whether partly accidental or not it was certainly a wonderful performance and placed Col. Berdan at once in the foremost rank of rifle experts. On the 28th of November, the day set apart by the governors of the loyal states as Thanksgiving Day, shooting was indulged in by different men of Co. F and other companies for a small prize offered by the field officers, the terms being two hundred yards, off hand, the shortest string of two shots to win. The prize was won from a large number of skillful contestants by Ai Brown of Co. F—his two shots measuring 4-1/4 inches, or each within 2-1/8 inches of the center.

On the 7th of December another regimental shooting match took place; the prize going this time to a Michigan man, his string of three shots, fired off hand at two hundred yards, measuring six inches. These records are introduced here simply for the purpose of showing the wonderful degree of skill possessed by these picked marksmen in the use of the rifle. But it was soon found that there were objections to the use in the field of the fine guns so effective on the target ground. The great weight of some of them was of itself almost prohibitory, for, to a soldier burdened with the weight of his knapsack, haversack and canteen, blanket and overcoat, the additional weight of a target rifle—many of which weighed fifteen pounds each, and some as much as thirty pounds—was too much to be easily borne.

It was also found difficult to provide the proper ammunition for such guns in the field, and finally, owing to the delicacy of the construction of the sights, hair triggers, etc., they were constantly liable to be out of order, and when thus disabled, of even less use than the smooth-bore musket, with buck and ball cartridge of fifty years before. Manufacturers of fine guns from all parts of our own country, and many from Europe, flocked to the camp of the sharp shooters offering their goods, each desirous of the credit of furnishing arms to a body of men so well calculated to use them effectively, and many fine models were offered. The choice of the men, however, seemed to be a modified military rifle made by the Sharpe Rifle Manufacturing Co., and a request was made to the war department for a supply of these arms. At this early day, however, the departments were full of men whose ideas and methods were those of a half a century gone by; and at the head of the ordinance department was a man who, in addition to being of this stamp, was the father of the muzzle loading Springfield rifle, then the recognized arm of the United States Infantry, and from him came the most strenuous opposition to the proposal to depart from the traditions of the regular army.

Gen. McClellan, and even the President himself, were approached on this subject, and both recognized the propriety of the proposed style of armament and the great capacity for efficient service possessed by the regiment when it should be once satisfactorily armed and fairly in front of the enemy. But the ordinance department was ever a block in the way; its head obstinately and stubbornly refusing to entertain any proposition other than to arm the regiment with the ordinary army musket; and, to add to the growing dissatisfaction among the men over the subject of arms, it became known that the promises made to them at the time of enlistment, that the government would pay them for their rifles at the rate of sixty dollars each, was unauthorized and would not be fulfilled; and also that the representations made to them with respect to telescopic breech loaders were likewise unauthorized. Discontent became general and demoralization began to show itself in an alarming form.

Some of the field officers were notoriously incompetent; the Major, one of those military adventurers who floated to the surface during the early years of the war, particularly so; he was a kind of a modern Dalgetty without the courage or skill of his renowned prototype, rarely present in camp, and when there of little or no service. The Lieutenant-Colonel, a man of rare energy and skill in his profession, and whose painstaking care had made the regiment all that it was at that time, fearing the after effects of this demoralization on the efficiency of the command, and seeing opportunity for his talents in other fields, resigned; and on the 29th of November, 1861, Wm. Y. W. Ripley of Rutland, Vt., was appointed Lieutenant-Colonel, and Caspar Trepp, Captain of Co. A., was made Major. Lieutenant-Colonel Ripley had seen service only as Captain of Co. K, First Vermont Volunteers. Major Trepp had received a thorough military training in the army of his native Switzerland, and had seen active service in European wars. The regiment remained at camp of instruction under the immediate command of Lieut.-Col. Ripley, employed in the usual routine of camp duty, drills, etc., during the whole of the winter of 1861–62, particular attention being paid to the skirmish drill, in which the men became wonderfully proficient; and it is safe to say that for general excellence in drill, except the manual of arms, they were excelled by few volunteer regiments in the service. All orders were given by the sound of the bugle, and the whole regiment deployed as skirmishers could be as easily maneuvered as a single company could be in line of battle. The bugle corps was under the charge of Calvin Morse of Co. F as chief bugler, and under his careful instruction attained to an unusual degree of excellence. All camp and other calls were sounded on the bugle, and the men found them pleasant little devices for translating curt and often rough English into music. They were bugled to breakfast and to dinner, bugled to guard mounting and bugled to battle, brigades moved and cavalry charged to the sound of the bugle.

The winter was an unusually severe one, and, as the enemy maintained a strict blockade of the Potomac, the supply of wood was often short, and some suffering was the result. The health of the regiment remained fairly good; measles, small pox, and other forms of camp diseases appeared, however, and Co. F, of course, suffered its share, losing by death from disease during the winter, Wm. T. Battles, Edward Fitz, Sumner E. Gardner and Geo. H. Johnson.

On the 20th of March, 1862, the regiment received orders to report to Major-Gen. Fitz John Porter, whose division then lay at Alexandria, Va., awaiting transportation to Fortress Monroe to join the army under McClellan. At this time the regiment was without arms of any kind, except for the few target rifles remaining in the hands of their owners, and a few old smooth-bore muskets which had been used during the winter for guard duty. Shortly before this time the war department, perhaps wearied by constant importunity, perhaps recognizing the importance of the subject, had so far receded from its former position as to offer to arm the regiment with revolving rifles of the Colt pattern, and had sent the guns to the camp for issue to the men with promise of exchanging them for Sharpe's rifles at a later day. They were five-chambered breech loaders, very pretty to look at, but upon examination and test they were found inaccurate and unreliable, prone to get out of order and even dangerous to the user. They were not satisfactory to the men, who knew what they wanted and were fully confident of their ability to use such guns as they had been led by repeated promises to expect, to good advantage. When, however, news came that the rebels had evacuated Manassas, and that the campaign was about to open in good earnest, they took up these toys, for after all they were hardly more, and turned their faces southward. Co. F was the first company in the regiment to receive their arms, and to the influence of their patriotic example the regiment owes its escape from what at one time appeared to be a most unfortunate embarrassment.

The march to Alexandria over Long Bridge was made in the midst of a pouring rain and through such a sea of mud as only Virginia can afford material for. It was the first time the regiment had ever broken camp, and its first hard march. It was long after dark when the command arrived near Cloud's mills; the headquarters of Gen. Porter could not be found, and it became necessary for the regiment to camp somewhere for the night. At a distance were seen the lights of a camp, which was found upon examination to be the winter quarters of the 69th New York in charge of a camp guard, the regiment having gone out in pursuit of the enemy beyond Manassas. A few persuasive words were spoken to the sergeant in command, and the tired and soaked sharp shooters turned into the tents of the absent Irishmen.

—◦—

CHANCELLORSVILLE.

On the 25th of January Gen. Burnside was relieved from the command and Gen. Hooker appointed to succeed him. The army accepted the change willingly, for although they recognized the many manly and soldierly qualities possessed by Gen. Burnside, and in a certain way respected and even sympathized with him, they had lost confidence in his ability to command so large an army in the presence of so astute a commander as Lee. His manly avowal of his sole responsibility for the terrible slaughter at Fredericksburgh commended him to their hearts and understandings as an honest and generous man; but they had no wish to repeat the experience for the sake of even a more generous acknowledgement after another Fredericksburgh.

The remainder of the winter of 1862–3 was spent by the men of Co. F in comparative comfort, although severe snow storms were of frequent occurrence, and occasional periods of exceedingly cold weather were experienced, to the great discomfort of the men in their frail canvas tents. Both armies seemed to have had enough of marching and fighting to satisfy them for the time being, and even picket firing ceased by tacit agreement and consent.

Soon after assuming command, Gen. Hooker reorganized the army on a plan more consistent with his own ideas than the one adopted by his predecessor. The system of Grand Divisions was abandoned and corps were reorganized; some corps commanders were relieved and others appointed to fill the vacancies. The cavalry, which up to this time had had no organization as a corps, was consolidated under Gen. Stoneman, and soon became, under his able leadership, the equals, if not the superiors, of the vaunted horsemen of the South. In these changes the sharp shooters found themselves assigned to the first division of the Third Corps, under Gen. Sickles. The division was commanded by Gen. Whipple, and the brigade by Gen. De Trobriand. The detachments were called in and the regiment was once more a unit.

Under Gen. Hooker's system the army rapidly improved in morale and spirit; he instituted a liberal system of furloughs to deserving men, and took vigorous measures against stragglers and men absent without leave, of whom there were at this time an immense number—shown by the official rolls to be above eighty thousand. Desertion, which under Burnside had become alarmingly prevalent, was substantially stopped; and by the 1st of April the tone and discipline of the army was such as to fairly warrant Hooker's proud boast that it was "the grandest army on the planet."

The winter was not altogether devoted to sober work. Sports of various kinds were indulged in, one of the most popular being snowball fights between regiments and brigades. Upon one occasion after a sharp conflict between the first and second regiments of sharp shooters, the former captured the regimental colors of the latter, and for a short time some little ill feeling between the regiments existed, a feeling which soon wore away, however, with the opening of the spring campaign.

As the season advanced and the roads became settled and passable, preparations began on all sides for an active campaign against the enemy. "Fighting Joe Hooker" had inspired the army with much of his own confidence and faith in the future, and it was believed by the troops that at last they had a commander worthy in every respect of the magnificent army he was called to command.

On the 28th of April the Third Corps, to which the sharp shooters were now attached, moved down the river to a point some five miles below Falmouth to support Sedgwick's command which was ordered to cross the Rappahannock at or near the point at which Gen. Franklin had crossed his Grand Division at the battle of Fredericksburgh.

Some days prior to this all surplus clothing and baggage had been turned in. Eight days rations and sixty rounds of ammunition were now issued, and the "finest army on the planet" was foot loose once more. Sedgwick's crossing was made, however, without serious opposition, and on the thirtieth the Third Corps, making a wide detour to the rear to avoid the notice of the watchful enemy, turned northward and on the next day crossed the river at United States ford and took its place in the lines of Chancellorsville with the rest of the army.

This great battle has been so often described and in such minute detail that it is not necessary for us to attempt a detailed description of the movements of the different corps engaged, or indeed proper, since this purports to be a history of the marches and battles of only one small company out of the thousands there engaged. It will be remembered that the regiment was now attached to the Third Corps, commanded by Gen. Sickles, the First Division under Gen. Whipple and the Third Brigade, Gen. De Trobriand. At eleven o'clock A.M. on this day, being the first of May, the battle proper commenced, although severe and continuous skirmishing had been going on ever since the first troops crossed the river on the 29th of April. The Third Corps was held in reserve in rear of the Chancellorsville house, having arrived at that point at about the time that the assaulting columns moved forward to the attack.

Almost instantly the fighting became furious and deadly. The country was covered with dense undergrowth of stunted cedars, among and over which grew heavy masses of the trailing vines which grow so luxuriantly in that portion of Virginia, and which renders the orderly passage of troops well nigh impossible. To add to the difficulties which beset the attacking forces, it was impossible to see what was in front of them; hence the first notice of the presence of a rebel line of battle was a volley delivered at short range directly in the faces of the Union soldiers, whose presence and movements were unavoidably made plain to the concealed enemy by the noise made in forcing a passage through the tangled forest. Notwithstanding these disadvantages the Fifth Corps, with which the sharp shooters had so recently parted, struck the enemy at about a mile distant from the position now held by the Third Corps, and drove them steadily back for a long distance until, having passed far to the front of the general line, Meade found his flank suddenly attacked and was forced to retire. Other columns also met the enemy at about the same distance to the front and met with a like experience, gaining, however, on the whole, substantial ground during the afternoon; and so night closed down on the first day of the battle.

On the morning of the 2d of May a division of the Third Corps was detached to hold a gap in the lines between the Eleventh and Twelfth Corps which Gen. Hooker thought too weak. The sharp shooters, however, remained with the main column near the Chancellorsville house. Early on this day the Confederate Gen. Jackson commenced that wonderful flank march which resulted in the disaster to the Eleventh Corps on the right, later in the day. This march, carefully masked as it was, was, nevertheless, observed by Hooker, who at first supposed it the commencement of a retreat on the part of Lee to Gordonsville, and Gen. Sickles was ordered with the two remaining divisions of his corps to demonstrate in that direction and act as circumstances should determine. In this movement Birney's division had the advance, the first division, under Whipple, being in support of Birney's left flank. The sharp shooters were, however, ordered to report to Gen. Birney, and were by him placed in the front line as skirmishers, although their deployment was at such short intervals that it was more like a single rank line of battle than a line of skirmishers.

Sickles started on his advance at about one o'clock P. M., his formation being as above described. Rapidly pressing forward, the sharp shooters passed out of the dense thickets into a comparatively open country, where they could at least breathe more freely and see a little of what was before them. They soon struck a line of rebels in position on the crest of a slight elevation, and brisk firing commenced; the advance, however, not being checked, they soon cleared the hill of the enemy and occupied it themselves. Changing front to the left, the regiment moved from this position obliquely to the southeast, and soon found themselves opposed to a line which had evidently come to stay. The fighting here was very severe and lasted for a considerable time. The rebels seemed to have a desire to stay the advance of the Union troops at that particular point, and for some particular reason, which was afterwards made apparent.

After some minutes of brisk firing, the sharp shooters, by a sudden rush on their flank, succeeded in compelling the surrender of the entire force, which was found to consist of the Twenty-third Georgia regiment, consisting of three hundred and sixty officers and men, which had been charged by Jackson with the duty of preventing any advance of the Union troops at this point which might discover his march towards Hooker's right, hence the tenacity with which they clung to the position. The obstruction having been thus removed, the Third Corps, led by the sharp shooters, pressed rapidly forward to the southward as far as Hazel Grove, or the old furnace, some two miles from the place of starting, and far beyond any supporting column which could be depended on for early assistance should such be needed. It had now become apparent to all that Jackson, instead of being in full retreat as had been supposed, was in the full tide of one of the most violent offensives on record; and at five o'clock P. M. Sickles was ordered to attack his right flank and thus check his advance on the exposed right of the army. But at about the same time Sickles found that he was himself substantially cut off from the army, and that it would require the most strenuous efforts to prevent the capture or destruction of his own command. Furthermore, before he could make his dispositions and march over the ground necessary to be traversed before he could reach Jackson's right, that officer had struck his objective point, and the rout of the Eleventh Corps was complete.

The most that Sickles could now do, under the circumstances, was to fight his own way back to his supports, and to choose, if possible, such a route as would place him, on his arrival, in a position to check Jackson's further advance and afford the broken right wing an opportunity to rally and regain their organization, which was hopelessly, as it appeared, lost. In the darkness and gloom of the falling night, with unloaded muskets (for in this desperate attempt the bayonet only was to be depended upon), the two divisions of the Third Corps set their faces northwardly, and pressed their way through the tangled undergrowth to the rescue of the endangered right wing.

As usual, the sharp shooters had the advance, and received the first volley from the concealed enemy. They had received no especial orders concerning the use, solely, of the bayonet, and were at once engaged in a close conflict under circumstances in which their only superiority over troops of the line consisted in the advantage of the rapidity of fire afforded by their breech loaders over the muzzle loading rifles opposed to them. Closely supported by the line of Birney's division, and firing as they advanced at the flashes of the opposing guns (for they could see no more), they pushed on until they were fairly intermingled with the rebels, and in many individual instances, a long distance inside the enemy's line, every man fighting for himself—for in this confused melee, in the dense jungle and in the intense darkness of the night, no supervision could be exercised by officers and many shots were fired at distances no greater than a few feet. So they struggled on until, with a hurrah and a grand rush, Birney's gallant men dashed forward with the bayonet alone, and after ten minutes of hand to hand fighting, they succeeded in retaking the plank road, and a considerable portion of the line held by the left of the Eleventh Corps in the early portion of the day and lost in the tremendous charge of Jackson's corps in the early evening. Sickles had cut his way out, and more, he was now in a position to afford the much needed aid to those who so sorely required it. Both parties had fought to the point of exhaustion, and were glad to suspend operations for a time for this cause alone, even had no better reasons offered. But the Union army was no longer in a position for offense; the extreme left, with which we have had nothing to do, had been so heavily pressed during the afternoon that it had been with difficulty that a disaster similar to the one which had overtaken the right had been prevented on that flank, and in the center, at and about Hazel Grove and the furnace, which had been held by Sickles, and from which he had been ordered to the support of the right as we have seen, an absolute gap existed, covered by no force whatever. This, then, was the situation, briefly stated.

The left was barely able to hold its own, the center was absolutely abandoned, and the right had been utterly routed. In this state of affairs the Union commander was in no mood for a further offense at that time. On the other hand, the controlling mind that had conceived, and thus far had successfully carried out this wonderful attack which had been so disastrous to the Union army, and which bade fair to make the Southern Confederacy a fact among the nations, had been stricken down in the full tide of its success. Stonewall Jackson had been wounded at about nine o'clock by the fire of his own men. He had passed beyond the lines of his pickets to reconnoiter the Union position, and on his return with his staff they were mistaken by his soldiers for a body of federal cavalry and he received three wounds from the effects of which he died about a week later. So fell a man who was perhaps as fine a type of stout American soldiership as any produced on either side during the war.

The sharp shooters, with the remnant of the Third Corps, passed the remainder of the night on the plank road near Dowdall's tavern. Co. F had left their knapsacks and blankets under guard near the Chancellorsville house when they advanced from that point in the morning, as had the rest of the regiment. Under these circumstances little sleep or rest could be expected even had the enemy been in less close proximity. But with the rebel pickets hardly thirty yards distant, and firing at every thing they saw or heard, sleep was out of the question. So passed the weary night of the disastrous 2d of May at Chancellorsville.

During the night Gen. Hooker, no longer on the offensive, had been busily engaged in laying out and fortifying a new line on which he might hope more successfully to resist the attack which all knew must come at an early hour on the morning of the third. On the extreme left the troops were withdrawn from their advanced positions to a more compact and shorter line in front of, and to the south and east of the Chancellorsville house. The center, which at sunset was unoccupied by any considerable body of Union troops, was made secure; and at daylight Sickles, with the Third Corps, was ordered to withdraw to a position indicated immediately in front of Fairview, a commanding height of land now strongly occupied by the Union artillery.

It was not possible, however, to withdraw so large a body of troops from their advanced position, in the face of so watchful an enemy, without interruption. In fact, even before the movement had commenced, the enemy took the initiative and commenced the battle of that day by a furious attack upon the heights of Hazel Grove, the position so handsomely won by the Third Corps on the previous day and from which they were ordered to the relief of the Eleventh Corps at five o'clock on the preceding afternoon, as we have seen.

This height of land commanded almost every portion of the field occupied by the Union army, and from it Sickles' line, as it stood at daybreak, could be completely enfiladed. This position was held by an inadequate force for its defense; indeed, as it was far in advance of the new line of battle it may be supposed that observation, rather than defense, was the duty of its occupants. They made a gallant fight, however, but were soon compelled to retire with the loss of four guns. The rebel commander, quick to see the great importance of the position, crowned the hill with thirty guns which, with the four taken from the Unionists, poured a heavy fire on all parts of the line, devoting particular attention to Sickles' exposed left and rear.

At almost the same period of time the rebels in Sickles' front made a savage attack on his line. The men of the Third Corps fought, as they always fought, stubbornly and well, but, with a force more than equal to their own in point of numbers, flushed with their success of the previous afternoon and burning to avenge the fall of Jackson, in their front, and this enormous concentration of artillery hammering away on their defenseless left, they were at last forced back to the new line in front of Fairview.

In preparation for the withdrawal contemplated, and before the rebel attack developed itself, the sharp shooters had been deployed to the front and formed a skirmish line to the north of the plank road with their left on that highway, and thus received the first of the rebel attack. They succeeded in repulsing the advance of the first line and for half an hour held their ground against repeated attempts of the rebel skirmishers to dislodge them. The position they held was one of the utmost importance since it commanded the plank road which must be the main line of the rebel approach to Fairview, the key to the new Union line, and aware of this the men fought on with a courage and determination seldom witnessed even in the ranks of that gallant regiment. After half an hour of this perilous work, the regiment on their right having given way, the sharp shooters were ordered to move by the right flank to cover the interval thus exposed, their own place being taken by still another body of infantry.

Steadily and coolly the men faced to the right at the sound of the bugle, and commenced their march, still firing as they advanced. Necessarily, however, the men had to expose themselves greatly in this movement, and as necessarily their own fire was less effective than when delivered coolly from the shelter of some friendly tree, log or bank which skirmishers are so prone to seek and so loath to leave. Still the march was made in good order and in good time, for the sharp shooters had only just time to fill the gap when the rebels came on for a final trial for the mastery.

For a long time the green coated riflemen clung to their ground and gave, certainly as good, as they received. But the end of the long struggle was at hand; the regiment which had taken the position just vacated by the sharp shooters was driven in confusion, and to cap the climax of misfortune, the Union artillery, observing the withdrawal of other troops, and supposing that all had been retired, opened a furious fire of canister into the woods. The sharp shooters were now in a sad case—before them a furious crowd of angry enemies, on the left the rebel artillery at Hazel Grove sweeping their lines from left to right at every discharge, while, worst of all, from the rear came the equally dangerous fire of their own friends.

To retreat was as bad as to advance. The ground to their right was an unknown mystery and no hopeful sign came from the left; so taking counsel from their very desperation they concluded to remain just there, at least until some reasonable prospect of escape should present itself. Taking such cover as they could get, some from the fire of our own guns and some from those of the rebels, shifting from side to side of the logs and trees as the fire came hotter from the one side or from the other, but always keeping up their own fire in the direction of the enemy, they maintained the unequal fight until an officer, sent for the purpose, succeeded in stopping the fire of our own guns, and the sharp shooters willingly withdrew from a position such as they had never found themselves in before, and from a scene which no man present will ever forget.

They were sharply pressed by the advancing enemy, but now, being out of the line of the enfilading fire from Hazel Grove, and no longer subject to the fire of their own friends, the withdrawal was made in perfect order, the line halting at intervals at the sound of the bugle and delivering well aimed volleys at the enemy, now fully exposed, and even at times making countercharges to check their too rapid advance.

In one of these rallies there fell a man from another company whose death as well deserves to be remembered in song as that of the "Sleeping Sentinel." He had been condemned to death by the sentence of a court martial, and was in confinement awaiting the execution of the sentence when the army left camp at Falmouth at the outset of the campaign. In some manner he managed to escape from his guards, and joined his company on the evening of the second day's light.

Of course it was irregular, and no precedent for it could possibly be found in the army regulations, but men were more valuable on that field than in the guard house; perhaps, too, his captain hoped that he might, in the furor of the battle, realize his own expressed wish that he might meet his fate there instead of at the hands of a firing party of the provost guard, and thus, by an honorable death on the battle field, efface to some extent the stain on his character.

However it was, a rifle was soon found for him (rifles without owners were plenty on that field), and he took his place in the ranks. During all of that long forenoon's fighting he was a marked man. All knew his history, and all watched to see him fall; for while others carefully availed themselves of such shelter as the field afforded, he alone stood erect and in full view of the enemy. Many times he exhausted the cartridges in his box, each time replenishing it from the boxes of his dead or wounded companions. He seemed to bear a charmed life; for, while death and wounds came to many who would have avoided either, the bullets passed him harmless by. At last, however, in one of the savage conflicts when the sharp shooters turned on the too closely following enemy, this gallant soldier, with two or three of his companions, came suddenly upon a small party of rebels who had outstripped their fellows in the ardor of the pursuit; he, being in the advance, rushed upon them, demanding their surrender. "Yes," said one, "we surrender," but at the same time, as —— lowered his gun, the treacherous rebel raised his, and the sharp shooter fell, shot through the heart.

He spoke no word, but those who caught the last glimpse of his face, as they left him lying where he fell, knew that he had realized his highest hope and wish, and that he died content. The sequel to this sad personal history brings into tender recollection the memory of that last and noblest martyr to the cause of the Union, President Lincoln. The case was brought to his notice by those who felt that the stain upon the memory of this gallant, true hearted soldier was not fully effaced, even by his noble self-sacrifice, and would not be while the records on the books stood so black against him. The President was never appealed to in vain when it was possible for him to be merciful, and, sitting down, he wrote with his own hand a full and free pardon, dating it as of the morning of that eventful 3d of May, and sent it to the widow of the dead soldier in a distant state. It was such acts as this that made Abraham Lincoln so loved by the soldiers of the Union. They respected the President, but Abraham Lincoln—the man—was *loved*.

Upon the arrival of the retreating riflemen at the new line in front of Fairview, they found their division, the main portion of which had, of course, preceded them, in line of battle in rear of the slight defenses which had been thrown up at that point, where they enjoyed a brief period of much needed repose, if a short respite from actual personal encounter could be called repose. They were still under heavy artillery fire, while musketry was incessant and very heavy only a short distance away, the air above their heads being alive, at times, with everything that kills. Yet so great was their fatigue, and so quiet and restful their position in comparison with what it had been for so long a time, that, after receiving rations and a fresh supply of ammunition for their exhausted boxes, officers and men alike lay down on the ground, and most of them enjoyed an hour of refreshing sleep. Their rest was not of long duration, however, for the rebels made a desperate and savage attack on the line in their front and the Third Corps soon found itself again engaged. The enemy, under cover of their artillery on the high ground at Hazel Grove, made an assault on what was now the front of the Union line (if it could be said to have a front) while the force which the sharp shooters had so long held in check during the early part of the day made a like attack on that line now the right of the entire army.

So heavy was the attack, and so tenaciously sustained, that the Union troops were actually forced from their lines in front and on the flank of Fairview, and the hill was occupied by the rebels, who captured, and held for a time, all the Union guns on that eminence. It was at this stage of affairs that the Third Corps was again called into action, and charging the somewhat disorganized enemy they retook the hill with the captured guns, and following up the flying rebels, they drove them to, and beyond, the position they had occupied in the morning. Here, however, meeting with a fresh line of the enemy and being brought to a check, they were ordered again to retire; for Hooker, by this time intent only upon getting his army safely back across the river, had formed still another new line near to, and covering, the bridges and fords by which alone could he place his forces in a position of even comparative safety.

To this line then the Third Corps, with the tired and decimated sharp shooters, retired late in the afternoon, hoping and praying for a respite from their terrible labors. For a little time it looked, indeed, as if their hopes would be realized, but as darkness drew on the corps commander, desiring to occupy a wooded knoll at some little distance from his advanced picket line, and from which he anticipated danger, ordered Gen. Whipple, to whose division the sharp shooters had been returned, to send a brigade to occupy it. Gen. Whipple replied that he had one regiment who were alone equal to the task and to whom he would entrust it, and ordered the sharp shooters to attempt it.

Between this wooded hill and the position from which the regiment must charge was an open field about one hundred yards in width which was to be crossed under what might prove a destructive fire from troops already occupying the coveted position. It was a task requiring the most undaunted courage and desperate endeavor on the part of men who had already been for two full days and nights in the very face of the enemy, and they felt that the attempt might fairly have been assigned to a portion of the forty thousand men who, up to that time, had been held in reserve by Gen. Hooker for some inscrutable purpose, and who had not seen the face of an enemy, much less fired a shot at them; but they formed for the assault with cheerful alacrity.

To Co. F was assigned the lead, and marching out into the open field they deployed as regularly as though on their old drill ground at camp of instruction. Corps, brigade and division commanders were looking on, and the men felt that now, if never before, they must show themselves worthy sons of the Green Mountain state. Led by their officers, they dashed out into the plain closely supported by the rest of the regiment. Night was rapidly coming on, and in the gathering gloom objects could hardly be distinguished at a distance of a hundred yards.

Half the open space was crossed, and it seemed to the rushing men that their task was to be accomplished without serious obstructions, when, from the edge of the woods in front, came a close and severe volley betraying the presence of a rebel line of battle;

how strong could only be judged by the firing, which was so heavy, however, as to indicate a force much larger than the attacking party. On went the brave men of Co. F, straight at their work, and behind them closely followed the supporting force. In this order they reached the edge of the forest when the enemy, undoubtedly supposing from the confidence with which the sharp shooters advanced that the force was much larger than it really was, broke and fled and the position was won.

From prisoners and wounded rebels captured in that night attack it was learned that the force which had thus been beaten out of a strong position by this handful of men was a portion of the famous Stonewall brigade, Jackson's earliest command, and they asserted that it was the first time in the history of the brigade that it had ever been driven from a chosen position. The sharp shooters were justly elated at their success and the more so when Gen. Whipple, riding over to the point so gallantly won, gave them unstinted praise for their gallant action. In this affair the regiment lost many gallant officers and men, among whom were Lieut. Brewer of Co. C and Capt. Chase, killed, and Major Hastings and Adjt. Horton, wounded. In Co. F Michael Cunningham, J. S. Bailey and E. M. Hosmer were wounded.

Major Hastings had not been a popular officer with the command. Although a brave and capable man, he was of a nervous temperament, and in the small details of camp discipline was apt to be over zealous at times. He had, therefore, incurred the dislike of many men, who were wont to apply various opprobrious epithets to him at such times and under such circumstances as made it extremely unpleasant for him. Such were the methods adopted by some soldiers to make it comfortable for officers to whom they had a dislike.

In the case of the Major, however, this was a thing of the past. On this bloody field the men learned to respect their officer, and he, as he was borne from the field, freely forgave the boys all the trouble and annoyance they had caused him, in consideration of their gallant bearing on that day. Adjt. Horton, also a brave and efficient officer, received a severe wound—which afterwards cost him his good right arm—while using the rifle of J. S. Bailey of Co. F, who had been wounded.

Co. F, which, it will be remembered, had been acting as skirmishers, were pushed forward in advance of the main portion of the regiment to further observe the movements of the enemy and to guard against a surprise, and shortly afterwards were moved by the flank some two hundred yards to the right, and were soon after relieved by a force of infantry of the line which had been sent up for that purpose. While retiring toward the position to which they were directed, they passed nearly over the same ground which they had just vacated when they moved by the right flank, as previously mentioned, and received from the concealed rebels, who had reoccupied the line, a severe volley at close range. Facing to the right, Co. F at once charged this new enemy and drove them in confusion from the field. Lying down in this advanced position they passed the remainder of the night in watchful suspense.

At day break on the fourth day of the battle, Co. F was relieved from its position on the picket line and returned to the regiment, which was deployed as skirmishers, and led the van of Whipple's division in a charge to check movements of the enemy which had for their apparent object the interposition of a rebel force between the right wing of the army and its bridges. Firing rapidly as they advanced, and supported by the division close on their heels, they drove the enemy from their rifle pits, which were occupied by the infantry of the Third Corps, the sharp shooters being still in front. Here they remained, exchanging occasional shots with the rebel sharp shooters as occasion offered, for some hours. Hooker was not minded to force the fighting at Chancellorsville; preferring to await the result of Sedgwick's battle at Salem Church, which had raged furiously on the preceding afternoon until darkness put an end to the strife, and the telltale guns of which even now gave notice of further effort.

Lee, however, pugnacious and aggressive, determined to renew his attack on the right, and, if possible, secure the roads to the fords and bridges by which alone could the defeated army regain the north bank of the river. With this view he reenforced Jackson's (now Stuart's) corps, and organized a powerful attack on the position of the Third Corps. The force of the first onset fell on the sharp shooters, who fought with their accustomed gallantry, but were forced by the weight of numbers back to the main line. Here the fighting was severe and continuous. The one party fighting for a decisive victory, and the other, alas, only bent on keeping secure its last and only line of retreat; but the incentive, poor as it was, was sufficient, and the rebels were unable to break the line. After four hours of continued effort they abandoned the assault and quiet once more prevailed. In this fight Gen. Whipple, the division commander, was killed. He was a gallant and an able soldier, greatly beloved by his men for the kindliness of his disposition. He had an especial liking for and confidence in the sharp shooters, which was fully understood and appreciated by them, and they felt his death as a personal loss.

To add to the horrors of this bloody field, on which lay nearly nine thousand dead and wounded Union soldiers and nearly or quite as many rebels, the woods took fire and hundreds of badly wounded men, unable to help themselves, and hopeless of succor, perished miserably in the fierce flames. Nothing in the whole history of the war is more horrible than the recollection of those gallant men, who had been stricken down by rebel bullets, roasted to death in the very presence of their comrades, impotent to give them aid in their dire distress and agony.

It was reserved for the *wounded* to experience the agonies of a ten-fold death. Hour after hour the conflagration raged, until a merciful rain quenched it and put an end to the horrible scene. The Third Corps remained in their position during the night, the sharp shooters, oddly enough as it seemed to them, with a strong line of infantry behind works between them and the enemy. Nothing occurred to break their repose, and for the first time for seven days they enjoyed eight hours of solid sleep unbroken by rebel alarms.

At day break on the morning of the 5th of May they were aroused by the usual command of "sharp shooters to the front," and again found themselves on the picket line confronting the enemy. The day passed, however, without serious fighting, one or two attacks being made by rebel skirmishers, more, apparently, to ascertain if the Union troops were actually there than for any more serious business.

These advances were easily repulsed by the sharp shooters without other aid, and at nine o'clock P. M., after seventeen hours of continuous duty without rations—for the eight days rations with which they started from their camp at Falmouth had long since been exhausted, and the scanty supply they had received on the afternoon of the third was barely enough for one meal—they were relieved and retired to the main line. The company lost on this day but one man, Martin C. Laffie, shot through the hand. Laffie was permanently disabled by his wound, and on the 1st of the following August was transferred to the Invalid Corps and never rejoined the company.

Several prisoners were captured by the men of Co. F on that day, but on the whole it was, as compared with the days of the preceding week, uneventful. On the 6th the army recrossed the Rappahannock by the bridges which had been preserved by the stubborn courage of the Third Corps, and the battle of Chancellorsville passed into history. The sharp shooters returned to their old camp at Falmouth as they had returned to the same camp after the disastrous battle of Fredericksburgh. It seemed as though they were fated never to leave that ground to fight a successful battle. Only eight days before they had marched out with buoyant anticipations, full of courage and full of hope. They returned discouraged and dispirited beyond description.

At Fredericksburgh the army had marched to the attack without hope or expectation of victory, for their soldiers' instinct told them that that was impossible. At Chancellorsville, however, they felt that they had everything to hope for—a magnificent army in full health and high spirits, an able and gallant commander, for such he had always shown himself to be, and a fair field. The thickets of the wilderness, it is true, were dense and well nigh impassable for them, but they were as bad for the enemy as for themselves, and they had felt that on anything like a fair field they ought to win. Now they found themselves just where they started; they had left seventeen thousand of their comrades dead, or worse than dead, on the field, and fourteen guns remained in the hands of the rebels as trophies of their victory; guns, too, that were sure to be turned against the federals in the very next battle. Twenty thousand stand of small arms were also left on the field to be gathered up by the victors. It was a disheartening reflection, but soldier-like the men put it from their thoughts and turned their minds and hands to the duties and occupations of the present.

CHAPTER 30

Vicksburg during the Trouble

By Mark Twain

There seem to be few subjects about which Mark Twain did not take up pen, and the Civil War was no exception. In his classic Life on the Mississippi, *as he steams past Vicksburg, Mississippi—well known for its famous caves—he recounts the story of a couple who lived through the city's shelling between May and July of 1863.*

—Lisa Purcell

We used to plow past the lofty hill-city, Vicksburg, down-stream; but we cannot do that now. A cut-off has made a country town of it, like Osceola, St. Genevieve, and several others. There is currentless water—also a big island—in front of Vicksburg now. You come down the river the other side of the island, then turn and come up to the town; that is, in high water: in low water you can't come up, but must land some distance below it.

Signs and scars still remain, as reminders of Vicksburg's tremendous war experiences; earthworks, trees crippled by the cannon balls, cave-refuges in the clay precipices, etc. The caves did good service during the six weeks' bombardment of the city—May 8 to July 4, 1863. They were used by the non-combatants—mainly by the women and children; not to live in constantly, but to fly to for safety on occasion. They were mere holes, tunnels, driven into the perpendicular clay bank, then branched Y shape, within the hill. Life in Vicksburg, during the six weeks was perhaps—but wait; here are some materials out of which to reproduce it:

Population, twenty-seven thousand soldiers and three thousand non-combatants; the city utterly cut off from the world—walled solidly in, the frontage by gunboats, the rear by soldiers and batteries; hence, no buying and selling with the outside; no passing to and fro; no God-speeding a parting guest, no welcoming a coming one; no printed acres of world-wide news to be read at breakfast, mornings—a tedious dull absence of such matter, instead; hence, also, no running to see steamboats smoking into view in the distance up or down, and plowing toward the town—for none came, the river lay vacant and undisturbed; no rush and turmoil around the railway station, no struggling over bewildered swarms of passengers by noisy mobs of hackmen—all quiet there; flour two hundred dollars a barrel, sugar thirty, corn ten dollars a bushel, bacon five dollars a pound, rum a hundred dollars a gallon; other things in proportion: consequently, no roar and racket of drays and carriages tearing along the streets; nothing for them to do, among that handful of non-combatants of exhausted means; at three o'clock in the morning, silence; silence so dead that the measured tramp of a sentinel can be heard a seemingly impossible distance; out of hearing of this lonely sound, perhaps the stillness is absolute: all in a moment come ground-shaking thunder-crashes of artillery, the sky is cobwebbed with the crisscrossing red lines streaming from soaring bomb-shells, and a rain of iron fragments descends upon the city; descends upon the empty streets: streets which are not empty a moment later, but mottled with dim figures of frantic women and children scurrying from home and bed toward the cave dungeons—encouraged by the humorous grim soldiery, who shout "Rats, to your holes!" and laugh. The cannon-thunder rages, shells scream and crash overhead, the iron rain pours down, one hour, two hours, three, possibly six, then stops; silence follows, but the streets are still empty; the silence continues; by-and-bye a head projects from a cave here and there and yonder, and reconnoitres, cautiously; the silence still continuing, bodies follow heads, and jaded, half smothered creatures group themselves about, stretch their cramped limbs, draw in deep draughts of the grateful fresh air, gossip with the neighbors from the next cave; maybe straggle off home presently, or take a lounge through the town, if the stillness continues; and will scurry to the holes again, by-and-bye, when the war-tempest breaks forth once more.

There being but three thousand of these cave-dwellers—merely the population of a village—would they not come to know each other, after a week or two, and familiarly; insomuch that the fortunate or unfortunate experiences of one would be of interest to all?

Those are the materials furnished by history. From them might not almost anybody reproduce for himself the life of that time in Vicksburg? Could you, who did not experience it, come nearer to reproducing it to the imagination of another non-participant than could a Vicksburger who did experience it? It seems impossible; and yet there are reasons why it might not really be. When one makes his first voyage in a ship, it is an experience which multitudinously bristles with striking novelties; novelties which are in such sharp contrast with all this person's former experiences that they take a seemingly deathless grip upon his imagination and memory. By tongue or pen he can make a landsman live that strange and stirring voyage over with him; make him see it all and feel it all. But if he wait? If he make ten voyages in succession—what then? Why, the thing has lost color, snap, surprise; and has become commonplace. The man would have nothing to tell that would quicken a landsman's pulse.

Years ago, I talked with a couple of the Vicksburg non-combatants—a man and his wife. Left to tell their story in their own way, those people told it without fire, almost without interest.

A week of their wonderful life there would have made their tongues eloquent forever perhaps; but they had six weeks of it, and that wore the novelty all out; they got used to being bomb-shelled out of home and into the ground; the matter became commonplace. After that, the possibility of their ever being startlingly interesting in their talks about it was gone. What the man said was to this effect:

"It got to be Sunday all the time. Seven Sundays in the week—to us, anyway. We hadn't anything to do, and time hung heavy. Seven Sundays, and all of them broken up at one time or another, in the day or in the night, by a few hours of the awful storm of fire and thunder and iron. At first we used to shin for the holes a good deal faster than we did afterwards. The first time, I forgot the children, and Maria fetched them both along. When she was all safe in the cave she fainted. Two or three weeks afterwards, when she was running for the holes, one morning, through a shell-shower, a big shell burst near her, and covered her all over with dirt, and a piece of the iron carried away her game-bag of false hair from the back of her head. Well, she stopped to get that game-bag before she shoved along again! Was getting used to things already, you see. We all got so that we could tell a good deal about shells; and after that we didn't always go under shelter if it was a light shower. Us men would loaf around and talk; and a man would say, 'There she goes!' and name the kind of shell it was from the sound of it, and go on talking—if there wasn't any danger from it. If a shell was bursting close over us, we stopped talking and stood still;—uncomfortable, yes, but it wasn't safe to move. When it let go, we went on talking again, if nobody hurt—maybe saying, 'That was a ripper!' or some such commonplace comment before we resumed; or, maybe, we would see a shell poising itself away high in the air overhead. In that case, every fellow just whipped out a sudden, 'See you again, gents!' and shoved. Often and often I saw gangs of ladies promenading the streets, looking as cheerful as you please, and keeping an eye canted up watching the shells; and I've seen them stop still when they were uncertain about what a shell was going to do, and wait and make certain; and after that they sa'ntered along again, or lit out for shelter, according to the verdict. Streets in some towns have a litter of pieces of paper, and odds and ends of one sort or another lying around. Ours hadn't; they had iron litter. Sometimes a man would gather up all the iron fragments and unbursted shells in his neighborhood, and pile them into a kind of monument in his front yard—a ton of it, sometimes. No glass left; glass couldn't stand such a bombardment; it was all shivered out. Windows of the houses vacant—looked like eye-holes in a skull. Whole panes were as scarce as news.

"We had church Sundays. Not many there, along at first; but by-and-bye pretty good turnouts. I've seen service stop a minute, and everybody sit quiet—no voice heard, pretty funeral-like then—and all the more so on account of the awful boom and crash going on outside and overhead; and pretty soon, when a body could be heard, service would go on again. Organs and church-music mixed up with a bombardment is a powerful queer combination—along at first. Coming out of church, one morning, we had an accident— the only one that happened around me on a Sunday. I was just having a hearty handshake with a friend I hadn't seen for a while, and saying, 'Drop into our cave to-night, after bombardment; we've got hold of a pint of prime wh—.' Whiskey, I was going to say, you know, but a shell interrupted. A chunk of it cut the man's arm off, and left it dangling in my hand. And do you know the thing that is going to stick the longest in my memory, and outlast everything else, little and big, I reckon, is the mean thought I had then? It was 'the whiskey is saved.' And yet, don't you know, it was kind of excusable; because it was as scarce as diamonds, and we had only just that little; never had another taste during the siege.

"Sometimes the caves were desperately crowded, and always hot and close. Sometimes a cave had twenty or twenty-five people packed into it; no turning-room for anybody; air so foul, sometimes, you couldn't have made a candle burn in it. A child was born in one of those caves one night. Think of that; why, it was like having it born in a trunk.

"Twice we had sixteen people in our cave; and a number of times we had a dozen. Pretty suffocating in there. We always had eight; eight belonged there. Hunger and misery and sickness and fright and sorrow, and I don't know what all, got so loaded into them that none of them were ever rightly their old selves after the siege. They all died but three of us within a couple of years. One night a shell burst in front of the hole and caved it in and stopped it up. It was lively times, for a while, digging out. Some of us came near smothering. After that we made two openings—ought to have thought of it at first.

"Mule meat. No, we only got down to that the last day or two. Of course it was good; anything is good when you are starving."

This man had kept a diary during—six weeks? No, only the first six days. The first day, eight close pages; the second, five; the third, one—loosely written; the fourth, three or four lines; a line or two the fifth and sixth days; seventh day, diary abandoned; life in terrific Vicksburg having now become commonplace and matter of course.

The war history of Vicksburg has more about it to interest the general reader than that of any other of the river-towns. It is full of variety, full of incident, full of the picturesque. Vicksburg held out longer than any other important river-town, and saw warfare in all its phases, both land and water—the siege, the mine, the assault, the repulse, the bombardment, sickness, captivity, famine.

The most beautiful of all the national cemeteries is here. Over the great gateway is this inscription:

"Here Rest In Peace 16,600 Who Died For Their Country In The Years 1861 To 1865"

CHAPTER 31

The Red Badge of Courage
By Stephen Crane

This excerpt from Stephen Crane's masterpiece, The Red Badge of Courage, *takes place during the climatic portions of the Civil War novel, when Crane's protagonist—identified throughout the story only as "the youth"—faces the ultimate horrors of combat.*

Published in 1895, the novel brought to the general public of that time the most wrenching battlefield images since the photographs of Matthew Brady that had been taken and exhibited during the war. Brady's photographs and his own research, talent, and imagination were the creative impetus that led Crane to produce his stirring portrait of courage under fire. The popular writer Ambrose Bierce said of Crane: "This young man has the power to feel. He knows nothing of war, yet he is drenched in blood. Most beginners who deal with this subject spatter themselves with ink."

—LISA PURCELL

THE YOUTH STARED AT THE LAND IN FRONT OF HIM. ITS FOLIAGE NOW SEEMED TO VEIL powers and horrors. He was unaware of the machinery of orders that started the charge, although from the corners of his eyes he saw an officer, who looked like a boy a-horseback, come galloping, waving his hat. Suddenly he felt a straining and heaving among the men. The line fell slowly forward like a toppling wall, and, with a convulsive gasp that was intended for a cheer, the regiment began its journey. The youth was pushed and jostled for a moment before he understood the movement at all, but directly he lunged ahead and began to run.

He fixed his eye upon a distant and prominent clump of trees where he had concluded the enemy were to be met, and he ran toward it as toward a goal. He had believed throughout that it was a mere question of getting over an unpleasant matter as quickly as possible, and he ran desperately, as if pursued for a murder. His face was drawn hard and tight with the stress of his endeavor. His eyes were fixed in a lurid glare. And with his soiled and disordered dress, his red and inflamed features surmounted by the dingy rag with its spot of blood, his wildly swinging rifle and banging accoutrements, he looked to be an insane soldier.

As the regiment swung from its position out into a cleared space the woods and thickets before it awakened. Yellow flames leaped toward it from many directions. The forest made a tremendous objection.

The line lurched straight for a moment. Then the right wing swung forward; it in turn was surpassed by the left. Afterward the center careered to the front until the regiment was a wedge-shaped mass, but an instant later the opposition of the bushes, trees, and uneven places on the ground split the command and scattered it into detached clusters.

The youth, light-footed, was unconsciously in advance. His eyes still kept note of the clump of trees. From all places near it the clannish yell of the enemy could be heard. The little flames of rifles leaped from it. The song of the bullets was in the air and shells snarled among the tree-tops. One tumbled directly into the middle of a hurrying group and exploded in crimson fury. There was an instant's spectacle of a man, almost over it, throwing up his hands to shield his eyes.

Other men, punched by bullets, fell in grotesque agonies. The regiment left a coherent trail of bodies.

They had passed into a clearer atmosphere. There was an effect like a revelation in the new appearance of the landscape. Some men working madly at a battery were plain to them, and the opposing infantry's lines were defined by the gray walls and fringes of smoke.

It seemed to the youth that he saw everything. Each blade of the green grass was bold and clear. He thought that he was aware of every change in the thin, transparent vapor that floated idly in sheets. The brown or gray trunks of the trees showed each roughness of their surfaces. And the men of the regiment, with their starting eyes and sweating faces, running madly, or falling, as if thrown headlong, to queer, heaped-up corpses—all were comprehended. His mind took a mechanical but firm impression, so that afterward everything was pictured and explained to him, save why he himself was there.

But there was a frenzy made from this furious rush. The men, pitching forward insanely, had burst into cheerings, moblike and barbaric, but tuned in strange keys that can arouse the dullard and the stoic. It made a mad enthusiasm that, it seemed, would be incapable of checking itself before granite and brass. There was the delirium that encounters despair and death, and is heedless and blind to the odds. It is a temporary but sublime absence of selfishness. And because it was of this order was the reason, perhaps, why the youth wondered, afterward, what reasons he could have had for being there.

Presently the straining pace ate up the energies of the men. As if by agreement, the leaders began to slacken their speed. The volleys directed against them had had a seeming windlike effect. The regiment snorted and blew. Among some stolid trees it began to falter and hesitate. The men, staring intently, began to wait for some of the distant walls of smoke to move and disclose to them the scene. Since much of their strength and their breath had vanished, they returned to caution. They were become men again.

The youth had a vague belief that he had run miles, and he thought, in a way, that he was now in some new and unknown land.

The moment the regiment ceased its advance the protesting splutter of musketry became a steadier roar. Long and accurate fringes of smoke spread out. From the top of a small hill came level belchings of yellow flame that caused an inhuman whistling in the air.

The men, halted, had opportunity to see some of their comrades dropping with moans and shrieks. A few lay under foot, still or wailing. And now for an instant the men stood, their rifles slack in their hands, and watched the regiment dwindle. They appeared dazed and stupid. This spectacle seemed to paralyze them, overcome them with a fatal fascination. They stared woodenly at the sights, and, lowering their eyes, looked from face to face. It was a strange pause, and a strange silence.

Then, above the sounds of the outside commotion, arose the roar of the lieutenant. He strode suddenly forth, his infantile features black with rage.

"Come on, yeh fools!" he bellowed. "Come on! Yeh can't stay here. Yeh must come on." He said more, but much of it could not be understood.

He started rapidly forward, with his head turned toward the men. "Come on," he was shouting. The men stared with blank and yokel-like eyes at him. He was obliged to halt and retrace his steps. He stood then with his back to the enemy and delivered gigantic curses into the faces of the men. His body vibrated from the weight and force of his imprecations. And he could string oaths with the facility of a maiden who strings beads.

The friend of the youth aroused. Lurching suddenly forward and dropping to his knees, he fired an angry shot at the persistent woods. This action awakened the men. They huddled no more like sheep. They seemed suddenly to bethink them of their weapons, and at once commenced firing. Belabored by their officers, they began to move forward. The regiment, involved like a cart involved in mud and muddle, started unevenly with many jolts and jerks. The men stopped now every few paces to fire and load, and in this manner moved slowly on from trees to trees.

The flaming opposition in their front grew with their advance until it seemed that all forward ways were barred by the thin leaping tongues, and off to the right an ominous demonstration could sometimes be dimly discerned. The smoke lately generated was in confusing clouds that made it difficult for the regiment to proceed with intelligence. As he passed through each curling mass the youth wondered what would confront him on the farther side.

The command went painfully forward until an open space interposed between them and the lurid lines. Here, crouching and cowering behind some trees, the men clung with desperation, as if threatened by a wave. They looked wild-eyed, and as if amazed at this furious disturbance they had stirred. In the storm there was an ironical expression of their importance. The faces of the men, too, showed a lack of a certain feeling of responsibility for being there. It was as if they had been driven. It was the dominant animal failing to remember in the supreme moments the forceful causes of various superficial qualities. The whole affair seemed incomprehensible to many of them.

As they halted thus the lieutenant again began to bellow profanely. Regardless of the vindictive threats of the bullets, he went about coaxing, berating, and bedamning. His lips, that were habitually in a soft and childlike curve, were now writhed into unholy contortions. He swore by all possible deities.

Once he grabbed the youth by the arm. "Come on, yeh lunkhead!" he roared. "Come on! We'll all git killed if we stay here. We've on'y got t' go across that lot. An' then"—the remainder of his idea disappeared in a blue haze of curses.

The youth stretched forth his arm. "Cross there?" His mouth was puckered in doubt and awe.

"Certainly. Jest 'cross th' lot! We can't stay here," screamed the lieutenant. He poked his face close to the youth and waved his bandaged hand. "Come on!" Presently he grappled with him as if for a wrestling bout. It was as if he planned to drag the youth by the ear on to the assault.

The private felt a sudden unspeakable indignation against his officer. He wrenched fiercely and shook him off.

"Come on yerself, then," he yelled. There was a bitter challenge in his voice.

They galloped together down the regimental front. The friend scrambled after them. In front of the colors the three men began to bawl: "Come on! come on!" They danced and gyrated like tortured savages.

The flag, obedient to these appeals, bended its glittering form and swept toward them. The men wavered in indecision for a moment, and then with a long, wailful cry the dilapidated regiment surged forward and began its new journey.

Over the field went the scurrying mass. It was a handful of men splattered into the faces of the enemy. Toward it instantly sprang the yellow tongues. A vast quantity of blue smoke hung before them. A mighty banging made ears valueless.

The youth ran like a madman to reach the woods before a bullet could discover him. He ducked his head low, like a football player. In his haste his eyes almost closed, and the scene was a wild blur. Pulsating saliva stood at the corners of his mouth.

Within him, as he hurled himself forward, was born a love, a despairing fondness for this flag which was near him. It was a creation of beauty and invulnerability. It was a goddess, radiant, that bended its form with an imperious gesture to him. It was a woman, red and white, hating and loving, that called him with the voice of his hopes. Because no harm could come to it he endowed it with power. He kept near, as if it could be a saver of lives, and an imploring cry went from his mind.

In the mad scramble he was aware that the color sergeant flinched suddenly, as if struck by a bludgeon. He faltered, and then became motionless, save for his quivering knees.

He made a spring and a clutch at the pole. At the same instant his friend grabbed it from the other side. They jerked at it, stout and furious, but the color sergeant was dead, and the corpse would not relinquish its trust. For a moment there was a grim encounter. The dead man, swinging with bended back, seemed to be obstinately tugging, in ludicrous and awful ways, for the possession of the flag.

It was past in an instant of time. They wrenched the flag furiously from the dead man, and, as they turned again, the corpse swayed forward with bowed head. One arm swung high, and the curved hand fell with heavy protest on the friend's unheeding shoulder.

When the two youths turned with the flag they saw that much of the regiment had crumbled away, and the dejected remnant was coming back. The men, having hurled themselves in projectile fashion, had presently expended their forces. They slowly retreated, with their faces still toward the spluttering woods, and their hot rifles still replying to the din. Several officers were giving orders, their voices keyed to screams.

$\sim\!\!\sim$

"Where in hell yeh goin'?" the lieutenant was asking in a sarcastic howl. And a red-bearded officer, whose voice of triple brass could plainly be heard, was commanding: "Shoot into 'em! Shoot into 'em, Gawd damn their souls!" There was a mêlée of screeches, in which the men were ordered to do conflicting and impossible things.

The youth and his friend had a small scuffle over the flag. "Give it t' me!" "No, let me keep it!" Each felt satisfied with the other's possession of it, but each felt bound to declare, by an offer to carry the emblem, his willingness to further risk himself. The youth roughly pushed his friend away.

The regiment fell back to the stolid trees. There it halted for a moment to blaze at some dark forms that had begun to steal upon its track. Presently it resumed its march again, curving among the tree trunks. By the time the depleted regiment had again reached the first open space they were receiving a fast and merciless fire. There seemed to be mobs all about them.

The greater part of the men, discouraged, their spirits worn by the turmoil, acted as if stunned. They accepted the pelting of the bullets with bowed and weary heads. It was of no purpose to strive against walls. It was of no use to batter themselves against granite. And from this consciousness that they had attempted to conquer an unconquerable thing there seemed to arise a feeling that they had been betrayed. They glowered with bent brows, but dangerously, upon some of the officers, more particularly upon the red-bearded one with the voice of triple brass.

However, the rear of the regiment was fringed with men, who continued to shoot irritably at the advancing foes. They seemed resolved to make every trouble. The youthful lieutenant was perhaps the last man in the disordered mass. His forgotten back was toward the enemy. He had been shot in the arm. It hung straight and rigid. Occasionally he would cease to remember it, and be about to emphasize an oath with a sweeping gesture. The multiplied pain caused him to swear with incredible power.

The youth went along with slipping, uncertain feet. He kept watchful eyes rearward. A scowl of mortification and rage was upon his face. He had thought of a fine revenge upon the officer who had referred to him and his fellows as mule drivers. But he saw that it could not come to pass. His dreams had collapsed when the mule drivers, dwindling rapidly, had wavered and hesitated on the little clearing, and then had recoiled. And now the retreat of the mule drivers was a march of shame to him.

A dagger-pointed gaze from without his blackened face was held toward the enemy, but his greater hatred was riveted upon the man, who, not knowing him, had called him a mule driver.

When he knew that he and his comrades had failed to do anything in successful ways that might bring the little pangs of a kind of remorse upon the officer, the youth allowed the rage of the baffled to possess him. This cold officer upon a monument, who dropped epithets unconcernedly down, would be finer as a dead man, he thought. So grievous did he think it that he could never possess the secret right to taunt truly in answer.

He had pictured red letters of curious revenge. "We are mule drivers, are we?" And now he was compelled to throw them away.

He presently wrapped his heart in the cloak of his pride and kept the flag erect. He harangued his fellows, pushing against their chests with his free hand. To those he knew well he made frantic appeals, beseeching them by name. Between him and the lieutenant, scolding and near to losing his mind with rage, there was felt a subtle fellowship and equality. They supported each other in all manner of hoarse, howling protests.

But the regiment was a machine run down. The two men babbled at a forceless thing. The soldiers who had heart to go slowly were continually shaken in their resolves by a knowledge that comrades were slipping with speed back to the lines. It was difficult to think of reputation when others were thinking of skins. Wounded men were left crying on this black journey.

The smoke fringes and flames blustered always. The youth, peering once through a sudden rift in a cloud, saw a brown mass of troops, interwoven and magnified until they appeared to be thousands. A fierce-hued flag flashed before his vision.

Immediately, as if the uplifting of the smoke had been prearranged, the discovered troops burst into a rasping yell, and a hundred flames jetted toward the retreating band. A rolling gray cloud again interposed as the regiment doggedly replied. The youth had to depend again upon his misused ears, which were trembling and buzzing from the mêlée of musketry and yells.

The way seemed eternal. In the clouded haze men became panic-stricken with the thought that the regiment had lost its path, and was proceeding in a perilous direction. Once the men who headed the wild procession turned and came pushing back against their comrades, screaming that they were being fired upon from points which they had considered to be toward their own lines. At this cry a hysterical fear and dismay beset the troops. A soldier, who heretofore had been ambitious to make the regiment into a wise little band that would proceed calmly amid the huge-appearing difficulties, suddenly sank down and buried his face in his arms with an air of bowing to a doom. From another a shrill lamentation rang out filled with profane illusions to a general. Men ran hither and thither, seeking with their eyes roads of escape. With serene regularity, as if controlled by a schedule, bullets buffed into men.

The youth walked stolidly into the midst of the mob, and with his flag in his hands took a stand as if he expected an attempt to push him to the ground. He unconsciously assumed the attitude of the color bearer in the fight of the preceding day. He passed over his brow a hand that trembled. His breath did not come freely. He was choking during this small wait for the crisis.

His friend came to him. "Well, Henry, I guess this is goodby—John."

"Oh, shut up, you damned fool!" replied the youth, and he would not look at the other.

The officers labored like politicians to beat the mass into a proper circle to face the menaces. The ground was uneven and torn. The men curled into depressions and fitted themselves snugly behind whatever would frustrate a bullet.

The youth noted with vague surprise that the lieutenant was standing mutely with his legs far apart and his sword held in the manner of a cane. The youth wondered what had happened to his vocal organs that he no more cursed.

There was something curious in this little intent pause of the lieutenant. He was like a babe which, having wept its fill, raises its eyes and fixes them upon a distant toy. He was engrossed in this contemplation, and the soft under lip quivered from self-whispered words.

Some lazy and ignorant smoke curled slowly. The men, hiding from the bullets, waited anxiously for it to lift and disclose the plight of the regiment.

The silent ranks were suddenly thrilled by the eager voice of the youthful lieutenant bawling out: "Here they come! Right on to us, b'Gawd!" His further words were lost in a roar of wicked thunder from the men's rifles.

The youth's eyes had instantly turned in the direction indicated by the awakened and agitated lieutenant, and he had seen the haze of treachery disclosing a body of soldiers of the enemy. They were so near that he could see their features. There was a recognition as he looked at the types of faces. Also he perceived with dim amazement that their uniforms were rather gay in effect, being light gray, accented with a brilliant-hued facing. Moreover, the clothes seemed new.

These troops had apparently been going forward with caution, their rifles held in readiness, when the youthful lieutenant had discovered them and their movement had been interrupted by the volley from the blue regiment. From the moment's glimpse, it was derived that they had been unaware of the proximity of their dark-suited foes or had mistaken the direction. Almost instantly they were shut utterly from the youth's sight by the smoke from the energetic rifles of his companions. He strained his vision to learn the accomplishment of the volley, but the smoke hung before him.

The two bodies of troops exchanged blows in the manner of a pair of boxers. The fast angry firings went back and forth. The men in blue were intent with the despair of their circumstances and they seized upon the revenge to be had at close range. Their thunder swelled loud and valiant. Their curving front bristled with flashes and the place resounded with the clangor of their ramrods. The youth ducked and dodged for a time and achieved a few unsatisfactory views of the enemy. There appeared to be many of them and they were replying swiftly. They seemed moving toward the blue regiment, step by step. He seated himself gloomily on the ground with his flag between his knees.

As he noted the vicious, wolflike temper of his comrades he had a sweet thought that if the enemy was about to swallow the regimental broom as a large prisoner, it could at least have the consolation of going down with bristles forward.

But the blows of the antagonist began to grow more weak. Fewer bullets ripped the air, and finally, when the men slackened to learn of the fight, they could see only dark, floating smoke. The regiment lay still and gazed. Presently some chance whim came to the pestering blur, and it began to coil heavily away. The men saw a ground vacant of fighters. It would have been an empty stage if it were not for a few corpses that lay thrown and twisted into fantastic shapes upon the sward.

At sight of this tableau, many of the men in blue sprang from behind their covers and made an ungainly dance of joy. Their eyes burned and a hoarse cheer of elation broke from their dry lips.

It had begun to seem to them that events were trying to prove that they were impotent. These little battles had evidently endeavored to demonstrate that the men could not fight well. When on the verge of submission to these opinions, the small duel had showed them that the proportions were not impossible, and by it they had revenged themselves upon their misgivings and upon the foe.

The impetus of enthusiasm was theirs again. They gazed about them with looks of uplifted pride, feeling new trust in the grim, always confident weapons in their hands. And they were men.

Presently they knew that no fighting threatened them. All ways seemed once more opened to them. The dusty blue lines of their friends were disclosed a short distance away. In the distance there were many colossal noises, but in all this part of the field there was a sudden stillness.

They perceived that they were free. The depleted band drew a long breath of relief and gathered itself into a bunch to complete its trip.

In this last length of journey the men began to show strange emotions. They hurried with nervous fear. Some who had been dark and unfaltering in the grimmest moments now could not conceal an anxiety that made them frantic. It was perhaps that they dreaded to be killed in insignificant ways after the times for proper military deaths had passed. Or, perhaps, they thought it would be too ironical to get killed at the portals of safety. With backward looks of perturbation, they hastened.

As they approached their own lines there was some sarcasm exhibited on the part of a gaunt and bronzed regiment that lay resting in the shade of trees. Questions were wafted to them.

"Where th' hell yeh been?"

"What yeh comin' back fer?"

"Why didn't yeh stay there?"

"Was it warm out there, sonny?"

"Goin' home now, boys?"

One shouted in taunting mimicry: "Oh, mother, come quick an' look at th' sojers!"

There was no reply from the bruised and battered regiment, save that one man made broadcast challenges to fist fights and the red-bearded officer walked rather near and glared in great swashbuckler style at a tall captain in the other regiment. But the lieutenant suppressed the man who wished to fist fight, and the tall captain, flushing at the little fanfare of the red-bearded one, was obliged to look intently at some trees.

The youth's tender flesh was deeply stung by these remarks. From under his creased brows he glowered with hate at the mockers. He meditated upon a few revenges. Still, many in the regiment hung their heads in criminal fashion, so that it came to pass that the men trudged with sudden heaviness, as if they bore upon their bended shoulders the coffin of their honor. And the youthful lieutenant, recollecting himself, began to mutter softly in black curses.

They turned when they arrived at their old position to regard the ground over which they had charged.

The youth in this contemplation was smitten with a large astonishment. He discovered that the distances, as compared with the brilliant measurings of his mind, were trivial and ridiculous. The stolid trees, where much had taken place, seemed incredibly near. The time, too, now that he reflected, he saw to have been short. He wondered at the number of emotions and events that had been crowded into such little spaces. Elfin thoughts must have exaggerated and enlarged everything, he said.

It seemed, then, that there was bitter justice in the speeches of the gaunt and bronzed veterans. He veiled a glance of disdain at his fellows who strewed the ground, choking with dust, red from perspiration, misty eyed, disheveled.

They were gulping at their canteens, fierce to wring every mite of water from them, and they polished at their swollen and watery features with coat sleeves and bunches of grass. For a time the men were bewildered by it. "Good thunder!" they ejaculated, staring at the vanishing form of the general. They conceived it to be a huge mistake.

Presently, however, they began to believe that in truth their efforts had been called light. The youth could see this convention weigh upon the entire regiment until the men were like cuffed and cursed animals, but withal rebellious.

The friend, with a grievance in his eye, went to the youth. "I wonder what he does want," he said. "He must think we went out there an' played marbles! I never see sech a man!"

The youth developed a tranquil philosophy for these moments of irritation. "Oh, well," he rejoined, "he probably didn't see nothing of it at all and got mad as blazes, and concluded we were a lot of sheep, just because we didn't do what he wanted done. It's a pity old Grandpa Henderson got killed yesterday—he'd have known that we did our best and fought good. It's just our awful luck, that's what."

"I should say so," replied the friend. He seemed to be deeply wounded at an injustice. "I should say we did have awful luck! There's no fun in fightin' fer people when everything yeh do—no matter what—ain't done right. I have a notion t' stay behind next time an' let 'em take their ol' charge an' go t' th' devil with it."

The youth spoke soothingly to his comrade. "Well, we both did good. I'd like to see the fool what'd say we both didn't do as good as we could!"

"Of course we did," declared the friend stoutly. "An' I'd break th' feller's neck if he was as big as a church. But we're all right, anyhow, for I heard one feller say that we two fit th' best in th' reg'ment, an' they had a great argument 'bout it. Another feller, 'a course, he had t' up an' say it was a lie—he seen all what was goin' on an' he never seen us from th' beginnin' t' th' end. An' a lot more struck in an' ses it wasn't a lie—we did fight like thunder, an' they give us quite a sendoff. But this is what I can't stand—these everlastin' ol' soldiers, titterin' an' laughin', an' then that general, he's crazy."

The youth exclaimed with sudden exasperation: "He's a lunkhead! He makes me mad. I wish he'd come along next time. We'd show 'im what—"

He ceased because several men had come hurrying up. Their faces expressed a bringing of great news.

"O Flem, yeh jest oughta heard!" cried one, eagerly.

"Heard what?" said the youth.

"Yeh jest oughta heard!" repeated the other, and he arranged himself to tell his tidings. The others made an excited circle. "Well, sir, th' colonel met your lieutenant right by us—it was damnedest thing I ever heard—an' he ses: 'Ahem! ahem!' he ses. 'Mr. Hasbrouck!' he ses, 'by th' way, who was that lad what carried th' flag?' he ses. There, Flemin', what d' yeh think 'a that? 'Who was th' lad what carried th' flag?' he ses, an' th' lieutenant, he speaks up right away: 'That's Flemin', an' he's a jimhickey,' he ses, right away. What? I say he did. 'A jimhickey,' he ses—those'r his words." Having stirred this prodigious uproar, and, apparently, finding it too prodigious, the brigade, after a little time, came marching airily out again with its fine formation in nowise disturbed. There were no traces of speed in its movements. The brigade was jaunty and seemed to point a proud thumb at the yelling wood.

On a slope to the left there was a long row of guns, gruff and maddened, denouncing the enemy, who, down through the woods, were forming for another attack in the pitiless monotony of conflicts. The round red discharges from the guns made a crimson flare and a high, thick smoke. Occasional glimpses could be caught of groups of the toiling artillery-men. In the rear of this row of guns stood a house, calm and white, amid bursting shells. A congregation of horses, tied to a long railing, were tugging frenziedly at their bridles. Men were running hither and thither.

The detached battle between the four regiments lasted for some time. There chanced to be no interference, and they settled their dispute by themselves. They struck savagely and powerfully at each other for a period of minutes, and then the lighter-hued regiments faltered and drew back, leaving the dark-blue lines shouting. The youth could see the two flags shaking with laughter amid the smoke remnants.

Presently there was a stillness, pregnant with meaning. The blue lines shifted and changed a trifle and stared expectantly at the silent woods and fields before them. The hush was solemn and churchlike, save for a distant battery that, evidently unable to remain quiet, sent a faint rolling thunder over the ground. It irritated, like the noises of unimpressed boys. The men imagined that it would prevent their perched ears from hear-ing the first words of the new battle.

Of a sudden the guns on the slope roared out a message of warning. A spluttering sound had begun in the woods. It swelled with amazing speed to a profound clamor that involved the earth in noises. The splitting crashes swept along the lines until an intermina-ble roar was developed. To those in the midst of it it became a din fitted to the universe. It was the whirring and thumping of gigantic machinery, complications among the smaller stars. The youth's ears were filled up. They were incapable of hearing more.

On an incline over which a road wound he saw wild and desperate rushes of men perpetually backward and forward in riotous surges. These parts of the opposing armies were two long waves that pitched upon each other madly at dictated points. To and fro they swelled. Sometimes, one side by its yells and cheers would proclaim decisive blows, but a moment later the other side would be all yells and cheers. Once the youth saw a spray of light forms go in houndlike leaps toward the waving blue lines. There was much howling, and presently it went away with a vast mouthful of prisoners. Again, he saw a blue wave dash with such thunderous force against a gray obstruction that it seemed to clear the earth of it and leave nothing but trampled sod. And always in their swift and deadly rushes to and fro the men screamed and yelled like maniacs.

Particular pieces of fence or secure positions behind collections of trees were wran-gled over, as gold thrones or pearl bedsteads. There were desperate lunges at these chosen spots seemingly every instant, and most of them were bandied like light toys between the contending forces. The youth could not tell from the battle flags flying like crimson foam in many directions which color of cloth was winning.

His emaciated regiment bustled forth with undiminished fierceness when its time came. When assaulted again by bullets, the men burst out in a barbaric cry of rage and pain. They bent their heads in aims of intent hatred behind the projected hammers of their guns. Their ramrods clanged loud with fury as their eager arms pounded the cartridges into the rifle barrels. The front of the regiment was a smoke-wall penetrated by the flashing points of yellow and red.

Wallowing in the fight, they were in an astonishingly short time resmudged. They surpassed in stain and dirt all their previous appearances. Moving to and fro with strained exertion, jabbering the while, they were, with their swaying bodies, black faces, and glowing eyes, like strange and ugly fiends jigging heavily in the smoke.

The lieutenant, returning from a tour after a bandage, produced from a hidden receptacle of his mind new and portentous oaths suited to the emergency. Strings of expletives he swung lashlike over the backs of his men, and it was evident that his previous efforts had in nowise impaired his resources.

The youth, still the bearer of the colors, did not feel his idleness. He was deeply absorbed as a spectator. The crash and swing of the great drama made him lean forward, intent-eyed, his face working in small contortions. Sometimes he prattled, words coming unconsciously from him in grotesque exclamations. He did not know that he breathed; that the flag hung silently over him, so absorbed was he.

A formidable line of the enemy came within dangerous range. They could be seen plainly—tall, gaunt men with excited faces running with long strides toward a wandering fence.

At sight of this danger the men suddenly ceased their cursing monotone. There was an instant of strained silence before they threw up their rifles and fired a plumping volley at the foes. There had been no order given; the men, upon recognizing the menace, had immediately let drive their flock of bullets without waiting for word of command.

But the enemy were quick to gain the protection of the wandering line of fence. They slid down behind it with remarkable celerity, and from this position they began briskly to slice up the blue men.

These latter braced their energies for a great struggle. Often, white clinched teeth shone from the dusky faces. Many heads surged to and fro, floating upon a pale sea of smoke. Those behind the fence frequently shouted and yelped in taunts and gibelike cries, but the regiment maintained a stressed silence. Perhaps, at this new assault the men recalled the fact that they had been named mud diggers, and it made their situation thrice bitter. They were breathlessly intent upon keeping the ground and thrusting away the rejoicing body of the enemy. They fought swiftly and with a despairing savageness denoted in their expressions.

The youth had resolved not to budge whatever should happen. Some arrows of scorn that had buried themselves in his heart had generated strange and unspeakable hatred. It was clear to him that his final and absolute revenge was to be achieved by his dead body lying, torn and gluttering, upon the field. This was to be a poignant retaliation upon the officer who had said "mule drivers," and later "mud diggers," for in all the wild graspings of his mind for a unit responsible for his sufferings and commotions he always seized upon the man who had dubbed him wrongly. And it was his idea, vaguely formulated, that his corpse would be for those eyes a great and salt reproach.

The regiment bled extravagantly. Grunting bundles of blue began to drop. The orderly sergeant of the youth's company was shot through the cheeks. Its supports being injured, his jaw hung afar down, disclosing in the wide cavern of his mouth a pulsing mass of blood and teeth. And with it all he made attempts to cry out. In his endeavor there was a dreadful earnestness, as if he conceived that one great shriek would make him well.

The youth saw him presently go rearward. His strength seemed in nowise impaired. He ran swiftly, casting wild glances for succor.

Others fell down about the feet of their companions. Some of the wounded crawled out and away, but many lay still, their bodies twisted into impossible shapes.

The youth looked once for his friend. He saw a vehement young man, powder-smeared and frowzled, whom he knew to be him. The lieutenant, also, was unscathed in his position at the rear. He had continued to curse, but it was now with the air of a man who was using his last box of oaths.

For the fire of the regiment had begun to wane and drip. The robust voice, that had come strangely from the thin ranks, was growing rapidly weak.

The colonel came running along back of the line. There were other officers following him. "We must charge'm!" they shouted. "We must charge'm!" they cried with resentful voices, as if anticipating a rebellion against this plan by the men.

The youth, upon hearing the shout, began to study the distance between him and the enemy. He made vague calculations. He saw that to be firm soldiers they must go forward. It would be death to stay in the present place, and with all the circumstances to go backward would exalt too many others. Their hope was to push the galling foes away from the fence.

He expected that his companions, weary and stiffened, would have to be driven to this assault, but as he turned toward them he perceived with a certain surprise that they were giving quick and unqualified expressions of assent. There was an ominous, clanging overture to the charge when the shafts of the bayonets rattled upon the rifle barrels. At the yelled words of command the soldiers sprang forward in eager leaps. There was new and unexpected force in the movement of the regiment. A knowledge of its faded and jaded condition made the charge appear like a paroxysm, a display of the strength that comes before a final feebleness. The men scampered in insane fever of haste, racing as if to achieve a sudden success before an exhilarating fluid should leave them. It was a blind and despairing rush by the collection of men in dusty and tattered blue, over a green sward and under a sapphire sky, toward a fence, dimly outlined in smoke, from behind which spluttered the fierce rifles of enemies.

The youth kept the bright colors to the front. He was waving his free arm in furious circles, the while shrieking mad calls and appeals, urging on those that did not need to be urged, for it seemed that the mob of blue men hurling themselves on the dangerous group of rifles were again grown suddenly wild with an enthusiasm of unselfishness. From the many firings starting toward them, it looked as if they would merely succeed in making a great sprinkling of corpses on the grass between their former position and the fence. But they were in a state of frenzy, perhaps because of forgotten vanities, and it made an exhibition of sublime recklessness. There was no obvious questioning, nor figurings, nor diagrams. There was, apparently, no considered loopholes. It appeared that the swift wings of their desires would have shattered against the iron gates of the impossible.

He himself felt the daring spirit of a savage, religion-mad. He was capable of profound sacrifices, a tremendous death. He had no time for dissections, but he knew that he thought of the bullets only as things that could prevent him from reaching the place of his endeavor. There were subtle flashings of joy within him that thus should be his mind.

He strained all his strength. His eyesight was shaken and dazzled by the tension of thought and muscle. He did not see anything excepting the mist of smoke gashed by the little knives of fire, but he knew that in it lay the aged fence of a vanished farmer protecting the snuggled bodies of the gray men.

As he ran a thought of the shock of contact gleamed in his mind. He expected a great concussion when the bodies of troops crashed together. This became a part of his wild battle madness. He could feel the onward swing of the regiment about him and he conceived of a thunderous, crushing blow that would prostrate the resistance and spread consternation and amazement for miles. The flying regiment was going to have a catapultian effect. This dream made him run faster among his comrades, who were giving vent to hoarse and frantic cheers.

But presently he could see that many of the men in gray did intend to abide the blow. The smoke, rolling, disclosed men who ran, faces still turned. These grew to a crowd, who retired stubbornly. Individuals wheeled frequently to send a bullet at the blue wave.

But at one part of the line there was a grim and obdurate group that made no movement. They were settled firmly down behind posts and rails. A flag, ruffled and fierce, waved over them and their rifles dinned fiercely.

The blue whirl of men got very near, until it seemed that in truth there would be a close and frightful scuffle. There was an expressed disdain in the opposition of the little group, that changed the meaning of the cheers of the men in blue. They became yells of wrath, directed, personal. The cries of the two parties were now in sound an interchange of scathing insults.

They in blue showed their teeth; their eyes shone all white. They launched themselves as at the throats of those who stood resisting. The space between dwindled to an insignificant distance.

The youth had centered the gaze of his soul upon that other flag. Its possession would be high pride. It would express bloody minglings, near blows. He had a gigantic hatred for those who made great difficulties and complications. They caused it to be as a craved treasure of mythology, hung amid tasks and contrivances of danger.

He plunged like a mad horse at it. He was resolved it should not escape if wild blows and darings of blows could seize it. His own emblem, quivering and aflare, was winging toward the other. It seemed there would shortly be an encounter of strange beaks and claws, as of eagles.

The swirling body of blue men came to a sudden halt at close and disastrous range and roared a swift volley. The group in gray was split and broken by this fire, but its riddled body still fought. The men in blue yelled again and rushed in upon it.

The youth, in his leapings, saw, as through a mist, a picture of four or five men stretched upon the ground or writhing upon their knees with bowed heads as if they had been stricken by bolts from the sky. Tottering among them was the rival color bearer, whom the youth saw had been bitten vitally by the bullets of the last formidable volley. He perceived this man fighting a last struggle, the struggle of one whose legs are grasped by demons. It was a ghastly battle. Over his face was the bleach of death, but set upon it were the dark and hard lines of desperate purpose. With this terrible grin of resolution he hugged his precious flag to him and was stumbling and staggering in his design to go the way that led to safety for it.

But his wounds always made it seem that his feet were retarded, held, and he fought a grim fight, as with invisible ghouls fastened greedily upon his limbs. Those in advance of the scampering blue men, howling cheers, leaped at the fence. The despair of the lost was in his eyes as he glanced back at them.

The youth's friend went over the obstruction in a tumbling heap and sprang at the flag as a panther at prey. He pulled at it and, wrenching it free, swung up its red brilliancy with a mad cry of exultation even as the color bearer, gasping, lurched over in a final throe and, stiffening convulsively, turned his dead face to the ground. There was much blood upon the grass blades.

At the place of success there began more wild clamorings of cheers. The men gesticulated and bellowed in an ecstasy. When they spoke it was as if they considered their listener to be a mile away. What hats and caps were left to them they often slung high in the air.

At one part of the line four men had been swooped upon, and they now sat as prisoners. Some blue men were about them in an eager and curious circle. The soldiers had trapped strange birds, and there was an examination. A flurry of fast questions was in the air.

One of the prisoners was nursing a superficial wound in the foot. He cuddled it, baby-wise, but he looked up from it often to curse with an astonishing utter abandon straight at the noses of his captors. He consigned them to red regions; he called upon the pestilential wrath of strange gods. And with it all he was singularly free from recognition of the finer points of the conduct of prisoners of war. It was as if a clumsy clod had trod upon his toe and he conceived it to be his privilege, his duty, to use deep, resentful oaths.

Another, who was a boy in years, took his plight with great calmness and apparent good nature. He conversed with the men in blue, studying their faces with his bright and keen eyes. They spoke of battles and conditions. There was an acute interest in all their faces during this exchange of viewpoints. It seemed a great satisfaction to hear voices from where all had been darkness and speculation. The third captive sat with a morose countenance. He preserved a stoical and cold attitude. To all advances he made one reply without variation, "Ah, go t' hell!"

The last of the four was always silent and, for the most part, kept his face turned in unmolested directions. From the views the youth received he seemed to be in a state of absolute dejection. Shame was upon him, and with it profound regret that he was, perhaps, no more to be counted in the ranks of his fellows. The youth could detect no expression that would allow him to believe that the other was giving a thought to his narrowed future, the pictured dungeons, perhaps, and starvations and brutalities, liable to the imagination. All to be seen was shame for captivity and regret for the right to antagonize.

After the men had celebrated sufficiently they settled down behind the old rail fence, on the opposite side to the one from which their foes had been driven. A few shot perfunctorily at distant marks.

There was some long grass. The youth nestled in it and rested, making a convenient rail support the flag. His friend, jubilant and glorified, holding his treasure with vanity, came to him there. They sat side by side and congratulated each other.

The roarings that had stretched in a long line of sound across the face of the forest began to grow intermittent and weaker. The stentorian speeches of the artillery continued in some distant encounter, but the crashes of the musketry had almost ceased. The youth and his friend of a sudden looked up, feeling a deadened form of distress at the waning of these noises, which had become a part of life. They could see changes going on among the troops. There were marchings this way and that way. A battery wheeled leisurely. On the crest of a small hill was the thick gleam of many departing muskets.

The youth arose. "Well, what now, I wonder?" he said. By his tone he seemed to be preparing to resent some new monstrosity in the way of dins and smashes. He shaded his eyes with his grimy hand and gazed over the field.

His friend also arose and stared. "I bet we're goin' t' git along out of this an' back over th' river," said he.

"Well, I swan!" said the youth.

They waited, watching. Within a little while the regiment received orders to retrace its way. The men got up grunting from the grass, regretting the soft repose. They jerked their stiffened legs, and stretched their arms over their heads. One man swore as he rubbed his eyes. They all groaned "O Lord!" They had as many objections to this change as they would have had to a proposal for a new battle.

They trampled slowly back over the field across which they had run in a mad scamper.

The regiment marched until it had joined its fellows. The reformed brigade, in column, aimed through a wood at the road. Directly they were in a mass of dust-covered troops, and were trudging along in a way parallel to the enemy's lines as these had been defined by the previous turmoil.

They passed within view of a stolid white house, and saw in front of it groups of their comrades lying in wait behind a neat breastwork. A row of guns were booming at a distant enemy. Shells thrown in reply were raising clouds of dust and splinters. Horsemen dashed along the line of intrenchments.

At this point of its march the division curved from the field and went winding off in the direction of the river. When the significance of this movement had impressed itself upon the youth he turned his head and looked over his shoulder toward the trampled and débris-strewn ground. He breathed a breath of new satisfaction. He finally nudged his friend. "Well, it's all over," he said to him.

His friend gazed backward. "B'Gawd, it is," he assented. They mused.

For a time the youth was obliged to reflect in a puzzled and uncertain way. His mind was undergoing a subtle change. It took moments for it to cast off its battleful ways and resume its accustomed course of thought. Gradually his brain emerged from the clogged clouds, and at last he was enabled to more closely comprehend himself and circumstance.

He understood then that the existence of shot and countershot was in the past. He had dwelt in a land of strange, squalling upheavals and had come forth. He had been where there was red of blood and black of passion, and he was escaped. His first thoughts were given to rejoicings at this fact.

Later he began to study his deeds, his failures, and his achievements. Thus, fresh from scenes where many of his usual machines of reflection had been idle, from where he had proceeded sheeplike, he struggled to marshal all his acts.

At last they marched before him clearly. From this present viewpoint he was enabled to look upon them in spectator fashion and to criticize them with some correctness, for his new condition had already defeated certain sympathies.

Regarding his procession of memory he felt gleeful and unregretting, for in it his public deeds were paraded in great and shining prominence. Those performances which had been witnessed by his fellows marched now in wide purple and gold, having various deflections. They went gayly with music. It was pleasure to watch these things. He spent delightful minutes viewing the gilded images of memory.

He saw that he was good. He recalled with a thrill of joy the respectful comments of his fellows upon his conduct.

Nevertheless, the ghost of his flight from the first engagement appeared to him and danced. There were small shoutings in his brain about these matters. For a moment he blushed, and the light of his soul flickered with shame.

A specter of reproach came to him. There loomed the dogging memory of the tattered soldier—he who, gored by bullets and faint for blood, had fretted concerning an imagined wound in another; he who had loaned his last of strength and intellect for the tall soldier; he who, blind with weariness and pain, had been deserted in the field.

For an instant a wretched chill of sweat was upon him at the thought that he might be detected in the thing. As he stood persistently before his vision, he gave vent to a cry of sharp irritation and agony.

His friend turned. "What's the matter, Henry?" he demanded. The youth's reply was an outburst of crimson oaths.

As he marched along the little branch-hung roadway among his prattling companions this vision of cruelty brooded over him. It clung near him always and darkened his view of these deeds in purple and gold. Whichever way his thoughts turned they were followed by the somber phantom of the desertion in the fields. He looked stealthily at his companions, feeling sure that they must discern in his face evidences of this pursuit. But they were plodding in ragged array, discussing with quick tongues the accomplishments of the late battle.

"Oh, if a man should come up an' ask me, I'd say we got a dum good lickin'."

"Lickin'—in yer eye! We ain't licked, sonny. We're going down here aways, swing aroun', an' come in behint 'em."

"Oh, hush, with your comin' in behint 'em. I've seen all 'a that I wanta. Don't tell me about comin' in behint—"

"Bill Smithers, he ses he'd rather been in ten hundred battles than been in that heluva hospital. He ses they got shootin' in th' nighttime, an' shells dropped plum among 'em in th' hospital. He ses sech hollerin' he never see."

"Hasbrouck? He's th' best off'cer in this here reg'ment. He's a whale."

"Didn't I tell yeh we'd come aroun' in behint 'em? Didn't I tell yeh so? We—"

"Oh, shet yer mouth!"

For a time this pursuing recollection of the tattered man took all elation from the youth's veins. He saw his vivid error, and he was afraid that it would stand before him all his life. He took no share in the chatter of his comrades, nor did he look at them or know them, save when he felt sudden suspicion that they were seeing his thoughts and scrutinizing each detail of the scene with the tattered soldier.

Yet gradually he mustered force to put the sin at a distance. And at last his eyes seemed to open to some new ways. He found that he could look back upon the brass and bombast of his earlier gospels and see them truly. He was gleeful when he discovered that he now despised them.

With the conviction came a store of assurance. He felt a quiet manhood, non-assertive but of sturdy and strong blood. He knew that he would no more quail before his guides wherever they should point. He had been to touch the great death, and found that, after all, it was but the great death. He was a man.

So it came to pass that as he trudged from the place of blood and wrath his soul changed. He came from hot plowshares to prospects of clover tranquilly, and it was as if hot plowshares were not. Scars faded as flowers.

It rained. The procession of weary soldiers became a bedraggled train, despondent and muttering, marching with churning effort in a trough of liquid brown mud under a low, wretched sky. Yet the youth smiled, for he saw that the world was a world for him, though many discovered it to be made of oaths and walking sticks. He had rid himself of the red sickness of battle. The sultry nightmare was in the past. He had been an animal blistered and sweating in the heat and pain of war. He turned now with a lover's thirst to images of tranquil skies, fresh meadows, cool brooks—an existence of soft and eternal peace.

Over the river a golden ray of sun came through the hosts of leaden rain clouds.

CHAPTER 32

An Artilleryman's Diary
By Jenkin Lloyd Jones

A boy from Pennsylvania becomes a man under fire.

—LAMAR UNDERWOOD

WHATEVER VALUE THIS PUBLICATION MAY HAVE, LIES IN THE FACT THAT IT OFFERS A typical case—a small cross section of the army that freed the slave and saved the Union.

The Editor of the Commission's publications has asked me to state briefly something about myself. I am one of the multitude of "hyphenated" Americans, born across the water but reared under the flag. I am a Cambro-American, proud of both designations, and with abundant heart, loyalty, and perhaps too much head pride in both. Introduced to this world in Llandyssul, Cardiganshire, Wales, November 14, 1843, I celebrated my first anniversary by landing at Castle Garden, in New York City. My parents were sturdy "come-outers" who, after the manner called "heresy," even among Protestants, worshipped the God of their fathers. They came from what in orthodox parlance was known as the "Smwtyn Du" the heretical "black-spot" in Wales. I am the third Jenkin Jones to preach that liberal interpretation of Christianity generally known as Unitarianism. The first Jenkin Jones preached his first heretical sermon in his mother's garden way back in 1726, ninety-three years before Channing preached his Baltimore sermon (1819), from which latter event American Unitarianism generally dates its beginning.

My father was a prosperous hatter-farmer—making hats for the local markets during the winter months, tilling his little ten-acre farm during the summer time. My parents were lured to America by the democracy here promised. In our family, freedom was a word to conjure by. Hoping for larger privileges for the growing family of children, they brought them to the New World, the world of many intellectual as well as material advantages. The long sea voyage of six weeks in a sailing vessel, interrupted by a dismantling storm which compelled the ship to return for repairs after two weeks sailing, brought them into the teeth of winter, too late in the season to reach their objective point in the West. So the journey was suspended and the first winter spent in a Welsh settlement near Steuben, New York.

May, 1845, found us in the then territory of Wisconsin. The broad, fertile, and hospitable open prairie country in southern Wisconsin was visited and shunned as a desert land, "a country so poor that it would not grow a horse-switch." And so, three "forties" of government land were entered in the heavy woods of Rock River valley, forty miles west of Milwaukee, midway between Oconomowoc and Watertown, which then were pioneer villages. The land was bought at $1.20 an acre, then were purchased a yoke of oxen and two cows; and when these were paid for, there remained one gold sovereign ($5) to start life with—father, mother, and six children.

Trees were felled for the log house which for the first six months was roofed with basswood bark, for the shingles had not only to be made, but the art of making them had to be acquired. In this log house were spent the first twelve remembered years of my life. In it four more children were born. In the log school-house, built in the middle of the road because it was built before the road was there—we had arrived before the surveyor—I learned to speak, read, and love the English language. My first teacher was a Cambro-American who could by her bi-lingual accomplishment ease the way of the little Welsh immigrant children into English. I think I can remember crying when the teacher would speak to me in the then unintelligible English.

In 1856, my thirteenth year, the family began to realize that they had chosen a hard place in which to make a home. The battle would have been a grim one, with the tall trees and their stumps, the "hardhead" boulders, the marshes, the mosquitoes, and the semi-annual attack of ague, had it not been lightened with the blind hopes and the inspirations that bring to frontier lives the consolations and encouragements of the pioneer. So the home in Ixonia, that had welcomed the coming of the first plank-road and witnessed the approach of the La Crosse & Milwaukee Railroad as far as Oconomowoc, was sold, and in 1855 we moved to a farm of 400 acres in Sauk County.

The next year this was reached by the old Milwaukee & Mississippi Railroad and the village of Spring Green was established, adjoining the farm. Here I worked on the farm in the summer time, and during the winter time grew with the growing village school in Spring Green. During the spring term of school, in 1861, the boys were organized into the Spring Green Guards. "Billy" Hamilton, a clerk in George Pound's store, was excused by his employer during the noon hour and the recesses, to come over to drill us. The tresses, black or golden, were sacrificed. Our hair was "shingled" and we wore cadet caps. Of course the boys had been stirred when they heard of the humiliation preceding the inauguration of Lincoln, of the firing on Sumter; and in the autumn all of the Spring Green Guards who were ripe enough heard and heeded the call of Father Abraham. Captain "Billy" Hamilton went out as sergeant in the 6th Wisconsin Battery, and four years later came back as colonel at the head of the 36th Wisconsin Volunteer Infantry.

I was too young to go out in 1861. I cannot say that I panted for the fray. I dreaded the coming of the dire moment when conscience, not the government, would deliver me into a service that had no charm for me. Another winter's schooling in the Spring Green Academy, another sowing and harvest time, then leaving unstacked the hay that I had mown, and in the shocks the oats that I had cradled, I obeyed this "stern daughter of the voice of God"—to use Wordsworth's phrase—and turned my face to the South. I joined my old comrades of the Spring Green Guards in the 6th Wisconsin Battery, nine months or so after their first enlistment.

I was a "mother's boy," and with the exception of three months' district schooling at an aunt's house in Watertown, when a little lad, had never been away from home over night. I had not then and have not since owned a firearm of any description. As I approach my three-score-and-ten, I can say that I have never sighted a gun, or pulled the trigger on anything smaller than a cannon, and that only when ordered.

It seems necessary for me to state further, that throughout the three years of camp life, as through all the succeeding years, I have been a total abstainer from all forms of liquor and tobacco. The strictures throughout the Diary concerning the over-use of intoxicants were written from this standpoint, and perhaps were over stated. At least truth requires that I should at this distance testify that the bulk of the Union army, so largely made up of boys, was of stern stuff, with their lives rooted in seriousness and committed to sobriety, as the subsequent careers of those who were allowed to return amply prove. Many things set forth in this Diary were necessarily untrue to fact, but there is nothing but what was true to the thought and feeling of the writer at the time. The simplicity of the narrative and the lapse of time, will, I hope, take all the barbs out of any random shafts that may have been fired by a battery boy.

The monotonous story of this battery boy is told in long meter in the Diary here published. The only remarkable thing about the record is, that it exists and is still available fifty years after the writing. Of course every soldier lad started to keep a diary. Very few persisted to the end; rare is the private who did not outlast his own diary. And then again, the vicissitudes of the camp, the hopeless carelessness of the American people to contemporary history, have carried to oblivion most of such records. These ten little memorandum books would doubtless have suffered a like fate, were it not for the vigilance of the home folk, to whose care the successive volumes were promptly consigned. And then many years after, there was the loving, unsolicited persistency of a faithful amanuensis, who, unbeknown to me, in the "cracks of time," patiently and faithfully transcribed the entire story, which was fast becoming illegible in the original camp- and battle-stained little books, to the clear, typewritten sheets which made them available to the Wisconsin History Commission.

~⌒~

Spring Green, Wis., Thursday, Aug. 14, 1862. I enlisted under Lieutenant Fancher for the 6th Battery, Wisconsin Artillery.

Madison, Wis., Monday, Aug. 25. I bade good-bye to friends, relatives and companions most dear, and at 8 o'clock embarked for Madison to begin my soldier's life. Arrived at camp at 12 M. and slept my first night on the lap of mother earth with Uncle Sam's blanket for a coverlid and a few rough boards raised about four feet in the center for a roof. I laid down; my eyelids were heavy and demanded sleep but the mind wandered and the stars shone bright and it was long ere sleep threw her curtain over the scene.

Madison, Tuesday, Aug. 26. I got partially rested by my short sleep, but I was awake long ere the rising of the sun. I awoke to a different scene to which had hitherto been my lot. Instead of the lowing of cattle and the bleating of sheep, was the rattle of the drum and the "hooray" of the volunteers. To-day we were examined by the surgeon and went up-town for the purpose of drawing our bounty money, but the press of business was too large, and we were put off till the next day. In the evening I had to bid good-bye to my brother John, who had accompanied me to camp. It was a difficult task—my constant companion in labor, my adviser and counsel in everything. I had to part. It seemed as if I was like a ship on sea without a compass, without other safeguard than my own firmness and weight.

Madison, Wednesday, Aug. 27. I had to pass through the regular scramble-game for my rations, and drew the bounty in the afternoon, went around town and bought my outfit, ready to leave.

Enroute, Thursday, Aug. 28. To-day we were informed that we were to be sent on in the evening. I wrote my first letter home and in the evening we started for "Dixie" at 10 P. M. It was dark and we could not see anything to attract our attention so our minds had free scope to wander home to loved ones, and it was a saddening thought that we were to leave all of these, to meet at best a very uncertain fate. We passed on to Milton where our car was uncoupled and taken up by the Janesville R.R., and off we rocked for another four or five hours' ride, half asleep, and by this time somewhat fatigued. At Janesville we changed cars for Chicago, it being about 1 A.M.

Enroute, Friday, Aug. 29. The day dawned just in time to see the suburbs (Chicago). We being about five miles from town received a magnificent view of the Western metropolis. The immense clouds of smoke issuing from the massive stacks of manufacture, and the countless rigging of the vessels lying at the dock were great sights to my country eyes. We arrived at the end of the line at 6:30 A.M. We were immediately formed in line, and forward march to the depot of the I[llinois] C[entral] R.R. about a mile distant. We were no sooner there than the shrill whistle told us we were again on a ride of three hundred and sixty-five miles to Cairo, without intermission. We crossed an arm of Lake Michigan having a fine view of the lake. Of our travel across the almost boundless prairies of Illinois I will not try to describe, but suffice it to say, we arrived at Cairo at 4 A.M.

Rienzi, Sunday, Sept. 7. Arose to the sound of the bugle at 3 A.M. Prepared for a general inspection, but Captain, apprehending a move, did not call us out. Drew good bunks from the old camp of 2nd Missouri. After roll call at 9 P.M. I went to bed hoping to have a good night's rest, but I was doomed to disappointment, for ere two hours had elapsed, we were awakened by Corporal Dixon telling us to pack up all our clothing and be in readiness to march. We of course obeyed and waited for further orders, when about midnight, "Strike your tents" was given. This done, the mules began driving in, loading was commenced, the horses harnessed, and by one o'clock all was ready to march. That which could not be taken was piled up ready for the march, but the order did not come, so we were obliged to pick our place and lay down for a short and uneasy sleep.

Rienzi, Monday, Sept. 8. To-day was spent in anxious waiting. I stood guard for the first time while we were momentarily expecting orders to leave; slept in the open air.

Rienzi, Tuesday, Sept. 9. Another day dawned without any orders. Some of the boys pitched their tents. I went out foraging in the afternoon.

Rienzi, Wednesday, Sept. 10. This was another day of idle waiting; most of the boys slept in tents last night, and it was supposed we would have to stay here. I went out foraging in the morning.

Rienzi, Thursday, Sept. 11. I answered the summons of the reveille, but I did not feel very well; had an attack of the ague but got over it by dinner. Nothing to break the monotony of camp life. Reinforced by one regiment of infantry.

Rienzi, Friday, Sept. 12. Spent the morning as usual in suspense of leaving, but finally the orders came to send all the baggage train to Clear Creek, a distance of ten miles to the west, and that we were to be stationed as an out-post. Detailed to go a-foraging, brought in two loads of corn from the south. The 1st Section were ordered out to the front. Had the first rain storm in the evening, and ere the morning I had a regular old shake of the ague.

Rienzi, Saturday, Sept. 13. The 3rd Section, Lieutenant Hood, went out in front and the first fell back to its old grounds. Foraging party brought in two loads of corn, three neat cattle, one sheep, twelve geese, seven hens, two or three bushels of sweet potatoes.

Rienzi, Sunday, Sept. 14. Was begun with another of the "strategic moves." We were told to hitch up with the greatest speed—all our baggage, knapsacks, etc. were put in a wagon, nothing was left to encumber us from a rapid and a desperate fight [in] which we were expected to share. The 3rd Section, two regiments of infantry, one of cavalry, started at 3 A.M. But all rumors of the enemy's presence proved false, and after lying in the shade, horses hitched, for an hour, we returned, unharnessed and lay quiet all day. The 3rd Section returned at 4 P.M. without seeing any enemy.

Rienzi, Monday, Sept. 15. To-day we began business in the old way. We had to sweep up for the first time in a week. I stood guard for the second time.

Rienzi, Tuesday, Sept. 16. We were aroused this morning with the same story of march and ordered to cook three days' rations and be ready to march at 1 P.M., but did not go and all quieted down again. The 3rd Section went out in the afternoon and stationed itself at bastion No. 5 at 9 P.M. Dispatches were brought around to the effect that McClellan had captured the rebel army of Virginia including General Lee. Nothing could induce us to restrain our joy but the fear of its being false.

Rienzi, Wednesday, Sept. 17. Was begun by a heavy shower of rain at about 9 A.M. I joined the foraging party and we started on the Corinth road. We had scarcely started before it began to rain and a perfect torrent poured until we returned, pretty well drenched. The rest of the day was spent inside of the tent as the rain continued nearly all day.

Rienzi, Thursday, Sept. 18. We awoke in a wet bed, it having rained very hard the latter part of the night. We received orders to march for Jacinto at 3 A.M. but countermanded before doing any harm save the usual harnessing up by the drivers about 9 A.M. The prisoners captured at Danville, twenty-three in number, including two captains, were marched to headquarters.

Rienzi, Friday, Sept. 19. On roll call the Captain told us that Burnside had captured the whole of Longstreet's command at Harpers Ferry after their first capturing the place and the whole army under Colonel Miles. Three cheers were given with a spirit. No mail. Went after berries in the afternoon.

Rienzi, Saturday, Sept. 20. There was nothing to break the monotony of camp life. Wrote two letters. Washed clothes. In the evening news of another battle at Iuka. They cleaned Price out and chased him four miles; 400 killed on both sides.

Rienzi, Sunday, Sept. 21. Was another repetition of that a week ago only on a little larger scale. The horses were harnessed at 1 A.M. and we went out on the Ripley road three quarters of a mile, laid there half an hour waiting for the enemy, then filed left on our drilling ground, drilled half an hour, then came home and unharnessed. Received new gun-carriages and caissons in the afternoon. Report of another great battle at Iuka in which 1,000 of our men were killed in twenty-five minutes. Colonel Murphy of the 8th put under arrest for withdrawing his men. Stood guard duty.

Rienzi, Monday, Sept. 22. To-day I felt very weak, there was no local pain, but a general debility.

Rienzi, Tuesday, Sept. 23. To-day I felt but a little better, got some milk and corn bread. With the secesh [women] had an encounter before I left.

Corinth, Miss., Sunday, Oct. 5. As it is seen from the last date, I have not written any for some time and I must write of the past from memory. Not getting any better, I went to the Company hospital on September 24 and there was treated for fever of which I had but a very slight touch. On the morning of October 1 every man that could not join his platoon was to be sent to Corinth as the Battery was going to move, so I and four others were put in the ambulance and driven to the depot, but the cars did not come till 2 P.M. When they came, they loaded all the commissary stores in the rooms. E. R. Hungerford and myself were lucky enough to get into the box car. We got to Corinth in about two hours, and after waiting an hour we were taken in a mule wagon to the Seminary Hospital situated on a hill about one mile and a half from Corinth. We were put in a comfortable tent and lay there unmolested until the 3rd, when early in the morning heavy firing was heard and continued all day. We learned that the cannon had been attacked by the rebels consisting of Price, Breckinridge, Van Dorn and one other commander. In the afternoon we had to move down under the hill, we being right in the range of the guns should they open fire in that direction at night. We were ordered to have everything packed so as to leave at a moment's notice.

At about 12 o'clock at night we were ordered out on the road, while the tents were struck and cots piled. Presently the teams began driving in and loading men and cots. At last our turn came, but not until the rebs had opened fire on the town with three guns throwing shells. We had to pass under the fire. The shells whistled over our heads in every direction, while off went the mules as fast as they could trot. It certainly was a rough ride. They drove us through town and left us on the east of it about 1/2 mile. By this time it was nearly daylight and the guns used by the rebs throwing shells were taken. About 9 o'clock the engagement became general. The noise of the musketry, occasionally broken in upon by the loud peal of artillery, made it truly terrific. The fight lasted about three hours, when the rebs were obliged to skedaddle.

All of this time we had heard nothing from the Battery. We supposed that it had been engaged, when at 12 o'clock Dr. Miller came around and told us that the Battery had been engaged that morning, and had been taken and retaken, but he could not give us a list of the casualties. We heard nothing more from the Battery until to-day, G. M. Spencer came with a list of casualties. He informed us that the sick and wounded were gathered in a Company hospital about a quarter of a mile to the south.

Corinth, Tuesday, Oct. 7. The doctor came to take our names to be sent to a Northern hospital as they had no room for us [in the general hospital]. I asked permission to join the Company hospital, which was granted, so in the afternoon we joined our comrades; found the wounded all in good spirits.

Corinth, Saturday, Oct. 11. The Battery returned from its chase after the retreating rebs, of a week in length. In the evening the Captain and Sergeant Simpson rode into our camp, the Battery being in camp two and one half miles out.

Corinth, Sunday, Oct. 12. To-day it was a little warmer, the rain of the last two days having cleared. My anxiety to visit the Battery was such that I was induced to start out on foot in order to see them. The walk was rather fatiguing as it was rather warm, but we found them at last on a ridge in a shady grove. But it did not look much like the camp of the 6th Battery, as they had no tents pitched and were quartered in brush bivouacs or under tarpaulins; I found them all well but somewhat reduced by the march. I remained with them for an hour, then retraced my steps alone through the solitary woods. I enjoyed pleasant thoughts of the good times to come. I reached camp by sunset well pleased with my walk and not as fatigued as I expected.

Corinth, Monday, Oct. 13. The troops on the outskirts of the town were all moved in, among which were the 6th Battery. They passed our encampment at about 8 A.M.; their designation was unknown but supposed not to be far. Quartermaster-Sergeant Simpson brought new clothing to camp in the afternoon. I drew one jacket, pair of pants and a hat.

Corinth, Tuesday, Oct. 14. Having learned the locality of our Battery, it being encamped on the south side of the town, the wounded men were removed to the general hospital, and the sick were taken to the Battery, with the exception of N. B. Hood and Byron Babcock.

Corinth, Thursday, Oct. 16. I joined my Platoon, went into tent with E. W. Evans and T. J. Hungerford as before. Owing to my weakness I was not put on full duty immediately, being excused from mounted drill, etc.

Corinth, Friday, Oct. 17. Resolutions relative to those who fell in battle on the 4th inst. were offered by H. S. Keene and unanimously adopted by the camp on roll call P.M.

Corinth, Saturday, Oct. 18. Roll call in the evening. —— made an explanation as to his whereabouts on the day of battle, and the orderly read a certificate from the commander of the 11th Ohio Battery, corroborating his statement.

Corinth, Sunday, Oct. 19. To-day we were told the sad news of the death of one of our number, John Haskins, who died during the night of chronic diarrhea. We had an inspection at 9 A.M. and in the afternoon we paid the last tribute of respect which one man can pay to another, to the remains of our comrade, Haskins. He was buried by the side of the brave five that fell in the battle of Corinth.

Corinth, Monday, Oct. 20. To-day we had to police the entire camp ground as it was reported that General Rosecrans was going to inspect camp. The ground was shoveled and swept over, but no Rosecrans came.

Corinth, Tuesday, Oct. 21. Finished policing around the guns. In the afternoon after the Company was formed for drill, as Orderly Hayward was returning after reporting to the Captain, his horse stumbled, falling on him, spraining his right ankle and fracturing the cap bone.

Corinth, Wednesday, Oct. 22. While on drill in the afternoon, I, in attempting to mount, lost my balance and fell, the hind wheel of the caisson running over my left ankle, luckily without any dislocation. After drill I was taken to the hospital, my foot being very painful during the night.

Corinth, Thursday, Oct. 23. The weather turned very windy and cold, water freezing in the night 1/4 inch in thickness.

Corinth, Friday, Oct. 24. My foot was a little easier. Dr. Arnold of the 12th Wisconsin Battery dressing it and keeping it cool by water. The weather still cold.

Corinth, Saturday, Oct. 25. We were moved from the tent this morning to an old deserted house a quarter of a mile from camp. In the afternoon it snowed and by night the earth was clothed in white.

Corinth, Sunday, Monday, Tuesday, Wednesday, etc. The troops were engaged in fortifying. All the buildings on the outskirts were torn down regardless of worth and hauled away by the troops to build stables, barracks, etc.

Corinth, Saturday, Nov. 1. Orders were given to Battery to cook three days' rations in their haversacks and three days' in the wagons, all ready to march on the following morning.

Corinth, Sunday, Nov. 2. I walked up to the Battery, the farthest I had walked since my lameness. Saw the boys off; they left their tents standing, their knapsacks etc. under charge of Lieutenant Simpson, and those unfit for the march. The inmates of the hospital were taken to the general hospital under Dr. Arnold, nine in number, viz: Orderly J. G. S. Hayward (fractured ankle), Corporal G. B. Jones (chronic diarrhea; waiting for discharge); W. W. Wyman (waiting for discharge); G. W. Benedict (diarrhea); E. W. Evans (fever); David Evans (convalescent); Alex. Ray (convalescent); E. R. Hungerford (chronic diarrhea); Jenk. L. Jones (bruised ankle), remained in the hospital until

Corinth, Sunday, Nov. 9. Learning that the Battery had gone to camp at Grand Junction, Tenn., Sergeant Hamilton was sent back to bring forward the baggage, etc., etc. and was to start by train in the morning. E. W. Evans, David Evans and myself procured a dismissal from the hospital and bade good-bye to our comrades (who were all doing well except E. R. Hungerford, who was very low) at 6:30 A.M. and reported at the depot. We found the boys and baggage on the platform, but owing to the rush of troops we could not get off to-day. We laid around all day, exchanged our tents, drew some quartermaster stores.

Corinth, Monday, Nov. 10. We were again disappointed, the train leaving us behind and nothing to do but wait another twenty-four hours. In the afternoon E. W. Evans and I went to the hospital where we learned that our comrade E. R. Hungerford had died at about 2 P.M. Sunday, and was to be buried in the evening.

Corinth, Tuesday, Nov. 11. Lay on the platform all day, and at night we were furnished a car to load our baggage. We loaded it by 12 P.M.

Grand Junction, Tenn., Wednesday, Nov. 12. It having rained during the night, the dust was converted to mud. Ate a breakfast of cold beef and bread, filled our canteens with water, when we scrambled on top the freight cars in order to procure transportation. It was raining, and when the train was in motion the smoke and cinders were torturing. Arrived at Jackson at 1 P.M. Waited an hour for dinner, then took Mississippi Central R.R. for Grand Junction. Remained at Medon Station till 6 P.M. when G. M. Spencer and I spread our blankets and laid down; awoke at Grand Junction at 3 A.M.

Grand Junction, Thursday, Nov. 13. Lieutenant Simpson went in search of the Battery early and left us to unload and guard the baggage. The teams arrived from the Battery 3 P.M. We loaded and started out about three miles and encamped where the team that left Corinth on the 8th had bivouacked for the night.

Davis Mills, Miss., Friday, Nov. 14. Reached the Battery about 10 A.M., it being situated one mile south of Davis Mills in an open field; church and cemetery hard by.

Davis Mills, Saturday, Nov. 15. Heard from home. Received two letters, from John and Thomas, which eased my anxiety. Listened to the first sermon [in camp].

Davis Mills, Sunday, Nov. 16. 10 A.M. we had a general inspection by U. S. Grant and General Quinby of the 3rd Division.

La Grange, Tenn., Monday, Nov. 17. Awoke to hear the rain pattering briskly on the Sibley [tent] above me. We were called out, and with expectations to march, we drew three days' rations in our haversacks. 8 A.M. the rain cleared off and the column of infantry began to move by on the road leading to Holly Springs. At 9 A.M. we fell in rear of column. We marched west about three quarters of a mile, then turned north toward La Grange; travelled through very pretty country. We halted at Wolf River to water our horses, fill our canteens and ate a dinner of hard crackers and sugar. Ascended a steep hill, half a mile in length, on the top of which was situated La Grange, when we turned westward and travelled until 7 P.M. Encamped on a hill. Killed a beef for supper.

Moscow, Tenn., Tuesday, Nov. 18. Up at 4 A.M., cooked our breakfast and again on the road by 6 o'clock, and after a four hours' march through a broken country, well cleared, persimmons plenty, we arrived at Moscow, where we went into camp for the time. Rode to water through a town completely deserted, no trace of a citizen. I, as could be expected, was bothered on the march by my foot and could not have kept up, were it not for S. E. Sweet, who allowed me to ride his colt part of the time.

Moscow, Wednesday, Nov. 19. To-day, ordered to pack our knapsacks, mark them preparatory to turning them over, and take them to be stored until we were to be permanently camped.

Moscow, Thursday, Nov. 20. Mail arrived to-day. Received two letters; weather rather cold. Went foraging in the morning; returned with fresh pork, beans, corn and fodder in plenty.

Moscow, Friday, Nov. 21. Weather cold and frosty. 2 P.M. bugle sounded the assembly, "Fall in," when we were given orders to prepare to march immediately. The horses were harnessed, everything packed ready for further orders which after an hour waiting, came, to unharness. It proved to be an alarm caused by a party of guerrillas making a dash upon our foraging train, capturing some seventy mules, then skedaddling before the escort could come up.

Moscow, Saturday, Nov. 22. Griffith Thomas, E. W. Evans and myself went to the spring in woods, washed our clothes and returned by one o'clock. Weather warm and pleasant during the day but very cold nights.

Moscow, Sunday, Nov. 23. Laid in tent all day. Mail arrived in the afternoon. Received two very welcome letters from home and Thomas L.

Moscow, Monday, Nov. 24. I felt rather unwell, having had a lusty old shake with the ague. In the night went to the doctor, had four pills and an excuse from duty. Foraging party brought in twenty-five bushels sweet potatoes, four hogs, a hive of honey and two loads of corn.

Chattanooga, Monday, June 26. That for which we have so long waited, for which so many hard words have been uttered because of its long delay, for which so many officers have been roughly abused for its being withheld—We are ordered to the States. To be mustered out. Hurrah!! Hurrah!!!

Boys went out grazing as usual this morning. 9 A.M. here comes an orderly which set the Captain a-jumping, Lieutenants a-crowing and privates run wild. In less time than it takes to write, all hands, cooks and negroes included, were at work cleaning off the guns so that they will be received by ordnance officers. Water, brush and rags and every available cleanser used until they would pass. Boys came in with horses at noon and another stock of good feelings passed around. Afternoon well spent in cleaning, counting and gathering harness and other stores. Commence turning them over to-morrow. Never since we last threw up works in front of the enemy, did the boys work with such a will. All past grievances forgotten in pleasant anticipations of the future.

Chattanooga, Tuesday, June 27. Daylight found us in our boots and stirring. 7:30 A.M. the Battery moved out followed by battery wagons, forge and four wagon loads of ordnance. I on detail along. Ordnance officer ready to receive us. Lieutenant A. Sweet superintended the counting of everything by the clerk, which is a very tedious job. Captain Simpson disposed of ammunition. I was on duty with Lieutenant Sweet and rode fast and heavy as orderly for him, bringing reports, etc. to and from camp. To-night everything is gone except the horses, which will be turned over to-morrow.

Great anxiety is expressed by all to reach home by the Fourth of July, which at present looks very probable. Camp looks forlorn and disorganized, everything upside down, boxes being made to be carried by express, knapsacks packed as though there was no time to do it to-morrow, but nobody notices it. All of the reserve are under home orders to-day. Fortune smiled on us this time in being first; aye, it laughed outright upon us. But, dear Journal, I cannot write, I feel too *good*.

After almost three years' absence, I found my valley home at dusk on the third of July, 1865. And what a happy union it was. Father, mother, sisters and brothers, all together. The circle unbroken during the terrible three years that had rolled over us since I parted to try my fate in a soldiers' camp. The bitter tears of anguish then, were replaced by those of unbounded joy. All the hardships and privations of my campaign were amply repaid at this joyful union.

Madison, Tuesday, July 18. The rolls have returned with Lieutenant Colonel Giddings' (mustering officer) signature annexed, and the military tie which bound us together as the 6th Battery has ceased to exist. 10 A.M. we assembled once more and in the yard in front of Captain Simpson's office, in the city of Madison, signed the final pay rolls, and received the much-coveted scrip "Discharge," bearing date of July 18. "Mustered out of United States service on the 3rd of July." It was not an hour of noisy demonstration, but happiness too sweet for utterance prevails, the emotion of thankfulness filling the dullest breast, "Free! Free!" was the exclamation of many as they became possessors of the prizes.

But to me it brought many dark and serious thoughts to mind. Yes, free, but for the first time in my life I am my only dictator as to what course to pursue. Have arrived at age with life's issue fairly before me, and undecided what course to pursue. Inclination and duty seem strangely at variance. The importance of such questions is almost oppressive.

But I must strive to attain the highest good that lies in my power. The dictates of conscience shall be my guide. To-night I retrace my steps to my quiet valley home. The many tender ties which bind me to my comrades of the march, battle and camp, are more than likely forever broken on this earth. And the diary which I have kept unbroken is hereby ended with the end of my service, having lived two years and eleven months in the service of my country. Three of the best years of my life have been lost to self-instruction, and the plans and hopes of my childhood have been ruthlessly toppled down, but the time has not been lost. I have no regrets for the way it has been spent. My prayer is that the remainder of my life may be as usefully spent. So, dear Diary, good-bye!

CHAPTER 33

A Night

By Louisa May Alcott

The battlefield combatants were men (with a few exceptions), but women were no less affected by the war. Many women volunteered as nurses, cooks, and even spies. In 1863 Louisa May Alcott, most famous for her book Little Women, *published* Hospital Sketches, *which chronicles her wartime experiences as a nurse in Washington, D.C. Although written with humor and a light touch, there is no disguising the pain of trying to save the lives of the shattered young soldiers who poured regularly into the wards, or of watching helplessly as one of them dies. Alcott's stint as a nurse was brief—only six weeks. While on duty, Alcott contracted typhoid pneumonia, from which she nearly died and never fully recovered; nurses were no less susceptible to the diseases that swept through hospital wards than were the patients.*

—LISA PURCELL

BEING FOND OF THE NIGHT SIDE OF NATURE, I WAS SOON PROMOTED TO THE POST OF night nurse, with every facility for indulging in my favorite pastime of "owling." My colleague, a black-eyed widow, relieved me at dawn, we two taking care of the ward, between us, like the immortal Sairy and Betsey, "turn and turn about." I usually found my boys in the jolliest state of mind their condition allowed; for it was a known fact that Nurse Periwinkle objected to blue devils, and entertained a belief that he who laughed most was surest of recovery. At the beginning of my reign, dumps and dismals prevailed; the nurses looked anxious and tired, the men gloomy or sad; and a general "Hark!-from-the-tombs-a-doleful-sound" style of conversation seemed to be the fashion: a state of things which caused one coming from a merry, social New England town, to feel as if she had got into an exhausted receiver; and the instinct of self-preservation, to say nothing of a philanthropic desire to serve the race, caused a speedy change in Ward No. 1.

More flattering than the most gracefully turned compliment, more grateful than the most admiring glance, was the sight of those rows of faces, all strange to me a little while ago, now lighting up, with smiles of welcome, as I came among them, enjoying that moment heartily, with a womanly pride in their regard, a motherly affection for them all. The evenings were spent in reading aloud, writing letters, waiting on and amusing the men, going the rounds with Dr. P., as he made his second daily survey, dressing my dozen wounds afresh, giving last doses, and making them cozy for the long hours to come, till the nine o'clock bell rang, the gas was turned down, the day nurses went off duty, the night watch came on, and my nocturnal adventure began.

My ward was now divided into three rooms; and, under favor of the matron, I had managed to sort out the patients in such a way that I had what I called, "my duty room," my "pleasure room," and my "pathetic room," and worked for each in a different way. One, I visited, armed with a dressing tray, full of rollers, plasters, and pins; another, with books, flowers, games, and gossip; a third, with teapots, lullabies, consolation, and sometimes, a shroud.

Wherever the sickest or most helpless man chanced to be, there I held my watch, often visiting the other rooms, to see that the general watchman of the ward did his duty by the fires and the wounds, the latter needing constant wetting. Not only on this account did I meander, but also to get fresher air than the close rooms afforded; for, owing to the stupidity of that mysterious "somebody" who does all the damage in the world, the windows had been carefully nailed down above, and the lower sashes could only be raised in the mildest weather, for the men lay just below. I had suggested a summary smashing of a few panes here and there, when frequent appeals to headquarters had proved unavailing, and daily orders to lazy attendants had come to nothing. No one seconded the motion, however, and the nails were far beyond my reach; for, though belonging to the sisterhood of "ministering angels," I had no wings, and might as well have asked for Jacob's ladder, as a pair of steps, in that charitable chaos.

One of the harmless ghosts who bore me company during the haunted hours, was Dan, the watchman, whom I regarded with a certain awe; for, though so much together, I never fairly saw his face, and, but for his legs, should never have recognized him, as we seldom met by day. These legs were remarkable, as was his whole figure, for his body was short, rotund, and done up in a big jacket, and muffler; his beard hid the lower part of his face, his hat-brim the upper; and all I ever discovered was a pair of sleepy eyes, and a very mild voice. But the legs!—very long, very thin, very crooked and feeble, looking like gray sausages in their tight coverings, without a ray of pegtopishness about them, and finished off with a pair of expansive, green cloth shoes, very like Chinese junks, with the sails down. This figure, gliding noiselessly about the dimly lighted rooms, was strongly suggestive of the spirit of a beer barrel mounted on corkscrews, haunting the old hotel in search of its lost mates, emptied and staved in long ago.

Another goblin who frequently appeared to me, was the attendant of the pathetic room, who, being a faithful soul, was often up to tend two or three men, weak and wandering as babies, after the fever had gone. The amiable creature beguiled the watches of the night by brewing jorums of a fearful beverage, which he called coffee, and insisted on sharing with me; coming in with a great bowl of something like mud soup, scalding hot, guiltless of cream, rich in an all-pervading flavor of molasses, scorch and tin pot. Such an amount of good will and neighborly kindness also went into the mess, that I never could find the heart to refuse, but always received it with thanks, sipped it with hypocritical relish while he remained, and whipped it into the slop-jar the instant he departed, thereby gratifying him, securing one rousing laugh in the doziest hour of the night, and no one was the worse for the transaction but the pigs. Whether they were "cut off untimely in their sins," or not, I carefully abstained from inquiring.

It was a strange life—asleep half the day, exploring Washington the other half, and all night hovering, like a massive cherubim, in a red rigolette, over the slumbering sons of man. I liked it, and found many things to amuse, instruct, and interest me. The snores alone were quite a study, varying from the mild sniff to the stentorian snort, which startled the echoes and hoisted the performer erect to accuse his neighbor of the deed, magnanimously forgive him, and wrapping the drapery of his couch about him, lie down to vocal slumber. After listening for a week to this band of wind instruments, I indulged in the belief that I could recognize each by the snore alone, and was tempted to join the chorus by breaking out with John Brown's favorite hymn:

"Blow ye the trumpet, blow!"

I would have given much to have possessed the art of sketching, for many of the faces became wonderfully interesting when unconscious. Some grew stern and grim, the men evidently dreaming of war, as they gave orders, groaned over their wounds, or damned the rebels vigorously; some grew sad and infinitely pathetic, as if the pain borne silently all day, revenged itself by now betraying what the man's pride had concealed so well. Often the roughest grew young and pleasant when sleep smoothed the hard lines away, letting the real nature assert itself; many almost seemed to speak, and I learned to know these men better by night than through any intercourse by day. Sometimes they disappointed me, for faces that looked merry and good in the light, grew bad and sly when the shadows came; and though they made no confidences in words, I read their lives, leaving them to wonder at the change of manner this midnight magic wrought in their nurse. A few talked busily; one drummer boy sang sweetly, though no persuasions could win a note from him by day; and several depended on being told what they had talked of in the morning.

Even my constitutionals in the chilly halls, possessed a certain charm, for the house was never still. Sentinels tramped round it all night long, their muskets glittering in the wintry moonlight as they walked, or stood before the doors, straight and silent, as figures of stone, causing one to conjure up romantic visions of guarded forts, sudden surprises, and daring deeds; for in these war times the hum drum life of Yankeedom had vanished, and the most prosaic feel some thrill of that excitement which stirs the nation's heart, and makes its capital a camp of hospitals.

Wandering up and down these lower halls, I often heard cries from above, steps hurrying to and fro, saw surgeons passing up, or men coming down carrying a stretcher, where lay a long white figure, whose face was shrouded and whose fight was done. Sometimes I stopped to watch the passers in the street, the moonlight shining on the spire opposite, or the gleam of some vessel floating, like a white-winged seagull, down the broad Potomac, whose fullest flow can never wash away the red stain of the land.

The night whose events I have a fancy to record, opened with a little comedy, and closed with a great tragedy; for a virtuous and useful life untimely ended is always tragical to those who see not as God sees. My headquarters were beside the bed of a New Jersey boy, crazed by the horrors of that dreadful Saturday. A slight wound in the knee brought him there; but his mind had suffered more than his body; some string of that delicate machine was over strained, and, for days, he had been reliving in imagination, the scenes he could not forget, till his distress broke out in incoherent ravings, pitiful to hear. As I sat by him, endeavoring to soothe his poor distracted brain by the constant touch of wet hands over his hot forehead, he lay cheering his comrades on, hurrying them back, then counting them as they fell around him, often clutching my arm, to drag me from the vicinity of a bursting shell, or covering up his head to screen himself from a shower of shot; his face brilliant with fever; his eyes restless; his head never still; every muscle strained and rigid; while an incessant stream of defiant shouts, whispered warnings, and broken laments, poured from his lips with that forceful bewilderment which makes such wanderings so hard to overhear.

It was past eleven, and my patient was slowly wearying himself into fitful intervals of quietude, when, in one of these pauses, a curious sound arrested my attention. Looking over my shoulder, I saw a one-legged phantom hopping nimbly down the room; and, going to meet it, recognized a certain Pennsylvania gentleman, whose wound-fever had taken a turn for the worse, and, depriving him of the few wits a drunken campaign had left him, set him literally tripping on the light, fantastic toe "toward home," as he blandly informed me, touching the military cap which formed a striking contrast to the severe simplicity of the rest of his decidedly undress uniform. When sane, the least movement produced a roar of pain or a volley of oaths; but the departure of reason seemed to have wrought an agreeable change, both in the man and his manners; for, balancing himself on one leg, like a meditative stork, he plunged into an animated discussion of the war, the President, lager beer, and Enfield rifles, regardless of any suggestions of mine as to the propriety of returning to bed, lest he be court-martialed for desertion.

Anything more supremely ridiculous can hardly be imagined than this figure, scantily draped in white, its one foot covered with a big blue sock, a dingy cap set rakingly askew on its shaven head, and placid satisfaction beaming in its broad red face, as it flourished a mug in one hand, an old boot in the other, calling them canteen and knapsack, while it skipped and fluttered in the most unearthly fashion. What to do with the creature I didn't know; Dan was absent, and if I went to find him, the perambulator might festoon himself out of the window, set his toga on fire, or do some of his neighbors a mischief.

The attendant of the room was sleeping like a near relative of the celebrated Seven, and nothing short of pins would rouse him; for he had been out that day, and whiskey asserted its supremacy in balmy whiffs. Still declaiming, in a fine flow of eloquence, the demented gentleman hopped on, blind and deaf to my graspings and entreaties; and I was about to slam the door in his face, and run for help, when a second and saner phantom, "all in white," came to the rescue, in the likeness of a big Prussian, who spoke no English, but divined the crisis, and put an end to it, by bundling the lively monoped into his bed, like a baby, with an authoritative command to "stay put," which received added weight from being delivered in an odd conglomeration of French and German, accompanied by warning wags of a head decorated with a yellow cotton night cap, rendered most imposing by a tassel like a bell-pull. Rather exhausted by his excursion, the member from Pennsylvania subsided; and, after an irrepressible laugh together, my Prussian ally and myself were returning to our places, when the echo of a sob caused us to glance along the beds. It came from one in the corner—such a little bed!—and such a tearful little face looked up at us, as we stopped beside it! The twelve-year-old drummer boy was not singing now, but sobbing, with a manly effort all the while to stifle the distressful sounds that would break out.

"What is it, Teddy?" I asked, as he rubbed the tears away, and checked himself in the middle of a great sob to answer plaintively:

"I've got a chill, ma'am, but I ain't cryin' for that, 'cause I'm used to it. I dreamed Kit was here, and when I waked up he wasn't, and I couldn't help it, then."

The boy came in with the rest, and the man who was taken dead from the ambulance was the Kit he mourned. Well he might; for, when the wounded were brought from Fredericksburg, the child lay in one of the camps thereabout, and this good friend, though sorely hurt himself, would not leave him to the exposure and neglect of such a time and place; but, wrapping him in his own blanket, carried him in his arms to the transport, tended him during the passage, and only yielded up his charge when Death met him at the door of the hospital which promised care and comfort for the boy. For ten days, Teddy had shivered or burned with fever and ague, pining the while for Kit, and refusing to be comforted, because he had not been able to thank him for the generous protection, which, perhaps, had cost the giver's life. The vivid dream had wrung the childish heart with a fresh pang, and when I tried the solace fitted for his years, the remorseful fear that haunted him found vent in a fresh burst of tears, as he looked at the wasted hands I was endeavoring to warm:

"Oh! if I'd only been as thin when Kit carried me as I am now, maybe he wouldn't have died; but I was heavy, he was hurt worser than we knew, and so it killed him; and I didn't see him, to say good bye."

This thought had troubled him in secret; and my assurances that his friend would probably have died at all events, hardly assuaged the bitterness of his regretful grief.

At this juncture, the delirious man began to shout; the one-legged rose up in his bed, as if preparing for another dart, Teddy bewailed himself more piteously than before: and if ever a woman was at her wit's end, that distracted female was Nurse Periwinkle, during the space of two or three minutes, as she vibrated between the three beds, like an agitated pendulum. Like a most opportune reinforcement, Dan, the bandy, appeared, and devoted himself to the lively party, leaving me free to return to my post; for the Prussian, with a nod and a smile, took the lad away to his own bed, and lulled him to sleep with a soothing murmur, like a mammoth humblebee. I liked that in Fritz, and if he ever wondered afterward at the dainties that sometimes found their way into his rations, or the extra comforts of his bed, he might have found a solution of the mystery in sundry persons' knowledge of the fatherly action of that night.

Hardly was I settled again, when the inevitable bowl appeared, and its bearer delivered a message I had expected, yet dreaded to receive:

"John is going, ma'am, and wants to see you, if you can come."

"The moment this boy is asleep; tell him so, and let me know if I am in danger of being too late."

My Ganymede departed, and while I quieted poor Shaw, I thought of John. He came in a day or two after the others; and, one evening, when I entered my "pathetic room," I found a lately emptied bed occupied by a large, fair man, with a fine face, and the serenest eyes I ever met. One of the earlier comers had often spoken of a friend, who had remained behind, that those apparently worse wounded than himself might reach a shelter first. It seemed a David and Jonathan sort of friendship. The man fretted for his mate, and was never tired of praising John—his courage, sobriety, self-denial, and unfailing kindliness of heart; always winding up with: "He's an out an' out fine feller, ma'am; you see if he ain't."

I had some curiosity to behold this piece of excellence, and when he came, watched him for a night or two, before I made friends with him; for, to tell the truth, I was a little afraid of the stately looking man, whose bed had to be lengthened to accommodate his commanding stature; who seldom spoke, uttered no complaint, asked no sympathy, but tranquilly observed what went on about him; and, as he lay high upon his pillows, no picture of dying statesman or warrior was ever fuller of real dignity than this Virginia blacksmith. A most attractive face he had, framed in brown hair and beard, comely featured and full of vigor, as yet unsubdued by pain; thoughtful and often beautifully mild while watching the afflictions of others, as if entirely forgetful of his own. His mouth was grave and firm, with plenty of will and courage in its lines, but a smile could make it as sweet as any woman's; and his eyes were child's eyes, looking one fairly in the face, with a clear, straightforward glance, which promised well for such as placed their faith in him. He seemed to cling to life, as if it were rich in duties and delights, and he had learned the secret of content. The only time I saw his composure disturbed, was when my surgeon brought another to examine John, who scrutinized their faces with an anxious look, asking of the elder: "Do you think I shall pull through, sir?" "I hope so, my man." And, as the two passed on, John's eye still followed them, with an intentness which would have won a clearer answer from them, had they seen it. A momentary shadow flitted over his face; then came the usual serenity, as if, in that brief eclipse, he had acknowledged the existence of some hard possibility, and, asking nothing yet hoping all things, left the issue in God's hands, with that submission which is true piety.

The next night, as I went my rounds with Dr. P., I happened to ask which man in the room probably suffered most; and, to my great surprise, he glanced at John:

"Every breath he draws is like a stab; for the ball pierced the left lung, broke a rib, and did no end of damage here and there; so the poor lad can find neither forgetfulness nor ease, because he must lie on his wounded back or suffocate. It will be a hard struggle, and a long one, for he possesses great vitality; but even his temperate life can't save him; I wish it could."

"You don't mean he must die, Doctor?"

"Bless you there's not the slightest hope for him; and you'd better tell him so before long; women have a way of doing such things comfortably, so I leave it to you. He won't last more than a day or two, at furthest."

I could have sat down on the spot and cried heartily, if I had not learned the wisdom of bottling up one's tears for leisure moments. Such an end seemed very hard for such a man, when half a dozen worn out, worthless bodies round him, were gathering up the remnants of wasted lives, to linger on for years perhaps, burdens to others, daily reproaches to themselves. The army needed men like John, earnest, brave, and faithful; fighting for liberty and justice with both heart and hand, true soldiers of the Lord. I could not give him up so soon, or think with any patience of so excellent a nature robbed of its fulfillment, and blundered into eternity by the rashness or stupidity of those at whose hands so many lives may be required. It was an easy thing for Dr. P. to say: "Tell him he must die," but a cruelly hard thing to do, and by no means as "comfortable" as he politely suggested. I had not the heart to do it then, and privately indulged the hope that some change for the better might take place, in spite of gloomy prophesies; so, rendering my task unnecessary. A few minutes later, as I came in again, with fresh rollers, I saw John sitting erect, with no one to support him, while the surgeon dressed his back. I had never hitherto seen it done; for, having simpler wounds to attend to, and knowing the fidelity of the attendant, I had left John to him, thinking it might be more agreeable and safe; for both strength and experience were needed in his case. I had forgotten that the strong man might long for the gentle tendance of a woman's hands, the sympathetic magnetism of a woman's presence, as well as the feebler souls about him. The Doctor's words caused me to reproach myself with neglect, not of any real duty perhaps, but of those little cares and kindnesses that solace homesick spirits, and make the heavy hours pass easier. John looked lonely and forsaken just then, as he sat with bent head, hands folded on his knee, and no outward sign of suffering, till, looking nearer, I saw great tears roll down and drop upon the floor. It was a new sight there; for, though I had seen many suffer, some swore, some groaned, most endured silently, but none wept. Yet it did not seem weak, only very touching, and straightway my fear vanished, my heart opened wide and took him in, as, gathering the bent head in my arms, as freely as if he had been a little child, I said, "Let me help you bear it, John."

Never, on any human countenance, have I seen so swift and beautiful a look of gratitude, surprise and comfort, as that which answered me more eloquently than the whispered—

"Thank you, ma'am, this is right good! This is what I wanted!"

"Then why not ask for it before?"

"I didn't like to be a trouble; you seemed so busy, and I could manage to get on alone."

"You shall not want it any more, John."

Nor did he; for now I understood the wistful look that sometimes followed me, as I went out, after a brief pause beside his bed, or merely a passing nod, while busied with those who seemed to need me more than he, because more urgent in their demands; now I knew that to him, as to so many, I was the poor substitute for mother, wife, or sister, and in his eyes no stranger, but a friend who hitherto had seemed neglectful; for, in his modesty, he had never guessed the truth. This was changed now; and, through the tedious operation of probing, bathing, and dressing his wounds, he leaned against me, holding my hand fast, and, if pain wrung further tears from him, no one saw them fall but me. When he was laid down again, I hovered about him, in a remorseful state of mind that would not let me rest, till I had bathed his face, brushed his "bonny brown hair," set all things smooth about him, and laid a knot of heath and heliotrope on his clean pillow. While doing this, he watched me with the satisfied expression I so liked to see; and when I offered the little nosegay, held it carefully in his great hand, smoothed a ruffled leaf or two, surveyed and smelt it with an air of genuine delight, and lay contentedly regarding the glimmer of the sunshine on the green. Although the manliest man among my forty, he said, "Yes, ma'am," like a little boy; received suggestions for his comfort with the quick smile that brightened his whole face; and now and then, as I stood tidying the table by his bed, I felt him softly touch my gown, as if to assure himself that I was there. Anything more natural and frank I never saw, and found this brave John as bashful as brave, yet full of excellencies and fine aspirations, which, having no power to express themselves in words, seemed to have bloomed into his character and made him what he was.

After that night, an hour of each evening that remained to him was devoted to his ease or pleasure. He could not talk much, for breath was precious, and he spoke in whispers; but from occasional conversations, I gleaned scraps of private history which only added to the affection and respect I felt for him. Once he asked me to write a letter, and as I settled pen and paper, I said, with an irrepressible glimmer of feminine curiosity, "Shall it be addressed to wife, or mother, John?"

"Neither, ma'am; I've got no wife, and will write to mother myself when I get better. Did you think I was married because of this?" he asked, touching a plain ring he wore, and often turned thoughtfully on his finger when he lay alone.

"Partly that, but more from a settled sort of look you have; a look which young men seldom get until they marry."

"I didn't know that; but I'm not so very young, ma'am, thirty in May, and have been what you might call settled this ten years; for mother's a widow, I'm the oldest child she has, and it wouldn't do for me to marry until Lizzy has a home of her own, and Laurie's learned his trade; for we're not rich, and I must be father to the children and husband to the dear old woman, if I can."

"No doubt but you are both, John; yet how came you to go to war, if you felt so? Wasn't enlisting as bad as marrying?"

"No, ma'am, not as I see it, for one is helping my neighbor, the other pleasing myself. I went because I couldn't help it. I didn't want the glory or the pay; I wanted the right thing done, and people kept saying the men who were in earnest ought to fight. I was in earnest, the Lord knows! But I held off as long as I could, not knowing which was my duty; mother saw the case, gave me her ring to keep me steady, and said 'Go': so I went."

A short story and a simple one, but the man and the mother were portrayed better than pages of fine writing could have done it.

"Do you ever regret that you came, when you lie here suffering so much?"

"Never, ma'am; I haven't helped a great deal, but I've shown I was willing to give my life, and perhaps I've got to; but I don't blame anybody, and if it was to do over again, I'd do it. I'm a little sorry I wasn't wounded in front; it looks cowardly to be hit in the back, but I obeyed orders, and it don't matter in the end, I know."

Poor John! It did not matter now, except that a shot in the front might have spared the long agony in store for him. He seemed to read the thought that troubled me, as he spoke so hopefully when there was no hope, for he suddenly added:

"This is my first battle; do they think it's going to be my last?"

"I'm afraid they do, John."

It was the hardest question I had ever been called upon to answer; doubly hard with those clear eyes fixed on mine, forcing a truthful answer by their own truth. He seemed a little startled at first, pondered over the fateful fact a moment, then shook his head, with a glance at the broad chest and muscular limbs stretched out before him:

"I'm not afraid, but it's difficult to believe all at once. I'm so strong it don't seem possible for such a little wound to kill me."

Merry Mercutio's dying words glanced through my memory as he spoke: "'Tis not so deep as a well, nor so wide as a church door, but 'tis enough." And John would have said the same could he have seen the ominous black holes between his shoulders; he never had; and, seeing the ghastly sights about him, could not believe his own wound more fatal than these, for all the suffering it caused him.

"Shall I write to your mother, now?" I asked, thinking that these sudden tidings might change all plans and purposes; but they did not; for the man received the order of the Divine Commander to march with the same unquestioning obedience with which the soldier had received that of the human one; doubtless remembering that the first led him to life, and the last to death.

"No, ma'am; to Laurie just the same; he'll break it to her best, and I'll add a line to her myself when you get done."

So I wrote the letter which he dictated, finding it better than any I had sent; for, though here and there a little ungrammatical or inelegant, each sentence came to me briefly worded, but most expressive; full of excellent counsel to the boy, tenderly bequeathing "mother and Lizzie" to his care, and bidding him good bye in words the sadder for their simplicity. He added a few lines, with steady hand, and, as I sealed it, said, with a patient sort of sigh, "I hope the answer will come in time for me to see it"; then, turning away his face, laid the flowers against his lips, as if to hide some quiver of emotion at the thought of such a sudden sundering of all the dear home ties.

These things had happened two days before; now John was dying, and the letter had not come. I had been summoned to many deathbeds in my life, but to none that made my heart ache as it did then, since my mother called me to watch the departure of a spirit akin to this in its gentleness and patient strength. As I went in, John stretched out both hands:

"I know you'd come! I guess I'm moving on, ma'am."

He was; and so rapidly that, even while he spoke, over his face I saw the gray veil falling that no human hand can lift. I sat down by him, wiped the drops from his forehead, stirred the air about him with the slow wave of a fan, and waited to help him die. He stood in sore need of help—and I could do so little; for, as the doctor had foretold, the strong body rebelled against death, and fought every inch of the way, forcing him to draw each breath with a spasm, and clench his hands with an imploring look, as if he asked, "How long must I endure this, and be still!" For hours he suffered dumbly, without a moment's respite, or a moment's murmuring; his limbs grew cold, his face damp, his lips white, and, again and again, he tore the covering off his breast, as if the lightest weight added to his agony; yet through it all, his eyes never lost their perfect serenity, and the man's soul seemed to sit therein, undaunted by the ills that vexed his flesh.

One by one, the men woke, and round the room appeared a circle of pale faces and watchful eyes, full of awe and pity; for, though a stranger, John was beloved by all. Each man there had wondered at his patience, respected his piety, admired his fortitude, and now lamented his hard death; for the influence of an upright nature had made itself deeply felt, even in one little week. Presently, the Jonathan who so loved this comely David, came creeping from his bed for a last look and word. The kind soul was full of trouble, as the choke in his voice, the grasp of his hand, betrayed; but there were no tears, and the farewell of the friends was the more touching for its brevity.

"Old boy, how are you?" faltered the one.

"Most through, thank heaven!" whispered the other.

"Can I say or do anything for you anywheres?"

"Take my things home, and tell them that I did my best."

"I will! I will!"

"Good bye, Ned."

"Good bye, John, good bye!"

They kissed each other, tenderly as women, and so parted, for poor Ned could not stay to see his comrade die. For a little while, there was no sound in the room but the drip of water, from a stump or two, and John's distressful gasps, as he slowly breathed his life away. I thought him nearly gone, and had just laid down the fan, believing its help to be no longer needed, when suddenly he rose up in his bed, and cried out with a bitter cry that broke the silence, sharply startling every one with its agonized appeal:

"For God's sake, give me air!"

It was the only cry pain or death had wrung from him, the only boon he had asked; and none of us could grant it, for all the airs that blew were useless now. Dan flung up the window. The first red streak of dawn was warming the gray east, a herald of the coming sun; John saw it, and with the love of light which lingers in us to the end, seemed to read in it a sign of hope of help, for, over his whole face there broke that mysterious expression, brighter than any smile, which often comes to eyes that look their last. He laid himself gently down; and, stretching out his strong right arm, as if to grasp and bring the blessed air to his lips in a fuller flow, lapsed into a merciful unconsciousness, which assured us that for him suffering was forever past. He died then; for, though the heavy breaths still tore their way up for a little longer, they were but the waves of an ebbing tide that beat unfelt against the wreck, which an immortal voyager had deserted with a smile. He never spoke again, but to the end held my hand close, so close that when he was asleep at last, I could not draw it away. Dan helped me, warning me as he did so that it was unsafe for dead and living flesh to lie so long together; but though my hand was strangely cold and stiff, and four white marks remained across its back, even when warmth and color had returned elsewhere, I could not but be glad that, through its touch, the presence of human sympathy, perhaps, had lightened that hard hour.

When they had made him ready for the grave, John lay in state for half an hour, a thing which seldom happened in that busy place; but a universal sentiment of reverence and affection seemed to fill the hearts of all who had known or heard of him; and when the rumor of his death went through the house, always astir, many came to see him, and I felt a tender sort of pride in my lost patient; for he looked a most heroic figure, lying there stately and still as the statue of some young knight asleep upon his tomb. The lovely expression which so often beautifies dead faces, soon replaced the marks of pain, and I longed for those who loved him best to see him when half an hour's acquaintance with Death had made them friends. As we stood looking at him, the ward master handed me a letter, saying it had been forgotten the night before. It was John's letter, come just an hour too late to gladden the eyes that had longed and looked for it so eagerly! Yet he had it; for, after I had cut some brown locks for his mother, and taken off the ring to send her, telling how well the talisman had done its work, I kissed this good son for her sake, and laid the letter in his hand, still folded as when I drew my own away, feeling that its place was there, and making myself happy with the thought, that, even in his solitary place in the "Government Lot," he would not be without some token of the love which makes life beautiful and outlives death. Then I left him, glad to have known so genuine a man, and carrying with me an enduring memory of the brave Virginia blacksmith, as he lay serenely waiting for the dawn of that long day which knows no night.

CHAPTER 34

The Rebel Army Life
By Carlton McCarthy

Cold, hungry, wet, worried, far from home. The agonies are unceasing for the men in gray.
*—*LAMAR UNDERWOOD

HAVE YOU EVER BEEN A SOLDIER? NO? THEN YOU DO NOT KNOW WHAT COMFORTS ARE! Conveniences you never had; animal consolations, never! You have not enjoyed the great exceptional luxuries which once in a century, perhaps, bless a limited number of men. How sad, that you have allowed your opportunity to pass unimproved!

But you have been a soldier! Ah, then let us together recall with pleasure, the past! once more be hungry, and eat; once more tired, and rest; once more thirsty, and drink; once more, cold and wet, let us sit by the roaring fire and feel comfort creep over us. So!—isn't it very pleasant?

Now let us recount, repossess rather, the treasures which once were ours, not forgetting that values have shrunk, and that the times have changed, and that men also are changed; some happily, some woefully. Possibly we, also, are somewhat modified.

Eating, you will remember, was more than a convenience; it was a comfort which rose almost to the height of a consolation. Probably the most universally desired comfort of the Confederate soldier was "something to eat." But this, like all greatly desired blessings, was shy, and when obtained was, to the average seeker, not replete with satisfaction.

But he did eat, at times, with great energy, great endurance, great capacity, and great satisfaction; the luscious slapjack, sweetened perhaps with sorghum, the yellow and odoriferous soda-biscuit, ash-cake, or, it might chance to be, the faithful "hardtack" (which "our friends the enemy" called "crackers") serving in rotation as bread.

The faithful hog was everywhere represented. His cheering presence was manifested most agreeably by the sweet odors flung to the breeze from the frying pan—that never failing and always reliable utensil. The solid slices of streaked lean and fat, the limpid gravy, the brown pan of slosh inviting you to sop it, and the rare, delicate shortness of the biscuit, made the homely animal to be in high esteem.

Beef, glorious beef! how seldom were you seen, and how welcome was your presence. In the generous pot you parted with your mysterious strength and sweetness. Impaled upon the cruel ramrod you suffered slow torture over the fire. Sliced, chopped, and pounded; boiled, stewed, fried, or broiled, always a trusty friend, and sweet comforter.

Happy the "fire" where the "stray" pig found a lover, and unhappy the pig! Innocence and youth were no protection to him, and his cries of distress availed him not as against the cruel purpose of the rude soldiery.

What is that faint aroma which steals about on the night air? Is it a celestial breeze? No! it is the mist of the coffee boiler. Do you not hear the tumult of the tumbling water? Poor man! you have eaten, and now other joys press upon you. Drink! drink more! Near the bottom it is sweeter. Providence hath now joined together for you the bitter and the sweet—there is sugar in that cup!

Some poor fellows, after eating, could only sleep. They were incapable of the noble satisfaction of "a good smoke." But there were some good men and true, thoughtful men, quietly disposed men, gentle and kind, who, next to a good "square" meal prized a smoke. Possibly, here begins consolation. Who can find words to tell the story of the soldier's affection for his faithful briar-root pipe! As the cloudy incense of the weed rises in circling wreaths about his head, as he hears the murmuring of the fire, and watches the glowing and fading of the embers, and feels the comfort of the hour pervading his mortal frame, what bliss!

But yonder sits a man who scorns the pipe—and why? He is a chewer of the weed. To him, the sweetness of it seems not to be drawn out by the fiery test, but rather by the persuasion of moisture and pressure. But he, too, is under the spell. There are pictures in the fire for him, also, and he watches them come and go. Now draw near. Are not those cheerful voices? Do you not hear the contented tones of men sitting in a cozy home? What glowing hopes here leap out in rapid words! No bitterness of hate, no revenge, no cruel purpose; but simply the firm resolve to march in the front of their country's defenders. Would you hear a song? You shall, for even now they sing:

> "Aha! a song for the trumpet's tongue!
> For the bugle to sing before us,
> When our gleaming guns, like clarions,
> Shall thunder in battle chorus!"

Would you hear a soldier's prayer? Well, there kneels one, behind that tree, but he talks with God: you may not hear him—nor I!

But now, there they go, one by one; no, two by two. Down goes an old rubber blanket, and then a good, thick, woolen one, probably with a big "U.S." in the center of it. Down go two men. They are hidden under another of the "U.S." blankets. They are resting their heads on their old battered haversacks. They love each other to the death, those men, and sleep there, like little children, locked in close embrace. They are asleep now—no, not quite; they are thinking of home, and it may be, of heaven. But now, surely they are asleep! No, they are not quite asleep, they are falling off to sleep. Happy soldiers, they are asleep.

At early dawn the bugle sounds the reveille. Shout answers to shout, the roll is called and the day begins. What new joys will it bring? Let us stay and see.

The sun gladdens the landscape; the fresh air, dashing and whirling over the fields and through the pines is almost intoxicating. Here are noble chestnut-oaks, ready for the axe and the fire; and there, at the foot of the hill, a mossy spring. The oven sits enthroned on glowing coals, crowned with fire; the coffee boils, the meat fries, the soldier—smiles and waits.

But waiting is so very trying that some, seizing towels, soap, and comb from their haversacks, step briskly down the hill, and plunge their heads into the cool water of the brook. Then their cheeks glow with rich color, and, chatting merrily, they seek again the fire, carrying the old bucket brimming full of water for the mess. All hands welcome the bucket, and breakfast begins. Now see the value of a good tin-plate. What a treasure that tin cup is, and that old fork! Who would have a more comfortable seat than that log affords!

But here comes the mail—papers, letters, packages. Here comes news from home, sweet, tender, tearful, hopeful, sad, distressing news; joyful news of victory and sad news of defeat; pictures of happy homes, or sad wailing over homes destroyed! But the mail has arrived and we cannot change the burden it has brought. We can only pity the man who goes empty away from the little group assembled about the mail-bag, and rejoice with him who strolls away with a letter near his heart. Suppose he finds therein the picture of a curly head. Just four years old! Suppose the last word in it is "Mother." Or suppose it concludes with a signature having that peculiarly helpless, but courageous and hopeful air, which can be imparted only by the hand of a girl whose heart goes with the letter! Once more, happy, happy soldier!

The artilleryman tarrying for a day only in a camp had only time to eat and do his work. Roll-call, drill, watering the horses, greasing caissons and gun-carriages; cleaning, repairing, and greasing harness; cleaning the chests of the limbers and caissons; storing and arranging ammunition; and many little duties, filled the day. In the midst of a campaign, comfortable arrangements for staying were hardly completed by the time the bugle sounded the assembly and orders to move were given. But however short the stay might be, the departure always partook of the nature of a move from home. More especially was this true in the case of the sick man, whose weary body was finding needed rest in the camp; and peculiarly true of the man who had fed at the table of a hospitable neighbor, and for a day, perhaps, enjoyed the society of the fair daughters of the house.

Orders to move were frequently heralded by the presence of the "courier," a man who rarely knew a word of the orders he had brought; who was always besieged with innumerable questions, always tried to appear to know more than his position allowed him to disclose, and who never ceased to be an object of interest to every camp he entered. Many a gallant fellow rode the country over; many a one led in the thickest of the fight and died bravely, known only as "my courier."

When the leaves began to fall and the wind to rush in furious frolics through the woods, the soldier's heart yearned for comfort. Chilling rains, cutting sleet, drifting snow, muddy roads, all the miseries of approaching winter, pressed him to ask and repeat the question, "When will we go into winter quarters?"

After all, the time did come. But first the place was known. The time was always doubtful. Leisurely and steady movement towards the place might be called the first "comfort" of winter quarters; and as each day's march brought the column nearer the appointed camp, the anticipated pleasures assumed almost the sweetness of present enjoyment.

But at last comes the welcome "Left into park!" and the fence goes down, the first piece wheels through the gap, the battery is parked, the horses are turned over to the "horse sergeant," the old guns are snugly stowed under the tarpaulins, and the winter has commenced. The woods soon resound with the ring of the axe; trees rush down, crashing and snapping, to the ground; fires start here and there till the woods are illuminated, and the brightest, happiest, busiest night of all the year falls upon the camp. Now around each fire gathers the little group who are, for a while, to make it the center of operations. Hasty plans for comfort and convenience are eagerly discussed till late into the night, and await only the dawn of another day for execution.

Roll-call over and breakfast eaten, the work of the day commences with the preparation of comfortable sleeping places, varying according to the "material" on hand. A favorite arrangement for two men consisted of a bed of clean straw between the halves of a large oak log, covered, in the event of rain, with a rubber blanket. The more ambitious builders made straw pens, several logs high, and pitched over these a fly-tent, adding sometimes a chimney. In this structure, by the aid of a bountiful supply of dry, clean straw, and their blankets, the occupants bade defiance to cold, rain, and snow.

Other men, gifted with that strange facility for comfort without work which characterizes some people, found resting-places ready made. They managed to steal away night after night and sleep in the sweet security of a haystack, a barn, a stable, a porch, or, if fortune favored them, in some farmer's feather bed.

Others still, but more especially the infantry and cavalry, built "shelters" open to the south, covered them with pine-tags and brush, built a huge fire in front, and made themselves at home for a season.

But all these things were mere make-shifts, temporary stopping-places, occupying about the same relation to winter quarters as the boarding-house does to a happy and comfortable home.

And now another night comes to the soldier, inviting him to nestle in clean straw, under dry blankets, and sleep. To-morrow he will lay the foundation of a village destined to live till the grass grows again. To-morrow he will be architect, builder, and proprietor of a cozy cabin in the woods. Let him sleep.

A pine wood of heavy original growth furnishes the ground and the timber. Each company is to have two rows of houses, with a street between, and each street is to end on the main road to the railroad depot. The width of the street is decided; it is staked off; each "mess" selects its site for a house, and the work commences.

The old pines fall rapidly under the energetic strokes of the axes, which glide into the hearts of the trees with a malicious and cruel willingness; the logs are cut into lengths, notched and fitted one upon another, and the structure begins to rise. The builders stagger about here and there, under the weight of the huge logs, occasionally falling and rolling in the snow. They shout and whistle and sing, and are as merry as children at play.

At last the topmost log is rolled into place and the artistic work commences, the "riving" of slabs. Short logs of oak are to be split into huge shingles for the roof, and tough and tedious work it is. But it is done; the roof is covered in, and the house is far enough advanced for occupancy.

Now the "bunks," which are simply broad shelves one above another, wide enough to accommodate two men "spoon fashion," are built. Merry parties sally forth to seek the straw stack of the genial farmer of the period, and, returning heavily laden with sweet clean straw, bestow it in the bunks. Here they rest for a night.

Next day the chimney, built like the house, of notched sticks or small logs, rises rapidly, till it reaches the apex of the roof and is crowned with a nail keg or flour barrel.

Next, a pit is dug deep enough to reach the clay; water is poured in and the clay well mixed, and the whole mess takes in hand the "daubing" of the "chinks." Every crack and crevice of house and chimney receives attention at the hands of the builders, and when the sun goes down the house is proof against the most searching winter wind.

Now the most skillful man contrives a door and swings it on its hinges; another makes a shelf for the old water bucket; a short bench or two appear, like magicians' work, before the fire, and the family is settled for the winter.

It would be a vain man indeed who thought himself able to describe the happy days and cozy nights of that camp. First among the luxuries of settled life was the opportunity to part forever with a suit of underwear which had been on constant duty for, possibly, three months, and put on the sweet clean clothes from home. They looked so pure, and the very smell of them was sweet.

Then there was the ever-present thought of a dry, warm, undisturbed sleep the whole night through. What a comfort!

Remember, now, there is a pile of splendid oak, ready cut for the fire, within easy reach of the door—several cords of it—and it is all ours. Our mess cut it and "toted" it there. It will keep a good fire, night and day, for a month.

The wagons, which have been "over the mountains and far away," have come into camp loaded with the best flour in abundance; droves of cattle are bellowing in the road, and our commissary, as he hurries from camp to camp with the glad tidings, is the embodiment of happiness. All this means plenty to eat.

This is a good time to make and carve beautiful pipes of hard wood with horn mouthpieces, very comfortable chairs, bread trays, haversacks, and a thousand other conveniences.

At night the visiting commences, and soon in many huts are little social groups close around the fire. The various incidents of the campaign pass in review, and pealing laughter rings out upon the crisp winter air. Then a soft, sweet melody floats out of that cabin door as the favorite singer yields to the entreaty of his little circle of friends; or a swelling chorus of manly voices, chanting a grand and solemn anthem, stirs every heart for half a mile around.

Now think of an old Confederate veteran, who passed through Fredericksburg, Chancellorsville, and the Wilderness, sitting in front of a cheerful fire in a snug log cabin, reading, say, "The Spectator!" Think of another by his side reading a letter from his sweetheart; and another still, a warm and yearning letter from his mother. Think of two others in the corner playing "old sledge," or, it may be, chess. Hear another, "off guard," snoring in his bunk. Ah! what an amount of condensed contentment that little hut contains.

And now the stables are finished. The whole battalion did the work, and the poor old shivering and groaning horses are under cover. And the guard-house, another joint production, opens wide its door every day to receive the unhappy men whose time for detail has at last arrived. The chapel, an afterthought, is also ready for use, having been duly dedicated to the worship of God. The town is complete and its citizens are happy.

Men thus comfortably fixed, with light guard duty and little else to do, found time, of course, to do a little foraging in the country around. By this means often during the winter the camp enjoyed great abundance and variety of food. Apples and apple-butter, fresh pork, dried fruit, milk, eggs, risen bread, and even cakes and preserves. Occasionally a whole mess would be filled with the liveliest expectations by the information that "Bob" or "Joe" was expecting a box from home. The wagon comes into camp escorted by the expectant "Bob" and several of his intimate friends; the box is dropped from the wagon to the ground; off goes the top and in go busy hands and eyes. Here are clothes, shoes, and hats; here is coffee, sugar, soda, salt, bread, fresh butter, roast beef, and turkey; here is a bottle! marked "to be used in case of sickness or wounds." Here is paper, ink, pen and pencil. What shall be done with this pile of treasure? It is evident one man cannot eat the eatables or smoke the tobacco and pipes. Call in, then, the friendly aid of willing comrades. They come; they see; they devour!

And now the ever true and devoted citizens of the much and often besieged city of Richmond conclude to send a New Year's dinner to their defenders in the army. That portion destined for the camp above described arrived in due time in the shape of one good turkey. Each of the three companies composing the battalion appointed a man to "draw straws" for the turkey; the successful company appointed a man from each detachment to draw again; then the detachment messes took a draw, and the fortunate mess devoured the turkey. But the soldiers, remembering that in times past they had felt constrained to divide their rations with the poor of that city, did not fail in gratitude, or question the liberality of those who had, in the midst of great distress, remembered with self-denying affection the soldiers in the field.

Not the least among the comforts of life in winter quarters, was the pleasure of sitting under the ministrations of an amateur barber, and hearing the snip, snip, of his scissors, as the long growth of hair fell to the ground. The luxury of "a shave"; the possession of comb, brush, small mirror, towels and soap; boots blacked every day; white collars, and occasionally a starched bosom, called, in the expressive language of the day, a "biled shirt," completed the restoration of the man to decency. Now, also, the soldier with painful care threaded his needle with huge thread, and with a sort of left-handed awkwardness sewed on the long-absent button, or, with even greater trepidation, attempted a patch. At such a time the soldier pondered on the peculiar fact that war separates men from women. A man cannot thread a needle with ease; certainly not with grace. He sews backwards.

In winter quarters every man had his "chum" or bunk-mate, with whom he slept, walked, talked, and divided hardship or comfort as they came along; and the affectionate regard of each for the other was often beautiful to see. Many such attachments led to heroic self-denials and death, one for the other, and many such unions remain unbroken after twenty years have passed away.

It was a rare occurrence, but occasionally the father or mother or brother or sister of some man paid him a visit. The males were almost sure to be very old or very young. In either case they were received with great hospitality, given the best place to sleep, the best the camp afforded in the way of eatables, and treated with the greatest courtesy and kindness by the whole command. But the lady visitors! the girls! Who could describe the effect of their appearance in camp! They produced conflict in the soldier's breast. They looked so clean, they were so gentle, they were so different from all around them, they were so attractive, they were so agreeable, and sweet, and fresh, and happy, that the poor fellows would have liked above all things to have gotten very near to them and have heard their kind words—possibly shake hands; but no, some were barefooted, some almost bareheaded; some were still expecting clean clothes from home; some were sick and disheartened; some were on guard; some *in the guard-house*, and others too modest; and so, to many, the innocent visitor became a sort of pleasant agony; as it were, a "bitter sweet." Nothing ever so promptly convinced a Confederate soldier that he was dilapidated and not altogether as neat as he might be, as sudden precipitation into the presence of a neatly dressed, refined, and modest woman. Fortunately for the men, the women loved the very rags they wore, if they were gray; and when the war ended, they welcomed with open arms and hearts full of love the man and his rags.

With the men who composed the Army of Northern Virginia will die the memory of those little things which made the Confederate soldier peculiarly what he was.

The historian who essays to write the "grand movements" will hardly stop to tell how the hungry private fried his bacon, baked his biscuit, and smoked his pipe; how he was changed from time to time by the necessities of the service, until the gentleman, the student, the merchant, the mechanic, and the farmer were merged into a perfect, all-enduring, never-tiring and invincible soldier. To preserve these little details, familiar to all soldiers, and by them not thought worthy of mention to others, because of their familiarity, but still dear to them and always the substance of their "war talks," is the object of this book.

The volunteer of 1861 made extensive preparations for the field. Boots, he thought, were an absolute necessity, and the heavier the soles and longer the tops the better. His pants were stuffed inside the tops of his boots, of course. A double-breasted coat, heavily wadded, with two rows of big brass buttons and a long skirt, was considered comfortable. A small stiff cap, with a narrow brim, took the place of the comfortable "felt," or the shining and towering tile worn in civil life.

Then over all was a huge overcoat, long and heavy, with a cape reaching nearly to the waist. On his back he strapped a knapsack containing a full stock of underwear, soap, towels, comb, brush, looking-glass, tooth-brush, paper and envelopes, pens, ink, pencils, blacking, photographs, smoking and chewing tobacco, pipes, twine string, and cotton strips for wounds and other emergencies, needles and thread, buttons, knife, fork, and spoon, and many other things as each man's idea of what he was to encounter varied. On the outside of the knapsack, solidly folded, were two great blankets and a rubber or oil-cloth. This knapsack, etc., weighed from fifteen to twenty-five pounds, sometimes even more. All seemed to think it was impossible to have on too many or too heavy clothes, or to have too many conveniences, and each had an idea that to be a good soldier he must be provided against every possible emergency.

In addition to the knapsack, each man had a haversack, more or less costly, some of cloth and some of fine morocco, and stored with provisions always, as though he expected any moment to receive orders to march across the Great Desert, and supply his own wants on the way. A canteen was considered indispensable, and at the outset it was thought prudent to keep it full of water. Many, expecting terrific hand-to-hand encounters, carried revolvers, and even bowie-knives. Merino shirts (and flannel) were thought to be the right thing, but experience demonstrated the contrary. Gloves were also thought to be very necessary and good things to have in winter time, the favorite style being buck gauntlets with long cuffs.

In addition to each man's private luggage, each mess, generally composed of from five to ten men, drawn together by similar tastes and associations, had its outfit, consisting of a large camp chest containing skillet, frying pan, coffee boiler, bucket for lard, coffee box, salt box, sugar box, meal box, flour box, knives, forks, spoons, plates, cups, etc., etc. These chests were so large that eight or ten of them filled up an army wagon, and were so heavy that two strong men had all they could do to get one of them into the wagon. In addition to the chest each mess owned an axe, water bucket, and bread tray. Then the tents of each company, and little sheet-iron stoves, and stove pipe, and the trunks and valises of the company officers, made an immense pile of stuff, so that each company had a small wagon train of its own.

All thought money to be absolutely necessary, and for awhile rations were disdained and the mess supplied with the best that could be bought with the mess fund. Quite a large number had a "boy" along to do the cooking and washing. Think of it! a Confederate soldier with a body servant all his own, to bring him a drink of water, black his boots, dust his clothes, cook his corn bread and bacon, and put wood on his fire. Never was there fonder admiration than these darkies displayed for their masters. Their chief delight and glory was to praise the courage and good looks of "Mahse Tom," and prophesy great things about his future. Many a ringing laugh and shout of fun originated in the queer remarks, shining countenance, and glistening teeth of this now forever departed character.

It is amusing to think of the follies of the early part of the war, as illustrated by the outfits of the volunteers. They were so heavily clad, and so burdened with all manner of things, that a march was torture, and the wagon trains were so immense in proportion to the number of troops, that it would have been impossible to guard them in an enemy's country. Subordinate officers thought themselves entitled to transportation for trunks, mattresses, and folding bedsteads, and the privates were as ridiculous in their demands.

Thus much by way of introduction. The change came rapidly, and stayed not until the transformation was complete. Nor was this change attributable alone to the orders of the general officers. The men soon learned the inconvenience and danger of so much luggage, and, as they became more experienced, they vied with each other in reducing themselves to light-marching trim.

Experience soon demonstrated that boots were not agreeable on a long march. They were heavy and irksome, and when the heels were worn a little one-sided, the wearer would find his ankle twisted nearly out of joint by every unevenness of the road. When thoroughly wet, it was a laborious undertaking to get them off, and worse to get them on in time to answer the morning roll-call. And so, good, strong brogues or brogans, with broad bottoms and big, flat heels, succeeded the boots, and were found much more comfortable and agreeable, easier put on and off, and altogether the more sensible.

A short-waisted and single-breasted jacket usurped the place of the long-tailed coat, and became universal. The enemy noticed this peculiarity, and called the Confederates gray jackets, which name was immediately transferred to those lively creatures which were the constant admirers and inseparable companions of the Boys in Gray and in Blue.

Caps were destined to hold out longer than some other uncomfortable things, but they finally yielded to the demands of comfort and common sense, and a good soft felt hat was worn instead. A man who has never been a soldier does not know, nor indeed can know, the amount of comfort there is in a good soft hat in camp, and how utterly useless is a "soldier hat" as they are generally made. Why the Prussians, with all their experience, wear their heavy, unyielding helmets, and the French their little caps, is a mystery to a Confederate who has enjoyed the comfort of an old slouch.

Overcoats an inexperienced man would think an absolute necessity for men exposed to the rigors of a northern Virginia winter, but they grew scarcer and scarcer; they were found to be a great inconvenience. The men came to the conclusion that the trouble of carrying them on hot days outweighed the comfort of having them when the cold day arrived. Besides they found that life in the open air hardened them to such an extent that changes in the temperature were not felt to any degree. Some clung to their overcoats to the last, but the majority got tired lugging them around, and either discarded them altogether, or trusted to capturing one about the time it would be needed. Nearly every overcoat in the army in the latter years was one of Uncle Sam's captured from his boys.

The knapsack vanished early in the struggle. It was inconvenient to "change" the underwear too often, and the disposition not to change grew, as the knapsack was found to gall the back and shoulders, and weary the man before half the march was accomplished. The better way was to dress out and out, and wear that outfit until the enemy's knapsacks, or the folks at home supplied a change. Certainly it did not pay to carry around clean clothes while waiting for the time to use them.

Very little washing was done, as a matter of course. Clothes once given up were parted with forever. There were good reasons for this: cold water would not cleanse them or destroy the vermin, and hot water was not always to be had. One blanket to each man was found to be as much as could be carried, and amply sufficient for the severest weather. This was carried generally by rolling it lengthwise, with the rubber cloth outside, tying the ends of the roll together, and throwing the loop thus made over the left shoulder with the ends fastened together hanging under the right arm.

The haversack held its own to the last, and was found practical and useful. It very seldom, however, contained rations, but was used to carry all the articles generally carried in the knapsack; of course the stock was small. Somehow or other, many men managed to do without the haversack, and carried absolutely nothing but what they wore and had in their pockets.

The infantry threw away their heavy cap boxes and cartridge boxes, and carried their caps and cartridges in their pockets. Canteens were very useful at times, but they were as a general thing discarded. They were not much used to carry water, but were found useful when the men were driven to the necessity of foraging, for conveying buttermilk, cider, sorghum, etc., to camp. A good strong tin cup was found better than a canteen, as it was easier to fill at a well or spring, and was serviceable as a boiler for making coffee when the column halted for the night.

Revolvers were found to be about as useless and heavy lumber as a private soldier could carry, and early in the war were sent home to be used by the women and children in protecting themselves from insult and violence at the hands of the ruffians who prowled about the country shirking duty.

Strong cotton was adopted in place of flannel and merino, for two reasons: first, because easier to wash; and second, because the vermin did not propagate so rapidly in cotton as in wool. Common white cotton shirts and drawers proved the best that could be used by the private soldier.

Gloves to any but a mounted man were found useless, worse than useless. With the gloves on, it was impossible to handle an axe, buckle harness, load a musket, or handle a rammer at the piece. Wearing them was found to be simply a habit, and so, on the principle that the less luggage the less labor, they were discarded.

The camp-chest soon vanished. The brigadiers and major-generals, even, found them too troublesome, and soon they were left entirely to the quartermasters and commissaries. One skillet and a couple of frying pans, a bag for flour or meal, another bag for salt, sugar, and coffee, divided by a knot tied between, served the purpose as well. The skillet passed from mess to mess. Each mess generally owned a frying pan, but often one served a company. The oil-cloth was found to be as good as the wooden tray for making up the dough. The water bucket held its own to the last!

Tents were rarely seen. All the poetry about the "tented field" died. Two men slept together, each having a blanket and an oil-cloth; one oil-cloth went next to the ground. The two laid on this, covered themselves with two blankets, protected from the rain with the second oil-cloth on top, and slept very comfortably through rain, snow or hail, as it might be.

Very little money was seen in camp. The men did not expect, did not care for, or often get any pay, and they were not willing to deprive the old folks at home of their little supply, so they learned to do without any money.

When rations got short and were getting shorter, it became necessary to dismiss the darkey servants. Some, however, became company servants, instead of private institutions, and held out faithfully to the end, cooking the rations away in the rear, and at the risk of life carrying them to the line of battle to their "young mahsters."

Reduced to the minimum, the private soldier consisted of one man, one hat, one jacket, one shirt, one pair of pants, one pair of drawers, one pair of shoes, and one pair of socks. His baggage was one blanket, one rubber blanket, and one haversack. The haversack generally contained smoking tobacco and a pipe, and a small piece of soap, with temporary additions of apples, persimmons, blackberries, and such other commodities as he could pick up on the march.

The company property consisted of two or three skillets and frying pans, which were sometimes carried in the wagon, but oftener in the hands of the soldiers. The infantrymen generally preferred to stick the handle of the frying pan in the barrel of a musket, and so carry it.

The wagon trains were devoted entirely to the transportation of ammunition and commissary and quartermaster's stores, which had not been issued. Rations which had become company property, and the baggage of the men, when they had any, was carried by the men themselves. If, as was sometimes the case, three days' rations were issued at one time and the troops ordered to cook them, and be prepared to march, they did cook them, and eat them if possible, so as to avoid the labor of carrying them. It was not such an undertaking either, to eat three days' rations in one, as frequently none had been issued for more than a day, and when issued were cut down one half.

The infantry found out that bayonets were not of much use, and did not hesitate to throw them, with the scabbard, away.

The artillerymen, who started out with heavy sabres hanging to their belts, stuck them up in the mud as they marched, and left them for the ordnance officers to pick up and turn over to the cavalry.

The cavalrymen found sabres very tiresome when swung to the belt, and adopted the plan of fastening them to the saddle on the left side, with the hilt in front and in reach of the hand. Finally sabres got very scarce even among the cavalrymen, who relied more and more on their short rifles.

No soldiers ever marched with less to encumber them, and none marched faster or held out longer.

The courage and devotion of the men rose equal to every hardship and privation, and the very intensity of their sufferings became a source of merriment. Instead of growling and deserting, they laughed at their own bare feet, ragged clothes and pinched faces; and weak, hungry, cold, wet, worried with vermin and itch, dirty, with no hope of reward or rest, marched cheerfully to meet the well-fed and warmly clad hosts of the enemy.

CHAPTER 35

A Woman's Wartime Journal

By Dolly Sumner Lunt

Women such as Alcott, Pember, and Edmonds chose to work in the thick of things, but staying at home was no guarantee of security for women, especially those in the South. With so many men away fighting the war, women were left on their own to run businesses, farms, and entire plantations without help from their husbands, fathers, or sons. Dolly Sumner Lunt, a widow who kept a plantation in Georgia with her small daughter, Sadai, and what was left of her slaves, details the terrifying days of Sherman's march to the sea that took the army through her hometown and her home.

—LISA PURCELL

November 17, 1864

Have been uneasy all day. At night some of the neighbors who had been to town called. They said it was a large force moving very slowly. What shall I do? Where go?

November 18, 1864

Slept very little last night. Went out doors several times and could see large fires like burning buildings. Am I not in the hands of a merciful God who has promised to take care of the widow and orphan?

Sent off two of my mules in the night. Mr. Ward and Frank took them away and hid them. In the morning took a barrel of salt, which had cost me two hundred dollars, into one of the black women's gardens, put a paper over it, and then on the top of that leached ashes. Fixed it on a board as a leach tub, daubing it with ashes. Had some few pieces of meat taken from my smoke-house carried to the Old Place and hidden under some fodder. Bid them hide the wagon and gear and then go on plowing. Went to packing up mine and Sadai's clothes. I fear that we shall be homeless.

The boys came back and wished to hide their mules. They say that the Yankees camped at Mr. Gibson's last night and are taking all the stock in the county. Seeing them so eager, I told them to do as they pleased. They took them off, and Elbert took his forty fattening hogs to the Old Place Swamp and turned them in.

We have done nothing all day—that is, my people have not. I made a pair of pants for Jack. Sent Nute up to Mrs. Perry's on an errand. On his way back, he said, two Yankees met him and begged him to go with them. They asked if we had livestock, and came up the road as far as Mrs. Laura Perry's. I sat for an hour expecting them, but they must have gone back. Oh, how I trust I am safe! Mr. Ward is very much alarmed.

November 19, 1864

Slept in my clothes last night, as I heard that the Yankees went to neighbor Montgomery's on Thursday night at one o'clock, searched his house, drank his wine, and took his money and valuables. As we were not disturbed, I walked after breakfast, with Sadai, up to Mr. Joe Perry's, my nearest neighbor, where the Yankees were yesterday. Saw Mrs. Laura in the road surrounded by her children, seeming to be looking for someone. She said she was looking for her husband, that old Mrs. Perry had just sent her word that the Yankees went to James Perry's the night before, plundered his house, and drove off all his stock, and that she must drive hers into the old fields. Before we were done talking, up came Joe and Jim Perry from their hiding-place. Jim was very much excited. Happening to turn and look behind, as we stood there, I saw some blue-coats coming down the hill. Jim immediately raised his gun, swearing he would kill them anyhow.

"No, don't!" said I, and ran home as fast as I could, with Sadai.

I could hear them cry, "Halt! Halt!" and their guns went off in quick succession. Oh Clod, the time of trial has come!

A man passed on his way to Covington. I halloed to him, asking him if he did not know the Yankees were coming.

"No—are they?"

"Yes," said I; "they are not three hundred yards from here."

"Sure enough," said he. "Well, I'll not go. I don't want them to get my horse." And although within hearing of their guns, he would stop and look for them. Blissful ignorance! Not knowing, not hearing, he has not suffered the suspense, the fear, that I have for the past forty-eight hours. I walked to the gate. There they came filing up.

I hastened back to my frightened servants and told them that they had better hide, and then went back to the gate to claim protection and a guard. But like demons they rush in! My yards are full. To my smoke-house, my dairy, pantry, kitchen, and cellar, like famished wolves they come, breaking locks and whatever is in their way. The thousand pounds of meat in my smoke-house is gone in a twinkling, my flour, my meat, my lard, butter, eggs, pickles of various kinds—both in vinegar and brine—wine, jars, and jugs are all gone. My eighteen fat turkeys, my hens, chickens, and fowls, my young pigs, are shot down in my yard and hunted as if they were rebels themselves. Utterly powerless I ran out and appealed to the guard.

"I cannot help you, Madam; it is orders."

As I stood there, from my lot I saw driven, first, old Dutch, my dear old buggy horse, who has carried my beloved husband so many miles, and who would so quietly wait at the block for him to mount and dismount, and who at last drew him to his grave; then came old Mary, my brood mare, who for years had been too old and stiff for work, with her three-year-old colt, my two-year-old mule, and her last little baby colt. There they go! There go my mules, my sheep, and, worse than all, my boys!

Alas! little did I think while trying to save my house from plunder and fire that they were forcing my boys from home at the point of the bayonet. One, Newton, jumped into bed in his cabin, and declared himself sick. Another crawled under the floor—a lame boy he was—but they pulled him out, placed him on a horse, and drove him off. Mid, poor Mid! The last I saw of him, a man had him going around the garden, looking, as I thought, for my sheep, as he was my shepherd. Jack came crying to me, the big tears coursing down his cheeks, saying they were making him go. I said:

"Stay in my room."

But a man followed in, cursing him and threatening to shoot him if he did not go; so poor Jack had to yield. James Arnold, in trying to escape from a back window, was captured and marched off. Henry, too, was taken; I know not how or when, but probably when he and Bob went after the mules. . . .

My poor boys! My poor boys! What unknown trials are before you! How you have clung to your mistress and assisted her in every way you knew.

Never have I corrected them; a word was sufficient. Never have they known want of any kind. Their parents are with me, and how sadly they lament the loss of their boys. Their cabins are rifled of every valuable, the soldiers swearing that their Sunday clothes were the white people's, and that they never had money to get such things as they had. Poor Frank's chest was broken open, his money and tobacco taken. He has always been a money-making and saving boy; not infrequently has his crop brought him five hundred dollars and more. All of his clothes and Rachel's clothes, which dear Lou gave before her death and which she had packed away, were stolen from her. Ovens, skillets, coffee-mills, of which we had three, coffee-pots—not one have I left. Sifters all gone!

Seeing that the soldiers could not be restrained, the guard offered me to have their remaining possessions brought into my house, which I did, and they all, poor things, huddled together in my room, fearing every movement that the house would be burned.

A Captain Webber from Illinois came into my house. Of him I claimed protection from the vandals who were forcing themselves into my room. He said that he knew my brother Orrington. At that name I could not restrain my feelings, but, bursting into tears, implored him to see my brother and let him know my destitution. I saw nothing before me but starvation. He promised to do this, and comforted me with the assurance that my dwelling-house would not be burned, though my out-buildings might. Poor little Sadai went crying to him as to a friend and told him that they had taken her doll, Nancy. He begged her to come and see him, and he would give her a fine waxen one.

He felt for me, and I give him and several others the character of gentlemen. I don't believe they would have molested women and children had they had their own way. He seemed surprised that I had not laid away in my house, flour and other provisions. I did not suppose I could secure them there, more than where I usually kept them, for in last summer's raid houses were thoroughly searched. In parting with him; I parted as with a friend.

Sherman himself and a greater portion of his army passed my house that day. All day, as the sad moments rolled on, were they passing not only in front of my house, but from behind; they tore down my garden palings, made a road through my back-yard and lot field, driving their stock and riding through, tearing down my fences and desolating my home—wantonly doing it when there was no necessity for it.

Such a day, if I live to the age of Methuselah, may God spare me from ever seeing again!

As night drew its sable curtains around us, the heavens from every point were lit up with flames from burning buildings. Dinnerless and supperless as we were, it was nothing in comparison with the fear of being driven out homeless to the dreary woods. Nothing to eat! I could give my guard no supper, so he left us. I appealed to another, asking him if he had wife, mother, or sister, and how he should feel were they in my situation. A colonel from Vermont left me two men, but they were Dutch, and I could not understand one word they said.

My Heavenly Father alone saved me from the destructive fire. My carriage-house had in it eight bales of cotton, with my carriage, buggy, and harness. On top of the cotton were some carded cotton rolls, a hundred pounds or more. These were thrown out of the blanket in which they were, and a large twist of the rolls taken and set on fire, and thrown into the boat of my carriage, which was close up to the cotton bales. Thanks to my God, the cotton only burned over, and then went out. Shall I ever forget the deliverance?

To-night, when the greater part of the army had passed, it came up very windy and cold. My room was full, nearly, with the negroes and their bedding. They were afraid to go out, for my women could not step out of the door without an insult from the Yankee soldiers. They lay down on the floor; Sadai got down and under the same cover with Sally, while I sat up all night, watching every moment for the flames to burst out from some of my buildings. The two guards came into my room and laid themselves by my fire for the night. I could not close my eyes, but kept walking to and fro, watching the fires in the distance and dreading the approaching day, which, I feared, as they had not all passed, would be but a continuation of horrors.

November 20, 1864

This is the blessed Sabbath, the day upon which He who came to bring peace and good will upon earth rose from His tomb and ascended to intercede for us poor fallen creatures. But how unlike this day to any that have preceded it in my once quiet home. I had watched all night, and the dawn found me watching for the moving of the soldiery that was encamped about us. Oh, how I dreaded those that were to pass, as I supposed they would straggle and complete the ruin that the others had commenced, for I had been repeatedly told that they would burn everything as they passed.

Some of my women had gathered up a chicken that the soldiers shot yesterday, and they cooked it with some yams for our breakfast, the guard complaining that we gave them no supper. They gave us some coffee, which I had to make in a tea-kettle, as every coffee pot is taken off. The rear-guard was commanded by Colonel Carlow, who changed our guard, leaving us one soldier while they were passing. They marched directly on, scarcely breaking ranks. Once a bucket of water was called for, but they drank without coming in.

About ten o'clock they had all passed save one, who came in and wanted coffee made, which was done, and he, too, went on. A few minutes elapsed, and two couriers riding rapidly passed back. Then, presently, more soldiers came by, and this ended the passing of Sherman's army by my place, leaving me poorer by thirty thousand dollars than I was yesterday morning. And a much stronger Rebel!

After the excitement was a little over, I went up to Mrs. Laura's to sympathize with her, for I had no doubt but that her husband was hanged. She thought so, and we could see no way for his escape. We all took a good cry together. While there, I saw smoke looming up in the direction of my home, and thought surely the fiends had done their work ere they left. I ran as fast as I could, but soon saw that the fire was below my home. It proved to be the gin house belonging to Colonel Pitts.

My boys have not come home. I fear they cannot get away from the soldiers. Two of my cows came up this morning, but were driven off again by the Yankees.

I feel so thankful that I have not been burned out that I have tried to spend the remainder of the day as the Sabbath ought to be spent. Ate dinner out of the oven in Julia's house, some stew, no bread. She is boiling some corn. My poor servants feel so badly at losing what they have worked for; meat, the hog meat that they love better than anything else, is all gone.

November 21, 1864

We had the table laid this morning, but no bread or butter or milk. What a prospect for delicacies! My house is a perfect fright. I had brought in Saturday night some thirty bushels of potatoes and ten or fifteen bushels of wheat poured down on the carpet in the ell. Then the few gallons of syrup saved was daubed all about. The backbone of a hog that I had killed on Friday, and which the Yankees did not take when they cleaned out my smokehouse, I found and hid under my bed, and this is all the meat I have. Major Lee came down this evening, having heard that I was burned out, to proffer me a home. Mr. Dorsett was with him. The army lost some of their beeves in passing. I sent to-day and had some driven into my lot, and then sent to Judge Glass to come over and get some. Had two killed. Some of Wheeler's men came in, and I asked them to shoot the cattle, which they did.

About ten o'clock this morning Mr. Joe Perry called. I was so glad to see him that I could scarcely forbear embracing him. I could not keep from crying, for I was sure the Yankees had executed him, and I felt so much for his poor wife. The soldiers told me repeatedly Saturday that they had hung him and his brother James and George Guise. They had a narrow escape, however, and only got away by knowing the country so much better than the soldiers did. They lay out until this morning. How rejoiced I am for his family! All of his negroes are gone, save one man that had a wife here at my plantation. They are very strong Secesh. When the army first came along they offered a guard for the house, but Mrs. Laura told them she was guarded by a Higher Power, and did not thank them to do it. She says that she could think of nothing else all day when the army was passing but of the devil and his hosts. She had, however, to call for a guard before night or the soldiers would have taken everything she had.

November 22, 1864

After breakfast this morning I went over to my grave-yard to see what had befallen that. To my joy, I found it had not been disturbed. As I stood by my dead, I felt rejoiced that they were at rest. Never have I felt so perfectly reconciled to the death of my husband as I do to-day, while looking upon the ruin of his lifelong labor. How it would have grieved him to see such destruction! Yes, theirs is the lot to be envied. At rest, rest from care, rest from heartaches, from trouble. . . .

Found one of my large hogs killed just outside the grave-yard.

Walked down to the swamp, looking for the wagon and gear that Henry hid before he was taken off. Found some of my sheep; came home very much wearied, having walked over four miles.

Mr. and Mrs. Rockmore called. Major Lee came down again after some cattle, and while he was here the alarm was given that more Yankees were coming. I was terribly alarmed and packed my trunks with clothing, feeling assured that we should be burned out now. Major Lee swore that he would shoot, which frightened me, for he was intoxicated enough to make him ambitious. He rode off in the direction whence it was said they were coming, Soon after, however, he returned, saying it was a false alarm, that it was some of our own men. Oh, dear! Are we to be always living in fear and dread! Oh, the horrors, the horrors of war!

CHAPTER 36

A Horseman in the Sky
By Ambrose Bierce

Newspaper columnist, satirist, essayist, short-story writer, and novelist Ambrose Bierce also chose to illustrate the consequences of divided loyalties in the haunting short story "A Horseman in the Sky." Bierce was himself a veteran of the war, fighting for the Union at several major battles, including Shiloh and Chickamauga, before he was severely wounded in the head at Kennesaw Mountain. "A Horseman in the Sky" is the tale of Carter Druse, a young Virginian whose conscience tells him he must fight for the Union. This is a heartbreaking decision for his proud Southern father, who can only tell him, "Well, go, sir, and whatever may occur do what you conceive to be your duty." For this one young man, however, following that advice costs him that which is most precious to him.

—LISA PURCELL

I

ONE SUNNY AFTERNOON IN THE AUTUMN OF THE YEAR 1861 A SOLDIER LAY IN A CLUMP of laurel by the side of a road in western Virginia. He lay at full length upon his stomach, his feet resting upon the toes, his head upon the left forearm. His extended right hand loosely grasped his rifle. But for the somewhat methodical disposition of his limbs and a slight rhythmic movement of the cartridge-box at the back of his belt he might have been thought to be dead. He was asleep at his post of duty. But if detected he would be dead shortly afterward, death being the just and legal penalty of his crime.

The clump of laurel in which the criminal lay was in the angle of a road which after ascending southward a steep acclivity to that point turned sharply to the west, running on the summit for perhaps one hundred yards. There it turned southward again and went zigzagging downward through the forest. At the salient of that second angle was a large flat rock, jutting out northward, overlooking the deep valley from which the road ascended.

The rock capped a high cliff; a stone dropped from its outer edge would have fallen sheer downward one thousand feet to the tops of the pines. The angle where the soldier lay was on another spur of the same cliff. Had he been awake he would have commanded a view, not only of the short arm of the road and the jutting rock, but of the entire profile of the cliff below it. It might well have made him giddy to look.

The country was wooded everywhere except at the bottom of the valley to the north-ward, where there was a small natural meadow, through which flowed a stream scarcely visi-ble from the valley's rim. This open ground looked hardly larger than an ordinary door-yard, but was really several acres in extent. Its green was more vivid than that of the enclosing forest. Away beyond it rose a line of giant cliffs similar to those upon which we are supposed to stand in our survey of the savage scene, and through which the road had somehow made its climb to the summit. The configuration of the valley, indeed, was such that from this point of observation it seemed entirely shut in, and one could but have wondered how the road which found a way out of it had found a way into it, and whence came and whither went the waters of the stream that parted the meadow more than a thousand feet below.

No country is so wild and difficult but men will make it a theater of war; concealed in the forest at the bottom of that military rat-trap, in which half a hundred men in posses-sion of the exits might have starved an army to submission, lay five regiments of Federal infantry. They had marched all the previous day and night and were resting. At nightfall they would take to the road again, climb to the place where their unfaithful sentinel now slept, and descending the other slope of the ridge fall upon a camp of the enemy at about midnight. Their hope was to surprise it, for the road led to the rear of it. In case of failure, their position would be perilous in the extreme; and fall they surely would should accident or vigilance apprise the enemy of the movement.

II

The sleeping sentinel in the clump of laurel was a young Virginian named Carter Druse. He was the son of wealthy parents, an only child, and had known such ease and cultivation and high living as wealth and taste were able to command in the mountain country of western Virginia. His home was but a few miles from where he now lay. One morning he had risen from the breakfast-table and said, quietly but gravely: "Father, a Union regiment has arrived at Grafton. I am going to join it."

The father lifted his leonine head, looked at the son a moment in silence, and replied: "Well, go, sir, and whatever may occur do what you conceive to be your duty. Virginia, to which you are a traitor, must get on without you. Should we both live to the end of the war, we will speak further of the matter. Your mother, as the physician has informed you, is in a most critical condition; at the best she cannot be with us longer than a few weeks, but that time is precious. It would be better not to disturb her."

So Carter Druse, bowing reverently to his father, who returned the salute with a stately courtesy that masked a breaking heart, left the home of his childhood to go soldiering. By conscience and courage, by deeds of devotion and daring, he soon commended himself to his fellows and his officers; and it was to these qualities and to some knowledge of the country that he owed his selection for his present perilous duty at the extreme outpost. Nevertheless, fatigue had been stronger than resolution and he had fallen asleep. What good or bad angel came in a dream to rouse him from his state of crime, who shall say? Without a movement, without a sound, in the profound silence and the languor of the late afternoon, some invisible messenger of fate touched with unsealing finger the eyes of his consciousness—whispered into the ear of his spirit the mysterious awakening word which no human lips ever have spoken, no human memory ever has recalled. He quietly raised his forehead from his arm and looked between the masking stems of the laurels, instinctively closing his right hand about the stock of his rifle.

His first feeling was a keen artistic delight. On a colossal pedestal, the cliff—motionless at the extreme edge of the capping rock and sharply outlined against the sky—was an equestrian statue of impressive dignity. The figure of the man sat the figure of the horse, straight and soldierly, but with the repose of a Grecian god carved in the marble which limits the suggestion of activity. The gray costume harmonized with its aerial background; the metal of accoutrement and caparison was softened and subdued by the shadow; the animal's skin had no points of high light. A carbine strikingly foreshortened lay across the pommel of the saddle, kept in place by the right hand grasping it at the "grip"; the left hand, holding the bridle rein, was invisible. In silhouette against the sky the profile of the horse was cut with the sharpness of a cameo; it looked across the heights of air to the confronting cliffs beyond. The face of the rider, turned slightly away, showed only an outline of temple and beard; he was looking downward to the bottom of the valley. Magnified by its lift against the sky and by the soldier's testifying sense of the formidableness of a near enemy the group appeared of heroic, almost colossal, size.

For an instant Druse had a strange, half-defined feeling that he had slept to the end of the war and was looking upon a noble work of art reared upon that eminence to commemorate the deeds of an heroic past of which he had been an inglorious part. The feeling was dispelled by a slight movement of the group: the horse, without moving its feet, had drawn its body slightly backward from the verge; the man remained immobile as before. Broad awake and keenly alive to the significance of the situation, Druse now brought the butt of his rifle against his cheek by cautiously pushing the barrel forward through the bushes, cocked the piece, and glancing through the sights covered a vital spot of the horseman's breast. A touch upon the trigger and all would have been well with Carter Druse. At that instant the horseman turned his head and looked in the direction of his concealed foeman—seemed to look into his very face, into his eyes, into his brave, compassionate heart.

Is it then so terrible to kill an enemy in war—an enemy who has surprised a secret vital to the safety of one's self and comrades—an enemy more formidable for his knowledge than all his army for its numbers? Carter Druse grew pale; he shook in every limb, turned faint, and saw the statuesque group before him as black figures, rising, falling, moving unsteadily in arcs of circles in a fiery sky. His hand fell away from his weapon, his head slowly dropped until his face rested on the leaves in which he lay. This courageous gentleman and hardy soldier was near swooning from intensity of emotion.

It was not for long; in another moment his face was raised from earth, his hands resumed their places on the rifle, his forefinger sought the trigger; mind, heart, and eyes were clear, conscience and reason sound. He could not hope to capture that enemy; to alarm him would but send him dashing to his camp with his fatal news. The duty of the soldier was plain: the man must be shot dead from ambush—without warning, without a moment's spiritual preparation, with never so much as an unspoken prayer, he must be sent to his account. But no—there is a hope; he may have discovered nothing—perhaps he is but admiring the sublimity of the landscape. If permitted, he may turn and ride carelessly away in the direction whence he came. Surely it will be possible to judge at the instant of his withdrawing whether he knows. It may well be that his fixity of attention— Druse turned his head and looked through the deeps of air downward, as from the surface to the bottom of a translucent sea. He saw creeping across the green meadow a sinuous line of figures of men and horses—some foolish commander was permitting the soldiers of his escort to water their beasts in the open, in plain view from a dozen summits!

Druse withdrew his eyes from the valley and fixed them again upon the group of man and horse in the sky, and again it was through the sights of his rifle. But this time his aim was at the horse. In his memory, as if they were a divine mandate, rang the words of his father at their parting: "Whatever may occur, do what you conceive to be your duty." He was calm now. His teeth were firmly but not rigidly closed; his nerves were as tranquil as a sleeping babe's—not a tremor affected any muscle of his body; his breathing, until suspended in the act of taking aim, was regular and slow. Duty had conquered; the spirit had said to the body: "Peace, be still." He fired.

III

An officer of the Federal force, who in a spirit of adventure or in quest of knowledge had left the hidden bivouac in the valley, and with aimless feet had made his way to the lower edge of a small open space near the foot of the cliff, was considering what he had to gain by pushing his exploration further. At a distance of a quarter-mile before him, but apparently at a stone's throw, rose from its fringe of pines the gigantic face of rock, towering to so great a height above him that it made him giddy to look up to where its edge cut a sharp, rugged line against the sky. It presented a clean, vertical profile against a background of blue sky to a point half the way down, and of distant hills, hardly less blue, thence to the tops of the trees at its base. Lifting his eyes to the dizzy altitude of its summit the officer saw an astonishing sight—a man on horseback riding down into the valley through the air!

Straight upright sat the rider, in military fashion, with a firm seat in the saddle, a strong clutch upon the rein to hold his charger from too impetuous a plunge. From his bare head his long hair streamed upward, waving like a plume. His hands were concealed in the cloud of the horse's lifted mane. The animal's body was as level as if every hoof-stroke encountered the resistant earth. Its motions were those of a wild gallop, but even as the officer looked they ceased, with all the legs thrown sharply forward as in the act of alighting from a leap. But this was a flight!

Filled with amazement and terror by this apparition of a horseman in the sky—half believing himself the chosen scribe of some new Apocalypse, the officer was overcome by the intensity of his emotions; his legs failed him and he fell. Almost at the same instant he heard a crashing sound in the trees—a sound that died without an echo—and all was still.

The officer rose to his feet, trembling. The familiar sensation of an abraded shin recalled his dazed faculties. Pulling himself together he ran rapidly obliquely away from the cliff to a point distant from its foot; thereabout he expected to find his man; and thereabout he naturally failed. In the fleeting instant of his vision his imagination had been so wrought upon by the apparent grace and ease and intention of the marvelous performance that it did not occur to him that the line of march of aerial cavalry is directly downward, and that he could find the objects of his search at the very foot of the cliff. A half-hour later he returned to camp.

This officer was a wise man; he knew better than to tell an incredible truth. He said nothing of what he had seen. But when the commander asked him if in his scout he had learned anything of advantage to the expedition he answered:

"Yes, sir; there is no road leading down into this valley from the southward."

The commander, knowing better, smiled.

IV

After firing his shot, Private Carter Druse reloaded his rifle and resumed his watch. Ten minutes had hardly passed when a Federal sergeant crept cautiously to him on hands and knees. Druse neither turned his head nor looked at him, but lay without motion or sign of recognition.

"Did you fire?" the sergeant whispered.

"Yes."

"At what?"

"A horse. It was standing on yonder rock—pretty far out. You see it is no longer there. It went over the cliff."

The man's face was white, but he showed no other sign of emotion. Having answered, he turned away his eyes and said no more. The sergeant did not understand.

"See here, Druse," he said, after a moment's silence, "it's no use making a mystery. I order you to report. Was there anybody on the horse?"

"Yes."

"Well?"

"My father."

The sergeant rose to his feet and walked away. "Good God!" he said.

CHAPTER 37

To the Sea: Sherman on the March
Dispatches of Major General W. T. Sherman

The way to victory for Lincoln's army was through Georgia—led by the man who made famous the expression "War is hell."

—LAMAR UNDERWOOD

HEADQUARTERS OF THE ARMY
WASHINGTON, December 18, 1864.
Major-General W. T. SHERMAN, Savannah (via Hilton Head).
My DEAR GENERAL: Yours of the 13th, by Major Anderson, is just received. I congratulate you on your splendid success, and shall very soon expect to hear of the crowning work of your campaign—the capture of Savannah. Your march will stand out prominently as the great one of this great war. When Savannah falls, then for another wide swath through the center of the Confederacy. But I will not anticipate. General Grant is expected here this morning, and will probably write you his own views.

I do not learn from your letter, or from Major Anderson, that you are in want of any thing which we have not provided at Hilton Head. Thinking it probable that you might want more field-artillery, I had prepared several batteries, but the great difficulty of foraging horses on the sea-coast will prevent our sending any unless you actually need them. The hay-crop this year is short, and the Quartermaster's Department has great difficulty in procuring a supply for our animals.

General Thomas has defeated Hood, near Nashville, and it is hoped that he will completely crush his army. Breckenridge, at last accounts, was trying to form a junction near Murfreesboro', but, as Thomas is between them, Breckenridge must either retreat or be defeated.

General Rosecrans made very bad work of it in Missouri, allowing Price with a small force to overrun the State and destroy millions of property.

Orders have been issued for all officers and detachments having three months or more to serve, to rejoin your army via Savannah. Those having less than three months to serve, will be retained by General Thomas.

Should you capture Charleston, I hope that by some accident the place may be destroyed, and, if a little salt should be sown upon its site, it may prevent the growth of future crops of nullification and secession.

Yours truly,

H. W. HALLECK, Major-General, Chief-of-Staff.

HEADQUARTERS OF THE ARMY
WASHINGTON, December 18, 1864.
To Major-General W. T. SHERMAN, commanding Military Division of the Mississippi.
My DEAR GENERAL: I have just received and read, I need not tell you with how much gratification, your letter to General Halleck. I congratulate you and the brave officers and men under your command on the successful termination of your most brilliant campaign. I never had a doubt of the result. When apprehensions for your safety were expressed by the President, I assured him with the army you had, and you in command of it, there was no danger but you would strike bottom on salt-water some place; that I would not feel the same security—in fact, would not have intrusted the expedition to any other living commander.

It has been very hard work to get Thomas to attack Hood. I gave him the most peremptory order, and had started to go there myself, before he got off. He has done magnificently, however, since he started. Up to last night, five thousand prisoners and forty-nine pieces of captured artillery, besides many wagons and innumerable small-arms, had been received in Nashville. This is exclusive of the enemy's loss at Franklin, which amounted to thirteen general officers killed, wounded, and captured. The enemy probably lost five thousand men at Franklin, and ten thousand in the last three days' operations. Breckenridge is said to be making for Murfreesboro'.

I think he is in a most excellent place. Stoneman has nearly wiped out John Morgan's old command, and five days ago entered Bristol. I did think the best thing to do was to bring the greater part of your army here, and wipe out Lee. The turn affairs now seem to be taking has shaken me in that opinion. I doubt whether you may not accomplish more toward that result where you are than if brought here, especially as I am informed, since my arrival in the city, that it would take about two months to get you here with all the other calls there are for ocean transportation.

I want to get your views about what ought to be done, and what can be done. If you capture the garrison of Savannah, it certainly will compel Lee to detach from Richmond, or give us nearly the whole South. My own opinion is that Lee is averse to going out of Virginia, and if the cause of the South is lost he wants Richmond to be the last place surrendered. If he has such views, it may be well to indulge him until we get every thing else in our hands.

Congratulating you and the army again upon the splendid results of your campaign, the like of which is not read of in past history, I subscribe myself, more than ever, if possible, your friend,

U. S. GRANT, Lieutenant-General.

HEADQUARTERS OF THE ARMY
CITY POINT, VIRGINIA, December 26, 1864.
Major-General W. T. SHERMAN, Savannah, Georgia.
GENERAL: Your very interesting letter of the 22d inst., brought by Major Grey of General Foster's staff; is fast at hand. As the major starts back at once, I can do no more at present than simply acknowledge its receipt. The capture of Savannah, with all its immense stores, must tell upon the people of the South. All well here.

Yours truly,

U. S. GRANT, Lieutenant-General.

HEADQUARTERS MILITARY DIVISION OF THE MISSISSIPPI
SAVANNAH, GEORGIA, December 24, 1864.
Lieutenant-General U. S. GRANT, City Point, Virginia.
GENERAL: Your letter of December 18th is just received. I feel very much gratified at receiving the handsome commendation you pay my army. I will, in general orders, convey to the officers and men the substance of your note.

I am also pleased that you have modified your former orders, for I feared that the transportation by sea would very much disturb the unity and morale of my army, now so perfect.

The occupation of Savannah, which I have heretofore reported, completes the first part of our game, and fulfills a great part of your instructions; and we are now engaged in dismantling the rebel forts which bear upon the sea-channels, and transferring the heavy ordnance and ammunition to Fort Pulaski and Hilton Head, where they can be more easily guarded than if left in the city.

The rebel inner lines are well adapted to our purpose, and with slight modifications can be held by a comparatively small force; and in about ten days I expect to be ready to sally forth again. I feel no doubt whatever as to our future plans. I have thought them over so long and well that they appear as clear as daylight. I left Augusta untouched on purpose, because the enemy will be in doubt as to my objective point, after we cross the Savannah River, whether it be Augusta or Charleston, and will naturally divide his forces. I will then move either on Branchville or Colombia, by any curved line that gives us the best supplies, breaking up in our course as much railroad as possible; then, ignoring Charleston and Augusta both, I would occupy Columbia and Camden, pausing there long enough to observe the effect. I would then strike for the Charleston & Wilmington Railroad, somewhere between the Santee and Cape Fear Rivers, and, if possible, communicate with the fleet under Admiral Dahlgren (whom I find a most agreeable gentleman, accommodating himself to our wishes and plans). Then I would favor an attack on Wilmington, in the belief that Porter and Butler will fail in their present undertaking. Charleston is now a mere desolated wreck, and is hardly worth the time it would take to starve it out. Still, I am aware that, historically and politically, much importance is attached to the place, and it may be that, apart from its military importance, both you and the Administration may prefer I should give it more attention; and it would be well for you to give me some general idea on that subject, for otherwise I would treat it as I have expressed, as a point of little importance, after all its railroads leading into the interior have been destroyed or occupied by us. But, on the hypothesis of ignoring Charleston and taking Wilmington, I would then favor a movement direct on Raleigh. The game is then up with Lee, unless he comes out of Richmond, avoids you and fights me; in which case I should reckon on your being on his heels. Now that Hood is used up by Thomas, I feel disposed to bring the matter to an issue as quick as possible. I feel confident that I can break up the whole railroad system of South Carolina and North Carolina, and be on the Roanoke, either at Raleigh or Weldon, by the time spring fairly opens; and, if you feel confident that you can whip Lee outside of his intrenchments, I feel equally confident that I can handle him in the open country.

One reason why I would ignore Charleston is this: that I believe Hardee will reduce the garrison to a small force, with plenty of provisions; I know that the neck back of Charleston can be made impregnable to assault, and we will hardly have time for siege operations.

I will have to leave in Savannah a garrison, and, if Thomas can spare them, I would like to have all detachments, convalescents, etc., belonging to these four corps, sent forward at once. I do not want to cripple Thomas, because I regard his operations as all-important, and I have ordered him to pursue Hood down into Alabama, trusting to the country for supplies.

I reviewed one of my corps to-day, and shall continue to review the whole army. I do not like to boast, but believe this army has a confidence in itself that makes it almost invincible. I wish you could run down and see us; it would have a good effect, and show to both armies that they are acting on a common plan. The weather is now cool and pleasant, and the general health very good. Your true friend,

W. T. SHERMAN Major-General.

HEADQUARTERS MILITARY DIVISION OF THE MISSISSIPPI IN THE FIELD, SAVANNAH, GEORGIA, December 24, 1864.
Major-General H. W. HALLECK, Chief-of-Staff; Washington, D.C.
GENERAL: I had the pleasure of receiving your two letters of the 16th and 18th instant to-day, and feel more than usually flattered by the high encomiums you have passed on our recent campaign, which is now complete by the occupation of Savannah.

I am also very glad that General Grant has changed his mind about embarking my troops for James River, leaving me free to make the broad swath you describe through South and North Carolina; and still more gratified at the news from Thomas, in Tennessee, because it fulfills my plans, which contemplated his being able to dispose of Hood, in case he ventured north of the Tennessee River. So, I think, on the whole, I can chuckle over Jeff. Davis's disappointment in not turning my Atlanta campaign into a "Moscow disaster."

I have just finished a long letter to General Grant, and have explained to him that we are engaged in shifting our base from the Ogeeohee to the Savannah River, dismantling all the forts made by the enemy to bear upon the salt-water channels, transferring the heavy ordnance, etc., to Fort Pulaski and Hilton Head, and in remodeling the enemy's interior lines to suit our future plans and purposes. I have also laid down the program for a campaign which I can make this winter, and which will put me in the spring on the Roanoke, in direct communication with General Grant on James River. In general terms, my plan is to turn over to General Foster the city of Savannah, to sally forth with my army resupplied, cross the Savannah, feign on Charleston and Augusta, but strike between, breaking en route the Charleston & Augusta Railroad, also a large part of that from Branchville and Camden toward North Carolina, and then rapidly to move for some point of the railroad from Charleston to Wilmington, between the Santee and Cape Fear Rivers; then, communicating with the fleet in the neighborhood of Georgetown, I would turn upon Wilmington or Charleston, according to the importance of either. I rather prefer Wilmington, as a live place, over Charleston, which is dead and unimportant when its railroad communications are broken. I take it for granted that the present movement on Wilmington will fail. If I should determine to take Charleston, I would turn across the country (which I have hunted over many a time) from Santee to Mount Pleasant, throwing one wing on the peninsula between the Ashley and Cooper. After accomplishing one or other of these ends, I would make a bee-line for Raleigh or Weldon, when Lee would be forced to come out of Richmond, or acknowledge himself beaten. He would, I think, by the use of the Danville Railroad, throw himself rapidly between me and Grant, leaving Richmond in the hands of the latter. This would not alarm me, for I have an army which I think can maneuver, and I world force him to attack me at a disadvantage, always under the supposition that Grant would be on his heels; and, if the worst come to the worst, I can fight my way down to Albermarle Sound, or Newbern.

I think the time has come now when we should attempt the boldest moves, and my experience is, that they are easier of execution than more timid ones, because the enemy is disconcerted by them—as, for instance, my recent campaign.

I also doubt the wisdom of concentration beyond a certain extent, for the roads of this country limit the amount of men that can be brought to bear in any one battle, and I do not believe that any one general can handle more than sixty thousand men in battle.

I think our campaign of the last month, as well as every step I take from this point northward, is as much a direct attack upon Lee's army as though we were operating within the sound of his artillery.

I am very anxious that Thomas should follow up his success to the very utmost point. My orders to him before I left Kingston were, after beating Hood, to follow him as far as Columbus, Mississippi, or Selma, Alabama, both of which lie in districts of country which are rich in corn and meat.

I attach more importance to these deep incisions into the enemy's country, because this war differs from European wars in this particular: we are not only fighting hostile armies, but a hostile people, and must make old and young, rich and poor, feel the hard hand of war, as well as their organized armies. I know that this recent movement of mine through Georgia has had a wonderful effect in this respect. Thousands who had been deceived by their lying newspapers to believe that we were being whipped all the time now realize the truth, and have no appetite for a repetition of the same experience. To be sure, Jeff. Davis has his people under pretty good discipline, but I think faith in him is much shaken in Georgia, and before we have done with her South Carolina will not be quite so tempestuous.

I will bear in mind your hint as to Charleston, and do not think "salt" will be necessary. When I move, the Fifteenth Corps will be on the right of the right wing, and their position will naturally bring them into Charleston first; and, if you have watched the history of that corps, you will have remarked that they generally do their work pretty well. The truth is, the whole army is burning with an insatiable desire to wreak vengeance upon South Carolina. I almost tremble at her fate, but feel that she deserves all that seems in store for her.

Many and many a person in Georgia asked me why we did not go to South Carolina; and, when I answered that we were enroute for that State, the invariable reply was, "Well, if you will make those people feel the utmost severities of war, we will pardon you for your desolation of Georgia."

I look upon Colombia as quite as bad as Charleston, and I doubt if we shall spare the public buildings there as we did at Milledgeville.

I have been so busy lately that I have not yet made my official report, and I think I had better wait until I get my subordinate reports before attempting it, as I am anxious to explain clearly not only the reasons for every step, but the amount of execution done, and this I cannot do until I get the subordinate reports; for we marched the whole distance in four or more columns, and, of course, I could only be present with one, and generally that one engaged in destroying rail-roads. This work of destruction was performed better than usual, because I had an engineer-regiment, provided with claws to twist the bars after being heated. Such bars can never be used again, and the only way in which a railroad line can be reconstructed across Georgia is, to make a new road from Fairburn Station (twenty-four miles southwest of Atlanta) to Madison, a distance of one hundred miles; and, before that can be done, I propose to be on the road from Augusta to Charleston, which is a continuation of the same. I felt somewhat disappointed at Hardee's escape, but really am not to blame. I moved as quickly as possible to close up the "Union Causeway," but intervening obstacles were such that, before I could get troops on the road, Hardee had slipped out. Still, I know that the men that were in Savannah will be lost in a measure to Jeff. Davis, for the Georgia troops, under G. W. Smith, declared they would not fight in South Carolina, and they have gone north, en route for Augusta, and I have reason to believe the North Carolina troops have gone to Wilmington; in other words, they are scattered. I have reason to believe that Beauregard was present in Savannah at the time of its evacuation, and think that he and Hardee are now in Charleston, making preparations for what they suppose will be my next step.

Please say to the President that I have received his kind message (through Colonel Markland), and feel thankful for his high favor. If I disappoint him in the future, it shall not be from want of zeal or love to the cause.

From you I expect a full and frank criticism of my plans for the future, which may enable me to correct errors before it is too late. I do not wish to be rash, but want to give my rebel friends no chance to accuse us of want of enterprise or courage.

Assuring you of my high personal respect, I remain, as ever, your friend,
W. T. SHERMAN, Major-General.

CHAPTER 38

Last Days of the Confederacy: Campfire and Battlefield

By General John B. Gordon, C.S.A.

When time was running out for the rebel army, the scene wasn't pretty.
—LAMAR UNDERWOOD

I WILL GIVE YOU FROM MY PERSONAL KNOWLEDGE THE HISTORY OF THE STRUGGLES that preceded the surrender of General Lee's army, the causes that induced that surrender—as I had them from General Lee—the detailed account of the last assault ever made upon the Federal lines in pursuance of an offensive purpose, and a description of the last scenes of the bloody and terrible civil war. This history has never been published before. No official reports, I believe, were ever made upon the Confederate side; for after the battle of Hare's Hill, as the attack upon Fort Steadman was called, there was not an hour's rest until the surrender. From the 25th of March, 1865, until the 9th day of April, my men did not take their boots off, the roar of cannon and the rattle of musketry was scarcely stilled an instant, and the fighting and marching was continuous. Hence no report of these operations was ever made.

You will remember the situation of affairs in Virginia about the first of March, 1865. The Valley campaign of the previous summer, which was inaugurated for the purpose of effecting a diversion and breaking the tightening lines about Richmond and Petersburg, and from which so much had been expected, had ended in disaster. Grant had massed an enormous army in front of Petersburg and Richmond, and fresh troops were hurrying to his aid. Our army covered a line of over twenty miles, and was in great distress. The men were literally starving. We were not able to issue even half rations. One-sixth of a pound of beef a day, I remember, was at one time the ration of a portion of the army, and the men could not always get even that. I saw men often on their hands and knees, with little sticks, digging the grains of corn from out of the tracks of horses, and washing it and cooking it. The brave fellows were so depleted by the time Grant broke our lines, that the slightest wound often killed them. A scratch on the hand would result in gangrene and prove fatal. The doctors took me to the hospitals and showed me men with a joint on their fingers shot off, and their arms gangrened up to the elbows. "The men are starved," they said, "and we can do little for them."

The sights that I saw as I walked among these poor, emaciated, hungry men, dying of starved and poisoned systems, were simply horrible. Our horses were in no better condition; many of them were hardly able to do service at all. General Lee had gone in person into Petersburg and Richmond, and begged the citizens to divide what little they had with his wretched men. The heroic people did all that they could. Our sole line of supplies was the railroad running into North Carolina and penetrating into "Egypt," as we called Southwest Georgia, which was then the provision ground for our armies. Such was the situation. My corps (Stonewall Jackson's old corps), after severe and heroic work in the Valley campaign, had been ordered back to Petersburg and placed upon the right wing of the army. I had general instructions to protect the flank of the army, prevent General Grant from turning it, and, above all, to protect the slender line of road from which solely we received our scanty supplies. We were almost continually engaged in fighting, making feints, and protecting our skirmish lines, which the enemy were feeling and pressing continually.

Before daylight on the morning of the 2d of March, 1865, General Lee sent for me. I mounted my horse at once and rode to the general's headquarters. I reached the house in which he was staying at about four o'clock in the morning. As I entered the room to which I had been directed, I found General Lee alone. I shall never forget the scene. The general was standing at the fireplace, his head on his arm, leaning on the mantelpiece—the first time I ever saw him looking so thoroughly dejected. A dim lamp was burning on a small center-table. On the table was a mass of official reports. General Lee remained motionless for a moment after I opened the door. He then looked up, greeted me with his usual courtesy, motioned me to the little table, and, drawing up a chair, sat down. I sat opposite him.

"I have sent for you, General Gordon," he said, "to make known to you the condition of our affairs and to confer with you as to what we had best do." The night was fearfully cold. The fire and lamp both burned low as General Lee went on to give me the details of the situation. "I have here," he said, "reports sent in from my officers to-night. I find, upon careful examination, that I have under my command, of all arms, hardly forty-five thousand men. These men are starving. They are already so weakened as to be hardly efficient. Many of them have become desperate, reckless, and disorderly as they have never been before. It is difficult to control men who are suffering for food. They are breaking open mills, barns, and stores in search of food. Almost crazed from hunger, they are deserting from some commands in large numbers and going home. My horses are in equally bad condition. The supply of horses in the country is exhausted. It has come to be where it is just as bad for me to have a horse killed as a man. I cannot remount a cavalryman whose horse dies. General Grant can mount ten thousand men in ten days, and move around your flank. If he were to send me word to-morrow that I might move out unmolested, I have not enough horses to move my artillery. He is not likely to send this message, however; and yet," smiling, "he sent me word yesterday that he knew what I had for breakfast every morning. I sent him word that I did not think this could be so, for if he did know he would surely send me something better. But, now, let us look at the figures. I have, as I have shown you, not quite 45,000 men. My men are starved, exhausted, sick. His are in the best condition possible. But beyond this there is Hancock, at Winchester, with a force of probably not less than 18,000 men. To oppose this force I have not a solitary vidette. Sheridan, with his terrible cavalry, has marched almost unmolested and unopposed along the James, cutting the railroads and canal. Thomas is approaching from Knoxville with a force I estimate at 30,000, and to oppose him I have a few brigades of badly disciplined cavalry, amounting to probably 3,000 in all. General Sherman is in North Carolina, and, with Schofield's forces, will have 65,000 men. As to what I have to oppose this force, I submit the following telegram from General Johnston. The telegram reads: 'General Beauregard telegraphed you a few days ago that, with Governor Vance's Home Guards, we could carry 20,000 men into battle. I find, upon close inspection, that we cannot muster over 13,000 men.'" (This, General Gordon said, was, as nearly as he could recollect, General Johnston's telegram.) "So there is the situation. I have here, say, 40,000 men able for duty, though none of my poor fellows are in good condition. They are opposed directly by an army of 160,000 strong and confident men, and converging on my little force four separate armies, numbering, in the aggregate, 130,000 more men. This force, added to General Grant's, makes over a quarter million. To prevent these from uniting for my destruction there are hardly 60,000 men available. My men are growing weaker day by day. Their sufferings are terrible and exhausting. My horses are broken down and impotent. I am apprehensive that General Grant may press around my flank and cut our sole remaining line of supplies. Now, general," he said, looking me straight in the face, "what is to be done?" With this he laid his paper down and leaned back in his chair.

I replied: "Since you have done me the honor to ask my opinion, I will give it. The situation as you portray it is infinitely worse than I had dreamed it was. I cannot doubt that your information is correct. I am confident of the opinion, therefore, that one of two things should be done, and at once. We must either treat with the United States Government for the best terms possible, or we should concentrate all our strength at one point of Grant's line—selecting some point on the right bank of the Appomattox—assault him, break through his lines, destroy his pontoons, and then turn full upon the flank of his left wing, sweep down it and destroy it if possible, and then join General Johnston in North Carolina by forced marches, and, combining our army with his, fall upon Sherman."

"And what then?"

"If we beat him or succeed in making a considerable battle, then treat at once for terms. I am forced to the conclusion, from what you say, sir, that we have no time for delay."

"So that is your opinion, is it?" he asked, in a tone that sent the blood to my face. I ought to have remembered that it was a way that General Lee had of testing the sincerity of a man's opinion by appearing to discredit it.

"It is, sir," I replied; "but I should not have ventured it, had it not been asked; and since you seem to differ from the opinion I hold, may I ask you what your opinion is?"

At once his manner changed, and, leaning forward, he said, blandly: "I entirely agree with you, general."

"Does President Davis and the Congress know these facts? Have you expressed an opinion as to the propriety of making terms, to President Davis or the Congress?"

General Lee replied to this question: "General Gordon, I am a soldier. It is my duty to obey orders."

"Yes," I replied; "but if you read the papers, General Lee, you can't shut your eyes to the fact that the hopes of the Southern people are centered in and on your army, and if we wait until we are beaten and scattered into the mountains before we make an effort at terms, the people will not be satisfied. Besides, we will simply invite the enemy to hunt us down all over the country, devastating it wherever they go."

General Lee said nothing to this for some time, but paced the floor in silence, while I sat gloomily enough, as you may know, at the fearful prospect. He had, doubtless, thought of all I said long before he sent for me. I don't wish you to understand that I am vain enough to believe for a moment that anything I said induced him to go to Richmond the next day. As I said before, he had probably decided on his course before he sent for me, and only feigned a difference of opinion or hesitation in order to see with what pertinacity I held my own. He did go to Richmond, and on his return sent for me again, and in reply to my question as to what had occurred, he said:

"Sir, it is enough to turn a man's hair gray to spend one day in that Congress. The members are patriotic and earnest, but they will neither take the responsibility of acting nor will they clothe me with authority to act. As for Mr. Davis, he is unwilling to do anything short of independence, and feels that it is useless to try to treat on that basis. Indeed, he says that, having failed in one overture of peace at Hampton Roads, he is not disposed to try another."

"Then," said I, "there is nothing left for us but to fight, and the sooner we fight the better, for every day weakens us and strengthens our opponents."

It was these two conferences that led to the desperate and almost hopeless attack I made upon the 25th of March on Grant's lines at Fort Steadman and Hare's Hill, in front of Petersburg. My corps was, as I tell you, at that time on the extreme right of General Lee's army, stretching from Hatcher's Run, southward along the Boydton plank road.

He proposed to transfer my corps to lines in and around Petersburg, and have me familiarize myself with the strong and weak points, if there were any weak ones, on Grant's line near the bank of the Appomattox River. He ordered my command into Petersburg to replace the troops which were there. I spent a week examining Grant's lines, learning from deserters and men captured the names of the Federal officers and their commands in the front. At last I selected a point which I was sure I could carry by a night assault. I so reported to General Lee.

It was in the last degree a desperate undertaking, as you will presently see; but it was the best that could be suggested—better than to stand still. Almost hopeless as it was, it was less so than the certain and rapid disintegration, through starvation and disease and desertion, of the last army we could ever organize. The point on my line from which I decided to make the assault was Colquitt's salient, which had been built by Governor Colquitt and his men and held by them, when, to protect themselves, they had to move under covered ways and sleep burrowed in the ground like Georgia gophers. I selected this point because the main lines here were closest together, being not more than two hundred yards apart, I should say, while the picket lines were so close that the Confederate and the Federals could easily converse. By a sort of general consent the firing between the pickets nearly ceased during the day, so that I could stand upon my breastworks and examine General Grant's. You can see at a glance how desperately strong was even this, the weakest point on Grant's line. It was close to Colquitt's salient where the fearful mine was sprung called the Crater. The whole intervening ground between Fort Steadman and Colquitt's salient, over which I had to make the assault, was raked not only by a front fire, but by flank fires from both directions from the forts and trenches of the main line.

An attack, therefore, by daylight would have been simply to have the men butchered, without any possibility of success, so that nothing but a night attack was to be thought of.

Between the main line of trenches and forts and the rear line of forts was a heavy line of Federal reserves, and the rear forts were placed with such consummate engineering skill as to command any point on that portion of Grant's line which might be captured. It was, therefore, necessary to capture or break through the reserves and take the rear line of forts as well as the front. This rear line of forts was so protected by abatis in front that the whole of General Lee's army could not have stormed them by a front attack, and the only possibility of securing them was to capture them from the rear, where there was an opening. This could only be done by stratagem, if it could be done at all.

I finally submitted a plan of battle to General Lee, which he approved and ordered executed. It was briefly this: To take Fort Steadman by direct assault at night, then send a separate body of men to each of the rear forts, who, claiming to be Federals, might pass through the Federal reserves and take possession of the rear line of forts as if ordered to do so by the Federal commander; next, then to press with my whole force to the rear of Grant's main line and force him out of the trenches, destroy his pontoons, cut his telegraph wires, and press down his flank. Of course, it was a most desperate and almost hopeless undertaking, and could be justified only by our desperate and hopeless condition if we remained idle. We both recognized it as the forlornest of forlorn hopes.

Let me particularize a little more. The obstructions in front of my own lines had to be removed, and removed silently, so as not to attract the attention of the Federal pickets.

Grant's obstructions had to be removed from the front of Fort Steadman. These obstructions were of sharpened rails, elevated to about breast high, the other end buried deeply in the ground, the rails resting on a horizontal pole and wrapped with telegraph wire. They could not be mounted or pushed aside, but had to be cut away with axes. This had to be done immediately in front of the guns of Fort Steadman. These guns were at night doubly charged with canister, as I learned from Federal prisoners. The rush across the intervening space between the lines had to be made so silently and swiftly as to take the fort before the gunners could fire. The reserves had to be beaten or passed and the rear line of forts taken before daylight. All this had to be accomplished before my main forces could be moved across and placed in position to move on Grant's flank, or rather left wing.

My preparations were these: I called on my division commanders for a detail of the bravest men in their commands. To rush over the Federal pickets and into the fort and seize the Federal guns, I selected a body of only one hundred men, with empty rifles and fixed bayonets. To precede these, to clear an opening to the fort, I selected fifty of the most stalwart and brave men I could find, and armed them with axes to cut down the obstructions in front of the fort. They were ordered to remove my own abatis, rush upon the Federal obstructions, and cut away a brigade front. The one hundred with empty rifles and fixed bayonets were to follow immediately, and this one hundred and fifty men were not to falter or fire, but to go into Fort Steadman, if they had to do it in the face of the fire from all the forts. Immediately after these axemen and the one hundred had cleared the way and gained the fort, three other squads of one hundred each were to rush across, pass through Fort Steadman, and go pell-mell to the rear, and right through the Federal reserves, crying as they went: "The rebels have carried our lines in front, captured Fort Steadman, and we are ordered by General McLaughlin, Federal commander of Fort Steadman, to go back to the rear forts and hold them against the rebels."

I instructed each commander of these last squads as to what particular fort he was to enter; and a guide, who had been raised on the ground, was placed with each of these three squads, or companies, who was to conduct them through the reserves and to the rear of the forts. If they were halted by the Federal reserves, each commander was instructed to pass himself off as one of the Federal officers whose names I had learned. I remember that I named one commander of one of the companies Lieutenant-Colonel Pendergrast, of a Pennsylvania regiment—I think that was the name and regiment of one of the Federal officers in my front. As soon as Fort Steadman should be taken, and these three bodies of one hundred men each had succeeded in entering the rear forts, the main force of infantry and cavalry were to cross over. The cavalry was to gallop to the rear, capture the fugitives, destroy the pontoons, cut down the telegraph wires, and give me constant information, while the infantry was to move rapidly down Grant's lines, attacking and breaking his division in detail, as they moved out of his trenches. Such, I say, was the plan of this most desperate and last aggressive assault ever made by the Confederate army.

General Lee had sent me, in addition to my own corps, a portion of Longstreet's corps (Pickett's division) and a portion of A. P. Hill's and a body of cavalry. During the whole night of the 24th of March I was on horseback, making preparations and disposing of troops. About four o'clock in the morning I called close around me the fifty axemen and four companies, one hundred each, of the brave men who were selected to do this hazardous work. I spoke to them of the character of the undertaking, and of the last hope of the cause, which was about to be confided to them. Around the shoulders of each man was bound a white strip of muslin, which Mrs. Gordon, who sat in a room not far distant listening for the signal gun, had prepared, as a means of recognition of each other. The hour had come, and when everything was ready I stood on the breastworks of Colquitt's salient and ordered two men to my side, with rifles, who were to fire the signal for attack. The noise of moving our own obstructions was going on and attracted the notice of a Federal picket. In the black darkness his voice rang out:

"Hullo there, Johnny Reb! what are you making all that fuss about over there?"

The men were just leaning forward for the start. This sudden call disconcerted me somewhat; but the rifleman on my right came to my assistance by calling out in a cheerful voice:

"Oh! never mind us, Yank; lie down and go to sleep. We are just gathering a little corn; you know rations are mighty short over here."

There was a patch of corn between our lines, some of it still hanging on the stalks. After a few moments there came back the kindly reply of the Yankee picket, which quite reassured me. He said:

"All right, Johnny; go ahead and get your corn. I won't shoot at you."

As I gave the command to forward, the man on my right seemed to have some compunctions of conscience for having stilled the suspicions of the Yankee picket who had answered him so kindly, and who the next moment might be surprised and killed. So he called out to him:

"Look out for yourself now, Yank; we're going to shell the woods."

This exhibition of chivalry and of kindly feelings on both sides, and at such a moment, touched me almost as deeply as any minor incident of the war. I quickly ordered the two men to "Fire."

Bang! Bang! The two shots broke the stillness, and "Forward!" I commanded. The chosen hundred sprang forward, eagerly following the axemen, and for the last time the stars and bars were carried to aggressive assault.

In a moment the axemen were upon the abatis of the enemy and hewing it down. I shall never know how they whisked this line of wire-fastened obstructions out of the way. The one hundred overpowered the pickets, sent them to the rear, rushed through the gap made by the axemen up the slope of Fort Steadman, and it was ours without the firing of a single gun, and with the loss of but one man. He was killed with a bayonet. The three companies who were to attempt to pass the reserves and go into the rear forts followed and passed on through Fort Steadman. Then came the other troops pouring into the fort. We captured, I think, nine pieces of artillery, eleven mortars, and about six hundred or seven hundred prisoners, among whom was General McLaughlin, who was commanding on that portion of the Federal line.

Many were taken in their beds. The prisoners were all sent across to our lines, and other troops of my command were brought to the fort. I now anxiously awaited to learn the fate of the three hundred who had been sent in companies of one hundred each to attempt the capture of the three rear forts. Soon a messenger reached me from two officers commanding two of these chosen bodies, who informed me that they had succeeded in passing right through the line of Federal reserves by representing themselves as Federals, and had certainly gone far enough to the rear for the forts, but that their guides had abandoned them or been lost, and that they did not know in what direction to move. It was afterward discovered, when daylight came, that these men had gone further out than the forts, and could have easily entered and captured them if the guides had not been lost, or had done their duty. Of course, after dawn they were nearly all captured, being entirely behind the Federal reserves.

In the meantime, the few Federal soldiers who had escaped from the fort and intrenchments we had captured had spread the alarm and aroused the Federal army. The hills in the rear of Grant's lines were soon black with troops. By the time it was fairly daybreak the two forts on the main line flanking Fort Steadman, the three forts in the rear, and the reserves, all opened fire upon my forces. We held Fort Steadman, and the Federal intrenchments to the river, or nearly so. But the guides had been lost, and as a consequence the rear forts had not been captured. Failing to secure these forts, the cavalry could not pass, the pontoons could not be destroyed, and the telegraph wires were not cut. In addition to these mishaps, the trains had been delayed, and Pickett's division and other troops sent me by General Lee had not arrived. The success had been brilliant so far as it had gone, and had been achieved without loss of any consequence to our army; but it had failed in the essentials to a complete success or to a great victory. Every hour was bringing heavy reinforcements to the Federals and rendering my position less and less tenable.

After a brief correspondence with General Lee, it was decided to withdraw. My loss, whatever it was, occurred in withdrawing under concentrated fire from forts and infantry. The fighting over the picket lines and main lines from this time to the surrender was too incessant to give me an opportunity to ascertain my loss. It was considerable; and although I had inflicted a heavy loss upon the enemy, I felt, as my troops reentered Colquitt's salient, that the last hazard had been thrown, and that we had lost.

I will give you here the last note I ever received from General Lee, and one of the last he ever wrote in his official capacity. It is as follows:

4.30 P.M., HEADQUARTERS, March, 24, 1865.

GENERAL: I have received yours of 2.30 P.M., and telegraphed for Pickett's division, but I do not think it will reach here in time; still we will try. If you need more troops, one or both of Heth's brigades can be called to Colquitt's salient, and Wilcox's to the Baxter road. Dispose of the troops as needed. I pray that a merciful God may grant us success, and deliver us from our enemies.

Very truly,

R. E. LEE, *General.*

GEN. J. B. GORDON.

P.S.—The cavalry is ordered to report to you at Halifax Road and Norfolk Railroad (iron bridge) at three A.M. to-morrow. W. F. Lee to be in vicinity of Monk's Corner at six A.M.

R. E. L.

I had very little talk with General Lee after our withdrawal. I recognized that the end was approaching, and of course he did. It will be seen from his semi-official note, quoted above, that he became very much interested in the success of our movement. While he had known as well as I that it was a desperate and forlorn hope, still we had hoped that we might cut through and make a glorious dash down the right and seek Johnston in North Carolina. The result of the audacious attempt that had been made upon his line, and its complete success up to the time that it was ruined by a mischance, was to awaken General Grant's forces into more aggressive measures. A sort of respite was had, for a day, after the night attack on Fort Steadman, and then the death-struggle began. Grant hurried his masses upon our starved and broken-down veterans. His main attack was made upon our left, A. P. Hill's corps.

Grant's object was to turn our flanks, and get between us and North Carolina. The fighting was fearful and continuous. It was a miracle that we held our lines for a single day. With barely six thousand men I was holding six miles of line. I had just one thousand men to the mile, or about one to every two yards. Hill and Longstreet were in not much better trim, and some part of this thin line was being forced continually.

The main fight was on my line and Hill's, as General Longstreet was nearer Richmond. Heavy masses of troops were hurled upon our line, and we would have to rally our forces at a certain point to meet the attack. By the time we would repel it, we would find another point attacked, and would hurry to defend that. Of course, withdrawing men from one part of the line would leave it exposed, and the enemy would rush in. Then we would have to drive them out and reestablish our line. Thus the battle raged day after day. Our line would bend and twist, and swell and break, and close again, only to be battered against once more.

Our people performed prodigies of valor. How they endured through those terrible, hopeless, bloody days, I do not know. They fought desperately and heroically, although they were so weakened through hunger and work that they could scarcely stand upon their feet and totter from one point of assault to another. But they never complained. They fought sternly, grimly, as men who had made up their minds to die. And we held our lines. Somehow or other—God only knows how—we managed day by day to wrest from the Federals the most of our lines. Then the men, dropping in the trenches, would eat their scanty rations, try to forget their hunger, and snatch an hour or two of sleep.

Our picket lines were attacked somewhere every night. This thing went on till the morning of the 2d of April. Early that day it became evident that the supreme moment had come. The enemy attacked in unusually heavy force, and along the line of mine and Hill's corps. It became absolutely necessary to concentrate a few men at points along my line, in order to make a determined resistance. This left great gaps in my line of breastworks, unprotected by anything save a vidette or two. Of course, the Federals broke through these undefended passes, and established themselves in my breastworks. At length, having repulsed the forces attacking the points I defended, I began reestablishing my line.

My men fought with a valor and a desperate courage that has been rarely equalled, in my opinion, in military annals. We recaptured position after position, and by four o'clock in the afternoon I had reetablished my whole line except at one point. This was very strongly defended, but I prepared to assault it. I notified General Lee of my purpose and of the situation, when he sent me a message, telling me that Hill's lines had been broken, and that General Hill himself had been killed. He ordered, therefore, that I should make no further fight, but prepare for the evacuation which he had determined to make that night.

That night we left Petersburg. Hill's corps, terribly shattered and without its commander, crossed the river first, and I followed, having orders from General Lee to cover the retreat. We spent the night in marching, and early the next morning the enemy rushed upon us. We had to turn and beat them back. Then began the most heroic and desperate struggle ever sustained by troops—a worn and exhausted force of hardly four thousand men, with a vast and victorious army, fresh and strong, pressing upon our heels! We turned upon every hilltop to meet them, and give our wagon-trains and artillery time to get ahead. Instantly they would strike us, we invariably repulsed them. They never broke through my dauntless heroes; but after we had fought for an hour or two, we would find huge masses of men pressing down our flanks, and to keep from being surrounded I would have to withdraw my men.

We always retreated in good order, though always under fire. As we retreated we would wheel and fire, or repel a rush, and then stagger on to the next hill-top, or vantage ground, where a new fight would be made. And so on through the entire day. At night my men had no rest. We marched through the night in order to get a little respite from fighting. All night long I would see my poor fellows hobbling along, prying wagons or artillery out of the mud, and supplementing the work of our broken-down horses. At dawn, though, they would be in line ready for battle, and they would fight with the steadiness and valor of the Old Guard.

This lasted until the night of the 7th of April. The retreat of Lee's army was lit up with the fire and flash of battle, in which my brave men moved about like demigods for five days and nights. Then we were sent to the front for a rest, and Longstreet was ordered to cover the retreating army.

On the evening of the 8th, when I had reached the front, my scout George brought me two men in Confederate uniform, who, he said, he believed to be the enemy, as he had seen them counting our men as they filed past. I had the men brought to my campfire, and examined them. They made a most plausible defense, but George was positive they were spies, and I ordered them searched. He failed to find anything, when I ordered him to examine their boots. In the bottom of one of the boots I found an order from General Grant to General Ord, telling him to move by forced marches toward Lynchburg and cut off General Lee's retreat.

The men then confessed that they were spies, and belonged to General Sheridan. They stated that they knew that the penalty of their course was death, but asked that I should not kill them, as the war could only last a few days longer, anyhow. I kept them prisoners, and turned them over to General Sheridan after the surrender. I at once sent the information to General Lee, and a short time afterward received orders to go to his headquarters.

That night was held Lee's last council of war. There were present General Lee, General Fitzhugh Lee, as head of the cavalry, and Pendleton, as chief of artillery, and myself. General Longstreet was, I think, too busily engaged to attend. General Lee then exhibited to us the correspondence he had had with General Grant that day, and asked our opinion of the situation. It seemed that surrender was inevitable. The only chance of escape was that I could cut a way for the army through the lines in front of me. General Lee asked me if I could do this.

I replied that I did not know what forces were in front of me; that if General Ord had not arrived—as we thought then he had not—with his heavy masses of infantry, I could cut through. I guaranteed that my men would cut a way through all the cavalry that could be massed in front of them. The council finally dissolved with the understanding that the army should be surrendered if I discovered the next morning, after feeling the enemy's line, that the infantry had arrived in such force that I could not cut my way through.

My men were drawn up in the little town of Appomattox that night. I still had about four thousand men under me, as the army had been divided into two commands and given to General Longstreet and myself. Early on the morning of the 9th I prepared for the assault upon the enemy's line, and began the last fighting done in Virginia. My men rushed forward gamely and broke the line of the enemy and captured two pieces of artillery. I was still unable to tell what I was fighting; I did not know whether I was striking infantry or dismounted cavalry. I only knew that my men were driving them back, and were getting further and further through.

Just then I had a message from General Lee, telling me a flag of truce was in existence, leaving it to my discretion as to what course to pursue. My men were still pushing their way on. I sent at once to hear from General Longstreet, feeling that, if he was marching toward me, we might still cut through and carry the army forward. I learned that he was about two miles off, with his face just opposite from mine, fighting for his life. I thus saw that the case was hopeless. The further each of us drove the enemy the further we drifted apart, and the more exposed we left our wagon trains and artillery, which were parked between us. Every line either of us broke only opened the gap the wider. I saw plainly that the Federals would soon rush in between us, and then there would have been no army. I, therefore, determined to send a flag of truce. I called Colonel Peyton of my staff to me, and told him that I wanted him to carry a flag of truce forward. He replied:

"General, I have no flag of truce."

I told him to get one. He replied:

"General, we have no flag of truce in our command."

Then said I, "Get your handkerchief, put it on a stick, and go forward."

"I have no handkerchief, General."

"Then borrow one and go forward with it."

He tried, and reported to me that there was no handkerchief in my staff.

"Then, Colonel, use your shirt!"

"You see, General, that we all have on flannel shirts."

At last, I believe, we found a man who had a white shirt. He gave it to us, and I tore off the back and tail, and, tying this to a stick, Colonel Peyton went out toward the enemy's lines. I instructed him to simply say to General Sheridan that General Lee had written me that a flag of truce had been sent from his and Grant's headquarters, and that he could act as he thought best on this information. In a few moments he came back with some one representing General Sheridan. This officer said:

"General Sheridan requested me to present his compliments to you, and to demand the unconditional surrender of your army."

"Major, you will please return my compliments to General Sheridan, and say that I will not surrender."

"But, General, he will annihilate you."

"I am perfectly well aware of my situation. I simply gave General Sheridan some information on which he may or may not desire to act."

He went back to his lines, and in a short time General Sheridan came forward on an immense horse, and attended by a very large staff. Just here an incident occurred that came near having a serious ending. As General Sheridan was approaching I noticed one of my sharp-shooters drawing his rifle down upon him. I at once called to him: "Put down your gun, sir; this is a flag of truce." But he simply settled it to his shoulder and was drawing a bead on Sheridan, when I leaned forward and jerked his gun. He struggled with me, but I finally raised it. I then loosed it, and he started to aim again. I caught it again, when he turned his stern white face, all broken with grief and streaming with tears, up to me, and said: "Well, General, then let him keep on his own side."

The fighting had continued up to this point. Indeed, after the flag of truce, a regiment of my men, who had been fighting their way through toward where we were, and who did not know of a flag of truce, fired into some of Sheridan's cavalry. This was speedily stopped, however. I showed General Sheridan General Lee's note, and he determined to await events. He dismounted, and I did the same. Then, for the first time, the men seemed to understand what it all meant, and then the poor fellows broke down.

The men cried like children.

Worn, starved, and bleeding as they were, they had rather have died than have surrendered. At one word from me they would have hurled themselves on the enemy, and have cut their way through or have fallen to a man with their guns in their hands. But I could not permit it. The great drama had been played to its end. But men are seldom permitted to look upon such a scene as the one presented here. That these men should have wept at surrendering so unequal a fight, at being taken out of this constant carnage and storm, at being sent back to their families; that they should have wept at having their starved and wasted forms lifted out of the jaws of death and placed once more before their hearthstones, was an exhibition of fortitude and patriotism that might set an example for all time.

CHAPTER 39

Decisive Maneuvers to End the War
By Ulysses S. Grant

The general who became president was a battlefield commander who knew his stuff. This excerpt from his autobiography shows him in action in critical last phases of the war.
—LAMAR UNDERWOOD

GENERAL MEADE AND I ENTERED PETERSBURG ON THE MORNING OF THE 3D AND TOOK a position under cover of a house which protected us from the enemy's musketry which was flying thick and fast there. As we would occasionally look around the corner we could see the streets and the Appomattox bottom, presumably near the bridge, packed with the Confederate army. I did not have artillery brought up, because I was sure Lee was trying to make his escape, and I wanted to push immediately in pursuit. At all events I had not the heart to turn the artillery upon such a mass of defeated and fleeing men, and I hoped to capture them soon.

Soon after the enemy had entirely evacuated Petersburg, a man came in who represented himself to be an engineer of the Army of Northern Virginia. He said that Lee had for some time been at work preparing a strong enclosed intrenchment, into which he would throw himself when forced out of Petersburg, and fight his final battle there; that he was actually at that time drawing his troops from Richmond, and falling back into this prepared work. This statement was made to General Meade and myself when we were together.

I had already given orders for the movement up the south side of the Appomattox for the purpose of heading off Lee; but Meade was so much impressed by this man's story that he thought we ought to cross the Appomattox there at once and move against Lee in his new position. I knew that Lee was no fool, as he would have been to have put himself and his army between two formidable streams like the James and Appomattox rivers, and between two such armies as those of the Potomac and the James. Then these streams coming together as they did to the east of him, it would be only necessary to close up in the west to have him thoroughly cut off from all supplies or possibility of reinforcement. It would only have been a question of days, and not many of them, if he had taken the position assigned to him by the so-called engineer, when he would have been obliged to surrender his army.

Such is one of the ruses resorted to in war to deceive your antagonist. My judgment was that Lee would necessarily have to evacuate Richmond, and that the only course for him to pursue would be to follow the Danville Road. Accordingly my object was to secure a point on that road south of Lee, and I told Meade this. He suggested that if Lee was going that way we would follow him. My reply was that we did not want to follow him; we wanted to get ahead of him and cut him off, and if he would only stay in the position he (Meade) believed him to be in at that time, I wanted nothing better; that when we got in possession of the Danville Railroad, at its crossing of the Appomattox River, if we still found him between the two rivers, all we had to do was to move eastward and close him up. That we would then have all the advantage we could possibly have by moving directly against him from Petersburg, even if he remained in the position assigned him by the engineer officer.

I had held most of the command aloof from the intrenchments, so as to start them out on the Danville Road early in the morning, supposing that Lee would be gone during the night. During the night I strengthened Sheridan by sending him Humphreys's corps.

Lee, as we now know, had advised the authorities at Richmond, during the day, of the condition of affairs, and told them it would be impossible for him to hold out longer than night, if he could hold out that long. Davis was at church when he received Lee's dispatch. The congregation was dismissed with the notice that there would be no evening service. The rebel government left Richmond about two o'clock in the afternoon of the 2d.

At night Lee ordered his troops to assemble at Amelia Court House, his object being to get away, join Johnston if possible, and to try to crush Sherman before I could get there. As soon as I was sure of this I notified Sheridan and directed him to move out on the Danville Railroad to the south side of the Appomattox River as speedily as possible. He replied that he already had some of his command nine miles out. I then ordered the rest of the Army of the Potomac under Meade to follow the same road in the morning. Parke's corps followed by the same road, and the Army of the James was directed to follow the road which ran alongside of the South Side Railroad to Burke's Station, and to repair the railroad and telegraph as they proceeded. That road was a 5 feet gauge, while our rolling stock was all of the 4 feet 8 1/2 inches gauge; consequently the rail on one side of the track had to be taken up throughout the whole length and relaid so as to conform to the gauge of our cars and locomotives.

Mr. Lincoln was at City Point at the time, and had been for some days. I would have let him know what I contemplated doing, only while I felt a strong conviction that the move was going to be successful, yet it might not prove so; and then I would have only added another to the many disappointments he had been suffering for the past three years. But when we started out he saw that we were moving for a purpose, and bidding us Godspeed, remained there to hear the result.

The next morning after the capture of Petersburg, I telegraphed Mr. Lincoln asking him to ride out there and see me, while I would await his arrival. I had started all the troops out early in the morning, so that after the National army left Petersburg there was not a soul to be seen, not even an animal in the streets. There was absolutely no one there, except my staff officers and, possibly, a small escort of cavalry. We had selected the piazza of a deserted house, and occupied it until the President arrived.

About the first thing that Mr. Lincoln said to me, after warm congratulations for the victory, and thanks both to myself and to the army which had accomplished it, was: "Do you know, general, that I have had a sort of a sneaking idea for some days that you intended to do something like this." Our movements having been successful up to this point, I no longer had any object in concealing from the President all my movements, and the objects I had in view. He remained for some days near City Point, and I communicated with him frequently and fully by telegraph.

Mr. Lincoln knew that it had been arranged for Sherman to join me at a fixed time, to co-operate in the destruction of Lee's army. I told him that I had been very anxious to have the Eastern armies vanquish their old enemy who had so long resisted all their repeated and gallant attempts to subdue them or drive them from their capital. The Western armies had been in the main successful until they had conquered all the territory from the Mississippi River to the State of North Carolina, and were now almost ready to knock at the back door of Richmond, asking admittance. I said to him that if the Western armies should be even upon the field, operating against Richmond and Lee, the credit would be given to them for the capture, by politicians and non-combatants from the section of country which those troops hailed from. It might lead to disagreeable bickerings between members of Congress of the East and those of the West in some of their debates. Western members might be throwing it up to the members of the East that in the suppression of the rebellion they were not able to capture an army, or to accomplish much in the way of contributing toward that end, but had to wait until the Western armies had conquered all the territory south and west of them, and then come on to help them capture the only army they had been engaged with.

Mr. Lincoln said he saw that now, but had never thought of it before, because his anxiety was so great that he did not care where the aid came from so the work was done.

The Army of the Potomac has every reason to be proud of its four years' record in the suppression of the rebellion. The army it had to fight was the protection to the capital of a people which was attempting to found a nation upon the territory of the United States. Its loss would be the loss of the cause. Every energy, therefore, was put forth by the Confederacy to protect and maintain their capital. Everything else would go if it went. Lee's army had to be strengthened to enable it to maintain its position, no matter what territory was wrested from the South in another quarter.

I never expected any such bickering as I have indicated, between the soldiers of the two sections; and, fortunately, there has been none between the politicians. Possibly I am the only one who thought of the liability of such a state of things in advance.

When our conversation was at an end Mr. Lincoln mounted his horse and started on his return to City Point, while I and my staff started to join the army, now a good many miles in advance. Up to this time I had not received the report of the capture of Richmond.

Soon after I left President Lincoln I received a dispatch from General Weitzel which notified me that he had taken possession of Richmond at about 8.15 o'clock in the morning of that day, the 3d, and that he had found the city on fire in two places. The city was in the most utter confusion. The authorities had taken the precaution to empty all the liquor into the gutter, and to throw out the provisions which the Confederate government had left, for the people to gather up. The city had been deserted by the authorities, civil and military, without any notice whatever that they were about to leave. In fact, up to the very hour of the evacuation the people had been led to believe that Lee had gained an important victory somewhere around Petersburg.

Weitzel's command found evidence of great demoralization in Lee's army, there being still a great many men and even officers in the town. The city was on fire. Our troops were directed to extinguish the flames, which they finally succeeded in doing. The fire had been started by some one connected with the retreating army. All authorities deny that it was authorized, and I presume it was the work of excited men who were leaving what they regarded as their capital and may have felt that it was better to destroy it than have it fall into the hands of their enemy. Be that as it may, the National troops found the city in flames, and used every effort to extinguish them.

The troops that had formed Lee's right, a great many of them, were cut off from getting back into Petersburg, and were pursued by our cavalry so hotly and closely that they threw away caissons, ammunition, clothing, and almost everything to lighten their loads, and pushed along up the Appomattox River until finally they took water and crossed over.

I left Mr. Lincoln and started, as I have already said, to join the command, which halted at Sutherland Station, about nine miles out. We had still time to march as much farther, and time was an object; but the roads were bad and the trains belonging to the advance corps had blocked up the road so that it was impossible to get on. Then, again, our cavalry had struck some of the enemy and were pursuing them; and the orders were that the roads should be given up to the cavalry whenever they appeared. This caused further delay.

General Wright, who was in command of one of the corps which were left back, thought to gain time by letting his men go into bivouac and trying to get up some rations for them, and clearing out the road, so that when they did start they would be uninterrupted. Humphreys, who was far ahead, was also out of rations. They did not succeed in getting them up through the night; but the Army of the Potomac, officers and men, were so elated by the reflection that at last they were following up a victory to its end, that they preferred marching without rations to running a possible risk of letting the enemy elude them. So the march was resumed at three o'clock in the morning.

Merritt's cavalry had struck the enemy at Deep Creek, and driven them north to the Appomattox, where, I presume, most of them were forced to cross.

On the morning of the 4th I learned that Lee had ordered rations up from Danville for his famishing army, and that they were to meet him at Farmville. This showed that Lee had already abandoned the idea of following the railroad down to Danville, but had determined to go farther west, by the way of Farmville. I notified Sheridan of this and directed him to get possession of the road before the supplies could reach Lee. He responded that he had already sent Crook's division to get upon the road between Burkesville and Jetersville, then to face north and march along the road upon the latter place; and he thought Crook must be there now. The bulk of the army moved directly for Jetersville by two roads.

After I had received the dispatch from Sheridan saying that Crook was on the Danville Road, I immediately ordered Meade to make a forced march with the Army of the Potomac, and to send Parke's corps across from the road they were on to the South Side Railroad, to fall in the rear of the Army of the James and to protect the railroad which that army was repairing as it went along.

Our troops took possession of Jetersville and in the telegraph office, they found a dispatch from Lee, ordering two hundred thousand rations from Danville. The dispatch had not been sent, but Sheridan sent a special messenger with it to Burkesville and had it forwarded from there. In the meantime, however, dispatches from other sources had reached Danville, and they knew there that our army was on the line of the road; so that they sent no further supplies from that quarter.

At this time Merritt and Mackenzie, with the cavalry, were off between the road which the Army of the Potomac was marching on and the Appomattox River, and were attacking the enemy in flank. They picked up a great many prisoners and forced the abandonment of some property.

Lee intrenched himself at Amelia Court House, and also his advance north of Jetersville, and sent his troops out to collect forage. The country was very poor and afforded but very little. His foragers scattered a great deal; many of them were picked up by our men, and many others never returned to the Army of Northern Virginia.

Griffin's corps was intrenched across the railroad south of Jetersville, and Sheridan notified me of the situation. I again ordered Meade up with all dispatch, Sheridan having but the one corps of infantry with a little cavalry confronting Lee's entire army. Meade, always prompt in obeying orders, now pushed forward with great energy, although he was himself sick and hardly able to be out of bed. Humphreys moved at two, and Wright at three o'clock in the morning, without rations, as I have said, the wagons being far in the rear.

I stayed that night at Wilson's Station on the South Side Railroad. On the morning of the 5th I sent word to Sheridan of the progress Meade was making, and suggested that he might now attack Lee. We had now no other objective than the Confederate armies, and I was anxious to close the thing up at once.

On the 5th I marched again with Ord's command until within about ten miles of Burkesville, where I stopped to let his army pass. I then received from Sheridan the following dispatch:

"The whole of Lee's army is at or near Amelia Court House, and on this side of it. General Davies, whom I sent out to Painesville on their right flank, has just captured six pieces of artillery and some wagons. We can capture the Army of Northern Virginia if force enough can be thrown to this point, and then advance upon it. My cavalry was at Burkesville yesterday, and six miles beyond, on the Danville Road, last night. General Lee is at Amelia Court House in person. They are out of rations, or nearly so. They were advancing up the railroad towards Burkesville yesterday, when we intercepted them at this point."

It now became a life and death struggle with Lee to get south to his provisions.

Sheridan, thinking the enemy might turn off immediately towards Farmville, moved Davies's brigade of cavalry out to watch him. Davies found the movement had already commenced. He attacked and drove away their cavalry which was escorting wagons to the west, capturing and burning 180 wagons. He also captured five pieces of artillery. The Confederate infantry then moved against him and probably would have handled him very roughly, but Sheridan had sent two more brigades of cavalry to follow Davies, and they came to his relief in time. A sharp engagement took place between these three brigades of cavalry and the enemy's infantry, but the latter was repulsed.

Meade himself reached Jetersville about two o'clock in the afternoon, but in advance of all his troops. The head of Humphreys's corps followed in about an hour afterwards. Sheridan stationed the troops as they came up, at Meade's request, the latter still being very sick. He extended two divisions of this corps off to the west of the road to the left of Griffin's corps, and one division to the right. The cavalry by this time had also come up, and they were put still farther off to the left, Sheridan feeling certain that there lay the route by which the enemy intended to escape. He wanted to attack, feeling that if time was given, the enemy would get away; but Meade prevented this, preferring to wait till his troops were all up.

At this juncture Sheridan sent me a letter which had been handed to him by a colored man, with a note from himself saying that he wished I was there myself. The letter was dated Amelia Court House, April 5th, and signed by Colonel Taylor. It was to his mother, and showed the demoralization of the Confederate army. Sheridan's note also gave me the information as here related of the movements of that day. I received a second message from Sheridan on the 5th, in which he urged more emphatically the importance of my presence. This was brought to me by a scout in gray uniform. It was written on tissue paper, and wrapped up in tin-foil such as chewing tobacco is folded in. This was a precaution taken so that if the scout should be captured he could take this tin-foil out of his pocket and putting it into his mouth, chew it. It would cause no surprise at all to see a Confederate soldier chewing tobacco. It was nearly night when this letter was received. I gave Ord directions to continue his march to Burkesville and there intrench himself for the night, and in the morning to move west to cut off all the roads between there and Farmville.

I then started with a few of my staff and a very small escort of cavalry, going directly through the woods, to join Meade's army. The distance was about sixteen miles; but the night being dark our progress was slow through the woods in the absence of direct roads. However, we got to the outposts about ten o'clock in the evening, and after some little parley convinced the sentinels of our identity and were conducted in to where Sheridan was bivouacked. We talked over the situation for some little time, Sheridan explaining to me what he thought Lee was trying to do, and that Meade's orders, if carried out, moving to the right flank, would give him the coveted opportunity of escaping us and putting us in rear of him.

We then together visited Meade, reaching his headquarters about midnight. I explained to Meade that we did not want to follow the enemy; we wanted to get ahead of him, and that his orders would allow the enemy to escape, and besides that, I had no doubt that Lee was moving right then. Meade changed his orders at once. They were now given for an advance on Amelia Court House, at an early hour in the morning, as the army then lay; that is, the infantry being across the railroad, most of it to the west of the road, with the cavalry swung out still farther to the left.

— ·~· —

The Appomattox, going westward, takes a long sweep to the south-west from the neighborhood of the Richmond and Danville Railroad bridge, and then trends north-westerly. Sailor's Creek, an insignificant stream, running northward, empties into the Appomattox between the High Bridge and Jetersville. Near the High Bridge the stage road from Petersburg to Lynchburg crosses the Appomattox River, also on a bridge. The railroad runs on the north side of the river to Farmville, a few miles west, and from there, recrossing, continues on the south side of it. The roads coming up from the south-east to Farmville cross the Appomattox River there on a bridge and run on the north side, leaving the Lynchburg and Petersburg Railroad well to the left.

Lee, in pushing out from Amelia Court House, availed himself of all the roads between the Danville Road and Appomattox River to move upon, and never permitted the head of his columns to stop because of any fighting that might be going on in his rear. In this way he came very near succeeding in getting to his provision trains and eluding us with at least part of his army.

As expected, Lee's troops had moved during the night before, and our army in moving upon Amelia Court House soon encountered them. There was a good deal of fighting before Sailor's Creek was reached. Our cavalry charged in upon a body of theirs which was escorting a wagon train in order to get it past our left. A severe engagement ensued, in which we captured many prisoners, and many men also were killed and wounded. There was as much gallantry displayed by some of the Confederates in these little engagements as was displayed at any time during the war, notwithstanding the sad defeats of the past week.

The armies finally met on Sailor's Creek, when a heavy engagement took place, in which infantry, artillery and cavalry were all brought into action. Our men on the right, as they were brought in against the enemy, came in on higher ground, and upon his flank, giving us every advantage to be derived from the lay of the country. Our firing was also very much more rapid, because the enemy commenced his retreat westward and in firing as he retreated had to turn around every time he fired. The enemy's loss was very heavy, as well in killed and wounded as in captures. Some six general officers fell into our hands in this engagement, and seven thousand men were made prisoners. This engagement was commenced in the middle of the afternoon of the 6th, and the retreat and pursuit were continued until nightfall, when the armies bivouacked upon the ground where the night had overtaken them.

When the move towards Amelia Court House had commenced that morning, I ordered Wright's corps, which was on the extreme right, to be moved to the left past the whole army, to take the place of Griffin's, and ordered the latter at the same time to move by and place itself on the right. The object of this movement was to get the 6th corps, Wright's, next to the cavalry, with which they had formerly served so harmoniously and so efficiently in the valley of Virginia.

The 6th corps now remained with the cavalry and under Sheridan's direct command until after the surrender.

Ord had been directed to take possession of all the roads southward between Burkesville and the High Bridge. On the morning of the 6th he sent Colonel Washburn with two infantry regiments with instructions to destroy High Bridge and to return rapidly to Burkesville Station; and he prepared himself to resist the enemy there. Soon after Washburn had started Ord became a little alarmed as to his safety and sent Colonel Read, of his staff, with about eighty cavalrymen, to overtake him and bring him back. Very shortly after this he heard that the head of Lee's column had got up to the road between him and where Washburn now was, and attempted to send reinforcements, but the reinforcements could not get through. Read, however, had got through ahead of the enemy. He rode on to Farmville and was on his way back again when he found his return cut off, and Washburn confronting apparently the advance of Lee's army. Read drew his men up into line of battle, his force now consisting of less than six hundred men, infantry and cavalry, and rode along their front, making a speech to his men to inspire them with the same enthusiasm that he himself felt. He then gave the order to charge. This little band made several charges, of course unsuccessful ones, but inflicted a loss upon the enemy more than equal to their own entire number. Colonel Read fell mortally wounded, and then Washburn; and at the close of the conflict nearly every officer of the command and most of the rank and file had been either killed or wounded. The remainder then surrendered. The Confederates took this to be only the advance of a larger column which had headed them off, and so stopped to intrench; so that this gallant band of six hundred had checked the progress of a strong detachment of the Confederate army.

CHAPTER 40

Appomattox: How the War Ended

By Ulysses S. Grant

Here are details and facts—not myths—on Lee's surrender, by the man who made it happen and was there. (Myth: Lee presenting sword; Grant handing it back. It never happened.)

—LAMAR UNDERWOOD

THIS STOPPAGE OF LEE'S COLUMN NO DOUBT SAVED TO US THE TRAINS FOLLOWING. LEE himself pushed on and crossed the wagon road bridge near the High Bridge, and attempted to destroy it. He did set fire to it, but the flames had made but little headway when Humphreys came up with his corps and drove away the rear-guard which had been left to protect it while it was being burned up. Humphreys forced his way across with some loss, and followed Lee to the intersection of the road crossing at Farmville with the one from Petersburg. Here Lee held a position which was very strong, naturally, besides being intrenched. Humphreys was alone, confronting him all through the day, and in a very hazardous position. He put on a bold face, however, and assaulted with some loss, but was not assaulted in return.

Our cavalry had gone farther south by the way of Prince Edward's Court House, along with the 5th corps (Griffin's), Ord falling in between Griffin and the Appomattox. Crook's division of cavalry and Wright's corps pushed on west of Farmville. When the cavalry reached Farmville they found that some of the Confederates were in ahead of them, and had already got their trains of provisions back to that point; but our troops were in time to prevent them from securing anything to eat, although they succeeded in again running the trains off, so that we did not get them for some time. These troops retreated to the north side of the Appomattox to join Lee, and succeeded in destroying the bridge after them. Considerable fighting ensued there between Wright's corps and a portion of our cavalry and the Confederates, but finally the cavalry forded the stream and drove them away. Wright built a foot-bridge for his men to march over on and then marched out to the junction of the roads to relieve Humphreys, arriving there that night. I had stopped the night before at Burkesville Junction. Our troops were then pretty much all out of the place, but we had a field hospital there, and Ord's command was extended from that point towards Farmville.

Here I met Dr. Smith, a Virginian and an officer of the regular army, who told me that in a conversation with General Ewell, one of the prisoners and a relative of his, Ewell had said that when we had got across the James River he knew their cause was lost, and it was the duty of their authorities to make the best terms they could while they still had a right to claim concessions. The authorities thought differently, however. Now the cause was lost and they had no right to claim anything. He said further, that for every man that was killed after this in the war somebody is responsible, and it would be but very little better than murder. He was not sure that Lee would consent to surrender his army without being able to consult with the President, but he hoped he would.

I rode in to Farmville on the 7th, arriving there early in the day. Sheridan and Ord were pushing through, away to the south. Meade was back towards the High Bridge, and Humphreys confronting Lee as before stated. After having gone into bivouac at Prince Edward's Court House, Sheridan learned that seven trains of provisions and forage were at Appomattox, and determined to start at once and capture them; and a forced march was necessary in order to get there before Lee's army could secure them. He wrote me a note telling me this. This fact, together with the incident related the night before by Dr. Smith, gave me the idea of opening correspondence with General Lee on the subject of the surrender of his army. I therefore wrote to him on this day, as follows:

HEADQUARTERS ARMIES OF THE U.S., 5 P.M., April 7, 1865.
GENERAL R. E. LEE Commanding C.S.A.
The result of the last week must convince you of the hopelessness of further resistance on the part of the Army of Northern Virginia in this struggle. I feel that it is so, and regard it as my duty to shift from myself the responsibility of any further effusion of blood, by asking of you the surrender of that portion of the Confederate States army known as the Army of Northern Virginia.
U. S. GRANT, Lieut.-General.

Lee replied on the evening of the same day as follows:

April 7, 1865.
GENERAL: I have received your note of this day. Though not entertaining the opinion you express on the hopelessness of further resistance on the part of the Army of Northern Virginia, I reciprocate your desire to avoid useless effusion

of blood, and therefore before considering your proposition, ask the terms you will offer on condition of its surrender.

    R. E. LEE, General.
    LIEUT.-GENERAL U. S. GRANT, Commanding Armies of the U.S.

This was not satisfactory, but I regarded it as deserving another letter and wrote him as follows:

April 8, 1865.
GENERAL R. E. LEE, Commanding C.S.A.
Your note of last evening in reply to mine of same date, asking the condition on which I will accept the surrender of the Army of Northern Virginia is just received. In reply I would say that, peace being my great desire, there is but one condition I would insist upon, namely: that the men and officers surrendered shall be disqualified for taking up arms again against the Government of the United States until properly exchanged. I will meet you, or will designate officers to meet any officers you may name for the same purpose, at any point agreeable to you, for the purpose of arranging definitely the terms upon which the surrender of the Army of Northern Virginia will be received.

    U. S. GRANT, Lieut.-General.

Lee's army was rapidly crumbling. Many of his soldiers had enlisted from that part of the State where they now were, and were continually dropping out of the ranks and going to their homes. I know that I occupied a hotel almost destitute of furniture at Farmville, which had probably been used as a Confederate hospital. The next morning when I came out I found a Confederate colonel there, who reported to me and said that he was the proprietor of that house, and that he was a colonel of a regiment that had been raised in that neighborhood. He said that when he came along past home, he found that he was the only man of the regiment remaining with Lee's army, so he just dropped out, and now wanted to surrender himself. I told him to stay there and he would not be molested. That was one regiment which had been eliminated from Lee's force by this crumbling process.

Although Sheridan had been marching all day, his troops moved with alacrity and without any straggling. They began to see the end of what they had been fighting four years for. Nothing seemed to fatigue them. They were ready to move without rations and travel without rest until the end. Straggling had entirely ceased, and every man was now a rival for the front. The infantry marched about as rapidly as the cavalry could.

Sheridan sent Custer with his division to move south of Appomattox Station, which is about five miles south-west of the Court House, to get west of the trains and destroy the roads to the rear. They got there the night of the 8th, and succeeded partially; but some of the train men had just discovered the movement of our troops and succeeded in running off three of the trains. The other four were held by Custer.

The head of Lee's column came marching up there on the morning of the 9th, not dreaming, I suppose, that there were any Union soldiers near. The Confederates were surprised to find our cavalry had possession of the trains. However, they were desperate and at once assaulted, hoping to recover them. In the melee that ensued they succeeded in burning one of the trains, but not in getting anything from it. Custer then ordered the other trains run back on the road towards Farmville, and the fight continued.

So far, only our cavalry and the advance of Lee's army were engaged. Soon, however, Lee's men were brought up from the rear, no doubt expecting they had nothing to meet but our cavalry. But our infantry had pushed forward so rapidly that by the time the enemy got up they found Griffin's corps and the Army of the James confronting them. A sharp engagement ensued, but Lee quickly set up a white flag.

On the 8th I had followed the Army of the Potomac in rear of Lee. I was suffering very severely with a sick headache, and stopped at a farmhouse on the road some distance in rear of the main body of the army. I spent the night in bathing my feet in hot water and mustard, and putting mustard plasters on my wrists and the back part of my neck, hoping to be cured by morning. During the night I received Lee's answer to my letter of the 8th, inviting an interview between the lines on the following morning. But it was for a different purpose from that of surrendering his army, and I answered him as follows:

HEADQUARTERS ARMIES OF THE U.S., April 9, 1865.
GENERAL R. E. LEE, Commanding C.S.A.
Your note of yesterday is received. As I have no authority to treat on the subject of peace, the meeting proposed for ten A.M. to-day could lead to no good. I will state, however, General, that I am equally anxious for peace with yourself, and the whole North entertains the same feeling. The terms upon which peace can be had are well understood. By the South laying down their arms they will hasten that most desirable event, save thousands of human lives and hundreds of millions of property not yet destroyed. Sincerely hoping that all our difficulties may be settled without the loss of another life, I subscribe myself, etc.,
    U. S. GRANT, Lieutenant-General.

I proceeded at an early hour in the morning, still suffering with the headache, to get to the head of the column. I was not more than two or three miles from Appomattox Court House at the time, but to go direct I would have to pass through Lee's army, or a portion of it. I had therefore to move south in order to get upon a road coming up from another direction.

When the white flag was put out by Lee, as already described, I was in this way moving towards Appomattox Court House, and consequently could not be communicated with immediately, and be informed of what Lee had done. Lee, therefore, sent a flag to the rear to advise Meade and one to the front to Sheridan, saying that he had sent a message to me for the purpose of having a meeting to consult about the surrender of his army, and asked for a suspension of hostilities until I could be communicated with.

As they had heard nothing of this until the fighting had got to be severe and all going against Lee, both of these commanders hesitated very considerably about suspending hostilities at all. They were afraid it was not in good faith, and we had the Army of Northern Virginia where it could not escape except by some deception. They, however, finally consented to a suspension of hostilities for two hours to give an opportunity of communicating with me in that time, if possible. It was found that, from the route I had taken, they would probably not be able to communicate with me and get an answer back within the time fixed unless the messenger should pass through the rebel lines.

Lee, therefore, sent an escort with the officer bearing this message through his lines to me.

April 9, 1865.
GENERAL: I received your note of this morning on the picket-line whither I had come to meet you and ascertain definitely what terms were embraced in your proposal of yesterday with reference to the surrender of this army. I now request an interview in accordance with the offer contained in your letter of yesterday for that purpose.
    R. E. LEE, General.
    LIEUTENANT-GENERAL U. S. GRANT Commanding U.S. Armies.

When the officer reached me I was still suffering with the sick headache, but the instant I saw the contents of the note I was cured. I wrote the following note in reply and hastened on:

April 9, 1865.
GENERAL R. E. LEE, Commanding C.S. Armies.
Your note of this date is but this moment (11.50 A.M.) received, in consequence of my having passed from the Richmond and Lynchburg road to the Farmville and Lynchburg road. I am at this writing about four miles west of Walker's Church and will push forward to the front for the purpose of meeting you. Notice sent to me on this road where you wish the interview to take place will meet me.
    U. S. GRANT, Lieutenant-General.

I was conducted at once to where Sheridan was located with his troops drawn up in line of battle facing the Confederate army near by. They were very much excited, and expressed their view that this was all a ruse employed to enable the Confederates to get away. They said they believed that Johnston was marching up from North Carolina now, and Lee was moving to join him; and they would whip the rebels where they now were in five minutes if I would only let them go in. But I had no doubt about the good faith of Lee, and pretty soon was conducted to where he was. I found him at the house of a Mr. McLean, at Appomattox Court House, with Colonel Marshall, one of his staff officers, awaiting my arrival. The head of his column was occupying a hill, on a portion of which was an apple orchard, beyond a little valley which separated it from that on the crest of which Sheridan's forces were drawn up in line of battle to the south.

Before stating what took place between General Lee and myself, I will give all there is of the story of the famous apple tree.

Wars produce many stories of fiction, some of which are told until they are believed to be true. The war of the rebellion was no exception to this rule, and the story of the apple tree is one of those fictions based on a slight foundation of fact. As I have said, there was an apple orchard on the side of the hill occupied by the Confederate forces. Running diagonally up the hill was a wagon road, which, at one point, ran very near one of the trees, so that the wheels of vehicles had, on that side, cut off the roots of this tree, leaving a little embankment. General Babcock, of my staff, reported to me that when he first met General Lee he was sitting upon this embankment with his feet in the road below and his back resting against the tree. The story had no other foundation than that. Like many other stories, it would be very good if it was only true.

I had known General Lee in the old army, and had served with him in the Mexican War; but did not suppose, owing to the difference in our age and rank, that he would remember me, while I would more naturally remember him distinctly, because he was the chief of staff of General Scott in the Mexican War.

When I had left camp that morning I had not expected so soon the result that was then taking place, and consequently was in rough garb. I was without a sword, as I usually was when on horseback on the field, and wore a soldier's blouse for a coat, with the shoulder straps of my rank to indicate to the army who I was. When I went into the house I found General Lee. We greeted each other, and after shaking hands took our seats. I had my staff with me, a good portion of whom were in the room during the whole of the interview.

What General Lee's feelings were I do not know. As he was a man of much dignity, with an impassible face, it was impossible to say whether he felt inwardly glad that the end had finally come, or felt sad over the result, and was too manly to show it. Whatever his feelings, they were entirely concealed from my observation; but my own feelings, which had been quite jubilant on the receipt of his letter, were sad and depressed. I felt like anything rather than rejoicing at the downfall of a foe who had fought so long and valiantly, and had suffered so much for a cause, though that cause was, I believe, one of the worst for which a people ever fought, and one for which there was the least excuse. I do not question, however, the sincerity of the great mass of those who were opposed to us.

General Lee was dressed in a full uniform which was entirely new, and was wearing a sword of considerable value, very likely the sword which had been presented by the State of Virginia; at all events, it was an entirely different sword from the one that would ordinarily be worn in the field. In my rough traveling suit, the uniform of a private with the straps of a lieutenant-general, I must have contrasted very strangely with a man so handsomely dressed, six feet high and of faultless form. But this was not a matter that I thought of until afterwards.

We soon fell into a conversation about old army times. He remarked that he remembered me very well in the old army; and I told him that as a matter of course I remembered him perfectly, but from the difference in our rank and years (there being about sixteen years' difference in our ages), I had thought it very likely that I had not attracted his attention sufficiently to be remembered by him after such a long interval. Our conversation grew so pleasant that I almost forgot the object of our meeting. After the conversation had run on in this style for some time, General Lee called my attention to the object of our meeting, and said that he had asked for this interview for the purpose of getting from me the terms I proposed to give his army. I said that I meant merely that his army should lay down their arms, not to take them up again during the continuance of the war unless duly and properly exchanged. He said that he had so understood my letter.

Then we gradually fell off again into conversation about matters foreign to the subject which had brought us together. This continued for some little time, when General Lee again interrupted the course of the conversation by suggesting that the terms I proposed to give his army ought to be written out. I called to General Parker, secretary on my staff, for writing materials, and commenced writing out the following terms:

APPOMATTOX C. H., VA.,
Ap 19th, 1865.
GEN. R. E. LEE, Comd'g C.S.A.
GEN: In accordance with the substance of my letter to you of the 8th inst., I propose to receive the surrender of the Army of N. Va. on the following terms, to wit: Rolls of all the officers and men to be made in duplicate. One copy to be given to an officer designated by me, the other to be retained by such officer or officers as you may designate. The officers to give their individual paroles not to take up arms against the Government of the United States until properly exchanged, and each company or regimental commander sign a like parole for the men of their commands. The arms, artillery and public property to be parked and stacked, and turned over to the officer appointed by me to receive them. This will not embrace the side-arms of the officers, nor their private horses or baggage. This done, each

officer and man will be allowed to return to their homes, not to be disturbed by United States authority so long as they observe their paroles and the laws in force where they may reside.

Very respectfully, U. S. GRANT, Lt. Gen.

When I put my pen to the paper I did not know the first word that I should make use of in writing the terms. I only knew what was in my mind, and I wished to express it clearly, so that there could be no mistaking it. As I wrote on, the thought occurred to me that the officers had their own private horses and effects, which were important to them, but of no value to us; also that it would be an unnecessary humiliation to call upon them to deliver their side arms.

No conversation, not one word, passed between General Lee and myself, either about private property, side arms, or kindred subjects. He appeared to have no objections to the terms first proposed; or if he had a point to make against them he wished to wait until they were in writing to make it. When he read over that part of the terms about side arms, horses and private property of the officers, he remarked, with some feeling, I thought, that this would have a happy effect upon his army.

Then, after a little further conversation, General Lee remarked to me again that their army was organized a little differently from the army of the United States (still maintaining by implication that we were two countries); that in their army the cavalrymen and artillerists owned their own horses; and he asked if he was to understand that the men who so owned their horses were to be permitted to retain them. I told him that as the terms were written they would not; that only the officers were permitted to take their private property. He then, after reading over the terms a second time, remarked that that was clear.

I then said to him that I thought this would be about the last battle of the war—I sincerely hoped so; and I said further I took it that most of the men in the ranks were small farmers. The whole country had been so raided by the two armies that it was doubtful whether they would be able to put in a crop to carry themselves and their families through the next winter without the aid of the horses they were then riding. The United States did not want them and I would, therefore, instruct the officers I left behind to receive the paroles of his troops to let every man of the Confederate army who claimed to own a horse or mule take the animal to his home. Lee remarked again that this would have a happy effect.

He then sat down and wrote out the following letter:

HEADQUARTERS ARMY OF NORTHERN VIRGINIA, April 9, 1865.
GENERAL:—I received your letter of this date containing the terms of the surrender of the Army of Northern Virginia as proposed by you. As they are substantially the same as those expressed in your letter of the 8th inst.,

they are accepted. I will proceed to designate the proper officers to carry the stipulations into effect.

R. E. LEE, General. LIEUT.-GENERAL U. S. GRANT.

While duplicates of the two letters were being made, the Union generals present were severally presented to General Lee.

The much talked of surrendering of Lee's sword and my handing it back, this and much more that has been said about it is the purest romance. The word sword or side arms was not mentioned by either of us until I wrote it in the terms. There was no premeditation, and it did not occur to me until the moment I wrote it down. If I had happened to omit it, and General Lee had called my attention to it, I should have put it in the terms precisely as I acceded to the provision about the soldiers retaining their horses.

General Lee, after all was completed and before taking his leave, remarked that his army was in a very bad condition for want of food, and that they were without forage; that his men had been living for some days on parched corn exclusively, and that he would have to ask me for rations and forage. I told him "certainly," and asked for how many men he wanted rations. His answer was "about twenty-five thousand;" and I authorized him to send his own commissary and quartermaster to Appomattox Station, two or three miles away, where he could have, out of the trains we had stopped, all the provisions wanted. As for forage, we had ourselves depended almost entirely upon the country for that.

Generals Gibbon, Griffin and Merritt were designated by me to carry into effect the paroling of Lee's troops before they should start for their homes—General Lee leaving Generals Longstreet, Gordon and Pendleton for them to confer with in order to facilitate this work. Lee and I then separated as cordially as we had met, he returning to his own lines, and all went into bivouac for the night at Appomattox.

Soon after Lee's departure I telegraphed to Washington as follows:

HEADQUARTERS APPOMATTOX C. H., VA., April 9th, 1865, 4.30 P.M. HON. E. M. STANTON, Secretary of War, Washington.

General Lee surrendered the Army of Northern Virginia this afternoon on terms proposed by myself. The accompanying additional correspondence will show the conditions fully.

U. S. GRANT, Lieut.-General.

When news of the surrender first reached our lines our men commenced firing a salute of a hundred guns in honor of the victory. I at once sent word, however, to have it stopped. The Confederates were now our prisoners, and we did not want to exult over their downfall.

I determined to return to Washington at once, with a view to putting a stop to the purchase of supplies, and what I now deemed other useless outlay of money. Before leaving, however, I thought I would like to see General Lee again; so next morning I rode out beyond our lines towards his headquarters, preceded by a bugler and a staff-officer carrying a white flag.

Lee soon mounted his horse, seeing who it was, and met me. We had there between the lines, sitting on horseback, a very pleasant conversation of over half an hour, in the course of which Lee said to me that the South was a big country and that we might have to march over it three or four times before the war entirely ended, but that we would now be able to do it as they could no longer resist us. He expressed it as his earnest hope, however, that we would not be called upon to cause more loss and sacrifice of life; but he could not foretell the result. I then suggested to General Lee that there was not a man in the Confederacy whose influence with the soldiery and the whole people was as great as his, and that if he would now advise the surrender of all the armies I had no doubt his advice would be followed with alacrity. But Lee said, that he could not do that without consulting the President first. I knew there was no use to urge him to do anything against his ideas of what was right.

I was accompanied by my staff and other officers, some of whom seemed to have a great desire to go inside the Confederate lines. They finally asked permission of Lee to do so for the purpose of seeing some of their old army friends, and the permission was granted. They went over, had a very pleasant time with their old friends, and brought some of them back with them when they returned.

When Lee and I separated he went back to his lines and I returned to the house of Mr. McLean. Here the officers of both armies came in great numbers, and seemed to enjoy the meeting as much as though they had been friends separated for a long time while fighting battles under the same flag. For the time being it looked very much as if all thought of the war had escaped their minds. After an hour pleasantly passed in this way I set out on horseback, accompanied by my staff and a small escort, for Burkesville Junction, up to which point the railroad had by this time been repaired.

After I left General Lee at Appomattox Station, I went with my staff and a few others directly to Burkesville Station on my way to Washington. The road from Burkesville back having been newly repaired and the ground being soft, the train got off the track frequently, and, as a result, it was after midnight of the second day when I reached City Point. As soon as possible I took a dispatch-boat thence to Washington City.

While in Washington I was very busy for a time in preparing the necessary orders for the new state of affairs; communicating with my different commanders of separate departments, bodies of troops, etc. But by the 14th I was pretty well through with this work, so as to be able to visit my children, who were then in Burlington, New Jersey, attending school. Mrs. Grant was with me in Washington at the time, and we were invited by President and Mrs. Lincoln to accompany them to the theatre on the evening of that day. I replied to the President's verbal invitation to the effect, that if we were in the city we would take great pleasure in accompanying them; but that I was very anxious to get away and visit my children, and if I could get through my work during the day I should do so. I did get through and started by the evening train on the 14th, sending Mr. Lincoln word, of course, that I would not be at the theatre.

At that time the railroad to New York entered Philadelphia on Broad Street; passengers were conveyed in ambulances to the Delaware River, and then ferried to Camden, at which point they took the cars again. When I reached the ferry, on the east side of the City of Philadelphia, I found people awaiting my arrival there; and also dispatches informing me of the assassination of the President and Mr. Seward, and of the probable assassination of the Vice President, Mr. Johnson, and requesting my immediate return.

It would be impossible for me to describe the feeling that overcame me at the news of these assassinations, more especially the assassination of the President. I knew his goodness of heart, his generosity, his yielding disposition, his desire to have everybody happy, and above all his desire to see all the people of the United States enter again upon the full privileges of citizenship with equality among all. I knew also the feeling that Mr. Johnson had expressed in speeches and conversation against the Southern people, and I feared that his course towards them would be such as to repel, and make them unwilling citizens; and if they became such they would remain so for a long while. I felt that reconstruction had been set back, no telling how far.

I immediately arranged for getting a train to take me back to Washington City; but Mrs. Grant was with me; it was after midnight and Burlington was but an hour away. Finding that I could accompany her to our house and return about as soon as they would be ready to take me from the Philadelphia station, I went up with her and returned immediately by the same special train. The joy that I had witnessed among the people in the street and in public places in Washington when I left there, had been turned to grief; the city was in reality a city of mourning. I have stated what I believed then the effect of this would be, and my judgment now is that I was right. I believe the South would have been saved from very much of the hardness of feeling that was engendered by Mr. Johnson's course towards them during the first few months of his administration. Be this as it may, Mr. Lincoln's assassination was particularly unfortunate for the entire nation.

About the Editor

Lamar Underwood's long-time editing and writing career includes fifteen anthologies he has edited for the Lyons Press. With titles ranging through such diverse subjects as survival, military history, aviation, and adventure, Lamar's anthologies also include his first mountain man book, *Tales of the Mountain Men*, published by Lyons in 2004. Books he has written include *The Quotable Soldier*, *The Quotable Warrior*, and *The Quotable Writer*—all Lyons Press—and the novel *On Dangerous Ground*, published by Doubleday in 1989. He is former editor-in-chief of both *Sports Afield* and *Outdoor Life* magazines and has written numerous articles published in a wide list of magazines.

Sources

"In the Ranks," by Reverend R. E. M'Bride, from *In the Ranks: From the Wilderness to Appomattox Court-House*, 1883.

"A Confederate Soldier Speaks His Mind," by Carlton McCarthy, from *Detailed Minutiae of Soldier Life in the Army of Northern Virginia, 1861–1865*, 1882.

"America's Deadliest Day: One Officer's Story" by Frederick L. Hitchcock, from *War from the Inside*, 1903.

"Lincoln at War: Prominent Letters and Papers," by Abraham Lincoln, from *The Papers and Writings of Abraham Lincoln, Volume Two, Constitutional Edition*.

"A Common Soldier," by Leander Stillwell, from *The Story of a Common Soldier of Army Life in the Civil War, 1861–1865*.

"The Soldier's Life: A Confederate View," by Carlton McCarthy, from *Detailed Minutiae of Soldier Life in the Army of Northern Virginia, 1861–1865*, 1882.

"Robert E. Lee in Command," by Captain Robert E. Lee (General Lee's son), from *Recollections and Letters of General Robert E. Lee*.

"Slaughterhouse at Fredericksburg," by Frederick L. Hitchcock, from *War from the Inside*, 1903.

"Among the Wounded," by Walt Whitman, from *The Wound Dresser*, 1898.

"On Confederate Battlefields," by Carlton McCarthy, from *Detailed Minutiae of Soldier Life in the Army of Northern Virginia, 1861–1865*, 1882.

"How Private George W. Peck Put Down the Rebellion (Or Funny Experiences of a Raw Recruit)," by George W. Peck, from his book of the same title, 1887.

"What I Saw of Shiloh," by Ambrose Bierce, from *The Collected Works of Ambrose Bierce, Volume 1*, 1909.

"Gettysburg: The Decisive Second Day," by Abner Doubleday, from *Chancellorsville and Gettysburg*, 1882.

"Gettysburg: Pickett's Charge," by Abner Doubleday, from *Chancellorsville and Gettysburg*, 1882.

"Gettysburg: Lee's Escape," by Abner Doubleday, from *Chancellorsville and Gettysburg*, 1882.

"The Truth about Gettysburg," by Helen D. Longstreet, from *The Story of Gettysburg: Lee and Longstreet at High Tide*, 1904.

"The Clash of Ironclad Titans: *Merrimac* vs. *Monitor*," by H. Ashton Ramsay, from *The "Monitor" and the "Merrimac": The Encounter at Short Range*, 1912.

"The Flag Bearer," by Theodore Roosevelt, from *Hero Tales from American History*, 1895.

"Love, Loss, and Army Life of the Common Soldier," by Leander Stillwell, from *The Story of a Common Soldier of Army Life in the Civil War, 1861–1865*.

"A Night Ride of the Wounded," by Randall Parrish, from *My Lady of the North*, 1904.

"The Unforgettable Private Peck: Further Adventures of a Raw Recruit," by George W. Peck, from *How Private George W. Peck Put Down the Rebellion (Or Funny Experiences of a Raw Recruit)*, 1887.

"Bull Run," by Joseph A. Altsheler, from *The Guns of Bull Run*, 1914.

"Andersonville: Confederate Prison Horror," by John L. Maile, from *Prison Life in Andersonville*, 1912.

"Chickamauga," by James R. Carnahan, from *Personal Recollections of Chickamauga*, 1886.

"An Occurrence at Owl Creek Bridge," by Ambrose Bierce, from *The Collected Works of Ambrose Bierce*, 1911.

"Army Life in a Black Regiment," by Thomas Wentworth Higginson, from his book of the same title, 1869.

"Drummer Boy from Maine," by George T. Ulmer, from *Adventurers and Reminiscences of a Volunteer Drummer Boy from Maine*, 1892.

"Suffering and Hatred," by Phoebe Yates Pember, from *A Southern Woman's Story*, 1879.

"Vermont Sharp Shooters," by W. Y. W. Ripley, from his book of the same title, 1892.

"Vicksburg during the Trouble," by Mark Twain, from *Life on the Mississippi*, 1883.

"The Red Badge of Courage," by Stephen Crane, from his book of the same title, 1895.

"An Artilleryman's Diary," by Jenkin Lloyd Jones, from his book of the same title, 1914.

"A Night," by Louisa May Alcott, from *Hospital Sketches*, 1863.

"The Rebel Army Life," by Carlton McCarthy, from *Detailed Minutiae of Soldier Life in the Army of Northern Virginia, 1861–1865*, 1882.

"A Woman's Wartime Journal," by Dolly Sumner Lunt, from her book of the same title, 1918.

"A Horseman in the Sky," by Ambrose Bierce, from *Tales of Soldiers and Civilians*, 1891.

"To the Sea: Sherman on the March," dispatches of Major General W. T. Sherman, from *The Memoirs of General W. T. Sherman, Volume 2*.

"Last Days of the Confederacy: Campfire and Battlefield," by General John B. Gordon, C.S.A., his chapter from the anthology of the same title, 1894.

"Decisive Maneuvers to End the War," by Ulysses S. Grant, from *Personal Memoirs of U. S. Grant, Volume 11*.

"Appomattox: How the War Ended," by Ulysses S. Grant, *from Personal Memoirs of U. S. Grant, Volume 11*.